Criminology

CRIMINOLOGY

SECOND
EDITION

RUTH SHONLE CAVAN
Professor of Sociology
on the Jane Addams Foundation
Rockford College

1958

THOMAS Y. CROWELL COMPANY · New York

FIRST EDITION

First Printing, August, 1948
Second Printing, August, 1949
Third Printing, April, 1950
Fourth Printing, April, 1952
Fifth Printing, November, 1952
Sixth Printing, May, 1953

SECOND EDITION

First Printing, March, 1955
Second Printing, July, 1956
Third Printing, August, 1958

MANUFACTURED IN THE UNITED STATES OF AMERICA
BY THE VAIL-BALLOU PRESS, INC., BINGHAMTON, N. Y.

Preface

This second edition of *Criminology* retains the basic point of view of the first edition. Thus, crime is used as a general term to refer to violation of criminal laws—any other definition is so vague that crime cannot be delimited. Nevertheless, despite the variety of actions covered by this broad definition, most criminal behavior can be and is here viewed as the result of the efforts of the individual to satisfy his needs in a social environment that either offers him criminal models of conduct or fails to give him a means of satisfaction, with the result that emotionally explosive behavior follows.

The two-part division of the book continues to reflect the author's two main purposes: first, to present a sociological analysis of the criminal and his behavior; second, to provide a detailed description and a critical evaluation of law-enforcement agencies and their methods.

Although the viewpoint and organization of this revision remain the same as in the first edition, several changes have been made. In Chapter 1 the theoretical approach is explicitly stated. In Part Two the discussion of prisons emphasizes postwar adoption of systematized prison systems and methods of rehabilitation. An historical survey of theories of criminality now forms Appendix A, and the definitions of crimes used by the Federal Bureau of Investigation have been added as Appendix B.

An innovation in college texts is a chapter on "Treatment of Offenders in the Armed Forces" and another on "European Adult Offenders and Prisons." The first of these chapters rounds out the discussion of prison systems in the United States. It is timely in that selective military service calls most young men into the service, where they must conform to military regulations. Also, the discussion, which centers on military correctional methods, is both theoretically and practically important to penology.

The chapter on European Adult Offenders and Prisons emphasizes techniques of treatment used in five countries, most of which have restated their philosophy of treatment since the end of World War II and are in the process of adapting their institutions and treatment to make the new principles effective. Here, too, are suggestions for penology in the United States.

Many people have given the author assistance. First, I would like to thank all the professors of sociology teaching classes in criminology who, by answering a questionnaire, provided many excellent suggestions for this revision. I am grateful to the following people for criticisms of portions of the original edition: Jordan T. Cavan, Rockford College; Stanley Erikson, Augustana College; Herbert O. Hardin, Sergeant in the Albuquerque Police Force; Bernice Olsen, policewoman of Rockford; and Henry D. McKay, Institute for Juvenile Research, Chicago. For assistance contributing to the second edition I wish to thank Eugene Zemans, Executive Director of the John Howard Association, Chicago, and the many jail, prison, and correctional school staff members who have either arranged field trips or granted personal conferences.

In preparation of the chapter on Treatment of Offenders in the Armed Forces, special help was given me by Austin MacCormick, University of California; Victor H. Evjen, United States Probation System; Colonel William C. Capehart, USMC, Director of the Corrective Services Division, Bureau of Naval Personnel; and George E. Foltz and Doyle Shackelford of the Air Force 3320th Retraining Center. Appropriate sections of the chapter were reviewed by the National Headquarters of the Selective Service System; the Office of the Judge Advocate General of each branch of the Armed Forces; the Army Staff Judge Advocate of the Fifth Army Headquarters; the [Army] Correction Branch, Office of the Adjutant General; the Corrective Services Division, Bureau of Naval Personnel; and the [Air Force] Enforcement Correction Division. Although none of these offices could give official approval, they were all most helpful in correcting errors of fact or interpretation and in providing suggestions for expansion or contraction.

The chapter on European Adult Offenders and Prisons benefited by the assistance of criminologists in Europe who arranged tours, granted conferences, or supplied reports and photographs: Charles Germain, Director of Penitentiary Administration in the Ministry of Justice, France; Jorunn Skeie, Counselor with the Department of Prisons, Ministry of Justice, Norway; Knut Sveri, cand. jur., Research Associate, Norwegian Council for Science and the Humanities, and Torsten Eriksson, cand. jur., head of a bureau in the Swedish Ministry of Justice.

To all these and others who have helped directly or otherwise I express deep appreciation, at the same time absolving them from any responsibility for the trend of the discussion.

RUTH SHONLE CAVAN

February 1, 1955

Contents

PART ONE

The Development and Prevention of Delinquent and
Criminal Behavior

1 CRIMINAL BEHAVIOR   3

Crime a legal concept, 3.   Concepts Allied to the Criminal Concept,
9.   A Theory of Criminal Behavior, 11.   Types of Criminals, 20.
Juvenile Delinquents, 29.   Crime and Criminals, 30.

2 CHARACTERISTICS OF CRIMINALS   32

Sources of Information, 32.   Limitations of Criminal Statistics, 35.
The Basis of Reports, 38.   Types of Crime, 40.   Urban and Rural
Rates, 41.   Age and Sex, 41.   Intelligence, 53.   Marital Condition, 56.   Race, 58.   Foreign-born Whites, 60.   Outcome of Delinquency and Crime, 64.   Summary of Characteristics of Criminals,
67.

3 CULTURAL AND SOCIAL BACKGROUNDS OF CRIMINALS   70

The Criminal Ethos of the United States, 70.   Social Disorganization and Crime, 75.   Transition Areas—An Example of Cultural
Deviation and Social Disorganization, 78.   Delinquency Patterns
in Disorganized Areas, 94.   Rural Background of Crime, 99.
Crime and Social Disorganization, 102.

4 FAMILY BACKGROUND OF THE CRIMINAL   106

Degree of Family Culpability, 107.   Economic Status of Families,
114.   Broken Homes, 115.   Interrelation of Factors, 120.   Relation of Family Influences to Community Background, 122.

5   THE DEVELOPMENT OF THE PROFESSIONAL CRIMINAL   125

The Professional Criminal, 125.   Transition from Juvenile Delinquency to Adult Crime, 126. The Criminal World, 137.

6   ORGANIZED CRIME   150

Organized Criminal Gangs, 151.   Criminal Syndicates, 154.
Racketeers, 159.   Political Graft and Corruption, 166.   Internal
Organization and Continuity of Organized Crime, 172.

7   CRIMINALS WHO LIVE IN THE NONCRIMINAL WORLD   180

The Casual Offender, 180.   The Occasional Offender, 181.   The
Episodic Offender, 189.   Segmental Crime, 190.

8   HABITUAL OFFENDERS   203

Personality of Habitual Offenders, 204.   Illegality of Habitual
Offenses, 207.   Relation of Habitual Offenders to Criminal Syndicates, 207.   Habitual Crime and Public Opinion, 208.   Drunkards,
210.   Drug Addicts, 216.   Habitual Sex Offenders, 220.   Gamblers, 223.   Vagrants and Related Types, 224.   Petty Thieves, 225.
Control of Habitual Crime, 226.

9   CRIMINALS WHO ARE SERIOUSLY MALADJUSTED   229

Maladjustment and Crime, 229.   Psychoses and Crime, 232.
Psychoneurosis, 238.   Psychopathic Personality, 240.   Incidence
of Maladjusted Criminals, 244.

10   PREVENTION OF DELINQUENCY AND CRIME   251

Community Reorganization, 254.   Family Reorganization, 274.
Adjustment of Emotional and Mental Disturbances, 275.   Public
Responsibility, 278.   Need for Unified Planning, 281.

PART TWO

Agencies of Law Enforcement and the Treatment of
Criminals

11   TREATMENT OF CRIMINALS—BACKGROUND   287

The Past in the Present, 288.   Imprisonment, a Recent Trend, 291.
Agencies of Law Enforcement, 293.   Failure of Past Methods, 297.
Scientific Approach to Reformation, 297.

12 THE POLICE   300

Relation of the Police to Criminals, 300. Number of Police, 301. Urban Police Systems, 301. The County Police System, 310. Coordination and Supplementation of Local Police Systems, 312. State Police, 315. Federal Police Systems, 316. The Criminal and the Police, 320. Criminal Investigation, 325. Evaluation of Police Activities, 330.

13 COURTS AND TRIALS   337

Courts of Inferior Criminal Jurisdiction, 337. Bail, 340. Grand Jury, 344. The Criminal Court, 345. The Trial, 346. The Prosecuting Attorney, 354. Criminal Defense, 358. Juvenile Courts, 362. Outcome of Legal Procedures, 369.

14 JAILS AND OTHER LOCAL INSTITUTIONS   376

Types and Functions of Jails, 376. Number of Jails and of Inmates, 377. Physical Condition of Jails, 377. Politics and the Fee System, 382. Offenders and Their Sentences, 384. Activities in Jails, 387. Release from Jail, 391. Suggestions for Improving the Treatment of Misdemeanants, 394.

15 PRISONS AND REFORMATORIES   398

Incidence of Penalties, 398. Development of Penal Institutions in the United States, 399. Prisons, 400. Prison Farms and Work Camps, 407. The Reformatory Movement, 413. Minimum Security Institutions, 415. Prison Systems, 419. State Systems, 426. Trends in Prison Development, 427.

16 LIFE IN PRISON: ADMINISTRATION AND CONTROL   431

Prison Population, 431. Prison Administration, 434. Guards, 437. Discipline, 440. Breakdown of Control, 446.

17 LIFE IN PRISON: SERVICES AND ACTIVITIES   456

Admission Systems, 456. Classification Systems, 457. Medical Services, 462. Psychiatric Services and Counseling, 464. Work for Prisoners, 466. Education for Prisoners, 476. Recreation in Prison, 482. Religious Services and Facilities, 485. Personal Relationships of Prisoners, 486. Effect of Imprisonment, 492.

18 THE WOMAN OFFENDER AND HER TREATMENT   499

Women in Jails, 499. Characteristics of Women Criminals, 500. Housing Women Criminals, 505. Women's Prisons and Reformatories, 506. Services and Activities, 508. Federal Reformatory for Women, 514. Comparison of Men's and Women's Penal Institutions, 517.

19 RELEASE OF THE CRIMINAL WITHOUT IMPRISONMENT   521

Difficulties of Readjustment, 521. Suspended Sentence, 522. Development of Probation, 523. Administration of Probation, 524. The Probationer, 527. The Federal Probation System, 529. Advantages and Disadvantages of Probation, 531. Results of Probation, 532. Evaluation of Probation, 535.

20 RELEASE OF THE CRIMINAL AFTER IMPRISONMENT   538

Methods of Release, 538. The Parole System, 539. The Parolee, 541. Preparation of the Prisoner for Parole, 546. Parole Supervision, 547. Advantages and Disadvantages of Parole, 548. Evaluation of Parole, 549. Pardons, 551. Unconditional Release of Felons, 552. Place of Probation and Parole in Rehabilitation, 554.

21 SUCCESS AND FAILURE OF THE RELEASED CRIMINAL   557

Extent and Types of Recidivism, 557. Factors Related to Recidivism, 559. Prediction of Noncriminal Behavior, 566. Reduction of Recidivism, 570.

22 TREATMENT OF OFFENDERS IN THE ARMED FORCES   573

Rejection of Criminals for Military Service, 574. The Uniform Code of Military Justice, 576. Military Police, 581. The Military Judicial System, 581. The Penal and Correctional System of the Armed Forces, 583. Wartime Military Acceptance of Criminals, 596. Characteristics of Military Offenders, 598. Military Justice Abroad, 604. Comparison of Military and Civilian Systems of Justice and Correction, 606.

23 EUROPEAN ADULT OFFENDERS AND PRISONS   611

Diffusion of Penal Methods, 611. General Observations, 613. Types of Offenders, 614. England and Wales, 618. France, 624. Denmark, 635. Sweden, 639. Norway, 642. Penological Comparisons, 652. Significant Procedures, 656. Cross-Fertilization, 658.

24 TRENDS AND FUTURE OBJECTIVES   662

Changes in Point of View, 662. Prevention of Crime, 664. Rehabilitation and Treatment, 664. Changes in Administration, 668. Community Responsibility, 671. Hindrances to Achievement of Goals, 673.

APPENDIX A: THEORIES OF CRIMINALITY   677

APPENDIX B: DEFINITIONS OF CRIMES   707

INDEX   711

Illustrations, Figures, and Tables

ILLUSTRATIONS

Map of ecological scheme of Chicago	79
Map of juvenile delinquency rates in Chicago, 1929–35	82
Map of residences of arrested females in Chicago, 1935	83
Map of first appearance in Boys' Court, Chicago, 1929–35	84
Map showing residences of arrested males in Chicago, 1935	85
Chicago slum showing street where children play	92
Skid row, West Madison Street, Chicago	93
Weapons seized from boys' gang in Los Angeles	130
Loot taken from house burglar	139
Murder in Little Italy, New York City	165
Checks representing a $780,000 swindle	188
"Cribs" in a southern city	209
Drunkard in doorway	213
Fireplace for use of boys' club, on roof of school building	263
Personal counseling in boys' club, Philadelphia	267
Basketball scene in boys' club, Philadelphia	268
Boys' club orchestra	269
Police training, Atlanta, Georgia	306
FBI training academy at Quantico, Virginia	318
FBI agents practicing with Thompson sub-machine gun	319
FBI agent preparing for a tool mark examination	325
Fingerprint files of FBI	327
Examination of typing by FBI agent	328
Antiquated county jail	379
Modern type of maximum security jail	382
Sing Sing in 1865	402
Steel cages in old-style southern road camp	409
Modern road camp in Virginia	409
Dormitory in a minimum security institution for men	417
Federal Reformatory, Chillicothe, Ohio	422
Illinois State Penitentiary, Stateville	422

Architect's plan for new penitentiary in New Mexico   427
Sweatbox in southern road camp   441
Overcrowding in a prison cell   451
X-ray equipment at Illinois State Penitentiary   463
Furniture factory at Illinois State Penitentiary   470
Maintenance work at Illinois State Penitentiary   473
Vocational training in federal prison   477
Barbershop at Illinois State Penitentiary   479
Library at the United States Penitentiary, Terre Haute, Indiana   484
Prison chapel at Illinois State Penitentiary   486
Inmate scrubbing floor of her room in reformatory for women   507
Federal Reformatory for Women, Alderson, West Virginia   515
Sewing shop at Federal Reformatory for Women   516
Women's prison in Paris (Maison d'Arrêt de la Roquette)   628
Dining room of women's prison in Paris   629
Central prison in Melun, France   630
Cell block in central prison, Melun, France   631
Recreation room at central prison, Melun, France   632
Shoe shop at central prison, Melun, France   633
Print shop at central prison, Melun, France   634
Women's prison, Oslo, Norway   646
Small living room, women's prison, Oslo   646
Inmate's room at women's prison, Oslo   647
Sewing room at women's prison, Oslo   648
Chapel at women's prison, Oslo   649
Central prison for men, Oslo   650
Woodwork shop at men's penitentiary, Oslo   651

FIGURES

1. Alternative types of integrated personalities   15
 2. The unsocialized personality   18
 3. Alternative types of frustrated personalities   19
 4. Percentage of two main types of major crime committed in 1952   42
 5. Percentage of each type of major crime committed in 1952   42
 6. Persons held for prosecution for major crimes, as a rate per 100,000
       population, 1952   44
 7. Persons held for prosecution for minor offenses, as a rate per 100,000
       population, 1952   45
 8. Age grouping of juvenile delinquents   46
 9. Arrests for specific crimes by age of offenders   48
10. Ratio of male to female arrests for theft, 1952   50
11. Ratio of male to female arrests for assault, 1952   51
12. Ratio of male to female arrests for minor violations, 1952   52
13. Marital status of federal male prisoners compared with the general
       population   57

14. Marital status of federal female prisoners compared with the general
    population   58
15. Percentage of 1,000 delinquent boys who were arrested during suc-
    cessive 5-year periods, from the time when their average age was
    14 until it was 29   65
16. Percentage of prisoners who were intoxicated, intemperate, or non-
    alcoholic at time of crime   216
17. Diagram of preventive methods   278
18. Percentage of offenses against the person cleared by arrest, 1952   331
19. Percentage of offenses against property cleared by arrest, 1952   331
20. Percentage of crimes cleared by arrest for cities of various popula-
    tions, 1952   332
21. Percentage of persons held for prosecution for serious offenses who
    were found guilty or not guilty, 1952   371
22. Percentage of persons held for prosecution for selected minor offenses
    who were found guilty or not guilty, 1952   372
23. Age distribution of women prisoners at admission   501
24. Distribution of offenses of women prisoners in reformatories   502
25. Percentage of women prisoners in each marital status   503
26. Percentage of juvenile delinquents who succeeded or failed during a
    15-year period that included probation   534
27. Percentage of prisoners with different kinds of release from state
    penal institutions, 1952   539
28. Percentage of men with success or failure in social relationships dur-
    ing postparole period who reformed or failed to reform   564
29. Percentage of parole violations of different types of criminals   567
30. Comparison of AWOL's and privates with reference to education   601
31. "In general, how do you feel most of the time, in good spirits or in
    low spirits?" (asked of AWOL's and privates)   602
32. "If it were up to you to choose, do you think you could do more for
    your country as a soldier or as a war worker?" (asked of AWOL's
    and privates)   602
33. "On the whole, do you think the army is giving you a chance to show
    what you can do?" (asked of AWOL's and privates)   603
34. "In general, how well do you think the army is run?" (asked of
    AWOL's and privates)   603

TABLES

1. Number and population of communities reporting to the Federal
   Bureau of Investigation, 1952   36
2. Offenses known to the police by size of city, 1952   43
3. Arrests by age groups, 1952, in 232 cities over 25,000 population   47
4. Incidence of crime per 10,000 for whites of native and foreign-born
   parentage, 15 years of age and over, for Buffalo and Detroit, 1930   63

5. Race and nativity of population and of juvenile delinquents, Chicago, 1929–35   64
6. Criminal records of 417 men, 15 years after expiration of parole from Massachusetts reformatory   66
7. Five hundred women 5 years after completion of term, Massachusetts State Reformatory for Women   66
8. Trends in offenses known to the police, for cities over 25,000 population   78
9. Comparison of crime rates with land use, Indianapolis   87
10. Delinquent boys and schoolboys from broken homes, by age   116
11. Percentage distribution of delinquents and nondelinquents, by type of home   118
12. Agencies appointing police chiefs, in cities over 25,000 population, for 1953   302
13. Percentage of different kinds of sentences given by different judges   352
14. Number of offenses and disposition of serious crimes for 208 cities over 25,000 population, 1952   370
15. Age of male prisoners admitted during 1 year to 4 state prisons   432
16. Sentences of male prisoners admitted during 1 year to 4 state prisons   432
17. Offenses for which male prisoners were sentenced to prison in 6 states   433
18. Recidivism among male prisoners admitted during 1 year to 5 state prisons   433
19. Marital status of male prisoners admitted during 1 year to 5 state prisons   434
20. Percentage of state and federal prisoners productively employed for different years   472
21. Value of production and number employed in state and federal prisons, 1923 and 1940   472
22. Educational level of male prisoners admitted during 1 year to 5 state prisons   481
23. Percentage of criminals placed on probation by type of crime   531
24. Percentage of prisoners released on parole from state prisons, by regions, 1952   538
25. Rating of prediction items, Joliet-Stateville and Menard divisions, Illinois State Penitentiary System   569
26. Experience table for 4,941 parolees, Joliet-Stateville and Menard divisions, Illinois State Penitentiary System, paroled 1940–45   570
27. Civilian and military prisoners, 1940–50   574
28. Principal offenses of Army and Air Force general prisoners   579
29. Record of Navy and Marine Corps offenders returned to duty   593
30. Educational level, Army and Air Force prisoner commitments, compared with educational level of enlisted men   599
31. General classification test scores of Army and Air Force prisoners and enlisted men   599
32. Attitudes toward being drafted expressed by soldiers and AWOL's in the United States, 1943–44   601

PART ONE

The Development and Prevention of Delinquent and Criminal Behavior

Criminal Behavior

Crime is a form of maladjustment whereby people fail to conform to certain standards of their society. In modern, urbanized society crime is a prevalent type of behavior, the study, prevention, and control of which absorbs the interest and efforts of a number of professional groups. The legislator formulates laws to embody the social standards; police, lawyers, and judges attempt to enforce the laws and to determine who the transgressors are; wardens of prisons, workhouses, and jails, together with their staffs, maintain custody and to some extent attempt to rehabilitate convicted criminals; psychiatrists, psychologists, and sociologists carry on research to unravel the network of causes of criminal behavior and, with social workers of all types, experiment with preventive and remedial programs. Finally, the public is intensely interested in criminal behavior, partly for its dramatic aspects, partly because it is often the victim, but also because through the force of public opinion and the financial provisions that people are ready to make for the prevention and control of crime, they are participants in crime even though they may never actually break a criminal law. The study of criminology and penology, therefore, is not only a specialty for professional groups alone but is also part of the preparation of all people for intelligent understanding of and participation in public life.

CRIME A LEGAL CONCEPT

Definition of Crime and Criminal

"Crime" and "criminal" are often loosely used to condemn any kind of behavior that the speaker regards as immoral or antisocial. A more exact use of the term reserves crime for acts that are a violation of criminal laws. These laws explicitly prescribe or prohibit certain types of behavior under threat of a specific penalty if the law is disobeyed. The justification of criminal laws is maintenance of the peace and security of the state. It follows

that the state takes the initiative in enforcing criminal laws and making public provision for apprehension, trials, and enforcement of penalties.   Crime,
therefore, is both a legal and a public concept.

"The criminal" is also carelessly used to designate anyone who shocks
one's sense of propriety or violates one's scheme of personal values, as well
as the person who disobeys criminal laws.   An exact definition of the criminal is the person who has confessed to or been convicted by a court of the
violation of a criminal law.   This definition is somewhat arbitrary, inasmuch
as a man who had committed a murder and not been detected would not be
a criminal; but after detection and conviction would be.   If he were never
convicted, even though he had committed the murder, he would not be a
criminal.   The distinction is not as artificial as it seems at first sight, for it
is part of our philosophy of justice that a man is innocent until convicted and
that the burden of conviction rests with the accuser.   Until the man is apprehended and has either confessed or been proven guilty in a trial, he is not
branded as a criminal nor can legal penalties be applied.   No matter what
his acts, he has the status and plays the role of a free citizen until proven
guilty.   Obviously this exact definition of criminal does not include the
body of men and women who secretively or openly commit crimes but are
not arrested or brought to trial.   Sometimes they are known but because of
prestige or protection are not accused of their crimes; sometimes it is simply
known that a crime has been committed but the offender is unknown.   For
this body of unapprehended violators we have no term.   They might be
called criminal deviants, legal nonconformers, or unofficial criminals.

The legal processes of apprehension, trials, and penalties are concerned
only with the accused or convicted criminal.   Preventive and remedial programs, however, often include the unapprehended criminal deviants.   Studies
of the etiology of criminal behavior also are as much concerned with unapprehended as with convicted criminals.

Traditional Crimes

Many crimes included in present-day criminal laws are heritages from the
distant past.   They are offenses that the crude tribes of early Europe branded
as wrong and that, before the time of criminal law, were the subject of private
vengeance on the part of the victim or his clan.   Such crimes include murder,
assaults and personal injuries, robbery, and burglary.   Even today when
criminal laws regulate a much wider array of behavior, these are the offenses
to which the citizen usually refers when he speaks of crime.

Because traditional crimes have had long and wide acceptance as wrongdoing, the consensus of public opinion condemning them is widespread and
all but unanimous.   When crimes clearly come under the categories of

murder, assault, robbery, or burglary, the legal processes run smoothly with the support of public opinion.

Crimes Growing Out of Change

When changes occur in society new situations arise that are not covered by the traditional laws inherited from past experience.   If the new situations offer opportunities for some individuals to exploit or injure others or if they interfere with the orderly operation of society, the safety and welfare of the society is threatened.   Modern societies meet these threats with the passage of new laws commanding or forbidding certain acts and attaching penalties to their violation.

Sometimes these new situations involve social relationships as groups are brought into a new juxtaposition.   The abolition of slavery created a new set of human relationships, for the regulation of which there were neither mores nor laws.   Traditionally Negroes had been slaves, controlled by their masters.   With abolition they acquired new rights and new relationships. Laws followed, sometimes to protect them (civil rights laws) and sometimes to limit their activities (forbidding of intermarriage with whites).

Another example of change in social relationships occurred with the Industrial Revolution.   When factories replaced home craftsmanship, previously independent workmen became subordinate to employers; large numbers of people working in one room replaced the small family group; children passed from the tutelage of their parents or, in the case of apprentices, their masters, to the control of impersonal supervisors.   As a consequence of the new relationships, many laws have been passed, such as those controlling child labor, workmen's compensation for injuries, safety devices, wages, and hours.

Other new situations not controlled by traditional laws arise from new material inventions whose use disturbs the old order and threatens injury to people or becomes a threat to public welfare.   The rapid adoption of the automobile was matched by equally rapid passage of laws to control its use.

The laws that arise out of new situations create new classes of criminals. Since the laws curb freedom, they are not always readily accepted or obeyed. Sometimes the law itself when first passed is declared unconstitutional by the courts.   For example, Roscoe Pound states that the highest court in New York held a workman's compensation act unconstitutional in 1911, and as late as 1920 a minority of the Supreme Court of the United States branded such acts as arbitrary, unreasonable, and unconstitutional.[1]   Even when a law is upheld by the courts, public opinion may reject it.   A minority and occasionally a majority of the public are quite likely not to approve of a newly passed criminal law.   Some people may obey a law upon principle, but in a democracy that has fostered individualism and independence of thought many feel that they have as great a right as the legislators to decide whether a certain relationship or act is or is not criminal. Some people disobey the law because it interferes with previously established habits or with their personal comfort or financial profit. Evasion of income tax laws, for instance, is practiced by many upright but protesting citizens. A few may regard a given law as an encroachment upon their rights and may disobey as a demonstration of their disapproval. Occasionally the state legislature itself will flaunt a federal act. An example of such failure to accept a federal act is the tendency of many southern states to pass laws to circumvent the Negro's constitutional right to vote. The most conspicuous recent example of inability to enforce new laws occurred in the 1920's and early 1930's in connection with prohibition laws. As a consequence, the Prohibition Amendment was repealed with the admission that public opinion opposed rather than favored it.

If the new situation continues and becomes part of the permanent social organization, a more unanimous public attitude toward regulation and control develops in time. With widespread acceptance and the passage of time, the law becomes part of the traditional heritage of criminal laws. Acceptance is often hastened by positive teaching of the values of the new law through such means as editorials, lectures, and indoctrination of school children.

Crimes Based on Emergencies

Often, in an emergency, it is necessary in the public interest to impose special regulations upon people. Lacking time in which to persuade people of the advisability of the regulations, public officials request legislators to pass laws backed by heavy penalties. Such laws are rather precipitately imposed upon the entire population. Since they almost always deprive people of rights or privileges that are considered legitimate, many protests and evasions follow. Examples of such laws and their violations are readily drawn from World War II, when gas, food, and shoes were rationed, and rents and prices controlled. Many normally law-abiding people temporarily became criminals and moreover condoned and catered to organized criminal groups that supplied them with coveted but forbidden articles through "black market" operations.

Usually these emergency laws are limited to the period of the emergency and are repealed or automatically become inactive with the end of the emergency. While they are in force, however, violators are handled through the criminal courts and are subject to fines or imprisonment.

Crime and Public Opinion

The discussion of new criminal laws suggests that crimes can be created or abolished with the passage or repeal of laws. In a heavily policed military state where laws are ruthlessly and uniformly enforced by physical dominance and severe penalties, such a situation may exist. In a democracy where individual opinion can express itself freely through speaking, writing, and elections, public opinion becomes the final arbiter in placing the opprobrium of crime upon a specific type of behavior. Even though laws are passed, it is impossible in the United States to enforce them through police action alone. Police forces are not sufficient in size; people move freely from state to state, finding new laws in each state to be compared with the laws of the earlier residence and rejected or accepted according to the judgment of the individual. In the face of some seemingly arbitrary designation of an act as criminal, people cling to their right to make independent decisions. When a law is not accepted, the police may attempt to enforce it against public opinion, but gradually the police yield to the pressure of public opinion, which they perhaps share. The law may remain on the statute books but be ignored by all. When public opinion supports the law, many pressures of an informal nature are brought against the violators to aid and lessen the police action.

Some Characteristics of Criminal Laws and Crime

The fact has already been mentioned that there is no one criminal law but a multitude of specific laws. Moreover, each state and the federal government has its own code of laws, no two of which are identical. Although the laws of many states or all states may designate specific acts as crimes, the definitions of these crimes and the penalties may differ widely. For example, murder is universally identified as a crime, but penalties vary from state to state, including life imprisonment, imprisonment for a term of years, and execution by hanging, electrocution, shooting, or in a gas chamber. Thus, even the old traditional crimes are not uniformly defined or penalized throughout the United States. More newly designated crimes are still less uniform in their inclusion in criminal codes. In addition to federal laws, we have, therefore, in the United States 48 autonomous legal systems, each independently arrived at by state legislative action and enforced by local or state courts. Furthermore, the military system has its own laws, police, courts, and penal institutions that operate in military reservations in independence of the laws of the state where the reservation is located.

Another characteristic of crime is that it refers to overt behavior—acts performed or threats expressed.   Usually, however, it is behavior backed up by intent to perform the act.   The purely accidental act is not crime, although gross negligence that results in injury to someone may constitute the act a crime.   An act of self-defense that is identical with a criminal act is not a crime, even though it leads to the death of a person.   A criminal act resulting from emotional stress makes the person less culpable than a premeditated act.   On the other hand, ignorance that one is violating a criminal law often cannot be used as a defense.   Thus, not only the act but the motivation is taken into account, although not uniformly for all crimes.   The situation may be illustrated by the act of killing someone.   Killing that is premeditated and carries the intent to kill is regarded as the most serious offense and draws the heaviest penalty.   Unpremeditated killing under the stress of emotion is less severely condemned and draws a lighter penalty. Killing another through negligence merits only a light penalty.   Purely accidental killing receives no penalty.   Killing in self-defense often is praised and approved.   Finally, to complete the series, police and men in the armed services are taught to kill in the interest of maintaining law and order and in public defense; awards are often conferred upon those who have killed conspicuously large numbers of the enemy.   This illustration shows how the overt act and the motivation are considered together in determining the criminality of an act.

The principle that crime consists of intentional acts implies understanding of the nature of the acts.   Two classes of people are exempted from criminal liability although they may commit criminal acts.   One class is children under the age of 7 years, who are assumed not to understand the nature of their acts.   The other is people of any age who are unable to distinguish between right and wrong by reason of insanity or feeble-mindedness.

Crimes are legally classified into certain categories.   The most highly condemned and severely punished crimes are called felonies.   They include murder, assaults, and the more serious forms of stealing; the penalty is usually death or a long term of imprisonment.   Misdemeanors are less injurious crimes punished by fines or short terms of imprisonment usually in jails or workhouses; typical misdemeanors are minor thefts, drunkenness, or disorderly conduct.   Juvenile delinquency applies to misconduct of children and youths under a stated age (usually 18 years) and includes many types of behavior thought undesirable for children, but not necessarily violations of criminal laws.

CONCEPTS ALLIED TO THE CRIMINAL CONCEPT

Nonconformity

Sociologists are interested in nonconformity, whether it is that of the criminal, the political rebel, or the creative inventor. Nonconformity is a relative term that implies a standard against which deviation may be measured. The usual standard is the values (ideal goals) or the norms (approved behavior) of a given society. The nonconformer deviates from one or both. His deviation is criminal if the standards are identical with criminal laws, but it is not *necessarily* criminal since the values and norms may not be incorporated into criminal laws. Values and norms define approved behavior in situations that have existed for a long period of time. In new situations and relationships, however, people may act impulsively or individually, since time is required for the slow growth and wide acceptance of values and norms. In the meantime, laws may be passed in an effort to control behavior—laws for which there are no corresponding values and norms. Consequently, there are then no values and norms from which to deviate, although violation of the law may constitute criminal behavior. Values, norms, and criminal law, therefore, are closely related but not necessarily identical.

When, with the passage of time, values, norms, and criminal laws have become co-ordinated and support one another, deviation from one is also deviation from the other two. For example, we believe a person's home should be safe from intruders (value); people are therefore taught to knock at doors and wait for permission to enter (norm); if there is no response or the householder refuses to admit the person, he is expected to leave peacefully. Criminal statutes explicitly define unlawful entering as criminal. A person who forceably or without permission enters someone's home violates our values, norms, and criminal laws, all of which uniformly protect the sanctity of the home.

Many values and norms, however, pertain to types of conduct whose violation does not constitute a crime. Keeping lawns and homes clean and neat, helping old people across the street, being courteous to strangers, sending children to religious school, and many other patterns of daily living are all widely held norms that reflect values; the deviant may be disapproved or informally reprimanded, but he has not violated a criminal law and does not run the risk of arrest, trial, and official penalty.

Values and norms differ from group to group and from institution to institution. Each ethnic group has values and norms that differentiate it from all other ethnic groups; rural values and norms differ to some extent from urban; and each region has some distinctive peculiarities. In the institutional realm, each religion has distinguishing values and norms; large universities differ in their ideals and methods from small colleges; business has values that differ from those of government. By adhering to the values and norms of one institution, a person may violate the values and norms of another. Great freedom in choice of subcultural groups and institutions is granted people; consequent deviations from the patterns of other institutions are to be expected. All such groups and institutions function, however, under the control of the criminal laws of the state or federal government. When a person, in conforming to the dictates of the small group, violates the criminal laws, he is treated as a criminal regardless of how sure he is of the rightness of the small-group values and norms. Thus, when members of the religious group known as Jehovah's Witnesses refused because of religious principles to register for the draft during World War II, they were tried in federal courts and sentenced to federal penitentiaries. In the eyes of their religious group they were honored martyrs; according to the federal laws they were criminals. When a group of people is convinced of the rightness of its views, members of the group often find the approval of their own consciences and of other members of the in-group a stronger motivation to behavior than the impersonal abstraction of the criminal law, even though winning the in-group approval is accompanied by criminal status in the community at large.

Sin

Sin is a religious concept that signifies disobedience of divine law. Specific sins vary from one religious system to another. Sins may be punished by the religious institution. If an act defined as sin by a religious institution is also defined as a crime in the criminal laws, a sinner would also be a criminal. Generally, in the United States adultery is regarded by religious groups as a sin; all states have some type of law making adultery a criminal act (although the laws are not rigorously enforced). Adultery might, therefore, be called both a sin and a crime. Some religions regard suicide or attempted suicide as a sin; but few states define suicide as a crime. Sin and crime therefore are two different concepts, both applying to disapproved behavior but receiving their meaning from different basic concepts. The fact that the same act may be both sin and crime does not make the two concepts identical.

Vice

Vice refers to behavior that is degrading or debased. Usually it connotes behavior primarily injurious to the person performing the act and only incidentally injurious to others. In the United States many personal vices are penalized by criminal laws, such as habitual drunkenness, many irregular forms of sex behavior, gambling, the use of narcotic drugs, and vagrancy. In any realistic approach to an understanding of crime, these forbidden personal vices must be distinguished from such crimes as murder, assaults, and stealing, which are injurious to other persons than the criminal. A vicious habit may be not only a crime if so defined by law but also a sin if some religious groups regard the vice as a violation of divine law.

A THEORY OF CRIMINAL BEHAVIOR

Criminal law sets aside certain types of behavior considered inimicable to public welfare and establishes penalties for violations. The objective of the penalties is partly to exact some suffering from the criminal for his misdeeds, partly to reform, and partly to deter others. As soon as attention shifts from the legal aspects of criminal law to the criminal, a multitude of new questions arises and new areas for study are opened. Why do people commit crimes? How may they be prevented from disobeying criminal laws? How may convicted criminals be set in the patterns of legal conventionality? The center of interest becomes the human being, his motivations for behavior, the processes by which he became a criminal nonconformer, and the methods of education and personality development by which he may be deterred or rehabilitated.

The Search for Causes

Many attempts have been made to find a single explanation for criminal behavior. In the past the attitude has usually been that conventional and moral behavior was normal and natural, and that deviations had to be explained. The explanations ranged over a wide field. To some, the criminal was a person who had allied himself with the supernatural forces of evil. Phrenology sought to account for specific types of crime according to the under- or over-development of certain portions of the brain. Early sociological studies in the nineteenth century began to connect criminal behavior with social and economic backgrounds and childhood experiences. These studies were superseded by those of Lombroso and Ferri, who became convinced that the criminal was a special biological type, a throwback to a primitive, savage stage of development. In time the atavistic theory was disproved, only to be followed by another unitary theory, that feeble-mindedness was the primary cause of criminal behavior. Careful use of mental tests dispelled this theory. With the greater development of sociology and the psychological sciences since 1915, two chief points of view have developed, both of which share a common theory that criminal behavior develops from previous experiences rather than from some inborn biological or psychological factor.   Sociologists tend to over-emphasize the social factors in experience; psychologists and psychiatrists the individual and mental factors. Obviously, a correlation of the two approaches is needed.

A detailed summary of theories of criminality is contained in Appendix A for those who wish a historical background to present conceptions.   The following discussion in this chapter states a theory based on both sociological and psychological concepts.

All Behavior Purposive

Criminal behavior springs not from the person's direct disregard for criminal laws or from a willful choice of wrongdoing; it is motivated by the desire or compulsion to satisfy inner drives, needs, and desires.   This statement rests on the theory that all behavior is purposive and has some value for the person—a theory applicable equally to conventional and criminal behavior.   The inner motivations that initiate the behavior may be simple biological drives, as the necessity for food; or socially acquired needs, as for higher education in a society where knowledge and skills lead to prestige and wealth.   Although the baby may seem to have few needs, the number of needs increases constantly with bodily maturing and widening of social experience.   Even the young child has many needs; the adult has a vast number.   The needs may be consciously felt by the person, who is then able to state his needs and to plan for their fulfillment; or they may be half-recognized or unconscious but still compulsive in nature, demanding satisfaction.   Finally, the needs fall into a hierarchy of urgency and importance to the individual; some must be satisfied at any cost to prevent unhappiness or even death, while others may more easily be discarded if not fulfilled. These needs may be thought of as internal physical or mental tensions whose normal release is found either in covert mental processes, such as imagination, or in overt behavior.   This general theory of the relation of behavior to internal needs is applicable to conventional behavior; to criminal behavior; and to neurotic, psychopathic, and psychotic behavior.

Learned Criminal Behavior

Much, perhaps most, criminal behavior is learned behavior.   Many groups of people customarily violate one, a few, or many criminal laws. Children who are reared in these groups learn the attitudes and behavior of crime through the process of socialization.

1. Socialization.   The explanation of the type of behavior that is learned lies in the relationship between inner needs and the external social environment in which the needs must find expression. This social environment defines needs through established values and norms, modifies their mode of expression, and provides institutional and other patterns through which satisfactions may be secured. Corresponding to the social patterns are behavior roles that individuals may follow, roles that help to organize their behavior. These roles consist largely of a self-conception and a set of personal habits that are both persistent in the individual and recognized and accepted by the community.

During childhood, needs are defined by the groups in which the individual has membership. These are usually the family, the informal playgroup, and any formal groups that the child may belong to, such as religious school or kindergarten. The child is expected to satisfy his needs according to the customs of his groups. Many new needs are created for the child through his identification with other (usually older) members of his groups and his desire for their approval and love. For example, on the biological level the child is taught toilet habits, table manners, and sleeping habits, through praise for accomplishments and penalties for failures. On the social level, he is taught to be competitive and to try to surpass his peers; he is commended for high grades in school, scolded for low ones. Moreover, the child's groups place needs in a hierarchy of values; some needs are more important than others and greater effort is expected of the child to achieve these highly valued needs. It is, for example, important for the child to have toys; but it is more important for him to be honest; therefore he is forbidden to steal toys even though he otherwise will have no toys. Thus, through the pressure of his immediate groups the child learns which needs he may express freely, which suppress; he learns the approved modes of expression; and he acquires a growing number of needs. If he learns well, he is rewarded by love, approval, and sometimes by tangible gifts; if he fails to learn, he is punished by disapproval, denial of privileges, and sometimes physical pain. As he accepts the social definitions of needs and how to fulfill them, he acquires a conscience.

The above statement gives the abstract process. Exactly what the child learns is dependent upon the groups of which he is a member—the specific family, play group, school, and so on. In a minority of families, honesty is not taught and the child may receive recognition and praise for dishonesty. In Shaw's account of the jack-roller, Stanley describes the parental approval of stealing in the neighborhood and his stepmother's practice of sending him with his older stepbrother, first to pick rags and bottles in alleys, later to break into box cars and steal food for the family's use, and, as an accomplished thief, to steal from stores and markets.[2] The process of socialization was the same as in a conventionally honest family, but the habits taught and the scale of values were very different. Another example of family teaching that led to delinquent behavior is found in the family of beggars described by Gilmore.[3] For over 60 years and through 5 generations, habits of dependency and skills of begging passed from parents to children. After a time, a philosophy of begging supported the way of life and the family lived in a beggars' social world without guilt or misgivings. In these and similar families children learn to satisfy their needs through delinquent behavior that receives the approval of family and neighborhood.

The influence of the neighborhood is strongly emphasized by McKay.[4] The child's play groups may follow patterns of delinquent behavior, with young children either learning the patterns from older children or developing them at random in an attempt to satisfy needs. In either case, the peer group gives approval and praise to each individual. Stanley, referred to above, stated that in his neighborhood in Chicago's slums, stealing was a common pastime of the boys, from little tots to adolescents. Boys who had served sentences in penal institutions were the heroes of streetcorner and alley. *The Gang* by Thrasher also shows how delinquent patterns become customary for boys' gangs with each new member being inducted into the activities and gaining prestige in accordance with his daring and skill.[5]

When, as sometimes happens, the family and the play group both approve delinquent behavior, the child is almost certain to accept such behavior as proper and normal. The school, church, community center, and police may all disapprove, but the primary groups of family and playmates usually are stronger in their influence and more pervasive in their contacts with the child than the more formal institutional organizations. Thus the child will accept a role that is approved in his immediate group, though disapproved by the larger society. His conception of himself, gained from his primary groups, will be that he is an upright person, and he will be uninfluenced by the opinion of the communal groups.

Delinquent behavior, therefore, is learned behavior when the child's most satisfying contacts are with delinquent groups. From these groups he learns to satisfy his needs in legally condemned ways, which are, however, approved by the groups whose praise is most important to him. He learns and follows the delinquent behavior without sense of guilt. When he is caught and punished by school officials or police, the punishment is something to be endured as stoically as possible. It makes little impression because the fundamental elements of a learning situation are absent: he has no identification with the school teacher or policeman and does not desire their love and approval. He does not strive to emulate their roles; he does not accept their conception of his personality.

Figure 1 diagrams the processes that lead to socially learned conventional and criminal behavior, as well as to maladjusted behavior.

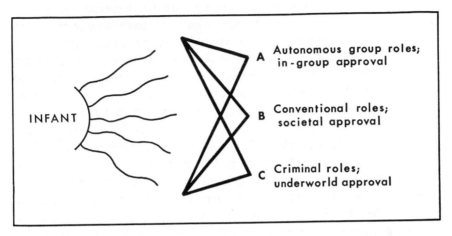

FIGURE 1

Alternative types of integrated personalities.   In all three types the person organizes his innate drives (shown by the wavy lines) into roles devised and approved by some definite group; by accepting the roles he secures status in the appropriate group.   The fact that his roles are condemned by one of the other groups does not greatly disturb him.   However, the strongest of the 3 groups may try to force compliance with its standards and roles through legislative and police action, fines, or imprisonment.   Thus, society as a whole (B) may penalize divergent religious or political groups (A) by passing laws that make at least some of their behavior illegal; through criminal laws, group C is constantly penalized for divergent behavior.

2. *Alternative satisfactions.*   As has been implied, society not only defines needs and their modes of satisfaction, but also provides approved means of satisfaction.   Prestige is approved and for the boy who yearns to stand above his fellows schools provide class offices, academic honors, and athletic awards.   Industriousness is also approved and the boy or girl finds that he can become productive through craft classes, part-time employment, or helping his parents.   There are many alternative ways of satisfying each need; the system of satisfactions is varied and flexible.

Many of the alternative patterns have social approval.   There are numerous choices as to how a person may make a living, where he may live, the type of home he builds, what recreation he will seek.   But systematic patterns of delinquent and criminal behavior also exist.   At the juvenile level a familiar systematic pattern includes persistent truancy, gang membership, stealing food, and sleeping in hallways; specialization of roles in stealing; knowledge of hideaways from the police; facile lying to parents, teachers, and police; and dependence on the gang for friendship, loyalty, and protection.   An adult system of criminal behavior is found among pickpockets, small groups of whom co-operate in stealing, each with a special role to play; the group is dependent upon a "fence" who buys stolen jewelry and often upon a co-operative patrolman who may be paid not to make arrests.   The pickpockets have prearranged meeting places where they come after their work is done; family life often is adjusted to the demands and dangers of their occupation.   Here is a complete mode of life providing for income, friends, security, and family life that is an alternative to a job and its accompanying conventional patterns of home, friendship, and protection. Here is a criminal social role ready and waiting for someone to fill it.

Many of these criminal patterns of behavior offer satisfactions without demanding as much effort or self-denial as conventional modes.   The gang boy may be highly lauded by his companions for a daring theft of a few moments' duration, whereas similar approval from schoolmates might come only after many weeks of athletic practice in order to kick a football over the goal line or shoot a ball through the basket.   The band of bank robbers may steal in a few minutes what it would take them a lifetime to earn.   True, such crimes require skill and daring, but the rewards often are high in relation to the time and effort involved.   Also, there is always some danger of detection and arrest; but the ratio of convictions to crimes is so low that the skillful criminal takes the chance of conviction in his stride.

Many people do not affiliate themselves completely with the criminal world but in a few areas find it less taxing and more satisfying to violate the laws than to follow them.   An otherwise law-abiding man may find the services of a prostitute, who makes only a financial demand, an easier way to satisfy sexual drives and the need for feminine companionship than marriage with its many responsibilities.   The bank clerk may be exemplary in his family and community conduct but regularly supplement his salary by stealing from the bank.

3. Roles and self-conceptions.   As the person becomes integrated into groups and institutions, he accepts habitual ways of acting, already existent in the group folkways and approved by the group.   Such recognized constellations of habits constitute social roles.   Roles define the functions that the person will play in the group and give him the specific duties and obligations that he must perform.   Roles, therefore, are not general but specific. For example, the leadership role is specific for each group.   In the family, the father exhibits leadership through support and protective authority.   In a club, leadership is vested in the president.   In the delinquent gang, the one who plans and directs activities is the leader.

Although the specific functions of a given role differ from group to group, the personal satisfactions may be the same. The responsible father, the successful club president, and the gang boy who leads his followers through a successful burglary may all feel the same glow of satisfaction and receive group approval. Similarly, the person who "lets down" his group—who plays the role of failure—feels his degradation, whether the group is the family, church, athletic team, or criminal gang.

Roles are composed not only of functions but also of self-conceptions. The person comes to believe that he is personally whatever his role indicates. He thinks of himself as leader, follower, a scholar, an athlete, or a criminal according to the role he plays. Since the group reacts to him in terms of his role, his self-conception is constantly reinforced, and he integrates his activities, attitudes, and interests around the dominant roles that he plays. Satisfaction accrues to the person to the degree that he fulfills his role and receives group approval, echoed by his own self-approval.

4. *The community and the criminal subgroup.* The delinquent or criminal who develops through membership in delinquent or criminal groups eventually finds himself the subject of two contrasting group conceptions. In the criminal group he may play a highly skilled and admired role (for instance, the skillful pickpocket); he may conceive of himself pridefully as a successful person. The conventional community, however, regards his role as reprehensible, degraded, criminal. The criminal maintains his self-respect, however, by confining himself to the criminal world, by rationalizing his conduct, and by depreciating the attitude of the conventional world. Thus he remains an integrated personality, but at the same time an unregenerate deviate according to community standards or the criminal law.

Among those who have accepted criminal roles we may expect as adequate integration of personality, as firm a conscience, as full acceptance of social roles as among noncriminals. The orientation, however, is to a subgroup—a criminal gang or an underworld—rather than to society at large. Somewhere in the process of socialization a criminally deviant group has taken precedence over conventional society as the dominant social milieu in which personality is formed.

Maladjustment as the Basis of Criminal Behavior

In addition to learned criminal behavior another general type of criminal behavior appears—criminal acts that result from the failure of a person to find satisfactions through any process of socialization, whether conventional or criminal. The emphasis in a discussion of crime emanating from personal maladjustment should be on the maladjustment; the criminal acts, although very harmful to the victims, are incidental to the basic maladjustment. Nevertheless, in the treatment of maladjusted criminals, the crime is usually the focus for whatever action is taken.   Only in a minority of cases, when a clearly defined psychosis is present, is the offender likely to be treated as a psychologically disturbed person rather than as a criminal. As with learned criminal behavior, the processes involved in maladjusted criminal behavior can be identified.   *Searchlights on Delinquency* analyzes a number of processes.[6]   It has been shown that needs demand satisfaction, although the satisfaction does not necessarily come through conventional channels.   Sometimes people are unable to secure satisfaction of one or more needs through any social relationship, conforming or delinquent. When a need is not satisfied, the person typically feels frustrated and un-

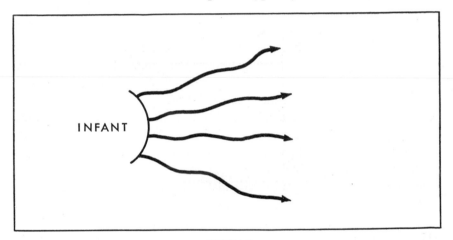

FIGURE 2

The unsocialized personality.   Here, as in Figure 1, the wavy lines represent urgent natural drives, which, without social definition and control, lead to behavior that is unfocused, contradictory, and socially disapproved.   A minority of persons falls into the category of unsocialized personalities and finds it difficult to accept social codes and social control.   These people live according to individual whims and impulses, rejecting restraints and authority.   The term *psychopathic* often is applied to certain types of unruly, unsocialized personalities.   Psychopathic persons frequently come into conflict with criminal laws and are among the most difficult of prisoners, since they cannot accommodate themselves to the regimentation of a penal institution and usually refuse psychiatric help when it is offered.

happy.   It is obvious that no one grows up without numerous frustrations; usually the child learns to dissipate some frustrations by concentrating upon the satisfaction of other needs or he accepts an alternative satisfaction to the one originally desired.   An important part of the process of personality development is learning how to handle frustrations without becoming disorganized.   Sometimes the child does not learn this important lesson or the frustrations are so long continued or so deeply seated that he cannot overcome them. One of several processes may then occur, the most common of which are illustrated in Figures 2 and 3.

Sometimes the person bottles up his tensions and seeks to allay them through withdrawing from traumatic relationships and experiences, or attempts to find satisfactions in daydreams. He may completely repress and succeed in forgetting his difficulties, although the tension remains as a factor in his behavior. People who thus try to solve their frustrations internally are maladjusted, but they are not delinquent.

Other people react overtly to unsatisfied needs. Their anxieties, hostili-

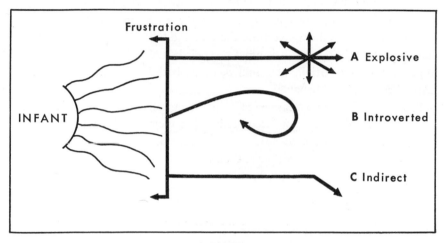

FIGURE 3

Alternative types of frustrated personalities. When innate drives are not organized and needs are not met in a realistic manner, the person may develop some habitual method of securing satisfaction outside of approved roles. Type A may habitually meet frustrations in an explosive and hostile manner that may take the form of anger, fighting, or murder. Type B withdraws from the harsh, frustrating world and takes refuge in daydreaming or, in extreme cases, in psychosis that permits him to construct an unreal but satisfying world. Type C finds indirect ways to satisfy needs, sometimes in socially approved activities, sometimes through neurotic reactions or compulsions. Any one of the three types may, in seeking satisfaction, injure another person, appropriate or destroy property, or violate mores or laws, thus calling down upon themselves criminal penalties.

ties, inferiority feelings, and other evidences of unsatisfied needs find outward expression of a destructive nature. As children these people often have been unable to ally themselves closely with any intimate group to which they could give loyalty and from which they could develop a conscience, a satisfying self-conception, or a suitable social role. Denied the opportunity for identification with a primary group or a friendly adult, such people are impulsive and unrestrained in behavior. Supremely egocentric, they have never had adequate motivation to curb their impulses, their hostilities, their hates. Inexperienced in love and security, they are unable to depend upon others or to give affection to others. They have no feeling of assurance that their needs will be satisfied by others or in any group relationship. Each stands alone, his back against a wall of fear, his hand raised against all others. The relationship to others is hostile, exploitative, defiant, and rejecting, a duplication of the treatment that these maladjusted people have received from others. They feel that any gratification they secure must be wrested by force from others—it will never be freely given. Although they are not necessarily criminal, from among them come a certain number of rebels, forever unable to fit themselves into the give and take of group relationships, continuously resisting and in conflict. Their behavior is individualistic and impulsive; it is not socially determined, as are both learned delinquency and learned conventional behavior.

Such persons have no clear conception of themselves and no definite social role to play. They are not integrated within themselves nor do they gain approval from either a conventional or a criminal group. They may crave identification with some group but their inner conflicts and tensions prevent both personal and social adjustment.

Basis of Criminal Behavior in Interaction

The foregoing discussion points up clearly that criminal behavior, like all behavior, is developed in interaction between the criminal and others; and that this interaction takes place in an active social situation that sets the standards and exerts pressures for conformity. Criminal behavior, like all behavior, is an effort on the part of the person to satisfy needs in a given social environment, or is a result of some failure in the normal process of need-satisfaction. No special theory is needed to explain criminal behavior. It is not necessary to posit criminal instincts, inherited criminality, abnormal physical anomalies, or special inborn mental quirks, to understand criminal behavior.

TYPES OF CRIMINALS

In the interactional process, no one sequence of acts will necessarily lead to delinquency or crime. Too many factors enter in to make a sure prediction of criminal behavior possible. Also, crime, as legally defined, includes so many different types of behavior that it would be unreasonable to expect all of them to have the same etiology. It is difficult, therefore, to relate types of crime to types of personality development. Nevertheless, in order to organize discussion in succeeding chapters it is desirable to make a tentative classification of criminals.   Since a person is not a criminal until he has been convicted of a crime, any classification must start with the crime itself and look backward to preceding factors.

Inadequate Classifications

Many classifications are in current use, each of which has a certain usefulness, none of which is adequate for an understanding of criminal behavior.

Class of crime: This classification usually divides crimes into those against the person (assaults and murder); those against property (various forms of stealing, vandalism, and destruction of property); and those against public safety (riots, treason, and so forth).   This classification shows in a general way which types of crime are prevalent in a given society and the trends that exist over a period of time.

Specific crimes: Classification by specific crimes (as murder, manslaughter, robbery, armed robbery, grand larceny, petty larceny, and so on) gives a more exact picture of criminal activities than does the more simple division into classes of crime.

Penalties: Penalties are usually capital punishment; imprisonment of varying lengths of time, sometimes combined with hard labor or solitary confinement; fines; and suspended sentence or probation.   When related to crimes, penalties show the seriousness with which society regards each crime.   They also show regional variations among the states.

Age: The chief legal division by age is into juvenile delinquents and adult criminals, with the laws of each state defining the age limits for juvenile delinquents.   In courts and institutions other age divisions are made.   Some cities have special courts for offenders above the juvenile court age but under 21, and some states have a series of institutions for juveniles, young adult offenders, and older offenders.   Age classifications are closely related to understanding of the development of criminal behavior as well as to provisions of adequate facilities for handling each age group.

Sex: Comparison of male and female offenders in number and type of offense raises many questions of differential factors in the etiology of criminal behavior among males and females.

Psychological reactions: This classification is useful in determining legal responsibility for crimes, since insane people are not held responsible for their crimes; among juvenile delinquents it is also used to study types of maladjustment and treatment.

Physical traits: From time to time efforts are made to classify criminals according to physical traits, but so far these classifications have not been of practical use and, in fact, are of doubtful validity.

A Socio-psychological Classification of Criminals

Although the law is content to prove that a crime has been committed by a specific person and to apply the stated penalty, both prevention of crime and rehabilitation of criminals demand a socio-psychological understanding of the origin and development of criminal behavior. The most useful classification for these purposes rests on the theory of criminal behavior already outlined. The chief factors in the classification are the degree of the person's withdrawal or exclusion from the control of the dominant social organization, and his inability to find satisfaction for his needs in that organization. It is probable that no one has been absolutely law-abiding at every moment of his life; nevertheless, most people seem able to manage their lives without disorganization to their own personalities or danger to those around them. With this group of essentially law-abiding people we are not concerned. Those whose violations occur often enough or are serious enough to provoke police attention fall into 5 types, with subtypes bringing the total to 12.

1. Conformers to a subcultural group. From time to time members of some subcultural group in the United States find themselves arrested and charged with violation of a state or federal law. Religious groups, cults, and experimental social groups sometimes make rules for their members that are contrary to criminal laws. In following the dictates of their group, members automatically disobey the criminal laws and are liable to arrest and prosecution as criminals. Usually, the group rules do not require malicious behavior toward the larger community, although they may violate social values as well as the laws of the larger society and thus shock or antagonize the public. The members of these small cultural groups in general conform to the laws of the larger society except in the few types of behavior where their small-group rules contradict the laws.

An example of such contradiction occurred in March, 1944, when 50 men were arrested in Utah by state and federal authorities. They were variously charged with violation of the Mann Act or with promoting polygyny. These people, members of a religious sect called the Fundamentalists, firmly believed that polygynous marriages were right and proper. The wives knew each other, and the husband supported his numerous dependents. According to their own beliefs polygyny was not a criminal offense although it was a violation of the state and federal code.

Since these groups are few in number and the criminal violations do not create a serious problem, they will not be discussed further.

2. Essentially law-abiding violators. Many people whose lives are organized conventionally nevertheless from time to time violate criminal laws.

Often valued members of the community, they are not able to bring their personal lives into complete conformity with restrictions upon their behavior; or under the pressure of some crisis, they burst forth with impulsive unplanned or violent behavior. In terms of the theory of criminal behavior previously set forth, some portion of their needs is not satisfied conventionally; or under stress they are not able to adjust conventionally to the demands of an unusual situation, but revert to individualized impulsive behavior. There are 3 subtypes.

The casual offender: The casual offender, who violates only minor laws and local ordinances, chiefly for his own convenience, is scarcely a criminal. He is well illustrated by the many arrests for violations of parking ordinances, failure to observe speed laws and traffic signs, destruction of property on Halloween, drunken driving on New Year's Eve, and rioting after football games.

The occasional criminal: The occasional criminal is essentially law abiding, but either once or occasionally commits a crime, usually of a minor nature. He does not justify his act with any philosophy of crime and may never repeat the offense, since he looks to the conventional world for satisfactions and tends to accept its definition of behavior. Therefore, he is ashamed and embarrassed when the community censures him, or casually accepts the discovery of his act and subsequent punishment if the community treats his crime lightly. This type of criminal is illustrated by the following cases.

A 16-year-old circus roustabout, aided by a friend, set fire to a large menagerie tent after he had been discharged for slow work. The two tossed lighted cigarettes into the dry straw with the intention of burning the circus, in revenge for the dismissal. The resulting fire destroyed both the tent and 39 animals with a loss of $200,000.

A man of 24 was fined $100 and costs, and his driver's license was revoked for 30 days, after the automobile he was driving had struck and injured a boy riding a bicycle. He was charged with leaving the scene of an accident and failing to give aid to the injured.

The episodic criminal: The episodic criminal, a term used by Ploscowe to describe the person who commits a crime, usually a serious one, when under some great emotional stress, is essentially a noncriminal.[7] Such a person lives in the conventional world and abides both by laws and unwritten mores. But for some reason he is unable to adjust satisfactorily to a specific crisis, usually of an emotional nature, and reacts in an explosive manner. The crisis may arise suddenly and produce an immediate reaction, as when a woman leaves her husband for another man and the husband shortly thereafter kills both wife and rival. Or the crisis may develop over a long period of time with the emotional conflict smoldering beneath the surface before it erupts into criminal action.

The case of Frank Fulton illustrates the episodic criminal. In a wild emotional outburst he killed 5 persons, against only one of whom he had a grudge. Armed with a shotgun he started out to hunt his divorced wife, whom he had abused and to whom he had to pay $25 a week alimony. Failing to find his wife, he vented his hatred against others. He killed 4 persons and wounded 2 at the house where he had believed he would find his wife. He then went to the home of the judge who had granted the divorce and shot and killed him as he stood in a window. He next proceeded to the police station where he wounded one man before he was disarmed.

In all 3 types, the criminal behavior is incidental and is not part of an organized criminal pattern of life. Casual, occasional, and episodic offenders do not follow a systematized criminal pattern of life, do not support a criminal philosophy, and are not members of criminal social groups. Their criminal activities do not constitute a continuous chain through the years but are isolated occurrences. Unfortunately, the episodic or explosive type of crime often is an assault upon another person and serious in its consequences.

3. *The segmental criminal.* The descriptive term, "white-collar criminal," has been applied to businessmen who, in the course of legitimate business, augment their profits through illegal activities. Like the casual, occasional, and episodic criminals, they live in the conventional world and uphold law and order, except with respect to certain business practices. Unlike casual, occasional, and episodic criminals, however, their illegal activities are not incidental but tend to become a regular part of their business operations. Their criminal attitudes and activities form a segmental part of their personalities and lives, unintegrated into the total personality. Disorganization over the seeming conflict in attitudes and behavior is prevented by confining illegal activities to one realm—business—and defending them by rationalizations. Since the illegal acts are sometimes carried out by corporations, a sense of personal guilt and responsibility is lessened.

In 1945, during the sugar shortage, the Office of Price Administration charged in a federal court that a certain corporation manufacturing ice-cream mixes, fruit flavors, and the like had violated its allotment of sugar by securing in addition a large supply of cane syrup. The sugar allotment was approximately 24,000 pounds; the syrup was the equivalent of an additional 40,000,000 pounds. The manufacturer argued that syrup was not sugar; hence he had committed no violation. The Office of Price Administration maintained that the syrup, made from sugar cane and usable by the manufacturer only when it had been reduced to sugar, was in fact sugar.

The court agreed with this view and issued an injunction restraining the manufacturer from acquiring more syrup.   Before buying the syrup the manufacturer had secured a legal opinion stating that contracting for it was not a violation of his sugar allotment.   The act was, however, an evasion of the rationing regulations, since the syrup otherwise could have been made into sugar and released for general public use.

In terms of our theory of criminal behavior, white-collar criminals are people to whom a strict ethical sense has not been taught or who find themselves affiliated with business organizations where respected members of the community follow criminal practices.   Often the simple rules of acceptable behavior learned in youth seem remote and inapplicable to the complex and impersonal business relationships.   The individual tends, therefore, to accept the attitudes and practices of the business organization.

4. *Professional criminals.*   Casual and occasional criminals verge into the class of full-time criminals whose personalities are integrated around a criminal philosophy of life and who find their roles and status among other criminals.   They are opposed to the conventional world, often finding their chief relationships in victimizing members of the conventional world and in evading the pressures brought by the conventional world through arrests, trials, convictions, and punishment.   Others, through bribery, make a working relationship with the forces of law and order and are no longer molested.   Very successful full-time criminals may lead a part of their lives in the conventional world but continue to make their money in unlawful ways.   Typically, criminal personalities are developed when family and companionship groups have permitted or encouraged the criminal when a child to find his satisfactions in delinquent behavior, and no institution has succeeded in developing conventional ethical standards or patterns of behavior.   The professional criminal is the end result of a process that leads away from conventional satisfactions to illegal ones.   The most fully developed criminal personality is found in the professional criminal.

Arthur Perry is a good example of the professional criminal.   His latest escapade was to represent himself as an official of a large motion picture company.   Moving into a first-class hotel in an Eastern city, he announced that a gigantic film would be made in the city soon, and that stars would arrive on certain dates.   Everyone believed this story and Perry was able to borrow money, cash worthless checks, and induce new acquaintances to pay the bills for entertainment.   After securing about $20,000, and apparently having a gay time for a week or two, he left just as suspicion was beginning to gather.   His criminal record revealed that for 23 years—from the time he was 20—he had perpetrated one swindle after another, each time under a different name.

The careers of a man of 49 named Blackmore, his wife, aged 35, and another man, Wilson, aged 44, are representative of professional crime. This trio confessed to a series of burglaries after they were arrested for larceny in a hotel. Their specialty was breaking into churches and schools. The thefts were small—in one place they took a number of articles including a radio, 2 watches, a penknife, and $10 in cash. They confessed, however, to thefts of similar nature in at least 6 small cities. Blackmore admitted to the police that he had served terms in 6 states for grand larceny and burglary, and in addition to "so many others" he could not remember them all.

Professional criminals often band together and develop an organized system of crime. They systematize their criminal activities much as some businesses are organized, with specialized personnel, permanent gradations of leadership, and bookkeeping systems. Gambling, bootlegging, houses of prostitution, confidence games, drug rings, automobile theft rings, and large-scale extortion are common examples of organized crime.

The story of bootlegging in Chicago during the life of the Prohibition Amendment (1920–33) shows the power of the organized criminal group and many of its techniques.[8] When prohibition was in force, many people, otherwise law abiding, wished to continue the use of liquor and were willing to overlook the lawlessness of its production and sale. Organized liquor rings developed to supply the demand. The men at the heads of these rings were old-time criminals, who previously had operated brothels, gambling halls, or handbook offices for betting on races, or had committed bank robberies and other forms of stealing.

At first, each gang operated in a small way in one section of Chicago or the suburbs in which it already had friendly affiliations. But soon the immense profits to be made from bootlegging induced the stronger gangs to try to expand their territory, which created rivalry that led to open conflict. The ensuing wars were settled according to gang methods—beating, torture, murder. Gang leaders killed not only competitors, but also those within their own ranks who became nervous and therefore susceptible to police questioning. The period between 1922 and 1926 has been called the "beer war," for during these years 215 gangsters were murdered by other gangsters, and another 160 were killed by the police in running battles, in the course of which policemen also were killed. Gradually all the various organized gangs were brought into one organization, with Al Capone at its head.

Within their own large group of employees, the bootlegging gangs were highly organized. In addition to a small controlling group at the top, they employed bodyguards for the protection of the leaders; bookkeepers for the elaborate accounting system; lawyers to avert arrest, or in the event of ar-

rest, to prevent the case either from coming to trial or resulting in conviction; doctors to treat wounded members; professional gunmen to eliminate
rivals; beer runners to carry liquor from the place of manufacture to the
retailer; and a host of supplementary persons.   The liquor sold by the gangs
was manufactured either in large breweries owned by the leaders, or in small
quantities in the homes of foreign-born families to whom its manufacture
did not seem wrong.

Since the liquor business was illegal, it became necessary to establish
special relationships with legal agencies that might normally interfere with
business operations.   At one time, according to newspaper reports, over 250
police were on the payroll of the Genna brothers, who paid sums for protection ranging from $10 per month to patrolmen to $800 per month to
bureau squads.   A police captain reported that he was offered a "commission" of $5 per barrel, on 200 barrels of beer a day, if he would permit the
beer to be moved.   Whenever possible, federal agents were also bribed to
prevent prosecution.   On one occasion the Federal Prohibition Administrator for Illinois, Indiana, and eastern Wisconsin reportedly received an offer
of $250,000 to permit a large alcohol plant to continue functioning.   In
1924, when gangsters were arrested for trying to move 13 truckloads
of beer from a brewery, a United States District Attorney reputedly was
offered $50,000 to prevent the case from coming to trial.   Although these
large offers were refused, evidently many bribes were accepted by law enforcement officials or the criminal organization could not have continued to
operate.   The tremendous size of the organization is indicated by the report
that the payroll for one week in 1923 of the Torrio-Capone gang for chauf-
feurs, truckmen, bookkeepers, guards, bombers, killers, lawyers and so on
amounted to $25,000.   In spite of these heavy expenses, the annual net
profit of the Capone organization was estimated to run well over a million
dollars.

The gangs also bought immunity from punishment by friendly acts toward
city and state governmental officials, which included contributions to campaign funds, rounding up votes on election day, invitations to elaborate parties staged by gang leaders (and attended by the officials as various newspaper photographs prove), and (by implication) direct contributions.   As
a result, arrests were rare, and cases often were not prosecuted by the State's
Attorney's office.   If cases actually came to trial, witnesses refused to testify,
sometimes revealing that they had been threatened with death.   In the event
that cases reached the jury, one or two jurors held out against a unanimous
verdict, and in some cases it was evident that they had been bribed.   Although a gangster was sometimes convicted, his sentence was eased by special

accommodations, permission to leave his cell and return to it, or by some means or other his term of imprisonment would be shortened.

The grip of Capone's group on Chicago was broken, not by local law-enforcement bodies, which during the 1920's had failed miserably to control the situation, but by federal agents. As it seemed impossible to secure a conviction for violation of the Prohibition Amendment, another device was tried. Capone was brought into court on the charge of defrauding the government of $1,036,654 in income taxes, and he was also charged with violation of the Prohibition Amendment. Although he attempted to make a deal for a short term in prison, the federal judge sentenced him in 1931 to 10 years in prison and $50,000 in fines. He served seven and a half years of his sentence, emerging a chronic invalid from a disease contracted before he entered prison. Although the Capone organization was not disbanded, its activities were less flagrant than in the days of Al Capone's rule.

The repeal of the Prohibition Amendment in 1933 brought an end to the beer barons, but it did not terminate organized crime. Gambling, book-making, control of unions, kidnaping, and extortion of money became the new businesses of the old gangs.

5. *Maladjusted criminals.* Maladjusted people vary from the overly anxious and tense individuals through those with persistent idiosyncrasies of behavior to the totally psychotic who intermittently or permanently lose their contact with reality. Maladjustment is not criminality and maladjusted people do not automatically become criminals. They come within the range of criminology, however, when their behavior conflicts with criminal laws.

Habitual offenders: Certain types of personal habits are treated by our criminal laws as crimes; for example, public drunkenness, drug addiction (illegal possession of drugs), vagrancy, petty thievery, prostitution, homosexuality, fornication, and adultery. Many people who persistently exhibit these types of behavior and especially those who allow their lives to be dominated by them have been found to be maladjusted. They suffer from some inability to find satisfactions in conventional ways or from inner tensions and conflicts. The law, which regards these behavior patterns as contrary to public welfare, takes little account of the inner motivations and imposes upon these people the same routine of arrest, trial, conviction, and penalty that is imposed upon all criminals. These habitual offenders account for a large proportion of the arrests of any city and, because their offenses are confirmed habits, reappear time and again for identical offenses. As a rule, they do no intentional harm to unwilling victims and thus are not in the same category as professional or white collar criminals.

Psychoneurotic criminals: Certain, but by no means all, psychoneuroses lead into criminal behavior. Uncontrollable compulsions may force the person to repeat one type of act. The act may be harmless, such as touching each fence post that is passed; or it may involve destruction of property through setting fires, or thefts of some one article. Occasionally the compulsion takes the form of repeated murders. Such psychoneurotics, normal in most of their behavior, markedly abnormal in a few aspects, create a serious problem when the judge and jury must decide whether to treat them as criminals or as mentally abnormal people.

Psychopathic criminals: The term psychopathic is loosely used to cover the behavior of social rebels, people who seem unable to fit into any ordered society, whether conventional or criminal. They are extremely hostile and egocentric, unable to accept supervision or authority. They strike back at police, prison officials, psychiatrists, and social workers with equal force, rejecting all restraints or efforts to help them. Their difficulties are deeply seated in personality and often have their roots in childhood problems.

Psychotic criminals: The psychotic person permanently or at intervals loses contact with reality and lives within an imaginary world of his own. Whether, within this unreal world, he commits crimes depends upon the nature of his malady. Most psychotics do not harm other people, but a few are tormented by delusions and fears that lead them to attack others or to destroy property, always with justifications that grow out of their delusions.

JUVENILE DELINQUENTS

Juvenile delinquents are boys and girls under a legally specified age (usually 18 years) who are either guilty of violation of the criminal laws or are following other patterns of behavior disapproved of for children or adolescents. Some of the usual types of prohibited behavior are incorrigibility to parents, running away, persistent truancy, roaming the streets at night, loitering in taverns, pool rooms, and other places where adult misdemeanants gather, and lewd or indecent actions. The purpose of juvenile delinquency laws is to place under control of the juvenile court boys and girls whose behavior is bringing them into contact with undesirable adults or seems to be paving the way for later criminal acts.

It would be possible to classify juvenile delinquents into many of the categories used in the preceding classification of adult criminals. It does not seem necessary, therefore, to break down the general classification into the subtypes. A study of criminology is incomplete however without some inclusion of juvenile delinquency, for the origin of much—perhaps most—adult crime lies in childhood.

CRIME AND CRIMINALS

Crime, the legal concept, is the province of police, court, and prison officials. Criminals, the human beings, are of primary concern to social scientists and psychologists, both after conviction of crimes and in the troublesome years when behavior is moving from conventional toward criminal but no specific crime has as yet been committed. In this text, criminals, the human beings, are given first consideration in Part I; the legal processes are reserved for Part II where they are discussed both in their administrative aspects and also as they impinge upon criminals.

QUESTIONS

1. What are the limitations of confining the study of crime to convicted criminals? Are there dangers in a less legalistic definition? Advantages?

2. Are people justified in disobeying recently passed criminal laws with which they do not agree?

3. From Appendix A trace the development of theories of criminality.

4. Many specialists are willing to accept only one theory of the origin of criminal behavior: it is learned; or it is the result of personal maladjustment. Can you reconcile the two theories?

5. Have you ever broken a criminal law? If so, in which category of criminals would you place yourself?

READINGS

Bettelheim, B., "On the Rehabilitation of Offenders," *Federal Probation,* 13 (Dec., 1949), 5–15. A discussion of the development of criminal behavior from the standpoint of individual psychology.

Clinard, M. B., "Criminal Behavior is Human Behavior," *Federal Probation,* 13 (Mar., 1949), 21–27. All behavior, including criminal, is the result of social interaction with other people.

———, "Sociologists and American Criminology," *Journal of Criminal Law and Criminology,* 41 (1951), 549–77. In this survey of the contributions of American sociologists to the etiology of crime, emphasis is placed on competing value systems of culture conflict.

McKay, H. D., "The Neighborhood and Child Conduct," *Annals of the American Academy of Political and Social Science,* 261 (1949), 32–41. This article explores neighborhood influences in delinquency—conflicts of values, especially in disorganized areas; excess leisure time; and the function of indigenous groups.

Sellin, T., *Culture Conflict and Crime* (New York: Social Science Research Council, 1938). Crime is considered as the violation of strongly held conduct norms that are supported by group sanctions.

Tappan, P. W., "Who is the Criminal?" *American Sociological Review,* 12 (1947), 96–102. Tappan gives a clear statement of the validity of limiting criminology to the study of legally convicted criminals and of excluding from the category of crime other types of nonconformity.

FOOTNOTES

[1] Roscoe Pound, *New Paths of the Law* (Lincoln: University of Nebraska, 1946), p. 16.

[2] Clifford R. Shaw, *The Jack-Roller* (Chicago: University of Chicago Press, 1930).

[3] Harlan W. Gilmore, *The Beggar* (Chapel Hill: University of North Carolina Press, 1940), pp. 168–82.

[4] H. D. McKay, "The Neighborhood and Child Conduct," *Annals of the American Academy of Political and Social Science,* 261 (1949), 32–41.

[5] Frederic M. Thrasher, *The Gang* (Chicago: University of Chicago Press, 1927).

[6] K. R. Eissler and Paul Federn (eds.), *Searchlights on Delinquency* (New York: International Universities Press, 1949).

[7] Morris Ploscowe, *Crime and Criminal Law,* The National Law Library, 2 (New York: Collier, 1939), 6–18.

[8] The material on bootlegging gangs is abstracted from a series of articles by James O'Donnell Bennett, which ran in the *Chicago Tribune* from February 3, 1929, to April 7, 1929, and from a series by Clem Lane published in the *Chicago Daily News* from June 3, 1943, to July 10, 1943.

2

Characteristics of Criminals

The spectacular crimes—murder, assault, and daring theft—are so thoroughly exploited as news items that one readily acquires a distorted impression of types of criminals and of crimes most frequently committed. Actually, assaults form only a small proportion of the total number of crimes; various forms of theft are much more common; and still more numerous are the offenses of the habitual criminal—disorderly conduct, prostitution, petty thievery, and the like. The more serious the crime, either from the point of view of personal injury or of the amount stolen, the less often does it occur. Therefore an examination of criminal statistics is necessary to present an accurate picture and to dissipate common misconceptions.

SOURCES OF INFORMATION

Criminal statistics are of recent origin in the United States, and at present they do not cover offenses for the entire nation. In order to understand the limitations of figures to be given later in this chapter, it is necessary first to survey the sources of information on crime and to understand some of the problems attending the collection of criminal statistics.

There are 3 chief sources of information: police departments and other local law-enforcement agencies, courts, and prisons. Reports from these sources are sent to certain federal agencies, which organize and publish the data. In addition, some states publish criminal statistics, and a few intensive studies of cities or states have been made, covering many phases of law enforcement and the disposition of criminals.

It is a common characteristic of all criminal statistics to use legal classifications, referring primarily to types of *crime,* rather than *criminals.* From these reports we may learn how many murders, larcenies, robberies, and so on were committed during a given period of time and some of the common characteristics of criminals, such as sex, age, and race; but we cannot learn much about the personalities of the men and women who committed the crimes. The classification tends to be legalistic rather than psychological or sociological. The reports tell what criminal acts were committed but give no hint of their motivation.

Federal Sources

The *Uniform Crime Reports* have been published by the Federal Bureau of Investigation since 1930. At first published as a monthly pamphlet, the reports became a quarterly in 1932 and during World War II a semi-annual publication. They cover crimes known to the police, either reported to the police by citizens and officials, or ascertained by first hand observation or investigation. The crimes are reported by police departments according to a uniform system, which divides criminal activities into two classes. Class 1 crimes include 7 serious offenses: criminal homicide (subdivided into [1] murder and nonnegligent manslaughter, and [2] manslaughter by negligence); rape; robbery; aggravated assault (assault with intent to kill or with a deadly weapon); burglary (breaking and entering); larceny (except automobile theft); and automobile theft. Class 2 crimes total 20 in number and include: assault (not aggravated); forgery and counterfeiting; embezzlement and fraud; stolen property (buying, receiving, or possessing); carrying and possessing weapons; prostitution and commercialized vice; sex offenses; offenses against the family and children; narcotic drug violations; liquor violations; drunkenness; disorderly conduct; vagrancy; gambling; driving while intoxicated; violation of road and driving laws; parking violations; other traffic violations; other violations of state and municipal ordinances with regard to traffic and motor vehicles; and suspicion. More complete definitions of these crimes are given in Appendix B.

National Prisoner Statistics, published since 1947 by the Federal Bureau of Prisons, gives the results of an annual census of prisoners in state and federal institutions. Prior to that date, essentially the same information was contained in *Prisoners in State and Federal Prisons and Reformatories,* by the Bureau of the Census, which had published annual reports since 1926. Before that year reports were issued at the time of each decennial census and at certain other times.

The Federal Bureau of Prisons, United States Department of Justice, publishes *Federal Prisons,* which is devoted to a discussion of organization and programs in the federal prisons and includes statistical information on federal prisoners.

Another federal report based upon juvenile court statistics is published by the Children's Bureau. Formerly issued as a numbered bureau publication entitled *Children in the Courts,* it has recently appeared in special statistical reports and in special issues of *The Child.*

State Sources

Certain states also publish reports through a central bureau. For example, statistics are published by the New York State Department of Correction, by the Bureau of Criminal Apprehension in Minnesota, and by the Department of Correction in Massachusetts. Since each state uses its own system of gathering statistics, the results are not always comparable. Police departments, courts, and probation departments of large cities also issue annual reports, but again it is difficult to make comparisons.

Surveys of Crime

Intensive surveys of criminal procedures have been made in a limited number of states or cities: the states of Illinois and Missouri, and the cities of Pittsburgh, Cleveland, Memphis, and Boston are examples. Since these surveys are concerned primarily with procedures after arrest, they do not contribute to the discussion at this point.

Limited Studies

A continuous stream of research reports and articles appears in professional journals, throwing light on some specific situation. Many of these reports will be referred to in later chapters. Recourse to the articles and book reviews in the following journals will keep the student abreast of current studies:

Journal of Criminal Law, Criminology and Police Science (Northwestern University Press, 357 East Chicago Avenue, Chicago)

Prison World (American Prison Association, 135 East 15th Street, New York)

Annual Proceedings of the American Prison Association.

National Probation and Parole Association Journal and *News* (National Probation and Parole Association, 1790 Broadway, New York.)

Federal Probation (Administrative Office of the United States Courts and Bureau of Prisons, United States Department of Justice, Washington, D.C.)

News Notes on Juvenile Delinquency (United States Department of Health, Education, and Welfare, Social Security Administration, Children's Bureau, Washington, D.C.)

LIMITATIONS OF CRIMINAL STATISTICS

Although a fairly accurate account of crime in one state or one city may be secured from local reports, it is extremely difficult to obtain a comprehensive record for the entire United States, presenting crime from the same point of view for all states.

Variation in State Laws

With the exception of a relatively small number of violations of federal laws, crimes are violations of the laws of different states. Although these laws are based on English common law, each state has developed its own criminal statutes. Hence an act that is criminal in one state may be legal in another; or the degree of misconduct that constitutes a felony (serious crime) in one state may be considered simply a misdemeanor (minor offense) elsewhere. The FBI, however, makes an effort to avoid these complicating facts in the *Uniform Crime Reports* by providing the police with detailed definitions of crimes as a guide to listing offenses regardless of state definitions.

Crimes reported from courts or prisons are not adjusted for differences in legal penalties. For example, in Michigan the penalty for murder is life imprisonment without parole. Over a period of time, therefore, the prisons accumulate a large number of murderers. In Illinois, however, the penalty for murder may be execution, life imprisonment, or imprisonment for a term not under 14 years. Consequently, Illinois prison statistics would tend to show a smaller number of murderers even had the number of murderers convicted in the two states been the same.

Incomplete Nature of Reports

A further limitation arises from the incompleteness of the federal reports, which results from the voluntary co-operation of local officials and institutions. This system of collecting information is inexpensive, since the federal government does not need to provide trained persons to gather the statistics. It is uncertain, however, since only estimates can be made of the total amount of crime in the United States, based upon the known amount in some communities. Also, officials vary in their ability to report with care and accuracy. Rural areas are especially likely to be underrepresented in the reports.

The FBI affords an excellent example of incomplete reporting in the *Uniform Crime Reports;* data are submitted voluntarily by local law enforcement agencies. Not all communities are included. In 1952 the communities reporting consisted of the classes shown in Table 1. Although the popula-

TABLE 1

Number and Population of Communities Reporting to the Federal Bureau
of Investigation, 1952

	Number	Population Represented
Cities over 250,000	39	
Cities 100,000–250,000	63	
Cities 50,000–100,000	123	
Cities 25,000–50,000	243	76,094,589
Cities 10,000–25,000	624	
Cities under 10,000	1,358	
Villages and rural areas serviced by		
County sheriffs, state police, etc.	1,780	40,691,017

Source: *Uniform Crime Reports for the United States and Its Possessions, 1952,* 23,
No. 2 (Washington: Government Printing Office, 1953), 92, 96.

tion of the United States in 1952 totaled well over 150 million, the *Reports*
cover only 116,785,606 people, or 78 per cent of the population.   Moreover, the *Reports* are weighted with urban data.   The cities included represent 85 per cent of the urban population whereas the rural areas include
only about 66 per cent of the total rural population.   The *Reports* are much
more representative now (1955) than in the past and it may be assumed
that they will become still more complete as more small communities are
induced to co-operate.   At present the uneven representation is partially
overcome by tabulating crimes according to the size of cities.

The juvenile delinquency reports made by the Children's Bureau are based
upon information from 350 to 425 courts located in one third to one half of
the states, although all states provide for juvenile courts.   City courts are
over-represented as compared with rural courts.

Unreported Legal Violations

One of the loopholes in crime reporting, most difficult to close, is the
known fact that many legal violations are not reported to the police.   Criminal statistics, in fact, are limited to cases that come to the attention of law
enforcing agencies.

Especially when children are concerned, people are reluctant to report
any except very serious or persistent delinquencies.   Parents make restitution to save their children from arrest.   Schools often handle acts of
theft or vandalism as institutional problems rather than as legal violations.
Children who seem to have some personality problem in addition to overt
delinquent behavior frequently are referred to case work agencies instead
of to the police or juvenile court.   Robison found that 32 per cent of behavior problems known to certain New York City agencies did not become

court cases.[1]   Murphy and associates found that out of 114 boys who were subjects of a special counseling program, only 13 had not been guilty of some delinquency.[2]   Of the 101 young offenders, only 40 had been the subjects of court complaints.   The total group had amassed 6,416 legal violations, but only 95 (1.5 per cent) had been reported to the juvenile court.   Porterfield, in a comparison of college students and juvenile delinquents, found that all the college students had committed offenses identical with offenses for which other young people were taken into court.[3]   The average number of offenses reported by college men for their precollege days was 17.6 and for their college years 11.2; and by college women in precollege days 4.7.

Many crimes of adults, also, are not reported to the police.   The injured person often does not seek the police when he feels that his prestige or well-being is better served by secrecy.   Thus the well-to-do man or woman who is exploited by a confidence man may prefer to suffer the monetary loss rather than reveal his naïveté or cupidity.   Retail businesses often do not report shoplifters apprehended by store detectives since to do so might reflect upon the good management of the store or, if the accusation could not be proved, might lead to a damage suit; such protection is accorded the amateur shoplifter more often than the professional criminal.   For example, a study by Arieff and Bowle states that in Chicago in 1945, 3,400 persons were apprehended for shoplifting but only 4.5 per cent were actually arrested.[4]   A Philadelphia report for 1928–33 by Sellin shows a yearly average of 5,151 thefts known to 3 large department stores, but only 1,190 arrests by store detectives and the very small number of 235 prosecutions and convictions.[5]   The average number of thefts known to the police for the entire city was 6,459 (including the 235 convictions), only slightly more than the thefts known to 3 stores but not reported to the police.

Personal vices that come under the criminal law usually are not reported, inasmuch as there is often co-operation between the "victim" and the criminal who supplies the forbidden services.   The drunkard, the drug addict, the patron of prostitution, the gambler, the woman who has an illegal abortion, and the girl who is below the age of consent for sex relations are not likely to co-operate with the police in locating and arresting the criminal vendors. Public opinion often fails to back up the police in trying to eliminate these activities; in fact, so lax is public opinion that the police may be criticized for stopping illegal indulgences.   The police often share the tolerant public opinion and please the public by refraining from arrests; they may, however, exact a fee from the criminal vendors.

An unknown number of criminals are never arrested because they make it financially profitable to police or political organization not to arrest them.

Organized criminal groups carry on their operations over many years of time with no or almost no arrests. Occasionally some bungling in their operations or the efforts of a zealous prosecuting attorney or special crime-investigation committee brings to light wide-spread criminal practices, as the probing of the Senate Crime Investigating Committee, popularly called the Kefauver Committee after its Chairman, Estes Kefauver, did in 1950–51.[6] In the long intervals between public exposures these criminal organizations operate unhindered and unreported.

Local and Sporadic Arrest Policies

Each police department establishes some individual policies of arrest.   In some cities, relatively few children are arrested and reported to the juvenile court, the police maintaining some type of juvenile bureau that handles minor cases.   Such cities seem to have a low delinquency rate when compared with cities in which police refer all cases to the juvenile court.   In some cities public and police are lenient toward certain types of crime, although they may be strict about other offenses.   In the "wide-open" town police arrest few proprietors of gambling or prostitution houses and close their eyes to all manner of violations.

On the other hand, when the public is aroused over some atrocious crime, the police throw out a "dragnet" and arrest all persons with a past criminal record whom they can find, although the prisoners must soon be released for lack of evidence against them.   The many arrests tend to pacify the public while the detectives make a more careful approach toward solving the crime.

Military Crimes

Since 1940 when the United States began to draft young men into the armed forces, reports of civilian offenses and of cases tried in the civil courts give an incomplete picture.   Many young men who would normally be tried by civil courts instead are tried by military courts.   In addition to the civil offenses incurred, there are the many purely military offenses created by military laws.   For a complete survey of crime, these offenses should be included.

THE BASIS OF REPORTS

Another problem in criminal statistics is the basis used in different reports in estimating the amount of crime.

Crimes Known to the Police

The *Uniform Crime Reports* are based on crimes known to the police. This definition raises a number of questions.   How often do people report that property has been stolen and then find that they have simply misplaced it? How much investigation should be undertaken by the police before assuming that a reported crime has been actually committed? How many assumed crimes are reported that later prove to be innocent acts, although this development is not reported to the police? Are police sometimes tempted to avoid recording all crimes in order to protect the name of their community, or to show a better ratio between crimes reported and arrests made than would be indicated by a true report? Although such questions must be considered in interpreting reports of crimes known to the police, this basis offers the most comprehensive picture of crime.

Number of Arrests

Another basis of reporting is arrests made by the police. The number of arrests differs from the number of offenses. A crime reported to the police may have been committed by one or a dozen persons. Thus, to clear up one crime, a dozen arrests might be necessary. On the other hand, the arrest of one person might account for a long series of crimes. For example, in Chicago the arrest of one 17-year-old boy was regarded by the police to have cleared up some 24 burglaries, 5 assaults, and 3 murders. The *Uniform Crime Reports* correlate the two bases of reporting crime by presenting both the number of crimes known to the police and the number of crimes cleared by the arrest of one or more persons. We do not know, however, the number of criminals who committed all reported crimes, for many crimes are never cleared by arrest.

Arrests may overstate the number of offenders. The same offender who is arrested and released after a fine, reprimand, or short period of detention may commit a second, third, or fourth offense within the year, each followed by an arrest. Similarly, the juvenile delinquent, placed on probation, may be brought into court several times during the year for different offenses. Each time, he is counted as an additional offender.

Number of Convictions

The number of arrests and court appearances cannot be assumed to refer only to actual criminals, since many suspects are arrested but are released when their cases come to trial. Adolescents are also brought into court but released as nonoffenders. Thus, a third basis for studying crime is the number of convictions secured. Although convictions are in part the result of guilt, they also depend upon the astuteness of the accused person's attorney and upon local policies. Official practices or local community opinion may lead to the release of persons accused of certain crimes in one community but may demand conviction for these same crimes in another. In addition, within the same community the percentage of convictions varies among judges.   Therefore, conviction is not synonymous with guilt.

Different Court Systems

Statistics on the amount of crime are further complicated by the fact that cases are tried in different systems of courts.   Felonies (serious crimes) are tried in one system of courts, whereas minor offenses, called misdemeanors, are brought before police judges, justices of the peace, municipal judges, or judges of other forms of lower or inferior courts.   Court statistics generally cover the felonies tried in the county or district courts but fail to include the minor offenses tried in the lower courts.

Number of Prisoners

There is a tendency to assume that all criminals who are a menace to the community are imprisoned.   Many discussions, as a result, are based upon the number of prisoners in state and federal prisons.   However, the difficulty with this choice of basis is that only a small proportion of crimes reported to the police actually result in imprisonment of the offenders (between 3 and 4 per cent of serious [class 1] crimes).[7]   Some persons who no doubt are guilty are not even tried because the evidence against them is insufficient for conviction.   Others, who are convicted, are merely placed on probation. Moreover, the many minor offenders are not sent to prison even if guilty; they serve short sentences in jail, are fined, or dismissed with a reprimand from the judge.   Therefore, the statistics on state and federal prisoners are limited to a highly select group, representing only a small proportion—and not necessarily the most dangerous members—of the total criminal population.

Estimates

In general, then, we may say that criminal statistics are incomplete and figures for the entire United States are only estimates.   In addition, the bases upon which they are made limit the statistics to a mere approximation of the number of offenders.   Bearing these many limitations in mind, we shall examine some statistics on the amount of crime in the United States.

TYPES OF CRIME

Serious (Class 1) Crimes

The most adequate material on the number of crimes committed comes from the *Uniform Crime Reports,* compiled by the FBI, which are described in the preceding section.

The 2,036,510 serious crimes of 1952 for which figures are available fall into two types: forms of stealing property and personal injury or assaults of some kind.   Figure 4 shows the extent to which stealing exceeds injuries and assaults.   Among all types of serious crimes, Figure 5 shows that the most frequent is larceny (theft of another's personal goods), with burglary (breaking and entering a residence or place of business to commit a crime) running a poor second.

Minor Offenses

The emphasis on serious crimes should not cause oversight of the many minor delinquencies and violations of law and order that occur.   In any community, most of the arrests are for minor delinquencies rather than for serious crimes.

The preponderance of minor offenses is shown by the report from 1,706 cities given in the *Uniform Crime Reports* for 1952 and shown graphically in Figures 6 and 7.   Well over one fourth of the population is arrested annually for violation of traffic and motor vehicle laws; various forms of drunkenness and disorderly conduct also have high rates.

URBAN AND RURAL RATES

Cities with population above 250,000 had the worst crime rate in 1952, according to Table 2.   For all types of crime the smaller cities have the lower rates, and for 6 out of 8 types, the smallest cities—those with less than 10,000 population—have the lowest rates.   In proportion to the population there are approximately twice as many cases of murder, burglary, and larceny in large cities as in small; about three times as many cases of manslaughter, rape, and automobile theft; and more than three times as many robberies and cases of aggravated assault.

In various types of personal assaults, rural communities tend to exceed small cities and to approach the rates of large cities.   For thefts, rural rates are much below those of cities.   Crimes that grow out of uncontrolled angers, hostilities, carelessness, or sex drives may flourish in rural as well as in urban areas.   Crimes that net the criminal financial gain are the truly urban crimes.   Cities offer many more opportunities for large gains and also the anonymity necessary for escape without recognition.

AGE AND SEX

Youthful Beginnings of Crime

Many children come into conflict with the law at a very early age, as Figure 8 shows for court cases reported to the Children's Bureau for 1946–49.

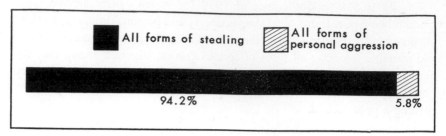

FIGURE 4

Percentage of two main types of major crime committed in 1952. Homicides, rapes, and felonious assaults, combined here under the title personal aggression, are rare forms of crime when compared with the many instances of stealing. (Based on *Uniform Crime Reports for the United States and Its Possessions, 1952,* 23, No. 2 [Washington: Government Printing Office, 1953], 73.)

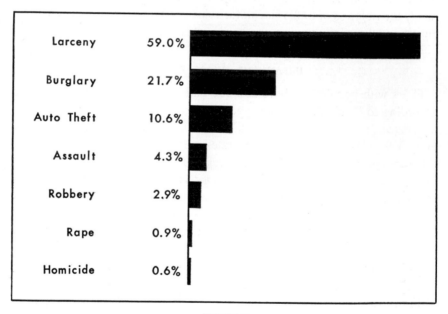

FIGURE 5

Percentage of each type of major crime committed in 1952. The most frequent types of crime are those that pose little threat to the personal safety of the victims. Most criminals wish to secure money or property with as great secrecy and as little injury to others and danger to themselves as possible. (Based on *Uniform Crime Reports for the United States and Its Possessions, 1952,* 23, No. 2 [Washington: Government Printing Office, 1953], 73.)

TABLE 2

Offenses Known to the Police by Size of City, 1952

(Rate per 100,000 of the population)

	Murder	Manslaughter by Negligence	Rape	Robbery	Aggravated Assault	Burglary	Larceny	Auto Theft
Cities over 250,000 (39)	6.52	4.26	17.45	102.8	119.2	482.6	1,021.4	245.6
Cities 100,000–250,000 (63)	6.40	4.15	9.10	47.2	75.8	457.4	1,122.1	220.7
Cities 50,000–100,000 (123)	3.97	3.27	7.59	32.8	77.9	346.9	983.9	163.1
Cities 25,000–50,000 (243)	3.55	3.24	6.59	22.8	47.4	317.9	991.8	137.8
Cities 10,000–25,000 (624)	2.95	1.46	5.90	17.4	36.3	267.8	874.0	106.7
Cities 2,500–10,000 (1,358)	2.73	1.47	6.18	14.6	26.0	210.3	555.8	78.9
TOTAL CITIES	5.05	3.39	11.51	59.6	81.5	391.5	961.6	187.0
Rural (under 2,500 and open country)	4.98	5.60	11.38	17.2	33.9	173.7	257.7	57.8

Source: *Uniform Crime Reports for the United States and Its Possessions, 1952, 23, No. 2* (Washington: Government Printing Office, 1953), 92, 96.

Some children under 12 years of age were referred to juvenile courts, and 60 per cent of all male and 62 per cent of all female juvenile delinquents who appeared in court were under 16 years of age. As these ages are for chil-

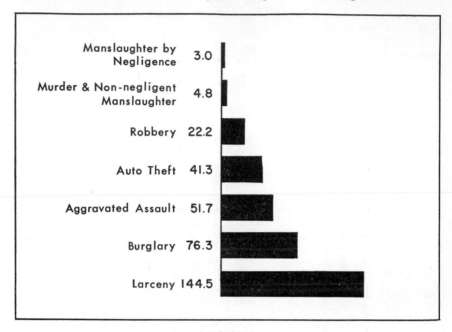

FIGURE 6

Persons held for prosecution for major crimes, as a rate per 100,000 population, 1952. Many criminals are not caught and, therefore, are not included in the rates for this graph. A comparison of Figure 6 with Figure 7 shows that minor violators held for prosecution far exceed the major criminals. Police and judges work primarily with minor offenders. (Based on *Uniform Crime Reports for the United States and Its Possessions,* 24, No. 1 [Washington: Government Printing Office, 1953], 50–51.)

dren arrested during one year rather than for the first offense, it is evident that the age of first arrest would be much lower for many of the children.

Reports from individual courts also show the extreme youth of some children when they first appear in the courts. In Passaic, New Jersey, among 761 children referred to the Passaic Children's Bureau during a 5-year period, 38 per cent of the boys and 20 per cent of the girls were 12 years of age or younger at the time of first referral.[8] Among the thousand boy delinquents studied by the Gluecks, 56.3 per cent had experienced their first arrest when not over 10, and 7.1 per cent had been arrested first when 6 to 8 years old.[9]

A special study for 1952 in the *Uniform Crime Reports,* covering both

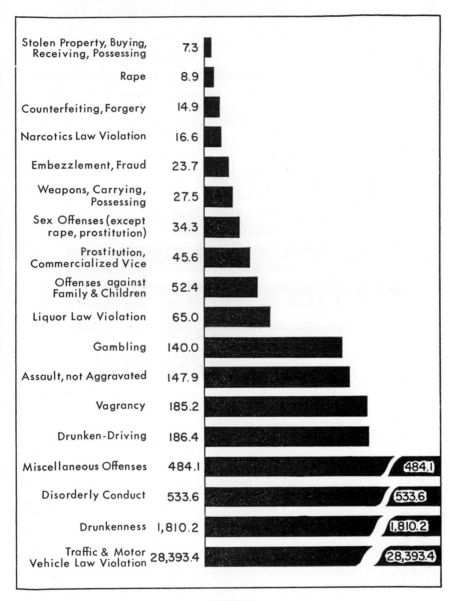

Stolen Property, Buying, Receiving, Possessing	7.3
Rape	8.9
Counterfeiting, Forgery	14.9
Narcotics Law Violation	16.6
Embezzlement, Fraud	23.7
Weapons, Carrying, Possessing	27.5
Sex Offenses (except rape, prostitution)	34.3
Prostitution, Commercialized Vice	45.6
Offenses against Family & Children	52.4
Liquor Law Violation	65.0
Gambling	140.0
Assault, not Aggravated	147.9
Vagrancy	185.2
Drunken-Driving	186.4
Miscellaneous Offenses	484.1
Disorderly Conduct	533.6
Drunkenness	1,810.2
Traffic & Motor Vehicle Law Violation	28,393.4

FIGURE 7

Persons held for prosecution for minor offenses, as a rate per 100,000 population, 1952. Disorderly conduct, drunkenness, and traffic and motor vehicle law violations far outnumber all other offenses, both major and minor. Major offenses do more damage, receive widespread publicity, and may occasion lengthy and expensive trials, but actually they are few in number when compared with certain minor offenses. (Based on *Uniform Crime Reports for the United States and Its Possessions,* 24, No. 1 [Washington: Government Printing Office, 1953], 50–51.)

juveniles and adults, shows that the age period with the greatest number of arrests is 25–29; the median age of arrests is 35.   This finding is in contrast with earlier and more fragmentary reports that placed the peak age for

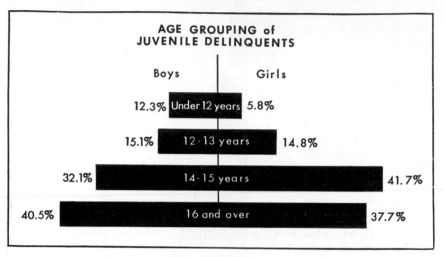

FIGURE 8

Although the teens are usually thought of as the juvenile delinquency years, 12.3 per cent of all boys and 5.8 per cent of all girls who appeared before 413 juvenile courts in 1949 were below the age of 12, and other early adolescent years are well represented.   (Based on 64,565 court appearances reported to the Children's Bureau and published in *Juvenile Court Statistics, 1946–1949,* Children's Bureau Statistical Series, No. 8 [Washington: Federal Security Agency, 1951], p. 13.)

arrests in the late teens or early twenties.   The 1952 report is based on arrests in 232 cities with more than 25,000 population.   Table 3 gives the percentage distribution by 5 year age periods.

Caution must be used in interpreting these figures, which are based on special reports tabulated for the first time in 1952.   Correspondence by the FBI with the reporting agencies showed that, although juveniles arrested are included, children handled informally are not—thus eliminating a large number of children with minor offenses.   Although the figures indicate a decline in number of criminals with age, nothing is shown about the rate of criminals in relation to the total population at each age in the cities covered. We know that the number of people who survive to middle and old age is less than the number of young people; therefore, the number of criminals would also be less, although the proportion of criminals to the total population might not have decreased appreciably.

TABLE 3

Arrests by Age Groups, 1952, in 232 Cities over 25,000 Population

Age	Number	Per Cent
Under 15	33,612	3.0
15–19	94,659	8.5
20–24	128,841	11.6
25–29	144,264	12.9
30–34	139,548	12.6
35–39	137,531	12.4
40–44	126,864	11.4
45–49	108,283	9.8
50 and over	195,529	17.6
Unknown	1,544	0.2
TOTAL	1,110,675	100.0

Median—35 years
Mode—25–29 years

Source: *Uniform Crime Reports for the United States and Its Possessions, 1952,* 23, No. 2 (Washington: Government Printing Office, 1953), 113.

Age and Type of Crime

Each age produces a characteristic type of crime. Few children commit serious offenses. Boys are brought into court on such charges as minor thefts, destruction of property, and other types of malicious mischief; girls are arrested for sexual offenses and incorrigibility.

Among adults, typical crimes change as one passes from youth to mature adulthood, to middle and old age. Figure 9 shows the high concentration of property thefts among criminals under 25 years old. The figures for automobile thefts are especially spectacular, with 80 per cent of all such thefts being made by persons under 25. Many types of theft require daring, the threat or use of force, physical strength, and lightning use of the hands; these are the attributes of youth. In contrast to burglary, robbery, and larceny are forgery, counterfeiting, embezzlement, and fraud—ways of obtaining money through skillful imitation of handwriting or printing, manipulation of accounts, and the outwitting of a victim. These crimes of manual skill and mental agility are most characteristic of the mature adult and to some extent of the middle and old-age group. The mature adult (aged 25–39) also is responsible for a disproportionate percentage of homicides and assaults, with the exception of rape, which is an offense of the young. Personal vices and catering to the vices of others also appear in the mature group—violation of the narcotic drug laws, prostitution, intoxication (while driving), and gambling. Personal vices are also common among offenders

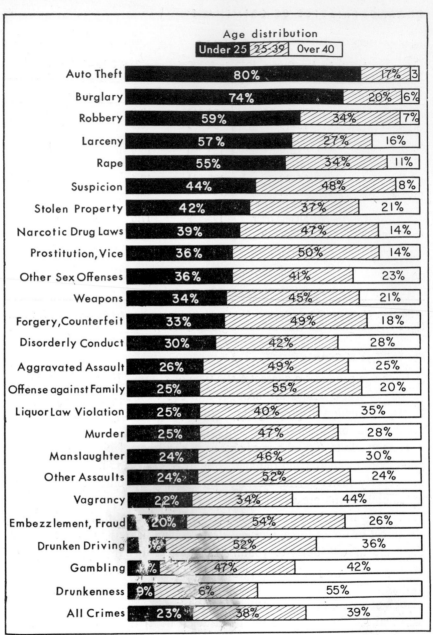

FIGURE 9

Arrests for specific crimes by age of offenders. So far as one may generalize, thefts requiring daring and speed are committed by the young; crimes of manual skill and some personal vices by the middle adult group; and crimes showing personality deterioration by the middle-aged and elderly. (Based on *Uniform Crime Reports for the United States and Its Possessions, 1952,* 23, No. 2 [Washington: Government Printing Office, 1953], 113–14.)

48

aged 40 and over, whereas few thefts of the type common to youth and few sex offenses can be attributed to this group.

The changing pattern with age raises interesting questions. What becomes of the bold thieves of the late teens and early twenties? Do they settle down into conventional citizens; become long-term inmates of prisons; or shift from forceful thefts into thefts of skill and manipulation of the victims? Are the vice-ridden mature persons the outcome of earlier thievery or are they persons who began life conventionally but for some reason drifted into drunkenness, vagrancy, or gambling? Statistical tables giving the age distribution cannot answer these questions; they must be left to longitudinal studies of criminals whose lives may be traced from childhood to old age. A limited number of such studies have been made, but not enough for generalizations.[10]

Sex Ratios

Every over-all statistical study shows that many more boys and men than girls and women are arrested and imprisoned. Among juvenile court referrals in 1951, the ratio of male to female was 4 to 1.[11] Studies of individual cities show sex ratios among juvenile delinquents varying from 4 males to 1 female in Chicago [12] to 1.6 to 1 in Houston.[13] For adults also, the ratio of males to females is high. In 1952 eight men were arrested for every woman in 232 cities of more than 25,000 population surveyed for the *Uniform Crime Reports*.[14] Although some juveniles are included, the tabulation is predominantly for adults.

Sex Ratios by Types of Crime

Figure 10 shows the number of men arrested for every woman for different types of theft, in 232 cities. Although men outnumber women for all thefts, they exceed women in greatest numbers in thefts requiring daring and force and exposing the criminal to most danger of physical harm if the criminal is detected. The embezzler or forger may be arrested but is not likely to be manhandled or shot as is the auto thief, burglar, or robber if discovered.

Figure 11 compares men and women arrested for assaults of various sorts. Men exceed women most in cases of manslaughter, carrying or possessing weapons, and minor assaults. Women who assault others tend to do so with murderous intent. No women are shown as guilty of rape. There are, however, marginal rape cases among men when the offense is statutory rape, the phrase used to designate cases in which the girl is below a certain age and assumed not to be responsible even though she has willingly participated in sex relations. Actually there may be little difference in the ages of man and girl.   In Illinois, for example, a male of 17 years or older is guilty of statutory rape if he has relations with a girl under 15.   There may, however, be little more than a year's difference in age and probably equal irresponsibility on the part of both.

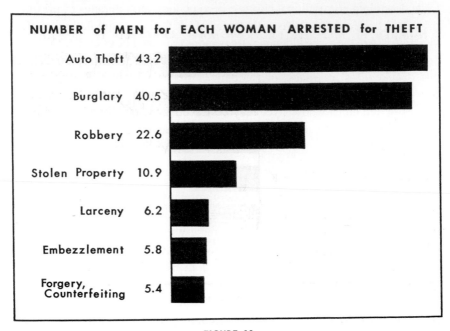

NUMBER of MEN for EACH WOMAN ARRESTED for THEFT

Auto Theft	43.2
Burglary	40.5
Robbery	22.6
Stolen Property	10.9
Larceny	6.2
Embezzlement	5.8
Forgery, Counterfeiting	5.4

FIGURE 10

Ratio of male to female arrests for theft, 1952.   Daring and dangerous thefts are more often committed by men, according to reports from 232 cities with population over 25,000.   (Based on *Uniform Crime Reports for the United States and Its Possessions, 1952,* 23, No. 2 [Washington: Government Printing Office, 1953], 116.)

Figure 12 shows the ratio of men to women for various personal vices that are illegal.   Prostitution and commercialized vice provide the only offenses in which women exceed men, and it should be noted that male patrons are not included; if they were the reverse ratio would be shown.

The difference in crime rates between men and women opens the way for speculations as to the reason.   Pollak [15] has brought together many possible reasons for the high arrest rates of men.   He contends that women have as great tendency toward crime as men, but that their crimes are of types that are difficult to detect.   He cites the ease with which domestic workers may make small, undetected thefts, the women shoplifters whom stores discover but do not report for fear of losing customers, the number of illegal abortions never reported, and blackmailing of men who prefer to be exploited rather than to have their sexual misdeeds exposed.   However, since many crimes of men also are not uncovered or reported, it is impossible to state with any reliability whether men or women are more inclined to criminal activity.

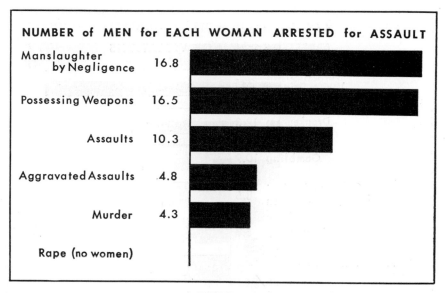

NUMBER of MEN for EACH WOMAN ARRESTED for ASSAULT

Manslaughter by Negligence	16.8
Possessing Weapons	16.5
Assaults	10.3
Aggravated Assaults	4.8
Murder	4.3
Rape (no women)	

FIGURE 11

Ratio of male to female arrests for assault, 1952.   Although men exceed women, the differences are less great than for some types of theft.   (Based on reports from 232 cities of 25,000 and over, *Uniform Crime Reports for the United States and Its Possessions, 1952,* 23, No. 2 [Washington: Government Printing Office, 1953], 116.)

Many of the sex differences seem related to the different roles of men and women and the different social worlds in which they live.   Among juveniles there is closer parental supervision of girls than of boys.   This supervision is especially characteristic of certain immigrant groups, and in general pervades western civilization.   Boys are permitted greater range in their adventures away from home and are allowed to remain out later at night. Girls more often entertain their friends (including boys) in their homes. Boys thus not only have more time in which to carry out delinquent activities, but also more opportunities to meet older delinquents and to acquire sophistication.   They are less closely questioned about their activities than are girls and in general are allowed independence at an earlier age.   If their freedom leads them into delinquent groups instead of well-organized groups, delinquent behavior will follow.

A less obvious reason is that boys, more than girls, turn to active forms of recreation—sports, camping, boating, and active games.   A careful reading of juvenile court cases reveals that many of the delinquencies of boys are in the nature of sport or are intended to provide athletic equipment or the means for camping or other outings.   There are numerous cases of boys

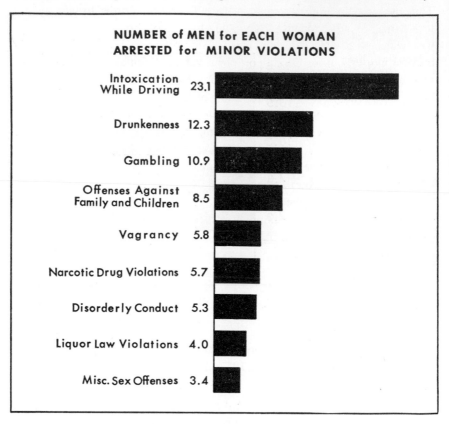

NUMBER of MEN for EACH WOMAN ARRESTED for MINOR VIOLATIONS

Intoxication While Driving	23.1
Drunkenness	12.3
Gambling	10.9
Offenses Against Family and Children	8.5
Vagrancy	5.8
Narcotic Drug Violations	5.7
Disorderly Conduct	5.3
Liquor Law Violations	4.0
Misc. Sex Offenses	3.4

FIGURE 12

Ratio of male to female arrests for minor violations, 1952.   The minor violations listed are primarily personal vices.   Women approach equality with men in some forms of vice, although in none of those shown in the graph do women exceed men.   For prostitution and commercialized vice, women outnumber men by a ratio of 32 to 1; it must be noted, however, that the male patrons are not included.   (Based on *Uniform Crime Reports for the United States and Its Possessions,* 23, No. 2 [Washington: Government Printing Office, 1953], 116.)

who begin a tour of the country in a stolen automobile; when it runs out of gasoline it is abandoned and another car is stolen.   The process is repeated until eventually the boys steal money or food or are arrested on suspicion and the trail of their delinquencies is traced.   They are then legally guilty of larceny of some 3 to 6 cars, but to them the purpose of the expedition was simply a cross-country tour.

Also, the fact should not be overlooked that when boys and girls become interested in joint activities, it is the male who provides the entertainment. Thus the young man may steal a car for an evening in order to take his girl to a dance; or gifts, ranging from candy to fur coats or jewelry; or money with which to pay for entertainment. The professional criminal steals not only for himself but for the support of his wife. A female as well as a male may benefit from the male's delinquencies, but the female is not guilty of a delinquency and, in fact, may not know of it.

Often there is actual participation of women in crimes but of a type that does not lead to arrest. The wife or mistress of a criminal may rent and preside over rooms or an apartment that becomes the headquarters of a criminal group. In her community contacts she learns when suspicion is centering upon the group and when a move must be made. She may investigate unobtrusively the possibilities of a store or bank for robbery. If members of the group are imprisoned, she may work for their parole or pardon and may provide a place to which they may come when released. But she may not have participated to such a degree that she can be found legally guilty of a crime. Thus, as in many other occupation groups, the man may take the active part and "make the living" while the woman remains in the background, although giving the man many forms of assistance.

INTELLIGENCE

Comparison of Criminals and Noncriminals

Several careful statistical studies establish the fact that criminals are not drawn from any one intelligence level but are drawn from all levels, in much the same proportions that these levels are found in the general population. Carl Murchison provided the first comparative study, in which the scores made by prisoners on the army alpha intelligence test were compared with scores made by men in the draft of World War I.[16] Murchison, who was Chief Psychological Examiner at Camp Sherman, Ohio, was invited by the warden of the Ohio Penitentiary to examine the prisoners, using the same test given to the soldiers; he later secured tests from inmates of 3 additional penal institutions in Ohio, 2 in Illinois, 2 in Indiana, 1 in New Jersey, and 1 in Maryland. Criminals and noncriminals were compared on the basis of race, country of origin, and state of residence.

In some instances Murchison found that the criminals had a range of intelligence superior to the range of intelligence for the army draft from the corresponding cultural group and state; in other instances, the range was al-

most identical or favored the draft.   It is therefore not possible to be dog-
matic in drawing a fine line between criminals and the draft group; but all the
evidence points to the fact that criminals are drawn from the entire range of
the population and that no one intelligence level contributes heavily to the
criminal group.   The seeming discrepancies that Murchison found could
probably be explained if more exact information were available about the
criminals and the draft.   It is known, for instance, that Negroes educated in
the North make higher scores on intelligence tests than do southern-bred
Negroes; that foreign-born whites make higher scores after a long residence in
this country than when they first arrive; that foreign-born groups with a
cultural background similar to that of America make higher scores than
those from a different cultural milieu.   Murchison found that men who were
incarcerated outside their home state made higher scores than those incarcerated within their home state.   A preponderance of any of these groups
in the criminal group as compared with the draft would affect the scores for
comparative purposes.

A later study by Tulchin for Illinois institutions supported the general
conclusion that prisoners in state penal institutions seem to approximate the
distribution of intelligence of noncriminals, as shown by the scores of
draftees in World War I.[17]

Certain classes of people are omitted from both army and prisons that
might modify the scores.   For example, certain industrial workers were
excluded from the draft; if they were of high intelligence their omission would
have lowered the scores for the soldiers; on the other hand, the omission of
obviously feeble-minded persons from the draft would have the opposite
effect.

Not all criminals are included in the prison population.   The derelicts
who are arrested for habitual drunkenness, vagrancy, prostitution, and the
like do not find their way to state penal institutions but to local jails, houses
of correction, or state farms for minor offenders.   The distribution of their
intelligence test scores might be very different from that of the general population.   The assumption is that many of these people are misfits unable to
adjust to normal social life, and low intelligence may be a factor in their nonadjustment.   But such an assertion cannot be made with conviction without
evidence from a comparative study.

Another group that does not reach the penitentiaries in large numbers is
composed of feeble-minded offenders.   During adolescence a number of
delinquents are weeded out and placed in institutions for the feeble-minded as
being irresponsible for their acts.   Another small group consists of the
mentally abnormal who when they commit crimes are sent to special institu-

tions for the criminal insane or to other institutions provided for the insane. This latter group may be of any range of intelligence.

Also, if white-collar crimes were handled as criminal cases rather than by injunctions or if white-collar criminals who escape arrest through legal evasions of the law were included, another twist might be given to the curve of intelligence test scores of criminals. Many of these persons operate businesses and it seems probable that few of them would fall into the inferior group intellectually. We might also ask what the effect would be of inclusion of those who indulge in political graft or of the leaders of criminal syndicates and rackets. In other words, it should be recognized that the figures quoted in this section refer only to men convicted of serious crimes and confined to state penal institutions. The mass of minor offenders is not included; nor is the sizable group that evades arrest and imprisonment because of legal technicalities or illegal alliance with law enforcement agencies; nor those who are placed on probation instead of imprisoned for their crimes.

Intelligence and Types of Crime

The studies of both Murchison and Tulchin show that those who commit fraud have a higher average intelligence than any other type of criminal. Fraud, which includes such manipulations as forgery, embezzlement, confidence games, counterfeiting, and passing fraudulent checks, calls for skillful planning, often a high degree of manual dexterity, and the ability to make a convincing personal approach to the victim. According to Tulchin, murderers have a high average score, relative to other criminals, among native-born whites, but a low average score among foreign-born whites and Negroes. Larceny, robbery, and burglary show varying ranks in the different groups but in general fall between fraud and murder at the upper end and sex crimes at the lower. The various forms of burglary, robbery, and larceny may demand careful planning before the crime is committed; on the other hand they may simply depend upon secrecy or upon the fear inspired by a revolver in the criminal's hand. None of them depend upon a personal approach to the victim and skill in persuading him to participate in the act, which are required in the execution of an intricate fraud.

In marked contrast to fraud are sex crimes. For instance, Tulchin shows that among native-born white criminals of native parentage in Illinois, the average score on the army alpha test for those convicted of fraud was 90 and for those convicted of sex crimes 49. Sexual criminals use force or approach children or indulge in unusual forms of sexual satisfaction because they are deficient in some respect and unable to establish a normal partner-

ship.   These studies indicate that lack of intelligence is one form of deficiency that prohibits normal sexual relationships.

MARITAL CONDITION

The life histories of criminals leave a clear-cut impression of the absence
of marriage and stability of family life.   Temporary liaisons, a succession
of marriages ended by divorce, or chance contacts with prostitutes seem
more characteristic of the confirmed criminal than stable married life.
Studies of groups of criminals throw some additional light on the situation.
In a follow-up study of 420 Chicago male delinquents, Healy and Bronner
state that when the average age of the group was 25 years, only 9 per cent
were married.[18]   In the general population, about 28 per cent of males between the ages of 20 and 24 and 60 per cent of males between the ages of
25 and 30 were married.   Of 255 female criminals, 47 per cent were married, as compared with about 60 per cent of the general population.   In
order to be completely valid, the comparison should be made between
delinquents and a nondelinquent group of the same cultural background and
economic level.   Information is not available, however, for such a comparison.

Among the 500 male criminals studied by the Gluecks, 54.5 per cent
were married at the time that their average age was 30.[19]   In the general
population in 1940 approximately 70 per cent of males were married by age
30.   By age 40 in this group—many no longer criminals—only 67 per
cent were married as compared with about 80 per cent in the general population.   Although it is difficult to make more detailed comparisons, it seems
evident from the data given by the Gluecks that marital instability and lack
of responsibility on the part of the husbands were greater than in the general
population.

Among prisoners who entered federal institutions in the year ending June
30, 1951, 56 per cent of the men and 77 per cent of the women had at some
time been married, although many were separated, divorced, or widowed.
Figures 13 and 14 show the excess of the latter categories as well as
of single criminals over corresponding categories in the general population.

The difficulty with all these comparisons is that many delinquents and
criminals, especially in larger cities, come from communities in which marital
instability is common.   Many of the criminals come from parental homes
characterized by dissension, desertion, or divorce.   It is therefore difficult
to determine whether the criminals exhibit more or less marital instability

than other groups in the same communities.   This problem is overcome in a study by Gillin in which prisoners in Wisconsin penal institutions were compared with their brothers.[20]   Gillin found fewer of the prisoners mar-

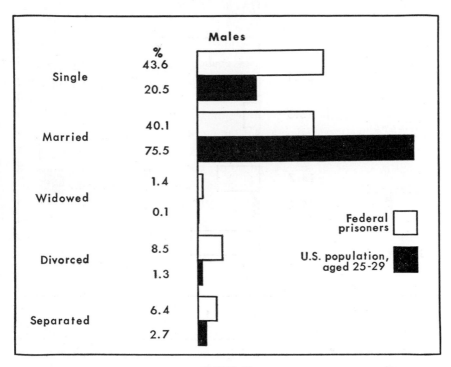

FIGURE 13

Marital status of federal male prisoners compared with the general population. When the marital status of prisoners in federal institutions is compared with that of the general population of approximately the same median age (28 years), the instability of married life for the prisoners is clear.   It should not be inferred that marital instability caused the criminal behavior, however.   It seems more likely that personal maladjustments or a generally unstable type of life organization has contributed both to crime and inability to marry or marital failure. (Based on *Federal Prisons, 1952* [Washington: Bureau of Prisons, U.S. Department of Justice, 1952], p. 75; and *Marital Status and Household Characteristics: April 1951, Current Population Reports, Population Characteristics,* Series P-20, No. 38 [Washington: Bureau of the Census, April 29, 1952], p. 10)

ried and more of them divorced than was true of their brothers.   Disharmony between husband and wife occurred more often among the prisoners and their wives than among the brothers and their wives.

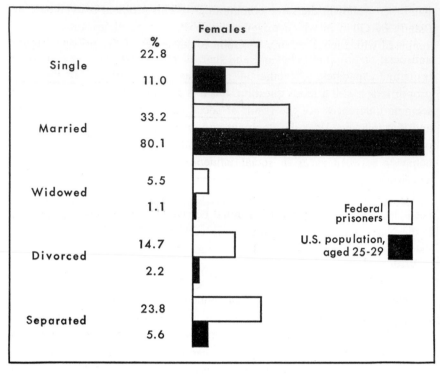

FIGURE 14

Marital status of federal female prisoners compared with the general population. Women offenders, even more than men, are heavily drawn from the widowed, divorced, and separated.   Both men and women prisoners have double the normal proportion of unmarried.   (Based on same sources as Figure 13.)

RACE

The relation of crime to race presents a delicate and complex problem that has not been fully explored.   It is closely tied to the prejudices that exist between racial groups and to the reflection of those prejudices in the administration of criminal justice.

Any discussion of crime with reference to race in the United States must take account of the fact that the whites are the dominant group, both among law-making bodies and among public officials that administer the law. Studies based on statistics of arrests and convictions therefore may give a false impression of the relative criminal behavior of different racial groups. The white policeman and the white judge may deal more harshly with a member of another race than with a white offender.   White legislators may make laws directed specifically at the activities of another race that are not regarded by members of that race as criminal.

It is generally accepted now that no race has an inherent tendency toward antisocial or criminal behavior, and that all races have the same array of traits and capacities. Whether all races have these attributes in the same proportions is still a moot question, but it is probable that they do and that seeming differences are the result of social experiences that begin at birth and that influence their development and expression. Hence, we shall expect to find most if not all of the explanation of differences in criminal behavior between races in social influences rather than in inborn characteristics.

The United States has a number of racial groups, not all of which have been studied with reference to criminal behavior. The largest numerically is the Negro group. Of importance in certain sections of the country are the various Oriental groups—Chinese, Japanese, Filipinos.

Negro Juvenile Delinquency

Official statistics of both juvenile delinquency and adult imprisonment generally show a higher rate of offenses for Negroes than for whites. In the summaries of numerous studies made by Frazier and Axelrad, it is shown that Negro children are brought before juvenile courts and are institutionalized 3 or 4 times as often as white children, in proportion to the number of each group in the population.[21]

As among white children, boys greatly exceed the girls in delinquency. Negro children become officially delinquent at a somewhat earlier age than do white children, which may indicate either that they actually escape family supervision earlier or that the police pick them up for minor misconduct at an age when they would overlook similar misconduct in white children.

Adult Negro Crime Rates

As with juveniles, adult crime rates for Negroes exceed those for whites, as judged by commitments to prison. This situation is true in all states at different periods of time and for all types of crime except embezzlement and fraud.[22] Undoubtedly, this excess in Negro rates is partially derived from discrimination by the courts, and inability of the Negro to employ adequate legal counsel or to pay fines and thus avoid prison sentences. Certain studies show that when a Negro offends against a white person, the percentage of convictions is much greater than when a Negro offends against a Negro or a white offends against a white. The lowest percentage of convictions in southern states occurs when a white offends against a Negro.[23] The trend has been toward less discrimination in length of prison sentences, but a greater proportion of Negroes who commit homicide receive the death sentence than is true for whites.[24]

Background of Negro Crime

Many special reasons have been suggested for such predominance of Negro crime as actually exists.   Some of them go back to the days of slavery and the traditions built up then that have been handed down from one generation to the next, especially in the rural South where the Negroes are isolated from contacts with white culture.   Slavery destroyed the Negroes' native culture and methods of social control but did not develop a substitute system.   Family life under slavery was a haphazard affair, a fact reflected still in the high rates of desertion and divorce among Negroes. Schools were not established during slavery, and those since established are far inferior to schools for whites.   Work habits were poorly developed and entrance into business and the professions was (and to a large extent still is) prohibited.   Thrift was unnecessary under a system of slavery, and it benefits the rural southern Negro slightly under the prevailing semipeonage system. These experiences have resulted in a failure on the part of the Negro to develop a high degree of self-respect and personal pride or of self-discipline and the ability to work.   He is inclined to feel dependent upon whites and often rationalizes thefts with the statement that the whites owe him a living.   Thus petty thefts, vagrancy, and abandonment of wives and children are to be expected.

When southern Negroes come to northern industrial cities, many of them are bewildered and unable to adjust to urban life.   Stealing may seem to be the way out.   Others may react to the release from white restraints found in the South by rowdiness and vandalism.   More aggressive Negroes may restrain themselves for a long period but eventually rebel against unjust discriminations, and their hatred and frustration may find expression in criminal acts directed against whites.   That not all Negroes thus react is evident in the relatively low rates of delinquency (and it may be assumed of adult crime) in well-organized Negro areas.   However, the tendency of well-adjusted and educated Negroes to withdraw into compact communities and to separate themselves from the less well-endowed members of their race contributes to increased crime in that it leaves the lower class Negroes leaderless.

FOREIGN-BORN WHITES

Until the 1930's much public anxiety was aroused by concern for criminal activities among the foreign-born.   The experience of social agencies and the police indicated high delinquency rates in the foreign areas of American cities, and it was common knowledge that many notorious criminals of foreign birth were active in organized crime. With the virtual cessation of European immigration following World War I and the passing of stringent laws to control immigration, attention has shifted to other areas of crime. Some of the findings of the earlier research on crime among the foreign-born have general significance for an understanding of criminal behavior, and also may give an understanding of the problems of law enforcement among such new arrivals as Mexicans and Puerto Ricans.

Rates by Nationality

When foreign-born groups were combined and their crime rates compared with the rates of native-born whites, the combined foreign-born rate was lower than the native-white rate in the majority of cities. This statement is based on a comprehensive study of 31 cities made by the National Commission on Law Observance and Enforcement,[25] in only 7 of which the foreign-born rate exceeded the native-white rate. In many cities, however, a few foreign-born groups exceeded the general foreign-born rate as well as the native-born rate. For example, in New York State in 1929 the rates for arrests for felonies and a group of related crimes per 100,000 of certain population groups stood as follows:

Native-born (whites and Negroes)	346.7
All foreign-born whites	207.8
Mexico	1,886.0
Greece	779.5
Italy	344.0

For all other foreign-born groups the rate was below the combined rate of 207.8 for all foreign-born white groups. Czechoslovakia (38.1), Germany (86.9), and Ireland (9.7) had especially low rates. In general, the groups that have excessively high rates are those that have most recently arrived in the United States, although there are some exceptions.

Crime and Age Distribution of Foreign-born

Further analysis shows that a large part of the difference between foreign-born and native-born rates may be accounted for on the basis of differences in the age distribution of the two groups. The foreign-born have become an "old" group. The restrictions on immigration have prevented large numbers of immigrants from coming in; since immigration usually consisted largely of young males, this restriction has reduced the proportion among the foreign-born of the group from which would come the highest

rates of crime.   When corrections are made for age differences between
foreign-born and native-born, the ratio of commitments to penal institutions
is 9 admissions of native-born men to 10 of foreign-born men, when each
group has spent its entire adult life in this country.[26]   The small difference
may be due to errors in estimates made in the course of computing the ratios,
or to chance.   Thus, although the fact still stands that criminality among the
foreign-born as a group is less than criminality among the native-born, it
does not indicate any greater tendency toward crime on the part of the native-
born group.   Rather, the tendency is much the same.

When the rates of native-born and foreign-born are computed by age
groups, it further appears that young foreign-born males have a higher rate
of commitments than have young native-born males.   For ages 15 through
29, foreign-born rates exceed native-born; for ages 30 through 34 the rates
are identical; for ages above 34 the native-born rates exceed the foreign-
born.   In the light of these differences in rates for different ages, it seems
significant that the higher rates are found among the foreign-born groups
that have most recently entered the United States, and which therefore contain the highest percentage of young males.

Social Factors

Sociological factors may also help to account for differences in rates among
nationality groups.   Probably members of the early immigration (chiefly
northwestern Europeans and British) came into established communities of
their own people in this country and were assimilated; a process that exerted
control over their movements and aided them in establishing themselves.
Also, since the native stock of America is descended primarily from these
same countries there is little prejudice against recent immigrants.   Americans accept immigrants from northern and western Europe and the British
Isles in friendly fashion.   The background of these immigrants and of the
native American stock is the same or similar, therefore there is little likeli-
hood of conflict or ridicule.

The newer immigrant stocks bring customs and carry names that set
them apart from the native-born group; their assimilation is difficult and opportunities for misunderstanding and conflict are numerous.   Moreover,
they do not have the advantage of absorption into a group of their own people long established in this country, which eases the problems of adjustment.
It is these newer immigrants, herded into the urban slums, who contribute
heavily to delinquency.

Sometimes the immigrants from central and southern Europe establish
customs that run counter to American mores and laws.   Drinking customs

vary, relations between the sexes are on a different basis, and customs of settling personal feuds without recourse to law deviate.

The rates of arrests and convictions by types of crime reflect to some extent these peculiarities of the social situation and differences in national customs, just as the arrests of Orientals on the west coast reflect their own customs. Thus, homicide, assault, rape, robbery, and illegal possession of weapons occur more frequently among Greeks and Italians than among other groups.[27]   Mexicans are guilty in high degree of these same offenses, as well as being drug violators.

Crime Among the Native-born of Foreign Parentage

When the native-born children of foreign parents are studied as a separate group, a distinctive pattern of criminal rates appears.   The rates shown in Table 4 for 1930, per 10,000 of the male population 15 years of age and

TABLE 4

Incidence of Crime per 10,000 for Whites of Native and Foreign-Born Parentage, 15 Years of Age and Over, for Buffalo and Detroit, 1930

| | Buffalo | | Detroit | |
	Serious Felonies	Less Serious	Serious Felonies	Less Serious
Native white				
Of native parentage	163.81	1264.74	53.06	274.96
Of foreign parentage	207.24	1016.31	51.00	142.99
Of mixed parentage	66.73	232.82	22.42	50.79
Foreign-born white	55.34	519.38	21.91	138.38

Source: *Report on Crime and the Foreign-Born,* No. 10 (Washington: National Commission on Law Observance and Enforcement, Government Printing Office, 1931), p. 158.

over for Buffalo and Detroit, show the contrast.   In each case those of foreign parentage exceed the foreign-born; persons with mixed parentage, however, have lower rates than the foreign-born.   In only one instance does the foreign-parentage group exceed the native-born native parentage.

Mowrer supplies some corroborative evidence for juvenile delinquents in Chicago for 1929 to 1935, shown in Table 5.

The usual explanation for the high crime rates of native-born persons with foreign-born parents, especially among juveniles, is that they stand halfway between the culture of the Old World and of America.   They are not thoroughly incorporated into either and therefore in a position subject to both social and personal disorganization.

TABLE 5

Race and Nativity of Population and of Juvenile Delinquents, Chicago, 1929–35

	Per Cent of Total Population	Per Cent of Juvenile Court and Boys' Court Cases
Native white		
Of native parentage	35	17
Of foreign or mixed parentage	37	52
Foreign-born white	20	3
Negro	7	25
Other	—	3

Source: Ernest R. Mowrer, *Disorganization, Personal and Social* (Lippincott, 1942), pp. 120–31, 584.

OUTCOME OF DELINQUENCY AND CRIME

How does crime run its course?   What proportion of youthful offenders reforms?   What proportion becomes thoroughly enmeshed in the criminal world?   The careers of two sets of brothers suggest the many possible outcomes.

Of the 6 Touhy brothers who flourished in the Chicago crime world during the years preceding and following World War I, all began their criminal careers as children or adolescents.[28]   As adult criminals they were safe-blowers, prohibition violators, and kidnapers.   One died in prison where he was serving a sentence for burglary and assault to kill; another was killed in 1927 at the age of 38 during a fight with a rival beer-running gang; a third was accidentally killed by his own gang in 1929 at the age of 35; a fourth is in prison serving a 23 year term that he received at the age of 44; a fifth is in prison with a 99 year term for kidnaping, to which he was sent when 37; the sixth decided at the age of 31 that crime "is a sucker's play," and turned to running a roadhouse in another state.

All 5 brothers described by Clifford R. Shaw in *Brothers in Crime* [29] began begging and stealing at an early age—some of them were even in their prechool years.   In spite of numerous arrests and detention in institutions for juveniles, they continued to steal until they were in their twenties.   John was last arrested at the age of 21 and was sentenced to prison, from which he was released when 24.   He passed the succeeding 10 years (until the book was published) without arrests and presumably without committing crimes.   Edward committed his last offense at 25; James at 24; Carl at 22. Michael was sentenced to the penitentiary for armed robbery when he was 21, and 6 years later was still serving his term.   Of the brothers who aban-

doned crime, 2 are married, and all are employed more or less steadily.
These men, however, were not "big shots" in the criminal world.

Many statistical studies have been made of the behavior of juvenile delinquents at intervals of 5, 10, or 15 years after referral by a juvenile court to a
psychiatric clinic, and of adult criminals after release from a penal institution.   These studies are based on the more serious offenders, inasmuch as
children reprimanded by police or judge without clinic referral and misdemeanants among adults are not included.   Three of the most thorough
studies have been made by Sheldon and Eleanor T. Glueck.

One thousand male juvenile delinquents who had been referred by the
juvenile court to the Judge Baker Foundation of Boston comprised the
initial group for one study.[30]   The records of as many of these boys as could
be located were checked at 5 year intervals from the time the average age of
the group was 13.5 years until the average age was 29.   More than half of
the boys had been arrested previous to their referral to the clinic; they were
not, therefore, novices at crime.   Figure 15 shows the percentage of boys at
each interval who had been arrested during the preceding 5 years.   Fifteen
years after the clinic referral, 57.9 per cent were still delinquent.

A second study by the Gluecks traces the experiences of 417 men 15 years
after the expiration of their parole from Massachusetts Reformatory.[31]

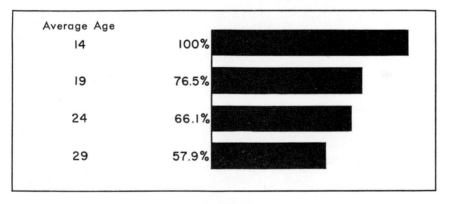

FIGURE 15

Percentage of 1,000 delinquent boys who were arrested during successive 5-year
periods, from the time when their average age was 14 until it was 29.   Recidivism was high among male juvenile delinquents who became court cases.   The
most marked return to conventional behavior came in the first five years after
the court appearance.   When the average age was 29, almost three fifths of the
number were still subject to arrests.   (Based on Sheldon and Eleanor T. Glueck,
Juvenile Delinquents Grown Up [New York: Commonwealth Fund, 1940],
pp. 16, 26, 43, 59.)

Their careers, summarized in Table 6, are predominantly criminal; two thirds remained either serious or minor offenders, or vacillated between conventionality and crime.

TABLE 6

Criminal Records of 417 Men, 15 Years after Expiration of Parole
from Massachusetts Reformatory

	Number	Per Cent
Became nondelinquent at some time during the 15 years and were still nondelinquent at the end of 15 years.	140	33.5
Persistently serious offenders throughout the 15 years	135	32.4
Serious offenders originally, but became and remained minor offenders	121	29.0
Became nondelinquent at some time during the first 10 years after discharge but relapsed into delinquency later	21	5.1

Source: Sheldon and Eleanor Glueck, *Criminal Careers in Retrospect* (New York: Commonwealth Fund, 1943), p. 121.   The percentages given here do not entirely agree with those given by the Gluecks.   Their percentages are computed on a basis of a total of 418 cases, although the correct total of their figures is 417.

Women, whose offenses are much less serious than those of men, have a very poor record of reform, according to the Gluecks' study.[32]   The records of 500 women who had served terms in the Massachusetts State Reformatory for Women were checked 5 years after the expiration of their terms.   According to Table 7, almost two fifths continued their offenses with an average

TABLE 7

Five Hundred Women 5 Years after Completion of Term,
Massachusetts State Reformatory for Women

	Number	Per Cent
Nondelinquent at the end of 5 years	94	23.6
Delinquent but never arrested	148	37.1
Delinquent and arrested one or more times	157	39.3
Situation not applicable or unknown	101	—
TOTAL	500	100.0

Source: Sheldon and Eleanor T. Glueck, *Five Hundred Delinquent Women* (Knopf, 1934), p. 504.

of one arrest every 15 months.   Approximately the same proportion had committed delinquencies for which they might have been arrested but were not.   Thus slightly over three fourths of the women were still pursuing delinquent careers 5 years after release from the Reformatory.

These studies show that among both male and female serious offenders more than half have not been diverted into conventional patterns by our present treatment of offenders.   Instead they have developed a life organization in which commission of misdemeanors and crimes is an integral part of their patterns of behavior.

SUMMARY OF CHARACTERISTICS OF CRIMINALS

It is evident that there is no one type of person who is destined for a life of crime and that crimes themselves vary greatly.   Nevertheless, certain generalizations can be made to show predominant types of crime and the classes of people most likely to become involved in crime.

Minor offenders (misdemeanants) are many times more numerous than serious criminals (felons).

Among felonies, thefts outnumber assaults.

Rural areas and small cities have the lowest rates of crime, medium-sized cities somewhat higher rates, and larger cities the highest rates.

The highest crime rate is in the young adult years.

Four to 8 times as many males as females are arrested and convicted.

Offenses differ with age and sex; the most serious crimes involving injuries to others are committed by young males; injuries to self (vices) are more common among women and older men.

On intelligence ratings, serious offenders represent a cross section of the comparable population.   It may be that misdemeanants and juvenile delinquents include a disproportionate number with subnormal intelligence.

A higher proportion of criminals than of the general population have not been married or their marriages have failed.

Negroes have a higher arrest and conviction rate than whites.

In general, foreign-born whites have the same rate of crime as native-born whites, although young foreign-born persons and native-born of foreign parentage have higher rates than older foreign-born or native-white of native parentage.

More than one-half of young delinquents and criminals continue their offenses into the adult years.

None of the characteristics of criminals just listed can be seized upon as a cause of crime.   No sex, age, racial, marital, or nativity group has within itself the seeds of criminal behavior.   Criminal acts arise out of the adjustment efforts of people within the mold of a specific social and cultural situation.   At most, the groups with high criminal rates may be thought of as those with the most difficult adjustment problems.

QUESTIONS

1. How could criminal statistics be made more reliable?
2. Secure annual police reports for your city and analyze them by age, sex,

and type of offense. Do the distributions corroborate those given in the text? If there are differences, try to explain them.

3. What is the relation of age to crime?

4. Are men more inclined to criminality than women? Read Otto Pollak, *The Criminality of Women* and give a critical evaluation.

5. In what racial and nativity groups is crime most likely to occur as indicated by arrests? Propose practical programs adapted to crime prevention in each group.

READINGS

Glueck, Sheldon and Eleanor T., *One Thousand Juvenile Delinquents* (Cambridge: Harvard University Press, 1934).

————, *Juvenile Delinquents Grown Up* (New York: Commonwealth Fund, 1940). In these 2 books, the Gluecks present their initial study of 1,000 boy delinquents during the first 5 years after release from treatment; and a further study 10 years later. The persistence of criminal behavior is clear.

————, *Five Hundred Criminal Careers* (Knopf, 1930).

————, *Later Criminal Careers* (New York: Commonwealth Fund, 1937).

————, *Criminal Careers in Retrospect* (New York: Commonwealth Fund, 1943). In 3 studies, the experiences in crime of 500 men are traced through 15 years following release from prison or parole. Many factors related to rehabilitation are revealed.

Hayner, N. S., "Social Factors in Oriental Crime," *American Journal of Sociology,* 43 (1938), 908–19. Cultural and social factors related to crime among Orientals in the United States are analyzed.

Pollak, Otto, *The Criminality of Women* (Philadelphia: University of Pennsylvania Press, 1950). This book explores the thesis that, although crime rates for women are much lower than those for men, nevertheless, women are in reality fully as criminally inclined in attitude and behavior as men.

Porterfield, A. L., "Delinquency and Its Outcome in Court and College," *American Journal of Sociology,* 49 (1943), 199–204. College students and court delinquents are compared with reference to amount and types of lawbreaking; interesting suggestions are given as to why some delinquent children come before the courts whereas others are spared this experience.

Tulchin, Simon H., *Intelligence and Crime* (Chicago: University of Chicago Press, 1939). This comparison of inmates of Illinois penal institutions with Illinois men in the draft of World War I shows that prisoners have virtually the same distribution of intelligence test scores as men in the draft.

FOOTNOTES

[1] Sophia Robinson, *Can Delinquency Be Measured?* (New York: Columbia University Press, 1936).

[2] F. J. Murphy, M. M. Shirley, and H. L. Witmer, "The Incidence of Hidden Delinquency," *American Journal of Orthopsychiatry,* 16 (1946), 686–89.

[3] A. L. Porterfield, "Delinquency and Its Outcome in Court and College," *American Journal of Sociology,* 49 (1943), 199–204.

[4] A. Arieff and C. Bowle, "Some Psychiatric Aspects of Shoplifting," *Journal of Clinical Psychopathology,* 8 (1947), 565.

[5] Thorsten Sellin, *Research Memorandum on Crime in the Depression,* Bulletin 27 (New York: Social Science Research Council), p. 69.

[6] Estes Kefauver, *Crime in America* (Doubleday, 1951).

[7] C. C. Van Vechten, "Differential Criminal Case Mortality in Selected Jurisdictions," *American Sociological Review,* 7 (1942), 833–39.

[8] W. C. Kvaraceus, "Chronological Ages of 761 Delinquents at Time of Initial Apprehension," *Journal of Criminal Law and Criminology,* 25 (1944), 166–68.

[9] Sheldon and Eleanor T. Glueck, *One Thousand Juvenile Delinquents* (Cambridge: Harvard University Press, 1934), p. 97.

[10] D. O. Moberg, "Old Age and Crime," *Journal of Criminal Law, Criminology, and Police Science,* 43 (1953), 764–76; P. L. Schroeder, "Criminal Behavior in the Later Period of Life," *American Journal of Psychiatry,* 92 (1936), 918.

[11] "A Few Facts about Juvenile Delinquency," *The Child,* 17 (1952), 63.

[12] Ernest R. Mowrer, *Disorganization, Personal and Social* (Lippincott, 1942), p. 581.

[13] *The Houston Delinquent in His Community Setting* (Houston, Texas: Council of Social Agencies, 1945), p. 2.

[14] *Uniform Crime Reports in the United States and Its Possessions, 1952,* 23, No. 2 (Washington: Government Printing Office, 1953), 116.

[15] Otto Pollak, *The Criminality of Women* (Philadelphia: University of Pennsylvania Press, 1950).

[16] Carl Murchison, *Criminal Intelligence* (Worcester, Mass.: Clark University, 1926).

[17] Simon H. Tulchin, *Intelligence and Crime* (Chicago: University of Chicago Press, 1939).

[18] William Healy and Augusta F. Bronner, *Delinquents and Criminals, Their Making and Unmaking* (Macmillan, 1926), 130–31.

[19] Sheldon and Eleanor T. Glueck, *Criminal Careers in Retrospect* (New York: Commonwealth Fund, 1943), p. 84.

[20] J. L. Gillin, "Backgrounds of Prisoners in the Wisconsin State Prison and of Their Brothers," *American Sociological Review,* 2 (1937), 210–11.

[21] E. Franklin Frazier, *The Negro Family in the United States* (Chicago: University of Chicago Press, 1939), p. 359. Chapter 17 of Frazier's book cites figures from various reports and also contains an excellent discussion of significant social influences in Negro delinquency. See also Mowrer, *op. cit.,* p. 120; S. Axelrad, "Negro and White Male Institutionalized Delinquents," *American Journal of Sociology,* 57 (1952), 569–74.

[22] Edward B. Reuter, *The American Race Problem* (Crowell, 1938), ch. 16; *Report on Crime and the Foreign-Born,* National Commission on Law Observance and Enforcement, No. 10 (Washington: Government Printing Office, 1931), pp. 100 ff.

[23] G. B. Johnson, "The Negro and Crime," *Annals of the American Academy of Political and Social Science,* 217 (1941), 93–104.

[24] T. Sellin, "Race Prejudice in the Administration of Justice," *American Journal of Sociology,* 41 (1935), 212–17; Reuter, *op. cit.;* Johnson, *op. cit.*

[25] *Report on Crime and the Foreign-Born,* pp. 100 ff.

[26] C. C. Van Vechten, "The Criminality of the Foreign-Born," *Journal of Criminal Law and Criminology,* 32 (1941), 139–47.

[27] *Report on Crime and the Foreign-Born,* p. 158.

[28] J. Fay and D. Anderson, "Story of the Terrible Touhys, Most Savage of Chicago Gangs," *Chicago Sun* (Feb. 14 through 24, 1943).

[29] (Chicago: University of Chicago Press, 1938).

[30] Sheldon and Eleanor T. Glueck, *Juvenile Delinquents Grown Up* (New York: Commonwealth Fund, 1940), pp. 16, 26, 43, 59.

[31] Sheldon and Eleanor T. Glueck, *Criminal Careers in Retrospect,* p. 121.

[32] Sheldon and Eleanor T. Glueck, *Five Hundred Delinquent Women* (Knopf, 1934).

3

Cultural and Social
Backgrounds of
Criminals

The theory set forth in Chapter 1 placed criminal behavior in the same category with all other behavior, as an effort on the part of the individual to satisfy needs within the confines, privileges, and frustrations of the cultural and social environment. In this chapter the cultural and social environment are further examined.

THE CRIMINAL ETHOS OF THE UNITED STATES

Although we have a plethora of laws to regulate behavior, crime is part of the cultural pattern of the United States. Whether people are rich, poor, old, young, white, Negro, foreign-born or native-born, intelligent or stupid, they are subject to certain general influences and attitudes that stimulate an interest in crime.

Interest in Crime

The criminal ethos of the United States is disseminated and perpetuated by the many secondary means of communication that make information common property of all people in all sections of the country. Motion pictures, radio and television programs, popular magazines, and certain types of "comic books" have all found crime a never failing source of dramatic interest to the public. The presentation may be purely fictional, a story of the life of some notorious criminal, or a serious discussion of juvenile delinquency, prison riots, or gambling syndicates. Whatever the form of presentation, the material, far removed from conventional life, is always dramatic and startling. On some programs the effort is made to show that "crime doesn't pay," by the simple expedient of having the criminal captured by the police, slain in the course of escape, or commit suicide. Nevertheless, the story that precedes the finale suggests a way of life that is exciting and daring, that brings quick rewards, and that opens the way to defiance of authority.

Many people recognize the artificiality of the endings and know quite well that few criminals are captured.   News stories certainly do not bear out the slogan that "crime doesn't pay."   The investigations of gambling rings by the Kefauver Committee showed that crime paid very handsomely and brought very few penalties.

The popularity of crime news and fiction is easily demonstrated.   In one week in Los Angeles, monitors who recorded types of television shows found that up to 9 P.M., 852 shows based on major crimes, including 167 murders, were shown.[1]   Eighty-five per cent of all crime shows were on the air before 9 P.M., during the hours when children form an eager audience; 78 per cent of all crime shows were on children's programs.   Radio programs and motion pictures find crime a certain means of attraction while all but the most sedate newspapers spread crime stories across much of the front page and more sensational papers print little except crime stories.   Perhaps nothing illustrates the fascination of crime for the public so well as the response to the televised public hearings carried out by the Kefauver Committee in 1950–51.   Men with criminal records and suspected operators of large-scale criminal operations were questioned before the television.   It was estimated that between 20 and 30 million people watched and heard these sessions of investigation.

The reasons for this avid interest in crime and some of the effects on behavior of the unremitting bombardment of crime stories are in part speculative.   Pending future research, several suggestions may be made.

Release of Repressions

The lawlessness typical of the opening of a new country is part of our immediate historical background.   During the period of settlement, social control was weak and each person determined the nature of his personal conduct for himself.   Many vagrant impulses found unbridled expression on the frontier through openly operated institutions of prostitution, gambling, and drinking.   As frontier settlements grew into organized communities, these institutions were repressed but not always destroyed; in many cities one famous, wide-open street remains where conventional controls may be forgotten.

At the same time that the frontier permitted open expression of elemental impulses, the mores of the United States dictated stern control of these same impulses.   From colonial days came a tradition of a strictly regulated personal life.   Idleness, lying, scolding, public demonstrations of affection, and many kinds of fun and recreation, as well as prostitution, gambling, drunkenness, and fighting, were forbidden as deviations from the temperate and controlled life that was the ideal.   Many of these repressions are still in force in modified form. For some people the wide-open street now grants, as the frontier granted in the past, relief from these repressions; for others who would never think of deviating from a temperate life, stories based on the past, and made more glamorous than the original events, afford vicarious satisfactions.   In the novel, the motion picture, the telecast based on the frontier, the conventional person may enjoy the thrill of forbidden pleasures while retaining his satisfaction in his personal purity.

Many of the news stories of present-day crimes seem to serve much the same purpose.   Daily life may be controlled, orderly, monotonous, but for a brief period the housewife, the highschool student, the business or professional man may share the hazardous adventures of a criminal.

Initiative and Daring

The rapid geographical expansion and economic development of the United States not only provided for great individualism in action but also called forth unprecedented initiative and daring.   At one extreme, men took advantage of the great freedom and murdered and stole for their own gain without making a contribution to the productivity of the country.   At the other extreme, law enforcement itself was often carried out with the same highhanded disregard for law and fairness.   The bands of vigilantes who tracked down and killed horse thieves and murderers; the frontiersman with his overhasty defense of his life, his family, and his property, which often resulted in the death of the aggressor; and the sheriffs in the Southwest who assumed dictatorial powers were all acting illegally in terms of the laws of the East.

Individualism, initiative, and forceful activity also marked the early industrial promoters.   Many of the great industries of the nineteenth century that now are the backbone of our economic system were established with scant regard for law or ethics.   The man who outwitted a competitor or the government might be criticized, but also was admired.   Although new laws and the settled condition of the country have outmoded the highhanded operations of the past, the basic qualities of individualism, initiative, and force are still a part of our economic systems and often conflict with legal procedures.

The Urge toward Success

We believe that all people are born with equal opportunities and that upward social mobility is the right of everyone.   We measure success in terms of wealth, symbolized by industrial position, place of residence, size of home, and make of car.   We also believe in competitiveness, with each person striving individually to better himself.   Theoretically, the accumulation of wealth and the upward climb are carried out according to the mores and laws of the nation.   Actually, many people grasp at either unethical or illegal ways of increasing their wealth or improving their social position.   From time to time new ways are invented to pile up wealth that are violations in principle of criminal laws, such as misrepresentation of manufactured products, adulteration of foods, or unsound holding companies.   Such practices become widespread and are adopted by one business concern after another.   Finally, the situation becomes so flagrantly unethical that new laws are passed to control it, often to be followed by a new method of circumvention that stays within the letter of the new law although violating the principles.   These attitudes and practices of gain at the expense of another become widely known and are a part of our general cultural heritage.   An investigation carried out by Cressey [2] to trace the origin of criminal behavior of 125 men imprisoned for trust violations failed to prove that the offenders had specific contacts with criminals from whom they learned the techniques of their crime or acquired criminal attitudes.   In fact, the only techniques used were ways of avoiding discovery of their thefts, and their attitudes were primarily rationalizations to protect themselves from feelings of guilt (for instance, they were merely borrowing the money temporarily).   These men were unable to say when or where they had acquired the idea of thefts or the rationalizations; no one specifically had taught them.   In other words, implicit in our culture is the attitude that personal gain may take precedence over strict honesty.

Ambivalence of Attitudes toward Crime

The cultural traditions of our country have produced contradictory attitudes toward crime.   In the abstract, crime is to be deplored; specific types of crime, however, may be not only tolerated but utilized.   Many types of self-indulgence are generally thought to be against public welfare and are treated legally as crime; but gambling, drug addition, and prostitution are tolerated generally, protected by the police, and patronized by enough people to make it profitable for someone to provide the services and take the risk of possible prosecution.   Honesty in the abstract is extolled, but sharp business practices are a part of accepted business procedures among many people.   Attitudes are ambivalent, also, with reference to the group committing the crime.   Murder usually meets with dynamic public opposition; however, murder within a criminal gang, or between competing criminal groups, does not arouse much anger in the community at large.

Although most Americans would condemn crime verbally, tolerance of specific crimes and deviant personal behavior show the great inconsistencies that exist.

Effect on Children

Paralleling the widespread interest in crime is an uneasy fear of the possible deleterious effects upon children of the many crime stories produced primarily for the consumption of children. Motion pictures, telecasts, and so-called comic books produce a steady stream of crime stories, explicit in detail, that are eagerly sought by children and adolescents. Although there have been a few objective studies and much speculation, a definitive answer can apparently not yet be given of the degree to which juvenile delinquency and crime may be attributed to these sources.

A number of psychologists and psychiatrists brush aside all suggestions that stories of murder, torture, exploitation, burglary, armed robbery, and the like will instill in a child the desire to carry out in overt behavior what he has seen in pictures or about which he has read. They maintain that the crimes of children are not traceable to pictures and stories of crime but are the result of emotional maladjustment that finds an outlet in attacks, vandalism, brutal play, and the like.

Full acceptance of the above point of view has implications for all the processes and techniques of learning. Schools depend upon books, motion pictures, radio programs, and posters to teach both attitudes and skills.[3] Propaganda, desirable and undesirable, also rests upon the use of audiovisual stimuli. Advertising uses many of the same techniques as education and propaganda. It is psychologically sound to expect crime stories in motion pictures, telecasts, and comic books to affect the attitudes and behavior of children. It is significant that the crime comic books use many of the techniques used in propaganda: repetition, attaching opprobrious names to police ("give those flatfeet a bellyful of lead"), use of such stereotypes as the successful gunman, and including among the crime comics legitimate advertisements or propaganda for philanthropic institutions.

A few objective studies have been made to attempt to measure the effect of audiovisual crime material on children's attitudes and behavior. The most extensive was a study of motion pictures carried out by Blumer and Hauser in which information was secured from delinquent and nondelinquent boys and girls in urban areas with low, medium, and high rates of delinquency.[4] The authors concluded that approximately 10 per cent of male and 25 per cent of female offenders had been affected by motion pictures. They admit that it is difficult to untangle influences that come from motion pictures from other threads of influence. Some results of motion pictures are difficult to trace. For instance, pictures of luxury may arouse the desire for large sums of money quickly and easily obtained; identification with a gangster or criminal hero may develop a spirit of bravado; on the other hand, the delinquent may take seriously the fact that in most crime pictures the criminal is caught or killed in the last few seconds.   It is significant that boys and girls living in areas with high delinquency rates were more affected by crime pictures than those who lived in areas of low delinquency rates—an indication that the former boys and girls already had their thoughts turned toward delinquency.   Many delinquent boys stated that they had learned definite techniques from motion pictures, for instance, prying a window open with a crowbar, cutting around the latch of a window with a glass cutter, opening a safe, unlocking an automobile with a hollow pipe slipped over the door handle, use of a gun, and making a safe getaway.

Since World War II a battle against comic books that depict crime has been waged by Fredric Wertham, a psychiatrist of New York City.   In his publications he describes and reproduces pictures of the brutal crimes that abound in certain comic books.[5]   From his experiences in clinic and juvenile court he firmly believes that much of the vandalism and many of the brutal crimes of juveniles are directly related to crime comic books—that is, that the attitudes and behavior patterns are directly learned and that they are not the result of emotional maladjustments.   He admits many opponents to his point of view.   Although his writings are provocative, he has not been able to make an objective study that proves his point conclusively.   Obviously, crime comics are not the only influence, since many children who read such books are not criminals.

The entire question of the influence of crime stories presented vividly and repeatedly on radio, television, in motion pictures, and in comic books is in need of careful study.   Such techniques when used educationally are thought to produce favorable results; careful research is needed to determine whether they may not also be teaching attitudes and skills favorable to criminal behavior.

SOCIAL DISORGANIZATION AND CRIME

Social organization refers to the co-ordination of folkways, mores, institutional functions, and laws.   Basic to social organization is acceptance of common values and support of generally accepted norms of conduct.   Social disorganization occurs when some break comes in this co-ordination.   Then the careful interlocking of the elements of social organization is replaced by conflict of some sort, or some function is not performed.   Through its social organization, a society places before its people the standards of conduct expected of them and also the means of satisfaction of personal needs.   When there is disorganization, standards of conduct are not clearly defined and satisfactions are not uniformly provided.   Under these conditions, small groups work out their own way of life, which may be at odds with more widely accepted mores and laws.   Or individuals abandon social dictates and follow the lead of individual impulses into irregular behavior.

Permanent Elements of Disorganization

The United States has many elements of disorganization that must be accepted as relatively permanent.   So long as people of other cultural backgrounds come into the United States, some divergence of culture and a period of unadjustment before the foreign group thoroughly accepts the American way of life must be expected.   Internal migration is also disruptive since it takes people away from their controlling groups and thrusts them as individuals into new communities.   Every new major invention destroys to some extent the efficacy of old mores and calls for the establishment of new, a process that requires time.   The trend from rural village to urban metropolis replaces the tight personal control of primary groups with impersonal and indifferent secondary controls.   Few Americans escape some contact with social disorganization.   Also, few Americans have been educated to maintain high ethical standards without the supporting pressure of society.   Caught in the maelstrom of social disorganization, many people drift into disorganized and perhaps criminal behavior.

Temporary Periods of Social Disorganization: Economic Depressions

Economic depressions with their widespread unemployment also constitute temporary periods of social disorganization.   When a depression is in an incipient stage, fearful predictions are often made of great increases in crime.   Studies made of the Great Depression of the 1930's [6] as well as of other periods of unemployment [7] show that crimes against property—larceny, robbery, and burglary—increase to some extent.   These crimes provide money and property to newly impoverished people.   Offenses that demand an expenditure of money—gambling, drinking, and prostitution—do not increase and may decrease.   Vagrancy also increases as the unemployed drift from city to city in search of work, often being urged on their way by local officials who do not want them added to the already swollen relief rolls.   Studies by Willbach for Chicago and New York City showed a decrease in crimes against the person during the Great Depression.[8]

In the 1930's the increase in crimes against property was checked while the depression was still in full force.   Various explanations have been offered.   It is probable that many of the depression criminals were unemployed people in need of food, clothing, or accustomed comforts.   The social organization failed to meet their needs and they turned to simple and direct methods, without regard to the property rights of owners.   It was relatively easy to rationalize that they had lost their jobs through no fault of their own, therefore that they were entitled to a "living" from some source; they took this "living" from those who had more than they.   But the forces of social reorganization were slowly marshaled against the disorganization caused by widespread unemployment.   Local relief was inadequate and unsatisfactory to persons who had always been self-supporting.   Local work-relief seemed the way out and by 1930–31 some 200 communities were experimenting with work-relief, paid by local public funds.   But these funds were soon exhausted.   The next step was the use of state funds and finally full-fledged federal aid both as direct relief through state agencies and as work-relief through such agencies as the Works Progress Administration, the Civilian Conservation Corps, and the National Youth Administration.   After these provisions were made, the attitudes of the unemployed changed.   Following a period of personal disorganization, many individuals adjusted themselves to the situation and accepted relief rationally and without too great humiliation; others were able to secure work-relief.   And with the establishment of federal aid, the relief funds were more ample and the inherent threat of insecurity in unstable local funds was removed.   Thus the pressure of need that caused persons not strongly motivated toward honesty to steal was relieved and the tendency to commit crime decreased.

Temporary Periods of Social Disorganization: War *

Like other forms of social disorganization World War II contributed to an increase in delinquency and crime.   The study of crime trends is always a difficult one and especially so during a period when many persons are removed from their customary places of residence, because it is difficult to compute an accurate population base for establishing rates.   Thus an apparent increase may be only the result of greatly increased population, such as occurred in many booming industrial centers.   Conversely, a decrease in criminal rates in another community may exist because part of the population has been drained off into industrial centers at some distance and part into the armed forces.   Also, certain types of crime decline whenever there is prosperity, and the war years were years of unprecedented prosperity.

In view of the multiple factors that influence crime rates, especially in wartime, it is not surprising that statistics do not show clearly defined trends. Table 8 shows major offenses known to the police in a selected group of cities for 3 periods: 1931–34 (the depression); 1935–39 (normal period); and 1940–44 (war).   The general trend is down except for rape, aggravated assault, and larceny; the increase for each of these offenses follows a distinc-

* For a discussion of crime among servicemen and the treatment of crime by the armed forces, see Chapter 22.

TABLE 8

Trends in Offenses Known to the Police, for Cities over 25,000 Population

Offense	Average Yearly Number of Offenses			Percentage of Increase or Decrease		
				1935–39 vs.	1940–44 vs.	1940–44 vs.
	1931–34	1935–39	1940–44	1931–34	1935–39	1931–34
Murder and non-negligent manslaughter	1,991	1,687	1,664	—15.3	—1.4	—16.4
Manslaughter by negligence	1,410	1,199	1,247	—15.0	+4.0	—11.6
Rape	1,681	2,222	3,060	+32.2	+37.7	+82.0
Robbery	24,125	17,022	15,142	—29.4	—11.0	—37.2
Aggravated assault	13,601	13,764	16,675	+1.2	+21.1	+22.6
Burglary	106,821	94,840	93,634	—11.2	—1.3	—12.3
Larceny	231,005	249,561	265,442	+8.0	+6.4	+14.9
Automobile theft	99,721	65,426	61,238	—34.4	—6.4	—38.6

Source: *Uniform Crime Reports for the United States and Its Possessions,* 16, No. 1 (Washington: Government Printing Office, 1945), 9.

tive pattern.   Without more information it is not possible to relate trends in crime closely to war.   Unfortunately, we do not have data indicating trends for minor offenses, such as drunkenness, prostitution, or petty thievery.

For juvenile delinquents, also, the trends are not clear.   A report from 82 cities showed a 51 per cent increase in delinquency between 1940 and 1943.[9]   Communities whose population had increased because of military or industrial expansion had a 55 per cent increase in delinquency.   Communities with decreased population showed a 44 per cent increase in delinquency.   There were, however, individual cities in which juvenile delinquency had decreased.   Increases were not consistent as between boys and girls.   In some areas the rate for girls increased and that for boys decreased; and in other communities the reverse was true.

TRANSITION AREAS—AN EXAMPLE OF CULTURAL DEVIATION AND SOCIAL DISORGANIZATION

In addition to the studies made of cultural factors and social disorganization in the United States as a whole, specific studies have been made of cities in which the transition areas or slums are contrasted with more stable neighborhoods.   The transition areas afford examples both of cultural deviation found in the invading foreign and rural people and of social disorganization resulting from the cultural conflicts and the general neglect of these areas on the part of the city itself.

Delinquency Areas in Chicago

When general studies of cities made in the 1920's showed wide variations between different local geographical areas, criminologists turned their attention to the relation of ecological areas to delinquency and crime.   Clifford Shaw was a pioneer in locating areas with high juvenile delinquency rates.[10]   So far above the average were the delinquency rates in certain areas

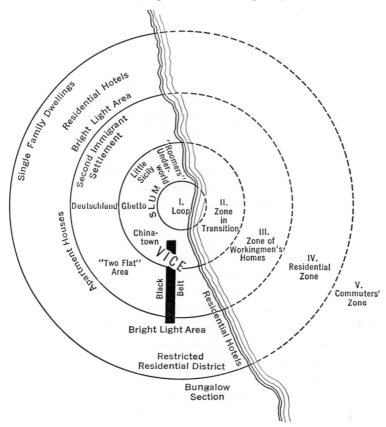

This map of the ecological scheme of Chicago shows by dotted lines the general pattern of a growing industrial city, with the central business district surrounded by a zone in transition in which business is supplanting old residential neighborhoods.   Successive residential zones of increasing socio-economic status lie beyond the zone in transition.   Some of the details of the zones in Chicago, as shown in the left-hand portion of the map, have changed since the 1920's when this map was first produced.   The general scheme of natural growth, however, remains the same.   In the zone in transition (the slums) typically a higher proportion of the population is delinquent or criminal than in any other zone. (Redrawn from Robert E. Park and Ernest W. Burgess, *The City* [University of Chicago Press, 1925], p. 55.)

that Shaw dubbed them "delinquency areas." Using square-mile areas, Shaw computed the number of delinquent boys as a percentage of all boys aged 10 to 16 living in each area. In his initial studies in Chicago, three measures of delinquency were used: alleged delinquents dealt with by police probation officers—the most comprehensive measure of delinquency; alleged delinquents brought before the juvenile court—the more serious cases; and delinquents committed by the juvenile court to correctional institutions —the limited number of boys thought unsuitable for handling in the community. All three series established essentially the same fact—that the delinquency rate was highest in the areas immediately surrounding the downtown business section, called the Loop.*

In these areas, the percentage of boys brought before the police in the year 1926 runs as high as 26 per cent in one square-mile unit, and 22 or 23 per cent in 3 other units. These high percentages indicate that in these neighborhoods, during a single year, 1 out of every 4 or 5 boys between the ages of 10 and 16 indulged in some form of behavior that brought them to the attention of the police. Outside the Loop the delinquency rate tends to decrease. For instance, in areas that are 3 or 4 miles away, the rate is from 5 to 18 per cent, and in the outlying residential sections of the city the rate is still lower, about 1 to 3 per cent. Three of the square-mile units in these districts had no delinquents for the year studied.

The uniform trend—a high rate near the central business section decreasing to a low rate in the outlying residential districts—fails to hold true in 2 situations. Wherever a well-organized and stable residential section extends into the area adjacent to the Loop, a condition that occurs along the lake on the north side of Chicago, the rate declines. However, when an industrial or business section encroaches on less stable residential areas, the rate increases. The well-ordered residential neighborhood tends to have a low rate of delinquency wherever it is found, while less stable sections adjacent to outlying as well as central industrial and business sections tend to have high rates of delinquency. It seems then that the location of an area in the city as a whole does not determine the delinquency rate, but rather proximity to an industrial or business section. The 3 sections of Chicago with the highest rates are near the downtown business section or Loop, near the stockyards, and near the South Chicago steel mills.

That the concentration of high juvenile delinquency rates near the business and industrial sections is not characteristic of only one particular period, is

---

* From the loop made by the elevated railway lines around the business section. At one time the entire business section of Chicago was confined to this area. Now, however, the business area has expanded outside the Loop.

borne out by another study made by Shaw for the years 1900–08.   During this earlier period also, high rates characterized these same areas near the business and industrial sections.   Moreover, a later study, for 1929–35, confirms these findings.[11]   Thus over widely separated periods of time the pattern of delinquency in Chicago remained the same—low rates in the out-lying residential areas, high rates near the central business district, and moderate rates near other commercial and industrial centers.

The difference in typical delinquencies of boys and girls raises the question whether the delinquency areas for girls coincide with delinquency areas for boys—whether sex delinquency of girls arises under the same social conditions as theft by boys.   Using all female offenders between the ages of 10 and 18 who were brought before the Juvenile Court of Cook County during the years 1917–23 inclusive, Shaw followed the same technique applied to his studies of boy delinquents, and computed the delinquency rates by square-mile areas.   Although areas with high rates of girl delinquency and areas with high rates of boy delinquency do not coincide exactly, their correspond-ence is close.   The correlation coefficient between the series of rates by areas for girls and the corresponding series for boys is +.79, which indicates a close correspondence.*

Delinquency Areas in Other Cities

A few years after Shaw completed his studies for Chicago he had an oppor-tunity to make similar studies for 6 other cities.[12]   In Philadelphia all boys brought before the juvenile court during the years 1926–28 were included in the study—a total of 5,859 boys.   In Philadelphia, an industrial city, the central business section is marked by the intersection of Market and Broad Streets.   The rates for individual small areas in this vicinity run as high as 22.6 per cent, while the rate for the total area adjacent to Market and Broad is 11.6.   The rates tend to decrease with distance from this central point until in some of the outlying sections of the city no delinquents were found for the years studied.   Variations of the rates are found primarily in high rates occurring in communities that once were independent cities but had

---

* The word correlation is familiar to most college students.   It means the degree of resemblance in the amounts of 2 characteristics possessed by each individual of a group. The coefficient of correlation is the number that expresses this degree of resemblance. In the instance above, the correlation coefficient shows the extent to which the rate of boy delinquency and of girl delinquency in each area correspond in degree.   The coefficient (usually expressed by the symbol r) can vary from +1.00, showing perfect agreement in the amounts of the two characteristics, to 0 showing no relationship, or to minus 1.00 for reversed relationship, that is, when a high amount of one characteristic is found with a low amount of the other and vice versa.   A correlation coefficient that is close to +1.00 (for instance .95 or .80) indicates a close association between the 2 characteristics, but it does not indicate at all that one caused the other.

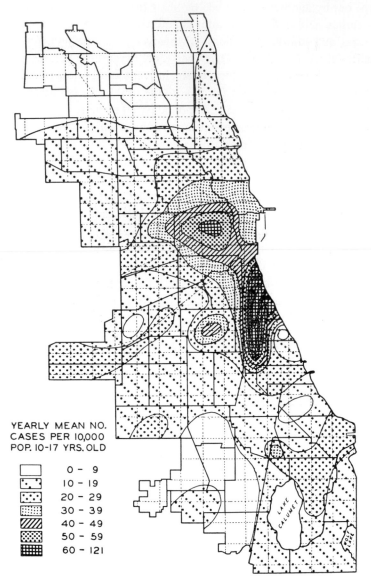

YEARLY MEAN NO.
CASES PER 10,000
POP. 10-17 YRS. OLD

	0 - 9
	10 - 19
	20 - 29
	30 - 39
	40 - 49
	50 - 59
	60 - 121

Map of juvenile delinquency rates in Chicago, 1929–35.   A comparison of this map and the 3 that follow with the ecological map on page 79 shows that the highest concentration of delinquents and criminals is in the transition or slum area.   (From Ernest R. Mowrer, *Disorganization, Personal and Social* [Lippincott, 1942], p. 130.)

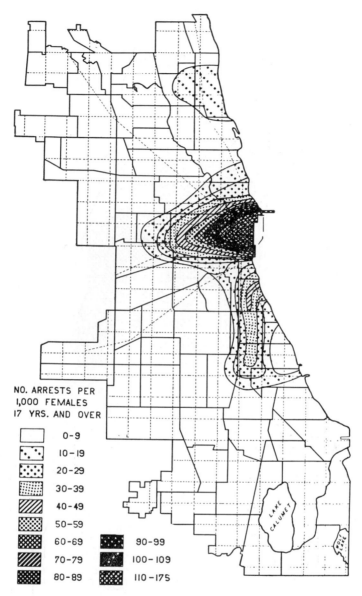

NO. ARRESTS PER
1,000 FEMALES
17 YRS. AND OVER

0-9	
10-19	
20-29	
30-39	
40-49	
50-59	
60-69	90-99
70-79	100-109
80-89	110-175

Map of residences of arrested females in Chicago, 1935. The usual offense is prostitution, a type of behavior associated only with the most disorganized neighborhoods of the city. In the vast majority of Chicago neighborhoods almost no women are arrested. Male offenders of all ages are more widely distributed throughout the city than are female offenders. (From Ernest R. Mowrer, *Disorganization, Personal and Social* [Lippincott, 1942], p. 145.)

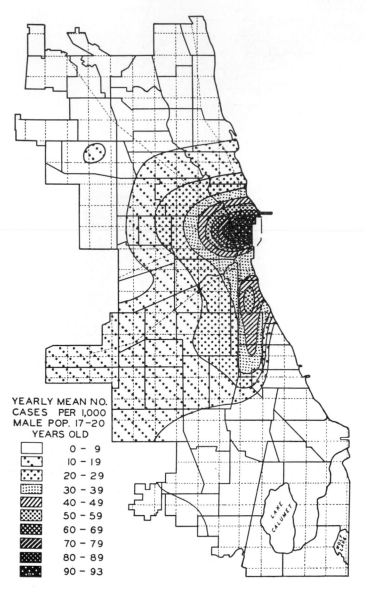

YEARLY MEAN NO.
CASES PER 1,000
MALE POP. 17-20
YEARS OLD

	0 - 9
	10 - 19
	20 - 29
	30 - 39
	40 - 49
	50 - 59
	60 - 69
	70 - 79
	80 - 89
	90 - 93

LAKE
CALUMET

WOLF
LAKE

Map of first appearance in Boys' Court, Chicago, 1929–35.   (From Ernest R.
Mowrer, *Disorganization, Personal and Social* [Lippincott, 1942], p. 129.)

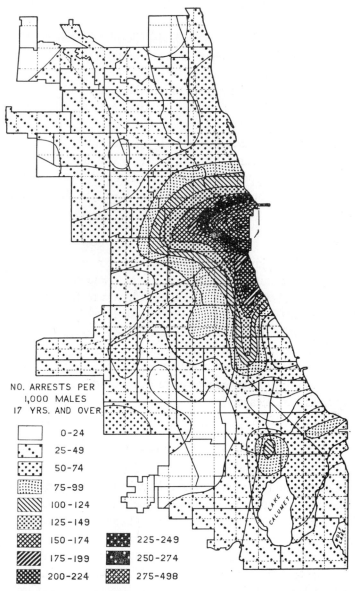

NO. ARRESTS PER
1,000 MALES
17 YRS. AND OVER

0-24	
25-49	
50-74	
75-99	
100-124	
125-149	
150-174	225-249
175-199	250-274
200-224	275-498

Map showing residences of arrested males in Chicago, 1935.   (From Ernest R.
Mowrer, *Disorganization, Personal and Social* [Lippincott, 1942], p. 146.)

been incorporated into the city of Philadelphia. Shaw does not discuss the reason for high rates in these communities nor does he discuss the rates near industrial sections.

The rates for the other cities studied—Cleveland, Denver, Birmingham, and Richmond—show corresponding distributions of rates with reference to business and industrial areas.

Various sociologists who have studied other cities find similar concentrations of delinquency in areas near business and industry and low rates in the more stable residential areas. Longmoor and Young confirmed Shaw's findings in a study of Long Beach,[13] and Hayner in studies of Seattle, Tacoma, Everett, and Bellingham.[14] In Houston, Texas, also, the characteristic delinquency pattern appeared with high rates in and surrounding the central business district and the lowest rates on the periphery of the city in residential areas.[15]

Adult Crime Areas

In areas where juvenile delinquency is common, adult crime also flourishes. Shaw studied the distribution of crime rates for young adult offenders brought before the boys' court of Chicago on felony charges.[16] He found that the distribution of rates corresponded closely with the distribution of rates for juvenile delinquency. When the two series of rates were correlated the coefficient was .90 $\pm$ .01, which indicates a very high degree of correspondence. In a more recent study, Mowrer found a correlation coefficient of .66 $\pm$ .06 between juvenile delinquency rates and adult arrest rates by areas for Chicago.[17]

Crime Rates and Land Use

These and other similar studies lead to a clear generalization: the highest rates of juvenile delinquency and crime are found in areas near the central business section and also in areas near heavily industrialized sections wherever located. A study by White of crime rates and percentages of land used for business purposes by areas for Indianapolis makes this statement concrete. The comparison is shown in Table 9.

White studied male felons (persons guilty of serious crimes) and male misdemeanants (guilty of minor crimes) in Indianapolis, by concentric circles radiating outward from the central business section. Circle, or zone, I included the business center; zone II was adjacent; zones III, IV, and V represented succeeding circular areas extending to the edge of the city. Table 9 shows an orderly downward progression, both in size of crime rates and in percentage of land used for business purposes, from the central business district to the periphery of the city.

TABLE 9

Comparison of Crime Rates with Land Use, Indianapolis

(Criminals per 1,000 males 15–74 years of age)

Zone	Felons	Misdemeanants	Per Cent of Land Used for Business
I	10.1	18.6	34.7
II	5.1	10.3	20.7
III	3.0	7.1	13.8
IV	1.9	4.7	6.4
V	1.5	2.9	3.1

Source: Several tables in R. C. White, "The Relation of Felonies to Environmental Factors in Indianapolis," *Social Forces,* 10 (1931–32), 498–509.   The crime rates are based upon 638 cases disposed of by the Marion County Court in 1930.

Physical Characteristics of Delinquency Areas

To the casual observer the most striking characteristics of the slum areas where delinquency thrives is the physical deterioration.   The central delinquency areas are in a process of transition from residential use to business use. The potential land value is high but the housing is usually old, poorly equipped with modern conveniences, and therefore undesirable as residences. Landlords are reluctant to make repairs and indeed often find it impossible to put the old buildings into really livable condition.   With the housing shortage of the 1940's, many of the apartments were subdivided by flimsy wallboard partitions so that an apartment building originally constructed with 6 apartments may have as many as 18 units, each housing a family, and with many families using the same toilet facilities.   The residents wage an unending and unsuccessful fight against rats, roaches, leaking water pipes, uncollected garbage, and gradual increase in deterioration of the buildings themselves.

In Chicago, the greatest concentration of houses condemned by the building department, to be either destroyed or repaired, directly overlies the areas with highest delinquency rates.   In Detroit, Carr correlated the percentage of delinquency found in each of 15 areas with the percentage of sub-standard housing in the same areas and secured a correlation coefficient of .95, which shows an extremely high degree of correspondence between delinquency and poor housing.[18]   In Houston, Texas, in the 5 census tracts with the highest delinquency rates, 65.6 per cent of the occupied dwelling units needed major repairs or had no private bathroom, whereas in the 5 tracts with the lowest rates only 3.9 per cent of the occupied dwelling units were in this condition.[19]   The coefficient of correlation between delinquency rates and the percentage of poor housing was .75 ± .06. Overcrowding was also more frequent in delinquency areas than in nondelinquency areas. The coefficient of correlation was .85 ± .04. The results of a study of housing and delinquency made by the Housing Division of the Federal Emergency Administration of Public Works confirm the link between delinquency and inferior housing.[20]

However, the relation of poor housing to delinquency is indirect. The connection may be due to poverty, which in turn may rest upon general inadequacy in meeting the demands of urban existence. Although poor housing may be responsible for overcrowding and consequent failure to provide home recreation, it does not cause delinquency. It is an element, however, of the social pattern in which delinquency develops.

Poverty

The people who live in deteriorated areas have one characteristic in common—they are poor. In Chicago, the areas in which the highest percentage of families received aid from the United Charities and the Jewish Charities in 1921 correspond almost exactly with the areas of high delinquency rates for the same period.[21] In Indianapolis, the cases known to the Family Welfare per 1,000 married and widowed women corresponded closely with the rates of felonies and misdemeanors, when the rates were compared by zones based on concentric circles.[22] In Zone I (business center), where the rate of felonies was 10.1 and of misdemeanors 18.6, the dependency rate was 30.0. In Zone V (periphery of city), however, where the rate of felonies had declined to 1.5 and of misdemeanors to 2.9, the dependency rate was only 3.2. Per capita gifts to the community fund showed the reverse trend, with the largest gifts coming from the zone at the edge of the city, the smallest from the residential area that included the central business area.

The study of Long Beach, California, showing 3 centers of delinquency, also indicated 3 centers of high dependency.[23] Although 1 dependency area coincided with a delinquency area, the other 2 were near but not identical with the other 2 delinquency areas. The coefficient of rank correlation by areas between delinquency and dependency rates was .47 which is fairly high for social data.

The Houston study shows higher correlations for certain indices of poverty, indicating close correspondence by areas between poverty and delinquency. The coefficients of correlation by census tracts between delinquency rates and indices of poverty are as follows: [24]

Average monthly rent —.53 ±.10
Percentage of professional and semi-professional workers, proprietors, managers and officials —.50 ±.11
Percentage of laborers and service workers except domestic workers +.50 ±.11

Number of families per 1,000 population known to the County Board of
 Public Welfare   +.87 ±.03
Number of families per 1,000 population on WPA referrals   +.87 ±.03

As with inadequate housing, poverty cannot be assumed to be a direct cause of delinquency. In may, however, be related to delinquency in 2 ways. Poverty may simply be a characteristic of groups not well adjusted to urban economic life and by implication not well adjusted in other respects. It may also cause certain persons to crave the luxuries or even the necessities that they see others enjoy, see pictured in motion pictures, or read about in advertisements. They may therefore steal as an easy way to obtain money to satisfy these needs and desires.

Mobility

Another characteristic of urban delinquency areas is the mobility of the population. For example, Long Beach had 4 areas with high rates of mobility, all adjacent to the areas with peaks of delinquency.[25] Shaw and McKay studied not only mobility, but decrease and increase of population for different areas.[26] They found that areas with a rapidly decreasing population had the highest delinquency rates; those with a slowly increasing population had medium rates; and those with rapid increases in population had low delinquency rates. A decreasing population was characteristic of those areas in which business and industry were expanding, and taking over territory formerly used for residences. Areas near the outer edge of the city that were essentially residential exhibited an increasing population.

Mobility among criminals themselves has been the subject of other studies. In Buffalo, criminals were found to be more mobile than noncriminals.[27] However, another study showed that although delinquents live in areas of high mobility they are not themselves mobile.[28]

Mobility is significant in relation to crime for several reasons. Shaw's study showed that communities with outward flow of population tend to have high delinquency rates. This type of mobility is indicative of the character of the community as a place where people do not want to live if they can escape from it. Moreover, areas with constantly shifting populations tend to have poorly organized neighborhood and community standards of conduct. Families do not become integrated into neighborhood life and neither take pride in nor feel responsible for it. Under such conditions, control of behavior is difficult.

Social Composition

The population of urban delinquency areas tends to consist of those at the bottom of the economic scale—unskilled workers, unadjusted newcomers to the city, groups subject to economic and social discrimination. The national and racial backgrounds of these people therefore vary in different cities and also at different periods of time.

In Chicago, for example, when Shaw made his studies the delinquency areas were populated by high percentages of the foreign-born, Negroes, and Mexicans.   At this time Negroes and Mexicans (in any large numbers) were newcomers to Chicago and low in the economic scale.   Transients, seasonal laborers, and hoboes also inhabited certain streets in delinquency areas, especially during the winter months.   Other streets constituted rooming-house districts.   Thus the residents represented a conglomeration of cultural patterns.   Some are foreign-born with standards of conduct that differ from those of the United States; others coming from rural areas either in this country or abroad find city life strange and difficult; still others are unaccustomed to settled and orderly living.

Obviously there is no single explanation for the high delinquency rates found in such diverse groups; nor do the same types of delinquency necessarily prevail in all sections of an area.   For instance, streets inhabited by transients and hoboes are the hangout of many habitual criminals whose offenses are of a minor nature, as well as those who prey on drunken men, who may easily be robbed.   Neighborhoods with high percentages of the foreign-born are conducive to the formation of boys' gangs that easily develop more or less serious delinquent habits.   Rooming-house areas with a shifting population encourage sex delinquency and prostitution.

Concentration of Adverse Community Influences

These statements regarding specific factors may be supplemented by brief descriptions which synthesize the factors into a unified picture of delinquency areas.   The community in Seattle with the highest delinquency rate is described thus by Hayner:

This is an interstitial neighborhood reflecting the northward push of the business center.   On the western rim of the area is Belltown, a rooming-house district with cheap hotels, secondhand stores, and houses of prostitution—a district in which "the pioneers gave way to the gold rushers, the gold rushers to the fishermen, the fishermen to the laborers."   The population of the area is composed largely of renters and is highly transient.   Of the pupils entering the Warren Avenue school during 1931–32, 62.7 per cent left school during the same year. Of all the schools in the city this was the highest percentage for mobility. "It is like teaching on a street car," said one of the instructors. . . . There is also a high family-dependency rate in the Warren Avenue District.[29]

The highest rate of delinquency in Everett, Washington, was in the Monroe district.   Of this district, Hayner writes:

All three series give the Monroe district, which includes the old Riverside business section, the highest rate for delinquency.   A special study of this neighborhood shows a declining population, many vacant stores, low rents, a relatively high percentage of foreign-born, 35 per cent annual turnover in the Monroe grade school population, no Camp Fire Girls or Boy Scouts, and many apartments or rooms of immoral repute.   This district has the highest rate in the series of chronic dependents. . . . According to the 1930 census data it had, with the Longfellow district to the south, the highest rate for unemployment.   It will be noted in contrast that the Washington district, a residential section, has consistently low rates in all the series.

Carr reports on a study wherein 11 indices of adverse community pressures or influences were worked into a rate, which was then correlated with delinquency rates for 41 areas in Flint, Michigan.[30]   The indices used were the following: lack of a telephone, lack of an automobile, houses without basements, families broken by death, desertion, or divorce, individuals without church affiliation, individuals not attending church every Sunday, individuals twenty-one to sixty years old not in industrial or professional organizations, individuals reading fiction instead of nonfiction, unemployment, illness, and families moving to their present address within a year.   When these indices were converted into one rate, the coefficient of correlation with delinquency rates by areas was .78.

All the characteristics of delinquency areas—poor housing, poverty, mobility, cultural differences with resulting confusion of standards—encourage community disorganization.   They also give rise to the development of institutions that lead to personal disintegration.   Pawnshops, burlesque shows, houses of prostitution, cheap saloons and taverns, flophouses, and drug peddlers offer a variety of demoralizing experiences that would not be tolerated in a more stable and homogeneous community.   These agencies cater to unregulated and unsatisfied cravings and no doubt help to create them.   The traditional institutions—church, school, and neighborhood group—cannot compete and are unable to exert control over personal conduct.

Personal disorganization is expressed in a variety of ways.   For example, in both Chicago and Peoria, Illinois, the areas that breed delinquency also have high divorce rates, a symptom of family and often of personal disorganization.[31]   Schroeder found a correlation coefficient of .69 in Peoria between areas with high divorce rates and areas with high delinquency rates.   Suicides also occur with high frequency in delinquency areas, as do deaths from alcoholism.[32]

Both the value and the limitations of the preceding data on delinquency areas must be recognized.   A study of correlation of 2 types of conditions expressed in rates *by areas* does not show causation, that is, it cannot be demonstrated conclusively that the existence of one condition is responsible for the existence of the other.   Thus, we cannot say from the preceding data

In this Chicago slum, the dark, narrow, trash-littered street with broken pavement is thoroughfare and playground, neighborhood gossip center and laundry drying-yard. Most large cities in the United States have many blocks of slums, inhabited by the newest and poorest comers. Many of the European immigrants who formerly lived in the northern slums have achieved enough economic status to move into better areas, and their places have been taken by Puerto Ricans, newly arrived southern Negroes, or Mexicans. Old or unsuccessful people of European background intermingle with the newer groups. Children are numerous, but the city and the landlord make little provision for their health or recreation. The conditions in the slums are in sharp contrast to the playgrounds and parks in better residential areas and the wide lawns and backyards of smaller communities. Without equipment or space for active games, boys easily succumb to opportunities for malicious mischief, vandalism, and petty thievery. (*Chicago Daily News* photograph)

that deteriorated housing, poverty, mobility, cultural conflicts, or divorce *causes* delinquency. We are not even sure that these factors are attributes of families that have delinquent members. The most we can say with certainty is that areas where all these factors are present are also the areas where delinquency and crime are found. Since the delinquency is committed by children and adolescents, it seems safe to say that these areas are breeding grounds for delinquents. Reckless expresses this relationship by saying that in areas of social disorganization the risk of delinquency is

West Madison Street in Chicago, termed a homeless-man area or skid row, duplicates similar areas found in most large cities. Cheap hotels, pawnshops, and missions abound. Employment offices advertise unskilled jobs, often unsuccessfully. Derelicts who have long since lost the ability or the desire to work loaf on the streets, beg from chance passing businessmen or curious visitors to the area, and drink. The photographer who took this picture commented that it showed more action than is typical, since many loafers tried to scurry out of range of the press camera. These men when drunk offer a temptation to youths to jackroll them for whatever small amounts of money they have. Police often bring them into nearby lockups by the wagonful, where they sober up overnight and are dismissed the following morning. They account for many arrest entries and much of the work of police courts in disorganized areas of large cities. (*Chicago Daily News* photograph)

greater than in more stable and well-organized areas.[33]   This statement is tantamount to saying that in such areas the influences that encourage social rather than individual motivation and the opportunities for conventional fulfillment of needs are less available and less potent than in more stable areas.   Community controls are weak, both because conventional institutions are weak or nonexistent and because pernicious institutions flourish in floundering, leaderless communities.

DELINQUENCY PATTERNS IN DISORGANIZED AREAS

Delinquency patterns that serve as models of behavior for boys and girls are easily developed in disorganized areas.   These patterns can be readily identified.

Influence of Adult Delinquency

The concentration of adult delinquency in delinquency areas permits adolescents to become more familiar with delinquency than is the case in better organized communities.   The young male adults studied by Shaw often must have been older brothers or near neighbors of adolescent delinquents. Many of the notorious gangsters of Chicago (and doubtless in other cities) either grew up in these disorganized areas or maintained headquarters in them.   They became successful, dressed well, drove expensive cars, and dispensed aid to distressed members of the community; thus they frequently furnished the only example of financial success known to residents of the districts. They tended to become the ideal of manhood toward which admiring adolescents strove.

Boys' Gangs

Loose familial control and the failure of family and community to provide recreational and social outlets make it easy for young boys to form play groups or gangs, which, without adult guidance, soon become predatory or otherwise antisocial in conduct.   The 1,313 Chicago gangs studied by Thrasher are found in the same areas in which delinquency rates are high— the areas fringing the business and industrial sections where familial and social control are weak.[34]   He also located the gangs of other cities—New York, Boston, Minneapolis, Cleveland, Los Angeles, and many others—in similar disorganized districts between business or industrial areas and the more stable residential sections.

The typical gang, as Thrasher describes it, is an undisciplined group alienated from family and community control and in conflict with the police. The activities of a gang known as the Dirty Dozen are representative.   Its members were loafers, young fellows from 16 to 22 years of age.   They spent their time swimming, playing baseball and football, shooting craps, and just sitting around and talking. Fighting was also a favorite occupation, and the gang deliberately provoked fights with rival gangs or with other racial groups.   In one such conflict a member of the Dirty Dozen was killed.   In retaliation this gang killed 2 and beat up 5 of the other race.   Leadership was determined by personal achievement in such admired activities as sports or fighting.   When the members of the gang earned money they spent it immediately on drinking parties and crap games.   At other times they secured money in devious ways—by delivering liquor during the prohibition period or by stealing.   Eventually this gang disbanded and the members became more or less integrated into conventional society.

Another gang described by Thrasher was nicknamed the Murderers. Every evening its 30 members congregated at their shack to loaf, smoke, chew, shoot craps, play cards and pool, and bowl.   Many of these boys were "bumming away from home," sleeping under sidewalks or in vacant lots. They liked to camp near the railroad tracks and were a nuisance to railroad detectives.   Food was stolen from delivery wagons or by breaking into box cars.   The boys stole wire cables and sold them for junk.   Telephone boxes were opened and the contents stolen.   Automobiles were "borrowed" for joy rides.   Most of the gang were truants, but the ones with outstanding prestige had been confined in the juvenile detention home or jail.

Descriptions and analysis of the Mexican-American juvenile gangs that operate in East Los Angeles emphasize the conflict of the gangs with police and community.[35]   Members of a minority group that experiences marked discrimination, the Mexican-American gangs vent their hostility against gangs from other backgrounds, which in turn often attack the Mexican-American gangs.   As with the gangs studied by Thrasher, the Mexican-American gangs secure the deepest loyalty of their members and create their most significant values, which are often opposed to those of the larger community.

Although not all gangs become delinquent, there is a definite tendency in this direction when the gang absorbs a great deal of the boys' time and usurps the place of the family and other agencies in directing activities and setting standards.

The importance of the gang as a factor in delinquency is evident when we realize that most delinquencies of boys are committed by pairs or small groups, rather than by single individuals.   Moreover, some of the most persistent adult criminals also work in small gangs, and extensive criminal operations are performed by organized gangs.   Studies of both Shaw and the Gluecks support the relationship of gangs to crime.[36]   In Chicago, among 8,484 offenders known to the courts or accomplices of boys known to the courts, only 12 per cent had committed their delinquencies alone, whereas 88 per cent had one or more companions.   Two or 3 boys working together was the most common combination and accounted for some 60 per cent of all offenses.   In only a small percentage of cases had 6 or more boys operated together.

The Gluecks report both on gang membership and companionship in the commission of crimes.   The definition of gang applied was somewhat rigid, since it involved a recognized leader, specific passwords or rules, meetings at stated places, and the planning of antisocial activities. They found that among 1,000 male juvenile delinquents in Boston only 7 per cent were members of such strictly organized gangs, and another 19 per cent met in loose street crowds without definite leadership or rules.   Companionship in crimes was very common, however.   When the offenses that brought the boys before the juvenile court were classified by the number of participants, 30 per cent of the boys had committed the delinquency alone, 28 per cent had 1 companion, 22 percent 2 companions, and 20 percent 3 or more.

Delinquency Patterns among Girls

Although girls do not escape from parental supervision, even in disorganized areas, as early as boys, there is ample evidence that girls in these areas find patterns of delinquency ready for imitation when they first begin to make contacts outside the family circle.   The study of 500 delinquent women who had served sentences in the Massachusetts Reformatory for Women, made by the Gluecks, traces the early childhood and adolescent contacts of these women.[37]   Slightly less than one fifth of the group had lived in childhood in neighborhoods that could be classified as good, that is, neighborhoods without street gangs or centers of vice and crime and possessing constructive recreational agencies, such as playgrounds and community centers.   Half came from fair neighborhoods, or ones in which gangs and vice were absent, but which lacked playgrounds and community centers.   A third of the women came from poor neighborhoods, or ones that contained active centers of vice and crime.   In adolescence, however, 44.3 per cent lived in poor neighborhoods, an increase due largely to the fact that some girls had left home and established themselves in such neighborhoods.

Although the childhood life of these women was difficult to trace, it was determined that at least 26.1 per cent had associated in childhood with other children whose influence was bad.   During adolescence, fully 87 per cent had unwholesome companions, such as streetwalkers, "drunks," "pickups," bootleggers, and persons known to the police as idlers.

Case studies by the Gluecks and others show that girls, as well as boys, are not solitary in their delinquencies. Girls may affiliate either with other already delinquent girls, or with men, or both. The inexperienced girl is quickly initiated into sex delinquency and stealing by these companions. The delinquent girl, like the delinquent boy, follows community patterns of delinquency readily available to her.

Influx of Criminals

Emphasis so far has been placed upon the community background in which juvenile delinquency appears, on the assumption that it breeds delinquency. We should not overlook the fact, however, that these disorganized areas also attract criminals from other areas. This statement applies especially to adult criminals. These in-migrant criminals come from various backgrounds, represent different types of offenders, and tend to reside in areas that cater to their particular needs and activities.

Criminals who move into a delinquency area may be drawn there because in a sense they have been forced out of some other area in the same city. Urban communities that are well organized and orderly are intolerant of criminal behavior; the members of the community and perhaps the criminal's own family disapprove and show their disapproval by social ostracism. If the criminal cannot meet the community standards he tends to drift to areas where criminality is tolerated and where he will find companionship among others engaged in crime.

In-migrant criminals may come also from other cities where they may have been reared in disorganized areas. The records of some notorious criminals, revealed when they finally came to trial, show that they moved from city to city, invariably seeking the same type of associates.

Other in-migrant criminals may come from rural areas and smaller cities, where their criminal careers have started, possibly in the counterpart to the urban areas of delinquency. The small community is neither a safe nor a profitable place for the confirmed criminal. He rapidly becomes known to citizens and police alike and is constantly harassed. Moreover, the small community does not offer enough opportunities for economic gain to appeal to criminals who wish to make large sums of money in one operation.

The criminals and minor offenders who move into the delinquency areas of the large city congregate in communities that permit or encourage their characteristic types of offense. Rooming-house areas near the centers of large cities cater to a transient group, usually employed, but restless and unassimilated into stable community organizations. Prostitution and illicit sex relations are characteristic offenses of such areas.

Most large cities have homeless-man areas, such as the Bowery in New York City or West Madison Street in Chicago. Detached men drift into these centers from all over the country. Some remain there permanently, finding cheap lodgings and living by begging, odd jobs, or petty thievery. Others come into the areas only during the winter and spend the summer elsewhere, perhaps at seasonal work. Vagrancy, petty thievery, drunkenness, and sex offenses are typical of these areas.

The slums that encircle the centers of large cities harbor varied types of criminals. Also, since slums are typically family communities, they draw families with criminal patterns of conduct, whose children find in their own parents adult criminal models who teach them the philosophy and techniques of such activities as begging, prostitution, or stealing.

Many hotels in and around the central business district of a large city are sought by criminals. In such places they can remain anonymous and can move quickly if necessary.

This list of types of communities that are attractive to criminals should not be interpreted to mean that all who live in rooming-house areas, homeless-man areas, and slums are delinquents and criminals. It is true, however, that these areas are tolerant of divergent conduct and hence attract persons who do not wish to conform to more orderly community standards. Also, these areas offer institutions that cater to delinquent and criminal activities. Some, such as houses of prostitution, merely satisfy personal vices that come within the criminal code. Others give aid to criminals, such as pawnshops, jewelry stores, or garages that accept stolen goods for sale; taverns that provide meeting places; and so-called athletic or political clubs that in reality carry on many criminal activities.

The criminals who enter the community tend to reinforce its character as a disorganized area that supports crime. The adult criminals become an element in the situation that provides criminal patterns for children who grow up in these areas, and their organizations are often ready to absorb young delinquents.

So far, the discussion has concerned movement of criminals into recognized delinquency areas. Another movement, away from these areas, should also be noted. When criminals become successful and when their crimes make a permanent residence possible, they follow the general pattern of successful people and tend to move away from the disorganized areas, although they may still return to them to perform their illegal activities. This group is limited in number, for the proportion of offenders who become wealthy through crime is small.

RURAL BACKGROUND OF CRIME

The rural background of crime has been less thoroughly studied than the urban background, no doubt because the problem is less acute in rural sections than in urban centers.

Regional Crime Rates

As we have already observed, many sections in large cities have low rates of crime, and in general delinquency and crime rates decrease with distance from the disorganized or slum areas around the central business section. When the rates are extended by zones beyond the outskirts of cities into the adjacent rural areas the same general decrease in crime rates continues, as studies of the metropolitan areas of Chicago, Detroit, and other cities clearly show.

The entire area within 200 miles of Detroit, studied for 1932–33, showed that for crimes against the person (murder, assault, rape, and robbery) the rate decreased consistently from the central part of the city to the periphery of the area studied.[38]   Crimes involving property failed to show a similar decrease.   However, when rates were computed against the amount of property rather than against the population, a decrease appeared.   Thus burglaries of chain stores decreased from 1.87 burglaries per store in the five-mile zone around the center of Detroit to .07 burglaries per store in the zone 44–55 miles from the center.   Thereafter the rate per store rose, probably because at this distance from Detroit large cities again appear, with increased opportunities for burglaries.

Studies for Chicago show similar results.[39]   For 1931 and 1932, 59.6 per cent of the stores belonging to a chain that were located in Chicago were burglarized, but burglaries were committed in only 29.8 per cent of the same chain of stores located in the suburbs within 25 miles of the center of the city. These burglaries continued to decrease when rates were computed by twenty-five-mile zones until a rate of only 6.2 per cent was found in the zone 100–125 miles from the center of Chicago.   Burglaries of a chain of drug stores showed a somewhat similar decrease with distance from the center of the city.   Bank robberies studied for Chicago, East St. Louis, and Wichita showed a slightly different pattern.   Robberies within the city occurred at a lower rate than in the suburbs, but outside this area the rate of robberies decreased.   The low rate in the city is probably explained by the recent precautions taken by urban banks against bank bandits, which caused criminals who specialize in this field to turn to less well-protected suburban banks. The rural banks are perhaps too far from their haunts and offer too small returns to attract many criminals.

Types of Rural Communities

When rural areas are studied without reference to their relation to urban centers, variations occur between types of rural communities. In Wisconsin, the counties with cities tend to have high rates of juvenile delinquency, as does the northern tier of counties, which includes many isolated logging communities.[40] In West Virginia, the mining communities have higher rates of crime than agricultural counties.[41] An analysis of a county in Ohio revealed 4 types of communities: urban (2 cities of 5,322 and 7,252 population); mining; transitional from decadent mining to agricultural; and agricultural.[42] The juvenile delinquency rates declined from community to community in the order given, with one exception—the boys' rate for mining communities. For boys the rates for the 4 communities, respectively, are 1.15 delinquents per 1,000 population, 1.26, 0.51, and 0.36. For girls the corresponding rates are 0.62, 0.59, 0.42, and 0.21.

A study of juvenile delinquency in Michigan for 1934–36 shows Wayne County (Detroit) with a rate more than double that of the southern agricultural counties.[43] The rate for the sparsely populated northern counties lay between the rates for the industrial and the agricultural counties.

A study of rural New York, made in 1918, revealed certain types of communities where delinquency tended to be prevalent.[44] One such community was the village with a decreasing population; another the country-crossroads settlement; a third the village on the edge of an urban industrial center. Two other types of villages with high rates undoubtedly suffered from cultural conflicts—the industrial village with a mixed foreign-born and native-born population, and the village with an influx of urban summer visitors.

These studies, which attempt to locate rural crime, again show higher rates in the communities where there is a mingling of persons of different cultural backgrounds, and also in communities where social organization is weak or where lawlessness is part of the cultural pattern. Industrial villages, villages on the edge of urban communities, and summer resorts are illustrations of the first type; mining and logging communities of the second. The latter communities—somewhat isolated from the larger social organization, generally peopled by persons of a rough and ready nature who must be able to face hardships and dangers—are likely to be places where local folkways and individual impulses override obedience to formal laws. Moreover, in mining communities, crime is frequently linked with efforts to unionize the miners or with struggles between employers and unions.

The situation that may arise in coal-mining areas is illustrated by the conflict in central and southern Illinois. In 1932, when the miners struck against a wage scale approved by the mine owners and the union, thousands of miners milled from one district to another, picketing mines to prevent any-one from working.   Hundreds of deputy sheriffs were appointed and units of the Illinois National Guard were called out.   At least 2 men were killed; one in the rioting and the other, a former union official, by someone who called him to an automobile by name and deliberately shot him.   Others were accidentally wounded by gunshot or were beaten.   A filling station and 2 houses were bombed.   When special deputies resisted the advance of the army of pickets a riot ensued, in which heads were clubbed and wounds were inflicted by broken windshield glass.   The presence of reporters and photographers from city papers aroused resentment, and these men were beaten and forced to destroy their camera plates.[45]

Rural Social Disorganization

The characteristics of rural life associated with delinquency and crime are to some degree similar to urban characteristics.   But several important differences exist.   As in many parts of the city, social controls in rural areas have tended to weaken.[46]   The automobile, in particular, has given young people mobility and resulting freedom from supervision by the family and the community church.   Taverns, dance halls, and rural filling stations may become centers for activities that run counter to the established rural folk-ways, and may permit novices to come in contact with more sophisticated persons.   Drinking to excess and sexual delinquencies are common results.

According to 2 studies, the more mature rural criminals, who have been committed to prisons, are persons who have become emancipated from the control of local institutions.   Failure to participate actively in these institu-tions, travel outside the community, and occupations such as trucking that involve separation from the local community seemed to characterize rural prisoners in both Iowa and Wisconsin.[47]

These studies also show an association of crime with poverty; possibly be-cause they are wholly or largely concerned with criminals who committed property crimes.   Another important finding is that the rural areas do not have definite criminal patterns or criminal gangs from which the amateur criminal may learn the finer techniques.   Rural crime tends to be associated with general emancipation from community controls and disorderliness; crimes are of a type and quality that the skilled urban criminal would scorn. Moreover, the rural offenders do not conceive of themselves as criminals, but rather as members of the conventional community who have committed a slight error in judgment.   After the expiration of their prison terms they expect to return to their normal round of living.

These studies fail to indicate one fact that seems obvious.   Rural of-fenders have little opportunity to become professional criminals who spend their lives in criminal activities.   Anonymity, which is essential to the professional criminal, is not provided by the small communities.   It is significant that many rural property crimes are carried out in areas other than the one where the offender lives.   Passing bad checks and minor forms of burglary, which seem to be popular rural offenses, are frequently performed in a small city some 25 miles from home—near enough to be reached easily without the offender being missed from his place of residence, and distant enough to enable the offender to pass unrecognized.   Probably a certain percentage of these small-time rural offenders become professionals, but not in the rural community.   Drifting to the larger cities, they become part of the urban criminal world.

The prevalence of delinquency in some mining communities has already been mentioned.   It is altogether possible for delinquency to become a part of the folkways of a rural community, just as it may become an accepted way of life in some urban communities.   Under these conditions we find the nearest approach to the professional criminal in rural areas.   The rural bootlegger in the South is a case in point.[48]   In many parts of the South small operators in rural areas secretly manufacture liquor without a license and without paying the tax required by federal law.   The liquor is transported to cities for sale to distributors who depend upon this supply.   Sometimes the manufacture of liquor is a sideline of farming, but in areas where farming is unprofitable, liquor manufacturing may become the chief occupation upon which families depend.   It is, however, regarded as a business rather than a crime and the folkways support rather than condemn it.   Techniques for secretly manufacturing, concealing, and transporting liquor are highly developed, as well as methods of evasion when the bootlegger is confronted by the representatives of the government.   The picture of rural crime under these conditions is different from that where crime occurs contrary to the customary methods of making a living and without the support of the local folkways.

CRIME AND SOCIAL DISORGANIZATION

With the development of individual psychotherapy, there has been a tendency to disparage the studies of delinquency areas that were the outstanding contribution of the 1920's and 1930's to the theory of delinquency. As often happens when a new insight into a problem is gained, overemphasis was at first placed upon the importance of social disorganization in the etiology of delinquency and crime.   Recognition of this overemphasis, however, should not lead to complete abandonment of the studies.   There is ample evidence of the existence of personal disorganization in socially disorganized areas and of the existence of criminal patterns of long standing, through which the restless and searching boy or girl may find satisfactions. Understanding of the individual mechanisms of criminal behavior is incomplete without an equal understanding of the social background.

QUESTIONS

1. Compare the techniques used in crime stories in motion pictures and crime comic books and on radio and television with known techniques of effective propaganda. Would you expect crime stories to develop favorable or unfavorable attitudes toward crime?

2. What are some plausible explanations of the fluctuations in crime during the 1930's?

3. How is the physical deterioration of slums related to high delinquency rates in these areas?

4. What factors in transitional areas are most conducive to delinquency: poor housing, poverty, high adult crime rates, or existence of boys' gangs?

5. Under what conditions does rural crime develop?

READINGS

Blumer, Herbert and Philip M. Hauser, *Movies, Delinquency and Crime* (Macmillan, 1933). In this careful study, the relationship of movies and delinquency is analyzed; movies are neither condemned nor given a clean bill of health.

Elliott, M. A., "Crime and the Frontier Mores," *American Sociological Review,* 9 (1944), 185–92. Although the frontier has long been closed, its individualistic, forceful life still influences our laws and behavior.

Josephson, Matthew, *The Robber Barons; the Great American Capitalists, 1861– 1901* (Harcourt, Brace, 1934). In this colorful story of the industrial giants who developed the material resources of the United States, many conflicts of values that still plague the nation are uncovered. Their ruthless exploitation of resources and men and their manipulation of governmental officials is balanced against their naive religious faith and their gifts to education and research.

Shaw, Clifford R., and Henry D. McKay, *Juvenile Delinquency and Urban Areas* (Chicago: University of Chicago Press, 1942). This book presents the studies of delinquency areas made in Chicago—the forerunners of many studies in other cities. Although it has since been contended that delinquency also exists in other areas, there is no doubt about the far greater percentage of children from disorganized areas than from other areas who are arrested, brought before the juvenile court, and sentenced to institutions.

Thrasher, Frederic M., *The Gang* (Chicago: University of Chicago Press, 1927). Although made a generation ago, this comprehensive study based upon firsthand observation and participation of the author in gang life, has never been duplicated. Interaction within the gang, the relation of the gang to other community institutions, and the modification of the gang as its members approach adulthood are all examined.

Wertham, Fredric, *Seduction of the Innocent* (Rinehart, 1953). This partisan presentation of objections to crime comic books grows out of the author's experience with delinquents and his personal conviction that crime comics motivate delinquent behavior. He is not always convincing to the reader inasmuch as he does not marshal objective data to support his contentions. The book, however, raises many questions in need of sound answers, and for this reason is recommended to the student.

FOOTNOTES

[1] "Current Notes," *Journal of Criminal Law, Criminology, and Police Science,* 43 (1952), 360.

[2] Donald R. Cressey, *Other People's Money: A Study in the Social Psychology of Embezzlement* (Glencoe, Ill.: Free Press, 1953).

[3] Wayland F. Vaughn, *Social Psychology* (New York: Odyssey Press, 1948), chs. 10, 17.

[4] Herbert Blumer and Philip M. Hauser, *Movies, Delinquency and Crime* (Macmillan, 1933).

[5] Fredric Wertham, *Seduction of the Innocent* (Rinehart, 1953).

[6] G. B. Vold, "The Amount and Nature of Crime," *American Journal of Sociology,* 40 (1935), 796–803; H. Willbach, "The Trend of Crime in New York City," *Journal of Criminal Law and Criminology,* 29 (1938), 62–75.

[7] H. A. Phelps, "Cycles of Crime," *Journal of Criminal Law and Criminology,* 20 (1929), 107–21; for a discussion of similar studies see Thorsten Sellin, *Research Memorandum on Crime in the Depression* (New York: Social Science Research Council, 1937), pp. 19–62.

[8] Willbach, *op. cit.;* "The Trend of Crime in Chicago," *Journal of Criminal Law and Criminology,* 31 (1941), 720–27.

[9] "Juvenile Court Statistics, 1943," *Social Statistics,* Supplement to Vol. 9, No. 12 (June, 1945) of *The Child* (Washington: United States Department of Labor, Children's Bureau), 19–20.

[10] Clifford R. Shaw, *Delinquency Areas* (Chicago: University of Chicago Press, 1929); Clifford R. Shaw and Henry D. McKay, *Social Factors in Juvenile Delinquency,* National Commission on Law Observance and Enforcement 2, No. 13 (Washington: Government Printing Office, 1931), 23–59, 140–88; and *Juvenile Delinquency and Urban Areas* (Chicago: University of Chicago Press, 1942).

[11] Ernest R. Mowrer, *Disorganization, Personal and Social* (Lippincott, 1942), p. 130.

[12] Shaw and McKay, *Social Factors in Juvenile Delinquency,* pp. 140–88.

[13] E. Longmoor and E. F. Young, "Ecological Interrelationships of Juvenile Delinquency, Dependency, and Population Mobility: A Cartographic Analysis of Data from Long Beach, California," *American Journal of Sociology,* 41 (1936), 598–610.

[14] N. S. Hayner, "Delinquency Areas in the Puget Sound Region," *American Journal of Sociology,* 39 (1933), 314–28.

[15] *The Houston Delinquent in His Community Setting* (Houston, Texas: Council of Social Agencies, 1945); *Houston Children and the Police* (Houston, Texas: Council of Social Agencies, 1946).

[16] Mowrer, *op. cit.,* p. 597.

[17] Shaw and McKay, *Social Factors in Juvenile Delinquency,* pp. 105–7.

[18] Lowell Juilliard Carr, *Delinquency Control* (Harper, 1941), p. 40.

[19] *The Houston Delinquent in his Community Setting,* p. 7.

[20] Mildred Hartsough and George Caswell, *The Relation between Housing and Delinquency,* Research Bulletin No. 1, Housing Division, Federal Emergency Administration of Public Works (Mar., 1936), p. 101.

[21] Shaw and McKay, *Social Factors in Juvenile Delinquency,* pp. 74–79.

[22] R. C. White, "The Relation of Felonies to Environmental Factors in Indianapolis," *Social Forces,* 10 (1931–32), 498-509.

[23] Longmoor and Young, *op. cit.*

24 *The Houston Delinquent in His Community Setting*, p. 11.

25 Longmoor and Young, *op. cit.*

26 Shaw and McKay, *Social Factors in Juvenile Delinquency*, pp. 71–74.

27 N. Carpenter and W. M. Haenszel, "Migratoriness and Criminality in Buffalo," *Social Forces*, 9 (1930), 254–55.

28 J. Stuart, "Mobility and Delinquency," *American Journal of Orthopsychiatry*, 6 (1936), 486–93.

29 Hayner, *op. cit.*, pp. 318–19, 325.

30 Carr, *op cit.*, pp. 105–7.

31 Ernest R. Mowrer, *Family Disorganization* (Chicago: University of Chicago Press, 1927), ch. 5; C. W. Schroeder, *Divorce in a City of 100,000 Population*, Private edition distributed by Bradley Polytechnic Institute Library, Peoria, Illinois (1939), p. 50.

32 Ruth S. Cavan, *Suicide* (Chicago: University of Chicago Press, 1928), pp. 81–105; C. F. Schmid, *Suicides in Seattle, 1914 to 1925* (Seattle: University of Washington Press, 1928), pp. 6, 14.

33 Walter C. Reckless, *The Etiology of Delinquent and Criminal Behavior* (New York: Social Science Research Council, 1943), p. 32.

34 Frederic M. Thrasher, *The Gang* (Chicago: University of Chicago Press, 1927).

35 S. Glane, "Juvenile Gangs in East Los Angeles," reprinted in Clyde B. Vedder, *The Juvenile Offender* (Doubleday, 1954), pp. 175–81, from *Focus*, 29 (Sept., 1950), 136–41.

36 Shaw and McKay, *Social Factors in Juvenile Delinquency*, pp. 194, 199; Sheldon and Eleanor T. Glueck, *One Thousand Juvenile Delinquents* (Cambridge: Harvard University Press, 1934), pp. 94, 100.

37 Sheldon and Eleanor T. Glueck, *Five Hundred Delinquent Women* (Knopf, 1934), pp. 69, 85.

38 S. Lottier, "Distribution of Criminal Offenses in Metropolitan Regions," *Journal of Criminal Law and Criminology*, 29 (1938), 37–50.

39 E. H. Sutherland, *Principles of Criminology* (Lippincott, 1939), pp. 135–36.

40 M. G. Caldwell, "The Extent of Juvenile Delinquency in Wisconsin," *Journal of Criminal Law and Criminology*, 32 (1941), 148–57.

41 H. L. Yoke, "Crime in West Virginia," *Sociology and Social Research*, 16 (1932), 267–73.

42 M. Phleger and E. A. Taylor, "An Ecological Study of Juvenile Delinquency in Athens County, Ohio," *Publication of the American Sociological Society*, 26 (1932), 144–49.

43 P. Wiers, "Juvenile Delinquency in Rural Michigan," *Journal of Criminal Law and Criminology*, 30 (1939), 211–22.

44 K. H. Claghorn, *Juvenile Delinquency in Rural New York*, Children's Bureau Publication No. 32 (Washington: United States Department of Labor).

45 From newspaper accounts.

46 H. M. Shulman, *A Study of Delinquency in Two Rural Counties*, for the Sub-Commission on Causes and Effects of Crime in the New York State Crime Commission, 1927.

47 M. B. Clinard, "Rural Criminal Offenders," *American Journal of Sociology*, 50 (1944), 38, 45; "The Process of Urbanization and Criminal Behavior," *American Journal of Sociology*, 48 (1942), 202–13; A. L. Wood, "Social Organization and Crime in Small Wisconsin Communities," *American Sociological Review*, 7 (1942), 40–46.

48 S. Winston and M. Butler, "Negro Bootleggers in Eastern North Carolina," *American Sociological Review*, 8 (1943), 692–97.

Family Background
of the Criminal

In the urban communities that are associated with a high incidence of crime, the proportion of persons who commit delinquencies and crime is naturally high.[1] The highest rates in Chicago were for adolescent boys who were brought before the police probation officer. In the areas with the highest percentage of boys delinquent in one year, 26.6 per cent of all boys between the ages of 10 and 16 were delinquent. In Philadelphia the number of boys brought before the juvenile court officially charged with delinquency (a more rigid definition of delinquency than the one given above for Chicago) were computed as a percentage of all boys in small areas who were 10 to 15 years of age; in the community with the worst record, 22.6 per cent were charged with delinquency during a 3 year period. In Richmond, Virginia, the community with the highest percentage of boys brought before the court on serious charges of delinquency in a 3 year period showed 25.1 per cent of the boy population delinquent. In Cleveland the highest delinquency rate was 29.6 per cent for a 3 year period; in Birmingham, 20.8 per cent; in Seattle, 24.0 per cent. Among young adult male felons in Chicago, the areas with the highest rates of delinquency for a 3 year period showed that about one fifth of the young adult male population was delinquent.

The rates for girl delinquents are lower than for boys. In Chicago, the area with the highest rate for girls during a 7 year period showed 9 per cent of the girls delinquent, or one girl out of eleven.[2] The highest areal rate in Everett found by Hayner, was 7.7 per cent, for approximately a 7 year period.[3]

These figures obviously are underestimates for the areas, since the figures represent only those whom the police arrested during the period of a few years. Nevertheless, it is evident that not all persons living in delinquency areas become delinquent. The disorganizing forces and the patterns of delinquency, prevalent as they are, do not affect everyone alike. One possible explanation is that the areas are not uniformly disorganized, but that disorganization is restricted to certain streets, so that only some of the persons living in the area are exposed to the full force of adverse influences. Another explanation is that other factors either counteract or supplement the community forces and thus help determine the delinquency rates.

The logical procedure, therefore, is to turn to studies, not of communities, but of delinquents and criminals themselves, and to press the inquiry back into the personal lives of these individuals. The logical thing is to turn to the family as a probable contributing factor, if not the primary agent, in the beginning of delinquency and crime.

The reasons for selecting the family as the point of attack are obvious. First, the family is the first social group in which the child normally has membership. It is therefore the most important in early training and in defining social situations. Consequently, we should expect to find that a boy or girl reared in a family that did not respect and exemplify community mores and morals would become a nonconformer of some type. Second, the family as an institution is assigned the task of providing for many of the everyday activities and interests of children and of supervising them. Without such provision and supervision, children are thrown upon community resources that may or may not be adequate. Third, and most important, the family is the first group to which the child attaches himself emotionally and from which he receives emotional satisfaction and the opportunity for normal emotional development from pleasure-loving babyhood to the controlled expressions of adulthood. The child's conception of his own personality and the type of relationship that he will later have with other people are determined in the home. The family, and especially the mother, is thus extremely important in establishing the role that the child will play both in the family and in society.

DEGREE OF FAMILY CULPABILITY

"The family is responsible for delinquency," "delinquency begins at home," and similar slogans are popular ways of expressing the recognition of the early beginnings of criminal behavior. The family's relationship to delinquency may be stated as follows:

1. Parents, because of personal and emotional difficulties of their own, are unable to give their children adequate personality training.

2. Parents, because of lack of education or unfamiliarity with the culture in which they live, may be unable to cope with destructive community forces.

3. Parents may be oriented to criminal behavior and find nothing wrong in condoning or actually training their children in similar patterns of attitude and behavior.

4. Parents never rear their children in isolation from the community. The neighborhood in which they live may reinforce conventional behavior through schools, churches, and neighborhood councils and may refuse to tolerate deviant behavior.   On the other hand, the community may have weak conventional institutions but strong criminal institutions or prevalent types of behavior that lead into delinquency.   Junk dealers and secondhand stores that encourage stealing, unsupervised boys' gangs and clubs, houses of prostitution, numerous taverns that admit youths, and groups of older criminals are examples of forces against which parents in some areas have to contend.

The prevalence of substandard family conditions and disorganized family relationships among delinquents is evident from a number of studies.   The Gluecks found among 1,000 male delinquents that only 8 per cent came from homes with both parents living at home and providing adequate supervision.   In 46 per cent of the families a parent had died or there had been separation or divorce; and in 46 per cent of the cases the family was characterized by such behavior as criminality of one or both parents, poor discipline, marked parental incompatibility, or absence of the mother from the home without provision of a substitute.[4]   Among the 500 delinquent women studied by the Gluecks, only 10 per cent came from homes where both parents were present and good family relationships existed.[5]

In a study of delinquent girls Lumpkin used as unfavorable home factors broken homes, contacts with social agencies, and "social defective tendencies." [6]   (This last term referred to the presence in the family of someone who was alcoholic, epileptic, mentally defective or diseased, guilty of sex irregularity, handicapped by serious physical disease, or who had a court record.) Only 10 per cent of the correctional school girls studied came from homes with none of these adverse features; 19 per cent came from homes with 1 of the 3 types; 35 per cent from homes with 2; and 36 per cent from homes with 3.

Emotionally Disturbed Families

Men and women often come into marriage and become parents without having previously achieved maturity or an integrated personality.   It is extremely difficult for such parents to assume the best parental roles toward their children.   Child psychologists vision the adequate parent as one who has found satisfactory outlets for his own needs on an adult level; whose personality is integrated around certain central interests or goals; and who therefore is able to give his children consistent and loving guidance.   Many parents fall short of this goal in some respects and a few are so disorganized that they are of little help to their children, who then often react with severe emotional and sometimes delinquent behavior.   A summary of family situations that hinder the best development of the child, based primarily upon the writings of Healy and Bronner [7] and Aichhorn [8] gives the following list:

Great severity on the part of one or both parents; excluding the child from the family, as in sending a reluctant child to summer camp or boarding school; forcing the child at too early an age into heavy responsibilities or independence. The child feels rejected, unloved, unwanted. He tends to slip back to an earlier stage of behavior and reacts as a younger child would, on the basis of immediate pleasure and without acceptance of responsibility. In certain types of cases, as severity of the father, the older child or adolescent may flare out in open rebellion.

Conflict within the family, especially between the parents, perhaps separation or divorce. The child is made the protagonist of one parent; the antagonist of the other. He may then rebel against all persons who resemble the hated parent, and he fails to find in that parent a standard against which to measure his own conduct.

Conflict in the family may take the form of differences in discipline. One parent may be severe; the other lenient. The child then clings to the lenient parent, seeking emotional protection. He tends to regress to infantile forms of behavior or to remain at a childish level.

Favoritism of the parents among the children. The slighted child may become extremely jealous of the favored brothers and sisters.

Mental conflict within the child because of some act or experience that conflicts with standards that he has been taught and has accepted. He may perform acts of delinquency that in some way are associated with his feeling of guilt, almost with a sense of compulsion, and may feel relief when punished.

Excess of love on the part of one parent, often the mother, who may substitute a son for the husband in her affections. She grants every wish of the son and protects him from the harsher aspects of reality. He begins to want recognition without making any effort and may rebel when in later years such recognition is withheld.

All of these situations cause emotional disturbances in the child—rebellion, conflict, fear, a feeling of dependence, and failure to develop into adulthood. Emotional disturbances are usually expressed in aberrant conduct, although such conduct is not necessarily delinquent or criminal. Obviously there is no single pattern by which emotional disturbances find their expression in delinquent behavior because of the great variety in types of emotional disturbance, differences in other personality traits of children, and the possibility of numerous kinds of aberrant behavior. The complexity of factors that may be involved has so far prevented any definite linking up of emotional disturbance with a resulting form of conduct, delinquent or otherwise. It is not possible to say that a boy who is rejected by his father and loved overmuch by his mother will necessarily react in a specific way. Nor can we say that a boy who steals clothing does so as a result of a definite emotional disturbance. But case by case a close analysis reveals a *certain proportion* of cases in which the emotional disturbance finds an outlet in delinquent behavior.

Healy and Bronner in a study of 105 delinquents found that 96 had severe emotional disturbances, some having more than one type. Most of these emotional dissatisfactions originated in the home or related to some other member of the family. The types of disturbance found and the number of children experiencing them are as follows: [9]

(a) Feeling keenly either rejected, deprived, insecure, not understood in affectional relationships, unloved, or that love had been withdrawn—46 cases.

(b) Deep feeling of being thwarted other than affectionally; either (a) in normal impulses or desires for self-expression or other self-satisfaction, (b) in adolescent urges and desires—even when (as in 5 cases) desire for emancipation had been blocked only by the individual's counteractive pleasure in remaining childishly attached—28 cases.

(c) Feeling strongly either real or fancied inadequacies or inferiorities in the home life, in school, or in relation to companionship or to sports—46 cases.

(d) Intense feelings of discomfort about family disharmonies, parental misconduct, the conditions of family life, or parental errors in management and discipline—34 cases.

(e) Bitter feelings of jealousy toward one or more siblings, or feelings of being markedly discriminated against because another in the family circle more favored —31 cases.

(f) Feelings of confused unhappiness due to some deep-seated, often repressed, internal mental conflict—expressed in various kinds of delinquent acts which often are seemingly unreasonable—17 cases.

(g) Conscious or unconscious sense of guilt about earlier delinquencies or about behavior which technically was not delinquency; the guilt sense directly or indirectly activating delinquency through the individual's feeling of the need of punishment (in nearly every instance this overlaps with the last category)—9 cases.

Sometimes parents establish satisfactory emotional relationships with some of their children but not with others, the difference often being based on events of early infancy. Healy and Bronner compared the 105 delinquents whom they studied with 105 nondelinquent brothers and sisters of approximately the same age. The external conditions of home and neighborhood were identical for the 2 groups. But their more intimate and intangible relationships and experiences were extremely different. For 100 pairs of delinquents and controls there were 113 incidents among the delinquents, but only 40 among the controls, of difficulties in infancy that would affect parent-child relationships. Such conditions as worry or sickness of the mother during pregnancy had occurred two and a half times as often where delinquents were concerned as among the controls. Three times as many delinquents as controls had been cross and fussy in babyhood, and two and a half times as many delinquents as controls had experienced difficulty in toilet habit-training—sometimes one of the most severe parent-child struggles.   A number of delinquents were underweight and had suffered many or severe illnesses or had injuries in childhood, although only a few of the controls were so handicapped.   Healy does not try specifically to relate these difficulties to delinquency but suggests some of the possible results of severe illness—irritability or restlessness, over protection or spoiling of the child, or the development of demanding and selfish attitudes.

The child whose parental relationships are unsatisfactory not only exhibits such specific emotional and delinquent behavior as has been indicated but fails to develop a socialized type of personality.   In *Searchlights on Delinquency,* a book dedicated to August Aichhorn, the effect of emotionally disturbed parent-child relationships is pointed out by many writers.[10]   The child who lacks parental warmth and affection remains self-centered and is unable to establish cooperative and friendly relationships with others.   Even minor frustrations by others unleash hostility and aggressiveness or lead to extreme withdrawal.   Feeling unloved and insecure, the child depreciates his own value and cannot give or accept love and friendliness.   He is unable to divert his impulses into conventional and acceptable channels and cannot accept social standards of behavior; he cannot believe that others will help him satisfy his needs.   His personality, therefore, lacks integration of native impulses and needs with cultural standards and is too self-centered to permit incorporation into group life.

The relationship between poorly adjusted parents and certain types of delinquency in children seems adequately established by the many clinical studies of disturbed and misbehaving children.   From other studies, already referred to in the preceding chapter, we know that personal and family disorganization is greater in the delinquency areas than in other parts of the city as shown by the abnormally high rates of alcoholism, suicide, vagrancy, desertion, and divorce.   These studies do not indicate whether the individuals involved are the parents of children and if so whether these children are delinquent.   From the studies of delinquency, such as those of Healy and Bronner and the Gluecks, we do know, however, that delinquents come in large numbers from families whose parents exhibit these and other traits of personal maladjustment.   It seems safe to assume, therefore, that one reason why delinquency rates are high in certain areas of cities is because of the disproportionate number of poorly adjusted families living in these areas whose children have poorly integrated and unstable personalities because of the maladjustment of their parents.

Parental Inability to Cope with Community Forces

Another factor in the etiology of delinquency is the inability of many parents to adapt themselves to the culture of the community in which they live and, therefore, their further inability to transmit to their children acceptable moral and ethical standards.   The burden upon the family is heavy, for the family is the institution that has been assigned the task of training the child to accept the mores—the approved ways of living.   The mores include both morals and daily living habits that are considered commendable and that contribute to the stability and organization of the person, the family, and the community.   Under morals may be listed such qualities as truthfulness, honesty in regard to material possessions, compliance with the sexual mores, and sobriety.   Under commendable living habits may be included regularity in school attendance; the inculcation of work habits in youth; habits of cleanliness; employment in adulthood as a means of support; acceptance of financial and other responsibilities; organization of time to provide for basic needs such as sleep, recreation, and work; and a host of other habits and systems of habits.   Failure on the part of the family to train children may result in the child's never learning these attitudes and habit-systems that are fundamental to orderly community living.   Consequently, children may become involved in delinquency and crime if their contacts outside the family are with delinquent groups.   The situation is especially acute for families that move into the already disorganized areas of a city from a very different culture to which they were adequately adjusted.   They face the double difficulty of adaptation to a new culture and the necessity of trying to withstand the destructive forces in the community.

Foreign-culture families form one group with marked problems of adjustment.   Areas of high delinquency coincide rather closely in the larger cities with immigrant areas of first settlement, in which foreign-born parents, still dominated by Old World and often rural patterns of culture, do not always understand the intricate economic system of the modern urban center. Without training in American mores regarding property rights and under the pressure of poverty, these foreign-born parents often give approval to forms of activity defined in America as illegal, or at least as undesirable in that they may easily lead to delinquency.   Stealing from coal cars is frequently found in poverty-stricken sections of cities.   Families that perhaps would not steal from the neighborhood grocer nevertheless send their boys to steal coal from the railroad, since taking coal that seems to be standing unused and with no visible owner does not seem to be particularly wrong. Their justification, if they are forced to make one, is their need for the coal. They may also teach their children to beg, an activity that quickly brings the children to the attention of the police and easily leads to petty thievery. Children are frequently permitted to sell newspapers on the streets at night, an occupation that can lead to participation in less legal activities.   Thus activities approved by the family and the neighborhood, which may also bring approval to the boy or girl because of the provisions or money brought home, are either directly defined as delinquent by the larger community or as undesirable in that they expose young people to the danger of becoming involved in actual crimes.

Deviant and Criminal Families

When deviation in ideals and conduct is measured, the standard of reference usually is the staid middle-class.   Lower-class families, who congregate in areas with high delinquency crime rates, have a system of culture in some respects quasi-criminal according to middle-class mores.   Children are taught to be hardfisted and aggressive in self-defense or in securing privileges that otherwise would be denied to them.   Sexual mores are more lenient and less repressive, and sexual prowess of the male may be a matter for open pride; the illegitimate child of a daughter is accepted more readily into the parental family than is true for the middle class.   Minor indirect thefts are condoned, such as slipping into the movies, riding on a crowded street-car or bus without paying the fare, or failing to return lost property that is found.   These deviations are part of the way in which hard-pressed people make their way and do not indicate that the lower class is a criminal society. Nevertheless, lower-class children or adults may be arrested for such conduct.

In some unfortunate instances, however, families themselves are criminal; that is, one or more members rather openly and persistently commit crimes and in extreme cases organize their lives with crime as a central pursuit. Children then may be encouraged in delinquency by their parents.   The Gluecks found among the delinquent women studied, that 45.5 per cent had parents or siblings who had been arrested for crime or immorality; an additional 31 per cent had parents or siblings who had committed acts for which they might have been arrested, although no arrest had taken place; and 4.2 per cent had near relatives who were known delinquents.[11]   Among the thousand delinquent boys studied by the Gluecks, 20 per cent had parents one or both of whom were criminals.[12]   Lumpkin in her study of girls in the Wisconsin correctional school found that 30 per cent came from families in which some member had a court record or had served a sentence in a penal or correctional institution.[13]   Although these data do not indicate that the parents deliberately taught their children methods of crime and delinquency, they do show that the example of a socially disapproved way of life was constantly before the children and that definite moral training was absent.

ECONOMIC STATUS OF FAMILIES

Poverty has often been singled out as a primary cause of juvenile delinquency.   Although in cities delinquency and crime rates are high in poverty-stricken sections, they are not limited to the poor nor to those who lack skills to earn an adequate income.   Healy and Bronner, in a study published in 1926 classified 675 juvenile delinquents as follows: destitute, 5 per cent; poverty-stricken, 22 per cent; normal income, 35 per cent; comfortable, 34 per cent; and luxury-class, 4 per cent.[14]

The Gluecks found that 8.1 per cent of the thousand delinquent boys whom they studied came from dependent homes; 68.2 per cent from homes in marginal circumstances; and 23.7 per cent from comfortable homes.[15] The classification differs from that used by Healy and Bronner, making direct comparison impossible, but apparently the Gluecks found a higher proportion of delinquents from homes with inadequate incomes than did Healy and Bronner.   The 500 reformatory men, whose subsequent careers were studied by the Gluecks, were classified as follows for the period prior to commitment, that is, during late adolescence or early manhood: dependent, 14.7 per cent; marginal, 56.4 per cent; and comfortable, 28.9 per cent.[16]   Moreover, the Gluecks found that the men who continued to exhibit criminal conduct during a period of 15 years following their release from the reformatory came more frequently from dependent homes than from those of economic adequacy.[17]   Economic status, however, was only one of some 15 factors that differentiated the reformed from the confirmed criminals—factors that included such conditions as broken homes, mental pathology, and conflict between parents.

Some of the values of these distributions of criminals by economic status of the parental home is lost because we do not have corresponding data for the communities at large.   Poverty can be considered a factor only if it is found in higher percentage among criminals than among comparable groups in the total population.   The Gluecks consider that the total population would not exhibit as high a percentage of families that were dependent or in marginal circumstances as the criminals do.

To the extent that poverty may be a factor in the beginning of delinquency, it operates indirectly.   Cases of juvenile offenders clearly demonstrate that many of the early depredations might not occur if the children had more spending money or were provided by their parents with more necessities or small luxuries of food, clothing, or play equipment.   Some typical delinquencies that grow out of poverty are stealing fruit or candy from street peddlers or stands, stealing beads and other ornaments from five-and-ten-cent stores, stealing athletic equipment, and sneaking into movies.   But the later, more serious and more professional types of delinquency and crime can scarcely be attributed directly to poverty. In periods of easy employment, adolescent boys and girls may refuse to work or may not be able to stick to a job in which money is earned slowly, if by a daring theft they can secure large sums or luxurious clothes or automobiles far beyond their means. Other factors than poverty operate in this instance. Some of them are the lack of supervision and training in establishing standards of honesty and good work habits; failure to secure vocational education; and the establishment of habits of delinquency. The quality of family relationships and family standards seem more important than poverty alone.

Once an individual is established in habits of crime, poverty appears to be a secondary matter. If it operates at all, it is influential only at the lower end of the scale among petty thieves in the vagrant class. Successful criminals continue in crime, just as successful businessmen continue to operate their businesses. Political grafters, racketeers, gangsters, operators of criminal syndicates, and professional thieves regard their operations as a way of making a living and of amassing a surplus. It should be remembered, also, that these groups are least often arrested and convicted; hence they do not appear in any great numbers in statistical studies based upon adult inmates of penal institutions.

BROKEN HOMES

The broken home has been a convenient symbol of the family that lacks the normal love and supervision that children need for their best development. For a long time broken homes were blamed in wholesale fashion for all kinds of juvenile problems and a large amount of juvenile delinquency.

Incidence of Broken Homes

Not until about 1929–30 were studies made on a comparative basis showing the incidence of broken homes among delinquents and nondelinquents. One of the most widely quoted studies is that by Shaw and McKay, in which delinquent and nondelinquent boys of the same areas were compared with reference to broken homes.[18]

Unfortunately, these sociologists used a crude definition of broken homes; simply, homes in which one parent was absent because of death, divorce, desertion, separation, or prolonged absence due to confinement in an institution. No account was taken of the fact that, from the point of view of the effect on children, there are several types of broken homes each of which creates a distinctive emotional situation. For example, the death of a parent usually causes grief, but often develops a closer unity and loyalty between the remaining members.   Later, the children may suffer financially or from lack of control, but a home broken by death does not necessarily denote family conflict or disorganization.   On the other hand, homes broken by separation or divorce have generally been arenas of quarrels and conflict, perhaps even of a physical nature.   The children in this type of broken home tend to line up with one parent or the other and to enter the conflict.

Shaw and McKay compared delinquent boys with schoolboys of the same ages, from the same areas, and of the same race or nationality composition. The delinquent group used in the study consisted of boys appearing before the juvenile court, described as being for the most part "serious gang offenders."   Boys involved in less serious offenses, who were handled by the police without a court appearance, were not included.   Among the delinquent boys, 42.5 per cent came from broken homes; among the schoolboys, whose age and nationality composition was the same as the delinquent group's, the percentage from broken homes was 36.1.   This difference is not wide, and does not account for a very large proportion of the delinquents.

TABLE 10

Delinquent Boys and Schoolboys from Broken Homes, by Age

Age	Delinquent Boys from Broken Homes (per cent)	Schoolboys from Broken Homes (per cent)	Ratio between Rates
10	50.0	26.7	1.87
11	40.0	30.5	1.31
12	40.8	33.3	1.22
13	40.1	33.3	1.20
14	43.1	35.3	1.22
15	41.1	37.0	1.11
16	45.7	39.3	1.16
17	42.0	38.5	1.09

Source: Clifford R. Shaw and Henry D. McKay, *Social Factors in Juvenile Delinquency,* National Commission on Law Observance and Enforcement, 2, No. 13 (Washington: Government Printing Office, 1931), 277.

This comparison of delinquents and schoolboys becomes more significant when each group is broken down by age.   Table 10 shows the percentage of delinquent boys and of schoolboys who came from broken homes at each age level.   Adjustments have been made so that the nationality composition of the 2 groups is the same.   At age 10, 50.0 per cent of the delinquent boys but only 26.7 per cent of the schoolboys came from broken homes, which is a ratio of 1.87.   At age 11 the delinquent group showed 40.0 per cent from broken homes and the schoolboys 30.5 per cent, a ratio of 1.31. In general the percentage of delinquent boys from broken homes decreased with the increased age of the boys, whereas the percentage of broken homes

among the schoolboys increased.   This increase with age among the schoolboys is to be expected, as in general the parents of the older boys are older
than the parents of the younger boys; therefore more of them have died
and more are divorced.   The significant feature is the decrease in percentage
of broken homes with age among the delinquents.   By age 17, the ratio
between the percentage of broken homes among delinquents and the school
group was 1.09, that is, almost the same percentage of both groups came from
broken homes and it may be assumed that broken homes are not a factor
in delinquency at this age.   Among the younger boys, broken homes are in
some way related to delinquency.

Types of Broken Homes

That Shaw's figures do not tell the whole story is evident from other studies
in which broken homes are classified by types.   Table 11 summarizes the
results of a number of studies, and compares the percentage of broken homes
among delinquents with the percentage of broken homes for a large sample
of public-school adolescents.   The latter figures are from a study made in
1930 for the White House Conference on Child Health and Protection, and
are based on information from 7,740 junior and senior high-school pupils in
many parts of the country and from all sizes of villages and cities.   Although
a comparison of delinquency figures with these general figures is not as
valid as comparisons made between delinquents and nondelinquents in the
same communities, nevertheless, the White House Conference figures give
one of the best indices available for general comparisons when community
comparisons are impossible.   The contrast between delinquent girls and
public-school pupils of approximately the same age is striking.   The Rockford figures show the least contrast, probably because the delinquent group
includes both girls brought before the county judge and girls handled informally in the probation office without a formal charge being placed against
them.   The latter girls were first offenders or were guilty of only minor in-
discretions and delinquencies.   The Indianapolis girls and the Spokane
girls were those brought before the juvenile court, the Wisconsin girls had
been committed to an industrial school, and the Massachusetts girls were
ones committed to the Reformatory for Women.   Among the juvenile court
and institutional cases only about half as many girls came from unbroken
homes as was true for the general girl population.   The number of girls
from homes broken by the death of one or both parents is double the number
of such girls in the general population.   The contrast for homes broken by
separations or divorce is especially marked; the delinquent girls of all types
come from such homes 3 to 5 times as often as would occur if the proportion
were the same as in the general girl population.

TABLE 11

Percentage Distribution of Delinquents and Nondelinquents, by Type of Home

Type of Home	Public School Boys and Girls[a]	Delinquent Girls					Delinquent Boys				
		Rockford, Illinois[b]	Wisconsin[c]	Spokane[d]	Massachusetts[e]	Indianapolis[f]	Rockford, Illinois[b]	Wisconsin[c]	Spokane[d]	Massachusetts[e]	Indianapolis[f]
Both parents home	75	51	36.5	31.9	38.2	34.0	66	62.6	60.4	54.5	58.4
Father dead	10	10					11				
Mother dead	6	7	40.0	30.9 [g]	39.2	34.8	7	26.6	16.4 [g]	26.7	22.0
Both parents dead	2	3					1				
Parents separated or divorced	7	29	23.5 [g]	37.2	22.6	31.2 [g]	15	10.8 [g]	23.2	18.8	19.6 [g]
NUMBER OF CASES	7,740	155	252	94	500	250	435	492	414	966	750

[a] Ruth Shonle Cavan, *The Adolescent in the Family* (for the White House Conference on Child Health and Protection), (Appleton-Century, 1934), pp. 322–23.
[b] From an unpublished study.
[c] M. G. Caldwell, "Home Conditions of Institutional Delinquents," *Social Forces*, 8 (1929–30), 390.
[d] H. A. Weeks, "Male and Female Broken Home Rates by Types of Delinquency," *American Sociological Review*, 5 (1940), 603.
[e] Girls' figures, Sheldon and Eleanor T. Glueck, *Five Hundred Delinquent Women* (Knopf, 1934), p. 451; boys' figures, Sheldon and Eleanor T. Glueck, *One Thousand Juvenile Delinquents* (Harvard University Press, 1934), p. 75.
[f] E. M. Bushong, "Family Estrangement and Juvenile Delinquency," *Social Forces*, 5 (1926), 75–83.
[g] Includes parents in institutions.

Among boys the contrast is evident but less marked.   In 2 series of figures, for Rockford and for Spokane, the proportion of delinquents and the proportion of public-school pupils from homes broken by death are almost identical, but for Wisconsin, Massachusetts, and Indianapolis the delinquents came slightly more often from homes broken by death.   In all cases the delinquents come more frequently than public-school adolescents from homes broken by separation or divorce, although the contrast is less marked than among the girls.

In another study of delinquency in Spokane, delinquent boys are compared with nondelinquents of the same age range.[19]   Seventy-three per cent of the nondelinquents and 60 per cent of the delinquents came from unbroken homes, 12 and 23 per cent, respectively, from homes broken by divorce or separation, and 13 and 15 per cent from homes broken by death.   A small percentage came from homes broken by other causes.

These studies corroborate the findings of Shaw and McKay—that there is some relationship between delinquency and broken homes, although experience in a broken home obviously is not the only factor present. The studies also lead to other conclusions: homes broken by divorce or separation are more often associated with delinquency than are homes broken by death, a situation that can be accounted for by the fact that divorce and separation often are preceded by disunity and conflict.   A much higher percentage of delinquent girls than of delinquent boys come from broken homes of both types.

Broken Homes and Types of Delinquency

Impressed with the striking difference between the percentage of boy and girl delinquents from broken homes, H. A. Weeks made a detailed investigation in which he related types of delinquency to broken homes.[20]   With delinquencies unclassified, he found that 68.1 per cent of the delinquent girls but only 39.6 per cent of delinquent boys came from broken homes in a series of cases from Spokane County, Washington.   Different types of delinquency, however, were unequally related to broken homes.   Weeks' conclusions follow:

For both boys and girls, ungovernability, running away, and truancy are more closely related to broken homes, especially those broken by divorce or separation, than to unbroken homes.

Property and traffic offenses and misdemeanors, primarily boys' offenses, are more closely associated with unbroken homes than with broken homes. These offenses are usually committed by unsupervised boys' gangs, and the gang rather than the home controls the situation.

Immorality among girls is only slightly more closely associated with broken than with unbroken homes. The broken homes usually are the result of divorce or separation, rather than of death.

These common offenses of adolescents differ in the degree to which boys and girls commit them. Few delinquent girls are involved in traffic or property offenses or misdemeanors—the offenses related to unsupervised gangs. Only 9.5 per cent of the girls in Weeks' series of cases as compared with 75.2 per cent of the boys were guilty of these three offenses. In contrast, many delinquent girls but few delinquent boys were charged with ungovernability, running away, or immorality—74.7 per cent versus 18.6 per cent. These offenses are related to broken homes.

Therefore, when like delinquencies are compared for boys and girls, a like relationship to broken homes is found. The gross totals imply a misleading conclusion (that girls are affected by broken homes more than boys), because the totals for boys include a high proportion of gang delinquencies not associated with broken homes, whereas girls' totals do not include such delinquencies.

This study does not answer an important question, however: why more boys than girls are delinquent. The Spokane series covered 414 boys and 94 girls. Boys exceeded girls in all types of delinquency except 2: equal numbers of boys and girls were classified as ungovernable; more girls than boys were guilty of immorality; a difference that may rest in part upon the tendency to condone irregular sex offenses among boys. Also, more boys than girls came from each kind of broken home as well as from unbroken homes, although the ratio of boys to girls was larger for the unbroken than for the broken homes (8.3 as compared with 2.6).

INTERRELATION OF FACTORS

A comprehensive study by the Gluecks brings many individual factors related to delinquency into focus and demonstrates their interrelatedness. The Gluecks selected 500 boys confined in a correctional school and compared them with 500 public-school boys as to type of neighborhood, age, ethnic heritage, and intelligence quotient.[21] Since the Gluecks were interested in discovering why some boys from deteriorated and disorganized neighborhoods become delinquent and some do not, both groups of boys were chosen from such neighborhoods. Highly trained specialists interviewed the boys and their families, administered physical and psychological tests, and analyzed the records of schools and other agencies.

The comparison between the two groups shows marked differences in the family relationships and attitudes. Mutual hostility or indifference between parents and children characterized the delinquents in a startling proportion of the cases: 60 per cent of the fathers of delinquents but only 19 per cent of the fathers of nondelinquents were indifferent or hostile.   Although mothers exhibited more affection than fathers, there was again a disproportionate number of indifferent or hostile mothers of delinquents.   Delinquent boys responded to parents with indifference or hostility, and only 17 per cent of delinquent boys found their fathers worthy of emulation, whereas 52 per cent of nondelinquents could place their fathers in this position.   Discipline was lax, erratic, or overly strict, rarely firm but kindly in the delinquent group and there was great dependence on physical punishment.   Underlying these unsatisfactory relationships were certain characteristics of the parents that appeared much more frequently among the parents of delinquents than of nondelinquents: emotional disturbances, drunkenness, criminal behavior, inability to manage economic affairs, and conjugal maladjustment.   Some of these same characteristics also typified the parents' parents, thus suggesting the transmission of a family pattern as well as the failure to develop well-balanced personalities in one generation after another under similar adverse conditions.

The delinquent boys emerged from these homes with certain characteristics that differentiated them from the public-school boys.   They were more assertive, defiant, resentful, suspicious and impulsive.   They had less self-control and less conventional acceptance of ideas or feelings; they were less co-operative and less dependent upon others.   At the same time, however, they tended to expect to receive many rewards without making an effort to secure them; they were interested in material things and in an immediate indulgence of appetites.   The delinquent boys tended to express themselves in extrovert ways, while the nondelinquents were more inclined to be introversive in solving their problems.

In the above paragraph we seem to have the typical unsocialized and restless delinquent boy, who, not finding full satisfactions in home and school, turns to nonconventional or delinquent activities.   Finally, the delinquent boys sought membership in gangs of boys like themselves; the nondelinquents, however, built up small groups of friends who were also nondelinquent.

Given a boy emotionally alienated from home and school, add the many opportunities for uncontrolled activities afforded by a slum neighborhood, and delinquency results.   On the other hand, boys in the same community environment who come from more stable and affectionate families and who find more satisfaction in school are better able to avoid delinquent activities and to meet conventional standards, despite adverse community conditions.

RELATION OF FAMILY INFLUENCES TO
COMMUNITY BACKGROUND

The relationship of inadequate families to disorganized communities is twofold. First, there are more inadequate families in disorganized communities than elsewhere. This situation is shown by the concentration of foreign-born families that often are unable to guide and control their semi-Americanized children. It is also shown by the amount of family disorganization symbolized by the high rates of divorce and desertion. Moreover, in these areas are concentrated the economically insecure families that are unable to provide recreation and often actual necessities. Because of these conditions the families in disorganized areas fail more frequently to provide emotional satisfaction, training, and supervision for their children than do families in other communities.

Second, the disorganized community does not supplement the family. Agencies to take over the functions neglected by disorganized families are few; and, what is perhaps more important, are usually imposed upon the disorganized community by outside groups that recognize its deficiencies and attempt to provide what families and the community cannot provide for themselves. Too often these agencies never succeed in becoming part of the community life and exert only a small amount of influence. Also, because it is disorganized, the community permits the growth of various agencies that contribute directly or indirectly to crime: the poolroom or tavern where criminals may congregate; pawnshops that act as receivers of stolen goods; junkmen who encourage boys to steal; and adult criminals who teach boys their crafts.

It is true that we are unable on the basis of present research to select the exact combination of personal, family, and community factors that will inevitably lead to a life of crime. A careful reading of cases suggests that although there are certain fairly common sequences, there is no single combination of factors. Rather, various situations exist that alienate the child from family control or cause the family to fail in establishing a satisfactory life for the child. The facts we seem to be sure of, however, are these:

Delinquency may arise when the family fails to provide a satisfying and progressive emotional development, so that as a result the child seeks satisfactions of a nonconforming nature.

Delinquency also may arise when the family fails to train the child or to provide interesting activities and supervision, without necessarily creating strong emotional disturbances.

Delinquency in these family situations is most likely to occur when the community is disorganized and affords patterns and opportunities for crime rather than influences that would counteract the family deficiencies.

QUESTIONS

1. How do emotionally disturbed parents fail their children?   Are their children necessarily delinquent?

2. What types of families are least able to cope with slum conditions?

3. Discuss the popular idea that broken homes cause delinquency.

4. Comparing the findings of Healy and Brunner, *New Light on Delinquency, and Its Treatment,* Eissler (ed.), *Searchlights on Delinquency,* and Glueck and Glueck, *Unraveling Juvenile Delinquency,* what do you conclude about the family that produces delinquents?

5. How are family factors and community factors interrelated?

READINGS

Eissler, K. R. (ed.), *Searchlights on Delinquency* (New York: International Universities Press, 1949).   This series of papers written in honor of August Aichhorn interprets maladjustment and misconduct in psychoanalytic terms. Many articles trace the origin of delinquency to early frustrating or loveless family relationships.

Glueck, Sheldon and Eleanor T., *Five Hundred Delinquent Women* (Knopf, 1934).   One of the few studies of delinquent women, this study traces the histories of 500 women who served time in the Massachusetts Reformatory for Women, bringing out background factors as well as conventional or deviant behavior after leaving the institution.

———, *Delinquents in the Making: Paths to Prevention* (Harper, 1952).   A popular version of *Unraveling Juvenile Delinquency,* listed below.

———, *Unraveling Juvenile Delinquency* (Cambridge: Harvard University Press, for the Commonwealth Fund, 1950).   A comparison was made of 500 delinquent boys with a matched group of 500 public-school boys, all selected from slum areas.   Outwardly, the boys all had the same disorganized social environment.   The study reveals many differences in personality, family relationships, and personal experiences that help to explain why some but not all boys in slum areas become delinquent.

Healy, William, and Augusta F. Bronner, *New Light on Delinquency and Its Treatment* (New Haven: Yale University Press, 1936).   A comparison of 105 delinquent children with their nondelinquent siblings brings out many subtle ways in which the family relationships of the delinquent children differed from those of their siblings.

Shaw, Clifford R., and Henry D. McKay, *Social Factors in Juvenile Delinquency,* No. 13, Vol. 2 of the reports of the National Commission on Law Observance and Enforcement (Washington: Government Printing Office, 1931).   Although much of this report assembles data on delinquency areas and their characteristics, chapters 9 and 10 discuss family relationships and chapter 11 coordinates many factors that play upon the life of a delinquent boy.

FOOTNOTES

[1] Clifford R. Shaw and Henry D. McKay, *Social Factors in Juvenile Delinquency,* No. 13, Vol. 2, of the reports of the National Commission on Law Observance and Enforcement (Washington: Government Printing Office, 1931), chs. 2, 5, pp. 106–7.

[2] Clifford R. Shaw, *Delinquency Areas* (Chicago: University of Chicago Press, 1929), p. 153.

[3] N. S. Hayner, "Delinquency Areas in the Puget Sound Region," *American Journal of Sociology,* 39 (1933), 317, 323, 325.

[4] Sheldon and Eleanor T. Glueck, *One Thousand Juvenile Delinquents* (Cambridge: Harvard University Press, 1934), p. 75.

[5] Sheldon and Eleanor T. Glueck, *Five Hundred Delinquent Women* (Knopf, 1934), p. 454.

[6] K. D. Lumpkin, "Factors in the Commitment of Correctional School Girls in Wisconsin," *American Journal of Sociology,* 37 (1931), 225–29.

[7] William Healy and Augusta F. Bronner, *New Light on Delinquency and Its Treatment* (New Haven: Yale University Press, 1936).

[8] August Aichhorn, *Wayward Youth* (New York: Viking, 1939).

[9] Healy and Bronner, *op. cit.,* pp. 56–57, 128–29.

[10] K. R. Eissler (ed.), *Searchlights on Delinquency* (New York: International Universities Press, 1949).

[11] Sheldon and Eleanor T. Glueck, *Five Hundred Delinquent Women,* pp. 72–73.

[12] Sheldon and Eleanor T. Glueck, *One Thousand Juvenile Delinquents,* p. 75.

[13] Lumpkin, *op. cit.,* p. 226.

[14] William Healy and Augusta F. Bronner, *Delinquents and Criminals, Their Making and Unmaking* (Macmillan, 1926), p. 263.

[15] Sheldon and Eleanor T. Glueck, *One Thousand Juvenile Delinquents,* p. 69.

[16] Sheldon and Eleanor T. Glueck, *Criminal Careers in Retrospect* (New York: Commonwealth Fund, 1943), p. 336.

[17] *Ibid.,* p. 127.

[18] Shaw and McKay, *Social Factors in Juvenile Delinquency,* pp. 261–84.

[19] H. A. Weeks, "Predicting Juvenile Delinquency," *American Sociological Review,* 8 (1943), 42.

[20] H. A. Weeks, "Male and Female Broken Home Rates by Types of Delinquency," *American Sociological Review,* 5 (1940), 601–9.

[21] Sheldon and Eleanor T. Glueck, *Unraveling Juvenile Delinquency* (Cambridge: Harvard University Press, 1950).

5

The Development of the Professional Criminal

As we have seen, juvenile delinquency develops from a background of family and community disorganization and deficiencies. Since one half to two thirds of these juvenile delinquents also have adult records as major criminals or minor offenders, we turn now to a discussion of these criminals, using as a classification 11 of the 12 types described in Chapter 1. It will be recalled that the basis of this classification was the degree to which the criminal has become incorporated into the criminal world. Wherever research has provided the data, the steps in the process by which the adult offender develops from the juvenile offender will be described. In order to emphasize the sharp contrast with noncriminals, the professional criminal who is completely incorporated into the criminal world will be discussed first, in this chapter as an individual and in Chapter 6 as a member of an organized criminal group.

THE PROFESSIONAL CRIMINAL

The professional criminal is the logical, final product of the social situations that permit and encourage criminal nonconformity. This "career man" of crime almost invariably practices some form of stealing or has an illegal occupation, which yields him an income. His relation to his trade and the degree to which his life is organized around it are comparable to the organization of the work and life of the banker, the doctor, the businessman, or the skilled craftsman; he too is a specialist. However, his activities are confined to the criminal world, whereas the professional or businessman lives in the conventional world.

There are at least 4 ways in which the professional criminal is differentiated from other types of criminals.

1. The professional criminal gets his living solely by the commission of crime. Since crime is his daily, full-time occupation, he makes no pretense

at having any other occupation unless it serves to further his criminal activities.

2. The professional criminal has acquired the skills necessary to commit one or several related types of crime. He tends to specialize in a particular type of crime.

3. The professional criminal organizes his life around his criminal specialty and subordinates other phases of his life to his money-making activities.

4. The professional criminal is an accepted member of the criminal world, to which he looks for social status and approval, and to whose disapproval and reproofs he responds.

There are many types of professional crime, such as picking pockets, burglarizing houses, stealing from hotel rooms, stealing automobiles, running confidence games, and kidnaping for ransom. Such crimes are performed by one person or a small group that may change its personnel from time to time, and that depends for its success upon anonymity of the criminal, which in turn requires mobility. The execution of the crime may take only a few minutes in the case of direct stealing, or a period of days or weeks in the case of elaborate confidence games. In other types of professional crime, a permanent organization is maintained, and the criminal activities become institutionalized, similar to the organization of legitimate business. Gambling establishments, houses of prostitution, bootlegging during prohibition, and rackets that prey on legitimate business, exemplify professional organized crime.

Men more often than women engage in professional crime, perhaps because it is a way of earning a living and women still look to men to support them. The professional criminal, probably in the majority of instances, has his origin in the disorganized areas of large cities. He is frequently a product of lack of family training in the mores of honesty and hard work plus the positive influences of unsupervised street gangs and of association with other criminals. It is true that criminals of this type sometimes have their origin in small cities or rural areas; however, the small community offers little opportunity for the resident professional criminal who soon finds his way to the city, completes his training with urban professional criminals, and becomes a member of the criminal underworld.

TRANSITION FROM JUVENILE DELINQUENCY
TO ADULT CRIME

Development of the Professional Criminal

The process by which the adult professional criminal develops has six steps.

1. A typical first step is the affiliation of a preadolescent with an unsupervised group of the same sex.   Among boys, this group is the gang; among girls, it is a clique.   The gang has been more completely studied, and the term has special connotations.   It differs from a play group: the play group is supervised either unofficially by parents or officially by a teacher or playground director; in contrast, the boys' gang is completely unsupervised. The gang may be large or may consist of only 2 or 3 boys.   Its essence is not in its size but in the importance it assumes for its members.   It is primarily a group of congenial spirits, usually composed of boys who like activity, fun, adventure, and risk.   The boy who likes to read, or who has a consuming hobby, may have friends and companions, but he does not have a gang. The gang is set for action.   Much of the action is adventurous in nature and takes the form of conflict with other gangs, families, the police, and stable community agencies.   Fighting with other gangs, evasion of family control and responsibilities, daring escapades, such as in "flipping" trains, stealing from fruit stands for excitement, tormenting the police, begging food or money, and collecting and selling junk for spending money are all characteristic of a well-developed boys' gang.   Its activities are rarely delinquent or criminal at this stage, and the boys are still living at home, with their parents providing necessities.

The gang thus supplies its members with excitement and adventure without the interference or supervision of adults.   Furthermore, it gives its members approval for their acts; physical prowess, devising new adventures, and daring are lauded.   It also furnishes its members with security of several kinds.   For example, the gang will protect a member from adult interference as long as it is able to do so; and by sharing food and money it makes possible relative independence of the family.

The girls' group differs somewhat from the boys' gang.   Ordinarily the girl does not affiliate with an unruly clique until adolescence, and such a clique exhibits a different pattern of conduct.   Nevertheless it is not certain that the motives of the 2 groups are dissimilar.   Instead of the excitement of flipping trains, stealing, or bumming away from home in some makeshift camp, the girl seeks the thrill and adventure of the dance hall, the forbidden automobile ride with a pick-up, the excitement of the first drink.   If sexual relations occur, they are merely incidental to the general adventure.   At this period the girl is still living at home and is considered a problem rather than a delinquent.

There are several possibilities in the future development of the young boys' gang or the girls' clique.   It may disintegrate as the boys and girls grow older and acquire other interests.   It may become conventionalized as an athletic, social, or school club; or a club affiliated with a community center.   Or it may develop into a delinquent group.   We are concerned with this last type only.

2. The gang activities begin to assume a quasi-delinquent aspect as the gang gains confidence and its members grow in years.   Among boys, begging is a means of acquiring money without any individual effort in the way of work.   Junking is also a borderline activity, since it is not always clear whether old rags, bottles, and metal collected and sold have been abandoned or still are the property of someone else.   Bumming rides in automobiles, flipping trains and riding without paying, collecting coal along the railroad right of way, getting slightly spoiled food at vegetable markets, going on long excursions to other cities, obtaining food and clean clothes for the whole gang from one member's house in his parents' absence, and playing truant from school are not strictly speaking serious delinquent activities.   But they are definitely on the borderline.   Such activities are still regarded as adventure, or they are carried out to get necessities for the gang or for home use.   At this stage boys will live at home and consider themselves part of the family group.   They are, however, usually suspected by police and teachers—representatives of a law-abiding society.

At this same stage girls extend their activities.   The sexual adventure satisfies not only the desire for excitement, but also becomes a method of obtaining gifts or money.   Petty stealing may also occur with some regularity from parents, at school, or in stores.   Staying out late at night, truancy, refusal to work, and general insubordination are common.

3. The next step in criminal development is the extension of activities into the definitely delinquent field.   Among boys, collecting junk in alleys and vacant lots is augmented by breaking into empty houses and tearing out the plumbing and other metal fixtures.   "Borrowing" automobiles for joy rides, until the gasoline gives out, replaces thumbing rides with others.   Breaking into freight cars or stealing coal from loaded cars replaces gathering coal from the right of way.   Burglary or picking pockets is an easy transition from begging.   Occasional truancy becomes chronic.   At this point the gang or certain members of it tend to stay away from home for weeks at a time, sleeping outdoors in summer and in vestibules or rented rooms in winter.   Although they are still officially schoolboys and nominal members of their families, their allegiance to the gang is fast replacing the hold of the family.   Among girls a similar progression takes place.

It should be noted that the motives of delinquency are essentially juvenile. Children must have food and clothing to live, they want adventure and recreation, but they prefer to steal what they need rather than to depend on their families.

4. Although at this stage many boys and girls are arrested for truancy,

stealing, disorderly conduct, and staying away from home, the general adult attitude toward them is either tolerance or despairing helplessness.   The delinquents are merely reprimanded by police officers or judges of the juvenile court and placed on probation with their families, who frequently do nothing to improve the situation.   However, if delinquent activities are not checked at this point, the future adult criminal is well advanced in the course of his development.

5. The next step is characterized by contact with older, more experienced criminals.   At first boys are often used as tools by irresponsible parents or minor criminals.   Thus the junk dealer may encourage boys to bring in material that they are unlikely to find without breaking into a house.   Needy parents overlook the origin of money and food that the boys bring home. But gradually the boy who continues his delinquent activities comes into contact with adult criminals.   Although the records of criminal careers do not indicate that a boys' gang of any size is adopted as a whole by adult criminals, 1 or 2 or 3 boys with experience as delinquents in childhood and early adolescence may be accepted by adult criminals as protégés or apprentices.   For a time the boys remain on the fringe of the adult criminal world.   At first they may be allowed only to play minor roles in major crimes, but by degrees they are taught the techniques necessary to a particular type of crime.   This instruction may be deliberate or casually acquired from association with criminals.   The adult criminals plan the crimes and assign boys to particular tasks in their execution.

A girl at this stage may be made use of by some man who takes her to live with him.   Sending other men to her, he retains the money himself from the ensuing prostitution.   Or 2 girls may combine forces, either stealing or practicing more or less regular prostitution.   Sometimes a girl marries a criminal and becomes a member of his gang to the extent that she helps dispose of stolen goods, hides his friends hunted by police, plans an escape for the gang, or otherwise aids without actually participating in the commission of crimes.   The girl may not be fully aware of the implication of her acts and may not have adopted a philosophy of crime.   She may simply follow the conduct of more experienced persons to whom she is attached by companionship or affection.

6. The final stage of development arrives when the delinquent begins to break off contacts with his family, the school, and other conventional groups. He definitely alienates himself from the family circle, sometimes deliberately losing himself by not communicating with his family or by adopting an assumed name.   He also evades contacts with the school if he is not yet past the age of compulsory school attendance.   For these conventional contacts the boy substitutes those of the criminal world and becomes an habitué of

the rooming houses, taverns, restaurants, and poolrooms where criminals congregate. The girl may become an inmate of a disorderly house, a hostess in a disreputable cabaret or dance hall, or she may affiliate herself with a criminal gang either of other women or of men. The youth abandons all thought of a lawful occupation or career, and chooses as his goal achievement in criminal activities. The successful criminal becomes his ideal, and he regards him with the same admiration that a boy or girl in another group would bestow upon the successful businessman or woman, the successful lawyer, or doctor. The juvenile delinquent has finally graduated from the class of delinquent adolescent to that of adult criminal.

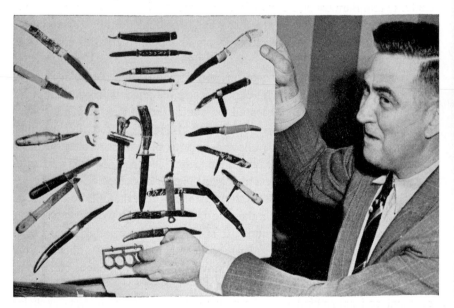

When boys' gangs have such dangerous weapons as brass knuckles, stiletto-sharp knives, and sharpened beer-can openers, their activities can no longer be classified as harmless play. The array of weapons shown above was seized during a police drive to end boy neighborhood gangs in an attempt to check hoodlumism in Los Angeles. (International News Photo)

Although these 6 steps may not be found completely developed in all cases, the general pattern occurs with almost monotonous regularity in the accounts of criminal careers. In the summaries of actual case histories that follow the numbers in parentheses indicate which step has been reached in the progress toward professional criminality.

Histories of Professional Criminals

A. The history of Rocco typifies the development of the professional criminal.[1]

(1) This boy, of Italian background, had a stern father and an indulgent mother who tried to protect him from his father's severity. As a young boy he attended school regularly and had his own play group.

(2) When the family moved to another neighborhood, Rocco began to play truant in order to return to the old neighborhood and visit his friends. Later he became a member of a group that bummed around and made trouble at school; some of the gang members stole.

(3) The gang began to steal shirts from clotheslines in a prosperous neighborhood, which were sold to older brothers or other young men. They also "robbed pennies" from peanut-vending machines. The money was used for various amusements including shooting craps. When the boys were about fourteen years old they stopped going to school. They progressed to stealing and selling bicycles. Encouraged by adults who wished to buy second-hand tires, they began to steal tires and maintained a small store where they dealt in them. At this time the boys began to have sexual relations with girls.

(4) Rocco was not arrested until he was 16 and had a long history of delinquencies. Although he was suspected of stealing, the charge was not proved and he was discharged. At 17 he was sent to St. Charles Reformatory for stealing cars.

(5) When Rocco was 18 he was invited by a group of older criminals to participate in some of their crimes. At first the younger boys did not share equally in the profits with the older and more experienced men, since they were in the position of apprentices. The older men gave them guns and taught them how to steal trucks of butter and eggs, which they unloaded and then drove into an adjoining police district. The butter and eggs were quickly and easily sold to various grocers. This gang had a lawyer to get them out of legal difficulties. These men also taught the younger boys to dress expensively and the various manners and customs of the successful adult criminal.

(6) Rocco quickly became an accomplished criminal. He carried out armed robberies of trucks and stores in association with older criminals. He spoke the language of the criminal world and looked back with amusement at his adolescent attempts at crime and sophistication. Although Rocco had not broken off his association with his family up to the age of 21, when this record ends, perhaps because of the protective attitude of his mother, nevertheless he was a full-fledged professional criminal.

B. Although the girl in the following extract was only 16, her record shows almost the complete progression from the nondelinquent little child to the confirmed adult criminal.[2]

(1) As a child, she lived in a 2 room basement apartment with her parents

and 4 brothers and sisters.   The back yard was used by a junkman and elevated tracks ran overhead.   After starting school she made friends first with
a girl called Bunny, then with another called Peaches.   Either in the company of these girls or alone she engaged in many unsupervised activities of
a doubtful nature.

(2) She collected junk and sold it, picked up coal along the tracks, and
sometimes seized the chance to "snitch" a bottle of milk or a loaf of bread.
When a gang of boys upset a pushcart she grabbed some of the fruit that
rolled off.   She begged in railroad stations and became truant from school.
By the age of eight she had learned not to beg too often in one station, and
to conceal her address if questioned by the police.

(3) With her two friends, Bunny and Peaches, she began to go to stores
in the main business section of the city where she lived, and was taught by
these girls to steal small articles, possibly for personal use.   She stole a string
of beads—the first thing of the kind she had ever had.   She also stole small
articles of clothing, either to wear or to sell.   She learned how to hide these
things in her clothing and also to avoid the floorwalker or store detective.
When she was 12 she and one of her friends began to have sexual relations
with boys.   At this time she also began to drink and to stay out half the
night.

(4) Her mother objected to the late hours she was keeping, but was unable
to control her.   Later, she influenced her mother to move to a better apartment and provided her with better clothing and food, which were accepted.

(5) With one of her friends, she associated with various men, from whom
the two girls demanded and received money for sexual relations.   She met a
man, named Darcy, who had an apartment, and stayed with him for 3
weeks.   When she and her friends got into trouble, they turned to Darcy.
He was a member of a group that had favorable connections and could "fix
things."   However, he was sent to prison for 2 years.   The girl's parents
objected strenuously to her activities and she left home.   She was then 14
years of age, and prostitution had made her independent financially.   She
rented 3 rooms in another neighborhood, not telling her mother where she
was.   Bunny joined her and the 2 girls began to work in a combination speak-
easy and brothel.   She had various adventures—wild automobile rides,
drunken episodes, and sexual experiences.   The gang she associated with
carried guns.   At last, "it didn't seem as if we were getting anywhere," and
she returned home and re-entered school.   But she persisted in her night life,
and school was of little interest in comparison.

(6) She continued to associate with her 2 girl companions and quickly
encountered several male criminals who planned crimes in the presence of
the girls.   Although the girls did not participate in these crimes, they spent

was published was in prison serving a sentence of 1 year to life for several armed robberies. Steps (1) and (6) do not appear.

(2) At the age of 4 Michael was picked up by the police for begging in the company of his older brothers. During the next 4 years he was brought to the police station once every few months for begging, usually with his brothers, occasionally alone.

(3) By the time he was 7 he was pilfering pennies from newsstands and playing truant with an older brother. He was sent to a training school for 2 years, but upon release reverted to his former conduct. When he was 11 he began to go to the beaches with older boys, where they stole pocketbooks from the clothing of persons who were swimming. He was caught and sentenced to the Chicago Parental School. A second commitment to this school was the result of his burglarizing 5 houses with his older brother. At the age of 12 he repeated this offense and was sent to the state training school for boys. By the time he was 12 he was associated with other boys in addition to his brother in burglaries and stealing automobiles. He was also staying away from home and school, sleeping every night for weeks at a time in a newspaper delivery truck.

(4) The family attitude was one of helplessness. The boys were beaten by the father whenever he learned of their stealing. The mother cried over their troubles and visited them when they were in nearby institutions.

(5) Michael's tutoring in crime was begun when he was about 9 years old by a boy about 4 years older than he. His contacts with this boy were resumed after each period of incarceration. When Michael was 15 he associated with boys of 17 and 18; one member of the group was 26. In company with these older delinquents he committed more serious crimes, such as frequent automobile thefts and armed robberies. At 16 Michael was committed to the state reformatory, where he remained for 5 years. Three months after his release he was again committed for armed robbery performed with a companion 4 years his senior.

Michael's career is incomplete. At the time of his last commitment he was engaged in adult types of crime, but he had not become a professional criminal. The crimes he and his companions committed were not well planned, and the group did not have the necessary contacts for avoiding arrest or escaping conviction that are typical of the professional criminal. Nor did Michael ever leave home completely or break off his attachment to his mother.

F. Alice, a professional criminal described by the Gluecks, followed the typical pattern.[6]

(1) She was the youngest of 5 children, pampered at home and a tomboy at play.

(2) At an early age she engaged in semidelinquent activities, indulging in sex play with an old man, writing filthy phrases at school, inciting other children to steal, and stealing from stores. Her mother and the neighbors accepted these stolen articles and when Alice was reported to the police her mother paid for them.

(3) In early adolescence Alice and a girl companion were stealing clothing from stores and money. Alice was already learning the techniques of crime, for she wore long, full skirts so that she might easily hide the things stolen. She and her friend also carefully planned in advance how to steal goods from the stores. She was also becoming familiar with boys and men.

(4) At this point the juvenile court placed her in a series of foster homes, in none of which she made a good adjustment for any length of time. From some of these homes she ran away, and upon one such occasion was found with a girl of bad reputation frequenting the cheap restaurants and cabarets where prostitutes and sailors gathered. Since attempts to place her successfully appeared to have failed, she was sent to a correctional school. Because of her incorrigibility she was transferred at the age of 16 to the reformatory for women, where she remained for almost a year.

(5) After her release from the reformatory she went to live with her parents in a neighboring town, but she soon returned to the city and her former girl companion, with whom she proceeded to steal from all the large department stores. By this time she had learned professional techniques of shoplifting from women met at the correctional school. Her friend was a pickpocket and between them they accumulated about $900 worth of goods in their room when they were arrested.

(6) Alice had almost completely entered the criminal world at this time. Not only was she a skilled shoplifter, but she boasted of an arrangement with store detectives so that they did not report her. At her trial she was represented by a lawyer and pleaded guilty to a charge of larceny, for which she was sentenced to the women's reformatory for a 5-year indeterminate sentence. She was then 18 years old. Upon her parole she rejoined her old gang, thus breaking her parole, and was recommitted. When again paroled she stayed with her sister for a short time, married a young man, and continued as a shoplifter, now training younger girls in the techniques of this form of crime. Her later career included several marriages, not all of which were legal, more and more skilled shoplifting of high-priced goods, and occasional sentences in jail. She had established various connections that always enabled her to secure bail and a light sentence.

In general the process of becoming a professional criminal may be described as a gradual alienation from loyalty to, and participation in, agencies that conform to the community mores, such as the family, church, school, and community organizations. Early in the process membership is acquired in a group that does not support the mores and whose activities verge on delinquency. For a time the individual is a member of both types of group—the conventional conforming group, and the nonconforming, semidelinquent group. Gradually, the strength of his relationship with the conventional group weakens and the hold of the nonconforming group grows stronger. When he arrives at the point of complete severance with the conventional group and organizes his life in terms of the criminal group he has become a full-fledged professional criminal.

THE CRIMINAL WORLD

The habitual criminal and the professional criminal, whose lives are organized around a pattern of crime, develop their own social organization with characteristic institutions, occupations, recreations, family life, language, codes, and philosophy. This social organization of criminals is termed the underworld.

The underworld presents some aspects of a distinct caste. Entrance into it and exit from it are perhaps not so difficult as in a genuine caste. However, the underworld is more than just a social class comparable to lower, middle, or upper-class groups in conventional society. The underworld is in a sense a world apart, with its own social classes, ranging from the hobo and streetwalker to the moneyed gangster or racketeer. The amateur delinquent who has adopted the underworld aspires only to rise in it, not to get out of it and into the conventional world. The successful criminal desires to become more successful in crime and not to enter conventional life, unless to retire on a stolen fortune. Moreover, once thoroughly indoctrinated in underworld codes and philosophy, once thoroughly incorporated into underworld life and institutions, it is difficult for the criminal to re-enter the conventional world, for he does not feel at home there. Also, if he has been imprisoned in a penal institution he is branded as a convict, and conventional people look askance at him in social groups and ban him from employment. The habitual and professional criminals can best be understood by comprehension of the nature of the underworld in which they live.

Habitat

Although criminal activities extend throughout the social organization, the residences and gathering places of criminals are usually located in special types of areas. They are found in areas where there is a great tolerance of conduct and little effort at formal control of illegal behavior. In every large city certain areas—the disorganized areas already discussed—are tolerant of crime and vice and lax in police control. Other such areas are found outside the limits of large cities but within easy transportation distance. To these areas the urban police system does not extend, and generally the county sheriff system is not adequate to police them. Hence they become a legal and moral no man's land. Within the city the areas include not only the slums but certain rooming-house districts and hotels that provide anonymity and tolerate criminal activities carried on within their walls. Hotels and rooming houses are important to criminals, since they make possible the mobility necessitated by frequent crimes. Only the more successful criminals, operating within a limited area and secure in their status, can afford to burden themselves with real estate, furniture, and the like.

Institutions

Criminals require a common meeting place, where a criminal newly arrived in a city may make contacts with others with whom he may wish to affiliate himself. Such a place also enables newly released prisoners to find friends; it provides a rendezvous for prisoners who make a pact in prison but who are released at different times; and it affords a protected place for planning crimes. A restaurant, a tavern, or a poolroom may fulfill these requirements. Successful organized gangs may have a specific headquarters limited to the activities of their own organization.

When property other than money, such as jewels, silverware, or clothing, is stolen, the criminal must have some means of disposing of it. The person who disposes of such stolen property is called a fence. He may be ostensibly a pawnbroker or a jeweler who remodels jewelry so that it cannot be recognized or removes stones from their settings. In the case of stolen automobiles, the fence attempts to remove or change the serial number before selling the car.

The institutions of crime also include the fix, or man who contrives the release of an arrested criminal. This man may be a minor politician who has contacts with both the political organization of a city and with the underworld. For an agreed sum of money the fix arranges with police or court for the criminal's release, which is accomplished by direct payment of cash, presents, or political favors. Everyone profits in some way from the transaction: the criminal obtains his freedom; the fix acquires money; and the police, judge, or other official receives cash, presents, or political security. Powerful criminals and permanently organized groups frequently employ lawyers to protect them.

The adult thief may acquire the remarkable variety of loot shown in this photograph.   In this case the thief, a cat burglar, jumped from a second-story window into the arms of waiting police.   His pockets were stuffed with such diverse articles as $20 bills and shoe laces.   Although the radio and the traveling clock would have brought only a fraction of their original cost, they could have been quickly pawned.   (International News Photo)

Recreation

Certain amusements are characteristic of the underworld.   The lack of formal education and the mobility of the group preclude numerous types of recreation.   The need for anonymity places further limits upon where criminals may go.   The lack of a normally organized family and emotional life also affects the choice of entertainment.   Moreover, criminals soon come to feel at home only among other criminals—just as college students feel most at home among other college students—therefore they find their recreation at common meeting places.   The saloon or tavern where drinking and gambling fill the time, the cabaret and house of prostitution that supply women, the private athletic club whose membership is composed largely of criminals, the burlesque show, and the cheap movie are typical forms of recreation.

Successful criminals frequently keep women to whom they are not necessarily married. They provide rooms or apartments for them, as well as jewels and clothes that are stolen, or bought from the thief. The automobile is another resource of the criminal, both for pleasure and for business. Delinquent boys often "borrow" cars for an evening's entertainment; mature criminals steal them to use in crime or to sell. However, successful criminals buy expensive makes of cars, often equipped with bulletproof glass. The few highly successful criminals own their homes, and occasionally (as in the case of Al Capone) have a winter home in the south as well as a summer home in the north.

Family Life

The professional criminal enjoys little family life, since the need for secrecy and mobility is too great. There is ample sex life, either with prostitutes, a mistress for a short period of time, a common-law wife, or sometimes a legal wife. But there are few children among the criminal group and few examples of settled married life.

Clark, whose story has been given in brief earlier in this chapter, never married, although he had contacts with women and mentions one girl with whom he lived, lavishing many luxuries upon her.[7] However, Eddie Jackson, a pickpocket of the early 1900's had prolonged associations with five women in addition to casual contacts with others.[8] The first was an older woman who operated a brothel; Jackson lived with her in her apartment, first as a roomer and then as her paramour; he had lived with her 7 years when their association was terminated by his imprisonment. Released from prison, he married a salesgirl who was never a criminal. This marriage lasted only 2 years; during this period Jackson did not stay at home much of the time, for his wife wanted him to reform. A child was born of this union. He then lived for 5 years with a woman whom he did not marry, an association again terminated by a prison sentence. After he left prison, this woman wanted him to reform; therefore he left her. He recovered from a drunken bout to find himself married to a woman with whom he then lived for 3 years. While he was in prison, she divorced him. Several years later he married again, and again his wife divorced him while he was in prison. She was unhappy after he went to prison and since his term was for a relatively long period, he stated that he urged her to get the divorce.

Conwell points out that the thief may consort with strange women in places where his identity is protected but that he takes to his home only a woman he knows and can trust, because of the danger of betrayal to the police.[9] He may or may not be married to the women who live with him, although the association is the equivalent of marriage, with the wife giving her husband loyalty and assistance, but not entering directly into his crimes. She may have been a thief or prostitute prior to her marriage, but subsequently she assumes the conventional wifely role and permits her husband to support her.

In a crisis, the wife is expected to help her husband.   If arrest is imminent, she is expected to select and prepare a new place to live.   If her husband is sent to prison, she is expected to keep him informed of important developments at home, and if he needs money to escape from prison, she arranges to get it from other thieves.   She frequently earns her living honestly, returns to her family, or becomes a temporary guest of other thieves; she is unlikely to indulge in criminal conduct in the fear that she also will be imprisoned, thus destroying her husband's contact with the world to which he will eventually return.

Language

Like other distinct social or professional groups, criminals have developed a language of their own, which pertains to their occupation.*   Several glossaries of the criminal argot have been published and life stories of criminals are replete with these terms.   A limited number of them are given here, not only because the terms demonstrate the professionalization of crime but because they reveal its ramifications and the degree of specialization in crime.[10]

Lowest in the criminal scale are the habitual criminals, many of whom are inefficient persons whose capacities have been further undermined by drink, drugs, and the lack of the physical necessities for a healthy life.   They may combine occasional employment with begging and forms of minor crime, such as petty thievery or obtaining small sums of money under false pretenses.

Among the terms employed in the vernacular of this group of habitual criminals are:

Stiffy: one who pretends that he is paralyzed in order to win sympathy while begging.

Dummy: one who poses as a deaf mute in order to enlist sympathy, which facilitates begging.

Jocker: one who teaches young boys to beg and to steal for him.

Grafter: one who exploits private and public charity organizations by telling fabricated stories of hard luck and illness.

---

* It is typical of any group that has close contacts and performs some specialized function within the larger society to develop a language of its own.   This language includes professional terms and also colloquialisms or slang that are often short cuts to longer professional terms.   The language facilitates communication between members of the group.   In time it tends to build morale and solidarity within the group, for it isolates them to a certain extent from other groups and gives a sense of distinction.

Jack-roller: a tramp or a young delinquent who rifles the pockets of a drunk either asleep or too drunk to resist. The jack-roller plies his trade chiefly in areas of large cities where hoboes, tramps, and bums congregate.

Criminals whose specialty requires planning and skilled techniques look down upon the beggars and jack-rollers. In this skilled group are the gun, dip, or cannon (pickpocket); the booster (shoplifter); the prowler (who burglarizes a house when the occupants are at home); the hotel worker (who steals from hotel rooms); the criminal who does slow work (or burglarizes a house during the daytime when the occupants are absent); the moll-buzzer (pickpocket who specializes in robbing women); the peterman (safeblower); the con man (who operates a confidence game); and various other specialists in different types of stealing.

In addition to general terms for stealing, each type of criminal operation has its own professional terms. For instance, the pickpockets work in mobs of 2 or 3 men. The man who actually takes the money or watch from the pocket of the victim is the hook, tool, or wire; his assistants are called stalls; the stall who conceals the movements of the hook's dukes or hands is called the dukeman. In the confidence game there is an outside man or steerer who makes the contacts with the victim and an inside man or spieler to whom the victim is brought for completion of a job. Often there is also a pay-off store or joint, which is a crooked gambling place or fake brokerage office, depending on the nature of the operation.

In gambling alone, more than 500 special terms are used, and commonplace words acquire new meanings: a cowboy is a reckless gambler; rats and mice are dice; to murder is to win money easily, quickly, and in large amounts; and Nina from Carolina is point nine in craps.

Other terms in general use and unrelated to any special type of crime are the following:

Hangout: place where a particular gang meets.
Poke: pocketbook.
Grand: one thousand dollars.
Right: trustworthy.
Broad or moll: woman.
To case: to survey a place, such as a bank or store, preparatory to planning a crime.

Other terms refer to relations with the police:

Dick: detective.
Around the horn: tour of police stations for purposes of identification after a criminal is arrested.
Lam: running away from imminent arrest.

Bum rap: arrest for a crime not committed.
Frame: false arrest.

Still other terms refer to jails and prisons, a part of the experience of every persistent criminal.   Among these expressions are bit and stretch for prison sentences; cop a heel for escape; hole for the place of solitary confinement; bank house for house of correction; jug for jail; and stir for penitentiary.

These examples are only a few of the many terms that comprise the criminal's professional language.   They refer to types of crime and criminals, the techniques and tools used in the commission of a crime, and the consequent relationships to other institutions.

Social Classes in the Underworld

It would be a mistake to classify all criminals alike if we wish to understand the social world in which they live.   The wealthy gangster or racketeer —who acquires an expensive automobile, a chauffeur, a bodyguard, a city home in the north, and a country home in the south—has no more in common with the petty thief than the wealthy industrialist in conventional life with the laborer.   The social gradations in the criminal world are based upon many of the same criteria of success as in the conventional world— daring in planning, ability to organize, skill in carrying out an operation, and amount of wealth obtained as a result.

Thus, at the lower end of the scale: the jack-roller is contemptuous of the stiffy, the dummy, the grafter, the beggar; and the jack-roller is in turn looked down upon by the various types of professional thieves.   In this group the degree of skill and the value of the amount stolen constitute status. The dip or pickpocket is low in the scale and the moll-buzzer who robs women is lowest among pickpockets.   However, the pickpocket who can steal from the left-front trouser pocket is highly respected by the fraternity, since this feat is difficult.   This attainment means more to pickpockets than the Phi Beta Kappa key to students.[11]   Next in rank to the pickpockets are the yeggs or safeblowers who specialize in country banks, the stick-up (holdup) men, and the prowlers.   Petermen or urban safeblowers rank highest in craftsmanship.   Thieves who neither use guns nor threats of personal violence take pride in this fact.   At the top of the underworld hierarchy stand the organized gangs, whose leaders or entrepreneurs occupy the pinnacle.

Techniques and Skills

Each type of crime requires special techniques and skills, which are handed down from the experienced to the novice, just as piano-playing is taught by a skilled pianist to a student.   The juvenile delinquent who detaches himself from conventional society and makes contacts with criminal groups usually has no thought of learning the techniques of crime.   However, as disapproval and punishment descend upon the young delinquent he is thrown into the criminal group.   If he is a promising boy a criminal gang will offer him some minor role, much as a businessman might offer a promising boy a job with the possibility of promotion.   If a girl is on the fringe of conventional society and has developed habits of casual promiscuity a house of prostitution may take her in; or some men's gang may accept her as the "moll" of one of the members, assigning certain duties to her that will aid them though not involving actual participation in crimes.

These inexperienced, and usually young, persons are in the nature of apprentices to experienced criminals.   At first they perform small tasks and are not fully admitted into the operations of the gang.   If they lack courage and cannot carry out their tasks, if they are clumsy and do not develop skill, or if they fail to abide by the criminal code, they are quickly dropped.   But if they can meet the rigid requirements of the particular type of crime they are learning, they become acknowledged members. Sometimes this training is deliberate.   A confidence man stated that a veteran in the gang "ran a school" in odd hours for new spielers and steerers, since it was necessary for each participant in the confidence game to become letter-perfect in his part.[12]   The man who supplied this information had worked without compensation for 6 weeks with an experienced confidence man in order to learn the particular game.

Many of the types of crime now prevalent are centuries old, and the techniques of execution have been transmitted not only from criminal to criminal but from generation to generation.   Modifications have naturally appeared as changing social conditions necessitated.   On the other hand, new crimes and new techniques for committing old crimes are constantly being devised.   The criminals who invent them are the creative geniuses of the criminal world.   The employment of the machine gun or tommy gun in crimes after World War I; the use of the automobile for quick transportation to and from the place of crime, and in the prosecution of such crimes as beer-running during prohibition and of kidnaping in the period following; and the use of the radio during World War II by saboteurs and spies; were new techniques and in effect created new types of crime.

Organization of Small Groups

Most types of professional crime are carried out by an organized group of some sort.   Such a group may be 2 or 3 persons who work together for a season and later disband, or it may be a permanent organization that endures year after year. It may have no formal leader or it may be highly stratified with various ranks of responsibility. But whether it is transitory or permanent, informal or formal in organization, each individual in the organization has a particular function. Only the combined corporate efforts of the group make the crime possible, since one person working alone could not perform it.

The organization of pickpockets is perhaps the best known. Three men make an ideal team. One man, the hook or tool, specializes in extracting the pocketbook. He is shielded by 2 assistants, called stalls, one of whom is known as the dukeman and has the special function of concealing the movements of the hook's duke or hand. Prior to the actual theft the stalls fan the victim or feel his pockets to locate his money. It may also be necessary to prat him or push him gently around to distract his attention and also to maneuver him into a good position for the hook. When the hook has withdrawn the pocketbook he passes it to his assistants, who as soon as possible retire to some place of concealment and remove the money, destroying or concealing the container.

The confidence game requires at least three men—all suave, well dressed, prosperous looking, and ready talkers—who have learned their parts down to the finest detail. The steerer picks out a stranger (the sucker) and in the course of a casual conversation discovers that he is wealthy. The steerer also pretends to be a stranger. The spieler claims that he is able to make some easy money on the stock exchange or by betting on races for both the steerer and the sucker. A make-believe exchange called the store is used, which may be used by numerous teams of con men; the man in charge is called the bookmaker. Over a period of several days the sucker is tantalized by the prospect of making money, until finally he arranges to produce the cash to be invested. When the cash is safely in hand, the sucker is told that his money has been lost because of an unfortunate error instead of being greatly increased as he had been promised. The spieler promises to refund the money and contrives to get him out of the city. A well-organized group of con men is frequently protected by the police when the victim realizes he has been robbed and appeals to them.[13]

Codes and Philosophy

The codes of conduct that have developed in the underworld are as compelling as those of conventional society and violations are as severely punished. Even young criminals, who are still on the fringe of the underworld, know and obey the code.

One rule requires criminals to be honest with other members of their gang. Money spent in the execution of a crime is first deducted from the amount obtained; often a certain sum is put away for fall money to pay the fix in case a member of the group is arrested; finally the money is divided equally or according to some other agreement. Small groups practice no formal accounting or bookkeeping; however, large, organized gangs may have elaborate systems of bookkeeping and pay regular wages or salaries to underlings Dishonesty in criminal gangs is dealt with by dismissal, ostracism, or death.

Another rule of conduct is loyalty to the underworld. Its importance is especially stressed when rival mobs or gangs operate in the same territory, and it is a vital element in maintaining security from the police. Violations of this rule are also summarily dealt with. The "double-crosser," the "snitcher," the "stool pigeon," and the "rat" are scorned and frequently killed. The rule of loyalty is obvious when one member of a mob is captured by the police who try to force him to reveal the names of his companions.

The powerful influence of this rule is evident in the case of the jack-roller whose story was recorded by Shaw in the book of that title.[14] At the age of 15 this boy was arrested for breaking into a hotel room and robbing a drunk (for the tenth time, in addition to being "picked up" by the police many times without formal action). Attempts were made to force him to reveal the names of his companions by "a clout on the ear" and a "general beating and razzing." But this boy refused to divulge the names of his partners. He wrote: "I would die first. My belief in the code was unbreakable. . . . Once a criminal violates it by turning against his partners in crime, he is branded as a rat by the underworld. . . . I regarded the rat as a snake in the grass."

The mode of life of the professional criminal is supported by a definite philosophy, based upon standards accepted in the underworld. This philosophy provides justification for his actions and prevents him from feeling remorse and regret. As a rule, an individual experiences a feeling of guilt and remorse only in the early stages of a criminal career, when he is still fluctuating between conventional and criminal society. At this point he is measuring his actions against conventional standards. However, as he progressively accepts the criminal life and isolates himself from conventional life he feels guilt and remorse less and less often. When he reaches the stage of complete immersion in the underworld and total acceptance of its standards he ceases to feel guilty or remorseful.

One of the attitudes that supports the criminal is the pretext that his career is primarily a business career. It is his way of earning a living and he goes about it as methodically and unemotionally as any businessman does. Although he may scorn some types of crime, just as the businessman would object to doing some kinds of business, nevertheless he regards himself as justified in earning a living in his own fashion. He further justifies his crimes by comparisons with the conventional business world, where he may find many examples of fraud and deceit performed in such a way that they are not labeled criminal, or carried out with immunity from legal prosecution.

He also justifies himself by the belief that noncriminals would commit crimes if they dared.   Most confidence games are based on the promise of securing enormous profits from the investment of a small sum of money, and the victims often know that the alleged methods are illegal.   They are willing to agree to these illegal methods in order to make a large profit. When the con man, instead of producing any profit for the victim simply makes off with his money, it is easy for the con man to justify his action by remembering that the victim was willing to participate in a crime to make money.

The criminal also has little sympathy for the person who is careless or naïve about his money.   Many thieves steal only from the rich, but do not steal from the poor or those with small wages.   The pickpocket does not make a distinction, which may be one reason why he is low in the social scale.   The justification is presented that the person who will condone dishonesty, who is careless with money, or who is wealthy either deserves to lose it or can afford the loss without hardship.

The professional criminal has a vague ambition to "get the big one," obtain a large sum of money, and retire.   But criminals rarely realize this aim. The sums they acquire are usually insignificant and come in irregularly. Because they are easily secured, they are quickly spent.   Money accumulated from a few important crimes may be squandered on pleasure trips, or used to fix an arrest and escape conviction and imprisonment.

It is difficult for the criminal to leave a life of crime and enter the legitimate business world.   Inquiries into his past reveal his criminal record and prevent firms from employing him.   Hence the criminal adjusts himself to the underworld and abandons the conventional world and its standards.

Adoption of the criminal philosophy of life indicates that the individual is not only a criminal in his way of making a living, but has also developed a criminal personality.   He has accepted a way of life, a role in a special type of social world, and a system of attitudes that are not easily subject to change. Imprisonment does not affect him because it is unable to break through this philosophy.   Imprisonment is evaded by the professional criminal to a surprising degree, but when it is imposed he accepts it unemotionally as a risk in his business, just as the manufacturer of raincoats and umbrellas accepts a drought as a bad year for which no one is to blame.

QUESTIONS

1. What are the six steps through which the juvenile delinquent becomes the adult criminal?

2. At what point in the transition from juvenile delinquency to adult criminality does it become difficult if not impossible to divert conduct into conventional patterns? Why?

3. Compare the professional criminal with members of such professions as medicine, dentistry, architecture, or law. What characteristics do professional criminals have in common with other professional groups? In which characteristics do they differ?

4. What is meant by saying that the underworld has some of the characteristics of a social caste?

5. What hindrances to stable family life exist in professional criminality?

6. What is the philosophy of the professional criminal? How does his philosophy act as a barrier to reform?

READINGS

Baarslag, Karl, *Robbery by Mail, the Story of the United States Postal Inspectors* (Farrar and Rinehart, 1938). Concerned primarily with successful apprehension and conviction of postal criminals, the book nevertheless gives an excellent picture of certain types of professional criminals.

Black, Jack, *You Can't Win* (Macmillan, 1926). The verdict of a professional criminal is that the criminal can't win.

———, "A Burglar Looks at Laws and Codes," *Harper's Magazine,* 151 (1930), 306–13. The criminal's code, as seen by an ex-burglar.

Clark, Charles L., and Earle E. Eubank, *Lockstep and Corridor: Thirty-five Years of Prison Life* (Cincinnati: University of Cincinnati Press, 1927). This book gives a detailed picture of the vicissitudes, successes, and failures of a professional criminal who was in and out of prison many times.

Shaw, Clifford R., *The Jack-Roller* (Chicago: University of Chicago Press, 1930). The life-story of a juvenile delinquent.

———, *et al., Brothers in Crime* (Chicago: University of Chicago Press, 1938). The careers of 5 brothers are traced from preschool begging to adult crime.

———, in collaboration with M. E. Moore, *The Natural History of a Delinquent Career* (Chicago: University of Chicago Press, 1931). Life story and analysis of the development of a young criminal.

Sutherland, E. H. (ed.), *The Professional Thief* (Chicago: University of Chicago Press, 1937). An inside view of the world of the professional thief.

Van Cise, Philip S., *Fighting the Underworld* (Houghton Mifflin, 1936). The story of professional swindling in a western city and its tie-in with politics.

FOOTNOTES

[1] J. Landesco, "The Life History of a Member of the '42' Gang," *Journal of Criminal Law and Criminology,* 23 (1933), 964–98.

[2] "Girl Delinquent, Age Sixteen," *Harper's Magazine,* 164 (1932), 551–59.

[3] Charles L. Clark and Earle Edward Eubank, *Lockstep and Corridor* (Cincinnati: University of Cincinnati Press, 1927).

[4] Edwin H. Sutherland (ed.), *The Professional Thief* (Chicago: University of Chicago Press, 1937), pp. viii–ix.

[5] Clifford R. Shaw *et al., Brothers in Crime* (Chicago: University of Chicago Press, 1938), pp. 34–42, 256–98.

[6] Sheldon and Eleanor T. Glueck, *Five Hundred Delinquent Women* (Knopf, 1934), pp. 32–38, 147–52.

[7] Clark and Eubank, *op. cit.*

[8] J. Landesco, "The Woman and the Underworld," *Journal of Criminal Law and Criminology,* 26 (1935–36), 891–902.

[9] Sutherland, *op. cit.,* pp. 154–58; Philip S. Van Cise, *Fighting the Underworld* (Houghton, Mifflin, 1936), pp. 249–55.

[10] Clark and Eubank, *op. cit.,* pp. 173–75; Sutherland, *op. cit.,* pp. 235–43; Frederic M. Thrasher, *The Gang* (Chicago: University of Chicago Press, 1927), pp. 266–69; Nels Anderson, *The Hobo* (Chicago: University of Chicago Press, 1923), ch. 7; Herbert Asbury, *The Gangs of New York* (Garden City, 1927), pp. 275–79; D. W. Maurer, "The Argot of the Dice Gambler," *Annals of the American Academy of Political and Social Science,* 269 (1950), 114–33.

[11] Sutherland, *op. cit.,* p. 48; on social status see also Clifford R. Shaw, *The Jack-Roller* (Chicago: University of Chicago Press, 1930); Clark and Eubank, *op. cit.,* p. 149.

[12] Van Cise, *op. cit.,* p. 268.

[13] *Ibid.,* pp. 268–300.

[14] Shaw, *The Jack-Roller,* p. 99.

6

Organized Crime

As we learned earlier, the small professional criminal groups or mobs that work together as pickpockets, shoplifters, or confidence men are organized in the sense that each person performs a distinct, specialized function directed toward accomplishing a common end. No single member could accomplish alone what the mob accomplishes by its precise interaction. The term organized crime, however, is reserved for a different type of organization, one that is more complicated and extensive than the small mob of 3 or 4 persons.[1] The chief characteristics of organized crime are these:

1. Control of all crime in a given geographic area, or at least of all crime of certain types, by a small central group, similar to the board of directors of a legitimate business organization. Sometimes the control is vested in the hands of one man. This controlling group dictates the conditions under which criminal activities are operated within the area. Support is granted to approved operators; outsiders who attempt to intrude or "muscle in" are ruthlessly threatened, tortured, or murdered. Thus a monopoly is established.

2. Standardized methods of conducting crime and rules of criminal conduct, which are sternly enforced on members of the organization.

3. Inclusion within the organization of personnel who perform services not essential to the commission of crime, but who contribute protection, such as lawyers, doctors, keepers of hideouts, and the like. These persons are attached only to one organization and do not serve other criminals.

4. Careful planning of each crime to achieve the maximum of success.

Four types of organized crime are observable in the United States at the present time: criminal gangs; criminal syndicates; rackets; corrupt political groups.

ORGANIZED CRIMINAL GANGS

Although the word gang does not imply violence in its derivation, in modern usage it has acquired this connotation. The gang is an intimate group bound by ties of friendship and loyalty that tends to establish its own folkways and mores, often in opposition to those of conventional society. It has some degree of cohesion and permanence. Its activities satisfy the immediate wants and interests of its members. Since the gang typically is composed of undisciplined youths its interests are likely to be directed toward adventure and thrill. In pursuing its activities the gang usually disregards the rights and interests of other groups. The gang thus implies a group that is not incorporated into the social structure and is often in conflict with it.

The Adolescent Gang and the Criminal Gang

Many gangs of youths cannot be termed professional criminal gangs.[2] They spend much of their time in athletics, roaming around, shooting craps, attending movies and dances, playing pool, and the like. As individuals the members are undisciplined; as a group they are relatively amorphous. When they indulge in criminal activities, such as jack-rolling, shoplifting, or burglary, they act by twos and threes rather than as a gang. These criminal activities are accessory to their main interests, which are essentially recreational in that they are seeking adventure and pleasure. For instance, during the race riots of 1919 between whites and Negroes in Chicago, the gangs of white youths molested and killed Negroes and destroyed Negro property. These acts neither developed from a pitched battle nor from the need for self-defense, but were motivated by the desire for sport.

Sometimes gangs of youths are organized into so-called athletic clubs, frequently sponsored by local politicians. They help organize the territory to vote for the politicians and in return receive protection from the police for minor depredations, petty thievery, general hoodlumism, and occasional major crimes. This type of activity undoubtedly is gang activity, but it is not the same as that carried on by the organized criminal gang.

The criminal gang exhibits some of the same characteristics as the youthful gang of hoodlums. It has the same close personal affiliation between members. In the commission of crime each member of the gang has a function to perform, and upon his ability depend both the success of the crime and the safety of all members. When a member is injured, perhaps wounded in the course of a crime, other members shield him and try to obtain medical aid. But if a member's conduct threatens the safety of the gang, he is disposed of by murder. The unity of the gang must be maintained whatever the cost to an individual member. The criminal gang also shares with the youthful gang its independence from conventional mores and its disregard for the rights of other persons. It makes its own laws and enforces them in its own way.

However, the criminal gang differs from the youthful gang in many important respects. It is organized specifically for crime, and all other activities are subordinate.[3] The criminal gang is unlikely to indulge in general hoodlumism, which would endanger its existence, since it does not care to call attention to itself unnecessarily. General excitement and adventure have no part in organized criminal gang activities. Such activities are carefully planned in advance and as carefully executed. For the time being each member of the gang subordinates his personal interests and safety to the plan of the gang as a whole. Thus the criminal gang, unlike the youthful gang, is a disciplined group. The criminal gang is also more thoroughly organized, with some one person as the leader, and with such accessories as lawyers, doctors, messengers, fences, and the like. When the gang is able to operate in one locale it has established definite protection for its members. But often the modern gang, equipped with automobiles, is mobile and shifts its headquarters from city to city, perhaps from one seaboard to the other, depending upon its own careful planning and cleverness in avoiding capture.

The Criminal Gang and the Mob

The organized criminal gang differs from the small mob, described in the preceding chapter, in several important respects. The first is its willingness to resort to physical force. Pickpockets, shoplifters, house burglars, and other types of thieves who depend upon their manual skill and upon secrecy usually pride themselves upon not using physical force or carrying a gun. Confidence men depend upon skillful psychological manipulation of their victims and also do not use force or threats of physical violence. They pride themselves upon the cleverness with which they can select a prospective victim, the finesse with which they lead him from step to step, and the decisiveness with which they leave the victim once his money has been taken. In contrast are the criminals who do not hesitate to kill their victims if this measure seems necessary in order to secure what they want. Thieves who use a gun in street hold-ups or in "sticking up" a store are of this class. They do not depend upon their skill entirely; sometimes not at all. Rather they depend upon their boldness and daring and the fear engendered by their guns. When criminals who use physical force and who are armed and prepared to kill, either in the prosecution of a crime or to avoid arrest, band together they form a criminal gang.

The gang is larger than the mob, less specialized in activities, and more mobile. Mobs that pick pockets or operate confidence games consist of 2 or 3 men; the gang may include a dozen or more. The mob usually specializes in one type of crime; the gang may specialize or it may carry on several types of criminal activities. The crimes of the mob are frequent and the gain from each crime is slight; thus a pickpocket mob may station itself on a corner where people transfer from one streetcar line to another and on a busy day steal from several dozen persons. Each theft may be small, although the aggregate will be large. The gang, in contrast, commits its crimes less frequently, but the gains are greater. One bank robbery may net the gang $100,000 or more. The mob may operate in one city indefinitely and even in one section of the city. The gang, because of the magnitude of its crimes, dares not concentrate in one area but must be prepared to move from one community to another to avoid detection and capture.

Mobility of the Criminal Gang

Since the criminal gang is predatory and tends to remain mobile, its headquarters are apt to be temporary in nature. Each crime usually requires a refuge, prepared in advance, or the scattering of the members of the gang until the hue and cry of pursuit have died down. The mobility of the criminal gang is well illustrated in the case of the Urschel kidnaping. The actual kidnaping occurred in Oklahoma; Urschel was held captive in a rural section of Texas; and the ransom money was paid in Missouri.[4] Part of the ransom money was exchanged in Minnesota and part was hidden in Texas. The kidnapers were captured in Colorado, Tennessee, Minnesota, Texas, and Illinois. The 7 states involved have an area of 683,000 square miles. Fifteen convictions were secured in this case, but before the captures were made the agents of the FBI had traveled through 16 states.

Typical Gang Crimes

The most frequent crimes of the criminal gangs are bank robberies, organized automobile stealing (the ring of automobile thieves), and kidnapings for ransom.* A few illustrations demonstrate the nature and extent of criminal gang activities.

The daylight bank robbery has largely replaced the old-time bank burglary. In the commission of a bank burglary the burglars entered the bank at night and an expert opened the safe. It was the ambition of the burglars to obtain the contents of the safe and escape without detection. Modern con-

---

* There is another kind of kidnaping, not discussed here—kidnaping by psychopathic persons, which often ends in the murder of the victim. The gang is only interested in securing a large ransom and having achieved its aim releases the victim, provided that doing so does not reveal the identity or whereabouts of the gang.

struction of safes, time locks, and burglar alarms in banks have made this procedure difficult. But a new method of stealing, the daylight robbery, has been made possible by the daring of gangs and the use of tear gas and machine guns to incapacitate and terrify bank officials and customers. Swift automobiles, possibly provided with bulletproof glass, have ensured escape. Since 1925 this method of bank robbery has been on the increase. Banks are not well prepared to defend themselves against such robberies, and if they are committed in small communities local police are not equipped to pursue and capture the robbers. A report of 27 robberies in which 140 bandits participated (an average of 5 bandits per robbery) shows that only 8 were convicted and 1 was killed. The loss was $5,206,467 (or approximately $193,000 per robbery), of which $1,067,000 was recovered.[5] The audacity of armed robbery is well illustrated by the twilight raid on the Boston branch of Brinks, Inc., on the evening of January 17, 1950.[6] Brinks, Inc. supplies armored car service for the transportation of large sums of money. On the evening in question, a number of their employees were working in the vault of the Boston branch when they were confronted with 6 or 7 masked men, identically clad in pea jackets. They were bound while the robbers made off with a million and a half dollars, most of it in cash. By the time the employees had succeeded in loosening their bonds and calling police, the robbers had disappeared completely, leaving behind inadequate clues for their detection.

Automobile stealing may be organized on a national or even international basis. The flagrancy of such thefts has caused automobile stealing to be made a federal offense if the stolen car is transported over a state line. In 1945 an ex-convict, aged 45, was taken into custody as leader of a ring of automobile thieves. According to newspaper reports it was thought that his gang was responsible for some 500 thefts. License plates were changed and the cars repainted before they were sold.[7] Other gangs have been arrested with 3 or more dozen cars in their possession or have disposed of 100 cars before being caught. Usually the engine and body numbers are effaced and new numbers stamped on corresponding to numbers of cars of similar makes in other states; these numbers are supplied by confederates. The automobiles are then taken to another state and sold.[8] Some gangs steal cars, strip them of all accessories and detachable parts and abandon the shell.[9] These parts can be sold easily and are more difficult to trace than the complete car.

CRIMINAL SYNDICATES

The criminal syndicate represents a completely different type of organization from the criminal gang. The gang is mobile, violent in treatment of its victims, and engaged in spasmodic, startling crimes. The syndicate, however, is a stable business organization, whose only violence is directed at unwelcome competitors. A syndicate is defined as a "combination of capitalists or financiers, entered into for the purpose of prosecuting a scheme requiring large resources of capital, especially one having the object of obtaining control of the market of a particular commodity." [10] The criminal syndicate is one whose object is illegal activity. Ordinarily the syndicate does not create a new type of crime; it simply co-ordinates crime previously carried out by individuals, small groups, or mobs of criminals. Its added danger to the community lies in the great power exerted by any powerful financial organization, criminal or otherwise, which obtains a monopoly of a commodity or of a particular type of service in the community.

Public Tolerance of Criminal Syndicates

Syndicated crime is frequently of the type that provides forbidden services or goods; such as illicit sex relations, narcotic drugs, alcohol in areas where it is prohibited, and, during World War II, stamps for gasoline and rationed foods. The syndicate is allowed to exist not only because it offers a service to some large section of the public, but because the entire public tolerates or is indifferent to the situation. The most glaring example of the denial of a pleasure that did not have public support was the prohibition of alcoholic beverages between the years 1920 and 1933. Many people thought the laws supporting the Eighteenth Amendment were unjustified, and otherwise law-abiding people stated both privately and publicly, in speeches and in writing, that they had no compunctions in violating the prohibition laws. Many persons who did not themselves indulge in alcoholic beverages thought the laws a violation of individual liberty and rights. World War II, because of the necessity of rationing foods and gasoline for motor vehicles, created another market in which criminals operated. Coupons to be used for gasoline were stolen, sometimes with the connivance of officials, or were counterfeited, to be sold at high prices. Food, especially meat, which was officially rationed, was sold without accounting for it in the regular channels for rationing, a situation called the black market. [11] Today, gambling is in somewhat the same position that prohibition was in the 1920's. [12] Supplying these commodities and other goods and services, forbidden by law but demanded by the public, becomes the field in which criminal syndicates function with relative impunity, for there is little public demand for their suppression.

Activities of Criminal Syndicates

The desire of people for wealth without work is at the base of other syndicates that operate various types of swindles or gambling. One of the most interesting criminal activities, which approaches out-and-out stealing but which may be syndicated, is the confidence game. Confidence men offer quick and fabulous wealth in return for a small investment of real cash. The victim deliberately gives his money to the confidence man, whom he believes to be a businessman, in order (as he believes) to gain large profits. Sometimes he is even told that the profits will be secured by unethical or illegal methods, to which he agrees. By a devious process, however, he is made to lose his money, apparently by legitimate accidents or business losses. The appeal of the confidence man is to the desire for great wealth, and the victim enters into the game willingly.

Some confidence men work in small groups but in certain cities all confidence men are under the control of one man or a few men who provide equipment and arrange for police protection. Such an organization falls into the classification of criminal syndicates.

Syndicates have also acquired control of many gambling devices, such as slot machines, betting on races, and the numbers game.[13] Even when the gambling game is operated honestly, the person who gambles has little chance to win. Sometimes the operator fixes the game so that the gambler cannot possibly win. In either case, here is a fertile and often illegal field in which the criminal syndicate operates. In some cases, as with pin-ball machines and the numbers game, local businessmen are forced by threats to act as operators of the machines or to sell numbers. The syndicate then becomes a racket, for the criminal syndicate proper offers an illegal service to the public but does not force legitimate business to co-operate with it.

The syndicates usually operate in large cities, partly because there are numerous customers for their services and commodities, and the financial involvements of the syndicate demand large-scale operations. Also, the city offers an impersonal setting and the typical indifference of the urban citizenry to a wrong that does not affect them personally. Then, too, the personnel of the syndicate may remain relatively anonymous in the city. In a smaller community, concealment is difficult, and profits are not sufficiently attractive.

Syndicates and Law-Enforcement

Because of the public tolerance, officials charged with enforcing the laws suppressing pleasures are especially susceptible to bribery of various sorts, in return for which they permit the syndicate to operate. But even when law-enforcing agencies are strict, syndicates continue to operate, for they are clever in hiding their operations. If they are forced out of one city, they may resume operation in another. If leaders are convicted and sentenced to prison, it is not long before the same or a similar syndicate is operating under new leadership.   As long as there is a public demand for the forbidden article, means will arise to supply the demand.   The law-enforcement agencies alone, even at their best, find it almost impossible to eliminate syndicates permanently without public support and public refusal to patronize the illegal establishments.

Organization of the Syndicate

The syndicate develops by a process of ruthless competition.   It begins when one powerful operator of a criminal activity (the vice lord of journalistic slang) extends his activities to include all similar activities within a pre-scribed territory.   Weaker competing operators are forced out of business, often by threats of personal violence, bombings or murder, or are brought in as subordinates.   The syndicate thus becomes a "trust" that monopolizes all the activities of a given type within one territory.   The territory may be a section of a city.   Thus at one time in the 1920's Chicago was divided into three vice territories; the South Side, West Side, and North Side, each with its own syndicate that controlled houses of prostitution, gambling, and, especially, the distribution of liquor to small establishments.   A series of wars went on between the three factions until all were brought under the central control of Al Capone's gang.

In 1940 a group called the Combination (which journalists dubbed Murder, Inc.) came to light in Brooklyn.[14]   This organization was an outgrowth of bootlegging; the repeal of the Prohibition Amendment had left a small group of criminals with wealth but no business.   The Combination was formed to eliminate competition and intergang wars.   Money was loaned to certain men to finance criminal activities; men not influential enough to borrow money from the inner group became employees who were paid wages.   Strict control was maintained and men once affiliated with the organization were not allowed to leave it.   Competitors who did not want to come into the Combination might be murdered.   It is important in this connection to note that the assaults and murders committed were not per-formed on the public, but on competitors—that is, other criminals.   When an illegal service is offered the public, criminal syndicates treat the public with consideration, with the exception of exacting a high price for the com-modity.   The brutalities and cruelties are reserved for those who attempt to interfere with the establishment and operation of the illegal business.

The organization of a syndicate may extend beyond one city.   The Senate Crime Investigating Committee (1950–51) developed evidence that showed there was a loose but definite federation of criminal syndicates based in many different cities.[15]   No one criminal heads the entire network; each local group is autonomous.   A strong group of leaders, however, controls syndicate operations informally, through financial control, and by threats and violence.   The Committee further found evidence of an international criminal organization, called the Mafia, with headquarters in Italy.   Criminals questioned were uniformly reluctant to talk about the Mafia or denied knowing what the word meant; most of the evidence came from the Federal Bureau of Narcotics, whose work in tracing the importation of narcotics brings it into contact with international criminal rings.   The Mafia was credited not only with affording an international connection but with many brutal murders of criminals who in some way had angered superior members of the criminal organization.

Syndicates, nevertheless, are primarily business organizations.   Usually there is a definite headquarters that serves as an office, which may be a suite of rooms in a hotel or a gambling establishment.   Unless some unusual trouble is brewing, the leaders of the syndicate openly come and go, although they may conceal their relationship to the syndicate.   They establish permanent residences in the city where they have headquarters, own real estate, live in good residential communities, and even send their children to college. They do not depend wholly upon secrecy for protection, but also upon political protection and the pseudo-legality of certain activities.

In personality type, the leaders are organizers, financiers, businessmen. They may have a background of crime, perhaps even a prison conviction or two, but in their capacity as leaders of a syndicate they are entrepreneurs operating a complicated and extensive business.

The way in which a syndicate operates is illustrated by the activities of confidence men in Denver, as portrayed in *Fighting the Underworld*.[16] At the turn of the century the ruler of the Denver underworld was Lou Blonger, a man who had settled in the western mining camps as a boy.   In 1880 he appeared in Denver as a bartender and soon became the proprietor of a saloon with the usual accompaniments of girls, roulette wheels, and other gambling equipment.   From this position he progressed gradually to become a "fixer," working closely with the chief of police and dictating terms to newcomers in the Denver criminal world.

By 1905, Blonger was operating behind the scenes, with a man named Duff as his active lieutenant.   Blonger had an office with the word "Mining" on the door, but his business was controlling police and elective offices, such as those of prosecuting attorney and various judges, for the benefit of the underworld.   When Philip S. Van Cise ran for prosecuting attorney, Blonger offered to deliver 1,500 votes for him, but in return he demanded protection for his criminals; such favors as dismissing cases, or setting the bond at a low figure to enable the criminal to forfeit the bond and still make a profit from his crime.

Blonger's principal operations were confidence games, which found ready victims among the visitors to Denver. Many of these visitors were unsophisticated, well-to-do men from smaller cities, who could be easily persuaded that a moderate investment could be doubled or trebled within a few minutes on the stock exchange. Gambling establishments, houses of prostitution, bootlegging, and the illegal sale of narcotic drugs were all permitted to operate openly. Key men in the police department collected fees from these enterprises for permitting them to continue, which were readily paid. But the big money was to be made in confidence games, which Blonger controlled throughout the city. Sums taken from trusting victims usually ranged from $5,000 to $25,000. From 9 victims a total of $167,600 was taken. Occasionally as much as $200,000 was secured from one victim.

During the winter, the confidence men operated in southern resort cities. In the spring they wrote or telegraphed Blonger to inquire whether he needed any "salesmen." If Blonger did not accept them into his organization it was useless for them to attempt to operate in Denver, for they would have been arrested immediately. Those accepted did not operate independently but as a part of Blonger's organization, and Blonger exacted a portion of each deal. In return he supplied a big store or fake stock exchange and an operator for it, a place necessary for the successful operation of the confidence game.

Blonger also protected his men from being arrested. When victims complained to the police, Blonger was notified. The confidence men involved stayed off the streets. The police presumably tried to help the victims locate the fake stock exchange but actually never allowed them to come near it. Since the victims were strangers in Denver and usually remained there for only a short period, they did not often push a case. If an arrest was forced, the prosecuting attorney arranged for a low bond, which Blonger provided. The confidence man then left the city and the bond—always less in amount than the sum taken from the victim—was forfeited. In 1922, 75 confidence men were in Blonger's organization.

This case illustrates the efficient leadership, tight organization, and political protection typical of the successful syndicate.

RACKETEERS

The third type of organized crime that reaps large profits is racketeering. The terms racket and racketeer came into use during the 1920's and have been vaguely defined and loosely used. A racket can best be defined as an organized method of extorting money from those engaged either in illegitimate or legitimate enterprises, by illegal means often accompanied by threats of infliction of injury or destruction of property. The racketeer does not offer a service as does the criminal syndicate; nor does he brazenly take what does not belong to him by theft or ransom as does the criminal gang. Rather, the racketeer forces a group in business to make payments, or to operate the business in favor of his group by threats of personal or property damage or of decreased profits. The racketeer exists simply to make money for his group and gives nothing in return.[17]

Development of Racketeering

Extortion and coercion are not new activities. In this country, in the late nineteenth century gangs coerced businesses that were illegal or on the borderline of legality to pay tribute to them, in order to avoid personal injury and destruction of property. Houses of prostitution and gambling establishments were easy victims, since they were in no position to appeal for police protection. The greatest development of coercion, however, was in connection with the struggles of employers and labor to adjust their relations with each other. The lack of a code of conduct and the failure of laws and police to regulate employer-labor relations opened the way for each side to attempt to enforce its will by any means at hand. The original arrangement was for one side or the other, or perhaps both, to hire thugs and gangsters to enforce their desires. Thus the employer might import strike-breakers from some other city, who were in reality thugs, to maltreat striking workingmen, so that they would return to work, and to intimidate others, so that they would not strike. Unions, desiring to organize an unorganized industry, might hire gangsters to force reluctant workingmen into line.

Crude and illegal as these methods were, they served the purpose of regulating employer-labor relations and acted as a kind of extra-legal police force.[18] Unfortunately, they were never impartially applied but always favored one side or the other. Organizations developed to furnish these services. Some were organized as private detective agencies, which could be hired by employers to place operatives in the plants. Posing as workers, these operatives reported on union activities through the detective agency to the employer.[19] Some of these organizations did not hesitate to send in men to beat, otherwise injure, or even kill leaders among laborers who opposed the employers' policies.

Although this early use of illegal methods by individual employers, employers' associations, or unions was sometimes called a racket, it was not a racket, strictly speaking. The spies and thugs were paid wages for specific services that they performed and were actually employed by someone. It is true that their acts were illegal; but they were an outgrowth of the struggle between employers and labor, and were based upon the failure of employers, laborers, and the public to define and regulate these relations.

The racket, however, developed from such use of thugs and gangsters to enforce the dictates of one side or the other in labor disputes. The racket differs from the use of coercion in employer-labor relations in that it demands money without giving a service, legal or otherwise. One of the simplest forms of the racket is the organization of a protective association that forces employers in a certain business to join it and pay dues; if the employer refuses, his place of business is bombed, ostensibly by a rival gang but actually by the protective association itself. The employer finds it less expensive to pay the dues than to fight the gang. A Chicago butcher is reported to have been dynamited 3 times and finally ruined in business because he refused to join such an association. The association may go further and dictate who may be employed, what wages may be paid, and under what conditions the business may be operated.

Types of Rackets

Often the racket takes the form of control of a labor union, a situation in which the union is operated not for the benefit of its members but for the benefit of the small group that controls it. The members of the union are induced by persuasion or fear to elect the proper officers, or elections may be dispensed with; once in control of the union, the racketeers exert tremendous power. The laborers may be victimized by having to pay high initiation fees in order to enter the union, or by having to pay a certain amount in return for the privilege of holding their jobs. The money collected for fees and dues is not accounted for, but is spent by the "union leaders" for their own use; the simple entry in the records states that the money has been spent for "the good of the local." For example, a president of the International Building Service Employees Union was convicted of stealing $60,000 from this union by such methods.[20]

Money may be extorted from employers by union leaders threatening strikes. Thus convictions were secured against the racketeers who, through leaders placed in a union of theatrical stage employees, had extorted $550,000 from 4 motion picture companies by threatening a strike of 35,000 union employees.[21] These same men also collected for their own use some $1,500,000 from one motion picture theater chain for averting a strike (fomented by themselves) over wages, and $100,000 from theater owners in another city by threatening to put 2 operators in each projection room.

Sometimes the same group of racketeers succeeds in controlling both the employer and the employee groups. At one time this situation existed in the restaurant field in New York.[22]

The building trades have offered an especially fertile field for racketeers.[23] Many different skills are required in the construction of a building and hence many unions are involved. This circumstance has provided numerous opportunities for threatened strikes and for fomenting trouble between unions, which only the racketeer who has caused the conflicts can straighten out. Also, most construction of an important nature is carried out under an agreement that requires completion by a certain date; otherwise the contractor is penalized by receiving less money for the job. Under these conditions a strike is a serious matter, since it may delay the work and cause the imposition of the penalties. These abuses are not new but come to light from time to time when they become flagrant. After a strike has been arranged a union agent settles the threatened strike upon payment of substantial sums from the contractor. One such agent collected a million dollars in 2 years' time for his services.

Sometimes the individual sums received are small, but the total over a period of time is large. In the 1930's, the man who held the positions of president of the Painters Union and business agent of the Glaziers Union was sentenced to 1 to 5 years in the Ohio Penitentiary for his illegal activities.[24] Some of his extortions are illustrated by the following episodes. A contractor who merely wanted glass installed in a building was forced to make these agreements and payments: he let a contract for window cleaning to a union in which the union official was interested; he paid $50 before men were assigned to the job; he paid $300 in overtime wages; and $200 on completion of the job because the union official found fault with it and threatened to demand that it be done over. Another company that had scheduled a public opening for a certain date was forced to pay $1,000, in order to have windows installed in time for the opening. Another man paid $150 to get mirrors installed, since they were said to have been silvered by non-union labor. For none of these payments were legitimate services rendered. Other union leaders refused to allow their unions to work on a construction job unless all the materials were ordered from certain manufacturers and dealers, who were then able to increase the price of materials unjustifiably.

A case of the 1940's in the construction field is that of Joseph S. Fay, international vice president of the Union of Operating Engineers, and James Bove, vice president of the Hod Carriers Union, whose strategic positions gave them virtual control over all construction workers in the east.[25] Fay had been a power in the labor movement for 25 years and, supported by attorneys and politicians, seemed in an impregnable position. However, in 1943 Fay and Bove were charged with extorting $420,000 from contractors building the 85 mile Delaware Aqueduct for New York City. Their attorneys secured many delays, but when the case finally came to trial one contractor after another testified that they had been called to secret meetings with Fay and Bove in 1937 when work on the project began. They were asked for large sums, which they were to pay Fay and Bove to prevent labor trouble. They testified that they had paid installments of from $5,000 to $50,000. The jury found Fay and Bove guilty of extortion and conspiracy. Imprisonment did not, however, end the activities of these extortionists. During his first 5 years in Sing Sing Prison, Fay received 88 callers, among them such political figures as the acting lieutenant governor of New York, a mayor, and a former New York state supreme court justice. He was reported still to be "a power in labor circles." Revelation of his activities led to his transfer to another prison.[26]

Another form of racketeering is the formation of groups of middlemen who, under threat of violence or strikes, demand that the retailer buy from them instead of directly from the manufacturer. The middlemen in these cases serve no useful purpose but are able to raise prices in order to secure a profit for themselves. They operate most successfully in fields where products are scarce or perishable. The racketeer buys or otherwise secures control of all the product shipped into a certain area. He then can set the price that the local wholesaler must pay in order to secure it; in return he may guarantee that this wholesaler will be the only one to handle the product in a given territory. The retailer must then buy from this wholesaler at whatever price is set. Control is maintained by the use of force.

Perishable products, such as fish, green vegetables, milk, or fruits, are most easily made the means of racketeering. In the 1920's the artichoke market in New York was controlled by racketeers. They organized the wholesalers and then, rather than buy the limited supply of artichokes that were shipped in, simply arranged for the wholesalers to buy from certain carload dealers who paid the racketeers. The carload dealers received no service in return for the payments except the promise that they would have a monopoly of the market. This monopoly was maintained by the racketeers through their control of the laborers who handled the shipments. If a dealer tried to operate without paying the racketeer, the laborers neglected to unload his cars for a few days and the artichokes spoiled. Or if the dealer managed to get the shipment into trucks for delivery, the trucks were stopped and the artichokes sprayed with kerosene. A retailer who attempted to buy from a wholesaler not under the control of the racket was first warned, and if he persisted his store windows were smashed or other damage was done.   Retailers and wholesalers found that they either had to go out of business or submit to the racketeer.   The payments that the racketeer demanded necessitated increased prices and thus the consumer became the person who actually paid the toll.

Since rackets operate in legitimate businesses, they verge into legitimate activities and it is frequently difficult to prove their illegality.   Unions and employers' associations in and of themselves are not illegal; neither are middlemen who serve a useful purpose and who operate according to accepted business standards.   Only when these organizations come under the control of men who pervert their activities, and through the organization extort money for their own use, does a criminal racket exist.

Methods of Racketeers

Since the racket is a form of extortion and therefore illegal, it has no legal methods of enforcing its desires either on its members or its victims.   Murder is regarded as a justifiable means of eliminating a rebellious or careless member of the organization.   Murder of witnesses is also a recourse when the racket is in danger.   When the Combination was finally brought to bay and the leaders were captured, it was revealed that the organization was responsible for 80 murders.   Three members of the organization who turned state's witness confessed to 11, 6, and 6 murders respectively.   The leader of the group, Lepke, did not believe in indiscriminate killing, but did not hesitate to order a man murdered who failed to follow his orders or who threatened the safety of the organization.   If his victims showed indications of discontent, or were suspected of being about to complain of his extortions to the district attorney, he ordered acid thrown in their faces or on their products.[27]

The more powerful racketeers are not content with controlling one union or one industry.   The Combination controlled the clothing workers, leather workers, bakery and pastry drivers, motion picture operators, flour truckers, clothing truckers, fur dressers, and milliners in an Eastern city.   This group was broken up after long and persistent pursuit and 5 members, including the leader, Lepke, were executed for murder.   The racketeers who extorted money from the motion picture unions, theater owners, and producers not only controlled the unions of stage hands and projection operators; but also controlled unions of hod carriers, common laborers, building service employees, engineers, bartenders and waiters, truck drivers, laundry workers, and retail clerks, as well as the cleaning and dyeing business.

In Little Italy, on New York's East Side, a café proprietor was riddled with bullets. In the photograph above he lies in his doorway surrounded by a group of detectives and reporters, while the residents of the neighborhood hang out of their tenement windows enjoying "balcony seats at a murder." When the police attempted to question the neighbors, they met with blank silence. The Italian community preferred following its own code of conduct in solving its own problems to relying upon the law. (Acme)

POLITICAL GRAFT AND CORRUPTION

Political graft and corruption constitute the fourth type of organized crime. Political corruption is classifiable as organized crime not only because of the similarities between corrupt political practices and organized criminal activities, but also because of the interwoven relationships between the corrupt political organization and the types of organized crime already discussed.

Political graft and corruption are not the handiwork of any one public official. An individual official who misuses public funds in his trust is the equivalent of a bank officer who, without the knowledge of others in the bank, embezzles funds. Political graft and corruption, however, are the deliberate work of the corrupt political machine.

Causes of Political Corruption

The system of government in operation in the United States lends itself to the development of an extra-governmental political organization. The functions of government are divided into 3 branches (legislative, judicial, and executive), a system characteristic not only of the federal government but of state and city government as well. There is thus no one central office in which the various strands of government are concentrated. Also, the elective system of short terms is a constant threat to continuity of leadership. At the same time, the party system, with 2 or more parties competing for control of important governmental offices, demands organization and continuity of the party. Therefore, the centralization and continuity of leadership that are lacking in official government are vested in the political party.

The machine is the organization through which the political party operates; the "boss" is the head of the machine. The boss, whose position is not dependent upon elections, survives through many elections and many terms. The machine is even longer lived and may outlast several bosses. The machine decides upon the candidates to back and organizes the voting strength so that its candidates will be elected. When a political machine is powerful and there is little organized opposition, the machine's candidates win the election.

The assumption that underlies a democratic, representative system of government is that the elected officials and their appointive subordinates will perform their duties for the greatest benefit of the community they govern. But when the officials have been elected by a political machine, their allegiance is first to the machine and second to themselves; the public runs a poor third. Although the political machine is not necessarily corrupt, there is a tendency for it to become so. The political machine functions best in a large city, where government is complicated, where the public does not know personally any of the candidates for office, and where public supervision of the operation of government is difficult. Under these conditions the machine tends to become corrupt. The opportunities for acquiring personal wealth by graft are numerous and tempting, and the machine attracts persons who see in official positions not so much an opportunity to serve the community at a moderate salary but an opportunity to become wealthy by easy, though illegal, means. Through these elected officials the professional politicians, who compose the machine, secure control of funds and also of power to influence industries and business for their private benefit.[28]

Once in power the corrupt political machine grows in boldness until there is a public revulsion, and a more disinterested group develops a strong enough organization to overthrow the corrupt machine and establish a more ethical government, often called a "reform government." LaGuardia was such a reform mayor in New York City. Usually, however, the group that sponsored the reform is only locally and temporarily organized and before the next election has fallen apart. Meanwhile the machine continues to function and eventually returns to power, or it is replaced by another similar machine that in turn tends toward corruption.

Operation of the Corrupt Political Machine

The corrupt and illegal practices of the machine begin at the polls. The primary is especially important, as the machine must get its men elected as candidates. Then and at the time of election to office, many devious methods may be used to assure success. Some of the corrupt methods used at the polls are the following:

Fraudulent voting:

1. Bringing into a voting place individuals who vote in the names of dead persons or those who have moved away; these voters then move on to the next voting place and repeat the process, always voting for candidates of the machine.
2. Registration of the same voters in several precincts.
3. Persuading voters to vote for the machine or to round up voters for it, perhaps by intimidation, small favors, or the payment of a bribe.
4. Listing fictitious names in the registration books, so that hired voters may cast votes in these names.

Fraudulence on the part of election officials:

1. Failure to initial ballots of those known to be voting against the machine, thus making the ballots illegal.
2. Filling in blanks on ballots that have not been marked.

3. Casting ballots for persons who failed to vote.
4. Changing the totals when ballots are counted.
5. Substituting a false record sheet for the one made when watchers were present.

In return for voting as the machine desires, individual voters receive some small favor or compensation.   Those who organize the illegal voting in a precinct or ward expect a larger return.   Having manipulated the election of their candidate, they may in turn be appointed by him to an office through which they may make money; or they may be persons engaged in some illicit activity, such as the operation of a gambling house, and are given immunity from arrest or conviction; or if they are in a legitimate business, their taxes may be reduced.

Corruption and graft do not cease with the election of the machine's candidates to office.   The machine needs not only votes but money.   Heavy contributions to campaign funds come from persons and businesses that expect some favor in return.   The large-scale criminal may expect and receive protection from arrest or, if arrested, from conviction; he may even be allowed to operate without any molestation whatever from the police.   Legitimate businesses may make contributions in return for favorable municipal and state legislation; or for reduction of taxes or the granting of franchises.

Types of Political Corruption

Individuals in the machine who are placed in public office are interested not primarily in their salaries but in the chances for personal gain.   These opportunities arise in several ways.   Officials may accept outright payments of money from those in illegal occupations in return for protection; or from legitimate industries seeking favors outside the law.   They may take advantage of their office to favor businesses in which they have a financial interest and hence stand to benefit.   They may appoint friends to subordinate positions, who will pay for the privilege.

A few illustrations demonstrate the type of operation that occurs and the amounts of money involved.   The Seabury investigation of conditions in New York City affords many examples.[29]   Although the Seabury report dates back to the 1920's and 1930's and is limited to one city, less extensive investigations and incidental cases that are uncovered from time to time prove that the conditions revealed in this extensive report are not limited to any one city nor any one decade.

The Borough of Richmond planned to extend the bus service.   Two companies, one known to be reliable, the other unreliable, competed for the franchise.   The Borough President arranged for the franchise to go to the unreliable company.   In return this company bought from him a local newspaper in which he was interested and which was losing money.

The democratic leader of Queen's County was successful in having a certain man elected as Surrogate.   The Surrogate in turn appointed the county leader Chief Clerk at a salary of $8,000 per year.   It was brought out in the investigation that this Clerk did not perform any useful duties.   It was also shown that he was interested in an automobile agency, from which the various local politicians bought their cars and from which publicly owned cars were bought.

Sometimes the possibilities of gain are implicit in the office, but nevertheless illegal.   For example, the Deputy City Clerk of Manhattan was empowered to perform marriage ceremonies.   This function was part of his office, for which he received in 1928 a salary of $8,500 yearly.   However, the Clerk at that time accepted "gifts" for performing ceremonies.   He was able to deposit $384,788 between 1925 and 1931, of which he admitted that about $150,000 came from such gifts; he was unable to give the source of the other deposits.

Other rewards came from permitting illegal activities to operate and sometimes from participating directly in the profits.   During prohibition patrolmen were allowed to collect protection money from small speakeasies, although the larger speakeasies paid to superior officers.   One patrolman spoke of getting only the "crumbs" but was nevertheless able to make bank deposits of $99,000 in 10 years.   A police inspector deposited $35,000 in excess of the amount of his salary over a period of 6 years, and another inspector deposited $27,856 in 7 months' time.

A number of political figures, holding appointive offices as clerks, were dominant in political clubs.   Notorious gamblers were permitted to open gambling establishments in these clubs which were equipped with shuttered windows and heavy doors with peepholes.   The politicians either received a share of the profits, or were paid large sums in return for full protection of the operating gamblers and their patrons.   When arrests were made, the leader of the club (who was also a county or city official) immediately secured the release on bail of those arrested; and the Clerk of the Magistrate's Court then issued a form certifying that in his opinion there was insufficient evidence to convict, which resulted in the release of the defendants.

Enormous sums of money were acquired by these and similar methods. Thus between 1925 and 1931, the Sheriff of New York City, whose legitimate income for the period amounted to $90,000, actually deposited $360,660.34.   The deputy Sheriff, whose salary was $7,000 a year, deposited $662,311.11 in 6 years' time; and the Assistant Deputy Sheriff, an appointee of the Sheriff, deposited $20,890.55 in 4 months, although his salary was only $2,700 per year.

Philadelphia, Kansas City, Chicago, and other cities, especially under certain administrations, also present examples of corruption and graft.   In Chicago and Cook County during the 1920's and early 1930's, such practices as the following were commonplace.[30]

During the period 1921–26, the Forest Reserve District of Cook County bought 4,000 acres of land.   The illicit personal profits to politicians, accruing from this purchase, amounted to $1,250,000.   The land was secretly selected; dummies representing the politicians then secured options at normal prices on the land; these options were then sold to the Forest Reserve District at inflated prices.   The difference between the price of the option and the price paid by the Forest Reserve District was taken by the politicians.   Since the money to purchase the land came from taxes, the transaction represents a misuse of public funds.

In another instance, a lot owned by the School Board, which was located in the heart of Chicago's business district, was rented for $47,640 per year; it was then subleased for $301,789 yearly on a sixty-year lease.   The total rent of $15,000,000, which would have been paid to the School Board had the lease been made directly with the private user of the land, was acquired instead by the politician or friend of the party who was given the low-priced lease.

A system of tax rebates was developed in Chicago.   The Board of Assessors first placed an abnormally high valuation on property.   When the owner protested he was steered to an attorney specializing in taxes.   This attorney would then secure a reduction of the taxes through the Board of Review, sometimes lower than the normal rate.   The fee charged by the attorney amounted to one fourth of the amount of the reduction, a share of the fee going to members of the Board of Review.   Private citizens were also openly offered reductions if they agreed to buy coal from companies owned by the politicians.   Moreover, certain businesses paid taxes on only one fifth of the actual value of their property, in return for heavy contributions to campaign funds.

During this same period the Sanitary District of Chicago also had a bad record.   It constructed a bridle path at a cost of $1,062,430.   Free cinders were secured from the disposal plant of the Sanitary District.   These cinders were then sold back to the District for the construction of the path.   A contractor was paid $1.60 per cubic yard to remove the free cinders; the District then bought the cinders back for $1.95 to $2.25 per cubic yard, thus paying a total of about $3.70 per cubic yard for its own cinders.   The contractor was also allowed $50 per day for each truck used in hauling. This particular contractor was a member of the State Assembly.

These concrete illustrations from 2 cities show forms of political corruption during short periods of flagrant abuse. Such abuse occurs in some degree in many large cities at all times. Still other common types of misuse of public funds are padding payrolls with the names of friends of the machine, who receive ample salaries but do almost no work; placing public funds in certain banks without requiring the bank to pay interest; placing members of the state legislature on the public payroll of a city as "experts" or "investigators," although they perform no service in return; paying excessive prices for labor and material used on city contracts, which are given to companies in which politicians have a personal interest; using public funds for trips by officials to other cities, presumably on official business but actually for a rowdy type of pleasure.

Public Officials and Criminals

Sometimes the corruption and graft in politics are technically within the limits of legality; but more often they are actual violations of specific laws. These operations are on a level with those of professional criminals; indeed, some politicians are also involved in criminal activities unrelated to their public office. The system of graft and contributions for protection of criminals may affect every office in government—the policeman on the beat who accepts his small sums from the gambler, pickpocket, or prostitute; the officials in the police department who guarantee protection to the more prosperous establishments; the prosecuting attorney who finds reasons for not prosecuting a case; the judges of courts of all levels who dismiss cases or find defendants not guilty; heads of various departments who grant contracts; legislators who make unethical laws to conform to the desires of powerful corporations. The graft runs all the way from the smaller political units to federal officials. This statement does not imply that every governmental unit or every official is corrupt, but that corruption and graft are sufficiently widespread and highly organized to constitute a constant problem of crime.

Control of Political Corruption

Political corruption is a type of crime that is extremely difficult to control. The same forces whose duty it is to apprehend, try, and, if guilty, convict criminals are involved; and they will not incriminate themselves. Also, many of their transactions appear legitimate on the surface. Often the illegal aspect of the transactions is carried out in a disguised form; money is paid in the form of a gift rather than as a fee. Or a third person not obviously connected with the government or with the individual politician acts as a go-between.   It is usually only when some third party, such as an investigating committee of citizens or a commission appointed by some higher governmental unit, makes an investigation that the abuses are uncovered and corrected for a time.

The men who are involved in political corruption come from many backgrounds.   Some of them have come up from the ranks and are not far different from the professional criminals who make no pretense at legitimate pursuits.   Others are men in legitimate business activities who enter into graft in the form of contributions to campaign funds, gifts, or payments of bonuses in order to obtain favorable legislation, evasion of taxes, or assignment of contracts.   Their actual profits come from their regular business enterprises, but they are nonetheless parties to graft in that they pay for favors that are contrary to the public welfare although profitable to themselves.

INTERNAL ORGANIZATION AND CONTINUITY OF ORGANIZED CRIME

Internal Organization of Organized Crime

Although every type of organized crime—in fact, each criminal group—may have special forms of internal organization, there are many similarities between them.   After brief descriptions of individual forms of organization, these similarities are summarized.

The nucleus of the criminal gang is composed of a small, fairly permanent group, which plans the crimes and assigns the various tasks; one person is usually the leader of this small group.   Essential to the gang activities and safety is the "moll" or wife of one of the men, who often goes ahead of the gang and arranges for a place to live, and who also maintains neighborhood contacts in order to learn of possible danger.   Another important figure is the lawyer who advises the gang on methods of escaping punishment, and, under the latitude permitted attorneys, is under no legal compulsion to hinder the criminals.   A doctor is essential to provide medical care for the injured and frequently to alter fingerprints or facial appearance in order to prevent identification and capture of the gangster.   Still other necessary assistants are the runners or messengers who bring information of developments in other communities and of possible pursuit by the police, and persons who harbor criminals.   For example, Ma Barker's gang had more than 20 such accessories.

The syndicate, which does not depend primarily upon secrecy, mobility, and terrorism of its victims, is a tightly organized, business-like structure, usually established in permanent headquarters.   Its leaders usually prefer to remain anonymous and operate through "lieutenants" who obey their orders and supervise the actual criminal work of the syndicate, which is carried out by a larger number of subordinates.

Describing the permanently established rackets of New York, Lockwood stated that the internal organization includes a large number of petty criminals who are at the bottom of the scale. Next in rank is a smaller group of specialists such as bomb makers, acid throwers, saboteurs, arsonists, and killers. Superior to these criminals is a small group of lieutenants with limited authority; then the trusted aides, the fixers, advisers, and attorneys; and at the top the head of the organization who tries to remain inconspicuous.[31]

The corrupt political machine is as well organized as the more patently criminal groups. The organization is pyramidal in nature with a wide base in the precinct captains and a central head in the city or county boss. The precinct captain makes personal contacts with the voters and it is his job to "deliver the votes." The precinct captains are directly responsible to the ward boss who reports to the city boss. Sometimes a state boss controls the entire state.

Each type of organized crime has a small group of leaders who plan and control the activities of various grades of subordinates. These subordinates are often specialists whose co-ordinate activities are necessary to the success of the criminal project. The proceeds of the criminal activities usually go to the leaders; the subordinates are paid salaries or fixed fees as in any noncriminal business.

Relation of Organized Crime to Law-Enforcement Agencies

In large cities where highly organized and efficient criminal organizations exist, the fact of their protection by the police is common knowledge. Only occasionally are the details brought into the open. However, the system of co-operation between criminal and police breaks down when one or the other violates the agreement between them and an exposure takes place. In other instances, rival political factions are represented in the law enforcement agencies and one faction attempts to discredit the other by exposing its connections with the underworld; or a prosecuting attorney, uninvolved in the underworld and eager for advancement, ferrets out and exposes the activities of organized criminal groups.

The fundamental process by which criminals obtain police protection is regular payments to the policemen on the beat for failure to arrest them. But in the case of organized gangs, which are making large sums of money, such a simple method is usually replaced by permanent arrangements between the criminal groups and officials in the police department. Thus in the notorious case of the murder of Herman Rosenthal, proprietor of a gambling house in New York, the key person in the protection of vice establishments was Lieutenant Charles Becker of the Strong Arm Squad in the police department.[32] He earned a salary of $2,200 a year but was reported to have banked $58,845 in 9 months. Although his squad concentrated on the arrest of minor criminals, Becker did not molest the large gambling establishments unless they refused to pay financial tribute to him. It was a refusal of this sort that precipitated the quarrel between Rosenthal and Becker, which led to the murder of Rosenthal by 4 hired murderers. For this crime Lieutenant Becker and the murderers were convicted and executed.

On occasion the connection of organized crime is with elected officials of city government and the courts. In return for protection from prosecution for their crimes, criminals contribute money to campaign funds, help get out the votes, terrorize voters in certain sections, and supply fraudulent voters.

When District Attorney Van Cise cleaned up Blonger's gang in Denver he found it necessary to use special deputies and state rangers to make the arrests, and to hold the prisoners in a special place rather than in jail while arrests were in process. The local police were so thoroughly allied with the gang operations that their co-operation could not be counted upon.

The Chicago criminal organization that controlled the more profitable criminal activities in Chicago from about 1925 to 1943 was virtually immune from arrest in Chicago. Al Capone, head of the group, was finally convicted for a federal violation of income tax laws by a federal judge who could not be fixed. Capone's successors, a group of 7 important members of the syndicate, were not molested until they stepped outside their own territory and were convicted in New York for extorting money from the motion picture industry.

Background of Criminals in Organized Crime

Because they are relatively immune from imprisonment, the personal backgrounds of powerful criminals are more obscure than the backgrounds of minor criminals whose records are obtained as they pass through clinics and courts on their way to prison. Nevertheless, what is known of the group indicates that they are drawn largely from the group of professional criminals and from a background of juvenile delinquency. Some examples support the contention that organized crime develops from an underworld background.

Abe (Kid Twist) Reles, who testified against the Combination in 1940, began his criminal conduct in 1920 at the age of 13. In the succeeding 20 years he had been arrested 43 times, 5 of the arrests being for murder. On the witness stand he confessed to 18 murders.[33]

Big Jack Zelig was leader of a gang of thugs and murderers who could be hired to molest or murder the enemies of other gangs.[34]   Four of his men were convicted of the murder of Rosenthal, mentioned earlier in this chapter. Zelig himself was murdered shortly before the trial.

Zelig's real name was William Alberts.   He was born in New York of respectable Jewish parents; by the time he was 14 he had run away from home and become one of Crazy Butch's group of juvenile pickpockets.   He was soon operating independently as a pickpocket.   To secure protection from the police he joined a gang of thugs and soon became proficient in using a blackjack and revolver.   In time he became the leader of this gang.

Dopey Benny, for some years (about 1911–14) leader of a successful New York gang hired indiscriminately both by employers and by labor unions to harass their opponents, began his delinquent career when he was 10 years old.[35]   He lived on the East Side streets and stole from express and delivery wagons.   Soon he was stealing from people and he became an expert pickpocket.   In the course of time he affiliated himself with a gang and eventually developed into the most successful gang leader of his time.

Louis (Lepke) Buchalter, head of the Combination, who was executed in 1944 for murder, was born in New York's East Side slums, the child of immigrant parents.   His father died when he was 14 and his mother moved from the city, leaving him with an older sister.   From a petty criminal he rose to the head of the syndicate.   He was accused of being responsible for more than 20 murders and had been convicted of violation of the narcotics laws.   He was 47 years old when executed.

The 4 Barker brothers, who were involved in many crimes including the kidnaping of Charles F. Urschel, grew up in the poor section of a Missouri mining town; thence the family moved to Tulsa, Oklahoma, where the boys became members of a juvenile gang, indulging in rowdyism and petty thievery.   By the time the boys were adolescents all had been accused of some law violation.   With their mother as the central figure of the gang, they stole automobiles, robbed banks, and eventually kidnaped Urschel, a crime that proved their undoing.

Baby Face Nelson, who was killed by agents of the Federal Bureau of Investigation during a running battle, was engaged in stealing automobile accessories at the age of 14.   He later became a member of a gang specializing in bank robbery.

John Dillinger, also killed by the federal agents, came from a poor section of Indianapolis.   He was first arrested when about 20 years of age for a store robbery; later he was affiliated with a gang of bank robbers.

Alvin Karpis grew up in Chicago.   At the age of 19 he was sentenced to the reformatory for robbery.   He was later a member of a gang of bank robbers and participated in the Bremer kidnaping in Minneapolis.[36]

Although this list is fragmentary, it indicates that many of the criminals who in adulthood are members of organized criminal groups, as children and adolescents were members of juvenile delinquent groups and were early engaged in crimes sufficiently serious to lead to arrest. It seems probable that in most cases they followed in youth the progressive path from unsupervised leisure to incorporation in the criminal world already discussed in Chapter 5.

Continuity of Organized Crime

Organized crime is the most audacious type of crime and one of the most difficult to control.   The reasons for its continuity in society are numerous.

Syndicates and rackets, although primarily organized for the benefit of their members, often provide advantages to some other group. Thus wholesalers who in return for a fee are permitted to monopolize the market in a certain territory may be able to increase the price of their product and perhaps make additional profit.   The union member who is forced to pay exorbitant dues may be compensated by a small increase in wages forced from the employer by threats.   Also, it is frequently possible for the group that must pay the extortion to pass the cost of it on to someone else.   The price of foods may be passed down the line to the consumer in order to cover fees extorted from the wholesaler.   The consumer knows only that prices are high but is unaware of the cause.

Threats are potent reasons for the continuation of criminal syndicates and rackets.   They are not so often threats of personal injury as of loss of money.   Instilling fear of a strike in the employer, loss of a job in the laborer, property damage in the retailer are all effective ways of forcing compliance with demands and of maintaining silence.

The criminal groups are usually so powerful and extensive that they can secure the co-operation of corrupt law-enforcement agencies.   It is significant that in Chicago major criminals of the 1920's were almost never convicted of crimes, and not until some of them were convicted of income tax evasion in federal courts were the most flagrant bootlegging syndicates curbed. Thus even when complaints arise and proof is laid before police and prosecuting attorneys, arrests and convictions do not follow.

When the syndicate offers a service that is illegal, but demanded by the public, almost nothing is done to destroy the organization.   Only the most brazen flaunting of the law, and of public order and decency, leads to prosecution; and then perhaps merely because some small group of citizens has assumed responsibility for arousing public indignation.

This situation was the case in the early 1900's when many of the notorious red-light districts were broken up.   In some cities they had become a public scandal and groups of citizens forced the police to take action, in some instances by parades and demonstrations. However, if the demand for the illegal service persists (as it usually does) an organization to provide it springs up again, possibly in some less obvious form. Thus the demonstration against the red-light district in Chicago succeeded in closing these houses of prostitution, but resulted in the opening of less glamorous places in more widely scattered areas, which were operated with less publicity but enjoyed the same protection from the law-enforcement agencies as before.

Finally, like any organization, the syndicate has a tendency to endure even though individual members disappear. In Chicago, there is an unbroken succession in the organization controlling vice and crime since 1905, when Colosimo brought in Torrio to help him organize gambling and prostitution. Colosimo was murdered in 1920 and control was assumed by Torrio and Al Capone, members of his organization. They slowly brought a wide territory under their control, and bootlegging of liquor became the major business of the organization. After Al Capone was imprisoned for income tax evasion, Nitti became the leader, with a half dozen "lieutenants." Bootlegging was replaced by labor racketeering. In 1943 Nitti and his lieutenants were indicted for extortion from the motion picture producers. Nitti committed suicide, but his assistants were convicted. Although the leaders have been replaced in a crime organization extending over many years in Chicago, organized crime in that city has not ceased to exist. When an organization has become established, and has developed definite methods and contacts, it tends to persist despite changes of leadership.

The corrupt political machine may remain in power for a generation or more, exhibiting various shifts in leadership. It is difficult to break up a machine because it operates behind the scenes through elected officials. The machine is always able to sacrifice a few members, or to make a pretense of "cleaning up" a city, without vitally affecting the organization. Citizens have little firsthand knowledge either of the candidates they elect or of the operation of government. For example, in Chicago alone there are more than 300 elective officials and in Cook County more than 600.[37] In addition there are more than 50,000 office holders in the city. To complicate the situation further, Cook County has 34 separate and independent governmental units empowered to levy and collect taxes.[38] Only when exasperated citizens form a strong counterorganization, and sweep the adherents of the corrupt machine completely out of office, is any change expected from corruption to government for the benefit of the public.

QUESTIONS

1. What are the characteristics of organized crime? How do these characteristics compare with the characteristics of modern business organizations?

2. Compare the chief types of organized crime: criminal gangs, criminal syndi-

cates, racketeers, and political graft and corruption.   What features do they have in common?   In what ways is each distinctive?

3. Why does the criminal gang remain mobile?

4. In what ways does the public support and encourage the operations of criminal syndicates?

5. How does the system of government in the United States lend itself to the development of political machines?   When are such machines termed corrupt?

6. Why is it so difficult to control organized criminal groups?

READINGS

Asbury, Herbert, *The Gangs of New York* (Garden City Publishing Co., 1927). This is a colorful history of the marauding gangs that have infested New York for many years.

Clinard, Marshall B., *The Black Market, A Study of White Collar Crime* (Rinehart, 1952).   This study of the black market of World War II shows that criminals as well as businessmen sought a profit from illegal activities in the market.

Hoover, J. Edgar, *Persons in Hiding* (Little, Brown, 1938).   Kidnapers, burglars, and other criminals organized into gangs pass through this story of the work of the Federal Bureau of Investigation.   The organization and operation of the gangs are clearly shown.

Kefauver, Estes, *Crime in America* (Doubleday, 1951).   This book reports on the findings of the Senate Crime Investigating Committee, which uncovered widespread networks of criminals over the United States and the inevitable protective arrangements with political machines.

Loth, David, *Public Plunder: A History of Graft in America* (Carrick and Evans, 1938).   The history of public graft from 1617 on—the "black side of government," as one reviewer termed it—is here laid bare.

Ploscowe, Morris, and Edwin J. Lukas (eds.), "Gambling," *Annals of the American Academy of Political and Social Science,* Vol. 269 (1950).   The volume covers the legal status of gambling, its various forms, and gambling abroad. The gambler is analyzed from several points of view.

Salter, J. T., *Boss Rule: Portraits in City Politics* (McGraw-Hill, 1935).   After a discussion of the operation of political machines, the author presents sketches of 9 political bosses, and the ways in which they control voters through favoritism and pressures.

FOOTNOTES

[1] Herbert Asbury, *The Gangs of New York* (Garden City Publishing Co., 1927); M. Conboy, "Organized Crime as a Business, etc.," *New York University Law Review,* 7 (1929), 339–51; Herbert Corey, *Farewell, Mr. Gangster! America's War on Crime* (D. Appleton-Century, 1936); Estes Kefauver, *Crime in America* (Doubleday, 1951); J. Landesco, "Organized Crime in Chicago," *Illinois Crime Survey* (Illinois Association for Criminal Justice, 1920); A. R. Lindesmith, "Organized Crime," *Annals of the American Academy of Political and Social Science,* 217 (1941), 119–27.

[2] Frederic M. Thrasher, *The Gang* (Chicago: University of Chicago Press, 1927).

[3] J. E. Hoover, *Persons in Hiding* (Little, Brown, 1938).

[4] August Vollmer, *The Police and Modern Society* (Berkeley: University of California Press, 1936), p. 79.

[5] R. C. Sanders, "Syndicated Bank Robbery," *Journal of Criminal Law and Criminology,* 23 (1933), 797–805.   Note that the use of "syndicated" in the title does not correspond to the use of that word in this chapter.

[6] "The Million-Dollar Robbery," *Life,* 28 (Jan. 30, 1950), 26–27.

[7] News item, *Chicago Daily News* (Jan. 2, 1945).

[8] Vollmer, *op. cit.,* pp. 57ff.

[9] J. E. Bulger, "Automobile Thefts," *Journal of Criminal Law and Criminology,* 23 (1933), 806–10.

[10] *Oxford Universal English Dictionary,* 9 (Doubleday, Doran, 1937), 2112.

[11] Marshall B. Clinard, *The Black Market, A Study of White-Collar Crime* (Rinehart, 1952).

[12] Kefauver, *op. cit.*

[13] Morris Ploscowe and Edwin J. Lukas (eds.), "Gambling," *Annals of the American Academy of Political and Social Science,* 269 (May, 1950), 39–80.

[14] J. Freeman, "Murder Monopoly," *Nation,* 150 (1940), 645–49.

[15] Kefauver, *op. cit.,* pp. 12–14, 19–34.

[16] Philip S. Van Cise, *Fighting the Underworld* (Houghton Mifflin, 1936).

[17] M. I. Gurfein, "Racketeering," *Encyclopaedia of the Social Sciences,* 13 (Macmillan, 1931), 45–49.

[18] R. L. Duffus, "The Function of the Racketeer," *New Republic,* 58 (1929), 166–68.

[19] Leo Hubermann, *The Labor Spy Racket* (Modern Age, 1937), p. 195.

[20] M. Ploscowe, "Crime in a Competitive Society," *Annals of the American Academy of Political and Social Science,* 217 (1941), 107.

[21] Newspaper accounts, 1944, at the time of the grand jury investigation and trial of those involved.   Also, John Martin, "Who Killed Estelle Carey?"   *Harper's Magazine,* 189 (1944), 48–60.

[22] Ploscowe, *op. cit.*

[23] C. Stevenson, "Housing—A National Disgrace," *Atlantic Monthly,* 162 (1938), 835–45.

[24] *Ibid.*

[25] *Time,* 45, No. 13 (Mar. 26, 1945), 21.

[26] "How Labor Czar Held Court in Sing Sing," *Life,* 35 (Oct. 12, 1953), 60.

[27] M. Berger, "Lepke," *Life,* 13 (Feb. 28, 1944), 86–88, 90, 92, 95, 96, 98.

[28] E. M. Sait, "Machine, Political," *Encyclopaedia of the Social Sciences,* 9 (Macmillan, 1931), 657–61; J. J. Senturia and P. H. Odegard, "Corruption, Political," *ibid.,* 4, 448–55.

[29] Samuel Seabury, *Intermediate Report in the Matter of the Investigation of the Departments of the Government of the City of New York, etc., Pursuant to Joint Resolution Adopted by the Legislature of the State of New York, March 23, 1931* (Jan. 25, 1932).

[30] W. W. Liggett, "The Plunder of Chicago," *American Mercury,* 25 (1932), 269–79.

[31] P. E. Lockwood, "How State and City Governments Deal with Racketeering," *Journal of Criminal Law and Criminology,* 132 (1941), 130–38.

[32] R. McCarthy, "A Murder Has Been Arranged," *Harper's Magazine,* 170 (1935), 175–89; Asbury, *op. cit.,* pp. 325–43.

[33] Freeman, *op. cit.*

[34] Asbury, *op. cit.,* pp. 328ff.

[35] Asbury, *op. cit.,* pp. 362ff.

[36] Information on the Barker brothers, Nelson, Dillinger, and Karpis, from Hoover, *op. cit.*

[37] Liggett, *op. cit.,* p. 271.

[38] Senturia and Odegard, *op. cit.,* p. 452.

7

Criminals Who Live in the Noncriminal World

The conventional stereotype of the criminal is the professional criminal, a man—or, less often, a woman—whose chief social role is predatory, who consorts with other criminals, who is in conflict with society, and who is regarded as a "public enemy." In contrast with the confirmed criminal is the conventionally organized person who, nevertheless, occasionally lapses into criminal behavior or follows a criminal pattern in one area of his life at the same time that he fulfills conventional roles without a serious sense of guilt or mental conflict. As is true of professional criminals, some of the conventional criminals commit trivial offenses, while others are guilty of enormous exploitation of the public. Since 1940 persons in the noncriminal world who break criminal laws have received increasing study by sociologists, in part because of their depredations but more because their behavior seems to call for revision of some current theories of the origin of criminal behavior. Neither the theory of personal disorganization nor the theory of adoption of a criminal philosophy through childhood contacts in slum areas seems adequate. Several sociologists have attempted to find an inclusive theory applicable alike to both professional and conventional criminals. These suggested theories are discussed after consideration of criminals in the noncriminal society.

The first three types discussed—casual, occasional, and episodic—are the essentially law-abiding offenders of our basic classification; the fourth type illustrates the segmental criminal.

THE CASUAL OFFENDER

The casual offender commits the least serious of crimes. His offenses are usually carried out for his own convenience and rarely harm anyone else, although they may inconvenience others and occasionally may endanger them indirectly. In the group of casual offenders we place those who indulge in minor violations of municipal ordinances, such as disregarding parking signs or parking overtime.   In this category, we also include an occasional violation of a state law, for instance, breaking the speed laws in driving to and from a hunting trip when time is limited (but not the habitual reckless driving that needlessly endangers the lives of others).   Here belong the many persons who during World War II acquired a few extra gas coupons without much thought as to their origin, or occasionally bought meat on the black market without ration stamps.

The casual offender is usually a good citizen; he upholds the law and the constitution in general and does not think of himself as a delinquent or criminal even though his acts are technically punishable by a fine, jail sentence, or imprisonment.   He justifies his acts—if he feels that they need justification—by the simple philosophy that if he can get away with the violations they are not particularly wrong, that he is doing no one any harm, and that his need justifies his deciding right and wrong for himself.   If he cannot justify his acts he is filled with a sense of guilt and fear of discovery. The opportunities for small violations of social regulations are many and obvious, and it is primarily a matter of personal decision whether a person follows the social regulations, or evades them when the chances of detection and punishment are slight or when the pressure of circumstances is great.

Probably the worst offense of the casual offender is his lack of respect for law and social regulation as such.   He places his own convenience above the laws designed to regulate group behavior.   In so doing he makes a breach in the completeness of community control and to a slight extent undermines the social organization.   His evasion of the law and escape from punishment may form a justification of some other person in the commission of a more serious offense.

THE OCCASIONAL OFFENDER

The occasional offender, like the casual offender, is a law-abiding citizen who accepts the conventional attitude toward illegal acts.   He commits a crime once or several times, perhaps separated by long intervals of time.

Types of Offenses

Sometimes the crime grows out of an immediate situation and is wholly unplanned; indeed, it may not be thought of as criminal at the time of its commission.   Thus some cases of rape are unpremeditated and are non-violent attacks that occur as the climax of an evening that began as a romantic and innocent adventure.   Or a boy looking for companionship and adventure may find that his more experienced companions are embarking on a burglary and accompany them without much consideration of the nature of his act. In other instances the occasional crime is committed in the attempt to avoid a painful situation. The bank officer who has contracted a gambling debt that he cannot pay, or whose wife needs an immediate and costly operation, may embezzle funds in order to meet his immediate problem. He does not try to justify his crime other than by his need, and he fully intends to restore the money, overlooking the fact that this result will be difficult to accomplish, since he did not have the necessary funds in the first instance.

Other occasional offenders are persons employed in some business where thefts may easily be concealed. Accepted by employer and community as industrious and respectable people, they may follow a systematic pattern of thefts extending over many years. Some offenders are eventually detected, discharged, or arrested and prosecuted. The thefts of others presumably are never discovered. Lie detector tests have sometimes revealed extensive dishonesty in employees. An article by McEvoy in *Reader's Digest* states that when all employees in certain Chicago banks were given lie detector tests, 20 per cent were shown to have stolen bank property; and among a cross section sample of chainstore employees, 75 per cent had stolen merchandise or money from the store.[1] In 1953, in an Illinois mental hospital, a small group of employees was discovered to have systematically stolen thousands of dollars' worth of food and supplies over a period of years.

Occasional offenders are found also among persons who are quick to take advantage of an opportunity to defraud or steal. The housewife who seizes an opportunity to take some article from a store without paying for it; the returned traveler who manages to conceal some article purchased abroad and does not declare it or pay duty upon it; the customer who receives a $10 bill instead of a $1 bill from a salesgirl and does not return it—these are all occasional offenders.

Minor Offenses

The occasional offender does not necessarily come from a particularly disorganized background and may not be personally disorganized himself. He finds his associates and satisfactions in the conventional community among others of his kind. He does not associate with known criminals, speak in criminal argot, learn any special skills of crime, nor organize his life around his delinquent activities. His offenses are incidental to his conventional life organization and unimportant in his scheme of things. Many occasional offenders, even those who commit crimes punishable by imprisonment, are never discovered. Others, who are caught and convicted, pay their fines or serve their terms. Nevertheless, they still do not regard themselves as criminals and are not so considered by their families and friends.   They maintain that they took a chance and were caught and were thus unfortunate; or that they were foolish in having done something subject to arrest, but not antisocial.   Many return to their own communities on the completion of their sentences, and, resuming normal associations with their families, attempt to re-establish themselves in the community.

Many of the offenders in rural and village communities are of this type. They either commit numerous minor offenses not regarded as actually criminal by themselves or the community, or one slightly more serious offense that leads to arrest and conviction.   Clinard, in his study of rural Iowa offenders who had been sentenced to the state reformatory, brings out many of the characteristics that set the occasional offender apart from the full-time criminal.[2]   He does not use the term "occasional offender," but that type is essentially the same as the one he describes.   He demonstrates that only a small percentage of these prisoners had ever been arrested before they were 17 years of age; that the offenses were minor ones and not part of a progression to serious crimes; that they did not involve the use of unusual criminal skills; and that the crimes were not the chief means of livelihood.   Several brief descriptions from this report illustrate the types of occasional crimes that sent the offenders to the reformatory.

One of these young men, ill and unable to work, was worried about losing his car upon which a payment was due.   His family helped him pay his hospital bill, but they did not know of his other debt.   He forged a check on his father's bank account, soon after his father had made a deposit, and thus paid the installment on his car.   For this forgery he was sent to the reformatory.

Clinard cites another case, of a young man from a respectable family who characterized himself as always being honest.   He wanted to go to a dance; however, his family refused to give him the money necessary to repair his car.   He became angry and told his family he would steal a car.   At the moment he really did not care what he did, and he stole one that belonged to a neighbor.   Although in his own mind he seemed to regard the act as not far different from earlier occasions when he had used his father's car without permission, he was sent to the reformatory.

The chief differences that Clinard noted between the reformatory cases and noncriminals were the greater mobility of the delinquents and their sense of relative freedom from community mores and restraints.

Juvenile Occasional Offenders

Many juvenile delinquents come under the heading of occasional offenders. The Gluecks found that among the boys who were delinquent at the average age of 13, 25 per cent were not arrested in the succeeding 5 years.[3]   These boys undoubtedly would be classed as occasional offenders; so also would some of those who continued to be arrested occasionally throughout adolescence, but committed no offenses after reaching maturity.   Among the young women who had served reformatory sentences studied by the Gluecks, a fourth were not guilty of delinquencies during the 5 years following termination of their sentences and might properly be classed as occasional offenders.[4]

In some cases the occasional offense results from a temporary disorganizing experience that is potentially part of the progression toward a criminal pattern of life, but which may be checked.   Such an experience is most likely to happen to a young person whose attitudes and habits are not stabilized. The sexual activities occasionally discovered among groups of adolescents belong in this category, as do also some of the delinquencies of adolescents in association with experienced criminals.   The Gluecks give in detail the story of one such girl.[5]

Marie came from a home in which there were many sources of conflict. The parents were of different religious faiths, which resulted in dissension over the religious training of the children.   Moreover, the father was strict and abusive to his wife and children, although the mother was docile toward her husband and lenient with the children.

Several times Marie ran away, but was found by the father after a period of time and brought home.   Finally she left home and secured work as a companion to a wealthy woman.   Soon she affiliated herself with a young man met at a movie and lived with him, although he did not marry her.   He used her as a prostitute (she was then 15 years old), collecting the money for her services.   Later he took her to another town where he opened a fruit store, which she helped to tend.   One day he hastily married her, and on the next he was arrested for white slavery and burglary.   He had been for some time a member of an organized criminal group.   Marie denied that she knew of these activities, but she possessed the keys to a house recently burglarized and was in the act of helping her husband prepare to escape.   She was arrested and sentenced to the reformatory for 5 years. After 14 months she was released on parole, still insisting that she was innocent.   She was given training as a nursemaid and worked steadily. She obtained an annulment of her first marriage and eventually made a happy second marriage to a law-abiding husband.

The 2 following cases show the development of the occasional offense and the way in which it is checked by detection, family support, and the offender's own efforts.   The attitudes of these 2 young men not only toward their crimes but also toward the prison are essentially those of the conventional, rather than of the criminal, community.   They co-operated with prison officials, followed the routine, took pride in advancement in prison jobs, learned all they could, regarded their punishments as deserved, and upon release affiliated themselves with the conventional world.[6]

Jim was forced to begin work early as his father drank heavily, did not support his family, and finally died of alcoholism.   At the age of 16 Jim was earning about $35 a week.   He spent his leisure time with a club of boys, one member of which was a criminal.   This boy secured a gun and persuaded Jim to accompany him on his expeditions.   They performed 5 "jobs," stealing money and several watches.   As they were novices in crime, they did not know how to dispose of the watches and therefore sold them to members of the club, stating that they were stolen.   When word of the theft reached the police, Jim was arrested.   His parents and employer attempted to have him released but he was sentenced to prison, where he made a good work record.   Following his release Jim worked steadily.   He selected his associates from his fellow-employees rather than from the former community. He was fond of sports and always came home early in the evening.

The second case is that of a young man who left school in the sixth grade in order to work, as there were 19 children in the family.   Since he was unskilled, he held casual jobs, such as selling papers or shining shoes.   Soon he was staying away from home, sleeping wherever he could, and associating with older boys who initiated him into breaking into sheds to steal junk and, finally, armed with a gun, into holdups.   In the course of his first holdup he was caught and sentenced to prison.   He was then 20 years old.   During his 3 years in prison, he completed high school, sang in the choir and with a quartette, and worked steadily, although he did not learn a trade.   He thought that there were many pleasant features of the prison, that there were many good officers, but that the food was poor—possibly because the prisoners did not deserve better.   Upon his release he made it clear to his old companions that he was through with them.   His sister secured work for him.   Several years later he was working steadily, had married, and had a well-kept, comfortable home.

Incidence of Occasional Offenses Among Youth

The wide-spread incidence of occasional offenses among adolescents and youths is shown by a comparative study made by Porterfield of the offenses of a representative sample of college students and the offenses of juvenile-court cases.[7]   Fifty-five offenses with which children were charged in juvenile court were listed, and college students were asked to indicate which of these offenses they had committed prior to entering college and which after matriculation.   Not one of the 437 college students queried was guiltless and the average number of offenses reported by men in their precollege days was 17.6; by men after entering college 11.2; and by women in precollege days 4.7. There were only 2 of the court offenses of which some student had not been guilty; suspicious character and incorrigibility. Also, none of the students classified themselves as having been neglected or abused—a situation that brought some of the children into juvenile court.

The types of offenses most characteristic of the college students differed, however, from the offenses most frequently charged against the court cases. The college men in their precollege days were characterized by acts of public annoyance, traffic violations, and sex offenses; the boys brought into court were characterized by vagabondage and thefts, and to a certain extent by malicious mischief, dishonesty, personal affronts and injuries, and trespassing and encroaching upon the rights of others. Porterfield believes that minor violations of laws are a common occurrence, and that whether or not the young occasional offender becomes a confirmed delinquent and criminal or a law-abiding adult depends upon social factors.

Social Influences

Many studies support Porterfield's contention that social factors help to determine the future conduct of the juvenile occasional offender. His own study shows striking differences: Although the students represented all socio-economic classes, their families seem to have held a more respected status in the community than did the families of the juvenile delinquents. Store-keepers would have hesitated to report minor delinquencies of those who later became college students, but not of those children who became court cases. Three times as high a proportion of the delinquents tended to have their contacts restricted to persons and groups that in some way tolerated or encouraged continued delinquency, whereas the college students through their families and continued school contacts moved into progressively more stable groups. The court experience, Porterfield believes, tends to be an isolating experience and to set definite limits to types of social participation to which the delinquent will be admitted, whereas the college student enters into the respectable community and detaches himself from earlier question-able contacts.

Similar results were obtained by the Gluecks in a comparison of recidivists with nonrecidivists among a group of one thousand delinquent boys.[8] Boys whose delinquencies were easily and quickly checked—that is, who were occasional offenders—tended to come from homes with wholesome family relationships, sound discipline, and good conduct; to be well adjusted at school; and to have supervised leisure.

A third study, by Doshay, centers on juvenile sex offenders guilty of such offenses as exhibitionism, excessive masturbation, assault, incest, perverted practices, and normal but illicit relations.[9]   In a comparison of boys guilty of only the one type of offense (occasional offender) with those among whom the sex offense was merely part of a total pattern of juvenile delinquency, Doshay found marked differences.   Such influential factors as higher education of the parents, better-paid occupations of parents, home ownership, proper care of the home and children, and regular church attendance occurred approximately twice as often in the group of occasional offenders as among those with a general pattern of delinquent behavior.   In contrast, the generally delinquent group had criminal parents or brothers and sisters, were victims of poverty, and resided in poor neighborhoods almost twice as often as the occasional offenders.   The personal habits of the generally delinquent group were also marked by frequent association with gangs, keeping late hours, maladjustment in school, and demoralizing recreation; they. were described as rebellious, nervous, cruel, and aggressive.   Only small percentages of the occasional offenders exhibited these characteristics.

Thus among adolescents the occasional offenders form the great reservoir of delinquency from which develops the smaller number of confirmed delinquents and criminals, who continue their crimes into adult life.   The type of family and community life seems to be an important factor in determining which adolescents will become adult criminals.

Serious Occasional Offenders

The more serious occasional crimes, committed by adults instead of juveniles, are usually committed under pressure of some sort.   Embezzlement is likely to be an occasional crime.   Riemer in an analysis of embezzlement lists 6 types, 5 of which appear to be of the type here termed occasional crimes.   He emphasizes the existence of an opportunity to embezzle, which he calls the "social pull," coupled with an emergency situation, which he calls the "social push." [10]   Typical situations in which embezzlement of the occasional type occurs are the following:

1. Embezzlement occurs among persons entrusted with handling money in civil service or administrative positions who may be pressed by indebtedness to "borrow" money from the funds they handle, with the idea of restoring it.   When such restitution proves impossible, they borrow from some other source.   As they are never able to cover the loss, they are nervous and worried, always expecting discovery.

2. Embezzlement may occur when an inexperienced entrepreneur of a small business, pressed by hard times, embezzles money in an attempt to maintain his status as a proprietor.   To lose his business would mean a loss of status and an admission of personal failure.   Lack of experience in meeting business reverses may precipitate this type of embezzlement.

3. Embezzlement may occur also in the attempt of a family with downward social mobility to maintain its former status; or when a family must assume new financial responsibilities and tries to do so without a lowering of socioeconomic status.

4. Petty embezzlement may be attempted in ill-conceived plans by the feeble-minded or by those suffering extreme poverty who have become socially disorganized.

5. Finally occasional embezzlement may be carried out by persons desiring luxuries and amusements beyond their normal income.

This impressive array of 136 checks represents a $780,000 swindle uncovered in 1946.   A small group of professional criminals induced a cashier in a linotype company to participate in crime.   Involving an elaborate scheme of fictitious companies, false invoices, and fraudulent checks that were issued by the cashier and slipped in among legitimate ones, the swindle enabled the man to live for a time in a lavish and dissipated manner.   When the scheme was uncovered, he pleaded guilty to 202 counts of grand larceny and forgery.   After turning state's evidence he received a short prison sentence, but the professional criminals associated with him were given long terms.   At the trial the judge castigated the offender's wife because she had made no attempt to interfere with his activities, although she must have known that his salary could never have provided the luxuries she enjoyed.   (Johna Pepper—Pix)

In all these types, embezzlement is carried out under pressure of some sort—usually to maintain a certain social status that is threatened.   The crime occurs because an opportunity presents itself in the person's normal occupational contacts and is carried out in the vague belief that in some way the money will be restored before discovery.   Even though the embezzlement extends over a long period of time it still comes under the heading of occasional crime, for it is incidental to the person's life organization rather than essential.   These occasional offenders who commit serious crimes react with serious emotional disturbances when discovered.   The respected businessman who is discovered in a theft of this kind may commit suicide rather than face the disgrace of arrest and conviction; or he may run away, later returning to accept his punishment and thus in his own mind expiate his crime and open the way for a resumption of conventional life.   The following case is abstracted from an account given by R. C. Angell in *The Family Encounters the Depression.*[11]

Mr. Fleming, the head of a small, well-organized family, operated an automobile agency.   His home was worth $10,000 and his net income normally was about $3,000 a year.   He held a respected position in the community and was active in social affairs.   However, Mr. Fleming owed money to his former partner, whose interest in the business he had bought.   During a slack period he found himself unable to meet his debts and began to sell the discount company second mortgages on newly sold cars, without the knowledge of the owners, keeping up the payments on the mortgages from the money obtained by sales of new cars.   Eventually, this system broke down, as he was not able to sell enough new cars.   When the crisis came, he fled to Canada, leaving his family to face the situation.   Later Mr. Fleming decided to return and give himself up on the charge of using the mails to defraud.   After 6 months' imprisonment while he awaited trial, he pleaded guilty, but was released because of his past record and the support of his friends.   His subsequent life was devoted to an attempt to re-establish himself financially; there was no further dishonesty.

THE EPISODIC OFFENDER

The episodic offender is a special type of occasional offender.   The term is used by Ploscowe to identify a person who is generally law-abiding, but who under the stress of a particular set of circumstances or temptation commits a criminal act.   The circumstance may never arise again.[12]   The truly episodic crimes—those that occur once and are not likely to be repeated— tend to be acts that are highly charged with emotion and that do not provide any lasting satisfaction to the offender.

Stealing may be an episodic crime, if the person steals something of value more or less on the spur of the moment or under tremendous temporary pressure.   Such a crime is usually motivated by the sudden need of money, which the individual cannot secure in legitimate ways.   The money stolen relieves the pressure, but does not give the thief any future satisfaction or gain.   For example, if A had committed a moral indiscretion that he did not want known, B, who happened to know of the indiscretion, might threaten to reveal it unless A paid him a large sum of money.   A might not be able to secure this money except by theft, and under the fear of exposure might steal the money to pay B.   If B did not again try to blackmail A, it is probable that A would not again steal.

Perhaps more common episodic crimes than thefts are personal assault and murder. Some assaults and murders are elements in a complex of crime or are calculated methods of subduing people; such assaults are not episodic but are usually part of the repertoire of the professional criminal. Thus the criminal gang that deliberately kills a member, who is believed to be on the verge of exposing its secrets, or the thief who uses a gun in the course of habitual stealing are not guilty of episodic crimes. But the woman who has learned that her husband has taken a mistress and who as the climax of her jealous rage kills her rival, has committed an episodic crime. Most murders or assaults that result from emotional frustration are episodic in nature. They grow out of a peculiar situation that is not likely to be repeated in the individual's experience. They are frequently the culmination of months of suspicion and uncertainty, followed by certain knowledge that an intimate emotional relationship has been violated or that a desired relationship is impossible.

Sometimes the episodic crime is committed by a drunken person. In this case, the crime may grow out of a momentary controversy with a stranger or it may be committed against a friend or member of the family. There is some reason to believe that such crimes are not primarily the result of the effect of alcohol, but rather that underlying emotional tensions usually suppressed find expression when alcohol releases normal inhibitions.[13] This psychological state may be as true of the assault on a stranger as of the assault on a friend. The stranger may thwart the drunkard and thus symbolize for him social restrictions that he finds oppressive. He assaults the stranger with the same violence that he would like to use against social conventions to which he submits unwillingly.

The truly episodic criminal is not a great menace to the community, provided the emotional difficulty that led to the crime can be smoothed out. But there is always the danger that, as a result of committing the crime, the offender may be shut off from normal community life and thus turn toward continued criminal activities, becoming an habitual, or even a professional criminal. Also, there is the possibility that the crime is not motivated by a temporary emotional disturbance but represents the first manifestation of the permanent disorganization attendant upon a psychosis.

SEGMENTAL CRIME

As discussed in Chapter 1, segmental crime consists of criminal activities that have become part of the occupational life of a person and that are accepted as normal in the framework of that occupation. The person accepts the criminal activities as the customary or practical ways in which to operate in the occupation, although the principles involved may run counter to other ethical principles by which he controls his nonoccupational life.   The person's criminal acts are, therefore, merely one segment of his total personality, and in other relationships he is ethical, law-abiding, and opposed to crime.

The first sociological studies of segmental crime were made by E. H. Sutherland, who was interested in what he called white-collar crime, or crimes carried out in the course of legitimate business or professional operations.[14]   Essentially the same types of crime are also carried on by some labor unions and some government officials.   Whether segmental crimes occur in business, profession, union, or government, certain characteristics tend to distinguish them from other types of crime.

Characteristics of Segmental Crime

In his many writings on the subject, Sutherland gradually evolved a description of white-collar crime, which applies also to other types of segmental crime.   White-collar (segmental) crime is essentially a business or professional practice that is sharp and therefore unethical or actually illegal. As a rule, it is not a private crime of some one person in the organization, but is part of an accepted practice known and acceded to by the officers and top-ranking employees, all of whom tend to gain.   In a business, investors may also gain; in a union, members; in government, a selected group.   The segmental criminal tends to be a person of respectability and high status in his occupational group and in his community.

Most segmental crimes are financial in nature.   They are, moreover, in continuous operation, since they are part of the method by which a business, government office, or union is carried on.   They differ from many professional crimes, bank robbery, for instance, in which each crime is carefully planned, carried out, and definitively ended.   Segmental crime is similar to the operation of a criminal syndicate in that it is everyday operation of an organization.   However, the function of the organization is legitimate whereas in the criminal syndicate the business itself is forbidden by criminal law.

Some types of segmental crime are scarcely distinguishable from professional criminalism.   Goldman, in *You Pay and You Pay,* gives many illustrations of the criminal who operates through a seemingly legitimate business but deliberately violates the law.[15]   Thus there are loan sharks who, by trick contracts and personal threats, force small borrowers to pay exorbitant sums in interest, which are forbidden by law.   Another type of business criminal is the dealer who sells household furniture on installments and charges an exorbitant rate of interest.   He expects the buyer to default on his payments, and when he does so the dealer repossesses the furniture and sells it to a confederate for a small sum, although payments to cover the balance are still demanded from the original buyer. Income-tax evasion, practiced by falsifying statements of profit, is another type of business crime that is obviously illegal.

Another type of segmental crime verges into activities that are technically legal, although they are comparable to recognized criminal activities. Goldman cites the deputy collectors of poll and excise taxes who are compensated not by a fixed salary but by fees paid for collections. This method of payment is provided by law. However, by careful manipulation the collectors are able to pile up unjustified fees that the citizen must pay; often the amount of such fees is larger than the amount of the tax. Another form of legalized theft is found in the charging of exorbitant fees for special services. For instance, a public administrator of an estate with no known heirs may manage by unjustified fees to absorb it instead of turning it over to the state as provided by law. Still another example is the practice of some employers, who induce an injured employee to sign a release giving up compensation for the injury or an agreement to accept a small payment. There are many ways in which legal requirements may be technically observed, although evaded in actual performance.

A third type of segmental crime grows out of large organizations, such as business corporations, large labor unions, or certain governmental agencies. In his discussion of business crimes, Sutherland has included not only violations of criminal laws but also violations of other laws intended for the control of business practices. In a special study of 70 corporations he included the following: violations of laws regulating the restraint of trade; misrepresentation in advertising; infringement of patents, copyrights, and trademarks; unfair labor practices; rebates; financial fraud and violation of trust; and violations of war regulations.[16] Violations of these laws usually are investigated and regulated through commissions, such as the Federal Trade Commission, which, among other things, moves against misrepresentation in advertising; or by such administrative agencies as the Food and Drug Administration. Administrative agencies usually resort to courts only in the most flagrant cases of violation of laws or when the corporation refuses to stop the violation; thus many cases are settled without recourse to a criminal court and without stigmatizing the officers of the corporation as criminals. Still other legal violations are handled through civil courts, again without the shame of criminal stigma or danger of imprisonment. In a study of 980 adverse decisions against 70 large corporations because of violations of laws, Sutherland found that only 16 per cent of the decisions were made by criminal courts.[17]

Unethical or illegal practices in government also are often handled by investigating committees.   Sometimes local law enforcement officials follow up such investigations with legal prosecutions; but in other cases the irregularities lead simply to reprimand or dismissal from the service.   Since the end of World War II, a number of unethical or illegal practices have been flushed into the open, often as a result of probing by a Congressional investigating commission.   The practices resemble business crime, inasmuch as they are not the systematic procedure of a corrupt political machine, but center in one governmental official, often of high rank, or in one department. Public pride in the federal government was badly shattered by these disclosures.   Often the defection of the government official was linked with illegal activities of a business concern; in fact, Senator Paul H. Douglas suggests that the initiative for unethical or criminal conniving comes from private sources—businessmen who see a chance to increase their profits if they can control the actions of governmental officials.[18]   Allowing themselves to be persuaded by open or concealed bribes, officials use their powers to manipulate legislative or administrative actions for the benefit of the businessmen (and of themselves) but to the detriment of the public.

In the early 1950's irregularities were discovered in the practices of a number of district and subdistrict offices of the Bureau of Internal Revenue. Many collectors and employees were forced to resign, and several collectors were convicted of illegalities.   The evidence showed that some collectors had accepted money from individuals or corporations whose taxes were out of order; thereupon favorable settlements were made with the delinquent taxpayers.   In other cases, the collectors operated private insurance companies; men who bought insurance from the collectors were not required to meet their full tax obligations.

An investigation of the Reconstruction Finance Corporation disclosed that loans were made to businesses that were not sound financially and were headed for bankruptcy or that already had sufficient funds to tide themselves over a hard spot.   It often developed that the RFC official who had been responsible for the loan soon resigned from the RFC to accept a position at a much higher salary with a business that had been granted large sums unjustifiably.   For example, in one case the loan examiner recommended that a certain loan should not be made.   An RFC official nevertheless granted a large loan and within a month resigned his position to accept a position with the company so favored, at 3 times his salary with the RFC.[19]

Labor unions, swollen in size and commanding great power in the continuity of industrial operations, also have been guilty of unethical and illegal practices.[20]   The sitdown strikes of 1937 were condemned by the courts, both state and federal.   The secondary boycott, "featherbedding," and jurisdictional strikes were forbidden by the Taft-Hartley Act of 1947.   Ethical principles and fairdealing are slowly being demanded of powerful unions.

Is Unethical Behavior Crime?

The tendency to handle the illegalities of large organizations through commissions and civil courts raises an interesting problem.   Among the corporations studied, technically only the 16 per cent of violations tried in the criminal courts were crimes.   All others, although legal offenses, were not crimes.   Sutherland contends, however, that all are crimes in essence, although for special reasons they are not so treated.   The criteria that he uses for criminal behavior are: Is the prohibited behavior defined in law as socially harmful; is there legal (though not necessarily in criminal law) provision of a penalty for the act?   He found many types of prohibited behavior that met these criteria but that were regulated by commissions or civil courts rather than criminal courts.   In the history of the 70 corporations he found 980 adverse decisions for violations of noncriminal laws, 2 corporations having 50 decisions each and only 2 having but 1 violation. It is Sutherland's position that these business offenses, regardless of how they are handled, are comparable to such individual crimes as larceny, embezzlement, securing money under false pretenses, and the like.   If we accept Sutherland's argument, then business firms, accepted as reputable by the public, are in reality sometimes comparable in their behavior to many organized criminal groups, and indeed Sutherland states that "white-collar crime is organized crime."

Other sociologists, however, would categorize as crime only acts that are so defined by the criminal laws.   Tappan, who designates himself a lawyer-sociologist, points out the difficulties that arise when anti-social conduct rather than legally defined criminal acts are made the subject of study.[21] In the absence of nationally accepted standards of anti-social conduct, each sociologist, in fact every individual, feels free to establish his own standards. Consequently, there is no clear-cut delineation of the group to be studied. Tappan points out that anti-social conduct and violation of general conduct norms constitute an important field of study, but that only those people can be termed criminals who have been convicted of violation of criminal laws. Although laws vary from place to place and from time to time, in any given time and place they afford a definite standard of conduct.   Tappan does not accept Sutherland's definition of white-collar crime as inclusive of violations of civil laws.

Another opponent of the concept of white-collar crime as inclusive of violations of civil laws regulating business is E. W. Burgess.[22]   Burgess' objection differs from Tappan's, however, inasmuch as he feels that a purely sociological concept of crime should be upheld.   From this point of view, crimes are only those acts long regarded as antisocial in the mores and that are embodied in criminal laws; people who commit the long-accepted crimes regard themselves and are regarded by the public as criminals.   Burgess excludes from the criminal category both violations of traffic regulations and such wartime regulations as the Emergency Price Control Act and the Second War Powers Act that regulated many aspects of business during World War II.   He defends his statement by saying that the violators of these laws are not criminal in personality, do not move in the criminal world, and are not regarded by the public as criminals.   Acceptance of Burgess' concept of crime would tend to eliminate from the group of criminals not only those whose law violations are handled by commissions and civil courts but also offenders of criminal laws who customarily live in the conventional or non-criminal world.

Transition from Unethical to Criminal Behavior

The anomalous status of corporation and allied types of crime can best be understood by reviewing its development.   The growth of the United States has called for collective efforts on the part of business, labor, and government.   The result has been big business, big labor, and big government—massive organizations that operate on an impersonal level.   The change from personal relationships to impersonal organizations came too rapidly for personal ethical standards to be translated into controlling regulations for large organized groups.   As the General Counsel of the Ford Motor Company states, "bigness did not come to us complete with operating instructions.   There were no well-developed rules to govern the conduct of the new group personalities that comprise bigness.   In a very real sense, the large aggregations of capital that are big business, and the large aggregations of workers that are big labor, began their operations in a legal and moral vacuum." [23]

Some of the reasons for unethical or downright criminal practices carried out jointly by government officials and businessmen are similar to the factors that underlie illegal activities of corporations and business firms acting alone. Douglas points out that certain phases of government have grown to ponderous size involving enormous sums of money; there is, as a result, a constant temptation to manipulate government in order to divert some of the money from public to private uses. [24]   The impersonality of government at the federal level in a country of more than 150,000,000 people glosses over a sense of guilt.   The business manipulations of the federal government—letting of war-material contracts, granting of subsidies, and the like—comprise an area of greater potential corruption than the strictly service functions, such as education or social welfare.   Great fortunes and private gains may be made in connection with the business functions, and hence the temptation is great for both officials and businessmen.   Administrators often are given unrestricted authority to make decisions, a situation arising from the new-ness of some governmental functions; there are few precedents from past ex-perience.   Often ethical standards and safeguards have not been established to guide the administrator.

Another factor in the development of unethical or criminal organizational behavior is emphasized by Clinard, who studied black market operations during World War II.[25]   He calls attention to the lack of consensus of opin-ions as to social values and the tendency of each group in society to follow practices that benefit its members regardless of the public welfare, but at the same time to condemn similar practices of other groups.   This lack of uni-formity of opinion is inherent in a rapidly changing, impersonal, urban so-ciety.

The individualistic and materialistic emphasis of our society is also cited by Clinard as a factor.   It should be added that the individualism is linked with a belief in the value of upward social mobility, the degree of which is measured in part in terms of wealth and business success.   A strongly up-held value in the United States, therefore, might be stated as individual am-bition to be achieved through material success.   The individual businessman or the small group that composes the corporation may pull up with them a large retinue of employees and may benefit the consuming public.   But they do not necessarily do so.   Especially in their early years of growth, corpora-tions often oppressed the labor force, exploited the public, crowded smaller competitors out of business, and maneuvered laws to their own advantage. Laws now prohibit many of these activities.   Nevertheless, the emphasis is still on individual, materialistic success.

The desire for material success is not limited to businessmen; it motivates the entire public.   Just as the criminal syndicate could not exist without consumers to buy its wares, or the swindler could not operate without avari-cious victims, so much illegal business could not function without the co-operation of the public.   A startling example of the public's acquiescence in illegal activities came during World War II in the operation of the black market.   This term was applied to attempts to evade or mitigate the effects of governmental controls designed to establish equal distribution of scarce goods and to prevent inflation.   The regulations included rent controls, price controls, and rationing of essential but scarce goods, such as gas, certain foods and types of wearing apparel, and some construction and industrial materials.   Clinard's discussion shows that all along the line from manu-facturer or producer through wholesaler and retailer to the consumer there were violations, with each group trying to increase its supply above the prescribed amount or trying to boost prices above the ceiling.[26] No one group involved in the process could evade the regulations without the co-operation of other groups. Clinard points out that this grasping after more profits or more goods was carried out at a time when the United States was involved in the most tremendous national effort ever made to win a war. Nevertheless, immediate acquisitiveness outweighed the nonmaterial value of winning the war.

Need for Control

Whether the ruthless actions of large organizations are regarded as un-ethical or in essence criminal, there is need for control, in order to protect the public; to prevent social disorganization; and to offset the ease with which traditional criminals can rationalize their own crimes by citing the practices of corporations, unions, and government. These three reasons are ex-amined in more detail.

1. The trend from small to large business makes it increasingly imperative to protect the public in their role as customers. In small businesses, the proprietor deals personally with the customer. Such a relationship tends to become personal and the proprietor finds it difficult to betray his customer. In the large corporation, the officers or controlling board do not know many of the customers personally. Nor do the customers know the officers. The officers and board therefore do not have a personal feeling of guilt when some practice is adopted that will increase earnings at the expense of customers.

If the customer does feel that he has been unfairly treated, usually he can do no more than protest to a local agent, who did not make the policies and can do nothing more than forward a protest to his superiors, who may be several steps removed from the controlling board.

The customer, even when he suspects he is being cheated, has no way to prove it. Even if it were possible for him to examine the books of the cor-poration (which is usually prohibited by the charters of large corporations) he would not be in a position to understand and interpret what he saw. The crimes of corporations are known only to themselves and their lawyers; their discovery is usually the work of experts and specialists.

Because of the financial power of large corporations and the prestige in which businessmen are held in the United States, laws are often protective of corporations to the detriment of the public. Some large corporations bring pressure on state and federal legislators to pass laws favorable to their corporations even though they may be detrimental to the public welfare; or persuade them to refuse to pass laws that might curb practices that bring profit but are not for the public good. In this way certain corporations or industries are favored, perhaps to the detriment of competitors or the public.

2. Antisocial conduct on the part of any group represents a threat to the unity of a society and is a step toward social disorganization. We recognize this threat in the case of direct stealing by the professional criminal, in the gross exploitation of the rackets, and in the widespread activities of criminal syndicates. Many organizational crimes are concealed and operate under the guise of necessary business operations. They may, however, be opposed to the welfare of the public, as in misrepresentation of advertising, substandard quality of products, excessive demands of unions, or manipulation of government for private gain. It is true that the entire operation of the organization is not antisocial or in opposition to laws, as is true of many professional criminal activities. Nevertheless, to the extent that organizations practice and rationalize as necessary or valid activities that are antisocial or against public welfare, they constitute a threat. The fact that the same organizations may also benefit the public in other ways does not offset the injurious quality of segmental antisocial practices.

3. Complete autonomy of any group with reference to practices affecting public welfare is a step toward disorganization. Autonomy implies that any group may establish its own standards of right and wrong and may decide which laws it will support and which disregard. Such disregard of the law is often permitted criminal syndicates as well as legal business. In either case it is a movement toward ruthless individualism and disregard for the common good. As Clinard in his study of the black market during World War II points out, the logical conclusion of selective obedience to the law on the part of all groups would lead to a "complete breakdown of law and order and the termination of the democratic process." [27]

Business crime is often an indication of the failure to extend to large corporations principles well developed in the past for controlling crime on a personal basis. The basic criminal laws, derived from the common law of England, primarily concern the protection of the person and property from violations based on a personal or face-to-face relationship. In relation to these crimes, which are well entrenched in the mores, there is little uncertainty, either with regard to what constitutes the crime or what the punishment should be. New and complex social institutions—such as corporations—cannot be controlled by the old laws. New formulations of honesty and fair dealing are needed and new types of control. Usually the new laws, methods of inspection, and boards of investigation and control are not established until some abuse has become excessively injurious to the public. For example, the antitrust acts were passed only after certain monopolies had brought disaster to small competing companies; in a personal relationship, equivalent action would undoubtedly have been punished under the basic criminal laws. But no existent law controlled the action of corporations. New laws had to be enacted for that purpose. Similarly, wild speculation in stocks and the unlimited development of holding companies were not curbed until after the depression, in the early 1930's, had brought ruin to many unwise investors. It is therefore possible for many abuses to arise and become widespread before there are measures to control them.

4. Finally, semicriminal practices that are not controlled or are handled by civil means that do not damage the prestige of the offenders afford to professional criminals a rationalization for their own offenses. The professional criminal is not concerned with the justifications advanced by business to defend misrepresentation or exploitation, nor with the niceties of distinction between civil and criminal offenses. If he knows of sharp business practices, legal or illegal, he is able to defend his own crimes as similar in essence to them.

Means of Control

There are three possibilities of control. The present system of regulation through commissions, administrative groups, and civil courts may be continued. Sutherland regards such regulation as inadequate and also as protective of the officers and employees who set the irregular activities in motion, since they are not individually branded as criminals nor made to pay a penalty personally through fines or imprisonment.[28] These means, however, may be less disruptive of the economy than criminal action would be; also in a period when values are in a state of flux they may be more effective than criminal laws that might prove difficult or impossible to enforce without the backing of public opinion—as the war regulations of goods and prices were.

The present regulations might be converted into criminal laws and all violations tried in criminal courts. This move would bring some uniformity to standards applied to individuals and to organizations, and to the penalties applied for violation. Clinard lists 4 reasons why white-collar crimes are not brought under the criminal law; his reasons would also apply to some other types of organizational offenses.[29] He states, first, that public resentment against white-collar crimes is unorganized and lacks sufficient force to get criminal laws passed; second, the extent and consequences of white-collar crime are not recognized by the public; third, the diversity of opinion as to the seriousness of white-collar crime would make enforcement of a criminal law difficult, whereas civil laws can be enforced and thus provide regulation; and fourth, the lack of consensus of opinion arises from the complexity of violations, their concealment under normal business practices, their specialized character, and the failure of the press to give publicity to white-collar crimes.

A third possibility is self-control by organizations. Douglas, for example, believes there is a need for a code of ethics for men and women in government and for stated standards and rules of procedures.[30] Many professional and business groups now have codes, but they are not always sufficiently comprehensive nor self-denying to give the public protection.

The Development of the Segmental Criminal

Although much of the discussion on the segmental criminal has been given in terms of patterns of organizational crime, the offender himself is still central to the problem. Granted that business, professions, unions, and government offer many opportunities for unethical or criminal conduct and often have developed established patterns of such conduct, nevertheless, not all persons attached to large organizations are unethical and not all organizations tolerate or practice unfair methods of conducting their functions. We return, therefore, to the same question that arose when we found that in spite of high delinquency rates in slum areas, not all slum adolescents were delinquent. The conditions favorable to delinquency or crime and the rationalizations by which people justify their offenses are only part of the picture. Some selective process takes place by which certain people become lawbreakers while others abide by the law.

Personal disorganization and the overt expression of conflicts and frustrations through crimes constitute one theory often advanced to account for the selective factor in juvenile delinquency. This theory is less readily applied to the adult segmental criminal, whose total mode of life does not indicate personal confusion.

Sutherland advances another hypothesis, which he calls differential association, or the learning of illegal and criminal business practices through association with persons already skilled in these practices and with a business philosophy to justify them.[31] When a young person enters a business for the first time as an employee he may find illegal practices already well-established. He is expected to accept and conform to these practices. Higher salary and greater prestige accrue to the employee who conforms. This is essentially the same learning hypothesis that accounts for much of the growth of delinquent behavior in slum areas.

The actual evidence on the development of the segmental criminal at present is too fragmentary for any positive statement of the process by which the business or professional man, the union official, or the government official introduces crime into his work or accepts previously established criminal patterns when he affiliates himself with a large-scale organization.

QUESTIONS

1. Contrast the casual offender and the occasional offender with the professional criminal, with reference to their attitude toward their offenses and toward themselves as criminals.

2. Studies that compare occasional offenders with confirmed offenders reveal what differences in personal and social background?   Do these differences seem sufficient to account for the fact that some occasional offenders remain essentially law abiding, whereas others drift into the criminal group?

3. How do you account for the development of segmental crime as it is practiced in large organizations?

4. In what ways does the public encourage segmental crime?

5. How might unethical practices and segmental crime of large organizations be controlled?   Which method would be most effective at the present time?

READINGS

Callender, Clarence N., and James C. Charlesworth (eds.), "Ethical Standards in American Public Life," *Annals of the American Academy of Political and Social Science,* Vol. 280 (1952).   In 19 articles public ethics are discussed with reference to elections, governmental agencies, business, the press, churches, colleges, and other institutions.   Of special interest is the article by H. R. Bowen entitled "How Public Spirited Is American Business?"

Clinard, Marshall B., *The Black Market* (Rinehart, 1952).   This study of the black market during World War II brings out in sharp relief the conniving of business, criminals, and consumers to evade the laws controlling the sale of scarce materials.

Douglas, Paul H., *Ethics in Government* (Cambridge: Harvard University Press, 1952).   In this series of lectures, Senator Douglas reviews ethical practices in the federal government and states reasons why it is difficult in "big government" to maintain high standards.

Sutherland, E. H., *White-Collar Crime* (Dryden, 1949).   Through a study of legal violations by 70 corporations, Sutherland develops his thesis that businessmen and corporations, although highly respected, actually commit many criminal acts; he also states his theory of criminality in terms of differential association.

FOOTNOTES

[1] F. P. McEvoy, "The Lie Detector Goes into Business," *Reader's Digest,* 38 (Feb., 1941), 69–72.

[2] M. B. Clinard, "Rural Criminal Offenders," *American Journal of Sociology,* 50 (1944), 38–45.

[3] Sheldon and Eleanor T. Glueck, *Juvenile Delinquents Grown Up* (New York: Commonwealth Fund, 1940), pp. 16, 26, 43, 59.

[4] Sheldon and Eleanor T. Glueck, *Five Hundred Delinquent Women* (Knopf, 1934), p. 236.

[5] *Ibid.*, pp. 28–32, 142–47.

[6] A. A. Bruce, *et al.*, *The Workings of the Indeterminate-Sentence Law and the Parole System in Illinois* (Springfield: The State of Illinois, 1928), pp. 206–8.

[7] A. L. Porterfield, "Delinquency and Its Outcome in Court and College," *American Journal of Sociology,* 49 (1943), 199–204.

[8] Sheldon and Eleanor T. Glueck, *One Thousand Juvenile Delinquents* (Cambridge: Harvard University Press, 1934), pp. 179–80.

[9] L. J. Doshay, *The Boy Sex Offender and His Later Career* (New York: Grune and Stratton, 1943).

[10] S. H. Riemer, "Embezzlement: Pathological Basis," *Journal of Criminal Law and Criminology,* 32 (1941), 411–23. Riemer's sixth type is not discussed as it does not represent the occasional crime.

[11] R. C. Angell, *The Family Encounters the Depression* (Scribner's, 1936), pp. 70–85.

[12] Morris Ploscowe, *Crime and Criminal Law,* The National Law Library, 11 (New York: Collier, 1939), 6–18.

[13] J. H. Cassidy, "Personality Study of 200 Murderers," *Journal of Criminal Psychopathology,* 2 (1940–41), 296–304.

[14] E. H. Sutherland, *White-Collar Crime* (Dryden, 1949); "Crime and Business," *Annals of the American Academy of Political and Social Science,* 217 (1941), 112–18; "White-Collar Criminality," in *Dealing with Delinquency,* National Probation Association Yearbook (1941), pp. 138–55; "White-Collar Criminality," *American Sociological Review,* 5 (1940), 1–12.

[15] M. M. Goldman, *You Pay and You Pay* (Howell, Soskin, 1941).

[16] Sutherland, *White-Collar Crime.*

[17] *Ibid.*, pp. 22–24.

[18] Paul H. Douglas, *Ethics in Government* (Cambridge: Harvard University Press, 1952.)

[19] *Ibid.*, p. 112.

[20] W. T. Gossett, "The Law and Group Ethics," *The Law School Record* (University of Chicago Law School), 3, No. 1 (1954), 22–24.

[21] P. W. Tappan, "Who Is the Criminal?" *American Sociological Review,* 12 (1947), 96–102.

[22] E. W. Burgess, "Comment," on F. E. Hartung, "White-Collar Offenses in the Wholesale Meat Industry in Detroit," *American Journal of Sociology,* 56 (1950), 25–34.

[23] Gossett, *op. cit.,* p. 6.

[24] Douglas, *op. cit.*

[25] Marshall B. Clinard, *The Black Market* (Rinehart, 1952).

[26] *Ibid.*

[27] *Ibid.*, ch. 12.

[28] Sutherland, *White-Collar Crime.*

[29] M. B. Clinard, "Sociologists and American Criminology," *Journal of Criminal Law and Criminology,* 41 (1951), 549–77.

[30] Douglas, *op. cit.*

[31] Sutherland, *White-Collar Crime,* ch. 14.

8

Habitual Offenders

The types of criminals so far discussed have normal personalities on the whole. Some of them—the professional criminals—have organized their lives on a criminal basis; they accept crime as an occupation and as a way of life. They think rationally and direct their thinking toward a realistic goal; their emotions are the normal ones of love and hate, admiration and disgust, and these emotions are aroused and expressed in normal ways. Their way of life is not that of the conventional community, but it differs only in social relationships, traditions, and attitudes. The professional criminal is socially a criminal because he has learned the techniques and accepted the traditions and codes of crime. He is not mentally abnormal; his mind and his emotions function as do those of his more conventional fellow-man.

Similarly, the typical occasional offender and the white-collar criminal are not mentally or emotionally maladjusted. They live primarily in the conventional world and do not regard themselves as criminals, for they rationalize and justify their criminal activities so that they feel neither regret nor anxiety. This process is relatively simple because criminal activities shade into legal but unethical activities and these into legal and ethical ones; thus the perpetrator of a criminal activity can easily regard it as merely unethical or even as ethical. The situation is complicated by the fact that legal provisions are not always ethical, that is, they may be unjust to large groups of citizens. The conflicting standards of different cultural groups also make it easy to find justification in one group for acts that may be condemned by another. Thus the occasional offender and the segmental criminal may go serenely along, violating the law, but in a perfectly healthy state of mind.

The professional criminal, the occasional criminal, and the segmental criminal share one thing in common. Their crimes are usually financial. They steal, swindle, operate confidence games, gain money by graft or extortion, sell an illegal service, or violate a trust—all with the simple object of making money.   When violence occurs it is usually because someone has interfered with this money-making process.   In a legal business someone who obstructed operations would be arrested and fined, or a judgment brought against him to restrain his obstructive tactics.   But such recourse to law is not open to a criminal whose occupation is itself illegal.   Moreover, the process of law is slow and uncertain of outcome.   The criminal seeks a swift and sure method and the obstructionist is simply killed and thus eliminated.   This type of violence is unemotional, and is in fact usually performed not by the person who feels he has been obstructed but by a hired killer who may not even know his victim by sight.

The habitual offender differs from the professional, occasional, and segmental criminals in that his offense is not some form of extracting money illegally from others, but is a vice—a debilitating habit that affects his own integrity and efficiency.   The habitual offender comes close to the ranks of the mentally and emotionally disturbed offenders to be discussed in the next chapter.   In fact, some of them undoubtedly fall into the class of persons with psychoneurotic or psychopathic personalities.   The term habitual offender is here used to designate the person who has acquired some habitual behavior, harmful to himself, that is also forbidden by criminal laws.   The term should not be confused with the more technical term, habitual criminal, used in some statutes to single out for special penalties the criminal who has repeated his crime a certain number of times.

Habitual offenders are not the glamorous and spectacular criminals who make front-page news.   They do not commit the daring crimes that bring a gasp from staid citizens and spur the police and federal agents to pursuit.   Nor do they commit the technically skilled, financial crimes of the professional criminal, who has regular methods of disposing of his goods and of avoiding arrest or conviction.   The offenses of the habitual criminal are habits in the literal sense of the word, which have been made illegal.   Clear examples of habitual offenders are disorderly habitual drunkards, compulsive gamblers, drug addicts, vagrants, prostitutes, and certain types of male sex offenders.   Many habitual offenders also commit crimes, especially stealing, for one of the characteristics of most habitual offenses is that they are debilitating and in time incapacitate the individual for earning a living.   Often, also, one offense leads into another: the drunkard becomes a vagrant, the female drug addict a prostitute, or the prostitute a drunkard.

PERSONALITY OF HABITUAL OFFENDERS

The misdemeanors of habitual offenders are personal vices that, long continued, debilitate the offender.   As a consequence, the status of the habitual offender in both conventional and criminal worlds is low.   Often he lives on the border line, with respected status in neither world.   Criminals as well as non-criminals respect and applaud success.   A clever criminal receives acclaim from other criminals.   A successful worker, business executive, or professional man gains approval in the conventional world.   But the habitual offender has not achieved either type of success.   He may encounter either the disgust or the pity of the conventional world; he usually is scorned and shunned by successful criminals.   There is reason to believe that in many cases the habitual offender develops because he is not able to achieve success in competition with other persons, whether criminal or noncriminal.

Some writers regard the actions of the habitual offender as symptoms of physical or mental inferiority; others as the result of psychopathic personality; and still others as the result of patterns of social relationships, originally established within the family or in early vocational efforts, which in some way lead to the development of the habits of the habitual offender.   For example, an analysis of alcoholics by Harriet Mowrer points out that children and youth who later became alcoholics had ambiguous status within the family, uncertain or low with regard to certain members of the family but high with regard to others.[1]   Unable to maintain or to improve the high status on the basis of legitimate personal achievement, the individual tried first one symbol of status, then another, drinking among them.   When the drinking brought attention, pampering, pity, and plans for reform from the family, the habit became established as a way to achieve what realistic competition with other members of the family could not.

The psychopathological approach not only to alcoholism, but to drug addiction, vagrancy, and prostitution, links these habits to various inferiorities in the inherited or acquired personality that prevent successful social or vocational relationships.[2]   Dull mentality, emotional immaturity, emotional instability, dependence, pathological jealousy, and latent homosexuality are some of the traits variously assigned to habitual offenders, all of which prevent a satisfactory social adjustment.   Whether the basis of the difficulty is in innate traits or in social relationships—the point does not seem to be definitely settled—it seems certain that many habitual offenders are in some way unable to compete successfully with their fellow-men, whether conventional or criminal.

Many types of habitual offenses are in the nature of personal vices that undermine physical efficiency and self-confidence.   The habitual offender is often caught in a vicious circle: he cannot compete because of some shortcoming; he acquires a habit that seems to give relief from his inability, but which in reality increases it and renders him still more unable to compete.   For example, many girl sex delinquents come from the ranks of domestics or

low-paid unskilled workers.   They are generally poorly educated, many are
of low-grade although not subnormal intelligence, their earning power is
poor; some are detached from their families and are lonely, lacking normal
opportunities to meet boys or men under some supervision.   In order to
have fun and adventure or to increase her income, or both, such a girl begins
to have sexual relations, usually with men older than herself, who are able to
pay or give her gifts.   But the late hours, the occasional pregnancy, the
probability of venereal infections, the habituation to sexual stimulation, the
acquisition of a "bad name," all tend to decrease the probability of improving
conventional social contacts and legitimate earnings.   The girl, therefore,
turns more and more toward prostitution until it sets the pattern of her life
and she becomes unable to conform to the conventional routine of work
and social contacts, even if she so desires.   A vice debilitates the person who
indulges in it, and makes achievement by ordinary standards increasingly
difficult.

A vice also gives artificial satisfaction of a temporary nature, and often
establishes a permanent craving.   Thus the habitual offender satisfies himself through his offense and does not really seek to be "cured" of his bad
habits.   He adjusts himself to living with his vice and in time stops rationalizing or defending his position.   He becomes demoralized, that is, he no
longer tries to abide by the mores of the community, or to re-establish himself in the eyes of reputable people.   He narrows his needs to a few, chiefly
physical, and lives with the least possible effort.   Arrests have little or no
effect upon him.

The offenses of the habitual offender usually result in short jail terms or
fines, which he works out in jail.   At the end of the jail term he returns to
his old community and repeats the process.   Thus the matron of the Omaha
jail commented on the women arrested (primarily for disorderly conduct,
drunkenness, and prostitution) that most of them were recidivists.   Released
after a lecture or a short jail term they returned to their old haunts in rundown areas where rents were low.   Whatever friends they had were there,
and from them they could get help as well as companionship.[3]

The habitual offender is the most numerous in the criminal group.   He is
rarely represented in criminal statistics, which are usually limited to those
who commit felonies—the more serious crimes.   But the habitual offenders
account for the bulk of arrests made.   The statistics given in Chapter 2
show that for every arrest for a Class 1 crime there are 10 arrests for minor
habitual offenses.   These offenses are tried in police courts, before justices
of the peace, or in municipal or county courts.   The offenders may be reprimanded and released, fined, given a short jail sentence or—especially if
they have frequently appeared before the same judge—given a longer term

at a prison farm. These cases are routine, unspectacular, unknown to the public, but they comprise a large part of the work of the law enforcement machinery of the country.

ILLEGALITY OF HABITUAL OFFENSES

As was pointed out in Chapter 1, criminal laws have as their objective preservation of public safety and welfare. Therefore, laws prohibiting personal vices are based on the premise that any large proportion of degraded persons is a hindrance to the general public welfare. The safety and welfare of others may be threatened by the habitual offenders, either physically or because offenders cannot discharge family obligations. Offenders also become a drag on the community financially since they often are unable to support themselves. These are the ostensible justifications for classifying personal vices as criminal offenses. Actually, another motive enters into the thinking of legislators and the public: vices are immoral according to many ethical and religious standards and there is a tendency to confuse personal immorality with criminal acts that are harmful to others. Whatever the reasoning behind the laws, habitual offenders are identified with the criminal group and are subjected to the same routine of arrest, and fines or imprisonment as criminals.

Often, also, there is a gradation in the degree to which a person indulges in forbidden behavior. The mild drinker, the moderate user of drugs, the occasionally promiscuous woman, and the person who gambles in small amounts, although perhaps technically lawbreakers, actually are not likely to be arrested. When the habits become deep-seated, when they interfere with normal social obligations, when they become a public nuisance, and when others are in some way threatened, then the law is likely to be called into effect.

RELATION OF HABITUAL OFFENDERS TO CRIMINAL
SYNDICATES

Many habitual offenders are in some way dependent upon organized crime, in that they are customers for the goods or services supplied by criminal syndicates or they are the last link in passing these goods or services on to customers. Organized criminal groups illegally import narcotic drugs, which are then passed through various middlemen, with dilution of the drug at each transfer, finally to come into the possession of the anonymous drug peddler on the street corner who is also often an addict. The control of drug addiction is more nearly a problem of control of illegal importation and the elimination of organized syndicates than of arrests of innumerable peddlers who may easily be replaced so long as the supply of drugs is unchecked.   Gambling establishments also are the lucrative business of organized criminal groups. The little bookies as well as the thousands of people who place illegal bets or who gamble through policy games are dependent upon city- or nationwide activities of criminal syndicates.   Although a prostitute may operate individually, organized crime again has established houses of prostitution that give the prostitute the security of affiliation with an organization as well as protection from molestation by the police.   Wherever and whenever the manufacture and sale of alcoholic beverages are forbidden by law, criminal syndicates spring up to meet the demand for intoxicating drinks.   The corner tavern—the little retailer—depends upon the criminal syndicate for his supply.   Criminal syndicates may be compared to manufacturers or wholesalers who spread their wares through a vast network of retailers to whom customers come for supplies.   The drug addict, the gambler, the patron of prostitution, the illegal alcoholic have contacts with the retailers, but the source of goods and services is organized criminal groups.

The problem of the reduction of habitual crime, therefore, is threefold. The habitual offender himself must be controlled.   Since his offense often is in the nature of a personal vice (chronic drunkenness, habitual gambling, drug addiction, prostitution), he may need re-education or psychiatric assistance more than a jail sentence or fine.   The minor criminal who caters to the habitual offender must have his activities checked; this group would include the illegal liquor salesman, the local bookie or peddler of chances in a policy game, the drug peddler, and the panderer and operator of a house of prostitution.   Since many of these illegal vendors are also victims of the vice they sell, they may be in need of rehabilitation.   Finally, the organized criminal groups that systematize illegal services on a wide scale, that secure illegal alcohol or drugs, that supply the information on races, that arrange for protection from arrest and prosecution, must also be eliminated.

HABITUAL CRIME AND PUBLIC OPINION

The control and elimination of habitual vice are extremely difficult.   So long as there is a demand for alcohol, gambling, drugs, and prostitution, the need will be supplied.   The problem is complicated by the fact that many people enjoy moderate indulgence without noticeable personality breakdown; they defend their right to this indulgence.   It is difficult, if not impossible, to draw a clear line between moderate and harmful indulgence.   Public opinion ranges from support of no legal controls to belief that penalties should be made more and more severe for the vendors of vice, and that those who patronize vice should be subjected to penalties or to medical and psychiatric treatment on a compulsory basis. At present there is not a definite and consistent policy. The trend is for control of personal indulgences to follow a cycle from no control to ever more severe repression of the activity and, when that fails, back to moderate control or no control. The manufacture and sale of alcoholic beverages, once free of governmental control, were

Many communities today take the position that indulgence of personal vices is a personal rather than a public responsibility. Conforming to this attitude, they permit or even encourage gambling and prostitution. The photograph, taken in a southern city, shows "cribs" (the cheapest form of house of prostitution), of which there were many blocks. After long-drawn-out public protests, these houses were finally closed in the 1930's. Many people tend to use the confusion that exists in traditions and present-day attitudes to justify this and other types of non-conforming behavior. (Acme)

brought under moderate control; then complete repression was attempted through the Prohibition Amendment; when that failed, moderate controls were again established through taxing, licensing, and regulation of hours when liquor may be sold, age of persons to whom it may be sold, and many other details regarding the sale and use of liquor. Importation and sale of drugs have had increasingly severe controls established without eliminating illegal sales and nonmedical use. The trend is toward more strict laws, increased police action, and longer prison terms for convicted offenders. Divided public opinion is evident, however. An article in *Harper's Magazine* entitled

"Make Dope Legal" argues cogently for the establishment of public clinics where addicts might register and receive drugs with the hope of reduction in the amount required by the addict and perhaps eventual cure.[4]

Opinion is divided also as to whether gambling should be permitted or repressed. The May, 1950 issue of the *Annals of the American Academy of Political and Social Science* shows the vagaries of laws opposed to gambling whereby, for instance, some forms of gambling are prohibited by state laws but in the same state religious, charitable, fraternal, or nonprofit organizations are permitted to install slot machines.[5] Nevada, for more than 20 years, has permitted gambling under a system of licensing and the payment of local and state taxes. All other states have repressive laws, although most of them permit certain types of gambling under stated conditions. Minorities urge stricter repression on the one hand, and greater leniency on the other; many, perhaps most, people approve of laws in the name of public welfare but are very tolerant of evasions of the law. Meanwhile, organized criminal groups operate gambling establishments of various types and, in addition to breaking the laws prohibiting or regulating gambling, introduce many types of cheating so that the gambler lacks even the normal chance that he should have to win.

So far as public opinion is concerned, prostitution is in much the same position as gambling. There is probably a consensus of opinion that prostitution is against the public welfare, but at the same time there is an unwillingness to stamp it out. As a consequence, some communities attempt to segregate prostitution in certain areas, while others make all forms of prostitution illegal. The latter communities may not, however, enforce their laws rigorously. One of the complications is the shading off of prostitution into casual sexual contacts when the giving of a gift may replace outright money payments or, even further, into irregular sex activities without a commercial aspect. The growing public tolerance of nonmarital sex relations increases the difficulty of delimiting and controlling prostitution.

DRUNKARDS

Drunkenness is one of the most common of the habitual offenses. There is no single explanation as to why men and women begin to drink alcoholic beverages or of the conditions under which drinking becomes excessive. Drinking may be part of the social ritual of the family, clique, or occupational group to which they belong; it may be at first a part of major celebrations, such as the annual New Year's Eve party; or drinking may be initiated by a person's feelings of loneliness or inferiority, feelings that are alleviated by the effect of alcohol. But only when drinking leads to excessive and frequent indulgence associated with disorderliness that disturbs others does the drinking person become a public offender subject to arrest and punishment.   Forty states recognize such drunkenness as an offense and provide for its punishment; in 8 states municipalities regulate it.[6]   Usually the laws forbid boisterous or indecent conduct on the part of the drunkard, or loud or profane discourse in a public place or near a residence not the drunkard's own.   In addition, the laws may set special penalties for drunkenness of certain professional persons while on duty, such as doctors or nurses, and for driving an automobile while drunk.

Characteristics of the Alcoholic

The true habitual drunkard drinks persistently and craves alcohol for its own sake.   Since the person who is intoxicated over long periods of time is unfitted for work during these periods, he is soon in financial straits, and his failure to hold a job may lead to further drinking to bolster a decreasing sense of success.   Because a period of years is required before excessive drinking takes full effect, most habitual drunkards are middle aged or elderly.   Family life is often disrupted by alcoholism; either the habitual drunkard becomes a homeless vagrant, unable to work steadily and more and more dependent upon alcohol; or he is merely tolerated by family and neighbors.   If he is homeless he is unprotected when drunk, and his usual fate is arrest and a short period in jail.   A description of the former Women's Workhouse in New York City gives a striking picture of the habitual women drunkards who sink to a level of almost permanent intoxication.[7]

The admission routine this first year became abnormally heavy.   About 100 men and 25 women were admitted each morning.   If a woman had a 3 days' sentence, it worked out as follows: She was sentenced in the women's night court, and that was reckoned the first day.   The next morning, she was brought by boat to the workhouse, bathed, searched, given institution clothing, examined by the doctor, and assigned to a cell for the night.   This was the second day of her sentence.   The following morning she rose at 6, put on her own clothes, received her property if she had any, was put in a cell with the others who were being discharged, was fed, and then was taken by boat to 26th Street, where she was set at liberty.   That constituted the third day, and everyone had worked except the women who had been sentenced to the Workhouse.   Many of the women who were habitual drunkards and excitable when drunk were rearrested the day they were discharged, and returned on the boat the next morning to begin the round over again.   One woman . . . had not slept out of prison or jail for 6 years, having had an unbroken succession of 6 months' sentences for that length of time.   Another was serving her sixtieth sentence at the Workhouse, and several had been in and out nearly as many times as she . . . The largest category of women at the Workhouse was that of the chronic alcoholics who comprised most of the "rounders."   Sometimes an acute case on the verge of delirium tremens would be admitted, but most of our alcoholic cases were women who had spent only a few days at liberty before being rearrested.

Several short case excerpts illustrate by examples the type of person who is classed as the habitual drunkard. Ross Drew was a man of 50, who went on a spree about once every 2 or 3 months. Each drinking episode was preceded by several days of nervous moodiness, during which he continued to work. Then he disappeared from work for 3 or 4 days, a period spent in taverns; several additional days were required for him to sober up. He was a member of a family in Pittsburgh which operated a dry goods store, and as a younger man had operated his own store successfully and had married. It is not clear when or under what circumstances he began to drink. When the depression came his world crashed about him. He lost his savings in a bank that closed; lost the store; and lost his wife. Because of his drinking, which now became aggravated, his family refused to help him. He left Pittsburgh and settled in a smaller city some distance away, where in time he became a WPA employee. When he was sober he was a capable and dependable worker; he found a lodging house where his landlady took a personal interest in him, encouraged him in his work, and saw to it that he was always clean and neat in dress. Nevertheless, his periodic drinking continued. When he was sober he never talked about himself or his past, but when drunk he was garrulous and poured forth all his grievances against his family, his wife, the bank, and business conditions in general. He told glowing stories of his past business success and of the way in which he had indulged his wife and tried to please her. He said that he never wanted to see Pittsburgh again. When sober, all these difficulties, which he could not face and for which he could not accept personal responsibility, were repressed below the surface of verbal expression, perhaps to some extent below the level of consciousness. But periodically his conflicts and failures overwhelmed him and he again drank.[8] Only the tolerance and protection of his landlady and the WPA supervisors prevented him from becoming subject to frequent arrests.

An immigrant woman from Ireland had a long history of drunkenness.[9] She had married a man who was a persistent drunkard, with whom she often quarreled. Her 3 children died in infancy. She never had a steady home but worked as a chambermaid or charwoman in cheap hotels and lodging houses. She was well known to relief agencies. She had been alcoholic since she came to the United States and had a court record that extended over at least 26 years and probably longer; complete tracing of her early years was made impossible by the unavailability of records before 1898. In this year she was 34 years old and a confirmed drunkard. In the next 26 years she had been arrested at least 100 times, and was always found guilty. Although she was sometimes given a suspended sentence, she had served 49 sentences in penal institutions, had been in private reformatories 3 times, and on probation 14. When drunk she was violent and had twice been placed in a padded cell.

Drunkards, such as this one, are often taken to the city jail by the police, as much for their own protection as for their offense. The typical procedure is to release such a man the following day, whereupon he continues his delinquent behavior. (Acme)

Alcoholism as Illness

In a discussion of the habitual drunkard, the question may fairly be raised as to whether these people are criminal offenders in the same sense that automobile thieves or burglars are. Their "crime" is not a deliberate attempt to secure something for nothing, disregarding the rights of others. Rather, their antisocial behavior is a personal vice that slowly undermines their efficiency and releases actions and emotions that are usually inhibited. The offense to other persons is a by-product of this personal vice. Action by the police in many instances accomplishes little more than to remove the drunkard from public places until he has sobered up. Certainly fines or jail sentences of whatever duration do little to prevent the habitual drunkard from repeating his offense. Habitual drunkenness is more in the nature of an illness—both physical and mental—than a crime and should receive specialized treatment.

An attack on the problem of alcoholism is being made by the Yale Plan Clinics, 2 of which were established at New Haven and Hartford in 1944.[10] These clinics, staffed by psychiatrists, psychologists, and physicians, take the point of view that the real problem of the alcoholic is not that he is using alcohol; but that he has an underlying maladjustment for which alcoholism becomes the remedy. Insistence upon total abstinence is combined with diagnosis of the underlying problem and guidance to aid the alcoholic toward greater maturity and development of new interests and life habits.

Alcoholics Anonymous is an organization that also attacks chronic alcoholism as an illness rather than as a crime. This group came into existence in 1935 and now has a large membership and many branches. The members are former chronic alcoholics who have been cured of their disorder, through membership in the organization and the moral support given by other members. In addition to sponsoring social activities, the members always stand ready to help a member who fears he may be unable to resist the resumption of drinking. One policy of the organization is that the chronic alcoholic who really wishes to stop drinking should abstain completely and never take a drink; another is that only a former alcoholic can help an alcoholic. The membership is an intimate and sympathetic group and, acting on the expectation that each member will resist drinking, has accomplished many cures. Both the psychiatric approach and the self-help program of Alcoholics Anonymous are more promising methods of treatment for alcoholism than the imposition of short jail sentences.

Alcoholism and Crime

The relation of drinking to such crimes as assaults and thefts is not clear. When an arrest is made for such a crime the fact that the offender may be an habitual drinker, or under the influence of alcohol at the time of the crime, is often not recorded and hence does not appear in later statistical reports. It seems certain that crimes requiring careful planning, timing, and skill (as a bank robbery), or business management (as organized crime), or social suavity (as the confidence game) could not be carried on successfully by the chronic heavy drinker. This statement does not imply that such criminals do not drink, but that in view of the demands of their crimes they could not be successful if they drank sufficiently to impair their abilities. The crimes performed by drunkards are more likely to be of the unplanned type or of a petty nature.   Spontaneous drunken fighting or venting a grudge normally suppressed, are typical offenses of the habitual drunkard, and occur under the influence of alcohol.   Other offenses may be carried out during periods of sobriety, but are related to the inability of the drunkard to earn money regularly.   Thus petty thievery of an unskillful sort, which is easily detected, is fairly common.   Or a married man may find himself arrested for failure to support his children.   In other cases, unsatisfied impulses usually inhibited may find outlet; and the homeless drunken man or woman, deprived of normal family life, may be guilty of sexual indecencies and obscenities.

Some of the relationships between alcoholism and crime are brought out in a study of inmates of Sing Sing Prison.[11]   All men admitted in 1938–39, and also in 1939–40, were classified into three groups: primary intemperates or those whose alcoholism had led to the commission of their crime; secondary intemperates or those whose drinking had appeared long after their criminal habits were established; and nonalcoholics.   The percentage of prisoners in each of the three groups stood as follows:

	1938–39	1939–40
Primary intemperates	19.7	24.2
Secondary intemperates	25.1	27.8
Nonalcoholics	55.2	48.0
Number of prisoners	1,576	1,559

According to this tabulation only a fifth or a fourth of those committed to Sing Sing for felonies had committed the crime as the direct result of alcoholism.   In another fourth of the cases alcoholism was part of a generally disorganized life which included criminal habits, but in point of time criminality had appeared before alcoholism.

When intemperance is related to the type of crime, the Sing Sing study shows marked differences.   Figure 16 shows the percentage of prisoners committed for different crimes who fall into the primary intemperate group and also the percentage who were intoxicated at the time of their crime. The highest percentages of both intemperance and intoxication are found for those guilty of sex crimes, assaults, burglary, and homicides.

The felony of the alcoholic that causes his imprisonment often is preceded by a long history of petty offenses and arrests for intoxication.[12]   The alcoholic becomes demoralized over the years and the seriousness of his offenses increases.   In one instance, extreme in the number of arrests but showing a typical development, a man of 42 had been arrested 68 times, over a period of 23 years.   Of the first 21 arrests, 18 were for intoxication.   From then on, arrests for larceny became frequent.   Still later came an arrest for assault

and battery and one for breaking and entering.   When this man finally broke
into a business house while intoxicated he was sentenced to prison.

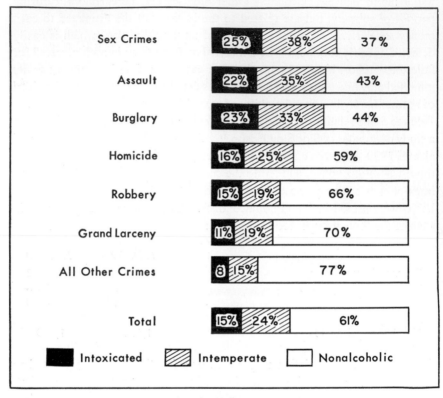

FIGURE 16

Percentage of prisoners who were intoxicated, intemperate, or nonalcoholic at
time of crime.   Intoxication at the time of the crime is a minor factor in all
types of crime.   In only 3 types of crime do the alcoholics (intoxicated and
intemperates) exceed the nonalcoholics.   (Based on R. S. Banay, "Alcoholism
and Crime," *Quarterly Journal of Studies on Alcohol,* 2 [1941–42], 688–89.)

DRUG ADDICTS

Drug addicts are fewer in number than habitual drunkards, but present a
somewhat similar problem.   In this case also, the individual is the victim of
a personal vice, which in its extreme form prevents normal social life and
impairs or destroys earning power.   Similarly, this vice has been made illegal.
The Harrison Narcotic Law of 1914 and its various amendments have made
the possession of certain narcotic drugs illegal under specific conditions and
have had the effect of making it a crime to use narcotic drugs for other than
authorized medicinal purposes.

Effect of Drug Addiction

The effect of drugs differs with the amount used. Drugs do not cause the nerve cells and fibers to degenerate as the excessive use of alcohol does.[13] Thus a person who uses only a small amount of a drug, and refrains from increasing the amount, may use it for years without any adverse effect on his personality or efficiency. The viciousness of the drug habit lies in the fact that many users do not take drugs in moderation and after they become accustomed to them must continue to take them or suffer great physical discomfort and perhaps acute illness. Also, the effect of drugs is such that an increasingly larger amount must be taken as time goes on, in order to secure the desired effect.

Not all drugs have the same effect on the user. Opium (including morphine and heroin) soothes and relieves tensions and inhibits violent impulses; but it also saps the user's vitality and reduces his ambition, so that he tends to become dependent upon others.[14] Cocaine, on the other hand, stimulates the user up to a certain point and temporarily creates confidence and courage. But after this phase has passed it produces fear and uncertainty. Marijuana, not widely used in the United States until about 1935, has a different effect.[15] It causes hallucinations and releases inhibitions, so that impulsive acts, sometimes of a criminal nature, easily follow the use of this drug.

Recently, barbiturates have been added to the list of drugs that should not be used indiscriminately. Barbiturates, commonly called sleeping pills, are sold, upon a doctor's prescription, under several trade names. Barbiturates differ from the narcotic drugs in that the user does not suffer physical distress if the habit is broken and therefore does not become dependent on the drug to avoid such distress. The danger lies, rather, in the possibility of death from overdoses.

Drug Addiction as Crime

The illegal possession of drugs is itself a crime. Thus the addict who buys narcotic drugs illegally, as well as the dope peddler who sells them to him, is liable to arrest and punishment even though he has not committed any of the crimes that injure other persons.[16] The large number of addicts who have not committed any other type of crime—or at least have not been arrested—is shown by the fact that of 13,000 felonies committed by 4,975 drug addicts in 1936, 65 per cent of the felonies were violations of the narcotic laws.[17] Only 10 per cent were grand larceny, 5 per cent burglary, 2 per cent felonious assault, 2 per cent highway robbery, less than 1 per cent each carrying concealed weapons and forgery, and 15 per cent miscellaneous.

Drug Addiction and Other Crimes

In addition to considering addiction itself as a criminal offense, which the law in effect declares it to be, we must consider the relation of drug addiction to other types of crime. The debate has waxed loud over the tendency of drug addicts to commit crimes because of the effect of the drug.[18] The more sober and well-considered statements show: (1) that some criminals are drug addicts, but that the addiction followed the onset of criminal habits and was merely part of the general pattern of a life of nonconformity; (2) that, because of the effects of the various drugs, professional criminals, who plan their crimes carefully and seek successful execution, are not drug addicts and will not associate with addicts not only because of their uncertain behavior, but because of the ease with which the police can extract confessions by withholding the drug, until the physical discomfort causes the addict to confess in order to secure it; (3) that occasionally a criminal, under the influence of one of the drugs that releases inhibitions, commits a crime, usually of a violent nature; (4) that many addicts, unable to earn money for the drug by legal employment, indulge in petty thievery.

Following are illustrations of each of these four situations.

1. The use of the drug may follow the onset of a criminal career and not be vitally related to the commission of other crimes. Kolb cites the case of a young man from an unstable family background; the father, a government employee, had stolen thousands of dollars in stamps; the mother had deserted her husband for another man. At the age of 14 the boy began to drink and was arrested 3 times. At 18, he took a girl to another city and used her to lure wealthy men into compromising situations. He then demanded money from them under the threat of exposure. He was arrested but was later released because of his youth. He began to use morphine, heroin, and cocaine, and stopped drinking. He was given 6 series of treatments but always relapsed. Several times he was arrested for possessing narcotics, and at the time Kolb talked with him was serving a year in jail for this offense.[19]

2. Chic Conwell, the professional thief who wrote of his experiences, stated that when professional thieves use drugs they start in secret.[20] They are ashamed to have their fellow thieves know of their failing and also fear that other thieves will not work with them, for the drug addict is regarded as unreliable and incapable. Conwell also gave in detail an account of a woman shoplifter (presumably a drug addict), who was so nervous and excitable that other shoplifters did not permit her to work with them.

3. Marijuana, which sometimes causes hallucinations and paranoid tendencies, was the drug in the following case. A young man under the influence

of this drug walked into a "whisky joint," where he saw a former friend, whom he believed was alienating his friends and acquaintances. He shot and killed this friend. When the toxic effect of the drug wore off, he no longer believed that the dead man had been persecuting him.

4. The most common crimes committed by drug addicts are petty; such as shoplifting, picking pockets, and other kinds of petty thievery. These crimes are of a minor nature and are committed to obtain money for living expenses and to buy drugs. Because drugs are sold illegally to addicts, their price is extremely high and the addict must have a ready supply of money if he is to continue to obtain them. The case of Florence is perhaps extreme, but it shows the slow progressive degradation that follows drug addiction.

Florence came from a family in which there was no want or evident family conflict.[21] Her mother was ill and neurotic and took morphine on prescription. At the age of 15 Florence left school because of ill health. She was a jolly, attractive girl, with a circle of friends. When she was 21 she was secretly married to a Jew, with whom she had had 3 years' secret courtship. She continued to live at home and told her parents about the marriage. Her husband's parents were not told, however, as they would have opposed the marriage of their son to a non-Jew. Several years afterward, Florence had an abortion and began to take morphine to ease the pain. She was soon habituated to the use of the drug, which her husband helped her to secure out of pity. When she had been married 6 years her mother died and she left her husband, moving to another community. Here she "married" another man, although she had not divorced her first husband. When she was 32, she was sent to a private hospital for the drug cure and her second husband disappeared. Following the cure, she worked as an attendant in a state hospital. She married a man 10 years her junior, who did not know of her past. She began to drink as a substitute for drugs and became subject to hallucinations. She was placed in a state hospital for treatment and her third husband deserted her. At this time she was 38 years old. Up to this point she had not been arrested, but she now stopped working and entered upon a career of minor crime in order to live and secure the drug. When she stole some prescription blanks and forged the names of physicians in order to obtain drugs, she was arrested and sent to the state reformatory for 15 months. After her release she was sent to a private sanitarium, but began again to use drugs when she left the institution. She violated her parole and was returned to the reformatory. Upon her release she became a drifter, begging and evading the payment of rent with hard luck stories. She developed the trick of renting typewriters and then pawning them. She also made a practice of ringing doorbells and saying she was ill. When she was admitted to the house, she looked around for something to steal or tried to induce the family to keep her for a few days.   In the 10 years after her release from the reformatory she was arrested 21 times for larceny, vagrancy, and drug addiction, and was constantly in and out of jails and hospitals.   Her family tried to have her permanently committed to an institution, but she was always found to be sane.

Youthful Drug Addicts

In 1951, primarily as a result of the investigations of the Senate Crime Investigating Committee (1950–51) and narcotics investigations by the State of New York and the mayor of New York City, many newspapers and magazines published sensational articles alleging widespread use of drugs by adolescents.   *Time,* on June 25, 1951, reported that New York City's superintendent of schools had testified before the state investigating committee that 1 out of every 200 high school students in the city used habit-forming drugs. Written and oral reports from students gave specific addresses of places where drugs were obtained, the amounts of money made by youthful drug peddlers, and the way in which use of drugs passed from one adolescent to another. Parents, school officials, and social workers the country over became deeply agitated and many local investigations were made.   When carefully carried out, most of these investigations failed to uncover any prevalent use of drugs by teenagers; in fact, in most cities few youthful addicts could be found.   An article in *Harper's Magazine,* based on interviews and a summary of published reports, states that where trouble spots were found they tended to be in cities that are large trade centers or ports, and within these cities use was localized in the slum sections where many types of crime and personal disorganization are found.[22]

HABITUAL SEX OFFENDERS

Sex offenders are among the more troublesome of deviants, partly because of our prohibitions and panicky fears surrounding sex and partly because so many types of sexual activities are forbidden by law and yet lumped in the public mind as emanating from one type of abnormal personality, often called the sexual psychopath.[23]

Types

The complexity of the question is shown by the following classification of sexual behavior, each type of which is illegal in at least some of the states.[24]

1. Normal sexual behavior between adults who are not married to each other, called fornication if between two unmarried people or adultery if between a married person and someone other than the spouse.   All states

have laws forbidding normal intercourse with a person other than the spouse, qualified in some states to instances where the illicit relationship is long continued or has become a public scandal.

2. Abnormal sexual relationships voluntarily carried out by adults, such as homosexuality and other perversions of the sex act.

3. Sexual acts that do no bodily harm but are a violation of public decency, such as exhibitionism, obscene talk, writing of obscene letters, or peeping in windows.

4. Sexual acts that are imposed by one person upon another through the use of force. Most conspicuous is forcible rape whereby sex relations are imposed by a man upon an unwilling and resisting woman, sometimes attended by gross physical injuries to the woman. Fortunately of rare occurrence are the extreme cases in which rape is accompanied by torture, mutilation, or even death. There is universal agreement that the latter type of case is the overt act of a disordered mind, although simple, forcible rape shades off into borderline cases where the woman has tantalized the man and is therefore to some degree responsible for the act.

5. Virtually any kind of sexual behavior, abnormal or normal, imposed upon children by adults with or without the child's consent. State laws specify the age (usually between 16 and 18 years) below which a girl cannot give consent to any type of sex relations. Some very anomalous cases arise in which a youth slightly above the juvenile court age may be technically guilty of statutory rape—a felony—because he had intercourse with a girl of 17 or 18, only a few years his junior and sometimes by the same state laws old enough to be married. When the man is mature, and the girl very young, public opinion is solidly behind the criminal laws.

6. Prostitution. Prostitution, a purely commercial transaction, shades off into intermittent and casual contacts where the woman's favor of sexual relations is rewarded by a gift or an evening's entertainment. When there is no commercial aspect at all, the relationship is that discussed under No. 1— fornication or adultery.

It is difficult to discuss so many types of behavior together. No. 1 may perhaps be omitted altogether, both because it is in the nature of a personal moral question and because the laws against it are rarely invoked unless there is a public scandal.

Male Offenders

Types 2 through 5 are primarily the offenses of men, often of men who are in some way maladjusted and unable to enter into normal sex relations with adult women. Some of the deviant relationships (notably No. 4 and No. 5) are harmful to women and little girls; others (Nos. 2 and 3) are not physically harmful unless a young boy is involved in homosexuality, but are psychologically shocking. All are very much condemned and any case that comes to light arouses consternation and fear.

Each type seems to be distinct; outlet for sexual interests seems to become set in a habitual pattern and the same general type of deviant behavior will appear repeatedly in one person. In this connection, however, it should be pointed out that many people commit one offense, are arrested and penalized, and do not become recidivists.

The conviction has been steadily growing that habitual sex offenders, especially types No. 2 through No. 5, should be provided with psychiatric treatment. Since the late 1930's a number of states have passed special laws singling out certain kinds of sex deviants for treatment. In general the laws have not been widely used, sometimes because it is difficult to single out the maladjusted person and sometimes because the state has not provided treatment facilities.[25] A brief summary of the case of a chronic sex offender shows the need for treatment.

Mr. L., who longed to be a hero, found satisfaction in the sexual mastery of little girls.[26] When he was found guilty for the fourth time at the age of 38, instead of being imprisoned or fined, he was placed on probation and arrangements were made for psychiatric treatment, which extended to 142 interviews. He was the sixth of 10 children and had had a domineering father and an over-solicitous mother. He had been married twice but his marital sexual experiences had not been satisfactory. His second wife tended to dominate him. His first experience with a little girl occurred a year and a half after his first marriage, and in the course of 15 years he had sought little girls 10 times, at intervals of a year or two. His dreams showed that he longed to be important and a hero; actually he had always given in to people. His intimacies with little or young girls gave him a sense of importance and were rationalized as not being wrong by a belief that he was giving them an enjoyable experience. Treatment included establishing self-confidence and self-respect. He was encouraged to assert himself and not to give in to his wife. Gradually Mr. L's opinion of himself changed, and he began to assert himself and to demand and receive more respect from others. Since he earned respect in other ways, he found it unnecessary to seek little girls and his relationship with his wife improved.

Prostitutes

Although prostitutes are perhaps not maladjusted in the same sense that the male sexual deviant is, they tend to fall into the general classification of habitual offenders, since the confirmed prostitute has organized her life around an illegal and demoralizing activity. Although a few prostitutes achieve some standing in the underworld if they are attached to night clubs or secure the patronage of some one man, most of them are tolerated rather than respected. Often they are girls who have not been able to meet competition in a legitimate occupation, or who have thoughtlessly entered into a sexual adventure at an early age and are gradually drawn into the ranks of the prostitutes. One writer finds 3 qualities in which prostitutes differ from other criminals of higher status.[27]

1. Most of them are of low middle-class origin, often from rural communities. They would still like to be respectable.

2. Most of them are socially inadequate, and as a consequence feel inferior. They attempt to compensate by the use of drink or drugs, by finery, and by claiming kinship or friendship with distinguished-looking persons whose photographs they possess.

3. Most of them are unintelligent; they are girls who have not been able to succeed in other occupations.

W. C. Reckless, who made a thorough study of prostitution in Chicago in the 1920's,[28] in a later article states that many girls are drawn into prostitution by association with prostitutes and that few are lured in by procurers.[29] For many, prostitution is simply a way of earning a living that is not regarded as especially degrading, and, in fact, may have as high status as the occupation from which the girl came; for instance, waitress in a cheap beer joint.

GAMBLERS

Gambling, or games of chance, covers a wide variety of activities: lotteries, roulette, policy games, betting on races or sports, card games, slot and pinball machines, and many variations of each of these. Gambling is condemned in the United States not only on moral grounds but because it readily becomes a social evil when not controlled, with many people in marginal circumstances steadily losing needed money in the vain hope of gaining great wealth. E. E. Blanche, a statistician who for 20 years has analyzed gambling games, states that the mathematical odds are so determined in all gambling games that in the continued conduct of the games, only the operator can be sure of continued winning, taking anywhere from 1.5 to 95 per cent of all the money wagered by players.[30] In addition, professional operators use many "fixes" or "gimmicks" so that the gambler has still less chance to win. In bingo, lottery, and raffle games the prize offered usually costs only a small part of the total amount paid for tickets, with the operator pocketing from 50 to 80 per cent of the money. Slot machines generally are fixed so that from 40 to 80 per cent of the money played in goes to the operator, and jack pots are few and small. Most gambling houses have roulette wheels controlled by mechanical or electrical devices so that winning numbers can be predetermined; thus the paying out of large sums of money is prevented. And so on through the list.

The occasional wealthy player may regard the sport as worth the money lost, but for the person in moderate circumstances gambling easily becomes a vice that devours money and tempts the loser to thefts, either to pay bets or to continue gambling. Among some gamblers, the urge to gamble becomes a compulsion, and all other considerations and obligations—family, job, civic responsibilities—are subordinated to the inner necessity to gamble. Psychoanalysts, whose studies are summarized by Lindner, have made several approaches to an analysis of compulsive gambling, linking it to unresolved infantile impulses.[31] The number of cases analyzed, however, is too few for any conclusions to be drawn as to the sequence of events leading to compulsive gambling. Often, also, gambling is found as one of a number of deviant types of behavior in unadjusted persons. Opposed to occasional and compulsive gamblers are the professional operators whose prime objective seems to be amassing money by unfair methods, and who fall into the criminal class.

Attempts to regulate gambling have been primarily through laws making various types of gambling illegal and through forcing professional gamblers out of business. Since interest in gambling is widespread and the laws are not at all consistent, a vast amount of gambling goes on at all times.

VAGRANTS AND RELATED TYPES

Bums, tramps, and hoboes are on the border line of the habitual offender. Bums have been defined both as persons who "drink and wander," and as stationary nonworkers; tramps have been called migratory nonworkers who dream and wander; and hoboes are migratory workers.[32]

Bums and tramps, the 2 nonworker groups, must have some way of securing money, food, clothing, and lodging. Begging, assistance from Salvation Army Missions and other charitable agencies, and occasional small jobs provide for them in part. However, petty thievery is not unknown to these groups. Tramps and hoboes, who wander over the country, habitually travel by hiding on trains and paying no fare. Trespassing on railroad property and riding without paying constitute offenses that the railroads constantly fight. They employ their own police and detectives who run the tramps and hoboes off the railroad property or turn them over to the police of the local community where they are found. Often tramps and hoboes go further and break into freight cars in search of food, clothing, or articles that can be sold to raise a little money. Also, stealing vegetables, fruit, and poultry from farms is frequently practiced.   Thus, although tramps and hoboes cannot be called habitual offenders because of their wandering or even their complete or partial idleness, a certain proportion of these vagrants are habitual offenders because of their methods of travel and attendant activities.[33]

A study of the men in Chicago shelters for the unemployed, established during the depression of the 1930's, throws light on the detached man who works periodically, has no reserve resources, and supplements what he earns or gets from charity with petty delinquencies.[34]   The study, made in 1935, covered some 20,000 men in 20 shelters.   About half of them had lived in the area immediately surrounding the Loop—the disorganized area in which hoboes, casual workers and nonworkers congregate.   Their average age was 45—an age at which most men are established as heads of families and are equipped with some skill or trade.   Among the shelter groups, 78 per cent were unskilled casual laborers.

In describing the life within the shelters, the authors state that petty thievery of articles that could be sold was common.   Men slept with their clothes on or under their heads to prevent their being stolen during the night, and carried all their possessions around with them during the day.   About a tenth of the residents were chronic alcoholics.   Whatever money they could get by stealing, begging, peddling, or by collecting and selling junk went for drink.   Gambling was a common pastime; when the men had a little cash they bet on the races or played cards among themselves.   Begging was common; the men begged for money on the streets, for food at restaurants, and for clothing at homes.   Sometimes the begging went on under the pretense of selling small articles.   These men avoided the police, but the police rarely arrested them, simply warning them to "move on."

PETTY THIEVES

In addition to the habitual offenders who shade off into personally disorganized and socially maladjusted types, there are those who stand midway between the occasional offender and the professional criminal.   These men and women are usually thieves of some sort who steal articles for their own use or to sell.   But they are amateurs both in executing the crime and in disposing of the goods.   Consequently they are easily caught, and, since they have no means of protection such as the professional criminal has established, are easily convicted.   They do not steal consistently, but as their reputation becomes known they find it more and more difficult to find employment and to live without criminal activity.

The woman described in the following newspaper item was such a thief, whose penalties were short jail terms.[35]

Mrs. May Sears, 53, expects to spend Christmas in jail—for the tenth time.

This time she is charged with violating the law which prohibits pickpockets from loitering in public places.   She got 100 days.

Police said Mrs. Sears was in jail at Yuletide in 1913, 1925, 1926, 1927, 1928, 1936, 1937, 1941, and 1942 on charges ranging from petty larceny to grand larceny.

CONTROL OF HABITUAL CRIME

Although most habitual offenders are still subjected to arrest and legal penalties, the trend is toward recognition of underlying psychological problems.   These problems increase and become intensified as the habitual offender finds himself less and less able to control his behavior.   Individual study of habitual offenders would probably reveal that many are definitely neurotic in personality.   The relation of neuroticism and more severe personality disorders to crime is discussed in the following chapter.

QUESTIONS

1. What kinds of offenders are typical habitual offenders?   Contrast them with professional criminals and with segmental criminals.

2. What justification is there for treating the habitual offender as a delinquent or criminal?

3. What is the relation of each type of habitual offender to serious crimes, such as assault or burglary?

4. Discuss the habitual offender as an inadequate person who cannot meet social responsibilities.

5. Suggest some alternatives to fines or jail as methods of dealing with habitual offenders.

READINGS

Anderson, Nels, *The Hobo* (Chicago: University of Chicago Press, 1923).   The ways of life of the hobo are discussed and illustrated by many case excerpts.

Bowman, K. M., "The Problem of the Sex Offender," *American Journal of Psychiatry,* 108 (1951), 250–57; Bowman and M. Rose, "A Criticism of Current Usage of the Term 'Sexual Psychopath,' " *American Journal of Psychiatry,* 109 (1952), 177–82; Bowman, *Sexual Deviation Research* (Sacramento, Calif.: Assembly of the State of California, 1952).   In these reports, Bowman discusses some general problems of sexual deviation and also reports upon investigations carried on in California.

Hampton, P. J., "A Descriptive Portrait of the Drinker," *Journal of Social Psychology,* 25 (1947): "The Normal Drinker," 69–81; "The Symptomatic Drinker," 83–99; "The Psychotic Drinker," 101–17; "The Stupid Drinker," 119–32; and "The Compulsive Drinker," 151–70.

Karpman, Benjamin, *The Alcoholic Woman* (Washington: Linacre Press, 1948).   Psychiatric case studies of women alcoholics.

Lindesmith, Alfred R., *Opiate Addiction* (Bloomington, Ind.: Principia Press, 1947).   Discussion of a theory of drug addiction.

Ploscowe, Morris, and Edwin J. Lukas (eds.), "Gambling," *Annals of the American Academy of Political and Social Science,* vol. 269 (1950). The many articles cover the legal aspects of gambling, organized crime and gambling, and the personality of the gambler.

Quarterly Journal of Studies on Alcohol (New Haven: Yale University Press). This Journal is devoted to reports on research in alcoholism.

Reckless, Walter C., *Vice in Chicago* (Chicago: University of Chicago Press, 1933). A study of prostitution and prostitutes after the breakup of the red light district and the dispersion of prostitution throughout the city.

Sutherland, Edwin H., and Harvey J. Locke, *Twenty Thousand Homeless Men* (Lippincott, 1936). This study of homeless men during the depression of the 1930's brings out many of the characteristics of vagrants.

FOOTNOTES

[1] H. R. Mowrer, "A Psychocultural Analysis of the Alcoholic," *American Sociological Review,* 5 (1940), 546–57.

[2] See, for example: J. H. Wall, "A Study of Alcoholism in Men," *American Journal of Psychiatry,* 92 (1936), 1389–1401; J. H. Wall, "A Study of Alcoholism in Women," *American Journal of Psychiatry,* 93 (1937), 943–53; O. Kinberg, "On So-Called Vagrancy," *Journal of Criminal Law and Criminology,* 24 (1933), 409–427, 552–83.

[3] T. E. Sullenger, "Female Criminality in Omaha," *Journal of Criminal Law and Criminology,* 27 (1937), 706–11.

[4] A. Stevens, "Make Dope Legal," *Harper's Magazine,* 205 (Nov., 1952), 40–47.

[5] Morris Ploscowe and E. J. Lukas (eds.), "Gambling," *Annals of the American Academy of Political and Social Science,* 269 (May, 1950), 1–38.

[6] J. Hall, "Drunkenness as a Criminal Offense," *Journal of Criminal Law and Criminology,* 32 (1941), 297–309.

[7] Mary Harris, *I Knew Them in Prison* (Viking, 1936), pp. 26–27, 47.

[8] From the author's files.

[9] S. S. Glueck, "A Tentative Program of Cooperation between Psychiatrists and Lawyers," *Mental Hygiene,* 60 (1925), 686–98.

[10] E. M. Jellinek, "Notes on the First Half Year's Experience at the Yale Plan Clinics," *Quarterly Journal of Studies on Alcohol,* 5 (1944–45), 279–302.

[11] R. S. Banay, "Alcoholism and Crime," *Quarterly Journal of Studies on Alcohol,* 2 (1941–42), 688–89.

[12] *Ibid.,* p. 694.

[13] L. Kolb, "Pleasure and Deterioration from Narcotic Addiction," *Mental Hygiene,* 9 (1925), 699–724; J. T. Fishman and V. T. Perlman, "Some Delusions about Crime," *Harper's Magazine,* 167 (1933), 36–45, 239–49.

[14] L. Kolb, "Drug Addiction in Its Relation to Crime," *Mental Hygiene,* 9 (1925), 74–89.

[15] P. O. Wolff, "Narcotic Addiction and Criminality," *Journal of Criminal Law and Criminology,* 34 (1943), 162–81; M. M. Hayes and L. E. Bowery, "Marihuana," *Journal of Criminal Law and Criminology,* 23 (1933), 1086–98.

[16] United States Treasury Department, Bureau of Narcotics, *Regulations No. 5* Relating to Importation, Manufacturing, . . . Opium or Coca Leaves . . . (Washington: Government Printing Office, 1938).

[17] A. R. Lindesmith, "Dope Fiend Mythology," *Journal of Criminal Law and Criminology,* 31 (1940), 199–208.

[18] See, for example, *ibid.;* the reply to this article by T. Michelson, "Lindesmith's Mythology," *Journal of Criminal Law and Criminology,* 31 (1940), 375–400; and Lindesmith's rejoinder, "The Drug Addict: Patient or Criminal?" *Journal of Criminal Law and Criminology,* 31 (1940), 531–35.

[19] Kolb, "Drug Addiction in Its Relation to Crime," *op. cit.*

[20] E. H. Sutherland, editor, *The Professional Thief* (Chicago: The University of Chicago Press, 1937), pp. 38–40; 161–62.

[21] Abstracted from Sheldon and Eleanor T. Glueck, *Five Hundred Delinquent Women* (Knopf, 1934), pp. 41–44; 157–60.

[22] J. Gerrity, "The Truth about the 'Drug Menace,' " *Harper's Magazine*, 204 (Feb., 1952), 27–31.

[23] Benjamin Karpman, "Considerations Bearing on the Problems of Sexual Offenses," *Journal of Criminal Law, Criminology and Police Science*, 43 (1952), 13–28; E. H. Sutherland, "The Sexual Psychopath Laws," *Journal of Criminal Law and Criminology*, 40 (1950), 543–54.

[24] Laws governing sexual behavior are found in the following: B. Johnson, *et al.*, *Digest of State and Federal Laws Dealing with Prostitution and Other Sex Offenses* (New York: American Social Hygiene Association, 1942, with supplement 1941–50); R. V. Sherwin, *Sex and the Statutory Law in All 48 States* (New York: Oceana Publications, 1949), Parts I and II.

[25] M. Guttmacher and H. Weihofen, "Sex Offenders," *Journal of Criminal Law, Criminology, and Police Science*, 43 (1952), 153–75.

[26] J. H. Conn, "The Psychiatric Treatment of Certain Chronic Offenders," *Journal of Criminal Law and Criminology*, 32 (1942), 631–35.

[27] D. W. Maurer, "Prostitutes and Criminal Argots," *American Journal of Sociology*, 44 (1939), 549–50.

[28] Walter C. Reckless, *Vice in Chicago* (Chicago: University of Chicago Press, 1933).

[29] Walter C. Reckless, "A Sociologist Looks at Prostitution," *Federal Probation*, 7 (April–June, 1943), 12–16.

[30] E. E. Blanche, "Gambling Odds are Gimmicked," *Annals of the American Academy of Political and Social Science*, 269 (May, 1950), 77–80.

[31] R. M. Lindner, "The Psychodynamics of Gambling," *Annals of the American Academy of Political and Social Science*, 269 (May, 1950), 93–107.

[32] Nels Anderson, *The Hobo* (Chicago: University of Chicago Press, 1923), p. 87.

[33] *Ibid.*, pp. 154–67.

[34] Edwin H. Sutherland and Harvey J. Locke, *Twenty Thousand Homeless Men* (Lippincott, 1936).

[35] *Chicago Daily News*, Dec. 19, 1945.

9

Criminals Who Are
Seriously Maladjusted

A small proportion of crimes are the outgrowth of, or are in some way related to, some form of serious mental abnormality. The man who, in a sudden orgy of killing and without previous criminal record, hammers to death his wife and children is in a different class from the criminals thus far discussed. So, also, is the kleptomaniac who steals small articles, apparently in an irrational manner and often without much effort to conceal his thefts. Or the chronic incorrigible who seems unable to submit to any form of orderly living and self-discipline. The motives of these persons are difficult for the layman to understand. Although few would condone the frauds, thefts, and conniving of the professional criminal or the careful lawbreaking of the segmented criminal, the money-making motives of these groups can be understood. We condemn the methods but comprehend the motives. It is also possible to understand the crimes that occur under great emotional stress, since most people at some time or other have conducted themselves in an unusual manner under the stress of anger, grief, or fear. However, a small group of persons commit crimes that cannot be attributed to motives that the normal person has experienced and therefore understands. These cases baffle attorneys and judges, and the usual methods of handling criminals do not seem to be effective.

MALADJUSTMENT AND CRIME

Hidden Psychological Motives

The reason that these apparently irrational cases are difficult to understand is because the motives for the crimes lie deeply buried within the mental and emotional make-up of those who commit them. The crimes are not committed to provide for physical needs (as crimes involving money), nor to satisfy the desire for a thrill (as many juvenile crimes), nor to provide luxuries and prestige (as many financial crimes). Rather, they give release to inner forces that demand outward expression.   Once the crime is committed, the person feels relief from these inner forces, at least temporarily.   He does not, therefore, experience normal regret as the person who commits an impulsive crime may do; nor does he always take precautions to conceal his crime, as the professional criminal does.   His crime is a part of a general mental or emotional maladjustment and can be understood only in its terms.

Tracing the process by which the personality becomes twisted and criminal behavior results is a slow procedure.   Usually when abnormal mental conditions are suspected, the court is concerned only with establishing legal insanity.   The test consists in demonstrating that the criminal was unable to recognize the nature and the quality of the act, or was unable to tell right from wrong, or that he was moved by an uncontrollable impulse and could not refrain from the deed even though he knew it was wrong.   The tracing of the process that led to the crime is not part of the court procedure.   But it is only by such an examination that the crime can be understood and the criminal perhaps helped back to a normal condition.

A revealing study of a crime committed under mental stress was made by Dr. Frederic Wertham under the title, *Dark Legend: A Study in Murder.*[1] This study concerns Gino, an Italian boy without a previous record of delinquency or crime, who apparently without cause killed his mother by stabbing her 32 times with a bread knife.   He was calm about the deed, reported it himself to the police, and maintained that he was not sorry he had done it as his mother had dishonored the family by various liaisons with men after his father's death.   Adjudged insane, he was committed to the state asylum for the criminal insane.   Gino's story as told to Dr. Wertham during the months following his commitment developed the following facts.   He was the oldest child in an Italian family in which the relationships seemed to be normal in terms of the low-income group represented.   While Gino was still a young boy his father died.   He attempted inadequately to operate the bakery that his father had owned, and thus to take his father's place in supporting the family.   As he identified himself strongly with his father at this time, he developed a special feeling of attachment for his mother.   Soon his mother began to see a great deal of a married man and neglected her children.   Gino resented her behavior and had the first impulse to kill his mother, a deed that he thought of in terms of vindicating the honor of the family.   At his father's grave he promised to avenge his name.   Later another man lived for a time with his mother, and then another.   Gino tried to bring himself to kill his mother by stabbing her in the back with a pair of scissors but could not do it. As he grew into adolescence he developed a strong aversion to women and to the idea of sexual relations with them; in his mind all women were bad. He played more and more with the idea of killing his mother and became moody, nervous, and forgetful. Although at this time his mother was not living with a man, Gino was consumed with thoughts of her past, of what he had seen her do, and of the disgrace to the family. Finally he killed her, calling her first by an Italian name that meant she had dishonored the family. Afterward he said he was glad he had killed her; he had no feeling of guilt.

This brief outline of events does not bring in all the emotional undertones of Gino's story, which were helpful in the diagnosis of the case. In reconstructing what went on in Gino's mind, the true significance of which was unrealized by Gino, Dr. Wertham came to the conclusion that Gino had developed a deep attachment to his mother, which was carried over into a period when most boys transfer their interest in women to girls of their own age. The death of his father had interfered with his normal development and he still identified himself with his father; he wanted the love of his mother as his father might have wanted it, and he felt cheated of that love by her affairs with other men. At the same time he was restrained from killing her by another phase of his concept of his father—that of the law-abiding man.

For 5 years Gino was torn between the two impulses, to kill his mother and to protect her. As he learned more about women he identified his mother with all women and developed the idea that they were sexually evil. He attempted from time to time to have some form of intimacy with girls but was always restrained. Eventually his growing maturity demanded that he should free himself from his infantile attachment to his mother and thus from his aversion to normal relationships with other women. The murder of his mother was a crude and violent way in which he freed himself from his infantile attachment; his belief that he did it for the honor of the family and to avenge his father was simply the rationalization that made the act seem justified.

During the course of the treatment, Gino came to see the true significance of his act and to regret it as unnecessary. Eventually he was pronounced cured and released.

This case well illustrates the psychological process that may lead to a violent crime that the court labels insanity. Although Dr. Wertham is unwilling to diagnose Gino's case as a definite form of insanity, he regards it as outside the normal and easily understood type of conduct. The motive for the act lay in events that had begun to happen years before and in Gino's interpretation of them; the true reason was hidden from the criminal himself; he felt only a compelling need to perform the act. His reaction to his crime was relief and happiness. These factors are indications of crimes that have a psychological rather than a financial motivation.

Types of Maladjustment

There is no criminal psychosis—no type of neurosis or psychosis or pathological personality that inevitably leads to crime. In fact, most criminals are not seriously maladjusted mentally, and most psychologically maladjusted persons are not criminals. But among the blind, hit-or-miss efforts, which the mentally disturbed person makes to relieve his tensions and conflicts, are some actions that are legally defined as crime. When the definitely psychotic person commits a crime, he usually is committed to a special institution for the criminal insane. Criminal psychoneurotics may be sent to such an institution or to a prison, depending upon how evident their maladjustment is. Criminal psychopathic persons are not as a rule classed as legally insane and are therefore committed to prison as normal persons. In all 3 types, the offenses and crimes that they commit are part of their attempt to satisfy powerful inner drives, which they have not been able to satisfy in the normal ways provided by society. They may or may not live in the underworld. But they are not the type of criminal that rationally and deliberately follows a career of crime as a money-making pursuit. Nor do seriously maladjusted persons become members of criminal mobs or participate in organized crime. They are not trusted by professional criminals; and they are not interested in the financial crimes carefully carried out by professionals. Crime is not a business to the mentally disturbed person; crime is an emotional debauch. The satisfaction produced by the crime is not in financial gains or in status among other criminals, but in the criminal's own inner emotional satisfaction and relief.

PSYCHOSES AND CRIME

The most serious type of personality maladjustment is found in the psychotic. Such a person is popularly referred to as insane or a lunatic. The psychotic divorces himself to some degree or completely from the world of reality. His responses do not arise from actual experiences and material objects in his environment, but from beliefs divorced from reality and false perceptions. For instance, he may have delusions of grandeur and believe that he is Napoleon or George Washington or God. He may have delusions of persecution and believe that some person that he knows or even strangers on the street are spying on him, or plotting to kill him. Hallucinations are also common; these apparent perceptions are false sense impressions, usually of sight or hearing. The psychotic may "hear a voice" that commands him to perform some act; or he may see visions, perhaps a dead member of the family or the devil. The thought processes of the psychotic are often confused and a logical train of thought cannot be maintained in writing or conversation.   In other cases, the psychotic sinks into persistent daydreams until the real world ceases to exist for him and he lives in an inner world of fantasy perhaps so completely that he cannot care for his physical needs. Again the psychotic may vacillate between moods of extreme violence, exultation or rage, and profound melancholia and depression.   Sometimes the psychotic condition affects only one area of interest; thus there are cranks and eccentrics who are psychotic in some phases of their thinking but not in other respects.   Manic-depressive cases and many other psychotics have intervals of normality between attacks.   But sometimes the trend is toward complete absorption of the personality in the psychosis and, as the individual travels further and further into the unreal world of his own concepts and interpretations, he loses contact with normal activities with the people about him and abandons himself to the satisfactions of his disease.   At this stage no reasoning can shake his beliefs; no appeal can be made to his emotions. He can no longer be expected to adjust to conventional life, nor can he be held accountable for his actions in terms of normal behavior.   His conduct is reasonable only if one accepts the basic tenets of his psychosis, which no one does except himself.

It should be emphasized that the psychotic may not exhibit his abnormalities at all times.   Periods of rationality are interspersed with periods of irrationality.   Or delusions may relate to only certain areas of experience and in other respects the person reacts in normal fashion.

A few types of psychosis are the result of organic conditions; for others no definite organic causes have been identified, and the presumption is that they develop from failure of a person to make adequate emotional and social adjustments as he develops from childhood to maturity, or from some later distressing personal experience.   The diagnosis of psychosis is often difficult to make, even when it is clearly recognized that a person is mentally ill.   This difficulty arises because the symptoms of the various types of psychoses overlap, and the question of whether an individual suffers from one or another form of mental illness may depend upon the dominance of some one symptom or upon a special combination of symptoms.   Clear-cut types, of course, are recognizable; the most common ones are listed and briefly described below.

Psychoses with an Organic Basis

Certain types of mental abnormality have an organic basis and stem from a diseased condition of the brain tissue.   The most common is paresis, which is the result of a syphilitic infection of the brain in which destruction of the tissue affects the individual's capacity for self-control and moral judgment.

Encephalitis (sleeping sickness) leaves aftereffects that may be related to delinquent behavior. This disease causes lesions in the central nervous system with the result that the person suffering from it may be lethargic, stultified mentally, and often extremely irritable. In other cases a person is restless, impulsive, and unpredictable in behavior. Epilepsy involves a period of automatism that follows the unconscious period in a severe attack, or which may occur alone in a minor attack. During this period the epileptic may do things normally inhibited and of which he later has no memory.

It should be noted that in none of these diseases is any specific type of criminal behavior a direct result of the disease. Rather the disease tends to lower self-control and to remove the inhibitions of earlier training and conventional habits. Under these conditions and in certain social situations the individual performs acts that are designated delinquencies and crimes, but which he does not recognize as such. There are no studies of the extent to which persons suffering from these diseases come into conflict with the law. Often their misconduct is of a minor variety that may simply make them family and neighborhood problems. The paretic becomes slovenly and careless in his work or about his person. He may drink heavily and indulge in excessive sexual activities. The misconduct of the epileptic too is often of a minor or nuisance variety, such as undressing in public. Post-encephalitic behavior involves quarreling and angry outbursts perhaps combined with violent destruction of property, some of which may be the response to demands from family or school that the individual attain standards that the aftereffects of the disease make impossible. Serious crimes, such as murder, rape, or theft, are committed more rarely by persons suffering from organic diseases of the brain.

Schizophrenia

Other psychoses seem related to disturbing experiences that an individual has been unable to assimilate, or to deep-seated conflicts between incompatible desires or between an innate drive and the social regulation controlling it. The most frequently found psychosis of this type is schizophrenia, often called dementia praecox because its onset usually occurs during youth or early adulthood. The chief characteristic of schizophrenia is gradual withdrawal into a world of fantasy and apathy of mental and emotional life, following often upon a childhood characterized by shyness and social isolation. In the completely developed case, the schizophrenic is extremely apathetic and requires physical care. In other stages, the apathy may be broken by periods of wild frenzy when attacks upon others may occur.   In mild cases the disease may not be recognized and the victim simply becomes unable to compete socially, at school, or at work and becomes a vagrant; or he becomes hypersensitive and reacts violently to seeming slights.

Among serious crimes, those most often committed by schizophrenics are murder and theft.[2]   Dr. Frederic Wertham states that assaults and homicides within the family circle are relatively frequent among the violent acts of schizophrenics.[3]   He adds that, according to current theories, infantile and unsocialized hatreds that children may harbor for other members of the family, and which normal persons outgrow, are still active in the mind of the schizophrenic and appear in undisguised form.   A case is given briefly below, unanalyzed so far as the psychological relation between the disease and the assault is concerned, in which the boy who committed the crime was diagnosed by the state psychiatrist as suffering from schizophrenia.*   This case not only exhibits the type of crime, but also some of the outward personality symptoms of the schizophrenic.

This boy, John, was one of the younger children in a family of 7 siblings. He left high school 2 weeks after entrance because other children made fun of him (withdrawal typical of the schizophrenic).   He had been in some minor difficulties and had been paroled to his brother-in-law, who lived in the country.   One day when he was left in charge of the children of his brother-in-law and sister he killed the older child, aged 5, with a hammer and then stabbed her body, leaving the knife plunged to the handle in it. He left a note on the child's body, which stated that he was "kill-crazy." Although he ran away to the home of his parents, he made no effort to conceal himself.   At first he pleaded not guilty but later changed his plea to guilty.   He was found to be of average intelligence, but was emotionally indifferent to his crime or to its effect on himself.   Stating that he did not care whether or not he was executed for the killing, he remained without emotional reaction during the examination of witnesses called to aid the judge in determining the length of sentence to be imposed; when his sentence of 207 years was pronounced; and when his mother wept at his departure (emotional indifference typical of the schizophrenic).   As he left the courtroom after being sentenced, he chuckled to himself (absorption in an inner world of fantasy that is more real than the outside world, typical of the schizophrenic).

* Regardless of this diagnosis, the 15-year-old boy involved was allowed to plead guilty, and was sentenced by the presiding judge to 207 years in the state penitentiary with every anniversary of the crime to be spent in solitary confinement. According to newspaper accounts, this sentence was the longest ever imposed on anyone sent to this particular state penitentiary.

Manic-Depressive Psychosis

Manic-depressive psychosis, another fairly common type, is characterized by alternating periods of great emotional display of violence or elation and periods of deep depression. Well-developed cases are usually recognized as abnormal and are placed under supervision. Mild cases are not always recognized and nuisance or criminal acts may result. One man brought a period of unpleasant practical jokes to a climax when he refused to show his commuter's ticket to the collector and upon insistence that he do so, became angry and brandished a pistol at the collector who fled in fear of his life. The man was arrested and it was discovered that the pistol was in reality a toy. This man regarded his action and various extreme practical jokes with great pride. He was suffering from a mild form of manic psychosis.[4] In another case, a man of 44 had an attack of the manic phase of manic-depressive insanity about once in 2 years. At these times he thought he had great wealth and became elated and expansive in manner. He would then pass bad checks and was twice arrested for grand larceny.[5]

During the depressive period the person may show suicidal tendencies. Sometimes he is remorseful over the poverty or illness of his family for which he rightly or wrongly feels responsible; sometimes, recognizing her illness, a mother may feel that she is unable to care properly for her children. Under those circumstances, the psychotic may kill or attempt to kill other members of the family and commit suicide. Often he succeeds in killing others but makes only an abortive suicide attempt; he may then be charged with murder unless the nature of his disease is recognized. An example is the young woman who after the birth of her first child felt an impulse to kill it. She reported her feelings to the doctor and her husband but was not taken seriously. The desire to kill the child left her after she stopped nursing it. During her second pregnancy she wanted to dispose of her unborn baby and some time after its birth she gave lysol to both children and to herself. One child died. The mother herself was only slightly indisposed and after 6 months' treatment recovered from her mental illness.[6] It should be noted that in most of these cases the motive for the killing as it appears to the perpetrator is altruistic and is designed to save the victim from some form of suffering. Manic-depressive psychosis does not lead to deterioration of the mental functions and often may be cured by proper treatment.

Involutional Melancholia

Involutional melancholia, a psychosis of middle age, is marked by profound anxiety, apprehension, delusions of sinfulness, and fear of illness and disease. Moreover, suicidal impulses are common and occasionally an attack is made upon someone else.

Paranoia

Paranoia, a somewhat rare type of psychosis, is marked by delusions of grandeur and of persecution, which are linked together. The paranoiac frequently believes that he is not receiving the prestige due him. He builds up an explanation satisfactory to himself; he is an important person (he may come in time to believe he is some specific notable) and therefore others envy him. For this reason they ignore him, and they try to do him harm and persecute him in various ways. Such delusions may extend to the belief that people on the street have been employed to spy upon him; or that some specific person is about to harm him.

The crimes of the paranoiac grow directly out of his delusion and are usually extreme in nature. The paranoiac may burn the house of someone whom he believes is working against him. Or he may attack, injuring or killing, one of his supposed persecutors. The crime may be either planned or impulsive. For example, a 27-year-old woman attacked the president of a relief society who had refused to give her financial assistance. This woman had showed mental symptoms for several years and thought she was the object of persecution. She believed that the president of the society had employed women to talk against her. Hence she bought a revolver for protection and the assault was the result.[7]

In its minor phases or early stages the disease may not be recognized. The paranoiac may commit a long series of minor aggressions, or he may simply be labeled as a crank or a troublemaker.

Treatment of Psychoses

Some psychoses are susceptible to treatment and cure; others are not. One reason for the difficulty of curing certain kinds is that the person resists treatment. The psychosis itself is a solution of his conflict; in the psychosis he finds justification for his feelings and actions or, as with the schizophrenic, he builds a fantasy world that satisfies him more than the real one. To leave these delusions and fantasies and return to the harsh reality of life is to face again the painful conflicts from which the psychotic is trying to escape. Hence, unconsciously, he resists attempts at treatment. Nevertheless, many psychotics, especially of the functional type, recover. The recovery may come after a period of institutionalization, during which the patient is removed from active life and sheltered from his difficulties. Specific types of therapy, such as the shock treatment, also aid in recovery.

PSYCHONEUROSIS

The maladjustment of the psychoneurotic is not so deep seated as that of the psychotic. He does not lose touch with the world of reality nor substitute his own delusions and hallucinations for actual events and experiences. He may laugh and cry immoderately, but he laughs and cries in response to appropriate situations. His intellect is not affected and he reasons in a normal manner, although he may allow his emotions to overrule his judgment. He may indulge in fantasies and daydreams but he recognizes them as such and does not mistake them for reality. He may cringe at meeting painful situations and may suffer from morbid anxieties and feelings of guilt; nevertheless he is usually able to make some degree of social adjustment.

Although in occasional cases obsessional compulsive psychoneurosis may develop into schizophrenia, it is generally true that psychoneurosis and psychosis are unrelated. That is, psychoneurosis is not the beginning stage of psychosis and does not evolve into it. Psychoneurosis and psychosis serve the same purpose—they are ways in which a person tries to solve his problems. They develop in different personality types, and the personality that tries to solve problems by psychoneurosis is not likely also to develop a psychosis.

Conflicts as Cause of Psychoneurosis

The psychoneurotic suffers from hidden emotional and mental conflicts. The conflict may arise from 2 codes of conduct that a person accepts but cannot reconcile. Or the basis of the conflict may be his inability to meet adult standards; he may be torn between his desire to achieve the status of the adult level and an equally strong desire to slip back into infantile types of behavior, which he finds more satisfying.

These conflicts are especially likely to develop around sexual conduct, a field in which individual desires are urgent and restraining social pressures and requirements are strong. In this case, the psychoneurosis is linked to our stern social taboos regarding forms of sexual expression.[8] When a person cannot conform to socially approved patterns whether of sex conduct or in some other field of experience, but nevertheless desires social approval, the conflict may become intense. Under these conditions the psychoneurotic may live in a constant state of frustration; he experiences anxieties, tensions, sense of inferiority, and, if he follows a nonsocial pattern of conduct, feelings of guilt. Often he becomes unable to make decisions and is in a continuous state of tension. These persons are unhappy and maladjusted but not criminal. In other cases, the repressed and unsatisfied desires find expression in action, whose meaning is disguised from the psychoneurotic.   This situation is true of compulsions, which drive a person to repeat the same action over and over without recognizing the reason for his act.   Possibly he must touch every telephone he passes, or wash his hands constantly, or step on every crack in the sidewalk.   Sometimes these compulsions lead to criminal behavior.   The various so-called manias are of this repetitive and disguised type and often bring the psychoneurotic into conflict with the law.

For example, a person may feel an irresistible impulse to wander.   Such wandering is a kind of flight or escape when the conscious personality is unable to meet the demands of the inner self.   Drug addiction and chronic alcoholism are also ways in which the psychoneurotic may seek relief from his conflict.*   Kleptomania or persistent stealing and pyromania, the repeated and seemingly unmotivated burning of buildings, are other forms of obtaining disguised satisfaction.   Gambling may be motivated by a desire to attain superiority, although it is not necessarily the case.   Occasionally the urge to satisfy an inner compulsion takes the form of repeated murders, usually performed in the same manner and without any previous history of animosity against the persons killed.   Many instances of habitual offenses, described in Chapter 8, undoubtedly are psychoneurotic in origin.

Characteristics of the Psychoneurotic Crime

The illustrations given indicate the disguised motives and the indirect relationship between motive and act that are characteristic of the psychoneurotic crime.   An English writer gives the following characteristics of the psychoneurotic crime:

1. It is the outcome of a conflict between a strong desire and the social conscience, although the social conscience may dictate action at the infantile level.
2. It is an act of compromise and not a direct expression of the desire.
3. It provides no material gain or at least such gain is not the object of the act.[9]

These 3 characteristics may be demonstrated by a hypothetical case.   A woman with strong sexual drives may be unmarried and thus is denied sexual experience of a type that is socially approved.   Her acquired inhibitions may make it impossible for her to seek sexual experience without marriage.   This situation contains the first characteristic—the conflict.   The woman develops into a kleptomaniac, stealing small articles from stores.   Perhaps she steals only one kind of article that for some reason symbolizes sex to her.   Or the general act of stealing may represent sexual satisfaction, in

---

* Although some writers regard all cases of drug addiction and chronic alcoholism as escape mechanisms of the psychoneurotic, this relationship has not been fully established as universal.

that she is taking something that does not belong to her and according to her code she has no right to sexual experience. This compromise act is the indirect expression of her conflict. It seems a less serious offense to such a woman to steal small articles than to accept sex experience. The articles she steals have little monetary or utilitarian value and often may be hoarded and not turned to any use. Furthermore she probably does not recognize the connection between her unsatisfied sexual desires and the stealing and may be worried and distraught because she cannot refrain from stealing. At the same time the pressure of her sexual desires is temporarily lessened by the act of stealing. Since these desires are not satisfied, however, they recur, followed by further stealing. It should be noted that because of the failure really to satisfy repressed desires, the crime that symbolizes satisfaction is repeated over and over in always more or less the same form.

Treatment of Psychoneurotic Criminals

In all cases of psychoneurosis resulting in criminal behavior (and most psychoneurosis does not so result) a direct attack upon the misconduct is futile. Such a person is often unable to tell why he does a thing and may be shocked and dismayed at his own actions. Jail sentences and punishments are useless. Two cases from English records are illustrative, and might be duplicated by cases in this country.[10] During a period of 18 years a man was convicted 13 times for indecent exposure. His punishment was invariably imprisonment, varying from 14 days to 1 year. His total imprisonment amounted to six and one-half years. During the time he was out of prison, this man was caught in the act about once a year, and it is of course not known how many other times he committed the offense without being arrested. In the second case a man was convicted 12 times in 25 years for indecent conduct. He was imprisoned from 5 days to 18 months for different offenses; his total imprisonment amounted to 5 years and 8 months. He therefore was arrested about once every year and a half.

Handled properly these cases may often be cured. Psychiatric treatment may disclose the conflict and give the psychoneurotic insight into his problem and an adequate way to solve it.

PSYCHOPATHIC PERSONALITY

From the point of view of misconduct, the psychopathic personality is the most baffling. The psychopath rarely reaches either the institution for the mentally abnormal or the institution for the criminal insane. Hence this type of personality organization has not been given the amount of study that has been devoted to some other forms of mental difficulties. Moreover, when psychiatrists attempt to study psychopaths they find themselves batter-ing against a stone wall of resistance; the psychopath refuses to co-operate with the psychiatrist or the psychoanalyst. He either will not or cannot reveal himself nor permit probing into his hidden motives. Hence, most attempts, either to understand the processes by which psychopathy develops or to help the psychopath to a reorganization of his personality, fail. His misconduct therefore tends to become chronic and he appears with startling frequency in jails and prisons, where he is universally a problem.

The term constitutional psychopathic inferior was formerly applied to the psychopath. Recent formulations have discarded the term, however, as it implies that the difficulty is constitutional, that is, inborn or organic. In line with current trends in psychiatry, the origin of psychopathy is now sought in the early experiences of an individual rather than in some innate defect. Indeed, the appellation may be further modified with study, as the term has been used to cover a wide variety of behavior patterns and perhaps several, instead of one, kinds of personality organization.

Symptoms of the Psychopath

The symptoms of the psychopath make a long and rather incongruous list. Most writers agree that first and foremost he is an undisciplined person who does not like to be restrained, and who finds it difficult or impossible to adapt himself to an orderly social existence. The published study of one case calls the psychopath a "rebel without a cause." [11] He seems to have an inner compulsion to rebel against all restraints even when such rebellion brings suffering on himself.

It is also agreed that the psychopath is self-centered and egotistical. On the one hand his motives of behavior are primarily selfish and he is willing to sacrifice others—even members of his immediate family—to gain his ends. On the other hand, he is not interested in the welfare of others and cannot work or co-operate with other people. He is impervious to their opinion and is satisfied with his own behavior.

The psychopath is also unable to set some distant goal and work toward it. He seeks immediate satisfaction for immediate needs. He is therefore unstable and undependable and cannot hold a job long. Moreover, the troubles of the psychopath begin early in life; his misconduct and his unco-operative attitude appear during childhood. His conduct seems unalterable. He is unable to modify it himself, and he does not yield to ordinary school training. Imprisonment makes no impression upon him. He refuses sym-pathetic or expert offers of help.

The psychopath's emotional life is distorted. He does not respond to the usual appeals of family or friends and seems to feel no sympathy for those close to him.   He does not establish normal family relationships. The psychopath may appear at any intellectual level, since the difficulty is not related to mental ability.

The psychopath differs from the psychotic in that he does not have delusions and hallucinations nor unrealistic emotional storms; he lives in the world of reality.   Nor does he have the obsessions and compulsions of the conflict-tortured psychoneurotic.   He is an aimless, undisciplined person, bound to be thwarted and frustrated in a society that demands ambition, planning, and orderliness.   His reaction to restraints is to escape from them; he may become a nomad, living by his wits; or a pathological liar seeking easy excuses for his shortcomings.   If he cannot escape, his reactions are aggressive and sometimes sadistic in effect.   He may simply become an agitator or be chronically quarrelsome; or he may do physical injury to others.

Legally, the psychopath is regarded in a different light from either the psychotic or the psychoneurotic, who may be impelled by compulsions or irresistible impulses and who may not be held accountable for their crimes. The psychopath is held legally responsible, for he (1) does not have an irresistible impulse to commit a crime, (2) does not have delusions or hallucinations, (3) has no memory defects, (4) has no loss of emotional capacity, and (5) has no organic disease of the central nervous system.[12]   Since he is legally held responsible he is punished by fines, jail, or prison sentences; since his difficulty is relatively incurable, he is a chronic offender and appears in court time after time for a variety of offenses.

Crimes of the Psychopath

Because of the variety of behavior that at present is classified under the term psychopathic, many different types of personality are found in the group and many types of crime.   The psychopath may be quarrelsome and generally aggressive and troublesome; he may be unable to work steadily and may resort to vagrancy or theft; he may try to get his own way by force and assault people who oppose him; he may misrepresent himself and obtain money fraudulently; he may set buildings on fire or do other damage in spite. The following lists the career of one person diagnosed as psychopathic.[13]

Enlisted in the army and was given an honorable discharge after being wounded in the knee.   Later he claimed he had been struck on the head and tried to secure compensation for the injury; no injury could be established.

Re-enlisted in the army; married a 15-year-old girl and secured his release on the plea that he had to support his wife; lived with his mother-in-law and allowed her to support him until she turned him out.

Cashed fraudulent checks but escaped punishment through the intervention of a sympathetic attorney who took him into his office and assisted him to enroll in a law class. When he failed to study, the attorney refused further help.

Had cards printed on which he claimed that he was associated with the attorney and that he handled ex-service men's claims.

Interfered with a client of the attorney and by representing himself as a lawyer who would handle the case for a smaller sum, was paid a fee.

Collected payments for a piano, although he did not represent the piano company.

Secured a false affidavit stating that he had completed two years in a law school.

Stole some of the attorney's letterheads upon which he wrote to clients making false representations.

Lied glibly when questioned about any of his misdeeds, always telling elaborate stories.

Courted a young woman without telling her he was married and when she learned of his marriage and left the city, followed and made threats against her and her family.

Misrepresented himself to this young woman as being a lawyer from a wealthy family. Sent her flowers and presents for which she later had to pay.

Was finally given treatment in a hospital for the mentally disturbed. He tried to establish claim to compensation on the basis of the head injury that he said he had received, but which could not be established. When this attempt failed and he was discharged from the institution, he wrote to the families of patients, making false accusations in a plausible manner about the treatment of the patients.

Pleaded guilty several months later to raising a U.S. Treasury check from $3.77 to $53.77, and was sentenced to a year and a day in jail. The further career of this man is not known.

An elaborate study of a psychopath—a man imprisoned in one of the federal penitentiaries—that employed a new technique to break through his resistance was made by Robert M. Lindner. This young man had a history of delinquency from his twelfth year, an irregular employment history, and a sullen attitude. He also had an eye defect that prevented complete vision, the cause of which was not known when Dr. Lindner undertook his study. He had repeatedly been diagnosed as a psychopath. The technique used by Dr. Lindner was a combination of hypnosis and psychoanalysis. Although psychopaths resist psychiatric or psychoanalytic probing, Dr. Lindner was able to secure the consent of his prisoner to an investigation under hypnosis. The published report of the case gives the method and the interviews in detail.[14] Through these interviews under hypnosis in which the prisoner was encouraged to talk freely, the origin of the psychopathic trouble was traced to an experience that had taken place when the prisoner was about 6 or 8 months old. Fear, linked to the father, turned the child toward the mother. The blinking of his eyes was an attempt to shut out or escape from his terrifying experience. His later delinquencies grew out of his fear of his father, his feeling of inferiority toward him, and his dependence upon his mother—feelings that he had been unable to overcome. Through the treatment he came to a new understanding of his problems with the result that his personality was reorganized and his eyes greatly improved. This study is an extremely important step in the understanding of the psychopath, for it opens the door to a technique that will aid the psychologist or psychiatrist to penetrate his resistance. It also indicates the hidden nature of the roots of the disease.

INCIDENCE OF MALADJUSTED CRIMINALS

The question of the incidence of maladjusted criminals has two sides. How many criminals suffer from one of the serious forms of maladjustment just described? What proportion of the seriously maladjusted become criminals? These questions are important, for crime and maladjustment are not synonymous terms. There is no crime-psychosis nor any other mental or emotional trait that inevitably causes crime. But a certain percentage of maladjusted persons commit crimes that are related to their mental disturbances and in order to understand and provide treatment for such criminals, it is necessary to comprehend the extent and nature of their crimes.

Proportion of Maladjusted Criminals

Several studies give fairly reliable answers to the first question—what proportion of criminals were suffering from a serious type of maladjustment at the time they committed their crimes. Complete reliance cannot be placed on the figures quoted because of the variability in diagnosis of a case of mental abnormality. Many cases are on record in which several psychiatrists have diagnosed a case within a short space of time and have given different reports. Also, the adequacy of the examining physicians varies from one state or city to another and this fact in itself would lead to disparities in the proportion of cases diagnosed as maladjusted. It is not surprising therefore to find some variation among cities and states in the percentage of criminals reported as abnormal mentally.

One of the most widely quoted early studies was by Bernard Glueck of the men in Sing Sing Prison.[15] He found 12 per cent who were mentally diseased or deteriorated and 19 per cent who had psychopathic personalities.

A summary of surveys made prior to 1931 by the National Committee for Mental Hygiene shows a wide variation in incidence of mental abnormality in prisons, reformatories, and houses of correction, and in jails in different parts of the country.[16] For nine states in the East, South, and Middle West the percentage of inmates of prisons, reformatories, and houses of correction diagnosed as suffering from mental diseases or deterioration varied from

0.9 per cent in Kentucky to 13.4 per cent in Georgia; the average of the percentages was 6.7. Among inmates of jails the percentage with mental disease or deterioration varied from 0.9 per cent for Arizona to 7.3 per cent for New York; the average of the nine percentages was 3.7. Psychopathic personality was the diagnosis for 5.5 per cent of the inmates of prisons, reformatories, and houses of correction in Georgia and for 35.3 per cent of the inmates in North Dakota. The other seven states stood between these extremes, with an average percentage for all nine states of 16.7. The percentage of psychopathic personalities in jails ranged from 3.0 per cent in Georgia to 45.3 per cent in Kentucky, with an average of 19.9 per cent. This extremely wide range for psychopathic personality is no doubt to be expected because of the lack of specific symptoms of this condition. The percentage of prisoners suffering from psychoneurosis was not given for all states. For those that reported, the average percentage of prisoners with psychoneurosis was 2.0 for prisons and 1.6 for jails. It is not clear whether all of these diagnoses refer to the condition of the offender at the time he committed his offense or whether in some cases the abnormality may have developed after his incarceration in the institution. Nor is the exact relation of the abnormality to the offense indicated, although it may be assumed that the abnormality was in some degree a causative factor if it existed prior to the offense.

A better controlled series of reports issued from the Court of General Sessions of New York City. All accused persons who come before this court are sent to the psychiatric clinic for an examination. Reporting on a total of 9,958 felons so examined between 1932 and 1935, Bromberg and Thompson state that 1.5 per cent were found to be psychotic, 6.9 per cent psychoneurotic, and 6.9 per cent psychopathic. A small group, 2.4 per cent, were feeble-minded. Although 82.3 per cent were classified as normal, three fourths of the normal group exhibited mild personality defects of various types, which had been a factor in the commission of their crimes.[17]

Another study of convicted felons from the same court shows a similar distribution of types of mental abnormality. Among convicted felons examined in the clinic of the Court of General Sessions in New York City in 1937, 1.6 per cent were afflicted with some form of psychosis, 4.2 per cent were neurotic, 7.3 per cent were psychopathic, 3.1 per cent were mental defectives (feeble-minded), and 83.8 per cent were normal.[18]

From these various reports it seems apparent that, when examinations are carefully made, a negligible percentage of those who commit serious crimes (felonies for which they may be committed to prison) are psychotic, whereas only moderate percentages are psychoneurotic or psychopathic. A conservative estimate would place from 15 to 25 per cent of felons in these classes. It seems probable that minor offenders who are punished by jail sentences or fines or are placed on probation might include a higher percentage of psychopaths, since many of them are of the drifter type and become guilty of minor offenses such as fighting, excessive drinking, vagrancy, and so forth.

Proportion of Maladjusted Who Commit Crimes

The problem may now be approached from the point of view of the second question posed at the beginning of this section. What proportion of the mentally abnormal commit crimes as a result of their abnormality?

A study of 1,262 male psychotic patients, in the Eloise State Hospital of Michigan showed that 21.1 per cent had criminal records and 4.4 per cent records of threatened or attempted crimes, or approximately one fourth had committed some crime. But of this group, 126, or 10.0 per cent of the total group, had committed the criminal act before the onset of the psychosis, or at least before it had been recognized; 197 or 15.6 per cent had committed the crime after its appearance. It is for this group alone that we can feel certain that the psychosis was a causative factor in the commission of the crime.[19]

In the state of Illinois, male criminals who are found to be psychotic (insane) at the time of conviction are committed to a special institution called the Illinois Security Hospital. Dunham studied the 543 males committed to this institution for the first time between 1922 and 1934. He found that this number was equivalent to 1.7 per cent of all males committed to hospitals for the mentally abnormal in the state. It is not established what proportion had committed the crime before the onset of the psychosis and what proportion as part of it. But regardless of the adjustment that should be made on this basis, it is obvious that only a small proportion of the psychotic persons committed to public institutions had been convicted of major crimes. The 543 criminals and mentally abnormal males were equivalent to only 1.3 per cent of the total number of male criminals committed to Illinois penal institutions during the same period.[20] This figure corresponds closely with the percentage of felons in New York City found to be psychotic. These figures indicate only a slight overlapping of the seriously criminal and the definitely psychotic groups; that is, few criminals are psychotic and few psychotics commit serious crimes.

Dunham discovered further that persons suffering from schizophrenia were most likely of all types of psychotic persons to commit crimes. He also found that a rather high percentage of the schizophrenics in the state (noncriminal) hospitals for the mentally abnormal had some kind of criminal record, not necessarily for serious offenses. For this analysis he used the records of 870 schizophrenics between the ages of 15 and 20, committed to state hospitals from Chicago between the years 1922 and 1934. The group was first classified into 2 subtypes; the catatonics, who show such traits as "seclusiveness, self-consciousness, anxiety qualities, feeling of difference, seriousness, submissiveness, conformity, and home attachment" and the paranoids who "display the first 5 traits indicated for the catatonic, but in addition, show certain differentiating traits such as aggressiveness, stubbornness, quarrelsomeness, suspiciousness, egocentricity, and home rebellion." [21]   Of the 525 seclusive catatonic schizophrenics, 1 had been a juvenile delinquent, 5 had adult police records, and 15.0 per cent of the group had records in the files of the bureau of identification.   Of the 345 quarrelsome paranoid schizophrenics, 2 were juvenile delinquents and 34.2 per cent were registered at the bureau of identification because of police records.   Most of the offenses were of a minor character.   Approximately 3 per cent of the catatonics and 7 per cent of the paranoids were sent immediately to the psychopathic hospital upon the commission of their crimes—an indication that the crimes were committed after the psychosis was developed.   Another indication of the relation of the crime to the psychosis lies in the fact that 11 per cent of the catatonics and 15 per cent of the paranoids committed their crimes after they had been treated in the state hospitals and released; it may be assumed that in many of these cases the psychosis had not been cured but was still a factor in the motivation of the individual.[22]   These figures are roughly comparable to those already given for the inmates of the Michigan hospital.

It should be noted that not too many inferences should be drawn from these figures in interpreting the relation of psychoses to crime.   In both studies an intensive search was made into the past of each individual studied to ascertain his criminal record.   We do not know what the results would be if a mentally normal group at large in the community of comparable age, education, and occupation were to be queried about their juvenile and adult records of delinquency and crime.   Would the mentally normal group show a higher or lower percentage than the psychotic group with a criminal record? Would the crimes of the normal group be more or less serious than those of the psychotics?   Until such a comparative study has been made we cannot conclude that psychotics are more or less criminal in conduct than normal persons.

If we try to untangle and sum up the incidence of mental abnormality among criminals we arrive at the following tentative conclusion: mental abnormality afflicts only a small proportion of those who commit major crimes (felonies) at the time the crime is committed; among minor offenders a larger proportion (perhaps 20 per cent) suffers from minor difficulties;

schizophrenics seem more likely than other types of psychotics to commit major crimes; when minor as well as major crimes are considered, inmates of state hospitals are guilty of such conduct before the onset of the psychosis in about 10 per cent of the cases and after the onset in about 15 per cent.

Importance of Studying Mentally Disturbed Criminals

In view of the rather small percentage of criminals who are mentally maladjusted, the question may be raised as to why a large amount of space should be devoted to their consideration. For 2 reasons this group of criminals merits more study than it has hitherto been given and should be brought under some type of control.

1. The more seriously affected persons—those with psychoses—often commit only one crime before they are taken into custody. But this crime is often of the spectacular and bizarre type that arouses public indignation and horror. It may seem unmotivated from a normal point of view, for the motivation may not lie in any real situation but in the fantasy world in which the psychotic lives. Dunham states that among the schizophrenic criminals that he studied murder was the most frequent crime, with larceny, burglary, and armed robbery next in order.[23] Assault with or without murder may occur over some imagined wrong. The abnormal manner in which some of the crimes are committed has some inner symbolism for the psychotic criminal. Not understanding the crime, the public often demands harsh punishment, and occasionally takes matters into its own hands and lynches the perpetrator of some horrifying crime. For the protection of the psychotic person as well as for his possible victims, more careful study of psychotics and adequate provision for their treatment are necessary.

2. Persons with psychoneurosis or psychopathic personality are less likely to commit spectacular crimes, but they are persistent offenders. Psychoneurosis is a fairly permanent feature of the personality unless a person is given early and adequate psychiatric treatment; the psychopathic personality is even more incurable, for psychopaths usually resist attempts of psychiatrists to assist them. Hence a psychoneurotic or a psychopath who tends toward criminal behavior may be a confirmed recidivist who appears in court time after time for reprimand, fines, or short jail sentences. Because the misdemeanor or crime is motivated from within, and satisfies a frustration or longing, these punishments are not effective. If such offenders could have their maladies understood and could be cured by psychiatric treatments, the police, prosecuting attorneys, and judges would be saved an enormous amount of time, and many habitual offenders would be enabled to lead normal, law-abiding lives.

QUESTIONS

1. Why does the maladjusted criminal feel no regret for his crime?

2. Is the person who is described as criminally insane essentially a criminal or a psychotic? In legal proceedings following a crime, which is he often considered?

3. Explain why some psychotics resist efforts to cure them.

4. Give the chief symptoms of schizophrenia, manic depressive psychosis, involutional melancholia, and paranoia. What behavior, typical of each, conflicts with criminal laws?

5. What is the relation of psychoneurosis to criminal conduct?

6. Why did Lindner call the criminal psychopath a "rebel without a cause"?

7. Approximately what proportion of felons (persons guilty of serious crimes) have mental abnormalities? Approximately what proportion of those committed to institutions for the insane have committed crimes? How great is the overlapping between the criminal and the insane groups?

READINGS

Alexander, Franz, and William Healy, *Roots of Crime: Psychoanalytic Studies* (Knopf, 1935). A psychoanalytic analysis of certain types of criminals.

Bromberg, Walter, *Crime and the Mind* (Lippincott, 1949). This book discusses the legal status of mental disorders as a cause of crime and also the relation of different types of disorder to crime.

Lindner, Robert M., *Rebel without a Cause* (New York: Grune and Stratton, 1944). This book consists of the analysis of the behavior of a criminal in prison; hypnosis was used to penetrate beyond the criminal's conscious defenses.

Wertham, Frederic, *Dark Legend: A Study in Murder* (New York: Duell, Sloan and Pearce, 1941). Analysis of motivations of adolescent boy who murdered his mother.

FOOTNOTES

[1] Fredric Wertham, *Dark Legend: A Study in Murder* (New York: Duell, Sloan and Pearce, 1941).

[2] H. W. Dunham, "The Schizophrene and Criminal Behavior," *American Sociological Review*, 4 (1939), 356.

[3] Wertham, *op. cit.*, p. 42.

[4] L. Radzinowicz and J. W. C. Turner (eds.), *Mental Abnormality and Crime*, English Studies in Criminal Science, 2 (London: Macmillan, 1944), 12–13.

[5] R. F. Yeomans, "Who are the 'Criminal Insane'?" *Mental Hygiene,* 14 (1930), 673–96.

[6] Radzinowicz and Turner, *op. cit.,* p. 15.

[7] Yeomans, *op. cit.*

[8] J. Wortis, "Sex Taboos, Sex Offenders, and the Law," *American Journal of Orthopsychiatry,"* 9 (1939), 554–64.

[9] Radzinowicz and Turner, *op. cit.,* ch. 3.

[10] *Ibid.,* pp. xvi and 115.

[11] Robert M. Lindner, *Rebel without a Cause* (New York: Grune and Stratton, 1944),

pp. 1–14. See also Robert M. Lindner, *Stone Walls and Men* (New York: Odyssey, 1946), ch. 10.

[12] H. S. Hurlbert, "Constitutional Psychopathic Inferiority in Relation to Delinquency," *Journal of Criminal Law and Criminology*, 30 (1939), 3–31.

[13] S. A. Silk, "Differential Diagnosis," in "The Psychopathic Individual: A Symposium," *Mental Hygiene*, 8 (1924), 183–86.

[14] Lindner, *Rebel without a Cause*.

[15] Bernard Glueck, "Concerning Prisoners," *Mental Hygiene*, 2 (1918), 1–42. Also quoted in C. B. Thompson, "Some New Aspects of the Psychiatric Approach to Crime," *Mental Hygiene*, 20 (1936), 531.

[16] Morris Ploscowe, *Some Causative Factors in Criminality*, No. 13, Vol. 1 of the reports of the National Commission on Law Observance and Enforcement (Washington: Government Printing Office, 1931), 51.

[17] W. Bromberg and C. B. Thompson, "The Relation of Psychoses, Mental Defect, and Personality Types to Types of Crime," *Journal of Criminal Law and Criminology*, 28 (1937), 70–89.

[18] P. Schilder, "The Cure of Criminals and Prevention of Crime," *Journal of Criminal Psychopathology*, 2 (1940–41), 152.

[19] M. H. Erickson, "Criminality in a Group of Male Psychiatric Patients," *Mental Hygiene*, 22 (1938), 459–76.

[20] Dunham, *op. cit.*, p. 355.

[21] *Ibid.*, p. 355.

[22] *Ibid.*, pp. 356–58.

[23] *Ibid.*, p. 356.

Prevention of Delinquency
and Crime

The cost of crime is enormous, in terms of both money and human productivity and happiness. Vast sums are spent each year to support
the law-enforcement machinery of the nation and to pay for the confinement of delinquents and criminals in correctional and penal institutions.
In addition huge amounts are lost through theft and embezzlement by persons
who make no productive return for the money they appropriate. On the
human side, the community loses whatever contribution the delinquents and
criminals might have made had they been law abiding; also families and often
criminals suffer unhappiness; and frequently human life is lost. If delinquency and crime could be prevented, a tremendous saving would be effected
in money and in the productivity, harmony, and happiness of the community
and its members.

Many suggestions have been made regarding the best way to prevent delinquent and criminal behavior from ever occurring in the community.
Some of them have been expressed by organized groups that have tried to
promote a single method of prevention. At one extreme are those who
advocate sterilization of criminals. Sterilization involves a physical operation upon the criminal to prevent procreation. The underlying assumption
is that criminality or traits that produce criminal behavior are inherited. In
terms of our present-day knowledge of crime this assumption is unwarranted.
No one trait leads to criminal behavior; in fact it is not clear that an innate
trait of any sort is involved in most cases but rather that early training and
processes of personality formation are the roots of later crimes. Feeble-
mindedness and psychoses, sometimes cited to justify sterilization, are not
directly related to crime; nor is sufficient known of their heredity to justify
sterilization. Although more than half the states have at some time passed
laws permitting sterilization under certain circumstances, in practice the laws
are not widely applied. The uncertainty of knowledge regarding heredity
of pertinent traits, as well as the feeling that the ability to reproduce is of

great value to the individual and the community, induce extreme caution in the application of these laws.

Supervised recreation has been the universal preventive advocated by many professional recreation workers, and many boys' clubs have based their claim to financial support from the community chiefly upon the unsupported statement that the work of the club prevents delinquency. Advocates of slum clearance, noting the concentration of delinquency in such areas, have set forth the hope that replacing deteriorated houses with modern and well-organized housing projects would reduce or eliminate delinquency. Character education in the schools, weekday religious education, visiting teachers, child-guidance clinics, and many other programs have been widely advocated as delinquency preventive programs from time to time.

Many, perhaps most, of these programs are valuable as delinquency prevention, and the continuance of most of them can also be justified on other grounds. But too often the program is not based on a well-rounded conception of the causes of delinquency, and too much is claimed for it. An adequate system of delinquency prevention should consider the following facts, all of which have been developed in the preceding chapters.

1. There are many types of delinquents and criminals: the casual delinquent who is essentially law abiding; the occasional criminal; the professional criminal; the habitual criminal whose crimes are really vices; the episodic criminal, who commits perhaps just one emotional crime; the respectable segmental criminal; and the mentally disturbed criminal. It is unreasonable to suppose that one type of prevention will suffice for all of them.

2. Criminal behavior begins during youth. This fact is obvious among confirmed and professional criminals whose crime careers have been traced. It is less obvious to the layman but well substantiated by psychiatrists in the cases of emotional and psychotic criminals. Once the delinquent habits have become established and form part of the personality, the problem is not one of prevention but of reorganization and reform—a subject to be discussed later. Preventive measures must be taken before criminal conduct appears, or in the early vague stages of digression from the mores before the criminal code and philosophy are closely woven into the personality. The same approach applies to the habitual offender who must be reached before his law-breaking vices become compelling habits. Similarly, the maladjusted person must be reorganized before he becomes psychotic. Therefore preventive measures pertain to the roving and unsupervised boy, the restless girl, the unhappy and brooding or rebellious adolescent. When the offender can be classified as an habitual or a professional criminal the time

for preventive work has passed. Then reform alone remains—a more difficult task. Preventive programs should primarily concern children and adolescents.

3. To be effective, a preventive program must by-pass the obvious symptoms of crime—the criminal acts—and discover the underlying causes. The causes, not the symptoms, must be the point of attack.

The causes of crime are so varied and some of them are so closely related to the basic organization of community and national life that the development of a preventive program is difficult. A brief review of some of the proved and assumed causes of crime provides a starting point for consideration of a preventive program.

One factor in the development of a criminal career is the existence of disorganized areas both in large cities and in the rural countryside that contain institutions directly encouraging the development of criminal conduct. Junk dealers who incite boys to steal metal fixtures from vacant houses, pawnshops that accept goods known or suspected to have been stolen, pimps or women who induce young girls to enter prostitution as a means of earning a living—all are examples of influences that encourage criminal conduct.

In these same areas other institutions cater to human desires that are regarded as better suppressed than exercised. In some instances, as among drug peddlers, the activity is criminal. In others, as saloons and taverns, the activity is supposedly regulated to prevent abuse. Houses of prostitution, disreputable dance halls, gambling establishments, clubs and poolrooms where adolescents meet older criminals or develop demoralizing habits are other examples of institutions that cater to undesirable human cravings. Disorganized areas also lack many of the more constructive community agencies and, what is more important, are deficient in local leadership that supports the mores of the conventional community.

Juvenile delinquency and hence adult crime are frequently nurtured in an unhappy family situation. The broken home is somewhat more likely to produce delinquent children than the unbroken home; its significance, however, lies not in the fact that one parent is absent but in the fact that broken homes more often are psychologically disorganized than are homes with both parents present.

Some delinquency seems to be related not to the emotionally disorganized home but to lack of training in accepted mores of orderly conduct, honesty, and respect for others. This deficient training is perhaps most common in families of foreign background in that the parents have least understanding of American folkways and mores.

Affiliation of both boys and girls with unsupervised play groups and gangs that tend toward delinquent behavior is another factor. These groups are most prevalent in disorganized areas of the city and affect most the children of poorly organized families.

Certain types of serious emotional disturbance may lead to the sudden outburst of some criminal act, usually of a violent nature and often injurious to another person. A minor percentage of crimes are committed by psycho-neurotic, psychopathic, or psychotic persons, as a part of the behavior pattern of the disease.

The successful careers of professional criminals offer disorganized and semidelinquent youth a ready example of crime without punishment. Similarly, the continued practice of graft on the part of public officials and of unethical or illegal activities on the part of business and professional men hold the promise of a rich return, and make difficult the task of educational and social agencies in training youth in more sober and slower methods of earning a living or accumulating wealth.

Another and perhaps the most deep-seated factor among the many causes of crime is the attitude of the public toward it. Tolerance of certain types of lawbreaking and apathy toward others insures the continued existence of criminal groups ready to accept the promising novice and to hold forth the assurance of large rewards for little work.

When these various factors are considered in relation to each other, we find four general situations that are closely related to the inception of delinquency and crime: disorganized local communities; families deficient in unity or in ability to train their children; emotional and mental disturbances of temporary or permanent nature; and the apathy of the larger community and the prevalence of attitudes permitting the continued operations of powerful criminal groups and criminal practices among certain business corporations. Preventive work now in progress is discussed under these four headings.

COMMUNITY REORGANIZATION

Community reorganization may require the revitalizing and adaptation of individual institutions; or may involve the community as a whole. Efforts of individual institutions to prevent delinquency are of longer standing than are attempts to reorganize entire communities.

Public Schools

The public schools of the nation have a unique opportunity to form strong characters, citizenship ideals, and to identify poorly adjusted children. Seventy-four per cent of boys and girls aged 14 to 17 are in secondary schools and a still higher percentage of younger children attend elementary schools.[1]

The schools, therefore, are in contact with children in the early stages of development, when preventive measures are most easily applied.

Not all schools make a positive approach to building character nor attempt to counteract the early stages of delinquent behavior. Vision and imagination as well as a knowledge of child psychology on the part of administrative officers and teachers are basic, and the school program must be organized to develop attitudes and conduct in conformity with community standards. The formal curriculum of academic subjects does not present much opportunity for character training, personality study, or remedial work. Cultivation of honesty, courtesy, fair play, and the like is somewhat incidental and often so closely linked with a repressive schoolroom atmosphere that the boy or girl thinks of these qualities as being part of the curriculum to be discarded and forgotten as soon as the school door is passed. When definite pre-delinquent situations arise the action of teachers and school officials is usually repressive. The occasional truant is tracked down, brought back, and punished for his actions without much attempt to understand why he did not want to come to school. Teachers and administrative officers are often outsiders who come into the community merely to teach, and who do not in any real sense become part of the community. This circumstance is true in the large city where the teachers in disorganized or slum areas have been reared in different types of communities and continue to live far distant from the sections in which they teach. It is also the case in many smaller cities, since teachers come in from other places but do not regard the city where they teach as home. Every vacation, during the school term as well as summer, is spent elsewhere; contacts are largely confined to other teachers, also from the outside, and the teacher does not really become a part of the community. She does not exert much influence beyond the formal schoolroom contacts.

Recognition is growing, however, on the part of teacher-training institutions, administrators, and teachers that they may make a two-pronged approach to delinquency prevention: constructive and positive training in responsible ethical conduct for all children; and special help for handicapped and poorly adjusted children, including those already delinquent.

The positive training for all children may be narrowly conceived as training for democratic citizenship or for obedience to laws, or broadly, as meeting the needs of youth with needs comprehensively defined to cover the child's current physical, personal, and social needs as well as preparation for the future.[2] With needs thus broadly defined, the teaching of individual academic subjects is no longer sufficient. Many school systems, therefore, are experimenting with the correlation of subjects, the building of a teaching program around problems rather than subjects, and the expansion of teaching from

the classroom into planned contacts in the community.   In addition to encouraging the pupil to face and deal with life-situations, the programs build
up a co-operative spirit between teacher and pupils and place the teacher in a
position to guide pupils without a sense of compulsion.

For a minority of children, more is needed than such a general program.
Proper placement of children in school is essential.   Children of dull or low
mentality may experience only a sense of failure and dissatisfaction as a result
of their inability to keep up with children of their chronological age.   If they
are not promoted and find themselves with younger children, the sense of failure is deepened.   Misconduct in school is one result of this unhappiness and
frustration.   Another is the seeking of satisfaction outside the school, perhaps playing truant in order to carry on satisfying but delinquent activities
with some other truant.   Larger cities usually have special programs for dull
children but in smaller cities where the number of dull children is small, the
problem of their education and personality development is often neglected.

Guidance and counseling of individual boys and girls are now emphasized,
a service that can be of special help to the incipient delinquent.[3]   The initial
counseling may come from the classroom teacher, who is supported by specially trained counselors to whom she may refer children.   These counselors
carry the process further but also may in turn refer the child or his family to
a specialized community agency, such as a child guidance clinic or family
service agency.   The school that is aware of the needs of children is in an
especially strategic position, since all children pass through the schools, and
children with emotional or conduct problems may be spotted long before
their difficulties become sufficiently serious to bring them to the attention of
clinic, police, or juvenile court.[4]

The public school systems of a few cities include a special school for predelinquents.   An example is the Montefiore School in Chicago, operated
since 1929 by the Chicago Board of Education.[5]   This school accepts boys
between the ages of 10 and 17 whose conduct has been such that they could
not be retained in the ordinary schoolroom.   Transfers from regular schools
to the Montefiore school are arranged through school authorities and every
effort is made to avoid the appearance of the boys in court.   The school is
organized into small classes of about 25 boys each, which are supervised by
specially trained teachers.   The Chicago Board of Health furnishes medical
and dental services; each boy is given a complete medical examination when
he enters the school.   A psychiatrist handles all severe cases of misbehavior
and a psychologist studies any mental handicaps or special abilities.   The
director of personnel and the truant officers carry on social work with the boy
and his family.   In placing the new boy many factors are considered; age,
mental level, educational achievements, mechanical aptitudes, educational

disabilities, interest in drawing, and personality characteristics.   About half the boys are mentally retarded or have some language or reading disability that lowers their test scores, and another 15 per cent are uneven in development and achievement.   Emphasis is placed on learning by activities as well as from books.

The school is well equipped for an activities program for it possesses a manual training room, electric and metal shops, provision for reed-weaving, rug-making, and mechanical and freehand drawing.   There is a science laboratory, library, music room, small gymnasium, and a game room.   Individual instruction is given in reading, arithmetic, and speech.   During the recreational period the boys are taught to co-operate in group play, an activity with which they often seem unfamiliar.   Academic work is emphasized wherever possible in order to bring each boy up to his highest achievement and, if possible, make feasible his transfer back to the regular school.

A report in 1935 stated that the attendance had been 90 per cent perfect, although 65 per cent of the boys were habitual truants before being transferred to Montefiore.   Less than 18 per cent were taken before the juvenile court and over 84 per cent of those returned to regular schools make good. Those who work in and write about the school are convinced that the converging of specialists upon the individual boy to help him solve his problems and the adjustment of the school program to his needs have saved many of the boys from becoming delinquents and criminals.

Schools have a unique opportunity for positive training in good citizenship and adjustment; they are also in a strategic position to discover and help children in early stages of delinquency and maladjustment.

Religious Training

Religious institutions as a rule play a double function: they provide for their members a creed regarding man's relation to the supernatural; and they support a code of morals, usually related both to their creed and to the mores of the environing society.   Occasionally a religious group advocates values and patterns of behavior that are contrary to the prevailing moral code of the larger society and consequently finds itself criticized or subject to criminal legal action.   Some examples of such groups were cited in Chapter 1.   By and large, however, churches, synagogues, and temples support the moral order of society, and have a function to play in delinquency prevention.

As with the programs of other institutions (schools, settlement houses, police systems), religious programs do not lend themselves easily to critical study of their preventive properties.   As the writer has pointed out in an article in *Federal Probation,* the values of religion and membership in religious institutions undoubtedly are a factor in the conforming behavior of many people.[6]   We do not know how many otherwise might become delinquents or criminals.   But mere affiliation with a religious group is not sufficient. According to the Gluecks' study of 1,000 juvenile delinquents, 93 per cent of the families had a nominal designation as Catholic, Protestant, or Jewish.[7] The weakness of the affiliation, however, is shown by the fact that 70 per cent of the families had low moral standards and 58 per cent included members with criminal records.   Another study of delinquents in Passaic, New Jersey, made by Kvaraceus, shows that most of the boys and girls had some religious affiliation, that 54 per cent attended services regularly and 20 per cent occasionally.[8]   A third study was made by Wattenberg of Detroit boys interviewed by police in 1946 after complaints had been made against them. Among 2,137 boys, 44 per cent were regular church attendants and 25 per cent were occasional attendants.[9]   In 1947, 672 of the same boys were again in trouble.   When the twice delinquent boys were compared with the nonrepeaters, it was found that 38 per cent of the repeaters as compared with 46 per cent of the non-repeaters were regular church attendants.   The church-going boys were a slightly better risk than the nonchurch boys, but the difference is not great.   It is evident that among church affiliates and attendants there are many who become delinquent, just as among school pupils or club members in community centers and settlements there are also many deviants.

Several careful studies made in the late 1920's sought to correlate fine character qualities with religious education.   The extensive tests made by Hartshorne and May demonstrated that there was no significant difference between Sunday school attendants and nonattendants where honesty is concerned and that academic teaching of morality did not make children more truthful and honest.[10]   Other studies, for example, by Hightower, supported their findings.[11]   These studies suggest the need for a different approach on the part of religious institutions than the academic one.

If teaching in religious values and morality is to be effective it must make the values an integral part of the child's personality.   The process by which a child achieves any system of values is social-psychological: the child accepts the values of people with whom he has close associations, whom he admires, and who reward him in some way for his compliance.   In time, the child accepts these socially taught values as his own and has a standard (or conscience) by which to measure his conduct.   This process is the same one by which the child becomes delinquent through close association with a delinquent gang or with older, admired delinquents, who may at times be members of his own family.   The religious institution often is not in a position to provide the conditions for the child's identification with religious leaders.   A few hours on one day a week are not sufficient to offset daily contact with delinquents during the remainder of the week. The religious program may rely too heavily on academic learning without bringing the moral principles into conjunction with the child's daily problems and needs. Religion may easily become segmental and not be integrated into the whole personality. The religious institution in a community with conflicting value-systems has an especially difficult task. The groups and institutions that tolerate or promote crime—the gangs, fences, corrupt police—offer easy solution to many needs, whereas the religious program may demand discipline, self-denial, and self-control. The rewards of delinquency often are immediate and tangible; the rewards of religion often are intangible or promised only for the future, sometimes a future as far away as life after death. Religion therefore struggles against many powerful antireligious influences in many communities.

In the deteriorated areas of large cities, some religious institutions supplement individual religious training by many types of group activities where, under supervision, moral principles may be put into practice. The church with a weekday recreational or club program, with a summer camp, or with classes in art and dramatics is moving in this direction. Some institutions also provide counseling for troubled individuals, either through a trained social worker or by a minister with special training in counseling. These institutions are not discarding religion but are seeking to make it vital in meeting people's needs.

The religious institution with the fewest problems is probably the one in a community in which the consensus of opinion on moral matters is uniform and where all major institutions share the same values. In such communities, parents, schools, religious institutions, newspapers, community centers, and the like all tend to co-ordinate their efforts and children are exposed to a steady pressure toward one pattern of conduct. Such communities exist, but they are not numerous in large cities, where there is great diversity within one community of religions, ethnic backgrounds, and moral standards. The efforts of religious groups may be thwarted by other groups or institutions in the community.

The Police

The police, like the public schools, are a pervasive institution, reaching into all corners of the community. They have a degree of coverage that few agencies possess. Traditionally the force that steps in after a delinquency or crime has been committed, the police have more recently realized their potential capacity for preventive work. The police as a crime-preventive agency involves a new conception of police duties. This function was first inaugurated in 1925 in Berkeley, California, by Chief of Police August Vollmer.   A special bureau of the police force, known as the Crime Prevention Division, was established under the direction of a psychiatric social worker.

Since that date, the police departments in many cities have added crime prevention to their list of duties, under a Crime Prevention Division, a Juvenile Bureau, or through policewomen.   In some cities, the same police officers also handle juvenile delinquents.   The line, then, between prevention of delinquency and control of delinquents becomes hazy, just as the line between mischievous and unsupervised play and definite delinquent acts is hard to define.   Each police department has its own conception of what constitutes preventive work.   In the original Crime Prevention Division, in Berkeley, the functions of the Division in 1936 were stated as follows: [12]

1. Working with adults; investigating and interviewing juvenile delinquents, that is, adolescent females, very young girls and boys up to 12 years of age (boys over 12 years are handled by an inspector of police who formerly did all the juvenile delinquency work); and deciding upon official disposition or unofficial probation.

2. Organization of predelinquency work; co-operation with community resources.

3. Changing the public attitude toward crime-prevention work in a Police Department through speeches and other forms of publicity.

4. Organization of community work, such as doing committee work and developing extensive volunteer service from the University of California and other sources for developing activities in connection with juvenile work.

5. Working still farther "upstream" so as to promote interest in the health, happiness and welfare of children.

The Youth Bureau of the Detroit Police Department combines control and preventive work.[13]   The Bureau is charged with the responsibility of investigating all complaints of misbehavior on the part of juvenile boys and girls. In 1952, this function of the Bureau brought the policemen and policewomen attached to it into contact with some 3,600 girls and 15,000 boys, two thirds of whom were interviewed during investigations of complaints but were found not to be involved, one third of whom were misconduct cases.   In addition, over 15,000 boys and girls, not offenders, met with police officers to obtain advice or assistance of some sort.   Among this vast total of almost 34,000 boys and girls with whom the police had direct contact, a small minority (about 6,000) were offenders.   The contacts with the other 28,000 might fall into the classification of general assistance and delinquency prevention.   In addition, the police attached to the Bureau patrol and inspect doubtful places where youth congregate, such as poolrooms, bowling alleys, theatres, confectioneries, and other hangouts, to enforce when necessary compliance with standards that will discourage delinquency.   Many contacts that the Bureau officers make with community agencies also come under the heading of prevention: they give thousands of talks to adult groups and make specific contacts with social agencies for boys in need of their assistance. The Bureau also sponsors both Girl and Boy Scout troops, providing police officers as leaders.   The Bureau does not carry its preventive work to the point of case work treatment of seriously disturbed children, but does screen out children to be merely reprimanded and returned to their parents, to be referred to the juvenile court, and to be referred to specific agencies.   In addition to control of actual delinquency and preventive contacts with both children and community groups, the program is calculated to change the traditional conception of the policeman as someone who threatens and punishes to acceptance of the police officer as a friendly and helpful person.

The New York City Police Department has gone further than any other city police department in the development of its work with youth.[14]   The Juvenile Aid Bureau handles both delinquents and "potential" delinquents or children who may commit delinquent acts if their behavior is not checked. In 1949, 17,447 boys and girls were referred to the Juvenile Aid Bureau, 81 per cent by its own officers or members of the regular police force, the remainder by parents, courts, schools, individuals, or social agencies.   The Bureau is empowered to handle all cases of delinquents and of children guilty of serious crimes up to age 16, and minor offenders from age 16 to age 21 (but not those guilty of felonies).   The Bureau carries a heavy responsibility and makes important decisions.   The officers handle the minor misconduct cases directly, sending the children home with admonitions, talking with the parents, or referring the child directly to some recreational program; they refer children with more serious problems to social agencies; they refer children whose cases do not seem to fit into the program of any available agency to the Bureau's own Service Unit, which then carries out case work treatment directly.   Two thirds of all cases are adjusted by the Bureau itself.   Only as a last resort does the Bureau refer a child to the juvenile court, priding itself upon keeping children out of court.   From this point of view, most of the work of the Bureau may be regarded as preventive, at least of serious delinquency on the part of younger children.   The efforts of the Bureau do not, however, forestall referrals to the court from other sources: the police, parents, school officials and others refer children directly to the juvenile court, sometimes children who are also on the active list of cases at the Bureau.

The New York Police Department has also carried its work into another area—group recreation.[15]   The Police Athletic League—known as PAL—was first organized by the Police Department.   Now, separately organized and operated by public contributions, the League is administratively staffed by members of the police department.   Approximately 300,000 boys and girls each year participate in the recreational programs carried out in youth centers, on streets, in playgrounds, and in summer camps.

The Juvenile Aid Bureau and PAL are both lauded and criticized. The specially staffed Bureau, whose officers are stationed in all parts of the city, is able to make immediate inspections and check-ups on incipient delinquent behavior and to adjust problems on the spot or refer them to other agencies. The Bureau thus takes the initiative in investigating doubtful behavior. Similarly, the activities of PAL extend into all parts of New York, after an earlier concentration in areas with high delinquency rates. The criticism is directed at two phases of the work. It is contended by critics that the attempt to do case work is inadequately handled, since the case workers are primarily policemen and women and secondarily trained in case work. The Bureau is also criticized for extending its work into the recreational field, clearly beyond the traditional function of a police department. The Bureau defends its position on both case work and PAL by pointing out that both services were established to fill in gaps left unserviced by other social and recreational agencies.

Many other cities have agencies similar to those of either Detroit or New York City. The possibilities of police departments for preventive work should not be overlooked. Along with the public schools, the police reach into every area of a city. They carry a type of authority sometimes needed by adults who exploit children and by youths who disregard the rights of others. They are, however, in a difficult position for preventive work inasmuch as authority must be curbed and friendliness and a relationship of confidence fostered between officer and youth if preventive work is to be anything except superficial.

Recreation and Group Work

Community houses, settlements, and varous types of boys' clubs are all popularly regarded as institutions that prevent delinquency. Thrasher's study of the Boys' Club in New York, failed to find proof that the club had prevented delinquency among its members.[16] In support of the clubs of this type, it should be emphasized that Thrasher's study was made when the club had been in its present location only four years, and it would perhaps be expecting a great deal for the club to have established its influence in that time. However, added significance is given to Thrasher's observations by Healy and Bronner in one of their studies of delinquents.[17] They found that the delinquent boys were more active in community agencies and took greater advantage of recreational facilities than did the control group of nondelinquents. Although this tendency of delinquent boys toward social participation might give the community agency a relatively high percentage of delinquents among its members, it opens an excellent opportunity to the agency. Some community agencies have deliberately taken advantage of the gang formation of delinquent boys by inviting the entire gang into the agency, and gradually substituting vigorous athletic sports for delinquent or disorderly activities.

City boys lack most of the outdoor opportunities of rural youth.   One club, sponsored by the board of education in a large city, has ingeniously installed a fireplace on the school roof.   Here boys may roast potatoes and hot dogs or cook other food.   Such fireplaces reduce the hazard from fires in alleys or vacant lots.   (Acme)

In contrast to these studies, which indicate a tendency for delinquents to join clubs, a more recent one made in Cincinnati showed that group work agencies drew their members primarily from among children under age 15 and rapidly lost members as they reached the middle and later teens—the ages where juvenile delinquents predominate.[18]   In the general population, 26 per cent of youths were aged 15–17; in the group work agencies, 22 per cent; and among juvenile court cases, 65 per cent.   There was also evidence that agency members came from families with more economic and social security than did the delinquents.   The report suggests that the program of the group work agencies studied did not appeal as strongly to delinquent youth as to younger children with more secure family backgrounds. It should be noted that many group work agencies no longer attempt to appeal specifically to delinquents but formulate their function as the development of leadership and democratically oriented character in youth drawn from all areas of the city.

Agencies that wish specifically to appeal to delinquents face the problem of making the supervised program sufficiently exciting and adventurous to provide a complete substitute for the excitement of robbing stores or over-turning fruit stands.

In some cities, for example, Philadelphia, a recreational agency appoints certain staff members to work with groups of boys or girls wherever they may be found without trying to entice them into the organized program of an agency.[19]   Some groups are well socialized within themselves—although it may be along delinquency patterns—but are wary of the motives of community centers or organized clubs.   A trained recreational or group work leader may be able to establish rapport on a personal basis and gradually influence the behavior and goals of the group.[20]

The development of group work as a special branch of professional social work has given a new significance to programs for groups of children and young people.   Group work is a combination of group recreation and case work.   Clubs, games, sports, and crafts become the medium through which the group work leader reaches children; the purpose, however, goes beyond the teaching of skills and good sportsmanship, beyond filling idle hours with constructive activity.   Group work has as its objective the development of well-balanced personalities through group participation.   The leader, there-fore, makes himself familiar with the needs and capacities of each child and seeks to guide the group in such a way that each child develops to the utmost.

Group therapy is an expansion of group work into the field of adjustment of socially and psychologically maladjusted people.   It is being used with seriously maladjusted people in mental hospitals on the one hand and with criminals in prisons and reformatories on the other.   It is also used with people in the community who have mild emotional or conduct problems. The groups with which the therapist works may be artificially formed, in contrast to the natural groups that the recreational and group work leaders supervise.   In children's groups, play and various activities form the ob-vious part of the program.   The leader, however, usually knows from previous individual studies made, perhaps by a clinic, what the problems of the individuals are.   He observes the reactions of each child, encourages, guides, if necessary restrains.   The groups are small in membership and the atmosphere is very permissive.   There is no planned program.   In this setting, children further reveal their difficulties and begin to find a solution. The boy with a domineering father may find in the leader a more friendly and just father substitute. The one who is hostile toward parents or siblings may be able to express this hostility in aggressive play or in rough and tumble play with other children without the feeling of guilt or fear of punishment that would accompany hostility in the family. The excessively shy child gradually finds a way to express himself when under no pressure. Hostility that has taken the form of vandalism in neighborhood or at school may be released through unchecked destruction of certain types of play materials. In severe cases individual therapy may be carried out concurrently with the group therapy, since the final result sought is a change of attitude.

Among adolescents and adults, group discussions replace play. Again the group is small and the leader very permissive; any subject may be discussed. The experience described by Beier is illustrative of group therapy with a gang of boys who were headed toward delinquent activities.[21] In a friendly and permissive atmosphere, the boys gradually were able to bring many personal problems into the open and through group discussion understand them better.

A shortcoming of many community agencies, settlements, and clubs is that they are grafted upon a local community or neighborhood. More often than not the neighborhood chosen by well-meaning people from prosperous communities in which to locate a community center is one whose residents are of foreign or rural extraction. Unless care is taken the agency merely becomes another means of breaking the allegiance of the boy or girl to the family without carrying them completely into the urban American way of living. In the absence of some means of interweaving the folkways and mores of the local community with those represented by the agency, its activities may become only a segment in youthful lives already divided by other diverse and sometimes conflicting influences. To be truly effective the agency needs to be thoroughly incorporated into the community organization. Members of the local community should serve on the board of directors and group leaders should be drawn largely from the local community and if necessary given special training in group work and leadership. The techniques of group work may be learned in the courses offered in universities; the language, folkways, traditions, and sentiments of the local community are less readily acquired without long residence in the neighborhood and acceptance as a member of the particular group.

Many persons regard recreation as the key to delinquency prevention. Park programs, numerous small playgrounds, swimming pools and beaches, and blocked-off streets in lieu of parks, are all advocated as methods of preventing delinquency. It is perhaps true that when boys are playing in these selected spots they are not getting into mischief, but it is not always so clear that recreation accomplishes more than to fill unoccupied time. If the recreation is under good leadership—and again leadership that understands the local folkways and mores—positive attitudes and behavior patterns may develop. If the play groups are more or less permanent so that a long-term program may be effected the chances of developing desirable attitudes and habits are greatly increased.* Group work that reaches beyond recreation and group therapy for the badly twisted personalities have great promise.

City-Wide Co-ordination

The long range trend of social and civic agencies has been toward ever finer specialization in function. Our philosophy of local autonomy has also led to the founding of many agencies within one city, each serving perhaps one small neighborhood and blinding its eyes to the needs of adjacent areas. Recently, the need for co-ordination has been recognized in order to give more complete and uniform service to all parts of a community.[22]

Some efforts at co-ordination have been formal and general—that is, they refer to all types of social agencies and not specifically to those working with delinquents and criminals. The Community Chest that collects and distributes funds for the use of privately supported agencies is one example. The social service exchange is another example; it registers individual cases reported by agencies and in turn on request informs a member agency which other agencies have already given service to a client.

More difficult is the co-ordination of the activities of social and civic agencies to increase coverage and prevent or eliminate overlapping of functions among agencies. Some co-ordinating efforts bring together agencies with many different functions, such as the community welfare council or the council of social agencies. Other efforts unite only agencies with identical or similar purposes. Illustrative are citywide youth councils in which young people and community leaders work for better youth programs; recreation councils; and delinquency prevention committees or councils. Through an over-all group, usually composed of representatives of different public and private agencies and often of churches, schools, and other institutions, a common effort is made to accomplish the objective of delinquency prevention, or, stated positively, of producing responsible young people.[23]

Several such efforts on a community or city level are here described.

---

* The criticism of community centers, parks, playgrounds, and the like as a means of preventing delinquency should not be taken as a criticism of these agencies per se. All of them can be justified on many grounds even though they may not prevent delinquency. Some of the justifiable bases for those that are adequately organized and staffed are: a meeting place for foreign and American cultures; healthful recreation; development of physical skills; growth of interest and ability in arts and crafts; and—not least—fun and relaxation.

1. Crime Prevention in Philadelphia. The co-ordination of effort devised by Philadelphia illustrates concretely a citywide prevention plan. The key organization is the Crime Prevention Association, established in 1932 and since 1943 under subsidization by the Community Chest.[24] At its request, the Police Department formed a Crime Prevention Division, now the Juvenile

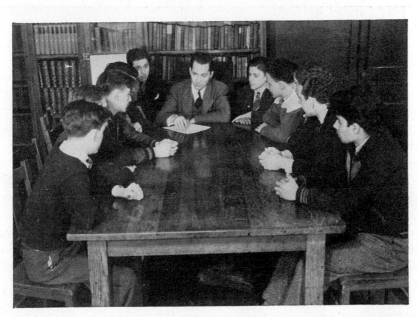

Club activities have great value in building well-adjusted youths by the provision of constructive outlets for their energies and by teaching them co-operation with others of their own age and also with adult leaders. However, group activities do not meet all needs of youth. Personal counseling in small groups therefore has a place in the well-rounded club program. In the above scene a counselor is discussing personal problems with the boys in one of the clubs connected with the Crime Prevention Association of Philadelphia. (Crime Prevention Association)

Aid Bureau, with a staff of 84 policemen and 25 policewomen in 1951. In addition to making 6,107 arrests of juveniles in 1952, the Bureau received, investigated, and adjusted 9,581 complaints directed against juveniles, and 2,427 additional arrests. Many of the juveniles who are on the edge of delinquency are directed to the referral service of the Crime Prevention Association, which handles serious cases itself and refers others to individual agencies or to area committees. These committees are regarded as of special significance since they are composed of representatives of both public and private agencies and responsible laymen, and thus in themselves are a way of bringing together a number of community forces. The Crime Prevention

Association also includes a recreation division, which in 1952 directed 41 full- or part-time recreation programs in the 5 clubs operated by the Association. Another phase of the work has been to enlist the interest of gangs of older adolescents to whom the usual club program does not appeal.

This basketball scene, from a championship play-off game of the Older Boys' League in a Philadelphia boys' club, shows an exciting moment in a favorite type of sport. The participation of both Negroes and whites in such activities fosters friendly relations instead of the racial clashes that too frequently occur between unsupervised gangs. (Crime Prevention Association)

Working with individual gangs of boys and groups of girls, staff members have made progress in inducing the members to reorganize their activities along more conventional lines and to assume some responsibility for their behavior. A research division makes regular reports on the state of delinquency and preventive programs. The Crime Prevention Association has also been active in furthering other co-ordinated attacks on crime and delinquency; for example, the Philadelphia Conference for the Prevention and Control of Juvenile Delinquency, organized in 1947 and continuing its work through a Continuing Committee. This Conference was composed of lay and professional representatives from 110 agencies. The Crime Commission of Philadelphia was organized in 1951 as a division of the Association, with representatives of city-wide organizations. On the basis of studies and surveys it makes recommendations for improving crime control. The Asso-

The boys' club orchestra learns co-operation as well as developing musical skill and appreciation. Leisure hours filled with constructive hobbies leave no time to seek outlets for violent adolescent energy in mischievous escapades. (Crime Prevention Association)

ciation is firm in its belief that the final responsibility for delinquency prevention lies with the citizens; hence at every step laymen and professionals from organized agencies are brought into joint participation in the program.

It is difficult to evaluate the work of such an agency as the Crime Prevention Association. Delinquency rates have declined and risen several times during the history of the Association. The rates are determined by many factors, such as changes in police policies, increased police personnel, the disturbances of war, and changes in population makeup. It is impossible to isolate the work of any agency. Nevertheless, the Association has definitely stimulated increased police activity, has established recreational programs in previously uncovered areas, has initiated a citywide referral system, and has brought together many individual agencies and laymen in a constant concern with delinquency prevention and control.

2. *The Chicago Area Project.* A new type of community approach to delinquency control was started quietly in Chicago in 1932 on an experimental basis, under the guidance of Clifford R. Shaw, of the staff of the Institute for Juvenile Research.[25] The Chicago Area Project, as the program is called, is a private corporation governed by a board of prominent citizens, organized to receive and distribute the funds needed to operate the delinquency-prevention program. The program itself is developed on a neighborhood basis and is operated almost entirely by local leadership, partly volunteer and partly paid. The work began in a small way in one area, a homogeneous Polish community. Now there are 6 projects in Chicago, each operated on the basis of a natural community of limited area and a population of about 10 to 50 thousand people.

The local community type of organization is a natural outgrowth of Shaw's intensive studies of delinquency areas. These studies were interpreted by him to indicate that delinquency is a natural result of the traditional patterns of conduct of a community, which are handed on from older to younger boys and which the community institutions are too weak or too indifferent to change. Outside institutions imposed on the community often have been ineffective, for they have rarely been accepted wholeheartedly. Shaw's idea was to stir up the community's own residents to a realization of the plight of their children and to find among them the leadership to change conditions and organize constructive activities.

To initiate a local community program it is necessary for someone from the outside to go in, become acquainted in an informal way, and be accepted by the community. At first youngsters and adults may be suspicious of the motives behind the actions of this person, but when they find that he can be trusted and that his interest is genuine he is gradually admitted into intimacy with neighborhood groups and even delinquent gangs. At the same time that this worker is gaining the confidence of the younger members of the community by sharing their recreation and not reporting their minor misdemeanors to the police, he is quietly talking with local leaders to the end that a local community council is formed that acts as the sponsoring agency for constructive community work. As rapidly as possible all responsibility is shifted to the committee. It is significant that the committees often represent not the "leading" citizens of the community, but the workingmen who make up the great bulk of the population and whose children are most likely to become delinquent. These groups have been most effective; they have managed to open summer camps; they have organized sport contests: they have drawn other agencies into the program.   Volunteer leaders from the community carry much of the work; paid workers are also usually from the local community.   These leaders often do not have formal training as recreational leaders nor as social workers; but they both know and share the traditions, sentiments, and problems of the community because they have been reared in it.

The work extends beyond providing recreation as a form of delinquency control.   The leaders in their association with groups or gangs of boys slowly impress upon these boys their own standards of honesty and fairness; they help them out of scrapes, sometimes even refunding stolen money in order to prevent the boys' arrest.   This procedure seems to make a marked impression on boys more accustomed to harsh treatment, and they respond by repaying the money.   Boys and men who have been in prison are helped to re-establish themselves in the community and in some instances have become excellent workers in its program, able to give special help to other delinquents.

The heart of the program is not in its activities, which do not differ greatly from those carried on by conventional agencies, but in the fact that the program is organized and operated by the local community.   Underlying it is the community's recognition of its own problems and its acceptance of responsibility for solving them.   Its effectiveness is not in formal action or threats of legal or police action, but in the gradual development of a community spirit that is intolerant of pernicious institutions and delinquency and that supports the more conventional standards of conduct and constructive agencies.   To develop such public opinion is a long, slow process that can be accomplished only by working from within the community.   The State Department of Public Welfare employs some of the men who serve as leaders, but they are usually local residents or persons long familiar with the community who are able to identify themselves with it.

Although one of the projects has been in operation for some 13 years, no extravagant claims are made regarding reduction in delinquency in the areas served.   It is true that delinquency rates have shown a greater decrease in some of these areas than in nearby areas without community projects, but Shaw and his associates are cautious in their claims and prefer to wait longer for a final answer as to the effect of these projects on delinquency rates.

3. *The People's Organization.*   In 1939, under the leadership of Saul Alinsky, a new type of community organization was initiated that has implications for the prevention and control of juvenile delinquency and crime.[26] The community in which this social experiment was first developed was the area near the stockyards in Chicago, known locally as "Back of the Yards." This is a workingman's residential area with a variety of national and religious

groups and typified by a high rate of juvenile delinquency.   In an urban community of this type, many independent programs are carried on by such groups as churches, social and athletic clubs, labor unions, industries, and political organizations.   These groups often work at cross purposes in trying to attain their individual objectives.   The total welfare of the community may be not only disregarded but hampered by the activities of local organized groups.   The organization fostered by Alinsky, which has been given the general title of the People's Organization, attempts to cut across organizational lines and bring together a representative group of community leaders who will be interested in the whole community and its problems.   The basis of membership rests upon local organizations, such as churches, clubs, societies, and unions.   Each organization is entitled to representatives in a Community Congress, the number of representatives being proportional to the membership of the organization.   This congress, which meets annually and also in emergency sessions, is responsible for policies, programs, and finances.   The congress functions through a board of directors composed of one representative chosen by each member-organization.   Major industries in the community are also represented on the board.   Thus, although the voting strength in the congress rests upon the size of the member organizations, in the board of directors each organization regardless of size has equal influence.   The board establishes special committees and employs an executive secretary.

The basic purpose of the People's Organization is not the control of delinquency but the development of a democratically minded people, interested in and informed about their own welfare, and organized for action to improve it.   Concrete action takes the form of an attack upon basic issues, which are listed as including the need for jobs, higher wages, economic security, housing, and health.   Recreation is secondary, but not disregarded. Money is raised for various projects, such as free dental clinics, recreational facilities, and sending children to summer camp.   In addition to its own projects, the People's Organization has worked with city-wide, state, and national projects for the betterment of the community.   In this way it has been instrumental in bringing into the community a station of the Infant Welfare Society and in establishing, through state and federal aid, free milk and hot lunches for school children.   Pressure has been brought upon city officials to remove fire and health hazards.   Inter-organizational and inter-group conflicts have decreased as organizations and groups have joined in community-wide projects.

It has been stated that control of delinquency and crime is not the primary purpose of the People's Organization since their prevention is only part of the total community welfare.   They are, however, closely related to more basic issues, such as a general condition of social disorganization, under-nourishment, disease, deterioration, and demoralization. As the basic issues are met and solved, the implication is that delinquency and crime will decrease.[27] Leaders in the Chicago project have organized the Industrial Areas Foundation on a national basis to promote similar projects in other cities.

The People's Organization is similar to the Chicago Area Projects in that it seeks local leadership and the stimulation of community pride and responsibility. It differs in that membership is wider—on the basis of all community organizations—and in that its primary purpose is an active community along all lines of welfare. Moreover, the Area Project makes delinquency control the focal point of other projects.

Residential Planning

The Chicago Area Project manipulates the life of a local community to the end that noncriminal attitudes and habits are developed. There are other, city-wide and nation-wide movements that must be initiated or encouraged for the total prevention of delinquency, in so far as such an end is possible.

One such movement is the physical reorganization of disorganized areas, in other words, slum clearance. The association between delinquency and poor housing has sometimes led to extravagant claims for good housing as a measure of delinquency prevention. The relationship, however, is indirect. Poor housing is prevalent in slum areas; so is delinquency. But this fact does not prove that poor housing creates delinquency. Rather, poor housing is found in certain areas because of their proximity to central business sections or to industry; the owners of the land expect business and industry to expand and absorb their property and they therefore are not interested in improving the houses on it. Or those who live in these areas are working men in low-wage industries who cannot afford to pay enough rent to merit improvements in housing. These same areas also attract persons who cannot compete economically with other groups, either because of a foreign background, racial handicap, inadequate education, or lack of ability. Also, for many of the same reasons, these people are frequently unable to meet the standards of the more prosperous and more favored communities in morals and conduct. They are often exploited by employers, politicians, and organized criminal groups and are helpless to resist. The relationship between delinquency and the poor physical make-up of the community lies in the disorganization that develops when ill-equipped persons because of poverty and ignorance crowd into a deteriorated section of a city. Nevertheless, one step toward reorganization of such a community is in its physical rehabilitation.   This process must include not only better housing but a community plan, for the basis of reorganization is in the community as a unit.   A sociologist's view of a neighborhood housing project most favorable for community organization is as follows: [28]

1. The area should be large enough to contain some natural unit of population, preferably adequate to maintain an elementary school.
2. The area should be residential in character with traffic streets routed around rather than through it.
3. Business houses should be located on the through streets at the periphery of the area.
4. A small park or playground should be located at the center of the area and around it should be grouped the neighborhood institutions of school, church, community center, and the like.

This plan would push the disorganizing and distracting influences to the edge of the area and the organizing and unifying influences to the center.   It would call for conscious planning, not on the part of one or two landowners, nor even on the part of a local community, but by the city as a whole.   It would also probably necessitate public funds for its prosecution.

FAMILY REORGANIZATION

Recognition of the importance of the family in the formation of the personality and habits of children places upon it a large share of the responsibility for juvenile delinquency and thus indirectly for crime.   But the problem is only outlined when it is stated that the family is responsible for the personality and habits of children.   Few parents do not wish happiness and material success for their children.   But there are relatively few parents equipped to provide these assets for their children unless they are able to maintain their own happiness and success and unless they have the co-operation of other community agencies.   The family per se is not a preventive agency.   It is an intimate group of persons, bound to each other by emotional ties, sometimes acting as a unit but often in a state of turmoil.   To make the family an instrument preventive of delinquency often requires positive action on the part of other community agencies.   Some of these bolstering supports are considered here.

Counseling centers for married couples are important aids.   There are relatively few such centers in the country, although the movement is growing. These centers provide expert assistance by physicians, psychologists, sociologists, and lawyers to husbands and wives who have failed to make a good adjustment to each other.   The domestic relations divisions of courts in some of the larger cities also offer help to married couples whose difficulties have reached the stage where they have been brought to court attention. Adjusting marital difficulties may seem a far cry from delinquency. It will be recalled, however, that the proportion of delinquents from homes broken by separation or divorce is greater than the proportion from unbroken homes. Healy and others have also amply demonstrated that the basic problem of a large amount of delinquency is an unhappy family situation in which the boy or girl feels insecure. It follows therefore that any aid given to maladjusted parents will indirectly act as a preventive of delinquency in the children. It seems doubtful whether at the present time many of the counseling centers reach those groups from which delinquents most often develop. Those connected with social agencies or working in close connection with them doubtless do, but many others reach only more privileged groups.

Parent-education groups are also important in the degree to which they reach parents most in need of understanding the problems of children and help these parents with their practical everyday problems. To be effective, such education must extend into the neighborhood and find the parents in need of help, and the training must be given in terms of the local culture. Greatly in need of assistance are rural families who have recently moved into cities and whose children snatch at the adventure of urban living. Negroes and Mexicans present many examples of such families. Although the restriction of immigration has decreased the problem, families of foreign culture usually need assistance in adjusting themselves to American ways of life and in helping their children find conventional satisfactions.

ADJUSTMENT OF EMOTIONAL AND MENTAL DISTURBANCES

The mass or community attack on delinquency undoubtedly solves many problems. For the boy or girl who needs help in organizing his energies and interests, the community center and similar agencies offer an effective means of assistance that may lead to an orderly and conventional instead of a delinquent life. Reorganization of the community to eliminate destructive institutions and to substitute constructive ones is important in offering proper patterns of conduct to the questing child. But not all delinquents are the result of failures in community organization. Some become delinquent primarily because of emotional tensions and conflicts that find expression in illegal conduct. Moreover, the criminal behavior may not appear until many years have passed after the occurrence of the initial cause of the conflict. Therefore, for all cases of personal maladjustment expert attention is needed, usually under psychiatric guidance.

The psychiatric clinics attached to juvenile courts are to a certain extent important in delinquency prevention. But too often they do not receive the child until the personality has become badly warped.   Also, the judge is not usually required to follow the advice of the clinics as to treatment of the child and may order a type of supervision or punishment that increases rather than decreases the maladjustment.   Most effective in preventive work are the clinics that have contacts with children at an early age, and are not related to another agency that traditionally metes out punishment for misconduct.   Clinics in connection with schools and those supported by some form of community philanthropy are examples.

The work of counselors in public schools has already been described. They help many children to make better school adjustment but usually refer seriously disturbed or delinquent children to more specialized agencies.   Few schools attempt to operate a clinic with a psychiatrist on the staff.

Community clinics have tended to increase in number, either in connection with some privately supported community agency or with support from taxation.   When the depression of the 1930's made financial demands upon local charities beyond their means, and financial relief was assumed by state and federal governments, the locally supported charities began to shift their work from giving financial relief to providing family adjustment services. Many family relief societies and charity organizations have changed their names to family consultation center.   The family may be referred or may come to the center because of any type of maladjustment; if the children are involved they are studied along with the other members and a more harmonious family adjustment is sought.

It should be noted that these various agencies and clinics that are not attached to the courts are rarely concerned primarily with preventing delinquency.   Their basic interest is in a child's mental and emotional problems and their fundamental aim is to correct them.   Delinquency may or may not be a manifestation of the underlying difficulty.   In any case, the clinic seeks the mental or emotional cause that lies back of whatever behavior manifestation is exhibited.   During the course of treatment delinquency, if it exists, may continue; in fact, it may temporarily become worse as the child struggles toward better adjustment.   Nevertheless, such clinics, dealing with all children showing personal or social maladjustment, would inevitably assist in the prevention of delinquency, since they would handle a certain percentage of cases in which, without treatment, delinquency would later occur.

Although the clinic approach is the most hopeful one in cases where delinquency is the outward manifestation of inner maladjustment, such clinics are available in only a limited number of communities.   In 1935 there were 617 psychiatric clinics in the United States that accepted children as patients; of these nearly half were located in cities of 100,000 and over. Nevertheless, a third of the cities of this size had no clinic, and extremely few smaller communities had such service.[29]   An attempt has been made to overcome this lack by providing traveling clinics under state support. The specialists on the staff of the traveling clinic remain in a community for a limited time, examining and diagnosing children referred to them by local agencies.   They then lay out a plan for remedial treatment, which must be carried out by these agencies.   This plan has not been wholly successful, as few of the agencies in the smaller communities have personnel trained in the handling of personality adjustments, and it has not been found possible to convert specialists in other fields into psychiatric social workers in a few easy lessons.   Recognition is now growing that the staff of the clinic must make its diagnosis and give detailed information on the patient's capacities, frustrations, and desires to the local agencies, which would then apply their own techniques.   The added knowledge, however, might enable them to adapt their methods to the greater benefit of the patient.[30]

Most of the discussion in this chapter has concerned agencies working with children or parents.   If delinquency is not checked in youth, the confirmed misdemeanant or criminal emerges and preventive work is replaced by penal and reformative measures.   These subjects form much of the discussion of Part Two.   For those persons who commit some one crime in adulthood after years of being law abiding the problem of crime prevention is extremely difficult.   In many emotional crimes of assault or murder or in isolated cases of embezzlement or larceny there may have been no previous signs of delinquency.   But usually such crimes are preceded by inner emotional tensions or conflict or by the pressure of crucial familial problems that a person feels he must solve.   Many people have such tensions and conflicts, such unsolved problems, but do not commit crimes in their attempt to reach a solution.   Some muddle along and conform to conventions; some become psychotic and require protective care in the family or an institution; some give up the struggle and find solace in a compensating vice; others receive help and make a genuine readjustment.   Unfortunately the sources of help are meager. Family consultation centers have been mentioned; they are to be found only in the larger communities and deal solely with family problems.   Physicians and ministers in smaller communities go as far as they can in helping their patients and parishioners; but neither is specifically trained in the diagnosis or solution of emotional and mental problems.   Psychiatrists are found almost exclusively in the larger cities and often do not receive patients until the processes of disorganization are well advanced. Mental hygiene clinics, which attend to minor difficulties and sometimes operate on a free basis, now exist in some cities and seem to offer a hopeful solution.   Before any of these agencies can work effectively, however, people must be educated to recognize the early symptoms of their own conflicts and to overcome the reluctance of adults to admitting their inability to meet their problems unaided.

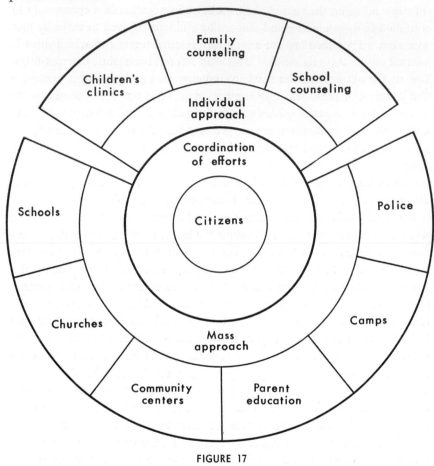

FIGURE 17

Diagram of preventive methods. The diagram shows that the citizens are central to a program of prevention. Citizens determine what values shall be preserved and create public opinion for their preservation. In the realm of practical prevention are some agencies with an individual approach, usually through counseling or clinical study and treatment. Other agencies use a mass approach through which large numbers of parents or children participate in such activities as classes, clubs, or camps. To be effective, each type must be co-ordinated into a well-integrated program covering all problems and all areas.

PUBLIC RESPONSIBILITY

The connection between crime and politics in large cities is an extremely serious hindrance to crime prevention. Although young adolescents do not have such connections, as soon as the juvenile delinquent is included in a mature criminal group he is incorporated into the system. Since the law-enforcement agencies are involved in arrangements whereby certain types of criminal pay for protection, it is not possible to look to these agencies as they now exist for a remedy to the situation. Responsibility for a change must lie with those who are directly responsible for the elected officers and indirectly for officers appointed by officials who are elected. It is notorious that in large cities the groups that find in public office an opportunity for private gain are highly organized; they often do not hold public office themselves, but they form the machine that puts in its chosen men, and which organizes the criminal and underworld voters to elect the nominees sponsored by it.

The urban groups that would like to have criminal practices in and out of politics cleaned up are not often strongly organized. Perhaps this circumstance exists because they do not receive a direct financial benefit from politics. Voters are frequently highly sensitive about public officials when there is a direct threat to their bank accounts but complacent when they fail to recognize such a threat. The mere prospect of living under an orderly and crime-suppressing government does not seem to furnish sufficient motivation for the law-abiding groups to organize and put on a vigorous campaign for honest government. There is of course a financial forfeit that every citizen pays for corruption, through greatly increased taxes to pay for political graft, high prices for food, goods, and services to cover sums extorted by racketeers, and in the expense of trials and prisons for the vast horde of minor criminals who exist in part because of the example of important and unpunished professional criminals. It does not seem possible that any plan of local community reorganization will be completely effective unless the profitable relationship between organized crime and politics is broken down and the successful criminals are removed as heroes that the young delinquent strives to emulate. The key to this problem is clearly in the hands of the voter who does not profit by such a relationship, and whose gain from clean government will be the indirect financial benefit of lowered taxes and retail prices and the positive emotion of pride in a well-organized local government.

The citizenry are also responsible for another failure in crime prevention by their complacence in regard to certain types of lawbreaking, those that occur when illegal services desired by many people are provided in defiance of the law. Prostitution, gambling, and the sale of narcotics and liquor when forbidden by law are examples. During World War II the illegal sale of gasoline, meat, and other foodstuffs without ration stamps (popularly termed the black market) existed because respectable people in the community wanted these products even though they, as well as the salesmen, were forced to break the law to secure them.   Police and prosecuting attorneys find it extremely difficult to eliminate this type of lawbreaking since there is a public demand for it and therefore tolerance of its existence.   Citizens must take the first step toward control.

Sometimes this popular demand for a legally forbidden service or article rests on the determination of wealthy people to gratify their desires regardless either of cost or legality.   They place their individual wishes above whatever idea of community good motivated the passage of the law.   This situation existed in regard to the black market.   Under rationing, no one in the United States needed to go hungry; but it was not always possible to secure legally the exact articles of food—especially meat—desired.   Those who did not themselves patronize the black market hesitated to report these activities among their friends or in their communities and thus condoned the illegal practices.

In other cases the breaking of laws regulating sale of certain articles rests upon personal habits that have become uncontrollable.   Much of the illegal sale of drugs is to addicts, who have so accustomed themselves to the use of drugs that they cannot stop using them.   Gambling and alcoholism are other such vices.   A part of the attitude of complacence of the community rests on the opinion that a mild indulgence in some of these habits is not particularly harmful and therefore that forbidding them by law violates personal rights.   Persons who take this view argue that the minority who indulge to their personal injury are medical, not criminal, cases and should be treated as though they were ill and given appropriate treatment.   Nevertheless until such treatment is provided and as long as repressive laws exist, violation of these laws is criminal conduct.

The public is also largely responsible for many of the unethical business practices that exist, as well as for various large-scale frauds.   As long as people are willing to tolerate or engage in dishonest practices because they expect to secure some financial gain, these practices will continue.   Many people who report to the police that they have lost large sums to a confidence man were willing to protect and co-operate with him in the expectation of large returns on their money even when they were told that his methods were illegal.   Only when the confidence man makes off with their money instead of returning it with a profit do they report him to the police.

It is necessary to make the public acutely aware of graft and illegal business practices wherever they exist.   Furthermore, the development of a sense of responsibility in each citizen for the continuation of these practices and the conditions that create them is essential.

NEED FOR UNIFIED PLANNING

Delinquency prevention is still handled sporadically and unsystematically. Although some efforts for over-all supervision have been made, the writer knows of no instance in which a city receives complete coverage in delinquency-prevention measures, comparable, let us say, to educational coverage. In a well-developed educational system, all phases of education are organized under one central policy-making body, a board of education, which has one administrator, a superintendent of schools. The typical system provides education for all children between the ages of 6 and 18 years; often, in addition, a kindergarten and sometimes nursery schools for younger children as a service of which parents may avail themselves at will; various types of vocational as well as academic education to meet differing needs; a 2 year junior college for further specialized training; and adult evening classes. Such a system reaches into all sections of a city and provides for many types of people. Education is accepted as a necessary attribute of every citizen and with few exceptions people value its advantages and submit to whatever restrictions it places upon their freedom. The question may be fairly asked whether a law-respecting and law-abiding citizenry is not fully as important as an educated citizenry and equally deserving of well-organized agencies for its development.

An adequately developed program of delinquency prevention would place its emphasis not upon the simple problem of preventing lawbreaking, but upon the more fundamental problem of developing well-adjusted children and adults who would be able to meet their responsibilities and who could find their satisfactions in socially approved and constructive channels. Such a program would be based on the following:

It would not be subject to the good intentions of small unstable private groups but would be under the guidance of some central body.

It would not receive its support from private sources alone but would have a definite and adequate sum allocated from public funds.

It would be based upon the needs of the city or region as a whole with distribution of efforts in all communities and among all groups in need of assistance.

It would exert pressure upon other phases of community organization, as political offices, business practices, and slum clearance, in order to eliminate some of the bases for delinquent conduct.

It would maintain experimental and research departments in order to develop better methods of adjustment, and to check the effectiveness of its own program.

It would approach the problem as a many-sided one and would provide for all the known institutions that function effectively in a preventive program. Seven important institutions are:

1. Psychiatric clinics working in close connection with the schools, so that any children in the community in need of assistance might be helped. The clinics would operate the year around, however, instead of during the school year only.

2. These clinics or similar ones should also be open to parents seeking assistance in child training.

3. Adult consultation centers, which might be operated in connection with the clinics for children, since many of the children's problems would have their roots in parental difficulties.

4. Parent education groups.

5. Recreation and group work centers for children and adults, widely scattered through the city, which would work in co-operation with the clinics, for a better adaptation of the club program to the needs of its members. Certain centers should have staff for group therapy.

6. Summer camps to continue the work of the recreation and group work centers.

7. Citizens' committees to provide constant vigilance against public graft and corrupt business practices.

QUESTIONS

1. What factors related to criminal behavior must be considered in planning a program of crime prevention?

2. What positive steps are some public schools taking to prevent delinquency?

3. Why are not the efforts of churches in delinquency areas more effective in reducing or eliminating delinquency?

4. There is some difference of opinion as to whether police departments should attempt specific work in delinquency prevention (such as the establishment of crime prevention bureaus or the organization of recreational programs). Discuss the matter pro and con.

5. What is the approach made in group therapy to delinquency prevention?

6. What different types of clinics are needed in a preventive program?

7. How would a city-wide delinquency prevention program be organized? What services should it include?

READINGS

Alinsky, S. D., *Reveille for Radicals* (Chicago: University of Chicago Press, 1946). Discussion of philosophy and organization of disorganized communities.

Hallowitz, E., "Camping for Disturbed Children," *Mental Hygiene,* 34 (1950),

406–22. This article discusses types of children who may be benefited by group therapy in a camp setting. The philosophy of group therapy is stated as well as practical details of organization.

Henry, Nelson B. (ed.), *The Forty-Seventh Yearbook of the National Society for the Study of Education,* Part I, "Juvenile Delinquency and the Schools" (Chicago: University of Chicago Press, 1948). This is an excellent series of articles on various ways in which public schools can prevent and reduce juvenile delinquency.

Kahn, Alfred J., *Police and Children* (New York. 1407 Broadway: Citizens' Committee on Children of New York City, Inc., 1951). A judicious discussion of the work of New York police with children that brings out general problems which would be found in other cities.

Konopka, Gisela, "Therapy Through Social Group Work," *National Conference of Social Work* (1946), pp. 228–36. Policies and practice of group therapy at the Pittsburgh Child Guidance Clinic.

Rinck, Jane E., "Supervising the Juvenile Delinquent," *Annals of the American Academy of Political and Social Science,* 291 (1954), 78–86. Written by a social worker, this article is a critical examination of the functions of social agencies and the police in delinquency cases.

Stroup, Herbert H., *Community Welfare Organization* (Harper, 1952), Parts II and III. The author discusses the structure of welfare agencies from the local to the international level. Processes of co-ordination, financing, and initiation of activities are included. The discussion is not limited to delinquency prevention.

Wattenberg, W. W., "Church Attendance and Juvenile Delinquency," *Sociology and Social Research,* 34 (1950), 195–202.

FOOTNOTES

[1] *Biennial Survey of Education in the United States, 1946–48,* "Statistical Summary of Education, 1947–48" (Washington: Government Printing Office, 1950), ch. I, p. 25.

[2] Nelson B. Henry (ed.), *The Fifty-Second Yearbook of the National Society for the Study of Education,* Part 1, "Adapting the Secondary-School Program to the Needs of Youth" (Chicago: University of Chicago Press, 1953).

[3] ———— (ed.), *The Forty-Seventh Yearbook of the National Society for the Study of Education,* Part 1, "Juvenile Delinquency and the Schools" (Chicago: University of Chicago Press, 1948).

[4] Robert C. Taber, "The Potential Role of the School Counselor in Delinquency Prevention and Treatment," *Federal Probation,* 13 (Sept. 1949), 52–56.

[5] E. H. Stullken, "How the Montefiore School Prevents Crime," *Journal of Criminal Law and Criminology,* 26 (1935), 228–34; Sheldon and Eleanor T. Glueck (eds.), *Preventing Crime* (McGraw-Hill, 1936), pp. 197–212; I. Dolton, "The Montefiore School, an Experiment in Adjustment," *Journal of Educational Sociology,* 6 (1933), 482–90.

[6] Ruth Shonle Cavan, "Replies to Father Coogan's Article, 'The Myth Mind in an Engineer's World,'" *Federal Probation,* 16 (June, 1952), 24–27.

[7] Sheldon and Eleanor T. Glueck, *One Thousand Juvenile Delinquents* (Cambridge: Harvard University Press, 1934), pp. 67, 79.

[8] W. C. Kvaraceus, *Juvenile Delinquency and the School* (New York: World Book, 1945), pp. 101–3.

[9] W. W. Wattenberg, "Church Attendance and Juvenile Delinquency," *Sociology and Social Research,* 34 (1950), 195–202.

[10] Hugh Hartshorne and Mark A. May, *Studies in Deceit* (Macmillan, 1928–30).

[11] P. R. Hightower, *Biblical Information in Relation to Character and Conduct* (Iowa City: State University of Iowa, 1930).

[12] Glueck, *Preventing Crime* (quotation reprinted with permission of the publisher), p. 240.

[13] Detroit Police Department, Youth Bureau, *Summary of Youth Bureau Annual Report for the Year 1952.*

[14] New York City Police Department, *Crime Prevention by a Police Department, the Juvenile Aid Bureau and the Police Athletic League of New York City,* undated; Alfred J. Kahn, *Police and Children* (New York, 1407 Broadway: Citizens' Committee on Children of New York City, Inc., 1951).

[15] Alan Hynd, "Pals—Cops and Kids," *Collier's,* Nov. 11, 1950.

[16] F. M. Thrasher, "The Boys' Club and Juvenile Delinquency," *American Journal of Sociology,* 42 (1936), 66–80.

[17] William Healy and Augusta F. Bronner, *New Light on Delinquency and Its Treatment* (New Haven: Yale University Press, 1936), pp. 71–72.

[18] Ellery F. Reed, "How Effective are Group-Work Agencies in Preventing Delinquency," *Focus,* 28 (Nov., 1949), 170–76.

[19] Crime Prevention Association of Philadelphia, *Crime Prevention in 1951,* unpaged.

[20] J. R. Dumpson, "An Approach to Antisocial Street Gangs," *Federal Probation* 13 (December, 1949), 22–29; Paul L. Crawford, D. I. Malamud, and J. R. Dumpson, *Working with Teen-Age Gangs* (Welfare Council of New York City, 1950).

[21] E. G. Beier, "Experimental Therapy with a Gang," *Focus,* 30 (July, 1951), 97–112.

[22] Herbert H. Stroup, *Community Welfare Organization* (Harper, 1952).

[23] Arthur Hillman, *Community Organization and Planning* (Macmillan, 1950).

[24] *Annual Report, Crime Prevention Association of Philadelphia,* 801 Administration Bldg., 21st Street and The Parkway, 1951 and 1952.

[25] For an interesting human-interest story of the Chicago Area Project, see J. B. Martin, "A New Attack on Delinquency," *Harper's Magazine,* 188 (1944), 502–12. For more formal statements see Clifford R. Shaw and Henry D. McKay, *Juvenile Delinquency and Urban Areas* (Chicago: University of Chicago Press, 1942), pp. 442–46; F. A. Romano, "Organizing a Community for Delinquency Prevention," in *Dealing with Delinquency,* National Probation Association Yearbook, 1940, pp. 1–12. The philosophy of the movement is ably stated by E. W. Burgess, J. D. Lohman, and C. R. Shaw, "The Chicago Area Project," *Coping with Crime,* National Probation Association Yearbook, 1937, pp. 8–28.

[26] Saul D. Alinsky, *Reveille for Radicals* (Chicago: University of Chicago Press, 1946).

[27] *Ibid.,* pp. 80–81.

[28] E. W. Burgess, in Shaw and McKay, *Juvenile Delinquency and Urban Areas,* p. xii.

[29] Helen L. Witmer, *Psychiatric Clinics for Children* (New York: Commonwealth Fund, 1940), p. 371.

[30] *Ibid.,* pp. 383–86.

PART TWO

Agencies of Law Enforcement and the Treatment of Criminals

11

Treatment of Criminals--
Background

Strictly speaking, the word criminal refers only to persons who have been legally convicted of committing a crime. Actually, however, the agencies charged with law enforcement become active as soon as a report is received that a crime has been committed, and may impose their authority on persons only mildly suspected of having committed the crime. The entire process of legal control of criminality extends from the report of the crime through investigations to find the probable perpetrator of the crime, the hearing and weighing of evidence to determine whether the suspected offender actually did commit the crime, his sentencing (if guilty) to punishment, the carrying out of punishment, and his final release as a free man. This involved process, which may be consummated in a few days' time or may last for many years or even for the natural lifetime of the convicted criminal, is carried out by a number of agencies. These agencies are listed below, with the duties usually delegated to each:

Police: assembling of evidence (detection), and apprehension of suspected offenders; detention in jail of the suspects until the time of trial, during trial, and if there is a conviction, until release on probation or transfer to prison; detention of convicted offender if sentenced to a short term in jail.

Courts: hearing of evidence according to legal regulations for trials; sentencing of convicted criminals.

Prisons and other penal and correctional institutions: custody of criminals sentenced to imprisonment, often including programs for re-education and rehabilitation.

Parole and probation agencies: supervision of prisoners during such portions of their sentences as they spend in the community instead of in prison.

Basic to the process is the criminal law, which designates what types of behavior are criminal in nature, that is, contrary to public welfare; what penalties may be assigned for each crime; and how the various agencies shall be organized and operated.

Part II is a discussion of the agencies of law enforcement in the order in which the criminal experiences them—police, courts, penal institutions, probation or parole. For an understanding of the total procedure, some background information is desirable. Such information as it applies to the entire procedure is given in this chapter; in addition, needed historical information relating to a specific agency is included in the chapter on that agency.

THE PAST IN THE PRESENT

Ideally, criminal laws should be closely correlated with the social conditions of a particular time and place and be subject to frequent change, in order to control new situations and employ new methods of rehabilitation. Actually, much of the explanation of criminal law and of the treatment of criminals must be sought in our historical past. As Kirchwey states, "all law is a growth, a matter of accretion and of development out of custom and habit" and cannot be accounted for "without harking back over the trail of its history to its beginnings." [1] The influence of earlier periods is found in our laws and penal systems, sometimes making them inadequate for maintaining the best standards of social welfare as we see those standards today.

Crime as Personal Injury

Prehistoric man, unable to write, left no record of his laws. The intricacy of the earliest written codes, however, is proof of a long preceding process of development of rules of behavior that had received the approval of the society. Enforcement of law as a duty of the state for the public good was preceded by the concept of injuries as a personal affair, with the injured person or his kinship group having the privilege of imposing upon the offender an injury identical with the injury received. Under the law of retaliation (*lex talionis*) as thus conceived, the person who lost the sight of an eye at the hands of another, might blind the offender. It was not necessary that the injury should have been deliberately or maliciously performed. Intent did not enter into the situation; it was sufficient that an injury had occurred. The reaction to the offense was not, however, one of unrestrained vengeance, since the mores decreed that the injured person could inflict only the kind and amount of injury that he had received; thus an element of justice entered into the situation, and the anger of the injured person could not lead him to go beyond his own injury. If he had lost one eye, he could blind the offender in one eye, but he could not completely blind nor kill him.

In time, the offender was allowed to substitute payments of money for the retaliatory injuries that might be inflicted upon him. These payments were not made to the state, as fines are today, but were paid to the injured person, or to the kinship group, as compensation. The amounts were fixed by the controlling power in each society and were equated to the status or rank of the injured person and to the specific type of injury. Men commanded greater compensation than women. Injuries to men of high rank called for higher payments than injuries to men of low rank. Conversely, penalties imposed were more severe for men of low rank than for those of high position, inasmuch as they showed greater audacity and defiance of authority. For example, laws attributed to the reign of Henry I in England (early twelfth century) set penalties for hunting deer in the king's forest as follows: the free man who paid rent for his land and helped the lord of the manor only in busy times, was to pay 10 shillings for violating the hunting law; the violator who was not a free man (that is, gave weekly labor to his lord), 20 shillings; and the serf, who was little better than a slave, was to "lose his skin." [2] Each injury had a stated amount of money compensation. Under Alfred the Great (871–900) the *bot* or amount paid to the victim for injuries was graded as follows for mutilation of the hand: if a man cut off an enemy's thumb, he was required to pay 35 shillings; the first finger, 15 shillings; the middle finger, 9; the fourth finger, 6; and the little finger, 5.[3]

Although we no longer impose upon the criminal a punishment that exactly duplicates his crime, the old idea of retaliation and vengeance has not entirely disappeared from public thinking nor from criminal law. In many states, the penalty for murder may be the same as the crime committed—the death of the offender. Criminal laws try to equate the severity of the penalty for other crimes to the degree of public condemnation of the offense; assaults receive longer prison terms than thefts, and a theft that endangers the life of the victim, such as armed robbery, is more severely penalized than burglary. The idea of "making the punishment fit the crime" is a survival of the old policy of retaliation.

Physical Punishments

The assumption by courts of the enforcement of criminal law did not eliminate brutal physical punishment. Death or capital punishment was widely used in England and Europe. France at one time applied the death penalty for more than 100 different offenses, and in England as late as 1820, there were 222 capital crimes, although by that time judges tended to avoid applying the death penalty for many minor offenses. In earlier periods the death penalty was frequently and cruelly applied. A French judge boasted of 800 executions by burning in the space of 16 years; in a quarter of a century, the public executioner at Nuremberg disposed of 1,159 persons; during the reign of Henry VIII in England, 70,000 criminals were put to death.[4]   During the struggle between Catholicism and Protestantism, heresy (belief in the religion not currently in favor) was stamped out by burning, and many were put to death for this religious crime as well as for civil crimes.   We think of capital punishment now in terms of swift and relatively painless methods.   The earlier forms were extremely painful and might consist of literally tearing the offender limb from limb, of burning the living offender to death, crushing him, throwing him into boiling oil, or impaling him on a sharp stake.   Sometimes a person was half killed, then revived, and again submitted to torture.

When the death penalty was not used, various forms of physical punishment were applied.   Flogging on the bare back was common, administered after tying a person to the end of a cart or to a whipping post.   Sometimes a criminal was ordered to leave a community and was whipped all the way to the next.   The ears might be cut off or the tongue slit and in early times hands or legs were cut off.   Boring the tongue with a red-hot spike was a punishment reserved for those who offended by their conversation or gossip. A letter signifying the crime might be branded on the person's cheek, forehead, or hand.   The ducking stool, in which the offender was placed and then plunged into a pond, and the stocks were in common use.   When vessels were propelled by oars, criminals were condemned to be galley slaves.

Many of these punishments have been abandoned.   Nevertheless, capital punishment is legal in 42 states and in many European countries.[5]   In Delaware the judge may still and sometimes does sentence a convicted offender to be whipped—so many lashes for each offense to be administered in a legally prescribed manner.   In many states that do not prescribe physical punishment for the crime committed, the warden of the prison is allowed to whip or otherwise physically punish criminals who fail to follow the strict prison rules.   Occasionally these punishments are so severe that the criminal dies.

When the death penalty and physical pain were the accepted methods of punishment, they usually were administered in public, under the belief that those tempted to crime would be deterred by the sight of suffering.   Spectators came in crowds, as for a holiday, and thieves busied themselves in the crowd, being not at all deterred by the sight of some other thief being put to death or flogged.   Today, in the United States the death penalty and, in Delaware, the flogging, are carried out within prison walls with only certain officials and perhaps a few others present.   Nevertheless, deterrence is still used as one justification for such punishments.   A second rationalization is that when someone commits a crime he must in some way pay for it by his life or by suffering.   Actually, such punishments are probably merely survivals from the past, reinforced by public anger and hostility toward criminals.

Banishment of the Criminal

Gradually, as public opinion turned against the severe physical punishments and with the development by European countries of colonies in remote places, a system of banishment of criminals was devised.[6]   England deported criminals to the American colonies until 1776 and then to Australia until 1840.   France began the deportation of criminals to its colonies in 1797 during the revolution and with various changes continued some use of deportation, chiefly to French Guiana, until the middle of the present century. Italy established penal colonies on her coastal islands.   For the most part, deportation and the establishment of criminal colonies has failed to do more than remove the criminals from the mother country.   The United States, having no colonies, has not attempted a system of banishment of criminals.

IMPRISONMENT, A RECENT TREND

The use of imprisonment as punishment for crimes is of recent origin. Prisons, however, have existed from early times.   Castles often had dungeons into which the king or lord could thrust prisoners taken in war or captured rivals; early courts also used prisons.   The purpose of imprisonment was custody until a sentence, such as death, could be carried out; or as a place of torture either by mechanical means or by the slow process of neglect and starvation.   The idea that an offender, and especially a major criminal, could be punished by loss of liberty and later restored to society as a free person was a concept that came to life in the period around 1800. It grew partly out of the acknowledged failure of previous methods of punishment and partly as an extension of methods used here and there for minor offenders.

In a few cities in Europe some form of compulsory institutionalization had been tried for minor offenders, vagrants, and prostitutes as early as the sixteenth century.[7]   In 1593, the Protestants of Amsterdam built a prison for women whom they hoped to reform by hard work and religious influences. Similar institutions were built in Germany and the Hanseatic towns.   In 1703, Clement XI erected a prison that became famous as an innovation in the treatment of young male offenders: St. Michel, at Rome.   Later in the same century, a workhouse was built at Ghent, Belgium, where it was hoped reformation could be achieved through hard work.   Felons as well as vagrants, beggars, and prostitutes were confined there, but were segregated, as were men and women.   England from the Middle Ages had local jails and a few institutions for debtors and those guilty of contempt of court.   In the middle of the sixteenth century, construction of workhouses or houses of correction was authorized, in order to give employment to "sturdy beggars" and the unemployed; in time these institutions housed petty offenders, a change recognized by an Act of Parliament in 1720.   Imprisonment as punishment for felons followed this earlier development of workhouses and houses of correction.

As the cell-block replaced the gallows, a new philosophy of criminology paralleled the change in punishment.   The criminal was slowly losing his role as an unbearable member of society who must be eliminated by torturous death or banishment, usually combined with such intolerable living conditions that early death resulted.   He was regarded as a rational being, who had a choice of good or evil in his conduct and who, under certain conditions, might choose to abandon the evil in favor of the good for his future behavior.   Reformation became the objective.   Hard work, moral and religious instruction, and, among the Quakers, solitude for contemplation and penitence were prominent in the programs instituted with the development of prisons.   Sociological and psychological theories and their application to penology did not appear for almost another century, and are still in the process of implementation.

Although many changes have come in the past centuries in criminal philosophy and penology, in accordance with the growth of knowledge and changing attitudes toward human nature, nevertheless, a surprising amount of the old philosophy remains to plague criminologists who are trying to apply our present fund of knowledge to the treatment of criminals.   No part of the old seems completely and universally eliminated.   Traces remain of the belief in retaliation; the victim of a criminal wishes the criminal to suffer as he has suffered, and sometimes he bypasses the courts and, as in the past, seeks his own revenge.   Often the courts exonerate the criminal act of the avenger or administer only nominal punishment.   For example, it is often difficult to induce a jury to convict a man who has murdered the rapist of his wife or daughter, even though the rape occurred some time in the past and the case is on its way through the courts.   Retribution, or the idea that a criminal must pay for his crime in suffering, is active in the minds of newspaper editors and the public when they demand severe punishment for criminals, although they themselves are not the victims.   Deterrence of others from crime is often used as an argument for capital punishment, with total disregard of the fact that history and present-day surveys alike fail to prove deterrence.   At the same time, newer ideas of reformation have also been widely diffused; often, however, they must fit into the framework of the past when hard work, physical hardships in prison living conditions, and severe punishment for infraction of prison rules were advocated.

Rehabilitation and re-education that employ current psychological and sociological knowledge and methods are slowly gaining a foothold. Their greatest obstacle is the medley of firmly held obsolete concepts that have come from the past. Their use is hindered also by the inheritance of antiquated prison structures that were built for the reformatory ideas of a century or more ago, which advocated isolation, restriction of free activity, repression of individual interests, and constant surveillance by guards.

AGENCIES OF LAW ENFORCEMENT

The process of criminal justice is a complicated series of steps whereby the suspected offender is passed along from one independent agency to another, from the moment of arrest by the police to final release from prison sentence, or—in a few cases—to death at the command of the state. Much of the system is predicated upon the old philosophy that the offender must be branded as guilty and punished for his offense. Confusion, delays, and contradictions in the process result from the assignment of different agencies to different units of government from the municipality to the federal government, and from the lack of any centralized control over local units.

The Process of Law Enforcement

The process of law enforcement operates like a series of loosely meshed gears. The initial contact with the suspected offender is usually an arrest, which may immediately follow the commission of an offense, if observed by the police or promptly reported to them. On other occasions, if the perpetrator is unknown, an offense is reported to the police or to the prosecuting attorney, who then undertake an investigation. If the police are able to attach suspicion to some person, they arrest him. It is also possible for a known offender to be brought before the court on a summons, but arrests are more common.

The succeeding process differs slightly according to the gravity of the offense. The law usually divides offenses into two categories: misdemeanors or minor offenses, and felonies or serious crimes. Sometimes the dividing line is the degree of injury inflicted: thus theft of $15 or less might be a misdemeanor but theft of a larger sum a felony. For some crimes, a first offense is defined as a misdemeanor, whereas a second offense is punished as a felony.

The law provides that the offender shall be brought before a magistrate without delay. The magistrate may be a police judge, a justice of the peace, a municipal judge, or other judge of an inferior or lower court. This judge is empowered with final disposition of misdemeanants. If there is insufficient evidence to convict the offender, who is termed the defendant, the judge dismisses him. If the evidence indicates his guilt, the magistrate imposes a fine or a short sentence in jail or house of correction. Probation or release of a convicted person conditional upon good behavior is not often granted to misdemeanants.

In the case of a felony, the magistrate hears the evidence against the arrested person and, if it is sufficient to warrant a trial, directs that he shall be held for the grand jury, or he may be released on bail. This process requires some relative or friend, or a professional bondsman, to sign a bond, supported by a listing of property, pledging himself to pay a certain sum of money to the trial court if the suspect does not appear before it when he is summoned to do so. A period of weeks or months may intervene between this preliminary hearing by the magistrate and the meeting of the grand jury.

The grand jury is a body of men drawn from a list of qualified voters whose duty is to decide whether the evidence is sufficient to hold the suspect for a trial. The function of the grand jury does not differ greatly from that of the magistrate. If the defendant is to be held for trial the grand jury brings in a true bill. If the defendant is to be released the grand jury brings in a no bill.

After the grand jury has brought in a true bill, another interval of time occurs before the trial, during which the defendant may be jailed or released on bail. The trial is held before a criminal court; either the judge or a jury renders the final decision of guilt or innocence. The prosecuting attorney, in the name of the state, presents the evidence against the defendant. A private attorney, employed by the defendant or appointed by the judge for an indigent defendant, presents the evidence in favor of the defendant, either to prove his innocence or to show mitigating circumstances and try to secure a light sentence.

The convicted defendant who is not satisfied with the decision of court or jury may appeal the sentence to a higher court. Again an interval of time elapses and again he may be held in jail or released on bail. After the final decision as to his guilt, the convicted person is sentenced by the judge. The penalty may be a fine, imprisonment, or both; or execution. The punishment for the crime may be fixed by law, or the judge may have the power to prescribe it within limits set by the law. The judge may also have power to suspend the sentence and place the defendant on probation, during a stated period of good behavior. The offender is then under the supervision of the probation officer. If he fails to observe the conditions of probation during this period, the sentence may be imposed immediately without further trial.

The defendant who is fined is released upon payment of the sum of money.

If he cannot pay it, however, he is confined in jail to "sit out" the fine, a certain amount being credited against it for each day in jail. The defendant who is sentenced to prison is usually taken there promptly by the local sheriff or other official and placed in charge of the prison warden.

Imprisonment may be a matter of months, of years, or for life. The exact length of time may be fixed by law or by the judge. Or the duration of imprisonment may be fixed by the parole board, dependent upon the background and the prison behavior of the convicted person. The well-behaved prisoner can shorten his sentence if the law allows a reduction for good conduct. The criminal who serves his full sentence is released unconditionally. The offender who is placed on parole is under the supervision of a parole officer for a predetermined period or until the expiration of his sentence; he may be returned to prison if he fails to observe the conditions of his parole. The convicted person who is sentenced to death is executed according to the method provided by the laws of the state.

This sketch is a brief résumé of a complex situation. With the exception of certain federal offenses that are uniform for the entire United States, crimes and the punishment of offenders are established by state laws. Hence, each state has its own system, which it changes from time to time. Certain fundamental principles underlie all these systems, however, and the basic process of arraignment, trial, conviction, and punishment obtains in all states. Most differences lie in the mechanics of operation of the system, rather than in fundamental assumptions of what constitutes a crime or how a criminal should be treated.

Complexity of Autonomous Units

Enforcement of criminal laws is a type of public service; it shares, therefore, in all the peculiarities of our democratic government. Our government gives autonomous authority to small units of population, which may be exercised over small geographical areas—the village, the city, the county. The state has enormous power, but it may not infringe upon the rights of the smaller units that compose it, nor impose its power over adjacent states. The federal government also has many powers, but may not usurp the authority of states or smaller units. The powers of each unit of government, large or small, extend to the making of laws or local ordinances, the establishment of independent systems of police, the formation of courts, and the construction and operation of penal institutions. Within any one community, therefore, exist law enforcement agencies established, controlled, and financially supported by each level of government. There are, for example, municipal police accountable to the city government; a county sheriff whose territory may include the city; state police who move freely from county to county; and federal police who are free to cross state lines.   Moreover, within each governmental unit, the police may be specialized or may be attached to different branches of government.   For instance, the state may maintain not only police who patrol the highways but also police for special services, as narcotics control.

A similar situation exists among courts.   The jurisdiction of the police magistrate and the municipal judge covers only the area of the city; the justice of the peace represents a township or some other small local unit; the county judge operates for the entire county; often the criminal judge has a jurisdiction that includes several counties; the state has a court that functions for the entire state.   The federal government has its own system of courts for offenses against federal laws, and for appeals from lower courts.

Penal institutions include the city jail, the county jail, sometimes regional jails or workhouses, state prisons of many types, and federal prisons, each under a different unit of government.

Laws or customs determine the boundaries within which each agency operates and the specific functions it performs.   The several systems of federal police each specialize in one type of crime and may not infringe upon each other's authority nor upon the local police.   State police often have their duties limited in such a way that they do not override municipal or county police officers.   The minor or lower courts have authority to settle only violations of local ordinances or of minor state laws, whereas the criminal courts enforce the major criminal laws of the state.

Nevertheless, different agencies often clash when the demarkation of authority is not clear or when it is capable of several interpretations.   In some states both the juvenile and the criminal court have jurisdiction when crimes are committed by a child.   Which has precedence?   Under what conditions may the Federal Bureau of Investigation enter a local criminal case?   The exact conditions are sometimes difficult to determine.   When a city has park police as well as city police, which group has authority to investigate a murder committed in a park?   Conflicts, competition, and jealousies thus often arise between agencies operating in the same area, and the furtherance of justice may be hindered rather than helped by a multiplicity of agencies.

More serious than the conflicts and confusion that may arise from overlapping or poorly defined functions, is the independence of agencies with reference to policies and practices in handling offenders.   The police may regard suspects as enemies and treat them with brutality; the judge before whom they are brought may find them guilty but secure information about the psychological and social factors involved, in an effort to sentence them in such a way that they will receive the most help; the prison to which he must send them may follow a repressive regime and may disregard the information secured by the judge.   In other words, one agency may establish and follow a program calculated to aid in rehabilitation, only to have its efforts negated by other agencies that in turn have control over an offender at an earlier or later period.   It is, therefore, possible to find, within one community or one state, outdated or cruel treatment of an offender in one agency, and enlightened and rehabilitative treatment in another agency. Since there is no central control over the autonomous agencies, many variations of criminological philosophy and types of treatment may be found, and a given offender may pass overnight from medieval cruelty to a program of education and personality adjustment.   Thus within one state, or one city, the worst and the best may be found, while among states provisions for criminals vary from severely punitive treatment to modern rehabilitation.

FAILURE OF PAST METHODS

All statistics of arrests and imprisonment show a high degree of failure in our traditional methods of handling offenders.   Even among juveniles, who receive the most promising treatment of all types of offenders, the rate of recidivism is high.   A few illustrations serve to demonstrate this point.

Among juvenile delinquents reported to the Children's Bureau, approximately 35 per cent have had previous court experience.[8]   The annual reports of 5 state prisons for a combined group of 5,000 prisoners show that 37 per cent of men admitted during one year had served sentences for previous offenses (See Table 18, page 433), and almost half of the recidivists had had 4 or more earlier commitments to penal institutions.   The various studies of the Gluecks, already discussed in Chapter 2, are the most conclusive.   They show that one half to two thirds of the offenders studied continued their criminal careers beyond the time of their first contacts with courts and reformatories, undergoing repeated arrests and periods of imprisonment.

SCIENTIFIC APPROACH TO REFORMATION

Against this congealed and inert background of punishment harshly applied to all offenders, of crude old prison structures, of complicated and unco-ordinated machinery of law enforcement, we may place present scientific knowledge of how to go about helping people to understand their adjustment problems, arousing a desire for personal readjustment, and motivating them toward better training in practical matters.   Psychology, psychiatry, and sociology have not found foolproof or final methods of retraining, but they offer the most hopeful approaches.   These sciences have been applied to child training, education for both normal and special classes of children, child adjustment, marital counseling, and parent-child relationships, to mention only a few areas in which progress has been made.   The contributions of these sciences, however, have scarcely begun to affect the treatment of criminals.   Here and there in individual prisons or correctional schools, in a few state prison systems, and in the federal prison system a definite movement has been made away from a punitive treatment toward education methods and personal rehabilitation.   In this newer approach, the following principles are observed.

1. The offender is the center of the retraining program.   Attention is focused not alone on the specific conduct that has brought him to public attention, but also upon his entire personality.

2. In the light of a study of the offender's personality and past experiences, an analysis or diagnosis is made of the causes of his misconduct.

3. A plan of treatment or retraining is devised, based upon underlying causes.   In order to activate the treatment, physical facilities are made suitable and some degree of integration is achieved among the many agencies that handle an offender.

4. The term of imprisonment or of probation or parole supervision is not fixed in advance but is adjustable to the progress in rehabilitation made by the offender.

5. Every effort is made to gain the co-operation of the offender in carrying out the program.

6. It is recognized that sometimes offenders do not come to the attention of specialists until their personalities and patterns of social behavior are so warped that they cannot be rehabilitated; for such individuals, custodial care is provided, perhaps for life.

7. Specially trained personnel make the diagnosis and supervise the retraining.   No single profession has a monopoly of the techniques that are useful.   These specialists include physicians, psychiatrists, psychologists, sociologists, and social workers—all of whom deal with aspects of human personality and social adjustment.

The succeeding chapters discuss in detail the various steps in the long process from the time of arrest until final release from custody.   Brief sketches of the development of the various agencies are given, since many of them are understandable only in terms of their historical background.   The present situation is described.   Trends are pointed out, since the vast mass of interlocked agencies is heaving in change and a transitional period has begun.   Finally, an attempt is made to evaluate the process in terms of the rehabilitative effect upon prisoners.   This evaluation is based upon objective studies as much as possible, but studies are not available for all phases of the process. Sometimes, therefore, evaluation is a matter of opinion, based upon established principles of rehabilitation.

QUESTIONS

1. After reading the article by Kirchwey (Readings), trace the development of criminal law.

2. Trace the changes in different methods of punishment from early times to the recent period. Discuss past philosophies and methods as a hindrance to present developments.

3. What would be the advantages of a unified system of law enforcement agencies, under one central authority for the nation? What disadvantages would there be?

4. Have traditional methods of handling criminals eliminated crime? Reformed criminals?

5. What are the main steps in scientific treatment of criminals?

READINGS

Barnes, Harry Elmer, *The Story of Punishment* (Boston: Stratford, 1930). An exposé of the more brutal forms of punishment applied to criminals over the centuries in Europe and America. Changes in methods and exchange of ideas between countries can be traced.

Kirchwey, G., "Criminal Law," *Encyclopaedia of the Social Sciences,* 4 (Macmillan, 1931), 569–79. The development of criminal law from earlier forms of personal vengeance is traced.

Ploscowe, Morris, *Crime and Criminal Law,* The National Law Library, Vol. 2 (New York: Collier, 1939). This book gives a thorough discussion of the development and characteristics of the criminal law. It is recommended as a background for Part II of this text.

Wines, Frederick Howard, *Punishment and Reformation* (rev. ed., Crowell, 1919). Chapters 3–10 trace changes in the philosophy and practice of penology from early historical times to approximately 1900.

FOOTNOTES

[1] George W. Kirchwey, "Criminal Law," *Encyclopaedia of the Social Sciences,* 4 (Macmillan, 1931), 569.

[2] Doris May Stenton, *English Society in the Early Middle Ages, 1066–1307* (Harmondsworth, Middlesex, England: Penguin Books, 1952), p. 108.

[3] Frederick Howard Wines, *Punishment and Reformation* (Crowell, 1919), p. 39.

[4] *Ibid.,* chs. 5, 6.

[5] F. E. Hartung, "Trends in the Use of Capital Punishment," *Annals of the American Academy of Political and Social Science,* 284 (1952), 10; P. P. Lejins, "The Death Penalty Abroad," *Annals of the American Academy of Political and Social Science,* 284 (1952), 137–46.

[6] "Deportation or Transportation," *Encyclopaedia Britannica,* 7 (Chicago: Encyclopaedia Britannica, Inc., 1948), 229–30.

[7] *Ibid.,* vol. 18, p. 514; Wines, *op. cit.,* pp. 122–23, 133–43; Negley Teeters, *World Penal Systems, A Survey* (Philadelphia; Pennsylvania Prison Society, 1944), pp. 48–52.

[8] "A Few Facts about Juvenile Delinquency," *The Child,* 17 (Dec. 1952), 63.

The Police

Police systems may be blackly condemned for inefficiency in crime detection, collusion with criminals, and police graft; or they may be extolled for praiseworthy methods of police selection, training, and law enforcement. Both pictures are true.   That both situations may exist at the same time is easily explained by the fact that in the United States there are some 40,000 independent and autonomous public law enforcement agencies.[1]   There are more than 16,000 municipalities, 19,000 townships, and 3,000 counties in addition to 48 states, the District of Columbia, several territories, and a number of departments of the federal government, each with its own law enforcement agencies.   In some of these agencies inefficient and dishonest police officers are found; in others the police forces operate at a high level of ethics and efficiency.

RELATION OF THE POLICE TO CRIMINALS

The primary duty of the police is to enforce the law and maintain order. Concretely, the police investigate complaints, seek to discover who committed crimes, and then find and arrest the suspected persons.   The policeman on the beat or in the roving squad car also endeavors to control any incipient disorder and makes firsthand investigations of suspected crimes. The police are not legally empowered to judge whether a person is guilty, to administer punishment, nor to retain custody of a prisoner for more than a minimum period unless directed to do so by a judge.   The limitations of their duties regarding crime should be clearly understood.   In addition to their relation to criminals, the police are assigned many other tasks, such as traffic control, supervision of parades, administration of first aid, and operation of ambulances.   These tasks must be performed but they are not closely related to the duties of the police with reference to crime control and prevention.

Recently, in some cities police have instituted positive programs of crime prevention (described in Chapter 10). At present, however, most crime prevention by the police is indirect and negative in nature. By supervision and control of minor disturbances they may prevent the commission of crimes, but they do not directly contribute to building up the type of personality that is law abiding as a matter of course.

Since contact with the police constitutes the first impact of law enforcement upon the delinquent or criminal, treatment by the police is important to his subsequent behavior. Harsh or abusive treatment will cause him to withdraw further from the mores of conventional society and to ally himself with the underworld. Consideration compatible with the conditions of the arrest opens the way for constructive work. The quality of the police force, therefore, is extremely important for the young offender or the adult at the time of his first apprehension.

The treatment that the police accord suspected criminals also affects the attitude of the public toward offenders. If the police treat them harshly, the public assumes that they are guilty, even though they are innocent. The public may ostracize the person who has been arrested and abused by the police and thus make his later integration into conventional society difficult. The offender or suspect in turn builds up resentment toward the public as well as toward the police.

NUMBER OF POLICE

The number of police is difficult to estimate because of the many independent police systems. The *Uniform Crime Reports* in 1951 received returns from 3,565 cities representing about half the total population of the United States; in these cities there were 147,000 employees of police departments, about 136,000 of whom were police officers and 11,000 civilian employees.[2] Among the 9 federal agencies with police, the Federal Bureau of Investigation alone has some 13,000 special agents, clerks, and technicians.[3] State police number about 18,000,[4] while sheriffs, constables, and marshals add another 80,000.[5] If all reports were complete, the total number would probably approach 400,000.

URBAN POLICE SYSTEMS

Origin of the Police System

Urban police systems in the United States have mushroomed out from the night watchmen of New England towns of the seventeenth century. From a duty imposed upon the citizens, the function of night watchman developed into a 24 hour, full-time paid position. Early conflicts arose between night watchmen and day police, who were under different officials. This conflict and the inefficiency of appointment of watchmen and police by wards led to concentration of both day and night police for all wards under a chief of police appointed by the mayor. After New York City took this step in 1844, other cities followed and the urban police force came into existence.

Organization

Various methods have been tried periodically in different states to provide adequate control of urban police systems: local police boards, state boards, chiefs of police appointed by and responsible directly to the mayor, and commissioners of police. Table 12 shows methods of appointment of police

TABLE 12

Agencies Appointing Police Chiefs, in Cities over 25,000 Population,
for 1953

Agency	Number of Cities
City manager	132
Mayor	124
City council	81
Police or safety board	70
Safety or service commissioner or director	38
Governor	2
Public, by election	4

Source: C. E. Ridley, O. F. Nolting, and D. S. Arnold (eds.), *The Municipal Year Book, 1953* (Chicago: International City Managers' Association, 1953), p. 415.

chiefs for 451 cities with more than 25,000 population. Although the city manager or mayor appoints 57 per cent of police chiefs, most popular head of police in large cities is the police or safety commissioner. He is not selected from the police force but presumably has an over-all view of community values. The commissioner appoints the chief of police, who has often worked his way up through the graded ranks of policemen. When a commissioner is not part of the system, the chief of police is responsible to the mayor or city manager, or to a board of public safety. The power and the responsibility of the chief are thus limited, since appointments of policemen, their advancement, and their dismissal may rest with the controlling officer or board.

The selection of the chief of police often has unfortunate legal limitations. A study of 300 cities showed that in 111 the chief is required to be a resident of the municipality and in 106 must be chosen from the police force.[6] Such limitations may prevent the best selection in some instances.   The chief may also have so many local ties and obligations that he cannot act freely and decisively in terms of his own best judgment.

The term of office of chief of police is usually short, frequently being 2 to 4 years or at the discretion of the appointing officer.   A change in political party often brings a change in police chief regardless of his merits; or the chief may be dismissed for displeasing his superior officer in some personal way.   Several studies show how brief the average tenure of office is in cities of different sizes.   A study of municipal police systems in Texas for a 20 year period ending in 1937 revealed that the average terms ranged from 4.5 years for cities of less than 1,000 to 2.9 years for cities of 100,000 or over.[7]   These short, uncertain terms are not conducive to high morale in the department, as the chief has no inducement to develop pride in his department nor time to build up a well-organized and adequately trained force.

The chief of police is in direct charge of the police force and translates the policies of the commissioner or other superior officer or board into the practical operations of the force.   Below the chief are the captain, who has charge of a police district or precinct; his assistant with the title of lieutenant; a number of sergeants under each captain, whose duty is to supervise a number of patrolmen, who do the actual work of walking a beat or supervising a limited geographic area.   This system is basic.   In most large cities the work of the department is organized on a functional basis into divisions, such as the Detective Division, Vice Division, Juvenile Division, Traffic Division, Patrol Division, and Auxiliary Services Division (records). When the volume of work demands, the division may be broken down into bureaus; for example, the Detective Division may be comprised of an Auto Theft Bureau, Homicide Bureau, Burglary Bureau, and so on.   Bureaus in turn may be subdivided into details.

Selection of Police

Although each police department may set its own standards for selection of recruits, the general movement has been toward increasingly rigid application of standards and the establishment of attractive conditions of work.[8]

In the past, police departments as a rule did not attract recruits of high quality.   For one thing, a policeman's job is not glamorous.   The patrolman, the starting grade, is out in the open in all kinds of weather, the year around, engaged in monotonous and tiresome work.   Many—in fact most —arrests are of vagrants, drunkards, or disorderly persons who are often unpleasant to handle.   When a major crime is committed the policeman faces possible injury or death.   In addition, many departments fail to set standards or provide training for the ambitious, and often make appointments and promotions on the basis of political affiliation rather than personal ability.

The trend, especially in the larger cities, and in state and federal units, is toward a more moderate working week, increase of pay, and pension provisions. Although the foot patrolman is still the largest group (33.2 per cent of the force in large cities), the use of motorcycles and squad cars has changed much of the character of police work.

Among cities of 10,000 and over, 21 years has become the minimum age for acceptance on the police force, and more than half of the cities require high school graduation. In some cities, however, standards are much lower —8th grade education or simply the ability to read and write English. Elimination of unsuitable candidates is achieved by many cities through the use of tests and examinations. Most large cities use civil service examinations given under an agency not connected with the police department. Such examinations frequently cover not only the initial selection of recruits but also all promotions, even to the chief of police. Civil service examinations select the better qualified men for appointment or promotion, prevent any feeling of unfairness, give a greater feeling of security of tenure, and in general promote better morale in the department. August Vollmer, a leader in better police training, regards civil service as a definite step forward and states that despite some corruption, owing to political appointment, a department under civil service is in a much better condition than one without it.[9]

Intelligence tests are used in many large cities and police aptitude tests in a few. Since the passing score is often low, the effect of the various tests is to eliminate the obviously unfit rather than to attract those best qualified to be policemen. However, as the position of policeman moves toward higher professional standards, a true selective process will develop.

Height and weight standards are also commonly applied, and fingerprints are checked with the national file maintained by the Federal Bureau of Investigation.

At each step of the testing and examining process applicants are eliminated. With the final group, personal interviews often are used, with the candidate being rated on such qualities as voice and speech, emotional stability, self-confidence, friendliness, temperament, and personal fitness for the position. In one program of selection that used various tests, examinations, and interviews, an initial list of 692 applicants was reduced to 74 who were accepted.[10]

Promotions

When inadequate selective methods for patrolmen are used, eventually the entire police force becomes mediocre, since the administrative positions of captain, inspector, deputy chief, and chief often are filled from the ranks below. MacNamara, Director of the Law Enforcement Program of the University of Southern California, urges selection of the officers in the higher ranks from among qualified men in other police systems or from the college-trained professional policemen who are now graduating from special university programs.[11] He compares these professional police officers to the army and navy officers who come through West Point and Annapolis, who receive training not required for men in the ranks. The criticism may be raised that such a system, rigidly adhered to, would condemn the capable and well-trained patrolman to that status for life; however, provisions could be made for patrolmen who had or gained necessary training to have opportunities for advancement. The point to be emphasized is the need for professionals at the top instead of the pushing upward of inadequately trained men through seniority, and the limitation of choice to the men in one force, none of whom may be good selections for the higher ranks.

Training

Except in the larger cities, the recruit does not receive much training after appointment, and often the training is inadequate for the responsibilities imposed upon policemen. In smaller cities, a few lectures by the chief of police and a kind of apprenticeship to an experienced officer are a substitute for a training course. More and more, police departments are turning to colleges and universities for assistance, both for professional training of men and women wishing to enter police work as a career and for short in-service courses. Three illustrations are here given of the growing number of degree-bearing college courses in police training.

For the career-minded student, San Jose State College in California offers a 4 year course designed for the policeman, parole or probation officer, or institutional worker. Students interested in police work are screened for the usual physical requirements demanded by police departments as to height, weight, and so forth. The student must be of good character and have appropriate personality qualities for the work. The course includes liberal arts as well as vocational courses specifically related to police work and penology. The vocational courses are given as follows in the *Circular of Information and Announcements of Courses* for 1953–54:

Police Agility Testing
Life Saving
First Aid
Administration of Criminal Justice
Gunnery

Judo
Criminal Identification
Police Sketching and Use of Plastics
Public Safety
Law of Arrest
Law of Evidence
Court Procedure
Crime Prevention
Traffic
Police Record Systems
Criminal Investigation
Police Organization and Administration
Criminology
Police Problems
Report Writing
Physical Evidence

Before the end of the course the student must pass a typing test.   The
student is required to have a minor in psychology and a second minor in
business or the Reserve Officers Training Corps.   In his last year of training he has field work.

The University of California, Berkeley, according to its *Bulletin* also offers
a 4 year program with many courses similar to those available at San Jose,
but with more emphasis on crime detection in such courses as Legal Medicine, Microchemical Testing of Physical Evidence, Comparative Microscopy,
Questioned Documents, and Interrogation and Detection of Deception.
Seminars carrying graduate credit are also given.

Michigan State College at Lansing in its *Catolog, 1953–54* outlines three
4 year programs in Law Enforcement carried out with the co-operation of
the Michigan State Police.   The student has a choice of three specialties:
General Police Administration leading to careers in law enforcement at
federal, state, or local levels of government or allied occupations in government, business, or industry; Police Science, preparing for scientific criminal investigation work for laboratory technicians; or Crime Prevention.
Courses are open to women as well as men.

Short inservice courses have also been established co-operatively by many
police departments and colleges or universities.   The Chicago Police Department and the faculties of Wright and Wilson (municipal) Junior Colleges have developed courses in Criminal Law, Human Relations, Practical
Psychology, Fundamentals of Speech, Report Writing, Typing, and Ad-

A police inspector shows a rookie of the Atlanta, Georgia, police force how to perform the "flying mare." Designed to throw an opponent flat on his back, this protective measure is only part of the intensive physical training required of each rookie in an effort to develop a highly efficient police force. The candidate must also study law, marksmanship, phases of traffic handling, and other police matters, as well as passing the severe physical examination. The entire program is designed to create for the city a force of men capable of meeting and overcoming every obstacle. (Acme)

vanced First Aid, described in the Department's *Annual Report* for 1951. Sixty carefully selected men from the police force enter the course each September and each February. In addition, the Chicago Police Department has courses for recruits, attended in 1951 by 353; inservice courses for detectives, attended by 1,228; a judo course taken by 39 policewomen; and a machine gun course attended by 41 detectives.

Inservice courses were also started in 1951 in Louisville as a co-operative effort of the University of Louisville and the State Director of Public Safety.[12] Three times annually, a course of 12 weeks' duration is given to 25 carefully selected police officers from the southern states.

An inservice training program that brings together the Federal Bureau of Investigation and the University of Minnesota was announced in 1953.[13] The University has revised courses offered by the FBI to meet University standards and has appointed the 6 special FBI agents who teach the courses to instructorships. For 45 hours of prescribed work, University credit in criminology is given, although the courses do not count toward a degree. These courses, given at various places throughout the state, are supplemented by short courses on the campus.

Juvenile delinquency is emphasized in the Delinquency Control Institute sponsored by police authorities and the University of Southern California at Pasadena.[14] Three months of intensive training with university credit is given to police, parole, and probation officers. Courses include child growth, psychology, public speaking, police techniques, and administration.

The courses cited are indicative of the trend toward professionalization that is spreading over the nation.

Another move for better police training is the 12 weeks' training school for local, county, and state law enforcement officers operated by the Federal Bureau of Investigation.[15] In order to attend the FBI National Academy, the men must be selected by the heads of their respective departments. The men pay their own expenses but are not charged a fee. By the end of 1952, 2,528 policemen had completed the course. Since the participants, upon return to their own departments, pass on their training to their colleagues a much greater number of policemen are benefited. A variety of subjects are covered: police organization and administration, records, teaching methods, public speaking, scientific crime investigation methods, fingerprinting, use of firearms, traffic regulation, and defensive tactics. In addition, attention is given to constitutional law, the Bill of Rights, history of law enforcement, and professional and ethical standards. On request, the FBI also aids state, county, and municipal police departments to operate schools for their own members, either new recruits or experienced men ready for inservice training. During the 1952 fiscal year, the FBI assisted in 2,350 such schools. Finally, the FBI held 131 law enforcement conferences during the same year, for the discussion of mutual problems of federal, state, county and municipal law enforcement officers.

Policewomen

Numbering approximately 1,000 for the entire United States, policewomen compose less than 1 per cent of all police officers.[16] In addition, some 2,000 women are engaged in law enforcement work as deputy sheriffs, or customs or immigration inspectors. From among several cities that vie for the honor of having had the first policewomen, Los Angeles emerges as the first to have used the title and to have assigned the normal police authority to the bearer of the title. Between 1910, when Los Angeles appointed its first policewomen, and 1953, 150 cities have added women to their police force.[17]

Policies controlling the duties of policewomen vary from city to city. In some cities they wear uniforms and walk beats. In others, for example, New York, they function as plain-clothes detectives on all types of crime—thefts, murder, shoplifting, prostitution, and drug-law violations.[18] Other policewomen are assigned chiefly to cases involving women and children or in preventive work. It is in the latter field that their function differs most from the main duties of policemen.

In Chicago officers in the Women's Division may have routine district assignments or permanent assignments in the detective bureau where they work on such cases as thefts, picking pockets, forgeries, or confidence games.[19] In working on violations of narcotics laws they may pose as addicts who wish to buy the drug. In addition the Division performs certain specialized duties such as investigation of missing women and girls and boys under the age of 12, guard duty at hospitals, and regular inspections of bus stations, railroad stations, public dance halls, motion picture theaters, hotels, and teen-age hangouts where girls are likely to become involved with men.

A summary of the work for the Woman's Division in Detroit states that in one year 15,084 complaints were received.[20] The noncriminal department investigates complaints of delinquency and neglect, and conducts the search for missing persons and runaways, which includes a routine check at the detention home, Receiving Hospital, county morgue, Traveler's Aid, Y.W.C.A., and other agencies, as well as interviews with interested persons. The work of the patrol and complaints department goes on day and night without a break. Routine checks are made of hotel registers for missing women and minors, taxi dance halls where each new girl hired must fill out registration cards, dance halls, beer gardens, penny arcades, movies, roller rinks, bus stations, depots, and other public places where missing persons or minors might be found. City parks and streets are patrolled regularly, often by a policewoman and policeman together. The crime complaints department handles felony and misdemeanor cases involving women, such as cases of indecent exposure, indecent liberties, assault and battery, bastardy, rape, pandering, and gross indecency.

The tendency for policewomen to concentrate much of their efforts on women and children, many of whose offenses are less indicative of crime than of personal maladjustment, gives them a close affiliation with welfare agencies, as well as with the courts. Many policewomen regard their duties as a type of social work, although they are not always accorded the status of social workers by professionally trained people in that field. In fact, tension may characterize the relationship between the two groups. The policewomen feel that they are best able to handle certain cases because they are familiar with the background through first hand contacts in patrol and investigative work; the professional social worker, however, regards this practical factual approach as of little value in comparison with the testing and interviewing that is carried out in clinic or interviewing office.

Most cities require high school education of applicants for the position of policewomen, but few require more than this.[21]   Also, in the majority of cities they must pass an examination.   Cities are about equally divided as to whether or not policewomen must attend a training school.

Political Appointments

It must be admitted that systems of selection, training, and promotion function only to the exent that those in power permit them to do so.   The degree to which a seemingly satisfactory system may be perverted is evident in a statement made in 1944 by the Operating Director of the Chicago Crime Commission:

> For years appointments to the police department have been based primarily on political considerations.   The influence of politicians, many times affiliated with racketeers and hoodlums in gambling, vice or other illicit enterprise, has been highly important in placing men on the police department.   The same ugly influence has been important in affecting assignments, transfers, and promotions. These facts were clearly demonstrated in the recent Cook County grand jury investigation, at which the Clerk of Cook County testified that Civil Service examinations for police promotions are largely "sham."   When asked about political interference with the police department he testified to the effect that "Everybody knows how promotions are made in the police department.   Most captains are appointed by the Mayor on recommendation of the Ward Committeemen.   Every Ward Committeeman knows that Civil Service examinations for promotions are mostly a sham—it's all handled through the Mayor." [22]

THE COUNTY POLICE SYSTEM

The Sheriff

Rural law enforcement traditionally rests upon the sheriff, an office inherited from England where the sheriff was a powerful representative of the crown.[23]   With the passage of time the authority of the sheriff decreased and his status declined.   At present (except in Rhode Island) the sheriff is elected, as an officer of the county or other small administrative unit.

The sheriff has police powers, the exercise of which has been greatly curtailed by the establishment of city police and in a few states by the assumption by state police of many functions in the rural areas.   The sheriff, in addition to such powers, has the duty of executing civil processes of the

law. Most important at the present time, however, is his function as jailer.
Although this duty is custodial rather than a police function, it is important
for it places the sheriff in authority over many persons who are being held
for trial but have not been proved guilty, as well as over many convicted
persons who are sent to jail to serve short sentences or who are serving
sentences in lieu of paying fines. Since this contact with suspected criminals and minor offenders places the sheriff in a strategic position, the office
should be filled with great care.

The sheriff is not selected, however, with consideration of his important
relation to offenders. As with most elective offices, the only qualifications
are those relating to age, residence, citizenship, and electoral status. The
sheriff receives no training for his position. Moreover, in most states the
legal term of office is brief, and in some states the sheriff cannot serve for
two successive terms; therefore, he cannot accumulate the wisdom of experience. Since his term is short he feels compelled to retain his connection with whatever work he did before he was elected and often continues his regular employment in addition to performing his functions as
sheriff.

In large cities, the sheriff often receives his nomination as a political reward. Because of the opportunities for large income, the office is highly
prized by machine politicians, and is awarded to some adherent who has
made some contribution to the party or who turns over to the party treasury
part of his fees. Moley stated that the office of sheriff "has lived only because it is a rich prize for a powerful party system. Its simple and perfunctory duties require no knowledge or skill, but its emoluments are
princely." [24] The position of sheriff in a large city is described by a remark of the late Alfred E. Smith, at one time governor of New York, and
some 30 years ago sheriff of New York County.[25] The sheriff, he stated,
has a difficult time finding anything of consequence to do. His own main
duty as sheriff was to collect approximately $70,000 yearly from salary and
fees. In smaller cities and rural areas, salaries are moderate and usually
are supplemented by fees for serving legal documents.

The Constable

The constable, like many other law enforcement officers, was inherited
from England where he was a town or parish officer with many duties, among
them the apprehension of criminals.[26] In the American colonies the constable was elected by the town meeting or the selectmen and had charge of
the local police. At present the constable serves as the village policeman.
Less than half the states provide for a constable, who is usually chosen by
election for a term of 2 to 4 years. With a few exceptions, the com-

pensation is derived from fees for serving civil processes.   There is little actual police work.

The growth of cities, the development of specialized groups of city and state police, and modern methods of transportation that carry a criminal quickly from place to place have outmoded both the constable and the sheriff as policemen.[27]   Many devices are coming into use to supplement rural police units.

CO-ORDINATION AND SUPPLEMENTATION OF LOCAL POLICE SYSTEMS

The administrative boundaries of urban police are the city limits and of the sheriff and his deputies the county lines.   Within large cities, the territory is divided into police districts each with its own station and perhaps local lockup under the control of a police captain who is assisted by lieutenants and sergeants who supervise a number of patrolmen.   Chicago, for example, has 39 districts in the 213 square-mile city area.   These small areas of operation were fairly adequate when a criminal depended for escape upon his own powers of locomotion or a horse.   They are a handicap now to the police who cannot legally follow the criminal as he speeds in automobile or airplane beyond the administrative limits of the police in whose territory he committed the crime.   Often the criminal is not caught and may not be heard of again until he commits another crime.   Various devices have been developed to correct this situation.

Mobility and Communication

To counteract the ease with which the criminal can disappear in a heavily populated area, police are now provided with motorcycles, automobiles, and, occasionally, airplanes.   Although the foot patrolman is still commonly used for traffic regulation and to walk a beat in business areas, motorcycles and automobiles are generally used for patrolling residential areas.   New York City has a Police Aviation Bureau, originally established in 1929 as a unit of the Emergency Service Division.[28]   The flying patrolmen perform many duties not related to crime—such as dusting marsh lands for mosquito control; but they have the same obligations as all patrolmen with reference to enforcing laws, preventing crime, and detecting and arresting law violators. Some of their work is directly related to the development of aviation; for example, they report violations of the rulings of the Civil Aeronautics Authority and of laws that forbid low flying over crowded areas and illegal landings.   They also aid in locating escaped criminals and may be sent to pick up a wanted or suspected criminal.

High mobility would be of little value without rapid means of communication. Mechanical devices in common use are street-call police boxes, and two-way radios for rapid communication between patrol car and police station or between cars. In 1950, 40,000 police cars were reported to use two-way radios, with 13,000 still to be equipped, a process whose completion was anticipated within a few years' time.[29]

The teletype system has made possible the co-ordination of the work of police over a wide area. The teletype sends a given message simultaneously to a number of cities, which in turn may communicate with each other directly or through a central point. Thus if a crime is committed in a city and the criminal escapes, immediate warning may be sent at the same time to all cities or villages in the teletype system. In 1934 five eastern states—New York, Pennsylvania, Massachusetts, Connecticut, and New Jersey—co-ordinated their teletype systems to cover 680 police points, to all of which a message could be sent within 30 minutes. Teletype, now used by many cities, is supplemented by radio communication between cities and a national police radio-relay system.

Centralization of Services

Within cities, decentralization in districts is beginning to give way to certain centralized services. Some cities have established centralized bureaus where all calls to police are now taken and from which instructions to police cars are given. When a call comes in that a crime has been committed, the central bureau, within a few minutes, may call the car nearest the place of the crime and give all available information. Similarly, the policeman who stops a man whose actions seem suspicious may call the central station for information about him. This central bureau, in addition to information on crimes of the moment, maintains a file on known criminals, a directory of all cars in the state with the name of the license holder, and other useful information.

Co-ordination of Police Forces

Two-way radios and teletyping can only partially compensate for the many autonomous police systems in and around large cities. The situation in Chicago and Cook County, Illinois, may be used to illustrate a situation typical of many large cities with extensive suburban and fringe areas. According to a report published in 1952, Cook County, which contains Chicago, has 90 law enforcement agencies with 8,100 law enforcement officials. Chicago itself has two systems of police, the city police and independent park police.[30] Sixty streets and boulevards and 136 parks are under the jurisdiction of the park police whose duty it is to investigate crimes committed in these areas, although their primary function as carried out is traffic control.   Often the city police as well as the park police investigate accidents and crimes occurring in parks or on boulevards.   There is duplication of effort as well as of administration, clerical staffs, records, and radio broadcasting systems.   In Cook County outside of Chicago the police of the 89 incorporated cities and villages do not have overlapping areas; the county sheriff, however, may and sometimes does enter the incorporated communities, although in general he confines his activities to the unincorporated areas.   The state highway patrol also functions throughout the county, although it also tends to avoid intrusion into communities with local police forces.   At times the State's Attorney (a county officer) sends the Chicago city police assigned to his office into rural areas under the sheriff's jurisdiction, when he feels that the sheriff is not enforcing the laws; gambling raids are an example.   The situation makes for confusion and often for competition or conflict between different law enforcement bodies or officials.

When the state rather than the metropolitan area is considered, a similar profusion of independent police forces appears, many operating over small areas.   For example, in 1934, Minnesota had 94 city police departments, 630 village police departments, one borough police department, 87 sheriffs and their deputies, a highway patrol unit, fire marshal's force, detective bureau in the office of the liquor commissioner, and a state bureau of criminal apprehension.[31]

Various methods of co-ordination have been attempted to bring under some central or co-ordinated control the criminal activities in metropolitan areas, where the criminal may easily slip from one jurisdiction to another, eventually evading all police forces.   Smith states that the criminal influence of Cincinnati in 1933 extended over six counties, which included within their boundaries 51 townships and 13 magisterial districts containing 12 cities and 65 villages.[32]   In this locale 147 police agencies operated independently within small geographic boundaries.   The areas of influence spread over 2,000 square miles populated by almost one million people. In lieu of consolidating the police systems a method of co-ordination and co-operation was developed involving training in identification, the establishment of crime records, and installation of radio and teletype equipment.

In other urban counties, uniformed police attached to the sheriff's office operate in the rural portions of the county.[33]   Their efficiency varies, depending in part upon whether appointments to the force are political in nature or rest upon careful selection.   In other communities county police to patrol the rural areas of urban counties are appointed by the county board, the county judge, or the governor.   Supplementary police forces are sometimes attached to some governmental unit, as to the park system for the purpose of patrolling parks and county boulevards in order to regulate traffic. Although county-wide police undoubtedly fill some of the gaps, the problem of co-ordination of these units with local constables and urban police still remains.

Uniform Laws

The ease with which criminals may now escape from local or state police has led to the first steps in measures to permit pursuing them across state lines. Uniform criminal laws that all state legislatures may pass as statutes are urged by such national groups as the Interstate Crime Commission, the National Conference of Commissioners on Uniform State Laws, the Department of Justice, the Council of State Governments, and the American Legislators' Association. The Uniform Act on the Fresh Pursuit of Criminals permits an officer in pursuit of a felon or suspected felon soon after the crime has been committed (that is, in fresh pursuit) to cross the state boundary into any state that has passed the act. The act provides that the state he enters authorizes the officer from the other state to catch and arrest the criminal. Without such provision the pursuing officer would have no authority once the state line was reached. Other acts concern uniform methods of extraditing a fugitive criminal; provision for returning escaped witnesses to the state where a trial is being held; certain conditions for supervision of parolees or probationers from another state; restrictions on the possession of firearms with penalties for violations; and control of narcotics.[34]

STATE POLICE

A recent development on a wider basis than the county is the state police system. In 1905, Pennsylvania established the first state police system of modern type. A few states adopted the idea, but not until the 1920's did the procedure of establishing state police systems become universal. Now all states have police units, although in 13 states their duties are largely confined to highway patrol.[35]

State police operate under a state superintendent responsible to the governor who appoints him, sometimes with the consent of the state legislature or a state board. The superintendent usually serves "at will," but actually terms are short. A study in 1939–40 showed that three fourths of the state superintendents had served less than 3 years.[36]

Applicants for state police are examined so that obviously unqualified persons are screened out, although especially desirable ones are not always secured. In some states the applicant is required to pass an intelligence test, and is made the object of a character investigation and an oral interview that enables officials to pass on his personal qualities.   Most states provide some training, although it is not always adequate.   The training usually includes instruction in the rules and regulations of the department, calisthenics and military drill, first aid, firearm practice and care of ordnance, accident inquiry, criminal investigation, and records and reports.   On the whole, the state police are better trained than municipal police; also they are free from the influence of local politics, although there is no assurance that the system may not be affected by state politics.

The basic duty of the state police in a fully developed system is to patrol the rural highways and enforce all state laws except within municipalities; often they are forbidden to interfere in industrial strikes or labor disputes, and in some states they do not enter a criminal case unless the local law-enforcement officer requests such action.   Free of the limitations of municipal or county boundaries, the state police may follow a criminal until they catch him, provided he does not pass into another state.   When not forbidden to do so, they assume most of the task of law enforcement outside the larger cities that have police departments, that is, they supersede the sheriff in rural areas.   They are better trained and have superior equipment, in addition to their greater mobility.   The state may also operate a bureau of identification with fingerprint files, descriptions, photographs of known criminals, and apparatus for laboratory crime detection; it may even have a staff of experts in handwriting and ballistics.[37]

FEDERAL POLICE SYSTEMS

Nine systems of federal police extend the unification of crime control still further, for they operate over the entire United States.   Their duties are limited, however, to enforcing federal (rather than state) laws.   Many of the 9 systems are attached to specific governmental agencies and confine themselves to the investigation of violations of laws pertaining to these departments.   Others, as the Coast Guard and Federal Bureau of Investigation, have more general duties.   The Federal Bureau of Investigation is of special interest from the point of view of co-ordination; recently certain crimes, difficult for local or state police to solve, were constituted federal offenses in order to place them under a police system that can operate across state lines.

The 9 federal police systems are the following: [38]

1. Federal Bureau of Investigation of the Department of Justice.   As the best known of the federal police, this bureau is discussed in some detail later in this section.

2. Secret Service Division of the Treasury Department.   This division

has jurisdiction over counterfeiting stamps, forging money orders and government pay checks, and similar offenses; it also protects the President of the United States.

3. Intelligence Unit of Bureau of Internal Revenue, which carries on tax fraud investigations.

4. Enforcement Division of the Alcohol Tax Unit of the Bureau of Internal Revenue, Treasury Department.

5. Customs Agency Service of the Bureau of Customs, Treasury Department. This service patrols the borders to prevent smuggling goods into the United States.

6. Bureau of Narcotics of the Treasury Department, which investigates violations of the laws controlling narcotics.

7. Coast Guard, Treasury Department. The Coast Guard covers general law enforcement on the seas and coast.

8. Immigration Border Patrol of the Immigration and Naturalization Service, Department of Justice. This patrol prevents the illegal entry of aliens.

9. Office of the Chief Inspector of the Post Office Department, which investigates the wrongful use of mails, losses, depredations, and so on.

In addition, the Army, Navy, and Air Force maintain police units.

The work of these various federal units is not co-ordinated and in some instances two of them are charged with the same duties, a situation that causes rivalry and confusion. Although efficiency might be increased by co-ordination, our democratic philosophy that permits each small governmental unit to maintain its own police force, also permits each federal department to maintain its police. The system encourages federal units to become specialists in certain types of crime detection and also prevents the building up of a powerful centralized police force that might conceivably work against democratic principles.

The level of efficiency of federal police is illustrated by Baarslag's interesting book, *Robbery by Mail,* in which he states that agents of the Inspection Service of the Post Office may spend years tracking down a criminal.[39] They do not bring an offender to trial until they are convinced that they have sufficient evidence to convict him; consequently 97.97 per cent of all cases brought to trial result in conviction within the same year as the arrest. About 30,000 criminal cases (and 70,000 noncriminal cases) are investigated each year. The criminal offenses include holdups, burglaries of post offices, thefts by employees, forgery of money orders and stamps, lotteries, obscene, threatening, and extortion letters, embezzlement, lewd and lascivious postal matter, the mailing of bombs, poisoned cakes and candies, and fraud—which alone has 31 classifications.

Best known of the federal police systems is the Federal Bureau of Investigation, founded in 1908 under the control of the Department of Justice.[40]   Until 1934 it was an investigative body only and arrests were performed by local police or the United States Marshal upon the basis of information supplied by the FBI.   Since that time the FBI agents have been empowered to make arrests.

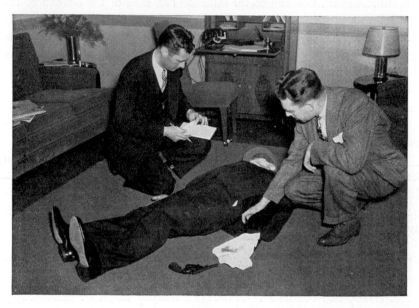

Among the techniques taught at the FBI training academy at Quantico, Virginia is how to examine the scene of a crime.   The future agent studies a hypothetical crime and learns to uncover all available clues.   Courses are given in federal law, accounting, fingerprint science, interviewing, photography, use of firearms, and jujitsu.

The modern development of the bureau began in 1924 with the administration of J. Edgar Hoover, who established the Identification Division in 1924 and the FBI laboratory in 1932, as well as a careful and elaborate system of training agents in crime detection.   Agents are meticulously selected; they must be between the ages of 25 and 40, above average in physical soundness, and graduates of recognized schools of law or accounting. They are expected to make the FBI their career.

With demonstration of efficiency on the part of the FBI, more and more functions have been assigned to it by Congress.   The FBI lists 42 specific statutes over which it has jurisdiction and states that the list is not complete.[41]   Most of the crimes involved fall into 6 loose classifications, as follows:

Generally recognized crimes that it is difficult for state laws to control.

such as certain types of bank robberies and burglaries, violation of the antitrust laws, frauds in connection with bankruptcies, and kidnaping.

Crimes that involve the government and government officers, as bribing,
assaulting, or killing federal officers, or thefts from the government.

Crimes that violate the rights of citizens, such as involuntary servitude,
depriving anyone of civil rights, or fraudulent elections.

Crimes that involve the jurisdiction of more than one state, as interstate
transportation of certain types of stolen property, women for immoral purposes, or obscene matter, or thefts from interstate shipments.

Crimes committed on the high seas or on Indian or government reservations.

Crimes involving the security of the nation, of increased importance
since 1940 and in some cases the result of newly passed laws.   Included
are such acts as espionage, sabotage, and subversive acts; treason; violations
of the Selective Service Act; and violations of the Atomic Energy Act and the
Internal Security Act of 1950.

The increase in the work of the FBI is indicated by the growth of its
staff from 1,035 persons in 1934 to approximately 5,400 special agents and
supervisors and 7,350 clerks and technicians in 1953.

Since FBI agents must be able to deal with professional, armed criminals, they
are taught to use firearms, including the Thompson sub-machine gun.   In
the photograph agents are firing the .45 caliber sub-machine gun, capable
of firing 600 rounds a minute.   They are firing full automatic and are forced to
lean into the gun in order to prevent it from climbing.   They also use the standard police .38-caliber revolver, learning to shoot with the left hand as well as
the right.   For their own protection, the agents are also taught how to disarm
criminals.

In general the quality of police improves in relation to the population unit covered. The rural county sheriff is least well qualified, holds his office for the shortest period of time and therefore gains least from experience, and is less trained than any type of police. Urban police represent marked improvement over the county sheriff. Although they are often not chosen because of any qualifications for the work or sound educational background, they remain longer in office and are beginning to receive training in crime detection. State police are better qualified and experience more rigid training. The various federal agents represent a highly selected and specially trained group who regard their work as a life profession.

THE CRIMINAL AND THE POLICE

The discussion in this section refers primarily to city police.

Police may legally arrest a person caught in the act of committing a crime or, in the case of a felony, anyone that the police feel reasonably sure might have committed it. Persons believed guilty of a misdemeanor, but not caught in the act, may be arrested only upon issuance of a warrant by a judge. In general, arrests on suspicion and dragnet raids are apt to be illegal. Certain restrictions on police action are designed to protect innocent people from imposition. A policeman may not search a person's home unless he has a warrant or has good reason to believe that criminal evidence will be found. The person arrested must not be held in jail for an undue length of time without being brought before a judge for a preliminary hearing. The police are not authorized to inflict punishment upon persons who are arrested, nor may they legally force a person to testify against himself in the form of a forced confession. In the face of these restrictions, police may circumvent or defy laws that limit their action.

Assumption of Judicial Powers

The police assume judicial powers under at least 3 circumstances, which are discussed below.[42]

1. When the police decide whether or not there is sufficient evidence that a person has committed a crime to justify arresting him. This decision is one that the policeman necessarily must make. Whether the decision is wise depends on several points: first, of course, upon the individual policeman's powers of deduction and sense of fair play; and second, upon his training, both psychological and practical, in detection. Sometimes, unfortunately, the policeman is open to bribe, either by the casual offender who slips him a ten-dollar bill to avoid a ticket for traffic violation or by the professional criminal who may be caught in the act of committing a

crime. Or a person of public prominence may not be arrested for some minor offense, whereas a person of a lower social class is taken into custody.

2. When minor offenses are settled without arrest. The police are called by many citizens when some minor neighborhood conflict arises; and in the course of their regular duties they encounter minor violations of law. The issue in a neighborhood quarrel may be some simple matter, as the right of thoroughfare through a driveway, the use of an alley for playing ball, running over newly seeded lawns, a noisy radio late at night, or other minor source of irritation. Often all that is needed to settle the matter is an explanation of the legal rights involved; a statement of what the legal penalties are for continued violation; or—in typical American fashion—a "good talking to." Children and adolescents may be innocent violators of law or they may indulge in mischievous play that gradually becomes malicious, involving the destruction of property or violation of personal rights. The policeman on the beat may check these tendencies before they become serious, without giving them the importance of being labeled as delinquencies or the youthful offender as a lawbreaker.

3. When minor offenders are arrested, taken to the city jail, held for a short time, and released without a trial. The offenders in these cases are usually drunk or disorderly persons or vagrants. The drunkard is held in jail until he becomes sober, the disorderly person until he calms down, the vagrant until he agrees to leave the city. Arrest and incarceration for 10 to 24 hours are punishment in that they constitute personal humiliation and inconvenience; they are also a way of protecting the public from a person who is not dangerous but is temporarily in a condition to injure someone. At the same time the offenses do not seem serious enough to merit a trial, a fine, or a longer jail sentence.

It is important that the police should exercise minor judicial powers. In a city where the policeman has long been assigned to a certain neighborhood, he is often familiar with the backgrounds, attitudes, and customs of the residents and can make a fair adjustment. Among youthful border-line delinquents he probably has more influence if he can control their activities without arresting them. Also, if all trivial cases subject to possible arrest were handled by arrest and court procedure, the courts would not have time for the more serious offenses. It would seem advisable to invest the police legally with wider discretionary powers and then to select men capable of exercising such authority and to train them for this important function.

Abuses of Power

In contrast to the commonsense overstepping of judicial powers in settling minor offenses, there are certain major abuses of power.[43]

A widespread practice that may lead to abuse is the custom of making illegal arrests on suspicion, although there is no actual evidence that a crime has been committed. The persons arrested often have a past record of petty offenses or are parolees. Such persons may be arrested if they are loitering on the street or if there has been a crime not yet solved. Sometimes public demand for action leads to wholesale arrests. An atrocious crime that arouses public fear or indignation leads to a clamor that the police "do something" about it. Persons connected in some way with the victim, especially if they have a past police record, may be arrested and perhaps held for days while the police seek for some clue to connect them with the crime. Although the law requires that an arrested person should be brought before a magistrate without unreasonable delay (a few hours or at most a few days), illegally arrested persons are not so brought since the magistrate would dismiss them if there were no real evidence against them. They may be held secretly in a police station, unable to communicate with family or a lawyer, while the police try to establish guilt. If no evidence of guilt can be found, the victim of this police activity is finally released.

Police defend the practice by pointing out that if they must bring the arrested person immediately before a magistrate he will be released; they must somehow detain him until they have had time to work on the case, and the only way they can do this is illegally and secretly. Some provision is needed for detainment or supervision of genuine suspects to prevent their leaving a city while the police have a reasonable length of time to work on a case. The present secretive practices may lead to further abuses.

When police are hardpressed to solve a case, they may turn to the third degree, a term applied to brutal methods by which a confession may be forced from a prisoner.[44] From time to time, an instance of severe injury to an accused person comes to public attention and receives headlines in local newspapers; occasionally, a person after release by the police will bring suit against certain policemen in the courts, presenting evidence of mistreatment; a few criminals in court repudiate confessions that they have signed, stating that the police beat or otherwise abused them until they signed the confessions. These occasional cases indicate that, under certain pressures, police may turn to the third degree to force a confession. Since use of the third degree is illegal and since many prisoners subjected to it do not report the fact for fear of retaliation by the police, the extent of this brutal practice is unknown. Some police departments do not tolerate it; in others, it is apparently a fairly common practice.

The third degree seems to have developed from 4 principal factors. 1) Many police are not sufficiently well-trained in detective methods to solve intricate crimes; forcing a confession, true or false, through fear and pain seems a simpler solution than the slower and more painstaking methods of scientific crime detection. 2) Many police are not trained to have high standards of ethics nor to have professional pride in their work. 3) The law forbids holding a suspect for a sufficient period of time to build up the evidence needed to demonstrate probable guilt; the police feel the pressure for a quick method. 4) Finally, newspapers and public demand a quick solution, which the police cannot provide except through a confession. The suspect is thus the victim of both the public and the police.

Many persons who have been subject to the third degree do nothing about it, although they are entitled to legal action against the police. Some of these persons have a history of minor offenses of which the police are aware; they may not want this history to be aired publicly. Or they may be afraid to protest, for fear of further brutality if they are again arrested. Also, proof is difficult, since many methods leave no physical trace, and the prisoner's word is pitted against the policeman's. Or the prisoner may have been made to face a wall during a beating and may not know who struck him. Usually physical abuse is administered by someone in a minor capacity on the police force, and even if action is brought against him it does not alleviate the system, so long as it is approved by police officials and condoned by the prosecuting attorney, who may be called in at the moment the prisoner is ready to confess although presumably ignorant of the methods employed.

The use of the third degree in its extreme forms is confined to a limited group of cases, usually when a notorious crime, such as a murder, has been committed. It is less likely to be a recourse in minor cases and is unnecessary when the offender is caught in the act. However, a certain amount of police brutality may occur in other instances, for the policeman often feels privileged to pummel and beat an offender in the process of arrest even when he encounters no resistance. The policeman's task is to bring the prisoner to the police station with only the minimum physical force necessary to accomplish the arrest. The policeman is not empowered to administer punishment, which should follow conviction before a judge.

Police Graft

Illegal arrests and forced confessions apply only to certain criminals. Professional criminals often make arrangements with the police, the prosecuting attorney, or the judges that render them immune from arrest or, if this situation is not possible, from punishment of a severity commensurate with their crimes. Working alone, in small mobs, or in organized gangs or syndicates, professional criminals operate over long periods of time in one city and regard their illegal activities as a full-time job by which they make their living sometimes to the extent of acquiring wealth. Continued activities necessitate some arrangement that insures no molestation by arrests or prison sentences. Money payments to the policeman on the beat or to his superiors insure freedom from police interference. Powerful criminals and especially those in organized groups do not deal with the police directly, but go directly to the heads of the local political machine. Large sums of money are at stake in securing protection Key, quoting various sources, gives estimates of revenue acquired by various notorious criminal organizations as $3,000,000 to $105,000,000 annually.[45] Much of the money that they receive comes from subordinates who operate gambling or vice resorts or offer other illegal services. These subordinates pay the organized criminals for protection; the organization in turn makes arrangements with the political machine or various officials of importance. The machine then passes the word down the line through judges, attorneys, and police, who owe it allegiance, not to interfere with the operation of the services carried on by the subordinates of the criminal gang. When arrangements for protection cannot be secured from the political machine in power the organized criminal group must depend on lower officials, perhaps precinct captains of police. This situation gives the criminal less security since at any time higher officials may interfere.

Need for Professionalization

Serious as some of the above shortcomings are, wholesale condemnation of police is not merited. Abuses of power are worse in large cities than in small ones; many communities are well protected from criminals. Moreover, even in cities riddled by corruption, the police perform their work well for the most part.

Solution of the abuses seems to lie in the greater professionalization of police work. Some trends toward professionalization of the police force have already been indicated. They include better methods of selecting policemen under civil service control; higher standards for intelligence and education of recruits; better training, not only in the routine features of police work, but in an understanding of sociological and psychological factors involved in the control of crime; elimination of political favoritism from the selection and promotion of policemen; destruction of the affiliation between police and criminals; certain legal provisions to give the police more discretion in handling minor offenses and to enable them to keep a suspect under supervision while an investigation is under way. Another trend, sufficiently important to merit special discussion, is the increasing use of scientific methods in detection of crimes and identification of criminals. Such methods will tend to eliminate some of the worst police abuses, such as illegal arrests and the third degree; at the same time they will contribute to the proportion of solved crimes.

CRIMINAL INVESTIGATION

An early scientific device used in criminal detection was photography, which made possible the establishment of a Rogues' Gallery of known

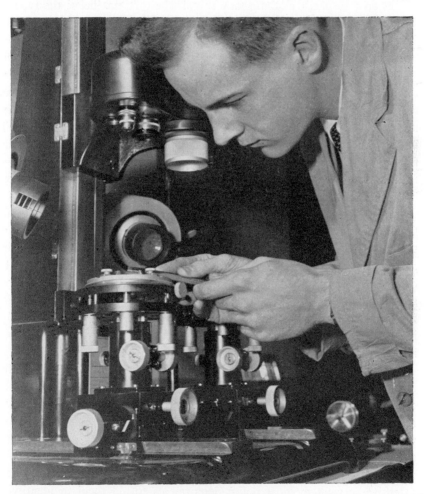

Modern science plays an important part in the daily routine of the agents of the FBI. The photograph shows an expert in the Firearms Section of the FBI Laboratory, Washington, D.C., preparing for a tool mark examination by means of a comparison microscope.

criminals in the New York City Police Department.   Photographs of criminals are still kept on file; in addition the camera is used in many other ways.   Detailed photographs of the scene of a crime are taken before anything is disturbed.   Photomicrography is used to photograph clues that cannot be seen with the eye.   The fluoroscope may be used to examine the contents of an unopened package—a valuable procedure for instance if the package is suspected to contain a bomb that might explode on opening it. The miscroscope is also used extensively.   Examination of fibers that have caught on a suspect's clothing may reveal where he has been; the type of dust in his clothes may indicate his occupation.   Scrapings from under fingernails may be subjected to microscopic examination and may disclose traces of blood.   Strands of hair caught on a suspect's clothing also may be studied under the microscope to prove whether they are human and whether they match the hair, let us say, of a murdered person.   Examination of hair reveals racial type as well as whether the hair has been dyed and whether it is naturally curly or artificially waved.   Although examination of hair is not always a definite means of identification, it may result in the elimination of certain suspects.   Chemical analysis also aids in crime detection, for instance, in determining the presence of poison in the organs of a dead body, or in determining stains or types of ink.

Fingerprinting has developed into an exact science.   Cities maintain fingerprint files and the Federal Bureau of Investigation has such a file containing 22,976,669 criminal prints.   Local police departments are encouraged to send fingerprints of criminals to the FBI for inclusion in the central file and for purposes of comparison with its records and hence possible identification of criminals.   If the FBI files show that the criminal has a past record, a copy of this record is sent to the police department supplying the fingerprints to aid them, the prosecuting attorney and the judge, in their disposition of the case.

Other types of records are maintained by some detective bureaus; for instance, a highly developed file of laundry marks has been built up in one city; other cities have *modus operandi* files, or records of the characteristic methods of known criminals, the techniques they usually employ, and any peculiarity in the way in which they carry out their crimes.   By reference to the *modus operandi* file, the list of suspects may be narrowed to a small number.   The FBI has assembled many reference collections, and offers extensive services to local police departments to aid them in identifying criminals.

The services offered by the FBI without cost to local law enforcement agencies, are here listed: [46]

Ashes: If paper ash is properly preserved, the restoration and reading of

The FBI Identification Division maintains files containing, in 1953, over 22 million criminal fingerprints representing approximately 10 million criminals, and more than 100 million noncriminal prints representing approximately 60 million persons. Police from all over the country are urged to send fingerprints of criminals to Washington, to increase the list of known criminals, as well as to bring records up to date. In return, the FBI searches its records for previous records of these criminals and sends a report of their offenses to the police, who then know whether they are dealing with a first offender or one of long-standing criminality.

printed material are possible. Many other materials have characteristic ashes that can be identified.

Blood: The FBI laboratory can determine whether a stain is from blood and if so, whether from human or animal blood, although it is not possible to identify the blood as having come from a specific person.

Bombs and explosives: A file is maintained containing information on the construction of various types of bombs, as well as a reference collection of dynamite wrappers, blasting caps, and fuses.

Casts: Casts of shoeprints, heelprints, and tire treads can be submitted to the laboratory for examination. A reference blueprint collection of tire treads and heel designs is on file.

Document examinations: Trained experts compare handwriting, handprinting, typewriting, printed matter, and papers. They can detect erasures and obliterated writing and often are able to make faded writing legible. A file of typewriter specimens makes possible the identification of make and

model of typewriter when a specimen of typing is at hand.   Files of water-
marks, paper samples, and rubber stamps are maintained.

Typewriting can be identified as having been typed on a particular machine by
a specific person.   In this photograph an FBI expert examines typewritten material for idiosyncrasies of the machine and personal variations of touch.

Firearms identification: Bullets and cartridges frequently can be linked
with the guns from which they have been fired.

Fraudulent checks: Bogus checks can be compared with thousands of
worthless checks on file in order to identify the passer on the basis of handwriting and other distinguishing features.

Glass fractures: From small fragments of glass from the car of a hit-and-
run driver, the make and model of the car often can be identified.   The
direction of a blow or bullet that has fractured glass can be determined in
many cases.

Hairs and fibers: Although hair cannot be identified as coming from some
specific person, by examining a small piece of hair found at the scene of a
crime it is possible to tell whether the hair is curly and whether the curl is
natural or artificial; dyeing can also be discovered.   Small shreds of fiber can
also be identified.

Metal examinations: Pieces of metal found at the scene of a crime, such
as pieces of wire or parts of automobiles, can sometimes be traced through
comparison with similar metal in the possession of a suspect.

Number restoration.   Serial numbers that have been obliterated from weapons or machines often may be restored and traced through the National Stolen Property Index.

Particles adhering to tools: Tools found on burglars often may be matched to tool marks at the place of a crime, or tiny fragments of material clinging to tools may be identified as coming from some specific place.

Paint comparisons: Tiny particles of paint found at the scene of a crime, especially when a car was involved, can be analyzed with specimens in the National Automotive Paint File.

Photography: The FBI is equipped for special types of photography.

Poisons: Body organs and fluids from the bodies of victims can be analyzed for the presence of specific poisons.

Powder patterns.   Examination of powder residues around a wound reveals information about close-range shootings.

Soil analysis: Soil carried away from a crime often may be exactly identified.   Such soil might come from the cuffs of a suspect's trousers, from fingernail scrapings, or from the soles of shoes.

Wood examinations.   Wood specimens can be identified with the aid of a file of North American woods.

Tool marks.   Every tool leaves a characteristic mark.   Chisels, pliers, hammers, wrenches, axes, and many other tools may be identified by comparing the test marks made by the tool with marks left at the scene of a crime.

The extensive use of the FBI laboratory is indicated by the fact that during the fiscal year 1952, 109,733 examinations were conducted.   Requests for examination came from all the states, several foreign countries, and other departments of the federal government.[47]

In addition to these many means of identification, other techniques aid the detective.   The lie detector makes use of the fluctuations in blood pressure, respiration, and action of the sweat glands of a person under stress. First developed through the efforts of W. M. Marston and John Larson, the lie detector records the normal reactions of a suspected person and also the fluctuations when the person lies to avoid confessing guilt.[48]   If the person is not guilty and therefore does not lie, only normal reactions are shown. The lie detector has some limitations, however.   Certain classes of persons seem immune to the emotional reactions of lying and hence their lying cannot be detected.[49]   These include the following 5 types: the unsophisticated person for whom lying has no significance; antisocial persons or permanent criminals without a sense of guilt about lying; pathological liars who cannot differentiate between truth and falsehood; persons who "forget" their crimes because they cannot accept responsibility for them; and some criminals who convince themselves by wishful thinking that they are not guilty of the offense.   Many courts will not admit the evidence of a lie detector, but the record may single out the guilty person from a group of suspects and thus narrow the search for admissible forms of proof.

Another aid to detection, whose use is not widely accepted, is scopolamine.[50]   By inhibiting the action of the higher cortical centers, this drug makes lying impossible for the person to whom the drug has been administered.   The results of questioning a suspect under the influence of scopolamine are not admitted in court, but again may lead the detective to identify a guilty person against whom other proof may be found.   It is not widely used both because it is difficult to administer, and because questioning the suspect while he is under the influence of the drug violates the rights of an accused person.

EVALUATION OF POLICE ACTIVITIES

Evaluation of police activities is extremely difficult.   There is no way of knowing how many misdemeanors are prevented by the efficiency with which police supervise the areas that they patrol; how many juveniles are deterred from delinquency by prevention programs of police; or how many neighborhood feuds that might come to a climax in crime are avoided by effective police action.   On the other hand, we do not know to what extent the efficiency of police in one city merely means an increase in crime in another owing to the movement of criminals from a well-policed city to a poorly policed one.   Uneven efficiency in police departments may only lead to a redistribution of crime rather than its prevention.

The percentage of crimes cleared by arrest is important, for by this means an offender is brought to official attention and arrest is the beginning of punishment or more effective rehabilitation, as the case may be.   The *Uniform Crime Reports,* in a survey for 1952 of 1,706 cities with a population of 61.6 million people showed that 26.1 per cent of offenses known to the police were cleared by the arrest of one or more offenders.   A comparison of Figures 18 and 19 reveals the unevenness of arrests for different types of felonies.

The highest percentages of arrest are found in cases of personal assault and injury.   If death does not occur, the injured person often is able to identify the offender, either from photographs of known criminals or from a line-up of suspects, or he may know the offender by sight or name.   Murder and manslaughter are considered our most serious crimes and a special effort is made by police and detectives to solve such cases.   The crimes that least often lead to arrest are primarily those that may be carried out in

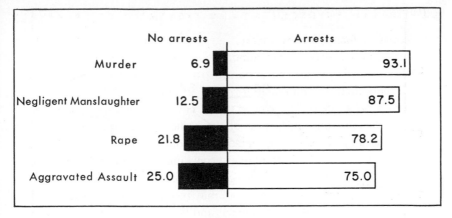

FIGURE 18

Percentage of offenses against the person cleared by arrest, 1952. A comparison of this Figure with Figure 19 shows that attacks upon people, most highly condemned of all crimes, are much more likely to lead to arrest than are property crimes. The police exert great effort to solve personal attacks and in addition except in murder the victim is often able to identify his attacker. Property crimes may easily be committed with no one catching a glimpse of the criminal. (Based on *Uniform Crime Reports for the United States and Its Possessions*, 24, No. 1 [Washington: Government Printing Office, 1953], 45.)

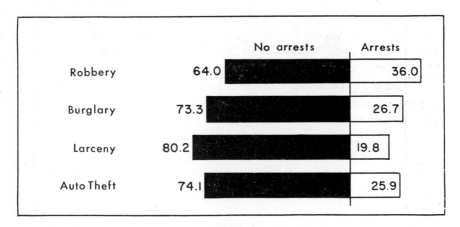

FIGURE 19

Percentage of offenses against property cleared by arrest, 1952. Offenses against property, more easily concealed than offenses against the person, lead to arrest in a much smaller percentage of cases. The robber, the burglar, the larcenist, and the automobile thief have more than an even chance of escaping without arrest. (Based on *Uniform Crime Reports for the United States and Its Possessions*, 24, No. 1 [Washington: Government Printing Office, 1953], 47.)

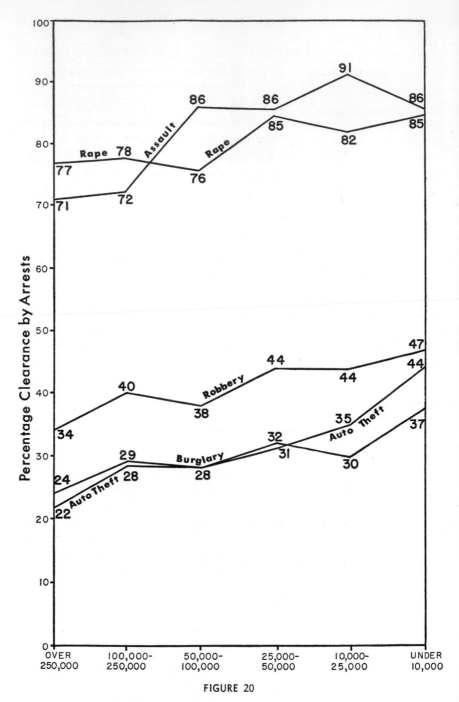

FIGURE 20

Percentage of crimes cleared by arrest for cities of various populations, 1952. Homicide and larceny, which do not appear in the Figure, show relatively little difference in arrest rates by size of city. In general, criminals are safer in large cities than in small. (Based on *Uniform Crime Reports for the United States and Its Possessions,* 24, No. 1 [Washington: Government Printing Office, 1953], 46.)

secret, often under cover of darkness, and unobserved. Hence it does not seem particularly surprising that the police are unable to discover who committed many of the relatively minor thefts and burglaries that occur. They often have no clue to the offender and perhaps have to wait until the stolen goods appear on the counter of some pawnshop or until a series of similar crimes gives them some information upon which to work. Also, since the police tend to concentrate on the more serious crimes, they often do not have time to follow up minor offenses. Nevertheless, it is probable that with more careful selection of policemen, especially of detectives, and with better training in crime detection, many more crimes could be solved than at present.

The percentage of crimes cleared by arrest varies as to the size of city, with the smaller cities in general having a decidedly higher proportion of arrests than the large cities. This is an extremely interesting finding in view of the more rigid standards of selection and training of police and detectives in large cities. It must be recognized, of course, that crime detection is much more difficult in large cities where people are unacquainted with each other and indifferent to irregular forms of behavior that they observe. The maze of city streets and alleys and crowds of strangers also enable the criminal to elude police and become lost among the hurrying throngs. Figure 20 shows the somewhat irregular increase in percentage of arrests with decrease in size of city.

Criticism should not be directed against policemen as individuals but rather against the present organization and administration of the police system. Policemen are not trained in an understanding of criminal conduct; abusiveness is often condoned or encouraged by superior officers and ignored by the public; in some cases the police department is part of a corrupt political machine. Remedial measures for these conditions would include specially trained heads of police departments; better selection and training of policemen; training of detectives in the best methods of detection; protection of the police from criticism and pressure during the time necessary to solve a crime and when advisable some method of holding a suspect while this process is carried out; and elimination of politics from the police system.

QUESTIONS

1. What is the primary purpose of the police force?

2. What different types of policemen or law-enforcement officers are there in the United States? About how many persons are contained in each group?

3. What are some of the problems involved in organizing an efficient police system?

4. What trends are apparent in selecting and training policemen that should improve the quality of men who enter the force?

5. What services do the state police offer?

6. In what ways does the Federal Bureau of Investigation supplement local police systems?

7. In what ways do uniform criminal laws in the different states aid the police?

8. Discuss illegal arrests, from the point of view of the person arrested and from the point of view of the police.

9. Why is the third degree tolerated or encouraged in some cities?

10. What scientific methods of crime detection are in use? How will the increased use of scientific methods change present police practices?

11. How successful are police in solving crimes?

READINGS

Floch, M., "Limitations of the Lie Detector," *Journal of Criminal Law and Criminology,* 40 (1950), 651–53. Excellent critical discussion of the possibilities and limitations of the lie detector.

Key, V. O., "Police Graft," *American Journal of Sociology,* 40 (1935), 624–36. Discussion of an ever-present problem.

MacNamara, Donal E. J., "American Police Administration at Mid-Century," *Public Administration Review,* 10 (Summer, 1950), 181–89. An objective statement of problems and trends.

Millspaugh, Arthur C., *Crime Control by the Federal Government* (Washington: Brookings Institution, 1937). A study of the various agencies for crime control, their organization, problems of conflict and overlapping of functions.

Muehlberger, C. W., "Interrogation under Drug Influence, the So-called 'Truth Serum' Technique," *Journal of Criminal Law, Criminology, and Police Science,* 42 (1951), 513–28. Report of experiments with questioning of subjects under the influence of drugs; consideration of the legal status of information so secured.

Report on Lawlessness in Law Enforcement, National Commission on Law Observance and Enforcement, No. 11 (Washington: Government Printing Office, 1931). Although progress has been made since 1931 in scientific methods of detection, numerous news reports indicate that the lawlessness reported in 1931 still operates.

Smith, Bruce (ed.), "New Goals in Police Management," *Annals of the American Academy of Political and Social Science,* Vol. 291 (1954). Although this series of articles is not limited to the crime-control activities of the police, many articles bear on this function. Articles by J. Edgar Hoover, P. L. Kirk, and E. W. Garrett are of special interest.

———, *Police Systems in the United States* (rev. ed., Harper, 1949). A standard book on the history, organization, and functioning of police systems in this country.

———, *Rural Crime Control* (New York: Institute of Public Administration, Columbia University, 1933). A comprehensive study of rural police.

Vollmer, August, and Alfred E. Parker, *Crime and the State Police* (Berkeley: University of California Press, 1935). State police are a relatively new development in the United States. This book gives the background needed for understanding their place in the total system of police functions.

FOOTNOTES

1 Donal E. J. MacNamara, "American Police Administration at Mid-Century," *Public Administration Review*, 10 (Summer, 1950), 181–89.

2 *Uniform Crime Reports for the United States and Its Possessions*, 23, No. 1. (Washington: Government Printing Office, 1952), 21.

3 *Testimony of the Director before the House Subcommittee on Appropriations on February 25, 1953 regarding the 1954 Appropriation Request for the Federal Bureau of Investigation* (Washington; Federal Bureau of Investigation, U.S. Department of Justice, 1953), p. 115.

4 *Statistical Abstract of the United States, 1952* (Washington: Government Printing Office, 1952), p. 371.

5 J. P. Shalloo, "Modern Police vs. Modern Society," *Prison Journal*, 25 (1945), 70–77.

6 Richard W. Morris, *Organization and Administration of a Municipal Police Department*, No. 30 (New York State Conference of Mayors and other Municipal Officials, Bureau of Training and Research, Albany, New York, 1934), pp. 9–10.

7 R. Weldon Cooper, *Municipal Police Administration in Texas*, No. 3843 (Austin: University of Texas, Nov. 15, 1938), p. 95.

8 C. E. Ridley, O. F. Nolting, and D. S. Arnold (eds.), *The Municipal Year Book, 1953* (Chicago: International City Managers' Association, 1953), section on Police; Bruce Smith, *Police Systems in the United States* (rev. ed., Harper, 1949).

9 August Vollmer, "Police Progress in the Past Twenty-five Years," *Journal of Criminal Law and Criminology*, 24 (1933–34), 161–75.

10 R. A. Kimball, "Civil Service Selection of Policemen in Denver, Colorado," *Journal of Criminal Law and Criminology*, 37 (1946), 333–45.

11 MacNamara, *op. cit.*, p. 186.

12 C. W. White, "A Few Trained Men Can Revitalize a Police Force," *American City*, 66 (Nov., 1951), 19.

13 "The University of Minnesota and the FBI Cooperate in Police Training," *School and Society*, 78 (July 25, 1953), 28.

14 "Child Study for Policemen," *Survey*, 86 (1950), 34.

15 *Report of John Edgar Hoover, Director, Federal Bureau of Investigation, Fiscal Year, 1952* (Washington: Federal Bureau of Investigation, 1952), pp. 23–25.

16 *The Outlook for Women in Police Work*, Women's Bureau Bulletin No. 231 (Washington: U.S. Department of Labor, 1949).

17 Ridley, Nolting, and Arnold, *op. cit.*, p. 413.

18 S. Frank, "Some Cops Have Lovely Legs," *Saturday Evening Post*, 222 (Dec., 24, 1949), 11–13, 39–40.

19 *Annual Report, 1951* (Chicago: Chicago Police Department, 1951).

20 Carol M. Williams, *The Organization and Practices of Police Women's Divisions in the United States* (Detroit: National Training School of Public Service, 1946), ch. 4.

21 Williams, *op. cit.*, ch. 2.

22 V. W. Peterson, "Chicago's Crime Problem," *Journal of Criminal Law and Criminology*, 35 (1944), 13.

23 Bruce Smith, *Rural Crime Control* (New York: Institute of Public Administration, Columbia University, 1933), ch. 2.

24 Raymond Moley, *Politics and Criminal Prosecution* (Minton, Balch, 1929), ch. 5.

25 Harold Zink, *Government of Cities in the United States* (Macmillan, 1939), p. 99.

26 Smith, *Rural Crime Control*, ch. 3.

27 Smith, *Police Systems in the United States*, pp. 89–104.

28 "What a Helicopter Can Do for a Police Department," *American City*, 67 (Jan., 1952), 123.

29 "40,000 Police Cars have Two-way Radio," *American City*, 65 (March, 1950), 17.

30 "Disorganization of Metropolitan Law Enforcement and Some Proposed Solutions," *Journal of Criminal Law, Criminology, and Police Science*, 43 (1952), 63–78.

31 Arthur C. Millspaugh, *Local Democracy and Crime Control* (Washington: Brookings Institution, 1936), p. 11.

32 Smith. *Rural Crime Control*, ch. 4.

[33] Smith, *Police Systems in the United States*, pp. 105–19.

[34] Interstate Commission on Crime, *Handbook of Interstate Crime Control* (Topeka: Kansas City Printing Plant, 1938), p. 111.

[35] *The Book of the States, 1952–53* (Chicago: Council of State Governments, 1953), pp. 282–83.

[36] David Geeting Monroe, *State and Provincial Police*, State and Provincial Section, International Association of Chiefs of Police and Northwestern University Traffic Institute, 1941.

[37] August Vollmer and Alfred E. Parker, *Crime and the State Police* (Berkeley: University of California Press, 1935).

[38] Arthur C. Millspaugh, *Crime Control by the Federal Government* (Washington: Brookings Institution, 1937).

[39] Karl Baarslag, *Robbery by Mail, The Story of the United States Postal Inspectors* (Farrar and Rinehart, 1938), pp. 3–9.

[40] J. E. Hoover, *Persons in Hiding* (Little, Brown, 1938); *Annual Reports* and other publications of the Federal Bureau of Investigation.

[41] *Services of the FBI* (Washington: Federal Bureau of Investigation, U.S. Department of Justice, undated); *Testimony of the Director before the House Subcommittee on Appropriation on February 25, 1953 regarding the 1954 Appropriation Request for the Federal Bureau of Investigation* (Washington: Federal Bureau of Investigation, U.S. Department of Justice, 1953), p. 115.

[42] S. B. Warner, "Investigating the Law of Arrest," *American Bar Association Journal*, 26 (1940), 151ff.; Jerome Hall, "The Law of Arrest in Relation to Contemporary Social Problems," *University of Chicago Law Review*, 3 (1936), 345ff.

[43] *Report on Lawlessness in Law Enforcement*, National Commission On Law Observance and Enforcement, No. 11 (Washington: Government Printing Office, 1931), pp. 3–4, 31ff.; O. K. Fraenkel, "From Suspicion to Accusation," *Yale Law Journal*, 51 (1941), 748–62.

[44] *Report on Lawlessness in Law Enforcement*, pp. 12–261; John Barker Waite, *Criminal Law in Action* (Harcourt, Brace, 1934), chs. 7, 8, 9.

[45] V. O. Key, "Police Graft," *American Journal of Sociology*, 40 (1935), 624–36.

[46] *Services of the FBI*.

[47] *Report of John Edgar Hoover, Director, 1952*, p. 18.

[48] F. E. Imbau, *Lie Detection and Criminal Investigation* (Williams and Wilkins, 1942); John A. Larson, *Lying and Its Detection* (Chicago: University of Chicago Press, 1932); W. M. Marston, *The Lie Detector Test* (Smith, 1938).

[49] M. Floch, "Limitations of the Lie Detector," *Journal of Criminal Law and Criminology*, 40 (1950), 651–53.

[50] C. W. Muehlberger, "Interrogation under Drug Influence, The So-called 'Truth Serum' Technique," *Journal of Criminal Law, Criminology, and Police Science*, 42 (1951), 513–28.

13

Courts and Trials

A person accused of committing a crime is brought into court either by an arrest or on a summons.* The process of arrest has been described in the preceding chapter. A summons, used when the complaint is made directly to the magistrate or the prosecuting attorney by the injured person, is an order from the judge to the accused commanding him to appear in court at a certain time. The police also may issue a summons to appear in court—a method followed in cases of minor traffic violations. Either the arrest or the summons brings the accused person before a judge and the process of determining guilt or innocence begins.

COURTS OF INFERIOR CRIMINAL JURISDICTION

Functions of Inferior Courts

Each state has several strata of courts, the lowest of which is known by such terms as police courts, justice of the peace courts, magistrates' courts, recorders' courts, mayors' courts, city courts, or municipal courts.[1] Minor criminal violations of state laws and violations of local ordinances, such as drunkenness, disorderliness, petty thefts, and traffic violations are handled by these courts. The suspected person is released if there is insufficient evidence to convict him. If he is found guilty by the magistrate (there is no provision for a jury in these courts), he is given a fine or short sentence in the county jail or house of correction. A defendant who feels that he has been unfairly treated may appeal his case to a higher court. Otherwise, he pays his fine or is taken immediately to the designated institution to serve his term.

When a person is suspected of a felony, usually punishable by imprisonment or death, he is brought before the magistrate of a lower court for pre-

* The courts discussed in this chapter have jurisdiction in both criminal and civil matters. The present discussion refers only to their duties in reference to crime.

liminary hearing. If the evidence seems to indicate guilt, the magistrate orders the case to go before the grand jury. A period of time intervenes between the preliminary hearing and the time that the case is presented to the grand jury, which is not in continuous session. Various methods are used to insure that the suspected person will not leave the jurisdiction of the court before the grand jury meets. He may be held in the county jail in charge of the sheriff, allowed to give bail bond, or released on his own recognizance. The latter method is used only for persons of responsibility and some standing in the community. When a person is released on bail, it is the duty of the magistrate to fix the amount of bail and approve the bondsman. Whatever method is used, the accused person passes out of the hands of the police and into the hands of county officers.

The preliminary hearing, in theory at least, is advantageous to both the suspect and the prosecuting attorney. When a suspected person is promptly brought before the magistrate he is saved from the possibility of third degree methods by the police or great pressure for a confession by the prosecuting attorney. He may be able to arrange for release on bail until the trial and thus avoid detention in jail during the period when he has not been proved guilty. The preliminary hearing also has several advantages for the state, which is the prosecutor in criminal cases. A long and expensive criminal trial is avoided for cases in which there is little or no evidence of guilt, since these cases are frequently dismissed by the magistrate. The state gains an interval in which to prepare the case. The state also learns who the witnesses are and what they have to say before they have forgotten the crime or been influenced not to testify. If necessary these witnesses may be held in detention until the trial. Despite their expediency, the lower courts have been severely criticized because of the ineptness with which they function and the quality of many judges found in them.

The Justice of the Peace

The justice of the peace is the traditional type of magistrate and still functions in rural areas and small cities, sometimes in conjunction with other magistrates, such as police judges. In most states the justice of the peace is an elected officer whose term is from 2 to 7 years; in a few states he is appointed by the governor.

In the rural areas the justice of the peace often has little or no legal training, since anyone may be elected. He is likely to be dominated by the prosecuting attorney, who may be eager to persuade him to hold a suspect for trial, or conversely, in the case of a friend or colleague, to release the suspect even though there is sufficient evidence against him to merit presentation to the grand jury. The justice of the peace may thus be merely a rubber stamp

according to the crime, and is fixed by the court of jurisdiction.   In the first instance this power rests with the justice of the peace, municipal court, or similar court.   For a few serious offenses bail is denied and it is mandatory that the accused person shall be held in jail until trial.

Bail is the outgrowth of an early English system whereby an accused person was released to a friend.   The friend who assumed responsibility for the prisoner was a kind of hostage who suffered the punishment meted out to the accused if found guilty, in case he failed to produce the convicted person. Later, instead of being regarded as a substitute for the prisoner, the friend was required to promise to pay a certain sum if he could not produce the prisoner at the trial.   The original purpose of bail was to avoid the difficulty and cost involved in imprisonment.   At present, the purpose is considered in terms of the right of the accused (but not convicted) person, who after all may be innocent, to retain his liberty until he has been proved guilty.

Advantages of Bail

Bail has the following advantages:

1. It permits the accused person with a business or vocation to continue to operate; unfortunately this opportunity is as available to the pickpocket or gangster as to the merchant or factory worker.

2. It permits the accused person to continue to support dependents while awaiting trial.

3. It reduces the number of persons who must remain in jail, usually an unpleasant experience.

4. It reduces the cost to the state, since jail prisoners are maintained at its expense.

Abuses of the Bail System

In the practical administration of bail many abuses are now found.   Some of these abuses are as follows:

1. The judge has wide discretion regarding the amount of bail or to whom it is granted.   If any personal animosity is involved, the judge may force the prisoner to remain in jail by setting the bail abnormally high.   On the other hand, the judge may release a notorious criminal with a long record of crime either because he is ignorant of the prisoner's background or because the prisoner has protective arrangements with the political forces.

2. Bail should be required only of persons whose character is such that they probably would not return for trial without a penalty for failing to do so.   In large cities the judges have no adequate system of learning about the personality of the prisoner.   They do not know and do not provide means

to find out which prisoners are reliable and which are not. Hence, reliable and unreliable alike are required to furnish bail or remain in jail until the time of the trial.

3. The poor find it difficult to provide bail. Usually, property must be listed as the basis for the bail bond signed by the bondsman, although sometimes cash may be deposited. If a poor prisoner has no wealthy friends, as is usually the case, he cannot easily obtain bail, and may be confined to jail although he is essentially a reliable person who has offended for the first time. However, the more dangerous criminal with wealth or influence may be released.

4. Many persons later released as innocent of illegal acts are held in jail to await trial because they cannot provide bail. They are dismissed because the evidence against them is insufficient, the offense is a minor one, or they have been considered guilty by mistake. Thus an innocent person may be held in jail because he could not afford bail. Beeley, in his study of the bail system in Chicago, presents many such instances.[6] For example, a German peddler with no previous criminal record was arrested on suspicion of intoxication and charged with disorderly conduct when a whisky bottle was found on his person. Bail was set at $400 or $25 cash bond. He remained in jail fourteen days and was then discharged without conviction.

5. Little provision is made for checking the security offered as the basis for bail. There are recorded cases in which a bondsman listed property that he did not own or greatly overvalued. This abuse is usually in connection with professional bondsmen, rather than friends of the accused; professional bondsmen make a business of providing bail in return for a fee.

6. The granting of bail is decentralized; each justice or judge acts independently of all others. This situation leads to two abuses. If one judge refuses to grant bail because he believes the prisoner is unreliable or the property insufficient, the prisoner's attorney may apply to another judge and perhaps secure it. Moreover, a person who makes a business of providing bail may use a small amount of property as the basis for the bond in one case after another, until the total amount of bail far exceeds the value of the property. Because there is often no central bureau where bail bonds are recorded, checking the number of bonds a bondsman had already signed might necessitate searching the records of three or four courts.

7. Few cities have adequate provision for collecting bail when the accused person disappears before trial, or for returning him to the jurisdiction of the court. Thus many persons who "jump bail" remain at liberty (and if they are professional criminals continue in crime); at the same time the court does not force collection of the bail so that no pressure is exerted on the bondsman to see that the accused returns to the court.

The Professional Bondsman

The fact that many accused persons, especially in cities, do not have friends with property who can sign the bail bond has encouraged the development of professional bondsmen. The original concept of the bondsman as a friend who would maintain the accused in friendly custody until trial is lost in the professional bondsman. Otherwise, he may meet the legal requirements in a situation where friendly custody is impossible. As the system has developed in connection with minor criminal cases, however, the professional bondsman has tended to become a pernicious character. He is frequently connected with the underworld and may have a criminal record of his own.

These bondsmen are especially active in two types of cases: professional criminals and the friendless who cannot secure bail otherwise.[7] They often work in conjunction with criminal lawyers and may frequent police stations to make contacts with prisoners who are brought in, not only to furnish bond but to provide a lawyer. Also, certain lawyers recommend particular bondsmen to their clients. The fees charged are often excessive and may run as high as 20 per cent of the amount of the bond. Sometimes the bondsman learns from the arresting policeman the amount of valuables that the prisoner has at the time and charges accordingly.

Needed Improvements

Recommendations to improve the bail bond system would give added protection to the state and the accused person.

1. A central bureau for investigation of each bondsman to determine whether he owns the property listed and its value.

2. A central bureau for recording all bonds granted, or a main agency to grant the bonds. The records should be kept in such a way that all bonds signed by one bondsman would appear on that bondsman's record. The value of these suggestions depends upon the willingness of judges to use the information thus made available.

3. Limitation of the fees that may be charged by professional bondsmen.

4. More vigorous prosecution of actions to collect forfeited bail.

5. Investigation of the background of prisoners applying for bail and release of many more than at present on their own recognizance, thus eliminating the necessity for either bail or jail detention.

6. Prompt trials especially of minor offenders so that bail does not become a necessity.

GRAND JURY

The person accused of a felony, as previously stated, is entitled to a preliminary hearing before the lower court, when the complaining witness, whether policeman or someone injured by the accused, is heard. If the judge thinks the evidence warrants proof of guilt, the accused person is held for the grand jury.[8]

The grand jury is a panel of citizens chosen by lot from among qualified voters to consider the evidence against the accused person. Under common law the number of persons on the grand jury was 12 to 24; when the number is fixed by statute, it is usually less. The origin of the grand jury lies in an old English practice whereby a group of men from the community investigated the circumstances of a crime and decided whether a trial was justified. At present in the United States the grand jury is simply another and perhaps unnecessary cog in the slow process of criminal procedure. The function of the grand jury is to decide whether there is sufficient evidence to hold the accused person for trial. Although a grand jury may originate an accusation, it rarely does so, for it has no means of investigation and would be dependent upon the prosecuting attorney to secure evidence. In practice, the prosecuting attorney presents to the grand jury an accusation against someone who has been held previously by the lower court. The grand jury may call witnesses and examine them under oath. It does not call the defendant or his attorney. If the grand jury decides that there is sufficient evidence to justify a trial, it brings in a true bill that authorizes the prosecution to proceed to trial. This accusation by the grand jury is called an indictment.

There are many criticisms of the grand jury as a clumsy anachronism. Since it does not sit continuously, but only at intervals, there is a delay in bringing an accused person to trial, which may permit witnesses to leave the city or to forget details of the crime, or occasionally to be bribed to forget. The delay also results in an innocent person's remaining under the accusation for a longer time, and in the case of a professional criminal, at liberty on bail, it allows him to continue his criminal career. The members of the grand jury have no knowledge of law and in fact none of the crime except what the prosecuting attorney presents to them or what they have read in the newspapers. Hence the grand jury develops into a rubber stamp for the prosecuting attorney. The work of the grand jury is in large measure a duplication of the work of the lower court; which, since it hears both the accused person and the witnesses against him, is in a better position than the grand jury to determine probable guilt.

A recent trend is to dispose of the grand jury system and to enable a prosecuting attorney to proceed directly from the lower court to the criminal court, by presenting an accusation in writing called an information.   More than half the states permit a case to come before the criminal court in this manner.   This method eliminates the duplication found in the grand jury system whereby the prosecuting attorney and witnesses against the accused must appear both before the lower court and the grand jury.   It also eliminates one more possible avenue of escape for the confirmed criminal.

The grand jury is still recommended as the means of inquiring into the record of public officers or other matters concerning the entire community. To make its work effective it should have the ability to conduct original investigations.

THE CRIMINAL COURT

The felony trial is held in a court having general criminal jurisdiction; these courts also handle civil cases.   They are established by state law and hence differ in name and organization from one state to another.   They are called by such names as Superior Courts, Courts of Oyer and Terminer, Quarter Session Courts, Criminal Courts, District Courts, and Circuit Courts.[9]   Each name has its own history.   For instance, the Circuit Courts take their name from the fact that, except in large cities, the judge travels a circuit from one county to another, holding court for a few days or weeks in each county and clearing up the accumulation of cases since his last visit. Oyer and Terminer, an Anglo-French term designating courts that originated in England, means literally to "hear and determine" an indictment.   The Quarter Session Courts are named from the practice of holding court four times a year.   Although duties vary from state to state, in general these courts have the power to call a grand jury, issue bench warrants for the arrest of a defendant who does not appear for trial, try felonies either with or without a jury, and dispose of cases appealed from the various lower courts.   For convenience, these courts are here called criminal courts.

Organization of Courts

The multiplicity of cases in large cities has led to the creation of a complex and sometimes overlapping series of special courts for different purposes, such as the juvenile court for boys and girls under a specified age (usually 18 years), a boys' court for older adolescents and youths, and a domestic relations, a traffic, and a morals court.   These institutions are in addition to the inferior courts previously described.   Also, one type of court may have several branches served by different judges.

Although the specialization of courts facilitates the handling of cases, the general lack of unification sometimes creates confusion and inconsistency. In general each judge even in co-ordinate branches is free to interpret the law independently and to use a large degree of personal latitude in fixing sentences. Thus one judge may be lenient and another strict with the same type of case. The lower courts and the criminal courts represent two different systems, and the judges of the two courts may differ widely in their interpretation of cases. Critics urge a reorganization to provide unification of courts into one system with an administrative head, who would either act as moderator over conferences of judges or who would have wide powers to assign judges to courts and cases to judges. Some advocates of unification urge not merely local centralization of authority but also a state-controlled system.[10]

Selection of Judges

In about three fourths of the states the judges of the criminal courts are chosen by popular election; in the remainder they are appointed by the governor or legislature. Selection by appointment for long terms seems advisable, although it does not necessarily secure good judges, since the appointments may be political in nature. One suggestion is to have an organization or committee of judges, lawyers, and laymen select a list of names of highly qualified candidates from which the governor would appoint judges to hold office for the period of good behavior.[11]

Elections, especially in the larger cities, are likely to tie the judge in with the local political machine. Since he is dependent upon the machine for election, he must give allegiance first to the political machine and second to justice. If politics are corrupt, he becomes involved in shady practices that favor criminals allied with the machine. Elections have the disadvantage also of diverting time and energy of the judge into campaigning.

THE TRIAL

Failure to Try Cases

Many cases of criminal prosecution started in the lower courts never reach trial. Some suspects are not held by the grand jury. Sometimes a case is settled out of court by agreement between the prosecution and the defense.

The prosecuting attorney may feel that he cannot get a conviction and hence may *nolle prosequi* the case, that is, decline to prosecute it. The defense attorney often moves to have the grand jury indictment quashed because of some defect in the wording of the indictment. On other occasions, he moves to have the case continued, a device that in the end often leads to no trial at all. After a number of continuances, witnesses are not easy to locate or are irritated by the frequent postponements and no longer can testify satisfactorily. The prosecutor, if he has more cases than he can handle, often agrees readily to such continuances in minor cases, centering his attention upon the more serious or more spectacular. With every continuance the chance of a trial and a conviction is greatly lessened.

Pleas of Guilty

A plea of guilty on the part of the defendant often makes a trial unnecessary. In 1943, of 31,690 convictions for felonies in 24 states, 26,027 or 82 per cent were based on pleas of guilt by the defendants.[12] Securing a plea of guilty therefore is an important part of the criminal procedure.

Prior to a plea of guilty, much bargaining goes on between the attorneys for the prosecution and defense, inasmuch as the prosecuting attorney has the power to recommend to the judge a light or a heavy sentence. Although the judge makes the final decision, in practice judges usually follow such recommendations. The prosecuting attorney therefore holds out to the defendant and his attorney the promise of a light sentence in return for a plea of guilty. The defense attorney, before he permits his client to confess, bargains for as lenient a sentence as possible. By securing pleas of guilty the prosecuting attorney is able to dispose quickly of many minor cases and thus gain time to concentrate on more serious matters. Also, when he is not sure he can secure a conviction, he is willing to compromise and recommend a light sentence in return for a confession. The guilty person, afraid of conviction in a trial and a possible heavy sentence, agrees to confess in return for leniency.[13]

The light sentence is often assured by permitting the accused person to plead guilty to a less serious offense than he has actually committed. A charge of grand larceny therefore may be changed to a plea of guilty to petty larceny; a charge of armed robbery to robbery; forgery to petty larceny; murder to manslaughter; or rape to assault or attempted rape. In 1952, in 208 cities over 25,000 in population covered by the *Uniform Crime Reports,* 13 per cent of convictions for serious crimes were for a less serious offense than the one for which the prosecution was originally instituted.[14]

The abuse of allowing the defendant to plead guilty to a lesser charge is most flagrant in the cases of professional criminals who are allied with a corrupt political machine and are able to escape all but a nominal penalty by this device, even though their crimes are extremely serious. It should not be thought, however, that all such arrangements are inimical to justice. With the present limited number of courts it would be physically impossible for all cases to be tried fairly. The acceptance of a lesser plea is an unofficial administrative device for disposing of cases without a trial. Often, also, it is a way in which judge, prosecutor, and defense attorney modify the law to fit the case when an exact application of the law would work a hardship. A study of 1,336 cases in which lesser pleas were accepted illustrates the types of cases and some of the philosophy that attends the device. The records studied were all filed in New York City in the summer of 1939 through the office of Thomas E. Dewey, then prosecuting attorney. There is no suggestion of corruption and the study therefore represents the system of accepting guilty pleas to lesser offenses when expediency and a desire to give justice are the main motives.[15]

1. In 241 cases the accused person was a second offender. In New York the penalty for an offense increases with each successive repetition. In a felony, the minimum penalty for the second or third offense is the maximum penalty for the first and the maximum penalty for the second or third is double the maximum for the first. For a fourth offense the penalty is still more severe. Nevertheless, the second or third offense may be minor in nature. Judge and attorney often feel that a light punishment, which the offender will feel is justified, serves better than a long incarceration that would cause embitterment and a closer affiliation with criminal groups. Therefore the person who has committed a second, third, or even fourth felony of a minor nature may be permitted to plead guilty to a minor offense.

2. In 357 cases the prosecuting attorney had what he considered a weak case, that is, he felt reasonably sure from his investigation that the person was guilty of an offense known to have been committed, but he was not sure that he could prove in court that the offense was as serious as had been charged. For example, in a conviction for grand larceny, it must be proved not only that the person stole but that the value of the property stolen was over $500. This point may be debatable, and rather than run the risk of the offender going free the prosecuting attorney may be willing to accept a plea of guilty to petty larceny and thus make sure that the offender receives some degree of punishment.

3. In 43 cases homicide was involved. First degree murder may be hard to prove since it involves premeditation; therefore a plea of guilty to manslaughter may be accepted.

4. In 58 cases the defendants had bad records, and it was felt that as a matter of general policy they needed punishment. Unable to build up a strong case, the prosecuting attorney and judge were willing to accept a plea of guilty to almost any felony in order to accomplish this end.

5. In 78 cases the crimes involved only small amounts of property and the legal provisions for punishment seemed too severe.

6. In 49 cases there was technically a felony but the person who committed it did not intend it as such. For example, a boy who borrows a

car for a joy ride is technically guilty of a felony, but it is often hard to get a conviction both because of the difficulty of proving the value of the car and because the boy may be young and without a previous criminal record.

7. In 145 cases the youth of the defendant was the chief reason for accepting a guilty plea to a lesser offense than the one committed.

8. Twenty-eight cases involved sex, often statutory rape.   Rape is hard to prove as it must be shown that physical force was used.   Statutory rape does not necessarily involve force, but refers to any sexual relation of a man with a girl under an age specified by state law.   If the girl is near the age of consent, the man also young, and no force was employed, it is difficult to secure a conviction, even though the man is technically guilty.

9. In 86 cases the defendant had no previous criminal record and hence was allowed to plead guilty to a lesser offense and thus receive a light punishment.

10. In 167 cases various conditions indicating leniency were involved, such as that the defendant had returned stolen property, had broken into a building without stealing, or was drunk when he committed the offense.

11. In 84 cases no reason for the plea could be found from the records.

It should be realized that in these cases the defendant is not allowed to go free; he is allowed to plead guilty to a less serious offense than the one with which he was originally charged but accepts the penalty for the lesser offense.   In the 1,336 cases summarized above, 700 of the pleas were to a lesser felony and 636 to a misdemeanor.

Jury Trial

If the case is actually tried, the trial may be held before a jury, or the judge alone may make the decisions.   This body is the petit jury, not to be confused with the grand jury that decides whether or not an accused person shall be held for trial.   The petit jury is selected from a list of qualified voters by the prosecution and the defense by a process of questioning.   Each attorney tries to retain persons thought to be favorable in attitude to his side of the case and to have dismissed those whose attitude would be unfavorable. In a notorious case days or weeks may be consumed in selecting a jury.

Many persons dislike jury duty as it entails absence from business or home, inconvenience to the family, loss of income, and perhaps the unpleasant duty of deciding whether a murderer is guilty.   Hence, persons of better socioeconomic status usually manage to escape jury service by pleas of other obligations, illness, and the like.   Many professional persons, as doctors and dentists, are not required to serve.   Hence, the jury selected is likely to consist of persons of little social or economic importance in the community and often with less than average educational background.

The task of the jury is to listen to the evidence of both sides and to the instructions of the judge on points of law, and then to decide on the facts (but not the law) of a case. Actually, the jury considers all phases of a case and is often swayed neither by the facts nor the law, but by its own ignorance, prejudices, and sympathies. The usual jury is not competent to judge the facts in cases involving complicated business procedures; insanity of the defendant; nor finely drawn legal distinctions between criminal and noncriminal conduct.

Prejudice may be a deciding factor when the defendant is of another religious or nationality group, a different race, or a different economic class against which the jurors may have deep-seated prejudices. Conversely, the sympathies of a jury may be drawn to an attractive young girl or a pathetic old woman, and such a defendant may be acquitted even when the evidence clearly indicates guilt.

To obtain a verdict of guilty or not guilty a jury must be unanimous in agreement. If one juror refuses to vote in harmony with the other eleven, a verdict is not obtained. A new trial is then necessary; however, it often is not held, and the defendant, although his name has not been cleared of the charge against him, is no longer under arrest. This situation sometimes enables a professional criminal to escape punishment by finding one juror who is willing, for a fee, to vote for acquittal.

In many states the defendant may waive jury trial and be tried by the judge. In practice the jury system is falling into disuse.[16] In many cities a minority of cases are now decided by a jury. Although this trend eliminates some of the shortcomings of the jury trial, it places greater responsibility upon the judge and opens the way to other difficulties involving the prejudices of the judge or his susceptibility to outside influences. Among convictions for major offenses in 1943 in 25 states, 10.2 per cent of the cases were tried before a jury and 7.7 per cent before a judge; 82.1 per cent of the defendants pleaded guilty.[17]

The Function of the Judge

The judge presides over the court. In the case of a jury trial, he supervises the selection of the jury by the attorneys, sees that evidence is presented according to the law, charges the jury with its duties, and outlines the law that applies to the case under consideration. If a verdict of guilty is brought in by the jury, he determines the sentence to be given the convicted person, within the limits set by the law. If there is a plea of guilty, the judge may hear evidence that will throw light on the reasons for the commission of the crime. He sentences the convicted person, often following the recommendation of the prosecuting attorney. When jury trial is waived, and there is no plea of guilty, the judge hears the evidence presented by both sides and determines whether or not the accused person is guilty. He then proceeds to sentence him. The judge also has the authority to place a convicted person on probation, within limits set by the law. He may not order a jury to convict a defendant, but he may order an acquittal, and he may grant a convicted person the right to a new trial. By these prerogatives and other authority granted him, his function is to see that the accused person has a fair trial and if found guilty is sentenced justly according to the law. Great responsibility therefore rests upon the judge. Although most judges are honest in discharging their duties, the ability of some judges to fulfill their responsibilities completely is limited by a number of factors:

1. No judge can free himself entirely from the biases and prejudices of his personal background. His own personal experiences and the convictions of the socioeconomic class to which he belongs color his conceptions of right and wrong. The judge therefore may be lenient toward one of his own social class, whose offenses he understands and forgives, but may be harsh toward someone of a lower or higher social class whose special temptations and attitudes he does not understand. He does not deliberately favor one class and condemn another but finds it impossible to free himself from his personal convictions. The difficulty is accentuated by the type of training judges experience. Judges usually have been lawyers before elected or appointed to office. They have been trained in the law but not in such disciplines as anthropology or sociology, which would tend to free them from class prejudices and promote an understanding of the varying standards of different social groups.

2. Some judges are susceptible to pressure from outside interested groups. An organized criminal gang may be able to operate because of the willingness of some judge to protect it from punishment, in return either for direct payments to himself or for indirect support of the political group to which he belongs.

3. Many judges who would not yield to direct bribes from criminals nevertheless are influenced by their connection with a ruling faction. When judges are elected for short terms they must play politics. In the urban situation, especially, the judge must maintain his affiliation with the political machine. To this end he may be called upon to deal lightly with graft, white-collar crime on the part of influential businessmen, or even with the more flagrant types of organized crime. In the case of crimes that do not affect their alliance with the machine that elected them, judges try to deal fairly with the situation.[18]

The personal idiosyncrasies and biases of judges are reflected in the sentences they give. Various studies have been provided of sentences given by judges in the same or similar communities for similar types of cases. Table 13 compares the sentences given by 6 judges sitting in Quarter Session

TABLE 13

Percentage of Different Kinds of Sentences Given by Different Judges

Sentence	Judge A	Judge B	Judge C	Judge D	Judge E	Judge F
PROPERTY OFFENSES						
Penal	37.3	57.4	52.3	58.1	43.4	33.9
Suspended sentence	32.5	23.1	27.7	17.9	28.9	35.9
Probation	29.6	18.1	19.6	23.8	26.3	29.4
Fines	0.6	1.4	0.4	0.2	1.5	0.9
Number of cases	1,119	1,141	1,569	492	346	1,637
PROPERTY OFFENSES AND VIOLENCE						
Penal	47.2	92.9	82.3	81.3	69.6	36.7
Suspended sentence	47.2	4.5	13.9	0.0	21.7	62.5
Probation	5.6	2.6	2.5	18.7	8.7	0.9
Fines	0.0	0.0	1.3	0.0	0.0	0.0
Number of cases	36	112	79	16	23	112
SEX CRIMES						
Penal	47.8	47.6	52.7	26.0	59.4	33.8
Suspended sentence	3.0	11.2	10.9	11.5	5.8	14.3
Probation	47.8	37.8	32.6	62.5	31.9	42.1
Fines	1.5	3.5	3.8	0.0	2.9	9.8
Number of cases	67	143	184	96	69	133
HOBART ACT (STATE PROHIBITION LAW)						
Penal	13.3	6.0	28.6	3.2	13.3	20.8
Suspended sentence	6.7	10.0	5.4	0.0	40.0	18.1
Probation	33.3	52.0	32.1	61.3	33.3	26.4
Fines	46.7	32.0	33.9	35.5	13.3	34.7
Number of cases	45	50	56	31	15	72

Source: F. J. Gaudet, "Individual Differences in the Sentencing Tendencies of Judges," *Archives of Psychology,* No. 230 (June, 1938).

or Special Session of the Court of Common Pleas of a New Jersey County. Cases were assigned to the judges in rotation. The percentages of penal sentences given, as contrasted with suspended sentences, probations, and fines, were 33.5 per cent for Judge F, 37.4 per cent for Judge A, 46.1 per cent for Judge E, 51.2 per cent for Judge D, 52.9 per cent for Judge C, and 57.4 per cent for Judge B. The inconsistencies become greater when sentences for special classes of crimes are examined. A judge who gave severe sentences for one type of crime might be lenient toward offenders who committed others.   Judge B, who was especially severe toward property and sex offenders, was extremely lenient toward prohibition violators.   Judge F, in contrast, was lenient toward both property and sex offenders but severe with prohibition offenders.

Psychiatric Examinations

Expert sociological and psychological analysis of factors in criminal cases is rarely employed in adult cases; both are used rather commonly in juvenile cases.   The most frequent use of these sciences appears when there is some evidence that the accused person may be psychotic.

State criminal laws are very inadequate in their definition of psychotic or insane.   Almost all states use the "right and wrong" test; if the accused person is capable of understanding that his acts were wrong, he is not insane.[19]   Some states have also included among the insane those whose acts are the result of irresistible impulse.   The "right and wrong" test goes back to a famous English case, the M'Naghten Case, which raised an issue over what constituted insanity.   The issue finally reached the House of Lords, which submitted questions to the Lord Justices.   The answers, representing the best judgment of the year 1843, established the "right and wrong" test for legal insanity.   The way in which this test was formulated gave it great prestige, which, with its seeming simplicity, has caused it to survive for well over 100 years.   The test is widely criticized now, since the development of psychiatry has demonstrated not only that such a test is inadequate to determine insanity, but also that there are many intermediate stages of maladjustment between normality and outright psychosis that are significant in criminal behavior.

State legislatures have been loth to provide for impartial psychiatric examinations of defendants in criminal trials, and judges have made little use of their perogatives in demanding psychiatric examinations.[20]   Psychiatric testimony is held in a certain degree of disrepute, both because of the many disagreements between schools of psychiatry and also of the uselessness of psychiatric examinations when authorized by one or both sides to the criminal trial—the prosecuting attorney or the defendant.

When a psychiatrist is privately employed by prosecutor or defendant, there is no check upon the qualifications of the psychiatrist, and all too often the psychiatrist testifies as his employer wishes.   The psychiatrist employed by the prosecutor states that the defendant was sane; but in the same trial, the psychiatrist employed by the defendant may testify that the defendant is insane and hence not responsible for his crime.   Such biased testimony obviously is worthless.

More authentic is the testimony of psychiatrists appointed by the judge of the criminal court to examine the defendant.   Some 20 states now have laws that permit the judge to follow this procedure.   This plan has 2 weaknesses: the judge, untrained in psychiatry, decides when such examination is advisable; and he has the power to select the psychiatrist to make the examination.

Other states provide that a defendant may be committed to a state mental hospital for observation, under certain conditions, for instance when mental disorder is pleaded as a defense for the crime.   This method increases the probability of securing qualified psychiatrists.

A few courts have psychiatric clinics, used primarily after conviction to aid the judge in passing sentence.   Among these courts are the Recorder's Court in Detroit, the Chicago Municipal Court, and the Court of General Sessions in New York City.

Massachusetts, in the Briggs Law, enacted in 1921, has gone further than other states in providing for impartial examination of defendants.   Only a few other states have followed her example, so that Massachusetts stands almost in isolation with an adequate plan for psychiatric testimony in criminal cases.   Pretrial examinations are provided by the State Department of Mental Hygiene for all persons indicted for a capital offense, those indicted for other felonies more than once, and those previously convicted of a felony. The report of the psychiatrist is filed with the clerk of the court and is open to the judge, probation officer, prosecuting attorney, and the defendant's lawyer.   It is not admissible as evidence during the trial, however, and hence is not given to the jury in a jury trial.   Nor are attorneys and judges compelled to make use of the reports.   Nevertheless, the Massachusetts plan provides for examination of all criminals in certain categories and thus eliminates spotty selection of criminals for examination; it also assures proper qualifications of the psychiatrists.

The failure to use fully the services of psychiatrists and the almost complete ignoring of the possibilities of social investigations are indicative of the continued dependence of lawyers and judges upon the old formulation of crime as an act of free will with punishment as the natural result.

THE PROSECUTING ATTORNEY

The prosecuting attorney has been termed the keystone in the arch of justice and the "pivot on which the administration of criminal justice in the States turns." [21]   Because of his influence with other branches of law enforcement it has been stated that "to a considerable extent he is police, prosecutor, magistrate, grand jury, petit jury, and judge—all in one." [22]   In general the function of the prosecuting attorney is to initiate and prosecute all actions, suits, indictments, and prosecutions, civil or criminal, in which the people of the state or county may be concerned. Violations of federal laws are tried in the federal courts and therefore the prosecuting attorney does not act in these cases. The activities of the prosecuting attorney are many and varied. One report states that he plays four roles: (1) He is a criminal investigator along with the police, sheriff, and coroner, and may work either in conjunction with these officers or independently with his own staff of investigators. (2) He performs the functions of a magistrate in that he decides which cases to bring to trial; he tends to dominate the lower court that made the first decision as to whether a suspect shall be held for trial; he presents the evidence to the grand jury for their decision; and he later decides whether to bring the case before the trial judge. (3) He acts as a solicitor in preparing cases for trial. (4) He is an advocate when he tries cases and argues appeals.[23]

Although the prosecuting attorney is in one sense a state officer in that he enforces the state laws, he is, nevertheless, a local officer in that he is elected by the populace of a small geographical unit, usually a county, and performs his duties within its confines.[24] In rural counties, the population served by the prosecuting attorney is very small, but in the largest cities a million or more people may live in the district served by this officer. It is evident that the office differs greatly between rural and urban areas.

The Rural Prosecuting Attorney

The typical prosecuting attorney in a rural county is a young man with relatively little legal experience. For instance, the Missouri crime survey showed that the median age of the prosecuting attorneys was 25 to 29 years and the median legal experience 1 to 4 years. The prosecuting attorney does not look upon the office as permanent, but rather as a stepping stone either to a good private practice or to a political career. He receives excellent advertising during his campaign; even if he loses he has brought his name before every family in the county. If he wins the election, he has a small assured income and gains experience as well as many contacts.

The county or district often suffers from the present arrangement. The small salary does not attract experienced men, and the inexperienced prosecutor often is no match for the better seasoned defense attorney. Also, the rural county rarely supplies the prosecuting attorney with needed lawbooks and clerical assistance.

One recommendation to improve the situation is to increase the size of the unit served by the prosecuting attorney; this change would make it possible to increase the salary and hence to attract more experienced men and retain them longer. Another recommendation is to have the prosecuting attorneys appointed perhaps by the judge of a superior court; this procedure would eliminate campaigning by the attorney for his own election but would not necessarily remove the office from politics especially if the judge who appointed him secured his office by election.

The Urban Prosecuting Attorney

In the large city the prosecuting attorney as an elected officer is usually allied with the local political party in power, and if local politics are corrupt he plays into the hands of the corrupt politicians.   Under these conditions he prosecutes (or fails to prosecute) many cases because of political and personal interests rather than for the public good.   The power he exercises in deciding which cases to bring to trial, and his influence in arranging for pleas of guilty to minor offenses when a major crime has been committed, make possible the existence of graft on the part of other office holders and also the continuation of illegal activities by professional criminals who contribute to the machine in money or votes or both.

The fact that the prosecuting attorney is a locally elected officer has other drawbacks, even when there is no corrupt political machine.   Campaigns for re-election divert time from official duties, and concessions to influential voting groups may be against the public welfare.

The short terms of office (2 to 4 years) are another handicap.   In even a small city the duties of the prosecuting attorney are many, and for the best results the office requires a strong organization and long familiarity with its obligations.   The prosecuting attorney may have no more than mastered the intricacies of his office when he is replaced.   Since each attorney may appoint his own assistants, a change may produce a complete turnover of personnel.   Thus at short intervals of time new persons, relatively inexperienced in the work, may assume control.   For example, in Chicago when a Republican prosecuting attorney was replaced by a Democrat, within 6 months all but 15 of some 85 assistants had been replaced and the clerical staff had experienced an almost complete turnover.

The salary of prosecuting attorney often compares unfavorably with the income of the attorney in private practice; and the political maneuvering that accompanies the office repels many men.   There are usually no official requirements of efficiency or moral character, of age or years of previous legal experience.

The staff of the prosecuting attorney may not be chosen for its legal ability. Many members are young men, seeking an opening, who have made themselves useful to the ward committeemen of their political party.   Since the prosecuting attorney selects his staff from persons recommended by the committeemen, the qualification for assistant prosecuting attorney may be loyalty to the party rather than legal ability.   In the large city office the entire staff may be required to campaign for the the re-election of the prosecuting attorney at election time—a task they are willing to assume both because of their adherence to the party and because their jobs depend upon it.

Authority of Prosecuting Attorney

Each prosecuting attorney is an authority in himself.   Although in some states the attorney general of the state is supposed to supervise the prosecuting attorneys he rarely does so.   Each attorney makes his own policies and his own decisions and only cases of the most flagrant neglect or misuse of office are investigated.   There is no check upon the efficiency nor the abuse of the office.   In general the prosecuting attorney feels that he must show many convictions in order to win re-election.   But many of these convictions are not based upon fair trials but upon pleas of guilty to lesser charges than those in the indictment; they are convictions secured on "bargain days." [25]   No one checks upon the number of really serious criminals who by these procedures may be permitted to continue in crime.

The prosecuting attorney decides which cases to present to the grand jury or directly to the court.   A case begun in the lower courts may be completely lost in the prosecuting attorney's office if he does not choose to carry it further.   Or if a complaint is made directly to the prosecuting attorney he may determine at his discretion whether to try to adjust the difficulty informally between the parties concerned, to ignore it, or to investigate and if a crime appears to have been committed prepare a case.   The prosecuting attorney may also enter a *nolle prosequi* prior to trial and cause the case to be dismissed.   He is not required to give reasons for this action unless he desires as the judge is helpless to stop it.

It is necessary that the prosecuting attorney should have some leeway, inasmuch as trials are as a rule slow and costly procedures.   If the major criminals are to be tried, then many minor difficulties must be settled without the formality of a trial.   The prosecuting attorney assumes this duty. Sometimes a threat of prosecution will cause an offender to right a wrong; sometimes asking a complainant in, say, a family conflict to return in a week's time will permit the family to "cool off" and work out its own adjustment. Sometimes, even when a crime has been committed and some evidence is secured, the prosecuting attorney may know from previous experience that he does not have enough of the right kind of evidence to secure a conviction.

Safeguarding the Office

There is no simple safeguard against abuses.   It seems impossible to place dependence upon the electorate, especially in large cities where abuses are most flagrant.   The political machine is too powerful and the public too apathetic.   One needed change, therefore, is to divorce the office from politics.[26]   In smaller places not a political machine but popularity, rather than merit, may control the election.   Alternatives to election would be selection perhaps by the governor; official requirements of training, experience, and character; or civil service appointments.   It should be recognized, however, that politics might enter into some of these methods.   An advantage would be longer terms of office to permit permanency of the attorney and his assistants and to provide better office organization and specialization.   Some supervision by a disinterested official or body also seems advisable to prevent failure in bringing serious criminals to trial and to promote justice.   The recommendation is sometimes offered that the grand jury should be retained in modified form to give this supervision or to investigate actions of the prosecuting attorney when necessary.

CRIMINAL DEFENSE

The attorney for the defense, whether he is paid by the public, the suspect, or some welfare agency, is part of the complex system of criminal justice.   A superficial examination of protective devices in the process of prosecution seems to indicate that the suspected person would not require a lawyer to defend him.   The assumption is that the suspected person is innocent until proved guilty.   Provision is made to bring the accused person promptly before a magistrate who dismisses him if the evidence does not indicate his guilt.   If he is held for trial, the assumption is that the prosecuting attorney will fairly present the facts in the case and that the jury or judge will come to a just decision.   Actually, the situation is radically different.   In practice the accused person is more likely to be treated as though he were guilty. Public opinion assumes guilt with arrest.   The policeman may try by illegal means to force a confession; or he may mistreat the prisoner during the arrest or afterward on an assumption of guilt, thereby exceeding his legal functions, which do not include punishment even though a person is guilty. The magistrate may order a person, still presumably innocent, to be held in jail unless he can furnish bail.   The prosecuting attorney is provided with a staff, funds, and official power for investigating and producing witnesses primarily to secure evidence against the accused.   The grand jury as a basis for determining whether to return a true bill hears only the prosecuting attorney, not the suspect.   At the trial the accused, especially if he has been in jail since his arrest, is not in as advantageous a position as the prosecutor to present witnesses.   Moreover, he is usually unfamiliar with the intricacies of the law and in no position to oppose the prosecuting attorney.   In other words, the accused person, who may be innocent and who in any case is entitled to present his side of the case, must be represented by an attorney if he is to have a fair trial.

The Defense Attorney Privately Employed

Usually the accused person, although assumed to be innocent by law, must privately employ an attorney in order to prove his possible innocence.   He must have the money to pay this attorney and perhaps also to pay the fees of investigators, handwriting or medical experts, or the expenses of witnesses who must be brought from other cities.

Defendants fall into four classes with reference to their capacity to provide for their defense:

1. Noncriminal persons who commit or are accused of committing some crime—perhaps the only violation of a lifetime.   These persons may or may not have the funds to provide for their own defense.

2. Professional criminals of all types, who generally have funds and who frequently employ lawyers on retainer to protect them from legal action.

3. White-collar or business criminals.   Legal fees are regarded as part of the expense of operating the business.   Corporations often pay large salaries to attorneys to interpret laws and to protect them in case of a lawsuit.   These attorneys do not regard themselves as criminal lawyers, however, as most of the lawsuits brought against large businesses are tried in civil courts.

4. Habitual offenders, whose crimes are usually minor and who may never come into the criminal court because their offenses fall within the jurisdiction of the lower courts; or only occasionally commit a felony that brings them into the criminal courts.   Usually habitual offenders have little or no funds with which to provide for their defense.

Lawyers also fall into rather definite classes with respect to the practice of criminal law.   Many lawyers specialize in civil law and will not take criminal cases.[27]   There are many reasons for this refusal: the intricacies of civil law are greater than those of criminal law and appeal to the intellectual interests of certain attorneys; the financial rewards are both greater and more certain, since the corporation lawyer, the patent attorney, or the lawyer who specializes in some type of financial activity eventually establishes permanent relationships with a limited number of firms whose legal business he always handles; he thus has financial security and, if he is competent, a comfortable income.   Many criminal cases have revolting details and are abhorrent to the average lawyer who shares the civilian attitude of disgust for certain crimes.   The ardor of the prosecuting attorney for convictions forces the attorney for the accused to work equally hard for an acquittal, so that the defense attorney in effect condones the crime; this situation is repulsive to many lawyers, who dislike being placed in a position where they seemingly tolerate murder, rape, abortion, assault, or theft.

A few lawyers, chiefly in large cities, specialize in criminal law and are eagerly sought by noncriminal persons with funds who have committed or are accused of committing some crime. These lawyers sometimes attain a nation-wide reputation and are called to distant parts of the country to defend the accused in a notorious case. The late Clarence Darrow is an example. His belief that criminals are the result of past personal experiences in a social matrix from which they cannot escape enabled him to defend criminals who had committed repulsive crimes without the accusation that he condoned the crime.

A few lawyers are permanently allied with criminal gangs or make a practice of defending professional criminals. Their greatest effort is exerted not in defending their clients during a trial, but in arranging that no arrest will occur or in the event of arrest arranging that the accused will be released at some step of the procedure before trial. Their task consists mainly of maintaining the right political connections and knowing how to operate the fix.

Finally, there are the "jail lawyers," who seek their clients among newly arrested petty offenders. Most of their clients are poor: habitual offenders or frightened first offenders. These lawyers glibly promise an early release and paint a dark picture of the offender's fate if they are not retained. Their fees are based upon what the prisoner is able to pay or what his family can be induced to pay by threats and promises. The lawyer is interested solely in the money he can extort. When the accused is clearly guilty, he may persuade him to plead not guilty in order to prolong the legal process as long as possible and thus secure larger fees. If the person is obviously innocent and in all probability would be dismissed by the magistrate, the jail lawyer, in order to secure a fee, nevertheless represents himself as necessary. Often when the petty offender appears before the magistrate he receives a small fine, but finds that the jail lawyer who has performed no useful service must be paid a larger sum.

In the process of securing private defense attorneys, the poor man caught in his first offense finds himself in the most precarious position.[28] Lacking both social position and funds, he is likely to be treated badly by the police when arrested and usually cannot afford to post a bail bond. Usually he does not know his legal rights or whether the charge against him carries light or serious penalties. If he has a job he is worried about losing it. He is the type most easily exploited both by the professional bondsman and the jail lawyer.

Attorney Provided by State

Various devices are used to provide lawyers for defendants without funds. For an indigent person accused of a capital offense the state usually provides an attorney who receives a fee and in some states money for such expenses as investigations and traveling. A competent attorney is readily secured under these circumstances, the appointment being made by the judge. More than half of the states provide that in other felony cases the judge may assign the case to an attorney if the defendant is unable to employ a lawyer. Since this lawyer is not always paid, the tendency is to give the assignments to inexperienced lawyers who are glad to accept them for the experience they offer but who may be no match for the more experienced prosecuting attorney; or to pass the assignments around among the lawyers who, in the press of their paying cases, give little time to the preparation of the assigned case. In some cities lawyers hang around the courts eager for such assignments, for they have developed ways of squeezing fees from the accused or his family. These men are usually of low caliber of the type already described as jail lawyers. If they find that they cannot extort a fee, they lose interest in the case or induce the defendant to plead guilty when often he should not do so.

Some states provide lawyers to indigent misdemeanants but in general only felony cases are allowed such assignments. Since the lawyers are not assigned until the trial opens in criminal court, the defendants do not have legal advice at the time of their preliminary hearing nor during the pre-trial period when preparation for the trial should be under way.

Voluntary Defenders

Within the past few decades several movements have developed to furnish defense to indigent persons, one of which is the voluntary defenders, consisting of some type of organization initiated by attorneys.[29] New York City's well-developed system is supported by voluntary public contributions. Established in 1917, by 1926 the organization maintained a paid staff of attorneys and social workers who investigated each case. Other cities, including Cincinnati, Pittsburgh, Philadelphia, and Boston, have organized similar systems. Certain limitations may be noted: the attorneys may decline to defend a doubtful case; also judges are not compelled to assign cases to these voluntary defenders and may continue to assign them to political friends.

Public Defenders

Under the public defender system some public body or official is legally empowered to appoint an attorney for indigent defendants, paying him from public funds.[30]   The creation of this office supports the principle of justice for all and avoids the situation whereby the state brings powerful forces to bear against an indigent person who is helpless in the intricacies of a lawsuit. The first public defender was appointed by the Board of Supervisors of Los Angeles County in 1913, from among persons passing a civil service examination.   In 1923 California provided for a public defender in each county. A limited number of other states have adopted similar plans, usually confined in practice to the larger cities.   Among cities that have used the public defender system successfully are Los Angeles, San Francisco, Oakland, Chicago, Bridgeport, New Haven, Hartford, Columbus (Ohio), St. Louis, and Tulsa.

Although both public and voluntary defenders fill a great need, certain drawbacks appear.   Under some types of appointments the public defender might become a political appointee who would abuse the privileges of his office.   Some lawyers refuse to support the public defender system, regarding it as a step toward socialization of law.   Moreover, in certain cities defenders—whether public or voluntary—function only in the criminal courts, although for effective defense, contact with an accused person should be made as soon after arrest as possible; otherwise, disreputable jail lawyers will have an opportunity to fleece the accused before the defender can help him.   However, appointment of a defender has tended to speed up court procedure, eliminate unnecessary trials when the person is clearly guilty and has no defense, bring mitigating circumstances to the attention of the judge when the defendant is guilty, provide a carefully prepared defense to the person whose guilt is doubtful, and abolish unethical practices.   The attorneys, becoming experts in handling criminal cases, present a skillful defense.   The general result is to give more dignity to criminal trials, make them more economical, and prevent neglect and abuse of the poor.   Further development of some system of free defense is needed, especially in large cities.

JUVENILE COURTS

A discussion of courts and trials, even though primarily concerned with those that handle adult offenders, is not complete without a brief description of juvenile courts.   In the first place, juvenile courts at their best have a point of view and use procedures that might well be extended to adult courts. In the second place, children who commit felonies often pose a serious problem of jurisdiction since in age they are juveniles but in behavior they are criminals.

Philosophy of the Juvenile Court

The philosophy upon which the juvenile courts rest is not new. It is a combination and extension of two long-established principles that came to the colonies from England. The two principles were (1) a protective attitude toward neglected and dependent children and (2) recognition that very young children should not be held accountable for their acts even though reprehensible. The genius of the juvenile court concept was to combine these two principles through expanding the classes of protected children to include delinquent as well as dependent and neglected children, and to extend the age of noncriminality to include most of the adolescent years.

Development of Juvenile Courts

Until the very end of the nineteenth century, delinquent children had the same legal status as adult criminals and were tried in the adult courts. In the background lay the English laws that permitted a child from the age of 8 on to be tried for felonies and if convicted to suffer the legal penalty, even to execution. Blackstone, writing in 1795, sets forth this principle and cites several earlier cases of children of 10 to 13 years of age who were executed (hanged or burned to death) for murder either as expiation for their crimes or as a deterrent to others. Such harsh punishment was not directed against children only; it was part of the general system of severe and often mutilating physical punishments used prior to the introduction of imprisonment. The significant point is that even very young children were held to the same degree of responsibility for their acts as adults were.

Our early court records also show occasional instances of children receiving the death penalty. Although such cases were exceptional, it was not at all unusual for children who committed minor delinquencies to be subjected to imprisonment in the same institutions as adults. Police records in New York City for the first quarter of the nineteenth century contain many entries of children from 11 to 14 years of age sentenced to 6 months in the penitentiary for such acts as begging, vagrancy, minor thefts, or (being homeless) sleeping on the sidewalks.[31]

During the nineteenth century there was a general tendency in both England and the United States to abate the more severe punishments for children. The belief grew that children should not be subjected to the same form of criminal trial as adults. In several states experiments in separate hearings for children were carried on; in 1899 sentiment in favor of differential handling of children found definite expression in the first juvenile court, organized in Chicago under a new Illinois law.   Gradually one state after another provided for juvenile courts, until in 1945 Wyoming became the last state to enact a juvenile court law.   Differing in details, the courts follow a general pattern of procedure and rest upon the same principles.

The juvenile court law transfers delinquent children below the age of 16 to 18 (in different states) from the criminal court to a court of chancery where equity is the object sought rather than conviction of a criminal.   The purpose of the juvenile court is to explore the background of each child, whether neglected, dependent, or delinquent, and make a plan for that child's future calculated not only to correct misconduct but to give the child the education and comforts that are regarded in the United States as the right of every child.

Juvenile courts stand halfway between criminal courts and welfare agencies, partaking of some of the attitudes and functions of each.   The juvenile court judge has the responsibilities of any judge—to hear evidence on the facts of the case and to make a decision as to the disposition of the case. The decision is binding upon the offender unless it is set aside in a rehearing or by a higher court.   The emphasis of the juvenile hearing, however, is somewhat different from the emphasis of a criminal trial; the welfare of the child (within the limits of public safety) is the paramount consideration rather than the proving of guilt and assigning of a specified penalty.   Typically in the juvenile court the attitude is that society has failed and must accept its responsibility to help the young offender; typically in the criminal court the attitude is that the criminal has failed and must make restitution through punishment.   The concept of rehabilitation dominates in the juvenile court with minor emphasis on punishment; in the criminal courts, the points of emphasis are reversed.

Juvenile Offenses

The laws defining a delinquent child instead of specifying exact offenses with their penalties, give broad classifications of behavior thought undesirable for children.   Often these same types of behavior on the part of an adult would not bring court action or even public disapproval.   In addition to the broad classifications the laws may also include violation of any of the laws of the state, including criminal laws.   In actual practice it is often difficult to distinguish between the three classes of children handled by juvenile courts.   The neglected child often is also the dependent child, and being neglected, he is very likely to misbehave.   The juvenile court is less concerned with punishing his past misdeed than with providing for his future well-being.

Types of behavior that bring a child before the juvenile court, in addition to the usual felonies, such as assault, stealing, and murder, are loitering on the street at night, incorrigibility, knowingly associating with older criminals, habitually spending time in places believed to inculcate undesirable habits, using obscene language, or sexually irregular conduct. The juvenile court law of Illinois, the first to be passed, defines a delinquent child as follows: [32]

"Delinquent Child" defined. Sec. 1. Be it enacted by the People of the State of Illinois, represented in the General Assembly: That for the purposes of this Act a delinquent child is any male who while under the age of 17 years, or any female who while under the age of 18 years, violates any law of this State; or is incorrigible, or knowingly associates with thieves, vicious or immoral persons; or without just cause and without the consent of its parents, guardian or custodian absents itself from its home or place of abode, or is growing up in idleness or crime; or knowingly frequents a house of ill repute; or knowingly frequents any policy shop or place where any gambling device is operated; or frequents any saloon or dram-shop where intoxicating liquors are sold; or patronizes or visits any public pool room or bucket shop; or wanders about the streets in the night time without being on any lawful business or lawful occupation; or habitually wanders about any railroad yards or tracks or jumps or attempts to jump onto any moving train; or enters any car or engine without lawful authority; or uses vile, obscene, vulgar, or indecent language in any public place or about any school house; or is guilty of indecent or lascivious conduct.

In order to carry out the purpose of the juvenile court laws it was necessary to separate children from adult offenders at all stages of the legal and rehabilitation process. Hence a separate system of institutions, and to some extent procedures, has evolved in the fifty-odd years since the first juvenile court was established. The pattern varies from state to state, in some places lending itself to a rehabilitative handling of all children and in others permitting some children still to be dealt with as criminals.

Procedures

Although children may be referred to the juvenile court by school authorities, irate citizens, or parents, most of them reach the court through the police. The child may be released in the custody of his parents or placed in detention—preferably in a special juvenile detention home—until the time for a hearing. In a fully staffed juvenile court this interval of time is used by a court social worker or probation officer to make a pre-hearing investigation. The inquiry extends beyond the misconduct into the conditions of family, school, friendship groups, and the community in which the child lives. In addition, the personality of the child is studied, if possible in a psychiatric clinic. The assets and weaknesses of his personal qualities and of his environment are assembled.

The judge then holds a hearing (the word trial is not considered good usage) attended by the child, his parents, the social worker and perhaps others intimately interested in the case. A representative of the prosecuting attorney may also attend. The child is entitled to a lawyer to represent him, but this action is discouraged as leading to the typical legal contest between the prosecuting attorney and the lawyer for the defendant. After hearing all the information assembled and the opinions of those present, the judge makes a plan for the child. The judge has wide discretion at this point: he may release the child in the custody of the parents, place him on probation, direct the probation officer or a social agency to find a foster home, or place him in a private or public training school. Often the hearings are held in a very informal manner in an office instead of in a courtroom, and sometimes in minor offenses only a confidential record is kept and no entry made on the public court records. The purpose is to establish a friendly relationship with the child, avoid the stigma of formal court trials, and at the same time make a long term plan for the child.

The degree to which a judge actually follows this line of procedure varies from one judge to another and from community to community. If the judge handles few juvenile cases he may tend to follow the procedure that he uses in criminal cases. In many small communities the judge does not have the services of a social worker or psychiatric clinic, or his only choice of disposal of a child who cannot be allowed to remain in his own home may be the state correctional school. In other communities, social workers and probation officers may be appointed by the juvenile court judge without the necessity of meeting high standards of training and experience; in fact, such appointments sometimes go to persons who have helped the judge secure the election. In general, however, the juvenile court plans for the welfare of the child.

Suggestions for Adult Courts

Regardless of the known shortcomings of many juvenile courts, the system has many suggestions for adult criminal courts. One suggestion is other specialized courts; in some cities such courts have been established, such as special courts for adolescents above the juvenile court age, traffic courts, family courts, and narcotics courts. Such courts permit specialization in one type of case and the building up of trained personnel who understand the cases with which they must work. Another suggestion is greater use of pretrial social investigations and when indicated, psychiatric examinations. There is, however, considerable controversy, even in the juvenile field, over pretrial investigations, since they may imply that the person is guilty before he has had a trial that may prove him to be innocent. Certainly, however, social investigations to throw light on the background of the offender would be useful before the judge pronounced sentence.   The effective use of such information by the judge would assume, of course, necessary training on the part of the judge to be able to interpret the findings and also legal provision for flexibility of sentencing.

The point of view of the criminal court would benefit by a change to the point of view of the juvenile court.   Interest in conviction and punishment could well shift to an effort to uncover the facts in the case and to investigate the social background and personality of the offender; the next step logically would be a genuine attempt to map out a plan of treatment that would both protect the public so long as necessary and actively bring the offender into a program of rehabilitation.

One criticism often made of the juvenile courts applies even more strongly to criminal courts—as the sociological and psychological sciences become more and more specialized, the judge with his legal training becomes less and less able to plan a rehabilitative program for the offender.   This criticism is now being met dramatically and decisively in a few states by the creation of a state agency that assumes control of the offender after the conviction but without sentencing by the judge.   In other words, the judge functions in the field in which he is trained, as a legal expert who sees to it that the trial is carried out fairly and that the rights of the accused person are protected.   Assigning of legal penalties fixed by law is superseded by the greater flexibility of a rehabilitative program in the hands of a new administrative staff originally called a Youth or an Adult Authority but now operating in different states under a variety of names.   In most of the states experimenting with this new procedure, the Authority is limited to children and older adolescents, but the plan is also being adapted to adult cases in a few states.   Further discussion of Youth Authorities is included in Chapter 17.

Juveniles in Adult Courts

Although in theory the juvenile court should hear all cases of juvenile offenders, in actual practice certain classes of youthful offenders are tried in adult courts.   Teeters and Reineman point out that many states issue driver's licenses to boys and girls of juvenile court age; traffic violations with which these youthful drivers are charged are tried in the traffic court along with adult cases.[33]   They raise the question whether these traffic violations should be tried in the juvenile court and given special treatment.   More serious, is the fact that in 21 states either felonies or capital offenses are excluded from the jurisdiction of the juvenile courts or the jurisdiction is shared with another court.[34]   In Illinois, for example, the criminal courts take prior jurisdiction in criminal charges against children over 10 years of age, a situation that could be changed only by a change in the state constitution. It devolves upon the prosecuting attorney to make the decision whether a given case shall be tried in the juvenile or the criminal court.

Opinion is sharply divided as to where the juvenile felon should be tried. The social worker's and psychologist's therapeutic point of view was expressed by Katherine F. Lenroot, Chief of the Children's Bureau, when she emphasized that criminal (as distinct from delinquent) children were especially in need of individual study and treatment and, therefore, should be tried in the juvenile court.[35] The Standard Juvenile Court Act of 1949 is explicit in its recommendation that first, when it is discovered in a criminal case in any court that the defendant is under 18, the court should at once transfer the case to the juvenile court; and second, that the jurisdiction of the juvenile court should be retained until the child becomes 21 years old.[36] It is also recommended, however, that a child of 16 or over charged with an offense that would be a felony at the adult level, may be certified by the juvenile court to the proper criminal court, if this transfer is believed for the best interest of the child and the public. The discretion would be in the hands of the juvenile—not the criminal—court.

But public opinion as reflected both in newspapers and in state legislatures often is reluctant to accept the juvenile court as the one to act when a serious crime has been committed by a juvenile. The reluctance is especially marked when the upper juvenile court age is defined as 18 or 20, since the older juveniles are in reality young adults who may be well confirmed in their criminal activities and past the malleable stage of the younger child. The hostility of the public toward criminals who assault, murder, and rob overrides the more lenient attitude toward the minor offenses of juveniles. Also, when a particularly atrocious crime occurs, or a series of crimes that threaten personal or property safety, a panic of fear often spreads throughout a community, and a sharp demand is made for severe punishment regardless of age of the offender or the opinion of the juvenile court.

Certainly the customary punitive methods of the criminal court do not promise much in the way of rehabilitation for the youthful offender (or the adult either); nevertheless, probation or the usual correctional school for the juvenile with its short term and early release are not geared to handle the serious offender. Clearly, here is an area for further study and experimentation.

Although the criminal court may have the jurisdiction over youthful felons, the judge often faces a serious dilemma when a boy or girl of 13 or 14 is convicted, since he may not be admissible to the correctional school for minor offenders and the adult prison for felons is obviously unsuited to a child. In a Chicago case in the 1940's, a boy of 12 confessed the murder of a playmate. He was held in the county jail (not the juvenile detention home) for 6 months before the trial; the judge sentenced him to 22 years in prison, after telling the boy that for his offense he could be sentenced to life imprisonment or to the electric chair. When the case was appealed to the state supreme court, the decision was reversed on the basis that the boy was too young to understand the import of his plea of guilty. After the lapse of a year from the time of the first trial, another criminal trial was held under a different judge, who found the boy not guilty (although there was no doubt that he had killed his playmate). By this move the judge avoided the necessity for a prison sentence and opened the way for treatment similar to that which might have been decreed by the juvenile court without the long delay and two criminal trials. The boy was placed under a guardian and sent to a private school for delinquent boys, from which he was released after a few years.

Although cases of felonies among juveniles are infrequent, in many states they constitute an unsolved problem. The juvenile court policies and procedures may not be adequate for public protection; the adult court and adult penal institutions are not geared for adolescents.

OUTCOME OF LEGAL PROCEDURES

In the long-drawn-out process that leads from arrest to trial there are 6 points at which a prisoner may be released either legally or by common practice: (1) by the police after questioning or (as in the case of a vagrant or a drunken person) after a night in jail; (2) when brought before the police judge or magistrate if there is insufficient evidence to make it seem probable that he is guilty; (3) after the grand jury hearing if it fails to hold him for trial; (4) when the prosecuting attorney fails to bring the case to trial because he fears that he cannot get a conviction; (5) at the time of trial, by a *nolle prosequi* submitted by the prosecuting attorney; (6) by a petition from the defense attorney to have the case dismissed for lack of evidence. If the prisoner is not released at any of these stages, he may either plead guilty or stand trial.

If the accused misdemeanant pleads guilty or is convicted in the magistrates' court he is sentenced immediately. The penalty usually is a fine or a short sentence that is served in the jail or a local workhouse or house of correction; or in some states the misdemeanant may be placed on probation and released. The offender who cannot pay a fine is confined to jail, each day canceling a certain amount of the fine. The accused felon who pleads guilty or is convicted in the criminal court, is sentenced by the judge. The sentence may be mandatory, if the law provides a specific penalty for a crime; or the law may set outside limits to the punishment, leaving the exact sentence to the discretion of the judge. The penalty may be a fine, imprisonment, or capital punishment according to the offense and the law of the state. Under certain circumstances the judge may place the prisoner on probation and release him. A prison sentence may be for a fixed number of years or may be indeterminate, that is, the sentence specifies a minimum and maximum number of years but the exact term served will depend upon the conduct of the prisoner while in prison and upon the action of the parole board.

Careful studies of the progress of cases through the courts show that only a small proportion of offenses result in conviction. The number of arrests for serious crimes and the disposition of cases for 208 cities are given in Table 14. Only 15.6 per cent of serious criminal offenses reported to the police were "solved" by convictions. The greatest gap is between offenses

TABLE 14

Number of Offenses and Disposition of Serious Crimes for 208 Cities
over 25,000 Population, 1952

		Per Cent of Offenses	Per Cent of Arrests	Per Cent of Those Charged
Total number of offenses known to the police	432,834	100.0		
Offenses cleared by arrests	138,161	31.9	100.0	
Charged (held for prosecution)	95,424	22.0	69.1	100.0
Found guilty of the crime charged	57,780	13.4 ⎫	41.8 ⎫	60.5 ⎫
		⎬ 15.6	⎬ 48.3	⎬ 70.0
Found guilty of a lesser offense	9,062	2.1 ⎭	6.5 ⎭	9.5 ⎭

Source: *Uniform Crime Reports of the United States and Its Possessions,* 24, No. 1 (Washington: Federal Bureau of Investigation, Government Printing Office, 1953), 57.

known to the police and the number of arrests; slightly less than a third of the known offenses being cleared by arrest. Somewhat over two thirds (69.1 per cent) of those arrested are held for prosecution, but only 48.3 per cent of arrests lead to convictions. Finally, of those held for prosecution, 30 per cent are released and 70 per cent convicted. The large numbers released at different steps may result from a number of different causes and do not necessarily signify inefficiency of lawyers or courts: arrests on inadequate evidence of guilt; later failure to find evidence to support the charge; in a few cases deliberate manipulations to secure the release of a

Figures 21 and 22 it should be noted that serious offenses much more often than minor offenses are likely to involve conviction of a lesser offense than the one charged, an indication often of a weak case or the belief that an injustice would be done the offender if he were sentenced for the more serious offense.

Distribution of Sentences

The Judicial Criminal Statistics, based on major offenses tried in courts of general jurisdiction in 25 states, show that of 36,766 convictions, 37.6 per cent of the convicted persons were sentenced to prison and 21.3 per cent to local jails or workhouses; 33.0 per cent were placed on probation or given suspended sentences; and 8.1 per cent received other penalties.[37]

It must be remembered that these figures refer only to persons convicted of felonies. The number fined or committed to jail or workhouse are in part felons who have been permitted to plead guilty to a misdemeanor, since a felony usually requires confinement in the penitentiary or death. In addition to the total picture of crime are the misdemeanants whose cases never go beyond the police court or the magistrate's court and who, if convicted, are fined or sentenced to jail or workhouse. During any single year approximately 10 persons are sentenced to county and city jails for every 1 sentenced to prisons or reformatories; but because of the short sentences given those sent to jail as compared with the sentences of those sent to prison, the number actually in jail at any one time is less than one third the number in prison.[38]

QUESTIONS

1. What special criticisms may be directed at courts of inferior criminal jurisdiction? How might these courts be improved?
2. What are the advantages and disadvantages of the present bail system?
3. Discuss the function of the grand jury in relation to the total criminal process?
4. What function does the judge serve in the criminal trial? What are some of the difficulties of his position?
5. How might the use of psychiatric examinations of defendants be made more valid and useful?
6. What are some of the difficult decisions that the prosecuting attorney must make?
7. Which provision for defense attorney seems to provide the greatest probability of justice to the defendant?
8. Discuss the relation of the juvenile court to the adult criminal court. How might the juvenile court be strengthened?
9. In the light of Table 14, does it seem to you that "crime does not pay"?

READINGS

Baker, N. F., and E. H. DeLong, series of articles in the *Journal of Criminal Law and Criminology:* "The Prosecuting Attorney, Provisions of Law Organizing the Office," 23 (1932–33), 926–63; "The Prosecuting Attorney—Powers and Duties in Criminal Prosecution," 24 (1933–34), 1025–65; The Prosecuting Attorney and His Office," 25 (1934–35), 695–720, 884–901; "The Prosecuting Attorney—the Process of Prosecution," 26 (1935–36), 7–21. The titles indicate the content of this excellent series of articles on the key official in criminal prosecution.

Chute, C. L., "Fifty Years of the Juvenile Court," *1949 Yearbook of the National Probation and Parole Association,* pp. 1–20. A critical evaluation of the juvenile court today.

Harno, A. J., "Some Significant Developments in Criminal Law and Procedure in the Last Century," *Journal of Criminal Law, Criminology, and Police Science,* 42 (1951), 432–36.

Kaplan, Benjamin, and Livingston Hall (eds.), "Judicial Administration and the Common Man," *Annals of the American Academy of Political and Social Science,* Vol. 287 (1953). Twenty-five articles covering public attitudes, the common man's case, the layman's part in the administration of justice, the costs of justice, and means of improvement. Although not limited to criminal cases, many parts are applicable.

Moley, Raymond, *Our Criminal Courts* (Minton, Balch, 1930). Discussion of criminal courts, their shortcomings, and possible improvement.

FOOTNOTES

[1] Raymond Moley, *Our Criminal Courts* (Minton, Balch, 1930), pp. 1–42; *Tribunes of the People, The Past and Future of New York Magistrate's Courts* (New Haven: Yale University Press, 1932); Morris Ploscowe, *Crime and Criminal Law,* National Law Library, 2 (New York: Collier, 1939), 207ff.; "The Inferior Criminal Courts in Action," *Annals of the American Academy of Political and Social Science,* 287 (May, 1953), 8–12; Bruce Smith, *Rural Crime Control* (New York: Institute of Public Administration, Columbia University, 1933).

[2] Moley, *Our Criminal Courts,* p. 36.

[3] Ploscowe, *Crime and Criminal Law,* p. 213.

[4] Moley, *Our Criminal Courts,* pp. 3–5.

[5] N. F. Baker and E. H. DeLong, "The Prosecuting Attorney—the Process of Prosecution," *Journal of Criminal Law and Criminology,* 26 (1935–36), 7–21.

[6] Arthur L. Beeley, *The Bail System in Chicago,* Social Service Monograph No. 1 (Chicago: University of Chicago Press, 1927), p. 19.

[7] *Missouri Crime Survey* (Macmillan, 1926), pp. 198–99.

[8] "Grand Jury," *Encyclopaedia of the Social Sciences* (Macmillan, 1931), 7, 148–50; Raymond Moley, *Politics and Criminal Prosecution* (Minton, Balch, 1929), pp. 127–48; *Report on Prosecution,* National Commission on Law Observance and Enforcement, No. 4 (Washington: Government Printing Office, 1931).

[9] Ploscowe, *Crime and Criminal Law,* pp. 207–13.

[10] Moley, *Our Criminal Courts,* pp. 75–90; Ploscowe, *Crime and Criminal Law,* pp. 207–13.

[11] Ploscowe, *Crime and Criminal Law,* pp. 222ff.

[12] *Judicial Criminal Statistics,* Department of Commerce, Bureau of the Census, (Washington, Government Printing Office, 1945), p. 4.

[13] Ploscowe, *Crime and Criminal Law,* pp. 257–60.

14 *Uniform Crime Reports for the United States and Its Possessions, 1953,* 24, No. 1 (Washington: Government Printing Office, 1953), 57.

15 R. G. Weintraub and R. Tough, "Lesser Pleas Considered," *Journal of Criminal Law and Criminology,* 32 (1941–42), 506–30.

16 Curtis Bok, "The Jury System in America," *Annals of the American Academy of Political and Social Science,* 287 (1953), 92–96; B. D. Meltzer, "A Projected Study of the Jury as a Working Institution," *Annals of the American Academy of Political and Social Science,* 287 (1953), 97–102.

17 *Judicial Criminal Statistics,* 1945, p. 4.

18 Louis P. Goldberg and Eleanore Levenson, *Lawless Judges* (New York: Rand School Press, 1934); John B. Waite, *Criminal Law in Action* (Harcourt, Brace, 1934).

19 A. J. Harno, "Some Significant Developments in Criminal Law and Procedure in the Last Century," *Journal of Criminal Law, Criminology, and Police Science,* 42 (1951), 432–36.

20 Winfred Overholser, "The Briggs Law of Massachusetts: A Review and an Appraisal," *Journal of Criminal Law and Criminology,* 25 (1935), 859–83; "Psychiatric Expert Testimony in Criminal Cases since McNaghten—A Review," *Journal of Criminal Law, Criminology, and Police Science,* 42 (1951), 283–99.

21 *Report on Prosecution,* p. 11.

22 Moley, *Politics and Criminal Prosecution,* pp. 476–78.

23 *Report on Prosecution,* pp. 11–16.

24 Most of the discussion of the prosecuting attorney is based on a series of articles by N. F. Baker and E. H. DeLong, published in the *Journal of Criminal Law and Criminology,* as follows: "The Prosecuting Attorney, Provisions of Law Organizing the Office," 23 (1932–33), 926–63; "The Prosecuting Attorney—Powers and Duties in Criminal Prosecution," 24 (1933–34), 1025–65; "The Prosecuting Attorney and His Office," 25 (1934–35), 695–720, 884–901; "The Prosecuting Attorney—the Process of Prosecution," 26 (1935–36), 7–21.

25 Roscoe Pound, *Criminal Justice in America* (Holt, 1930), p. 184.

26 Ibid., p. 188; *Report on Prosecution,* pp. 37–38.

27 J. W. Madden, "Is Justice Blind?" *Annals of the American Academy of Political and Social Science,* 280 (March, 1952), 60–66.

28 Justin Miller, "The Difficulties of the Poor Man Accused of Crime," *Annals of the Academy of Political and Social Science,* 124 (1926), 63–68.

29 Louis Fabricant, "The Voluntary Defender in Criminal Cases," *Annals of the American Academy of Political and Social Science,* 24 (1926), 74–80; "Voluntary Defenders in Criminal Cases," *Annals of the American Academy of Political and Social Science,* 205 (1939), 24–29; E.A. Brownell, "Availability of Low Cost Legal Services," *Annals of the American Academy of Political and Social Science,* 287 (1953), 120–26.

30 R. H. Smith, *Justice and the Poor,* Bulletin No. 13 (Carnegie Foundation for the Advancement of Teaching, 1919), pp. 117ff.; Mayer C. Goldman, *The Public Defender* (Putnam, 1917); "Public Defenders in Criminal Cases," *Annals of the American Academy of Political and Social Science,* 205 (1939), 16–23; Charles Mishkin, "The Public Defender," *Journal of Criminal Law and Criminology,* 22 (1931), 489–505.

31 Grace Abbott, *The Child and the State,* 2 (Chicago: University of Chicago Press, 1938), 347–48.

32 J. C. Cahill and F. D. Moore, compilers and editors, *Revised Statutes of the State of Illinois* (Chicago: Callaghan and Co., 1935), p. 1161.

33 Negley K. Teeters and John Otto Reinemann, *Challenge of Delinquency* (Prentice Hall, 1950), p. 306.

34 C. L. Chute, "Fifty Years of the Juvenile Court," *1949 Yearbook of the National Probation and Parole Association,* pp. 1–20.

35 K. F. Lenroot, "The Juvenile Court Today," *Federal Probation,* 13 (1949), 11.

36 *A Standard Juvenile Court Act* (New York: National Probation and Parole Association, revised, 1949).

37 *Judicial Criminal Statistics,* p. 5.

38 L. N. Robinson, *Jails* (Winston, 1944), p. 6.

14

Jails and Other Local Institutions

I n addition to the prisons and reformatories operated on a state or national basis for serious offenders, another series of institutions exists to receive persons immediately after arrest, detain them until trial, and, in the case of misdemeanants or minor offenders, provide a place where they may serve their sentences. These institutions are police lockups, jails, houses of correction, county work camps, and the like.

TYPES AND FUNCTIONS OF JAILS

The most prevalent type of jail is the county jail, which is operated by the county sheriff or under his supervision by a staff of wardens, guards, matrons for women, and so on. In rural areas where villages and small cities do not have police departments, the arrested person is placed in the county jail until time of trial and, if convicted of a minor offense, serves his sentence in the same jail. If he is found guilty of a serious crime, he is transferred to a state prison after conviction.

In cities the county jail is supplemented by the police lockup. Small cities have one police lockup; large cities may have many since the city typically is divided into districts, each with its own police station and lockup. Chicago, for example, has 39 police districts and as many lockups. The newly arrested person is brought to the police lockup where he is held for the next step that carries him toward release or trial, a process already discussed in Chapter 13. He may be released almost immediately, without a trial, if his offense is trivial; held in jail for appearance before a magistrate's court, or released on bail until this appearance; or sentenced for minor offenses to spend any amount of time up to one year either in the police jail or county jail. If, however, he is suspected of a serious offense that must be tried in the criminal court, he is transferred to the county jail after the preliminary hearing in the magistrate's court.   Police lockups and jails are municipal institutions under the control of the police department.

In addition, some cities or counties maintain houses of correction where the more substantial sentences for minor offenses may be served.   Houses of correction as a rule do not accept persons awaiting trial, but are strictly penal or correctional institutions.   The county road camps in the South mentioned in Chapter 15 also are penal institutions for minor offenders.

NUMBER OF JAILS AND OF INMATES

There are many more jails than prisons.   Virtually every county, urban or rural, has its own jail, and, in addition, cities have lockups and often city jails.   The Bureau of the Census in its last jail census in 1933, gave a total of 3,806, which included 130 houses of correction, road camps, and stockades.[1]   Robinson, in his special study of jails published in 1944, estimates that the number of jails is near 4,000.[2]   In addition there are many thousands of police lockups where arrested persons are held until their cases are heard by the lower court.

On the whole, jails are small and are equipped to hold only a few prisoners at one time.   A survey of 3,200 jails shows that 54 per cent are equipped to house under 25 prisoners; 37 per cent have a capacity of 25 to 99 prisoners; and only 9 per cent can accommodate 100 or more.[3] It should be noted, however, that among the large jails are 10 urban jails with capacity for 1,000 or more prisoners. The jail may provide a part-time job for the rural sheriff, or necessitate a large full-time staff in an urban center.

The official capacity of a jail tells little about the actual jail population. In many small rural jails the capacity is not met and only a few people are held at any one time; in many cities with rapidly increasing population, jails are badly overcrowded, with inmates sleeping on cots in the corridors. Also, account must be taken of the fact that most jail sentences are short and the total number of people who pass through a jail in a year exceeds the inmate capacity even when there is no overcrowding.   Robinson estimates that approximately 600,000 people spend some time in jail each year.   Jails, therefore, touch many more people than do prisons, but the length of the impact is shorter.

PHYSICAL CONDITION OF JAILS

Discussions of jails usually refer to the "jail problem."   One aspect of the jail problem is the generally unsavory and rundown physical condition of jails.   The results of several surveys show the tendency for jails to be more heavily represented at the lower end of the rating scale than at the upper end. The State of Indiana provides for state inspection of county jails with ratings on 5 basic essentials: strength to prevent penetration from the outside by either natural elements or riotous mobs; security provided by locks, bars, walls and the like to prevent escapes; safety against fire or other hazards; sanitation applied to sewage disposal, cleanliness, and food; and segregation by sex, age, and type of offense.[4] A classification in 1948 of Indiana's 89 county jails placed 19 in Group 1 with satisfactory fulfillment of all 5 requirements; 46 in Group 2 with fair equipment but in need of repairs and remodeling; and 24 lacking practically all of the 5 basic requirements—in fact the jails in this group are described as "neither safe nor suitable as places for the confinement of human beings as prisoners." Therefore, only one fifth of the jails were physically satisfactory. The rating does not include personnel or program.

The Federal Bureau of Prisons uses a more comprehensive rating scale based on personnel, administration and discipline, building and equipment, food, cleanliness, personal hygiene, employment and industry, medical service, education and recreation, and religious instruction.[5] In 1952, of 398 jails inspected, 42 per cent were given a rating of less than 60 per cent; that is, they had less than 60 per cent of the features of a satisfactory jail.

From many descriptions of individual jails, a general picture of the 25 to 50 per cent of unsatisfactory jails may be drawn. They are dirty and insanitary; vermin abound. Ventilation is poor, and cells are cold in winter and hot in summer. Plumbing is in need of repair and in some jails buckets substitute for flush toilets. Bathing facilities may be absent. Bedding is rarely washed, often being used until it is worn out, then discarded and new provided. Prisoners with infectious diseases mingle with healthy prisoners. Only rarely do the local boards of health inspect them; the federal reports indicate that 76 per cent are never so inspected.

Food is inadequate, monotonous, and poorly prepared.

Many city jails are overcrowded, with people sleeping on cots in the corridors or on the bare floor. Opportunities for exercise or to carry on activities are impossible.

Descriptions of a few jails, which could be endlessly multiplied, make clear the actual conditions. The first is of a county jail in southern Indiana in a county with a small city.[6] The jail is approximately 100 years old and has had no basic changes in that period of time; the original slate roof was replaced in 1949. The jail of the 1850's had 8 cells with solid walls and doors, built on the inside of a large room and separated from the outer wall by a corridor. What light and ventilation there was came from 8 windows cut into the wall approximately 18 feet above the floor level.   Coal stoves, with fuel in nearby bins, were in the corridor.   There were no bathing facilities for either men or women and no segregated sections for women or juveniles.   In 1950 a program of remodeling was begun to be completed in 5 years.   Much of the outer structure is being used, with additional win-

This county jail, in use for more than 100 years, shows the heavy construction. lack of windows, and use of stove for heating of an earlier period.   It is typical of antiquated and begrimed jails still found in all parts of the country.   (Indiana Department of Public Welfare)

dows at lower levels, central heating, and more adequate sanitary facilities. Cells and dormitory rooms are planned for two levels and in three separated units: men will be in cells on the ground floor, and women and juveniles in separate dormitory units on the second floor.

The city police lockups in Chicago's many district police stations were surveyed and the results widely published in 1947–49.[7]   Thirty-seven lockups were in use, and two condemned, some dating back to the 1870's. Since 1885 the lockups have been repeatedly surveyed and condemned, but continued in use with little change.   Of the 37 in use, only 6 new lockups and the women's lockup at the central station were given approval.   The survey, made by the John Howard Association,* classed only 7 lockups as good; 10 were rated fair, and 22 poor.   In 5 districts, the lockups were in basements; in a number the only toilet facility was an open trough that ran through all the cells with running water in it; wooden or metal benches or the floor were used for sleeping.   Ice boxes without ice, buckets of drinking water with tin cups, dirty floors, vermin, and leaking pipes were characteristic.   Many stations had given up the constant fight against vermin and dirt that must be carried on continuously for even moderate cleanliness, and those which attempted cleanliness were handicapped by open toilets, lack of paint, and the outmoded structure of the lockups.

One lockup is described as having 22 cells, each measuring 8 feet by 6 feet by 8 feet, and housing in all about 80 men on week days and 100 on weekends.   Wooden stairs that led to the basement cells were warped and worn; windows were dirty and cracked.   The stone floors in 2 cells were wet with water from a leaking ceiling pipe.   An open trough provided toilet facilities.   The tin drinking cups were rusty and dented.   There was no lighting equipment in the cells and a plank along one wall provided the only bed.

The lockups rated as good differed from the poor ones in being of more recent construction, with individual toilets in the cells, refrigerators for food, and running water for drinking purposes.   The premises were clean and frequent fumigations reduced or eliminated vermin.

Newspaper publicity given to the report of the John Howard Association and the subsequent pressure of public opinion and active co-operation between the Association and city authorities have achieved marked changes since 1947.   Basement lockups and some others in very poor condition have been closed.   Prisoners are sent to other lockups with better construction and more adequate sanitary facilities.   Three new stations have been built.   Year by year, cleanliness, care of food, and provision of toilet and washing facilities have improved, although conditions vary from one lockup to another.   One great lack is centralized control, which would impose uniform standards on all lockups.   Another lack is an inspection service, which would probably exist if there were centralized control.   In the absence of official centralized inspections, the John Howard Association has assumed the task of a yearly inspection of all lockups and a published report, with recommendations.   As an independent organization whose desire is not to condemn and fix blame for shortcomings but to assist in improving

* The John Howard Association of Chicago is a private agency whose functions include crime prevention through rehabilitation of released prisoners, prison reform, and public enlightenment.

conditions, the Association has been remarkably effective in bringing both to official and public attention changes that need to be made and ways in which such changes can be accomplished.

It is not necessary, of course, that jails should be dirty. They are so primarily because many jails are very old, built of materials that have absorbed dirt over the years in cracks and crevices, and still retain the sanitary facilities thought adequate 50 to 75 years ago. Another important factor is that many cities and states have failed to establish standards for jails or inspection services to maintain the standards. When an effort is made, jails can be modern in structure and sanitary in condition.

At the time that the survey of Chicago jails showed the deplorable situation described above, New York City jails offered a contrast. Representatives of certain Chicago groups visited New York City, where they inspected old and new police lockups.[8] They found cells of better construction than in Chicago, with satisfactory provision for light and air. Cells were occupied by only one person, and each cell was equipped with a flush toilet and drinking fountain. Cells were well-painted and clean. New York State has a jail inspection law and state and city inspections are made frequently.

In smaller cities and rural areas, state inspections also lead to pressure for improvement of jails. Indiana, one of the states that provides for inspections, carries out this work under the State Department of Public Welfare.[9] Between 1937, when a state survey was made, and 1950, 5 new county jails were built and in one fourth of the counties extensive remodeling was carried out. Subsequent inspections showed a greater effort toward cleanliness, with fewer reports of trash-littered cells, vermin-infested bunks, and unsegregated inmates. The Department of Public Welfare makes a practice of giving the results of its surveys and inspections to the local newspapers so that the public may be made aware of the condition of the jails, and often the pressure for improvement comes from the citizens of the county or city.

In Virginia, also, the state has assumed responsibility.[10] Virginia, which had typical insanitary jails in 1942, created a Department of Corrections to take charge of state and local prisons and jails. The fee system of paying sheriffs was abolished and a provision substituted for the state to pay two thirds and the county or city one third of the salary of sheriff or warden. A state inspector of jails was appointed and minimum standards for jail construction were developed. The state legislature appropriated funds for the construction of 2 jail farms during 1944–46. With this stimulation from the state, 25 substandard jails had been closed by 1952 and some 26 counties had built new jails or rehabilitated old ones.[11]

This modern type of maximum security jail is in Indiana. The steel construction is fire- and escape-proof, and easily kept clean. Such jails for the few dangerous prisoners who require maximum security should be supplemented by other jails, perhaps on a regional basis, allowing more freedom and a program of work and recreation planned for rehabilitation. (Indiana Department of Public Welfare)

POLITICS AND THE FEE SYSTEM

One basic difficulty in adequate administration of jails is the tie-up of sheriffs and police with the political structure; another is the fee system.

Politics

It has been pointed out in Chapter 12 that sheriffs are elected officials who usually serve short terms and often cannot be re-elected to succeed themselves. Consequently, there tends to be a high turnover in the officials in charge of county jails. With each change in sheriff may come also a change in jailers and other personnel necessary in the operation of a county jail of any size. High standards and professional pride are not built up among people who know their jobs may be only temporary.

Moreover, elective officers and appointees alike may be closely related to the political machine of a city or area. Sheriff and appointed staff may hold their jobs not by virtue of their training or suitability for the work to be done, but because they have given faithful support to the political machine. If those put in charge of jails are intelligent and conscientious, the jails may be well run; but with a change of administration, a totally inadequate staff may be placed in charge.

The same criticisms may be made of police, who operate the lockups. When they are political appointees, the standards of training and personal suitability for the work tend to be lost in the effort to reward those who have helped "get out the votes" for the election of higher officials. Civil service examinations lead to the selection of police interested in the work, make possible maintenance of higher standards, and by assuring tenure promote the trend toward professionalization.

The Fee System

The fee system is a method of compensating sheriff, police, or jailer by fixed fees for different services performed for the prisoners, including the provision of food. The total amount that the sheriff or jailer receives varies according to the number of prisoners and the length of time they remain in jail. There is an incentive, therefore, to keep the jail full. The amount allowed for food usually specifies so much money per day per prisoner; however, if the sheriff or jailer can feed the prisoners for less, he retains the unspent portion of the fee. The result is that prisoners are underfed.

A 1940 survey of Missouri jails illustrates the way in which the fee system can be manipulated by the sheriff to his advantage.[12] Despite a food allowance ranging from 40 to 75 cents per day per prisoner in the different counties, many sheriffs spent only 10 or 15 cents per day. In 1939, one sheriff reported that he had acquired for himself $13,000 from food fees alone. Such a large amount could be siphoned off only in an urban county, of course.

Various devices are used by some sheriffs to keep the jail full so that the maximum number of fees may be collected.   Trivial offenses may lead to arrest, even though the person will surely be released as soon as he comes before a magistrate; in the meantime the food fee and perhaps other fees are collected for the short period of time.   Some sheriffs receive a turnkey fee each time a prisoner is locked up or taken from jail, regardless of how short the period of imprisonment.

The fee system solves a practical problem for small cities or counties where the number of prisoners is small and varies so much that a system of ordering food on contract by the county or city government does not seem practical.   The same objection does not hold in an urban county or large city jail system.   When the fee system is maintained in urban communities it is primarily to permit sheriff, police, or jailer to profit personally.

OFFENDERS AND THEIR SENTENCES

Hearing

In cities the police lockup is the first institution to receive the arrested person, whether he is found drunk on the street or is suspected of or caught in the act of committing a murder.   The length of time that the suspect remains in the lockup depends primarily upon the speed with which the lower courts function to dispose of his case.   When the lower courts operate at night and on Sundays, as the magistrates courts of New York City do, arrested persons may be brought directly before the court and in many cases disposed of without detention in the police lockup.   When the lower courts operate for a brief number of hours on 5 days of the week, as they do in some cities, arrested people must remain in the lockup until their turn comes to be heard, even though this period of time may exceed the legal limit for holding a person in police custody before he has a hearing before a judge.   Especially on weekends, the lockups are full and it is at such times that the floors may be filled with men for whom no bunks are available.

Most of the men and women who pass through the lockups and lower courts are suspected or guilty of minor offenses and many are dismissed with a reprimand, or because the defendants do not appear, or at the request of the prosecuting attorney or the defendant who fails to enter a suit.   According to the *31st and 32nd Annual Reports of the Municipal Court of Chicago,* among a total of 6,700,000 cases heard from 1906 through 1939, only 313,000 involved felonies, the vast majority of offenses being misdemeanors or quasi-criminal offenses.   More than half of the total number of cases were dismissed at the time of the first hearing; approximately one third were fined; small numbers were held for criminal prosecution or committed to jail.

Fines

Many minor offenders (in Chicago, 32 per cent) are assessed a small fine, upon payment of which they are free. If, however, they are unable to pay the fine, they must be kept in jail, presumably to work for the city or county until the value of the work done equals the amount of the fine. Actually, the system rarely operates in such a way that the prisoner does productive work. Sometimes the jail or house of correction maintains a stone quarry or a small farm where the work is done, the prisoner being credited with a certain sum for each day's work. Sometimes "housekeeping" jobs around the jail constitute the only available work. Often the prisoner merely sits out the fine, accumulating credit for each day's imprisonment until the total equals the amount of the fine. During this period the city or county provides food and, of course, must maintain a sufficiently large jail and staff to care for the prisoners. Thus money is expended to imprison the offender who, according to his sentence, should be paying a fine to the city or county. In the meantime, if he has a job, he probably loses it, and if he has a family it is left without support. Nor is there any evidence that the method prevents a repetition of the offense. A sounder system would permit the person with a job to pay his fine on the installment plan while he continues to work. Those who have no source of income should not be fined in the first place.

Sentences

Although there are some exceptions due to differences in local practices, in general offenders sentenced to imprisonment for one or more years are sent to state prisons or reformatories, those with sentences of less than one year to city or county jails or similar institutions. Actually, according to Bureau of the Census reports of the 1930's (since discontinued), 70 per cent of jail sentences were less than 2 months: [13] 20 per cent were less than 10 days. Many chronic offenders (vagrants, drunks) are in and out of jail a number of times in one year.

The Offenders

The group sentenced to jail consists primarily of adult male minor offenders, often of the habitual variety. In 1933, the Census of jails showed that 70 per cent of the jail inmates for the United States were guilty of 4 offenses: disorderly conduct and drunkenness, larceny, vagrancy, and violation of liquor laws.[14] Seventy per cent were between the ages of 21 and 44; the largest group being between the ages of 21 and 24. There was one female to every 14 males. More than half—58 per cent—had previously been committed to jail.

A survey of Connecticut jails for one month in 1934 showed that the majority of both men and women were under 35 years of age.[15]   There was a higher proportion of Negroes than the proportion in the population, and two and one-half times as many unskilled laborers in jail as their proportion in the population.   One fifth were in poor health and two fifths of the men were chronic alcoholics and an additional 30 per cent were heavy drinkers. Forty-two per cent had been arrested 6 or more times and almost as high a percentage had served sentences in penal institutions 4 or more times.   It was estimated that 26 per cent were in need of permanent institutional care and an additional 6 per cent needed supervision.

A survey of the District of Columbia, for a limited period in 1937, showed that more than half the jail inmates were convicted of intoxication.[16]   The median age for men was 37.5 years.   About 85 per cent of the men had some serious disability or illness, and more than three fourths had served previous sentences.

In the 20 years since these reports were made, the quality of jail inmates has not changed.   Massachusetts may be used to illustrate the situation in 1950.[17]   During this year, 11,998 men and women were sentenced to the jails and houses of correction in 16 communities.   Half of the prisoners were sentenced to serve 1 month or less and 27 per cent between 1 and 6 months.   Only 6 per cent of the total number were women.   Drunkenness alone accounted for 64 per cent of the inmates.   Middle-aged and elderly people predominated, with 63 per cent being 40 years of age or older.

The state of Virginia reports similar facts for 1952.[18]   In addition to 22 police lockups and 45 town lockups, which are excluded from the statistical report, the state has 92 jails—county, city, and farm.   The daily average number of inmates is 2,801, or an average of 30 per jail; the total number imprisoned at sometime during the year, however, was 105,417.   Drunken and disorderly conduct caused the commitments of 44 per cent of the prisoners; offenses against decency and good order, and offenses against the public peace each brought 13 per cent to jail.   Thus a total of 70 per cent of commitments was because of drunkenness or some form of indecent or disorderly conduct.

The picture that one receives from these reports is of a constant stream of brokendown men and women passing through the courts and jails, a short period of incarceration, and release—with a repetition of the process.   It is doubtful whether anyone officially connected with the procedure really believes that these short idle periods behind bars in any way aid the prisoner. The custom of many years, public inertia, and the isolation of local institutions from the main stream of penal reform perpetuate an antiquated system.

Children in Jail

It is estimated that yearly 50,000 to 100,000 boys and girls of juvenile court age are held in jail, often unsegregated from the run-of-the-mill adult inmates.[19] Several situations bring teenagers into jails. In many small communities there are no special detention homes in which to place children until a trial or juvenile court hearing. There are too few delinquent children to justify the expense of a special detention home. Alternatives are to release the child in the custody of his parents or other responsible people until the trial, or to arrange with some one family to assume charge of all delinquents. Too often, however, the untried delinquent is already regarded as a criminal, or people fear to take into their home a delinquent, and he is placed in the jail. Sometimes the child is not even delinquent but is a waif awaiting admission to an orphanage.

Even in cities with juvenile detention homes, juveniles are sometimes placed in jail to await trial or to serve a sentence. In states where children who commit serious offenses may or must be tried in the adult criminal courts, such children typically are placed in the county jail to await trial. Reference has already been made in Chapter 13 to the Chicago boy of 12 years of age, who spent 18 months in the county jail while the criminal court took its slow process in deciding what to do with him for the murder of a playmate. Most of the offenses for which children are detained in jails when juvenile detention homes are available are felonies such as burglaries and robberies, with a much smaller number of assaults of all types.[20]

Objections to holding children in jails are quickly stated. Usually there are no segregated quarters for them and often they are placed in cells or mingle during the day in the bull pen (open common room) with adult jail inmates of all types. The young girl may find that her cell mate is a prostitute; the boy may be sexually accosted by depraved men. Education, provided in the larger juvenile detention homes, is rarely found in jails; the same statement may be made regarding recreation. In the jails, the juvenile is treated the same way as the adults; in juvenile detention homes usually an effort is made to provide constructive activities.

ACTIVITIES IN JAIL

Discipline

Discipline varies from jail to jail, depending largely upon the temperament of the official in charge of the jail. Some jails have a few cells with solid walls and doors, into which recalcitrant (or violently drunk) prisoners may be placed. Striking or beating the prisoner is resorted to in some jails, sometimes in the form of the third degree before a hearing (see pages 322–23) and sometimes for disciplinary purposes.

In some jails, discipline is left to the inmates, with the result that "kangaroo courts" develop, usually dominated by the most aggressive and brutal inmates, who form a controlling clique.[21]   This little group makes rules, presumably for the orderliness of the institution, but often of an arbitrary nature.   Examples are the prohibition of fighting, stealing, rowdyism, loud talking, and intruding when a fellow-prisoner has a visitor.   On the surface, these rules seem to indicate a desirable type of self-government, but the system does not so operate because of the dominance of the self-appointed rulers and the methods of punishment.   Fines are assessed for violations and if the newcomer is known to have entered jail with any money it is soon lost in arbitrary fines.   When there is no money, the offender is beaten or abused in some way.   Occasionally a prisoner is badly injured or killed and court action against the so-called "judge" of the kangaroo court follows.   Usually, however, the system operates without the knowledge of outsiders and with the connivance of the sheriff or jailer, who is thus saved the trouble of instituting an adequate system of discipline.

Medical and Psychiatric Care

Small jails do not have special medical facilities, but depend upon whatever the community offers for the care of ill or injured prisoners.   When a prisoner must be placed in a hospital, a policeman or county deputy often must guard the room day and night to prevent escape or undesirable contacts.   Large city and county jails provide an infirmary and medical care within their own walls, the adequacy depending upon the local situation. Psychiatric help is almost unknown.

Activities for Prisoners

In small jails there are virtually no planned activities.   Space is limited; there is no money for equipment or supervisors.   Trusties—often repeaters who depend upon the periodic security of the jail—may be permitted freedom around the grounds, to rake leaves, hoe flower gardens, wash officials' cars, and the like.   Within the jail, inmates may help with the maintenance by scrubbing floors, cooking meals, and doing the jail laundry.

In larger jails, workshops, outdoor work, or a jail farm may provide work for some prisoners.   In Cook County (Chicago) jail, which rated high on the Federal rating scale in the 1940's, wood, print, and shoe shops are operated.[22]   In the women's quarters is a sewing room.   Inmates are encouraged to carry on hobbies, the products of which are offered for sale, with half the proceeds going to the inmate.   An institutional library is open to the prisoners.   During the day, inmates are kept in large day rooms, where they may play cards (but not gamble), read, or talk.   The Board of Education provides classes for boys.

Nevertheless, a visit to the Cook County jail in the summer of 1954 gave an impression of idleness.   With some 20,000 men and women passing through the jail in one year, the daily average approximates 2,000 inmates. The jail is a large gray stone building, housing certain offices and jury facilities, but primarily given over to the incarceration of prisoners.   Cellblocks, kitchen, dining rooms, chapel, limited hospital facilities, workshops —all are in connected wings of the building.   There is no necessity for the prisoner ever to step foot outside of the building; some never do, while others have limited outdoor periods in a small fenced yard.   The workshops are small, and provide only for the needs of the institution.   Narcotics prisoners remain in their cellblocks at all times, without occupation or treatment.   Authorities fear that if they are in the exercise yard or mingle with other prisoners drugs will be surreptiously passed from hand to hand from outside the prison to the drug addicts.

In general, Cook County jail receives only violators of state laws; offenders against city ordinances and minor misdemeanants are placed in the House of Correction, operated by the City of Chicago.   When the first buildings of the House of Correction were constructed on the present site in 1871, the site was beyond the city limits.   Now a part of the city, nevertheless it still has adequate grounds.   Prior to a building program now under way, the cellblocks were all constructed between 1871 and 1909. The oldest of the cellblocks, still in full use with two men in most of the tiny dark cells, does not have flush toilets in the cells but depends upon buckets covered with a board for use during the long hours when the men are locked in the cells.   The 2 oldest cellblocks have the cells built down the middle of the building; in the newer cellblocks, the cells are built along the walls with outside windows.   All are maximum security cells, although 70 per cent of the inmates are tractable alcoholics and vagrants from Chicago's skidrow, many of whom are elderly or old.   Some shops and outdoor work are provided but it has not been possible to devise work for all inmates.   In the oldest cellblock scrubbing goes on all the time; the entire cellblock is scrubbed down by the inmates 3 or 4 times daily.   Admittedly it is difficult to keep clean and, as a guard said, "They have nothing else to do."   Women are closely confined within their own quarters.   Their cells are less crowded than those of the men and have been painted a bright light blue.   The women carry out maintenance in their own quarters, such as laundry.   Once each week they are permitted outdoor exercise.   Many of them, however, sit idly at long tables in the corridor of the cellblock.   Boys are segregated from older men and have a program of study adapted to their capacity and school placement, provided by the city Board of Education; they also have shop work and indoor and outdoor recreation.   Certain small groups, such as the homosexuals, are strictly segregated.   The House of Correction operates a 300 acre farm outside the city, to which 900 men are sent.   As in the main plant, there is insufficient work.   Chicago has provided $4,000,-000 for rehabilitation, with emphasis on a youth center outside the main institution but on the grounds, and a new hospital.   The oldest of the cell-blocks will be torn down upon completion of the new facilities.   Even with these improvements, the House of Correction will remain primarily a max-imum custody institution for inmates, most of whom could be handled with medium or minimum security.   No change in living quarters or activities has been announced for the women.

Another jail that serves an urban center is the Berks County Prison in Pennsylvania.[23]   This farm-type jail houses several classes of persons: those awaiting trial, convicted persons with short terms, and some prisoners from state institutions who are sent to the County Prison to complete their terms. Witnesses are also confined there.   This jail differs from many others both in its rural location and in the variety of occupations provided.   The inmates farm, manufacture and repair shoes, make tables and chairs, launder, work in a weaving shop, quarry stone, or do maintenance work.   A library, recreational program, sports, and movies are provided.   Other jails might be cited that have adequate physical structure and recreational and employ-ment programs.

In some states, the state itself has provided a correctional farm to which all counties may send misdemeanants sentenced to more than a few weeks time.   Virginia, for example, in addition to the jails described on page 381, operates a correctional farm as a minimum security institution for mis-demeanant jail prisoners.[24]   About 170 prisoners are incorporated into a beef-raising program, the meat being sold to other state institutions as well as used on the correctional farm.   Other agricultural products are raised for immediate use.   A lime grinding plant and automobile repair and blacksmith shops are operated; in 1952 money had been appropriated for the construction of a cannery and slaughter house.   A canteen serving the prisoners netted a profit of approximately $1,000 in 1951–52, half of which was used for the recreation and welfare of the inmates.   Virginia also main-tains a State Penitentiary Farm for men, which accepts both felons and mis-demeanants with sentences of 30 days or more.   A diversified work pro-gram of agriculture and mechanical trades is offered the prisoners.   State institutions overcome many of the handicaps of small jails and make possible an active program especially well suited to jail prisoners.   Questions might be raised about the mingling of misdemeanants and felons, unless the latter are carefully selected.

Houses of correction, or workhouses, are maintained in a few communities, the total not exceeding 130 for the entire country.[25]   Inmates tend to be limited to those serving sentences.   The institutional routine is built up around the philosophy of the value of hard work, with agricultural work provided when there is a farm, and various small shops or factories when the main type of work is industrial.   The manufacture of brooms, carpets, furniture, pottery, bricks, shoes, and clothing is typical.   The educational program is limited and often exists only in the learning that comes through the job done.   In general houses of correction surpass jails in the quality of physical structure, sanitation, ventilation, and food.   Many have a resident medical staff and a hospital, both necessary in institutions that often house a thousand or more people.

The small size of many jails and the typical short sentences are hindrances to a planned program of activities.   It often scarcely seems worthwhile to county or city to provide equipment for activities that would engage the time of the prisoner for only a few weeks or months.   A third and serious hindrance is the physical and mental condition of many inmates. Chronic alcoholism, venereal disease, malnutrition, and age incapacitate many of the jail prisoners for any effective industrial program.   Many of them are in need of medical and psychiatric attention, and others are no doubt beyond such help if it were available and can only be given custodial care.

RELEASE FROM JAIL

One group of penologists believes that one type of jail inmate should probably not be there at all—those imprisoned because they cannot pay their fines.[26]   Their imprisonment is a cost to city or county, and for the offender an idle period when nothing is gained and when a job, if he had one, usually is lost.   If the offender is unable to earn money, he should not be fined in the first place.   If he has a job, he should be allowed to keep it and meet his usual financial obligations as well as pay his fine.   It would be necessary to establish a collection system for fines, but such a system might be combined with probation, which is also more and more urged for a certain proportion of the jail population.

Suspended Sentence and Probation

Suspended sentences and probation both involve the release of an offender after conviction but without imprisonment.   If the offender misbehaves, he may be sentenced for the original offense. Probation, in addition to releasing the offender, places him under the supervision of a probation officer. Both suspended sentences and probation are discussed more fully in Chapter 19 in connection with persons guilty of felonies.

Probation is rarely employed with misdemeanants and the use of the suspended sentence varies. A survey of the jail inmates of Baltimore from January to March, 1940, showed that only 2.9 per cent received suspended sentences and probation.[27] The percentage in the District of Columbia for the same period was only 3.2. In Chicago, only 1 per cent of misdemeanants are placed on probation.

The suspended sentence for misdemeanants is common in other cities and does not involve probation and supervision. A survey of 100 cases of drunkenness that came before the Municipal Court of Cleveland showed that 96 were found guilty and that for 55 both sentence and court costs were suspended.[28] Many cities follow the practice of releasing drunkards before trial, or judges discharge them without a fine or jail sentence. Recidivists, however, are usually sent to jail.[29]

Probation, used widely for persons convicted of felonies, is gradually being advocated for disdemeanants as a substitute for jail, sometimes during the period when a fine is being paid. The National Parole and Probation Association is active in the endeavor to extend probation to misdemeanants. Certain problems are involved—one being the enormous number of misdemeanants each year, which would necessitate an increased probation staff. Another is the selection of misdemeanants to be placed on probation; many habitual offenders need more intensive treatment than probation can provide. These are practical problems that do not undermine the fundamental value of supervision of misdemeanants as a substitute for short jail sentences.

Milwaukee County, Wisconsin, has used probation for misdemeanants for a number of years.[30] A report covering the years from 1938 to 1950 states that out of a total of 11,323 persons on probation, 82 per cent completed the probationary period and were discharged; 18 per cent had their probation revoked. No further details are given as to types of failure nor of recidivism after the end of the probationary period. Some classes of offenders were more successful in completing the probationary period than others: 92 per cent of drunken drivers were successful; 87 per cent of those found guilty of assault and battery (often wife-beating) were successful; 85 per cent of minor sex offenders; 81 per cent of the drunk and disorderly; and 52 per cent of vagrants. More detailed studies that follow the misdemeanant beyond the end of the probation period are needed.

[28] M. H. Miller, "Arrests for Intoxication in Cleveland, Ohio," *Quarterly Journal of Studies on Alcohol,* 3 (1942–43), 34–44.

[29] E. H. L. Corwin and E. V. Cunningham, "Institutional Facilities for the Treatment of Alcoholism," *Quarterly Journal of Studies on Alcohol,* 5 (1944–45), 21.

[30] W. Oldigs, "Probation in Misdemeanant Cases," *Yearbook, National Probation and Parole Association* (1952), pp. 76–85.

[31] G. R. Bacon, "Service for the Short-termer," *Yearbook, National Probation and Parole Association* (1951), pp. 20–30.

[32] S. D. Bacon, "The Alcoholic and the Jail," *Journal of Criminal Law and Criminology,* 36 (1945), 189–91 (abstract of article in *Prison World,* May–June, 1945).

[33] *Quarterly Journal of Studies on Alcohol,* published at Yale University, reports many studies on alcoholism and its treatment.

[34] Mazie F. Rappaport, "Casework in Social Protection," *National Conference of Social Work* (1946), pp. 452–63.

[35] Alexander, *op. cit.,* p. 18.

[36] "The Regional Work Farm," *Jail Association Journal* (March–April, 1939), pp. 17ff.

[37] Alexander, *op. cit.,* p. 15.

15

Prisons and Reformatories

M en and women found guilty of felonies may be fined, imprisoned, or executed. If the offense is not serious and especially if the guilty person is not a chronic offender, probation may be granted.

INCIDENCE OF PENALTIES

Number in State and Federal Prisons

At the end of 1952 there were 167,374 men and women in state and federal prisons, for violations, respectively, of state and federal criminal laws.[1] During the year 1952, 86,886 prisoners were received and 84,470 discharged. The number of prisoners increased from 1934 to the end of 1939, but showed a decrease from 1940 through 1943. Later statistics show a resumption of the increase as a result of the return of the younger age group from the armed services and the postwar period of readjustment. The 1952 figure is much lower, however, than the 1939 figure. These figures do not include men imprisoned in military prisons. The bulk of the 167,374 prisoners were inmates of state prisons; on December 31, 1952, federal prisoners numbered 18,014.

The total number of persons in prison during at least a part of a given year is somewhat higher than these figures indicate. At the beginning of 1952, 164,896 men and women were in state and federal prisons. During the year, 86,886 additional prisoners were received from courts, as parole violators, or as returned escapees. Therefore a total of 251,782 persons were in prison sometime during 1952, although the average number or the number at any one time was not so high. By adding to this figure the 600,000 estimated to have been in jail sometime during the year, we arrive at approximately 852,000 persons who experience jail or prison confinement for some period yearly.

Capital Punishment

Although capital punishment is legal in most states, 6 states do not provide for it: Maine, Rhode Island, Michigan, Wisconsin, Minnesota, and North Dakota.[2] In 1952, capital punishment was imposed in only 23 states; in 19 states that provide for this punishment no executions occurred. Eighty-five persons were executed in 1952 and 105 in 1951. Executions are much less than 1 per cent of prisoners received from the courts. The death penalty usually is reserved only for premeditated murder and (in some states) rape, although only a small percentage of criminals convicted of these crimes are actually executed. A special issue of the *Annals of the American Academy of Political and Social Science* amply demonstrates that capital punishment may be considered a waning type of penalty.[3] Since it is indefensible from the point of view of reformation, other supporting arguments are commonly employed: permanent removal of a dangerous criminal from the community; expiation; and deterrent effect on others. Possibly public indignation and resentment toward certain types of crime and criminal may be more realistic motives in individual cases. Inasmuch as relatively few criminals are affected, the subject is not discussed further.

DEVELOPMENT OF PENAL INSTITUTIONS IN THE UNITED STATES

The American colonists applied the types of punishment common in England during the colonial period. Jails and workhouses were used for the imprisonment of drunkards, vagrants, prostitutes, and other minor offenders, who might pay fines as a substitute if they were able. The stocks, whipping, the ducking stool, branding, and minor physical mutilations were also in common use. Death was the penalty for 17 offenses. The Quakers in Pennsylvania, under William Penn's leadership, modified this system, reduced the severity of physical punishment, retained the death penalty for murder only, and increased the use of workhouses. Although, under later leaders, Pennsylvania tended to revert to the typical colonial system, nevertheless, this state was a pioneer in penal reforms after the Revolutionary War. Imprisonment was substituted for corporal punishment, and the death penalty was exacted only for murder.

The prison, as distinct from jail, was an early move toward specialization of institutions. Although some states with sparse population may have only a few types of penal institutions, the more populous states have added institutions for special classes of prisoners until now a typical listing shows detention homes and jails for those awaiting trial; public or private institutions for problem children; separate reformatories for boys and girls; reformatories for men convicted of minor offenses; reformatories for women; state prisons for adult male offenders; industrial and farm training schools; special institutions for the criminal insane and for defective delinquents; and road camps.　In addition, the jails and workhouses continue to operate. Including jails and workhouses some 4,000 penal institutions are estimated to exist in the United States.

These penal institutions may be operated as independent agencies, a situation especially true of locally controlled institutions, such as city or county jails or work camps.　Different types of state penal institutions often operate under different departments or boards, although the tendency is to bring penal institutions at the state level under central control, thus facilitating coordination of functions.　It is still generally true, however, as Ploscowe states, that many penal institutions represent as many "different examples of administrative arrangements, methods of control and of policy in dealing with the human material incarcerated in them.　We have no uniform practices except in a few places.　The whole stands as an unwieldy, unorganized, hit-or-miss system, which has grown up over hundreds of years of local policy making, local tradition and local objective.　Certain broad influences have made themselves felt, especially in the last hundred years, in the development of types of prison buildings, in the use of labor, in the scheme of discipline.　But, as a rule, even where general influences have appeared they have been so adapted, modified and absorbed into the older local pattern, as to leave our national penal system nearly as complex, varied and unstandardized as it was before these 'reforms.' " [4]　Not least of these complexities is the independent administration of penal institutions by all levels of government—city, county, state, and federal.　Under these circumstances it is difficult to obtain a concise picture of penal institutions, since type and condition vary from one community to another.　Nevertheless, a general discussion is attempted, which points out the prevailing conditions as well as the significance of innovations.　The order of discussion places prisons and men's reformatories first, as the key type of penal institutions housing offenders convicted of major crimes.　The institutions themselves are the subject of this chapter, while a discussion of their administration and programs composes the following 2 chapters.

PRISONS

Philosophy of Imprisonment

When men were imprisoned for a number of years instead of receiving physical punishment for their crimes, new concepts of the treatment of prisoners evolved.　Since imprisonment itself constituted the punishment and since criminals were conceived of as wicked and sinful, it was thought important to make certain that they could not escape.   Therefore, the first prisons were strongly built with heavy stone walls, small barred windows, and closely barred or solid doors to the cells.   Each prison was surrounded by a high, massive wall, with guard towers rising above the walls at fixed intervals of space, from which armed guards constantly surveyed the prison grounds.   When Central Prison, in Raleigh, North Carolina, was built in the 1870's the outer walls of huge granite blocks were built up to a height of 20 feet above the ground and were sunk 15 feet underground; they were made 4 feet wide at the top and 16 feet wide at the ground level.[5]   This prison is still in use.   In these fortress-like institutions, all prisoners were subjected to the maximum degree of custody to prevent escape.

The Federal Bureau of Prisons now estimates that only about 25 or 30 per cent of prisoners require the close custody typical of the nineteenth-century prison to prevent their escape and subsequent harm to the public.[6] Nevertheless, many of the old prisons are still in use and many new prisons conform to the basic maximum-custody pattern, although only a minority of the men to be imprisoned would require such rigorous restriction of activity and guard supervision.   A third of all prisons now in use were built over 70 years ago, and less than 20 prisons have been erected since 1900; many of these newer prisons repeat the basic pattern of the old structures.[7]

The nineteenth-century prisons were based on physical standards acceptable at that time but since discarded.   Standards of sanitation, heating, and light were very different from those of today.   Although some old prisons have been remodeled, it is almost impossible to bring many of them up to the minimum standards regarded as essential to human health and decency.

The old prisons were built also with certain types of programs in mind. Imprisonment implied some kind of reformation before the prisoner was released again to the community.   A hundred years ago, industriousness and hard physical labor were highly valued as curative agents for misconduct. In some prisons handcraft was provided for men who remained in their cells; in others, the congregate factory system was used.   Recreation was regarded as a frivolous pastime for anyone and as debilitating to criminals.   Playing fields, gymnasiums, and libraries were unthought of; such modern means of recreation as radios and motion pictures, of course, did not exist.   The educational level of the population in general was lower than at present. Compulsory schooling was unheard of and the only motivation for teaching criminals to read was so that they might read the Bible and, it was hoped, be converted to higher morals and better conduct.

In the effort to reform the men, many prisons insisted on absolute isolation

Sing Sing in 1865 shows the inmates in striped suits lined up prepared to move in lock-step formation.   The building in the background is one of the old cell blocks that was later condemned as unfit for human habitation.   (Culver Service)

of each prisoner, so that the men might not contaminate each other.   The Pennsylvania system, which was based on isolation, went so far in its efforts to prevent contacts, that small, individual exercise yards were built. In other prisons, when men were in physical proximity to each other, as in work rooms, they were forbidden to speak.[8]   When they moved from one building to another, they marched in single file in lockstep in complete silence.   Meals were served in the cells or in a dining room without the sound of a spoken word.   In the mess hall, if a prisoner wanted a second helping of bread he raised 1 finger; for an extra tin of soup he raised 2; and for another serving of potatoes, 3.   In the workshop, similar signs were used.   Guards carried clubs or guns to enforce the rules.   Severe punishments followed infractions.

Men were unable to adjust to these severe repressions, and disobedience was common. Frequent and severe punishment did not bring a decrease in the number of offenses. From time to time public indignation was aroused over the death of some prisoner from physical abuse, and reforms were demanded. Gradually, minor privileges were granted the prisoners. At Sing Sing, tobacco was allowed the prisoners for the first time in 1846; soon afterward they were allowed to receive a visit from relatives once in 6 months. A little later lights were installed in the cells so that prisoners might read. The lockstep was abolished in 1900 and as the years followed other privileges were acquired slowly: freedom of the yard on Sunday morning instead of confinement in cells for the entire weekend; later, freedom of the yard Saturday afternoon and all day Sunday; and the introduction of baseball.

Early Prison Models

Two prison systems, in Pennsylvania and New York, stand out as exemplifying early prison philosophies and as models for other prisons, even to the present time.

The Pennsylvania system, as carried out in the Eastern and Western Penitentiaries of Pennsylvania (opened in 1829 and 1826 respectively) emphasized complete solitary confinement of each prisoner. The forerunner of these prisons was a cell block built in the yard of the Walnut Street Jail in Philadelphia, to house felons, the old jail building being retained for suspects, witnesses, and misdemeanants. Following the pattern of the times, the old jail crowded everyone into one large room at all times, awake or asleep. The new cell block for felons provided individual cells, and the new prisons built in Pennsylvania adopted the cell system. The isolation of the prisoner was carried to extremes. He was blindfolded when he was brought into the prison to prevent his seeing any of his fellow-prisoners and recognizing them after release. He was placed alone in a cell measuring 8 by 15 feet, which was 12 feet high at the center of the vaulted roof. Each cell had an individual, walled exercise yard. The Eastern Pennsylvania Penitentiary was built with a central rotunda from which branched seven corridors like the spokes of a wheel. Each corridor was lined with cells on either side, and beyond the cells extended the walled exercise yards. An outer wall enclosed the entire structure, which was regarded as the most advanced type of prison.

The separate cells were designed to prevent plotting between prisoners and to encourage meditation and thus, it was believed, reform of character. The Bible was the only reading matter allowed. Labor was performed in isolation by each person in his own cell. The system was strongly advocated for other states by the Philadelphia Society for the Alleviation of the Miseries of Public Prisons, which had been instrumental in initiating it as a substitute both for idleness in the jails and for a degrading type of public labor. But it was costly to build prisons with individual cells and exercise yards and to provide individual labor. Consequently only the 2 prisons in Pennsylvania and 1 at Trenton, New Jersey, followed the system of isolation. Maryland constructed a prison at Baltimore with individual outside cells but soon abandoned the idea of solitary labor.

Meanwhile another system was being developed in New York. In 1796 a prison had been erected at Newgate, New York, patterned after the cell house at the Walnut Street Jail in Philadelphia, but with congregate rooms (where all prisoners were kept together) instead of individual cells. This prison was soon overcrowded and in 1816 construction was begun on a new prison at Auburn. The original construction was based on congregate rooms for the prisoners, but certain reformers induced the legislature to provide for solitary cells. In an economy effort, small cells measuring 3.5 by 7 feet were built on the inside of the structure. Without employment, the men confined in these narrow cells soon showed the deleterious effects of their isolation and a compromise was devised whereby the men worked together during the daytime and were alone at night and on nonworking days. Semi-isolation was maintained during the daytime as the men were required to walk in lockstep with downcast eyes, never to face each other, and never to speak to one another. A new cell block to accommodate 400 prisoners was built at Auburn, and when Sing Sing Prison was started in 1825 it was constructed on much the same plan, with 1,000 small cells. The Boston Prison Discipline Society, founded and dominated by a religious reformer, Louis Dwight, advocated the prison system begun at Auburn, of solitary confinement at all times except during working hours, and work in groups but without communication.

A contest developed between the Philadelphia Society for the Alleviation of the Miseries of Public Prisons and the Boston Prison Discipline Society, with each society urging the various states that were in the process of developing penal systems to adopt the system that it advocated. The Auburn system was less expensive, both for construction and provision of labor, and it appealed to many persons as more in keeping with the normal social habits of mankind. Therefore the Auburn system was adopted generally, and prison after prison was built with inside cells measuring 7 by 3.5 feet. Prisons originally built with outside cells in accordance with the Philadelphia plan were soon operating on the Auburn plan—confinement in the cells at night and work in groups during the day. A few of the prisons had established dining halls, but in most the prisoners were fed in their cells.

From these early beginnings our present array of prisons has developed.

The typical prison is still built with small individual cells into which the prisoners are locked except at stated times when they are engaged in specified activities.

The Prison Day at the Present Time

Descriptions of the routine followed in several prisons will give some conception of prison routines. It must be recognized that congregate living of any kind necessitates rules, regulations, and a certain amount of regimentation. The mere fact of a large group of people living together makes it necessary to designate certain hours for meals, for arising, for turning out lights at night, and rules regarding noise and occupations, what clothing may be worn, when and where smoking is permitted, and many others not required when a person lives in his private domicile or carries on independent work. These rules are necessary for safety, for the comfort of others in the group, and for efficiency in running the establishment. They are found in college dormitories, orphanages, homes for the aged, large factories, day nurseries, and armies—in fact, in all types of institutions where people live or work in groups. In addition to these customary regulations of congregate living, the prison requires others. These special restrictions grow out of the necessity of keeping prisoners within the prison and preventing conflict, riots, or escapes. Some of the regulations no doubt are necessary to achieve these ends. Others stem from the fears of guards and officials, fears justified by the conduct of a small proportion of prisoners but extended to embrace all of them. The primary object, therefore, is not a comfortable and orderly method of living, but the elimination of any free and uncontrolled time in which prisoners might try to escape. Thus, although the regulations of nonpenal institutions provide for certain necessary routines and permit a larger amount of freedom for the group, prison regulations prohibit free time and creative expression. Many of them are simply repressive in nature with no object other than to prevent freedom.

Although with the passage of time rules have been relaxed and more freedom allowed prisoners, the day still runs according to a strict schedule. For the 1930's the routine at Sing Sing is described as follows: [9]

The day begins at 6:30 o'clock, when the first bell is sounded for dressing and making beds. The night watch has already made its count. All prisoners accounted for by the night force are re-checked by the incoming morning shift.

At 7 o'clock the second gong signals to the officers on the tiers to open the brake that controls all the cell doors on each gallery. The prisoners step out of their cells and march to breakfast. It is Monday morning. The menu today is plain but wholesome. Cornmeal with fresh milk, granulated sugar, bread and coffee. The cereal is served hot, cafeteria style. The men line up holding their plates or bowls and the food is ladled out as they pass. On the long mess tables are pitchers of steaming coffee; a cup for each man.   The rule is that each man may have as much as he wants and needs, but waste is strictly forbidden.

Breakfast over, the men rise from their places, drop their utensils in waiting baskets at the door of the mess hall, and march down hill into the old prison for a half hour's recreation before the 8 o'clock whistle calls them to their appointed shops and tasks.

Prisoners who work in shops must then hurry to their respective shop buildings where they line up for the count.   Outside companies, assigned to construction or sanitation, line up in the yard.   Heads are checked, the count balances and the wheels begin to turn.   Sing Sing is now an active, busy community.

Sing Sing's industries manufacture about 70 articles for sale to State, County and City institutions and departments . . .

The visitor at the prison, viewing any of these shops in operation will see a normal factory at work.   The atmosphere is that of a busy industry with rules no harsher than those which prevail in outside factories.   Smoking during working hours is not permitted.   Men must pay strict attention to their tasks.   There is no loafing.   Yet there is an air of informality that speaks well for the normal human being and the utter absence of oppression or slave driving.   One sees an officer in uniform.   He is there to preserve the peace.   But he does not seem to be busy.   The telephone rings.   One of the prisoners is being called to another department on some special errand, or for a visit.   The officer makes out a pass for the man, which permits him to leave his work to go through the Key Room for his visit in the new Administration Building at the entrance of the prison.

The directing force of each shop is the civilian superintendent.   He is a civil service employee . . .

We hear a steam whistle.   It is 11:50 and the prisoners are being called to the noon mess. . . . The shops have emptied and every company is lined up in its accustomed place waiting for the blare of the prison band which guides the prisoners' march to the mess hall on the hill.   Few officers are in the yard.   They are posted along the line of march.   Each company stands at attention.   Deputy Sergeant prisoners, designated by the Mutual Welfare League, direct the order of precedence which is changed daily.   The music begins and the first column steps forward.   It marches the length of the courtyard . . . and winds its way through corridors to the mess halls.

The menu is well assorted.   Roast veal with mashed potatoes, turnips and brown gravy.   Bread and cocoa.   For dessert there is cornstarch pudding.

There is an air of homeliness.   Men talk.   You hear laughter.   Not suppressed and afraid, but open and free.   It helps digestion, our doctors say.   It is an aid, also, to morale and clears away the fog of hopelessness.   No finger language here.   If a man needs and wants an extra helping he asks for it. . . .

The men are leaving their tables to return down hill to the prison courtyard where they will spend a half hour in the open air. . . . We hear a prolonged whistle.   It is 12:50 and the prisoners are being called back to their shops and their work. . . . Before the routine can be resumed, every man must be checked.   Every officer satisfies himself that the entire company is present or accounted for. . . .

It is getting late. . . . The prisoners had returned from their supper and were scattered over the prison yard and in the athletic field for their 3 hours of outdoor recreation allowed them during the summer months before the evening lockup. . . .

A steam whistle blows loud and long.   It is 6:50 and the call for the evening lockup. . . . Men walk at ease and talk at will.

The typical summer schedule in a large middle western state prison in 1940 was arranged as follows: [10]

5:30 A. M.	A bell was rung to awaken the prisoners. As soon as they were up the guards counted them.
6:00	Guards were changed.
6:30 and 7:15	Prisoners ate breakfast in the mess hall in 2 shifts.
7:15 and 7:45	Prisoners marched to work.
7:30	Sick call.
10:45 and 11:30	Mid-day dinner, served in 2 shifts.
1:00 P. M.	Return to work.
3:30 and 4:30	Supper served, in 2 shifts.
5:00 to 5:30	Evening count.
6:00	Guards changed.
8:45	Warning bell.
9:00	Lights out.

At stated times the men in this Illinois prison might listen to radio programs or read.   The weekend schedule provided for certain periods of recreation.

During the fall, winter, and spring, prisons with an educational program allow groups to attend classes.   For example, at San Quentin prison 1,200 men are released from their cells 5 nights of the week between the hours of 6 and 10 to attend night school.[11]

The recent recognition of different types of prisoners and the construction of specialized institutions permit the segregation of prisoners who are not rebellious or incorrigible in suitable institutions and allow a greater amount of freedom.   As much freedom as possible in view of the necessity of keeping the prisoner confined leads not only to less discontent, but also offers the opportunity for officials to institute programs whereby prisoners may learn to control their own freedom, to plan their own activities, and hence to become better fitted for a return to the community.

PRISON FARMS AND WORK CAMPS

Many prisons, even of the maximum security type, maintain farms or work camps outside the prison walls.   These centers are used for several purposes.   Long-term men who can be trusted not to attempt to escape are assigned to camps or farms where they may enjoy a degree of freedom and certain comforts not possible in the main prison.   Some farms or camps are reserved for young offenders or for men whose crimes are minor in nature and who are thought not to merit the rigors of prison life. To other farms or camps may be sent men during the last few months before release from prison, as a way of gradually reintroducing them to the complete freedom of release. Farms are usually operated under the direction of prison officials; work camps may be under the supervision of some other agency, such as a highway or forestry department, although often the prison supplies officers to take charge of the prisoners during nonworking hours.

California Work Camps as an Illustration

The California Department of Corrections maintains a series of honor camps, which in 1952 totaled 21.[12]   These camps represent co-operation between the Department of Corrections and other agencies: 3 are road camps where the work is done under the supervision of the Division of Highways, and 8 are forestry camps under the Division of Forestry. In addition, during each summer some 10 camps are maintained under the direction of the United States Forest Service. Although the work is supervised by these special agencies, the custody of the men rests in the hands of representatives of the Department of Corrections. From the wages paid for their work is deducted the cost of their maintenance, and the remainder is credited to the men. Through careful selection of the men to be assigned to these camps and adequate supervision of their work and activities, the men not only escape the repressive atmosphere and mass relationships of prisons, but contribute to the welfare of the state, especially in fire prevention work, fire fighting, and reforestation. Men are assigned to camp only upon their own request. These camps cannot be placed in the same category with the work camps of some southern states, inasmuch as they are under the joint supervision of the Department of Corrections and specialized state or federal services; they are honor camps, open only to men who have previously demonstrated that they can benefit from the camps as well as contribute to the work; and the camps are operated under minimum security provisions.

Southern Road Camps

The southern states have long used road camps as substitutes for workhouses and prisons, originally without attention to rehabilitation. For many years the condition of road camps in the South was a national scandal, brought to public attention by such accounts as *I Am a Fugitive from a Georgia Chain Gang.*[13]   The term chain gang came from the practice, now obsolete, of hobbling convicts by a short chain fastened about the ankles, which permitted the convict to walk and work but not to run. At night a

The old-style southern road camp, shown in the upper picture, consists of movable steel cages that can be hauled from one site to another. The cages have barred walls, the only protection from storms being canvas curtains. Approximately 12 men are assigned to each cage, where they spend all nonworking time. In the lower right hand corner appear double stocks used in some camps for punishment. (Acme)

Fortunately, these portable camps are fast being replaced by permanent camps, similar to the one in the lower photograph, that permit more humane and rehabilitative treatment of prisoners. One of 7 such units in Virginia, this plant contains, on the first floor, classrooms and shops for activities during inclement weather, and shower and locker rooms. Living quarters for prisoners are on the second floor. At the rear of the main entrance—not visible in the picture— are dining room and kitchen, with cold storage and other storage rooms beneath.

long chain was often run through the leg chains and fastened at each end so that all the convicts in a barrack or cage were chained down for the night. With prisoners working in the open in the daytime and confined in crude shelters at night, the chains were defended as a way of preventing escapes.

Many of the more lurid descriptions of southern road camps refer to a period now fortunately passing away.   The use of movable steel or wooden cages in which the convicts were locked when not at work and in which they could be transported from place to place has almost disappeared. Some states have forbidden or curtailed the more inhuman punishments, such as the use of stocks and sweat boxes that sometimes resulted in the death of those locked into them, flogging, stringing a convict up by the thumbs, and other cruel physical punishments that often permanently crippled the convict and bred hatred.

One obstacle to further, needed improvement is that many camps are under the control of the county sheriff.   The men committed to road camps work on maintenance and construction of roads, tasks that are often a county responsibility.   In other states, however, the state highway departments operate the road camps, and in some the state constructs and maintains the main highways, and the county the lateral roads.   Unless the state assumes some control, each county may set its own standards (as with county jails) and there is virtually no possibility of installing trained supervisory personnel.   In either case—state or county control—the emphasis is likely to be on the amount of work accomplished rather than on rehabilitation of the prisoners.

Brief descriptions of road camps in several southern states show their present usage.   Many comforts and amenities are provided, in contrast to the older emphasis on work only, but there is little provision for such constructive rehabilitation programs as education or counseling.

Alabama operates 3 prisons and, in addition, furnishes some 1,700 criminals or about 30 per cent of the total to the State Highway Department, which operates 30 road camps, 5 of which are honor camps.   Each camp has an average of about 55 men.   The convicts are placed with the Highway Department on a contract basis, the state receiving about $30,000 per month from the Highway Department.[14]   The Department of Corrections feeds and clothes the prisoners and is also responsible for their custody, health, and welfare.   The Highway Department, however, selects all employees in the camps.   The road camps seem to be the depository for Negro prisoners; of 1,745 white male prisoners in 1953, 7 per cent were in road camps and the remainder in prisons; of 2,499 Negroes, 55 per cent were in road camps.[15]

In the early 1940's the Alabama road camps were described as clean and sanitary, with indoor toilets.[16]   Outdoor exercise yards were provided. One guard was assigned to each 20 men, and leg irons or chains were unnecessary; although about 10 per cent of the prisoners each year attempted to escape, they were usually caught, sometimes by dogs carefully trained to trail escaped prisoners.   Corporal punishment (since abolished) was used with the consent of the state prison director and the approval of a physician. Since Alabama has been in the process of reorganizing and improving its prison system, it may be assumed that improvements will continue to be made in the road camps.

Georgia may be used as an example of a state in the process of transition from neglect to rehabilitation, with lodging of authority in the state.

Georgia in the recent past had one of the most degraded systems of county road camps, to which were sent not only misdemeanants but most of the felons. In the 1930's only about 10 per cent of felons were in state institutions; these prisoners were the old, incapable, or incorrigible.[17] Of the 159 counties in Georgia, 125 maintained camps, in which at least three fourths of the prisoners were Negroes. The State Prison Commission, although empowered to supervise and inspect the camps, actually did not do so. This commission appointed the wardens and other officials, but the nominations and payment of salaries came from the counties. To all intents, therefore, the counties had charge of the camps, each with its own policy and standards. The camps are profitable to the counties and make low taxes possible. Since the state pays for the maintenance of the prisoners and the highway funds pay for road building, the county makes a profit on the operation of the camp. Also, if one county has more prisoners than it can use it may lease them to another county in need of more workers.

In 1937 the Georgia camps varied greatly in quality from county to county. Camp G was an old type road camp, housing 32 Negroes. The warden and guards lived in an old house and the convicts in steel cages with latticed sides and solid steel floors and roofs. Board sidings could be closed in case of rain. Each cage was 8 by 22 feet in size and was mounted on a steel truck. Equipment was limited to a small wood stove and a crude toilet. Water was carried from a well in buckets. There was one crude shower for the entire camp. The convicts ate in the cages or the yard.

In contrast, camp A was a modern structure and represented the new trend. The 2 story fireproof building of concrete was equipped with modern plumbing, steam heat, electricity, and an air-cooling arrangement. The men slept in dormitories that were provided with lockers. The hospital had 4 beds. The kitchen was equipped with modern utensils and running water. This camp, built to house 150 men, had 43 at the time of the report.

In the Georgia camps in 1937, punishment consisted of solitary confinement or the use of shackles. Of the prisoners covered by the report from which this information is taken, approximately one fourth were shackled. During the day there was one guard to 8 or 10 convicts; each guard was

armed with a shot gun loaded with buckshot.   Although the Prison Commission provided for 3 grades of status among prisoners, involving differences in privileges and work, the system was not in use.   All wore striped
clothing and all performed the same type of work.   Each camp was officially required to maintain a hospital unit, but the older camps did not
have such facilities.   No provision was made for education, recreation, or
religious services.   The convicts worked from sunrise to sunset five and a
half days a week.   If the camp had a stockade, they could spend the free
time in the open yard.   But if there was no stockade they were locked in
the sleeping quarters as soon as they returned from work and for the entire
weekend.   Since many such quarters in 1937 were still of the old type—
overcrowded cages or barracks sometimes with double-decker beds—the
situation verged on inhuman treatment.

In addition to the county road camps, Georgia in 1937 maintained 10
state highway camps in which were housed 206 white and 463 Negro felons.
The Prison Commission appointed the officers but the salaries were paid
by the State Highway Department.   Standards of the camps were extremely
low.   The situation was particularly bad, since the State Highway Department and the county camps were not compelled to accept felons and if the
Prison Commission attempted to enforce high standards these agencies
might refuse to accept them.   The Prison Commission had no adequate
place in which to house the number convicted each year.

In 1946 Georgia created a State Board of Corrections authorized to establish a classification system to apply to all prisoners.[18]   This Board is free
to assign prisoners to county or state road camps as well as to prison.   Rules
were set by the General Assembly for the operation of both state penal institutions and county work camps, with the State Board of Corrections in
supervision of the county camps.[19]   The act establishing the rules emphasizes individual attention to the prisoner and rehabilitation.   Article XI
states that "it shall be the purpose of the State Board of Corrections to make
available to all prisoners opportunity for self-improvement, including
planned recreation, educational courses, reading materials, assistance in
maintaining contact with their families, and in the solution of their personal
problems.   These services will be developed and sponsored by the county
camps.   The Wardens will be expected to co-operate fully in having these
programs carried out in their camps."   County wardens are also instructed
to provide for religious services.

The act creating the State Board of Corrections in Georgia expressly forbids the whipping of inmates and all forms of corporal punishment.[20]   Also
prohibited from all correctional institutions, including county and state high-

way camps, are shackles, manacles, picks, leg-irons, and chains as means of punishment; manacles may be used in transferring prisoners from one institution or locality to another to prevent escape.

Georgia counties are in the process of building new work camps, a movement that began in 1943 and it was anticipated would be completed during the 1950's.[21]

In Virginia, the Division of Corrections under the State Department of Welfare and Institutions has charge of the county road camps as well as of state penal institutions. Thus Virginia has been able to avoid many of the problems of county operation of camps. The 32 road camps house almost half the total prison population, with approximately 60 men in each camp.[22] Since Virginia uses a classification system, the road camps are integrated into the total prison system.[23]

The South is gradually bringing its road camps under state control or supervision, providing more adequate housing, and expanding activities to include a typical program of recreation, medical care, and religion. As yet, little seems to have been accomplished in the road camps in education or therapy and counseling.

The road camps are an important and probably permanent part of the prison system in the South. In an area slow in developing industrially, prisons have placed less reliance on industries for employment of prisoners than have those in other parts of the United States. The roads provided outdoor work suited to the many unskilled men among the prisoners and as first conceived did not demand a large outlay of money for buildings, equipment, or supervision. In addition, the road work reduced the expense of maintenance of roads and when one county leased excess prisoners to another provided a means of income to the county. The leasing of prisoners from the prisons to the state highway department similarly benefited both agencies: the prisons received an income for the labor of the prisoners and the highway department paid less than it would have for free labor. As living conditions and programs are improved and as emphasis shifts from the financial advantages of convict road labor to rehabilitation of the prisoners, the criticisms of southern road camps will likewise change.

THE REFORMATORY MOVEMENT

In time, the limitations of the early prisons were recognized by a few humane groups who sharply criticized prison officials for their stern repressive measures and severe punishments. The reformatory movement for young male offenders was one result.

Elmira Reformatory

The first reformatory for youths was opened at Elmira, New York, in 1876.   It was the fulfillment of the dream of Zebulon R. Brockway, a leader in prison reform, who had experimented with elementary education, popular lectures, and reading assignments at the Detroit House of Correction. Brockway became convinced that rehabilitation could be accomplished better through retraining and education than by repression and punishment. When the reformatory for young male offenders aged 16 to 30 was opened at Elmira, Brockway became the head and inaugurated a program that, for the time, was radical in philosophy and activities.   Officials and public spirited citizens from both the United States and abroad visited this first reformatory in the world and watched its progress with keen interest.

To support his philosophy of retraining, Brockway established both workshops and classes and inaugurated discussion groups and religious services.   A summer school, similar to the popular Chautauqua summer school of that period, was also organized.   Teachers were recruited from nearby schools and Elmira College.   Brockway was experimental in his approach.   When he found that some of his charges did not respond to academic instruction, he instituted industrial training.   Soon the trade classes were a year-round activity, housed in a special building, and including plumbing, tailoring, telegraphy, and printing.   For exercise and recreation, the youths had both military drill and organized sports.   The latter were developed to a high point in the belief that they would develop self-control and team spirit.   Although Elmira, in common with prisons of the time, used the contract and later the piece price system of labor, rehabilitation rather than amount of production was the main objective.   When the contract system was abandoned because of restrictive legislation, and work was less abundant, Brockway filled in the time with additional classes and an expanded program of physical education.

Brockway used an early form of classification, as offenders were graded and passed from one rank to another depending upon their conduct.   He also was instrumental in establishing the indeterminate sentence and the use of parole or release from prison under supervision prior to the end of the sentence.

In time the Elmira system became outdated as new theories of readjustment developed.   Now, the prisonlike cell blocks of Elmira are regarded as unsuitable in a reformatory.   Military drill, long emphasized at Elmira, is now used in few institutions.   Elmira itself has changed and modified its program, although it no longer holds the pre-eminence among reformatories that it did when Brockway turned from repression to a varied program of academic, vocational, and social re-education.

The Swell and Ebb of the Reformatory Movement

The fiery zeal of Brockway made converts among others interested in youthful offenders and soon other states were following the example of New York in building or converting prisons into reformatories. Michigan opened a reformatory in 1878. Four more were opened during the eighties, 5 during the nineties, 4 between 1900 and 1910, 2 between 1910 and 1920, and 7 between 1920 and 1939. The older of the institutions are structurally modeled after prisons, with cell blocks, high walls, and little provision for group or social activities. Although planned for young offenders, older men were often also sent to reformatories. Serious as well as minor offenders were placed in the same institutions. In some reformatories, Brockway's methods were rigidly followed without imagination on the part of officials and in complete disregard of changing social and psychological concepts regarding rehabilitation. Many institutions had more than 1,000 inmates, with little possibility of individual treatment of the men.

Thus for many years the program of men's reformatories tended to stagnate, but the basic concept of reform through an active retraining program continued to live and find root and growth in other types of institutions. Long after Brockway's period—in the 1930's and 1940's—special programs for young criminals again came into the lead in penal practices, but with a very different philosophy of treatment, based on current psychological and sociological principles. Also, the reformatory movement helped to loosen the repressive prison programs and slowly methods found useful in the reformatories were cautiously tried in the prisons. It was discovered that relaxation of rules and provision for recreation did not lead to unruliness but to better order. Meanwhile, the more creative reformatory wardens moved on toward new methods of rehabilitation and helped to lay the foundation for some of the best of modern programs.

MINIMUM SECURITY INSTITUTIONS

By the 1920's, penologists had conceded that the reformatory movement fathered by Zebulon Brockway had lost its vitality. A new movement started, in part under the leadership of the Federal Bureau of Prisons, which was experimenting with classifying prisoners according to the amount of security they needed to prevent escape and with corresponding programs.

The Federal Bureau of Prisons uses the term, maximum security, to describe those prisons built like fortresses, from which escape is very difficult. The traditional prison was a maximum security institution. Some new prisons are also built for maximum security to house incorrigible or dangerous criminals. The term medium security refers to prisons with less formidable structural barriers to escape and provision for more freedom of movement within the prison grounds. Minimum security institutions are unwalled institutions from which a prisoner could easily escape. Such institutions are planned for responsive men whose sense of obligation and desire for rehabilitation can be used as motivations for retaining them in the institution and incorporating them into a retraining program. The minimum security institution is planned for essentially the same type of men that Elmira Reformatory sought to serve. The philosophy of rehabilitation has changed, however, since the time when Elmira was the hope of prison reform.

The basic emphasis of the new movement for young offenders is on personality rehabilitation, that is, replacement of criminal attitudes with those of responsible conformity, joined with practical retraining to make it possible for the offender, when released, to accept the obligations expected of the adult in our society—support for himself and his family, acceptance of family responsibilities, participation in civic and community activities, and ability to fulfill his personal needs without violating the rights of other people. In support of these objectives, new types of physical construction and new programs are being experimented with, some in one institution, some in another. Some of the experimental procedures are too new for their worth to be known. It is clear, however, that they are based upon current social-psychological concepts and make use of modern techniques of personality development and education. It is to be hoped that they will not solidify due to over-optimism that the final methods have been found; these methods are the best that we have for the present, but they should be kept in a sufficiently fluid state that they may be changed as theoretical scientific knowledge changes.

Minimum security suggests first the unwalled institution, unlocked doors, freedom of movement on the institutional grounds, and work beyond the buildings under minimum supervision. Many localities resist the building of minimum security institutions, for they visualize the institution filled with vicious criminals intent upon escape and ready to rob or murder people living in the vicinity. A program that includes minimum security institutions also implies a selection of prisoners for such institutions who require no more than minimum security to remain in prison. Regardless of the type of institution to which a prisoner is sent, it is still the legal obligation of the institution to keep him in custody.

Minimum security institutions often construct dormitory cell blocks. The illustration shows a well-lighted and -ventilated dormitory in the Federal Prison System. The lack of privacy is offset by the opportunity for freedom of movement and for companionship.

Minimum security, therefore, refers to a certain type of prisoner who can live with the opportunity to escape and still not take advantage of that opportunity. Annandale Farms in New Jersey is illustrative; it is described as "a completely open institution with separate cottages and no fence or other barriers to escape, designed for first offenders between the ages of 16 and 30 who do not have deeply seated personality problems." [24] These restrictions are not rigidly adhered to, however, inasmuch as 25 per cent of the white youths and 45 per cent of the Negro youths between the ages of 16 and 19 have had previous commitments.[25] The California Institution for Men is planned for first offenders and other prisoners who give promise of social readjustment to community standards. Some of the men have served a part of their sentences in other prisons of the state and are regarded as readjusted, but cannot be released because of the length of the sentence imposed upon them at the time of their conviction in criminal court.[26] In general the men at this institution are of normal intelligence, in good physical condition, able to do hard work, not habitual criminals, and with a good prison record if they have served part of their term in another prison.

The federal correctional institutions and reformatories gather into their ranks chiefly young men, without vicious, antisocial traits, whose offenses merit short terms.

The minimum security type of prisoner, then, is one who is not a professional criminal; he has broken criminal laws but has not identified himself with the criminal underworld.   He has not shown himself to be rebellious to rules and officials; therefore, some degree of co-operation can be anticipated.   Usually his term is short; he looks forward hopefully to an early release.   Since he does not regard himself as a thoroughgoing criminal, he often welcomes some aid that will help him re-establish himself when he re-enters the community.

Two other factors should be mentioned.   The minimum security prison has material advantages over other types.   Usually cells or rooms are larger, more comfortably furnished, and unlocked.   Greater freedom of movement is allowed within the institution and at work.   Programs of recreation and social life are expanded and often the prisoners are allowed to participate in their planning.   There is a definite and immediate reward for co-operation and conformity on the part of the inmate of the minimum security institution.

The second factor is the converse of the first.   Failure of the prisoner to co-operate in the program brings a penalty.   Scudder, the superintendent of the California Institution for Men, emphasizes the necessity for fair but firm enforcement of rules, with infractions met in a quick and decisive manner.[27]   The Institution has a few isolation cells, really the same as other cells that are used but with locked doors.   After minor flaunting of rules, a prisoner is locked in one of these cells where he remains until he has made up his mind either to conform or be transferred to prison.   Serious irregularities and attempts to escape are met with immediate transfer to prison and loss of the opportunity ever to return to the Institution.   The Federal Correctional Institution at Danbury, Connecticut, is built with 4 types of quarters: a maximum security cellblock, 3 intermediate-security cellblocks, 6 dormitories, and a unit of honor rooms with unbarred windows and unlocked doors.[28]   Incoming men are placed in maximum security and gradually advanced to the degree of freedom that they are able to handle; unruliness brings a reversal of the process back to maximum security cells.

According to Scudder, minimum security not only permits a better type of training program but is itself an important factor in rehabilitation.   The relaxation of custody to the point where a man may escape without much difficulty places upon him the necessity for making a moral decision.   Each time that he resists the temptation he has strengthened his determination to conform.[29]

The men in minimum security institutions usually have been selected in part upon the basis of good or at least fair personality adjustment.   By and large, they are not in need of psychiatric treatment.   There is a tendency, therefore, to emphasize social training in such areas as co-operation, tolerance of others, protection of the rights of others, and incorporation into primary groups.

The unlocked cell or room doors and dormitory living throw upon each inmate the necessity of respecting the rights and property of other inmates. The general freedom about the institution also opens the way for thefts of various sorts. Although such thefts occur, it is part of the training program in many institutions that the men should be trusted until there is evidence that some of them have violated the trust. The California Institution for Men takes a middle ground between complete trust and no trust at all. In the early days of the institution, a "shakedown" or investigation of cells was made when the men were absent, in the search for forbidden objects. The men were discouraged over this seeming lack of trust on the part of the officers. A compromise was reached, whereby no inspection is made unless the men are present in their cells. Each Saturday morning there is a routine inspection, for which the men may prepare, and each day a surprise inspection of a limited number of cells, but always with the men present.

PRISON SYSTEMS

The chief types of adult penal institutions for men have been described. In addition, there are reformatories and prisons for women (described in Chapter 18). It is evident that certain types of institutions are interrelated. Southern road camps are adapted to able-bodied prisoners and depend upon prisons to care for the old and the ill. Minimum security institutions are suitable for only one type of offender and, furthermore, operate with the assurance that incorrigibles and escapees may be absorbed into a maximum security prison. The successful operation of diversified institutions rests upon some co-ordination between the different types of institutions. The Federal Bureau of Prisons has demonstrated the advantages of an integrated system under central control. A movement is now active among the states to bring state penal institutions under the control of a well organized state department of corrections, which is given authority to study convicted offenders as they come from the courts and place them in the most appropriate types of institutions.

Since the Federal Bureau of Prisons represents the most diversified and highly integrated system of prisons in the United States, it will be used as an example of integration.[30]

Development of Federal Prison System

The federal prison system, operated by the Federal Bureau of Prisons, represents a well-integrated series of institutions, planned to meet the needs of different types of criminals and incorporating many of the best methods of rehabilitation that have been devised.   It includes 30 institutions, spread over the entire United States, but under centralized control.   Except for a few prisons of the old type, most of the system has been developed since World War I, under expert leadership and in accordance with a definite plan for classification of criminals for treatment.

For approximately the first century of statehood, the United States continued a system used in the colonial period, of confining violators of federal laws in state and county penal institutions.   The increasing number of federal offenders and the inability of state prisons to find work for all their inmates forced the United States to establish special prisons for federal offenders.   The first prisons, at Leavenworth, Kansas, and Atlanta, Georgia, were typical nineteenth-century penitentiaries, built for maximum security of inmates and housing old and young, the hardened criminal and the first offender.   The federal government followed the trend of the times, adding a woman's reformatory and a reformatory for young men.   There was, however, no real planning either as to sites for the institutions nor for a complete and co-ordinated program.   Meanwhile, the need for prisons and reformatories continued, as the population grew and as new laws created additional federal crimes.

Under the newly organized Bureau of Prisons (1930), and following a special congressional investigation of federal prisons, a comprehensive program for providing an integrated system was charted.   The system rests upon a classification of offenders from young and impressionable to confirmed habitual criminals, with special provision for women offenders, narcotic-drug violators, and mentally disturbed criminals.   Keyed to this classification of offenders is a classification of institutions, with each institution planned to aid in the rehabilitation of a specific type of offender. Prisons and reformatories already built were fitted into the over-all plan at appropriate places, and new institutions were built to round out the system.

Prisons with Maximum Security

The oldest of the federal prisons, built on the nineteenth-century plan, are for maximum security, as are several newer institutions.   To these prisons are sent federal criminals from all parts of the United States who, it is felt, must be kept under close custody.   Alcatraz Prison, situated on an island off the coast of California, receives intractable male offenders— men with long criminal careers who do not respond to efforts at reform and often who have threatened the safety or morale of prisoners in other prisons. Habitual criminals who are thought to be capable of responding to training and treatment are sent to prisons at Atlanta, Georgia, and Leavenworth, Kansas.

Prisons with Medium Security

Criminals of a slightly more improvable character are sent to the federal prisons at Lewisburg, Pennsylvania, McNeil Island, Washington, and Terre Haute, Indiana.

Reformatories

The reformatories are for late teen-agers and men under 30 years old who are not major criminals and who are considered to be capable of rehabilitation. The four men's reformatories have all been opened since 1925, as medium security institutions. Barred cells are in use for some inmates, but in addition each institution has dormitories and, in some instances, individual rooms. Prisoners can be assigned to the type of living arrangement to which they are able to adjust. In addition to administration buildings, cell blocks and dormitories, each institution has provisions for medical care, religious services, and recreation of various types. A library and academic classes scaled to the status of the man are operated. Finally, each institution includes needed work shops and, if agriculture is included, fields and barns. Each institution, therefore, is a small community in itself, located in the country, and planned for group re-education.

The four institutions range in capacity from 600 to 1,288—numbers that make possible some individual attention and counseling. In addition, men are encouraged to accept personal and social responsibility through such devices as an open forum, an inmates' council, and participation in group recreational projects. When they leave they are, so far as possible, steered into jobs. During World War II the men were brought into the war effort through training for war industries after release, production of war materials in the institutional shops, and opportunities to contribute to the Red Cross and the blood bank. Brief descriptions of the four institutions point up differences in inmates and programs.

At Petersburg, Virginia, are gathered offenders whose best possibility for rehabilitation seems to be through agricultural work. To this reformatory, with a capacity of 600, are sent men whose chief offense is violation of the federal liquor laws. Most of them are illiterate or semi-illiterate young men from southern sections where textile mills, small farms, timber industries, and furniture factories offer the chief occupations. Although there are some shops of an industrial type, farming, a cannery, and a modern dairy are the central types of work.

The reformatories near Chillicothe, Ohio and El Reno, Oklahoma, each

The rectangular cell block with several tiers of cells is the most common type of prison housing. The wide corridor and barred fronts of the cells make supervision a simple matter for guards who patrol the corridors. The above photograph shows one type of cell block used at the Federal Reformatory at Chillicothe, Ohio, a training center for males between the ages of 17 and 30 who are not confirmed criminals.

Below, the maximum security prison at Stateville, Illinois, uses a circular type of cell block, called a panopticon (seeing all). Guards stationed on the first floor and at the top of the central guard tower are able to see into any cell at any time. Only a few prisons have circular cell blocks, first advocated by Jeremy Bentham in England in 1799.

with a capacity of slightly over 1,000 inmates, receive youths and men under the age of 30. In each institution, almost half of the inmates are guilty of violating federal laws related to transportation of stolen motor vehicles; the second most frequent offense (approximately 15 per cent) is some violation of the federal juvenile delinquency laws applying to boys under 18 years of age. Other offenses are widely distributed. The inmates are described as coming from limited social backgrounds that offered little in the way of vocational training; many have long prior records of delinquency; in general, they are potential life-long criminals. The program is an intensive effort to check the delinquency before it becomes a fixed pattern of life. Various types of classes are provided, recreation and sports are well developed, personal counseling is available, and the usual medical care and religious guidance are given. The heart of the program, however, is in industrial production and vocational training that have increasingly veered away from simply filling up time to specific types of training that may be put to use when the inmate leaves the institution. During the early 1940's, for example, Chillicothe organized an airplane mechanic's school and El Reno concentrated on welding and machine shop techniques. With the short term served and the training completed, the men in these programs were equipped to enter war industries.

Englewood Reformatory, in Colorado, receives boys between the ages of 12 and 21, primarily sentenced under the federal juvenile delinquency act. Their background is primarily rural and substandard economically and educationally. Therefore, education and vocational training are emphasized. The varied program includes both elementary and high school courses, business training, many skilled trades, and agricultural training.

Correctional Institutions

Planned for short-term, tractable, and nonhabitual offenders, the 7 correctional institutions of the federal system demonstrate the policy of the Federal Bureau of Prisons to emphasize a rehabilitation program and to reduce security to the minimum needed for a specific class of prisoners. The institutions tend to be self-enclosing, that is, the buildings themselves frame the institution rather than a high and forbidding wall. In the agricultural type, farms may extend beyond the enclosure. The capacity ranges from 350 to 600 inmates, with the actual population below capacity in many of the institutions. The small number facilitates personal study and counseling of the inmates. Dormitory rooms and individual honor rooms reduce the prison atmosphere and hold out a promise of fairly normal habits of living. Each institution is characterized by certain types of offenders to whom the program is adjusted.

The correctional institution near Ashland, Kentucky draws primarily from rural areas in the middle south. Approximately a fifth of the men have violated the federal liquor laws; these men are noncriminal in attitude, rural in experience, and often illiterate. During their short terms they are encouraged to learn to read and write and are taught improved agricultural methods. It is the hope of the institution to return them to their rural homes with better attitudes and methods of making a living.

The institution near Tallahassee, Florida receives a similar type of offender from the southeastern states. Two fifths of the inmates are liquor-law violators. Again, agriculture is the chief occupation; a modern laundry is also operated. When it was discovered that Puerto Ricans among the inmates were having difficult adjustments, a special educational program was initiated for them.

At LaTuna, Texas, 65 per cent of the inmates in the correctional institution are Mexican violators of immigration laws. They are young, noncriminal in attitude, and responsive to the program of scientific farming. When released, they are returned to Mexico.

The institutions at Texarkana, Texas, Seagoville, Texas, and Milan, Michigan have heavy proportions of violators of federal narcotic drug and marihuana laws—34, 27, and 55 per cent respectively. They also have many violators of immigration laws among men coming either from Mexico or Canada.

The Danbury, Connecticut institution receives men from New England and New York, whose offenses are primarily transporting motor vehicles across state lines, other larcenies, and men sentenced by military courts-martial.

Prison Camps

The federal prison system includes 9 prison camps located in the southern and western parts of the United States with the one exception at Allenwood, Pennsylvania. These camps are minimum security institutions, often with little structural provisions for security, especially in camps whose inmates are engaged in mountain road construction. Isolation and the necessity of moving the camp from time to time tend to transform prison camps into work camps.

The inmates tend to fall into two general types. Many are short-term prisoners who would be held in idleness in overcrowded jails if work camps were not provided. Two camps opened in Arizona during 1952 were especially designed for Mexicans who had entered the United States illegally. Other offenders are found in these camps also, but in one camp approximately 70 per cent and in the other about 20 per cent are immigration violators.   The second type of inmate is the long-termer who is nearing the end of his period of incarceration.   The camp with its relative freedom and normal working day gives preparation for release and complete freedom.

In addition to men who have broken immigration laws, there are many violators of federal liquor and drug laws and of laws related to transportation of motor vehicles.   Each camp includes also a miscellaneous group of offenders.   Men for the camps are carefully chosen, since successful operation depends upon the trustworthiness of the men and their willingness to respond to the program.

Women's Reformatory

The federal reformatory at Alderson, West Virginia, receives women offenders and girls sentenced under the federal juvenile delinquency act from all parts of the United States.   Opened in 1927, it represents the modern type of cottage construction and has a program that is a model for women's reformatories.

Other Federal Institutions

The Federal Bureau of Prisons also maintains a detention headquarters in New York City for males awaiting trial or serving short sentences.   Other than this jail, the Bureau of Prisons does not maintain jails, but inspects county jails and selects those that meet certain standards in which to place federal suspects before trial.   Federal narcotics offenders in need of treatment are sent to special institutions at Fort Worth, Texas, and Lexington, Kentucky, operated by the Public Health Service, which also operates St. Elizabeth's Hospital in Washington, D.C., to which mentally disturbed federal offenders are sent.   In Springfield, Missouri, is a Medical Center for physically and mentally disturbed male offenders.

Finally, the Federal Bureau of Prisons maintains training schools for boys in Washington, D.C. and in Virginia.

Advantages of the Federal System

The basic advantage of the federal system is that each prisoner may, after careful study, be placed in an institution best suited to his rehabilitation.   If he does not adjust in the institution to which he is first assigned, he may be transferred to another institution.   Only those prisoners who are dangerous and rebellious—whom, in short, we do not know how to help—are placed in maximum security institutions.   Criminals who respond to training and treatment programs and who learn to accept responsibility are given the opportunity to live under conditions with as little restriction as is necessary.

The system also facilitates the use of a trained staff that includes professionals from many fields and also a carefully selected and trained custodial staff who are in daily contact with the prisoners.

The standards of administration and operation are set by the Federal Bureau of Prisons, which functions under the leadership of outstanding penologists who view their task as one of rehabilitation of prisoners so that they may accept normal responsibilities when released from prison.

STATE SYSTEMS

Many states are moving toward diversified institutions integrated under a central state administration board. A central classification board is then necessary for the most effective operation of the system; the classification board replaces the judge in determining in which institution the prisoner will receive most benefit. California is credited with having perhaps the best developed state system, with institutions ranging from work camps and a minimum security correctional institution to maximum security prisons. The old maximum security prisons at Folsom and San Quentin are still in use, but modifications of plant and program have brought them into line with modern standards and made them part of the entire system. Prisoners from the courts are received at classification centers for study of their potential capacity for rehabilitation before they are assigned to a specific institution.

The greatest difficulty in developing a modern prison system is faced by states with few prisoners. In these states the expenditure of funds necessary for many small individual institutions hardly seems justified. Some states are meeting this situation by diversification within one institution. New Mexico, with approximately 675 prisoners, is an example. The new prison, occupied late in 1954, is adapted to many types of prisoners and contains possibilities for expansion as needed. The caption under the accompanying illustration explains the way in which various classifications of prisoners are segregated in the cell blocks, with centrally located administrative and service units to serve all groups. The chief objective of the new plant is rehabilitation and retraining. For assignment within the prison and planning of each prisoner's program, a classification procedure is used, with testing of each prisoner and careful study of his record and potentialities. The total plans for activities at the time the building was completed included an ambitious and diversified industrial program. Thorough vocational training is a part of the educational activities. The prison also operates a farm outside the walls for men who can accept a minimum of custody measures.

warden of Sing Sing, but traces the history of the prison and changes in treatment of prisoners from its beginning to the time of his book.

McKelvey, Blake, *American Prisons, a Study in American Social History Prior to 1915* (Chicago: University of Chicago Press, 1936). A well-documented history of various trends in prison administration in the different regions of the United States. Excellent for a background of present conditions.

Manual of Suggested Standards for a State Correctional System (rev. ed. New York: American Prison Association, 1954). Standards devised by the leading association interested in prison reform.

Proceedings of the American Prison Association. Published annually, the *Proceedings* contain a variety of articles on prison problems and procedures. The Association also publishes a journal called *Prison World*.

Scudder, Kenyon D., *Prisoners Are People* (Doubleday, 1952). An excellent description of methods used at a minimum security institution (California Institution for Men) and discussion of the philosophy of such an institution.

FOOTNOTES

[1] *National Prisoner Statistics*, No. 9 (Washington: Federal Bureau of Prisons, U.S. Department of Justice, Aug., 1953), Table 1.

[2] *National Prisoner Statistics*, No. 8 (Washington: Federal Bureau of Prisons, U.S. Department of Justice, April, 1953).

[3] Thorsten Sellin (ed.), "Murder and the Death Penalty," *Annals of American Academy of Political and Social Science*, Vol. 284 (Nov. 1952).

[4] Morris Ploscowe, *Crime and Criminal Law*, National Law Library, 2 (New York: Collier, 1939), 284–85.

[5] *North Carolina Prison Department* (Raleigh: North Carolina Prison Department, undated), p. 6.

[6] *Federal Prisons, 1952* (Washington: Federal Bureau of Prisons, U.S. Department of Justice, 1952), p. 2.

[7] Paul W. Tappan (ed.), *Contemporary Correction* (McGraw-Hill, 1951), p. 276.

[8] Lewis E. Lawes, *Twenty Thousand Years in Sing Sing* (New York: Long and Smith, 1932), pp. 74ff.

[9] Lawes, *op. cit.*, pp. 160ff.

[10] Donald Clemmer, *The Prison Community* (Boston: Christopher, 1940), p. 72.

[11] C. T. Duffy, "The Function of the Prison to Prepare for Freedom," *Proceedings of the American Prison Association* (1945), p. 131.

[12] *Biennial Report for the Period Ending December 1, 1952* (Sacramento: Department of Corrections, State of California, 1952), pp. 19–20.

[13] Robert E. Burns, *I am a Fugitive from a Georgia Chain Gang* (Vanguard, 1932).

[14] *Supplementary Report* (Montgomery, Ala.: Department of Corrections and Institutions, Oct. 15, 1948), p. 3.

[15] *Annual Report, 1952–53* (Montgomery, Ala.: Board of Corrections, State of Alabama, 1953).

[16] Malcolm C. Moos, *State Penal Administration in Alabama* (University, Ala.: University of Alabama, 1942).

[17] *The Prison Labor Problem in Georgia* (Washington: United States Prison Industries Reorganization Administration, 1937).

[18] *An Act of the Legislature of the State of Georgia Creating the State Board of Corrections. . . .* Senate Bill No. 284, Act No. 617, Approved Feb. 1, 1946.

[19] *Rules and Regulations Governing the Penal System* (Atlanta, Ga.: State Board of Corrections, State of Georgia, 1946).

[20] *An Act of the Legislature of the State of Georgia Creating the State Board of Corrections, op. cit.*, p. 4.

[21] *Annual Report of the State Board of Corrections* (Atlanta, Ga.: State Board of Corrections, State of Georgia, 1953), pp. 2–3.

[22] *Annual Report, 1951–52* (Richmond, Va.: Department of Welfare and Institutions, Commonwealth of Virginia, 1952), p. 40.

[23] *Classification Manual for Virginia Penal System* (Richmond, Va.: State Department of Welfare and Institutions, 1953).

[24] *State Correctional System in New Jersey,* Research Bulletin, No. 111 (Trenton, N.J.: Department of Institutions and Agencies, Nov. 1953), p. 5.

[25] *Delinquent Children and Youth in State Correctional Institutions in New Jersey,* Research Bulletin No. 110 (Trenton, N.J.: Department of Institutions and Agencies, Nov., 1953), p. 10.

[26] Kenyon J. Scudder, *Prisoners are People* (Doubleday, 1952).

[27] *Ibid.*

[28] *Gearing Federal Prisons to the War Effort* (Washington: Federal Bureau of Prisons, U.S. Department of Justice, 1942), p. 52.

[29] Scudder, *op. cit.*

[30] *Gearing Federal Prisons to the War Effort; Federal Prisons, 1953* (Washington: Federal Bureau of Prisons, U.S. Department of Justice, 1954); Tappan, *Contemporary Correction,* ch. 5.

16

Life in Prison: Administration and Control

The problem of housing several hundred or several thousand criminals in one institution requires a formal organization to carry out the traditional obligations of physical care and safe custody as well as the newer obligations of re-education and rehabilitation.

PRISON POPULATION

The population of the prison is important in a discussion of administration and program. Individual institutions may have as few as 50 prisoners, as is true of some southern road camps, or be the size of a small village with 3,000 prisoners, as Ohio Penitentiary, or 6,500 as in Southern Michigan Prison. For the larger prisons all the services of a village are needed to supply the normal human needs of any large aggregate of people, governmental, medical, dental, food, clothing, housing, religious, recreational, and employment. In addition, the nature of the prison population creates special needs and their attendant services.

The prison population is always composed of only one sex. When, as as is still true in some states, men and women are housed in the same prison, they are completely separated and have no contacts. Usually officers and attendants are of the same sex as the prisoners.

The age distribution is not normal. Correctional schools usually house all offenders of juvenile delinquency age; adult institutions begin with the age just above the juvenile delinquency age. Reformatories and minimum security institutions may have a preponderance of young adults, and prisons more than their proportion of older men. Nevertheless, a wide adult age range is typically found in prisons, as Table 15 shows, with predominance, however, in the young adult age.

Most prisoners are members of the prison community for less than 5 years. Table 16 shows 76 per cent in this group. A small percentage of men are

TABLE 15

Age of Male Prisoners Admitted during One Year to Four State Prisons

Age	Per Cent
Under 20 years	8
20–29	38
30–39	26
40–49	17
50–59	9
60 and over	2
Number	2,965

Source: Annual reports of admissions during one year to state prisons in 1 eastern, 1 middle western, 1 western, and 1 southern state. In this Table and Tables 16–19 reformatories, prison farms, and work camps are not included.

TABLE 16

Sentences of Male Prisoners Admitted during One Year to Four State Prisons

Length of Sentence	Per Cent
Under 1 year	8
1–5	68
6–10	14
11–20	4
Over 20	2
Life	4
Number	2,258

Source: Annual reports of admissions during one year from the courts to state prisons in 1 eastern, 1 middle western, 1 western, and 1 southern state.

sentenced to 20 or more years and some have life sentences. Since many are released on parole before expiration of their terms, the actual number of years in prison is less than the periods of time shown in the table. Most prisoners are, in fact, little better than transients.

This ever-changing male population has been guilty in most instances of some form of theft (Table 17), the most common types being burglary, forgery, and automobile larceny. These are crimes that usually involve little if any threat of bodily harm to the victims. Criminals who are deliberate killers are rare indeed and the entire group guilty of murder, manslaughter, and assaults equals only one fifth of the prison commitments. Sex offenders constitute only 5 per cent. The prison population, therefore, is primarily composed of men who did not respect other people's property, and not of vicious killers or rapists intent on bodily harm.

Although about one third of male prisoners are recidivists, two thirds

TABLE 17

Offenses for Which Male Prisoners Were Sentenced to Prison in Six States

Type of Offense	Per Cent
Property crimes	71
Assaults and homicides	19
Sex offenses	5
Other	5
Number	6,385

Source: Annual reports of admissions from the courts during one year to state prisons in 1 eastern, 1 middle western, 1 western, and 3 southern states.

are first offenders (Table 18). In reformatories, the percentage of first offenders would be even higher. However, 15 per cent of all incoming prisoners have had 3 or more—sometimes many more—previous commitments to jail, juvenile institution, or adult prison. This group poses a very different problem in rehabilitation from the first offender.

TABLE 18

Recidivism among Male Prisoners Admitted during One Year to Five State Prisons

Number of Commitments	Per Cent
One	63
Two	14
Three	8
Four or more	15
Number	4,983

Source: Annual reports of admissions from the courts during one year to state prisons in 1 eastern, 1 western, and 3 southern states.

Many prisoners come from disorganized marital backgrounds. Only 36 per cent of male prisoners were married and living with their wives at the time of their commitment to prison. Table 19 shows the unstable quality of their marital relationships.

Later data show that their educational background is poor—more than half having less than eighth grade education.

A generalized picture of the male prison inmate is of a young adult, poorly educated, unmarried or with a broken marriage, who has been dishonest, perhaps repeatedly, and who has been removed from normal society and imprisoned, partly as punishment and partly in the hope that he can be rehabilitated and returned to the community a normally conventional person.

TABLE 19

Marital Status of Male Prisoners Admitted during One Year to Five State Prisons

Marital Status	Per Cent
Single	42
Married	36
Widowed	2
Separated	8
Divorced	12
Number	3,434

Source: Annual reports of admissions from the courts during one year to state prisons in 1 eastern, 1 middle western, 1 western, and 2 southern states.

Reformatories and minimum security institutions would vary from this picture only slightly, with somewhat younger ages and fewer serious crimes. It is not only to punish but to meet the human needs of these men and to restore them to conventional ways of living that systems of prisons have been built and elaborate programs developed.

PRISON ADMINISTRATION

The trend in administration of state penal institutions has been to remove it from local to state control.[1]

Prison Boards

When state prisons were considered local institutions, local boards appointed by the governor of the state in turn selected the warden and acted as his adviser on matters of policy and administration. These boards were composed of leading citizens who served without pay. With the increase in number and size of prisons, opportunities for private profit developed, for the board determined purchases. Gradually supervision of prisons was centralized in state agencies, until now some form of state control is the accepted pattern.

Great variety exists in the methods of state control. In some states control is vested in a board or a department. This board or department may be in charge only of prisons or it may be in charge of a number of welfare agencies. The members may be paid or unpaid. In other states, a superintendent of prisons may be in charge of prisons or a director of welfare may control both prisons and other welfare agencies. In other states, in addition to a state board or department, individual institutions have local boards of trustees. Still other states have both a board or department and a director of welfare or superintendent in charge of prisons. The trend is toward centralized control in the hands of a paid board or a paid director. The board is usually appointed by the governor.

Although there is some controversy as to whether it is advisable to have the state control of prisons vested in a general welfare department or in an independent department, an independent board of control is recommended by the American Prison Association for states with a large prison population and numerous penal institutions. Such a board encourages the appointment of professional personnel and the integration of a variety of correctional functions. With its chief function the operation of prisons, the board may also include parole; in some states it has supervision over jails. A central agency with control over the various phases of correction is necessary for an integrated state system of correction.

In political affiliation, the boards may be members of one party, or they may be bipartisan and represent the two dominant parties, or nonpartisan in an attempt to have persons of a variety of backgrounds. The wholly partisan board has little continuity as a rule as it may be changed with each change of the political group in control of state offices. Bipartisan and nonpartisan boards remain in office longer and hence offer more continuity to prison policies and more stability to tenure of wardens. Bipartisan or nonpartisan control is found in only a few states.

With reference to individual prisons, the duties of the board of control usually are: [2]

1. Selection of a warden.
2. Formulation of general rules of administration.
3. Determination of the budget, including salaries.
4. Purchase of supplies and awarding of contracts.
5. Presentation of the requirements of the institutions to the governor and state legislature.

The quality of performance of the board of control in carrying out these duties depends upon the quality of the members of the board. Individual gain and political advantage may determine what is done in one state, while in another a high level of ethical standards may direct the action of the board, which then functions for public safety and prisoner rehabilitation.

The Warden

The prison is an autocracy whose ruler is the warden. Lewis E. Lawes, for a long time warden of Sing Sing Prison, has stated that prison administration "savors of the nature of a despotism." Lawes' attitude was that the successful prison administrator was the "benevolent despot as well as the understanding leader." [3] Officially, the warden's task is to retain the prisoner within the prison.   Much of what he does over and above this duty depends upon his interest, sense of humanity, and enlightenment.   Even when a state prison board outlines the broad penal policies of a state, or a classification committee makes recommendations, there is little check upon how the warden actually carries out the daily administration of the prison. Often his chief concern is to maintain order and prevent trouble; he may accomplish this purpose by a maximum of isolation of the prisoners in their cells and a minimum of social and educational opportunities.   He may also attain this end by imposing heavy penalties for even minor infractions of rules, such as solitary confinement, whipping, or other physical punishment, even though forbidden by law.   He makes the rules that the prisoner must obey, and he devises the means of enforcing obedience.

It should be clearly understood that prison rules and punishment have nothing to do with the original sentence given the prisoner for his crime; they are solely to maintain whatever degree of routine order the warden thinks is desirable.   Wardens who are more interested in the rehabilitation of their charges than in uniformity in all minute details of daily living introduce recreation, libraries, educational classes, and a certain freedom of communication.   But these amenities are simply "privileges" that the warden allows; they are not rights that the prisoner can expect or demand.   And if the prisoner disobeys regulations these privileges may be withdrawn at the warden's will.   This situation places enormous power in his hands.   When it is considered that most wardens are political appointees usually without training in either institutional administration or handling criminals, the danger of this concentration of power is apparent.   Some wardens, by experience and personal attributes have developed into efficient administrators and humane leaders of the men under their care, but many more are both inefficient and ignorant of how to handle men either for an orderly but unoppressive prison life or a return to normal community living.

Sanford Bates, formerly in charge of the Federal Bureau of Prisons, states what may be regarded as the enlightened warden's point of view toward his position.[4]

Many wardens have been heard to remark that the first requirement of a well conducted prison is discipline.   Everything must be subordinated to that end, and unless they are able to discipline their inmates they cannot control the prison. The first dictionary definition of "discipline" is: "To train to obedience, subjection or effectiveness; drill; educate."   The second meaning, "To punish or chastise."

Fortunate is the warden who can maintain his institution through the imposition of the educational type of discipline rather than the punitive.   When we are able to define prison discipline as punishment for the sake of training, and when we are clever enough to instill into the minds of the inmates some realization of this purpose of a prison, we shall have solved some of the most troublesome of the practical problems of prison management.

The deputy warden in most prisons is an absolute monarch. It is his duty to pass upon the reported infractions of the rules by inmates, to decide as justly as he can as to guilt or innocence and to mete out punishment. He must be neither too soft nor too harsh. He must be able to penetrate the subterfuge and artifice with which a thousand clever inmates cloak their peccadillos. He must not allow himself to be surprised. He must let the inmates know that he is always the master of the ship, and he cannot permit insolence, insubordination, or defiance. On the other hand, he must be fair. He must be just. He must understand the failings and the shortcomings not only of his prisoners but of his officers. Some officers have a knack of getting along with prisoners and never have to make a report, others are in trouble a great deal of the time. Sometimes it pays to overlook an infraction of the rules, provided doing so will not break down the morale of the institution.

The warden and his deputy in a modern penal institution must therefore rely on something more than brute force and punitive discipline. The day of the lash, the water cure, the paddle, the rack, and the torture chamber have gone from our American prisons. But the necessity for corrective discipline has not.

GUARDS

Although the warden makes the rules and grants the privileges, the guards, who operate under a deputy warden or a head guard, enforce the rules and are the representatives of the prison administration who have daily, first-hand contacts with the prisoners. Also, under the present penal system, the guards must be depended upon to carry out many of the recommendations of the classification committee in prisons where it functions. The guard, therefore, is in a strategic position.

Unfortunately, guards are rarely equipped, either by selection or training, to offer a constructive contribution to the prisoner's rehabilitation. The first obstacle to the choice of good men for guards arises in the method of selection.

Selection

Most guards are appointed by the warden. The warden, himself usually a political appointee, tends to choose those who have performed some minor service for the party he represents or who are relatives or friends of politicians. This system results in a short and uncertain tenure of office, as each election may produce a new warden and perhaps new guards.

In a few states civil service examinations are given to prospective guards.[5] This procedure does not necessarily assure appointment of men adequate to the task. Much depends upon the type of examination given; such examinations often merely screen out the obviously unfit, but do not draw to the occupation persons best fitted for the work.   Also, wardens may circumvent the purpose of the examination by making temporary appointments.

Undesirable Aspects of the Guard's Position

Long hours and low pay are characteristic of most prisons.   When the job is thought of primarily as one of custody, it is monotonous and unstimulating.   The guard as well as the prisoner is confined within a penal institution, and he is subject to strict rules regarding his conduct and his relationship to the prisoners.   In general, the guard is instructed not to have social contacts with prisoners, and to speak to them only when necessary. Therefore, although in physical contact with many men, he is in a peculiar condition of social isolation.

In the occasional time of riot, the guards must bring the mass of irrational men under control and herd them into their cells, where locked doors release the guards from danger.   In some riots, guards have been held for hours or several days as hostages, under constant threat of injury or death if demands of the rioters are not met by prison officials.   Escapes also place additional burdens upon guards.

New Concept of Prisoner-guard Relationship

In the federal prisons and in some reformatories the position of the guard is undergoing reformulation with emphasis on helpfulness to the prisoners rather than wholly on authoritarianism.   This statement does not mean that there are fewer guards but rather that their functions are redefined, and along with the change in functions has often gone a change in title.   The Federal Bureau of Prisons calls all its guards correctional officers and instructors and those of a higher rank, correctional supervisors; these people form the custodial service.   These officers have the responsibility of maintaining order and preventing escapes—the traditional guard duties—but in addition they provide on-job training of prisoners and give advice and counsel.[6]   The California Institution for Men calls guards supervisors and emphasizes a helpful relationship between men and guards.[7]   In his initial selection of supervisors when the Institution opened in 1940, Superintendent Scudder refused to accept anyone with previous experience as a prison guard.   When the work of guards is thought of in terms of a helpful, counseling relationship, selection and training become extremely important.   The guard has a difficult line to walk: he must maintain order and therefore represents authority to the prisoners; at the same time he must understand the men and their problems and try to help them, but always within the framework of the institution and without violating the degree of social distance found necessary in asserting necessary authority.

Training of Guards

When rehabilitation as well as custody is an objective of the prison, training is needed other than in the use of firearms and jiu jitsu.   The Federal Bureau of Prisons has experimented over many years to find adequate methods of selection and training of its correctional officers.[8]   Civil-service examinations are used to make the first selection of potential officers; a finer selection is made by the use of a standardized test of judgment that reveals two essential qualities, "a genuine feeling for people and good practical judgment."   New personnel are then enrolled in a 4 week basic training course, which results in the elimination of individuals not suited to correctional work.   The course consists of a week of group instruction and 3 weeks of instruction on 14 posts within the prison—in the dining room, shops, classroom, recreation areas, and so on.   Advanced training is offered a selected group of experienced officers and consists of a 5 day training conference followed by an independent investigation of some special prison problem, carried out on the officer's own time.   In 1953 a third training device was added, known as quarterly training; every 3 months each employee receives 4 hours of intensive instruction.   Employees are also encouraged to read professionally and each federal institution contains a staff library of professional books.

Promotions in the federal prison system are made on the basis of performance tests in various skills used by the staff and a 2 week trial assignment.

The most comprehensive state training programs are carried out in states that place the greatest emphasis on rehabilitation.   New Jersey is outstanding in having instituted a training program in 1930, which involved 300 hours of intensive training over a period of 4 weeks.[9]   New York organized the Central Guard School in 1936, but later was forced to curtail the program through failure of the state legislature to appropriate sufficient funds.[10]

California has had a system of in-service training of prison personnel since 1946, carried out in each institution under a full-time training officer.[11]   New correctional officers are allowed 53 hours of training and officers with one or more years of experience, 18 hours per year.   In addition, the new officer is started off on his work with a 40 hour orientation program.   During a 2 year period the courses of instruction cover the following subjects:

Introduction to institutional correction service
Custodial duties and techniques

Introduction to the psychology, guidance, and treatment of prisoners

Supervision techniques in state correctional service

Physical conditioning and self-defense methods

Firearms and chemical equipment

Institutional civil defense and first aid

Camp management

Food handling and sanitation

Control and treatment of the abnormal prisoner

Transportation of prisoners

Such training programs as these are of vital importance in the transformation of prisons from harsh, punitive institutions to correctional centers.

DISCIPLINE

Some definite system of external discipline is no doubt inherent in any prison system. Prisoners have been sent to prison because they have been unable to exert sufficient self-discipline to conform to the mores and laws of society. These men, many of them accustomed to living impulsively or by their own rules, are expected in prison to adapt to a much more rigid routine than they have followed in their private lives. For many, only the threat of punishment holds them to the prison rules and routines. Strict adherence to the rules is regarded by the officials as one of the most important phases of prison life. Any deviation from rules, any defiance of authority, immediately arouses fear that the prisoners will burst into rioting, and perhaps attempt mass escape. The small handful of guards maintains control over a vastly greater number of prisoners by enforcing strict obedience to rules usually through punishment or the threat of punishment. When a state places confirmed criminals and first offenders in one prison, this strict control is imposed upon all alike. In states with a graded system of institutions, the close control is exerted only in the maximum-security prisons with decreasing rigidity of external control in institutions with more amenable offenders.

Discipline by Force

Methods of enforcing order range in different prisons all the way from whipping to programs for prisoner self-government. Traditionally, discipline was enforced by physical punishment. In the restricted life of a prison only a few methods of punishment are possible; few privileges remain to the prisoner that may be denied him. In the past, whipping, physical torture of various sorts, and confinement in a solitary cell often with inadequate food and water were regular recourses when prisoners persisted in violating rules. Although in some prisons these methods have been eliminated or are used only sparingly, many instances of physical punishment are still found today.

Solitary confinement, called by convicts being sent to the "hole," is still in general use.*   The cells for solitary confinement are separate from the

Southern road camps often include small special punishment cells or small buildings.   The illustration shows one type, a sweatbox measuring about 7.5 feet square; in 1941 while 21 prisoners were shut up in this building, one suffocated to death.   Another punishment device is a one-man cell, so small that the prisoner is unable to lie down or even to sit down.   One southern state that prides itself on its construction of permanent road camps publishes in its annual report on road camps the official specifications for a punishment cell.   Built with solid wooden walls and door, the cell must measure 3 feet wide, 6 feet 6 inches long, and 7 feet high.   In the daytime a partition can be inserted to divide the cell in half, limiting the prisoner to floor space of 3 feet 3 inches by 3 feet.   Ventilation is provided by a screened vent at the top of the cell.

others; often they are completely dark, or narrow openings may allow some light to enter but are so arranged as to prevent the prisoner from looking out. Usually there is no furniture, and the prisoner must sleep on the floor.

* References to solitary confinement are made in most personal accounts of prison life written by ex-prisoners, in some prison reports, and in specifications for prison construction.

Solitary confinement is usually accompanied by a restricted diet and limited water allowance.   In the past—and no doubt still in some prisons—these restrictions were so severe as to cause great suffering from hunger and especially thirst.   The more modern prisons still use solitary confinement as a method of punishment, but they provide sufficient food and water to avoid illness or too great suffering and also provide that a physician shall visit the prisoner each day to check on his health.   While confined, the prisoner has no one with whom to talk, has no visitors, receives and writes no letters, and sees no one.   Solitary confinement is, therefore, not only physical isolation but also social isolation of an extreme type.   The mental suffering that may accompany it, the monotony, and the strain of having no means of verbal expression are extreme.

Discipline by Manipulating Privileges

Another method of discipline is by manipulating "good time" provisions, which were established more than a hundred years ago.   The early laws provided that for every month that the prisoner conducted himself with propriety, a certain number of days would be deducted from his sentence. At present, the practice is to credit the prisoner upon his entrance to prison with the maximum reduction of sentence that he might receive if he were well behaved throughout his term and then to deduct from his good time, that is, lengthen his sentence, each time he violates a prison rule.   This practice is thus definitely a disciplinary device, since obedience to the rules and the guards will guarantee a reduction of sentence automatically, regardless of whether or not any real change has occurred in the prisoner's attitudes.

The degree to which good time may reduce a sentence is marked.[12]   The reduction may be applied to the minimum period of an indeterminate sentence or to the maximum, or to a definite sentence, according to the laws of the state.   A typical provision is to deduct one month from the first year of the sentence, two months from the second year, and so on, up to five months for the fifth and each succeeding year.   Thus a three-year minimum sentence or a three-year definite sentence can be reduced to two years and six months; a ten-year sentence may be reduced to six years and eight months. The laws of some states provide for still greater allowances; in other states the good time is lower.   These deductions are sufficient to motivate the prisoner to good conduct.

Another incentive to good conduct is the method of the parole system in some states.   The parole board has the authority to release the prisoner under the supervision of the parole officer, before the expiration of his term, if the board feels that the prisoner will adjust to community life.   The prisoner may be eligible for parole after only a third of his minimum sentence has been served, and the period may be further reduced by a good time allowance.   Inasmuch as parole boards consider the prisoner's record before his last conviction, conduct in prison is only one factor in determining parole. But the hope of an early parole is usually sufficiently bright to cause a prisoner to conduct himself with circumspection in order to impress the board favorably.

Other methods of discipline in common use at the present time involve denying the prisoner certain privileges that the warden has permitted to all. These privileges vary from one institution to another.   In one western prison the following privileges were denied for disciplinary purposes.[13]

1. Freedom on Sunday—the prisoner remains locked in his cell all day Sunday on a diet of bread and water.

2. The prisoner's privilege card for a specified period, perhaps 30 days. This card gives the man admission to ball games, the use of the library, the privilege of mailing letters and buying small articles at the prison commissary, and so on.   Thus the loss of the card means a general denial of privileges.

Another device for securing adherence to regulations is the grading system, whereby prisoners are assigned to one of several grades, depending upon conduct.   Sometimes all prisoners upon entrance are assigned to the lowest grade and must then work their way up.   The higher grades carry more privileges than the lower and often entitle the prisoner to wear a different type of uniform.   If a high-grade prisoner violates some rule, he may be reduced to a lower grade and thus lose his privileges and prestige.

Most of the disciplinary methods thus far presented have been in the nature of punishment—some unpleasant experience imposed upon the prisoner because he has deviated from the level of conduct expected of all prisoners. These methods encourage only external temporary conformity and do not provide training in self-discipline or responsible community living.   Here and there experiments have been tried that throw some personal responsibility upon the prisoners for their own conduct and for community orderliness.

The Honor System

The honor system was one of the earliest methods that placed responsibility upon the prisoners.   A limited number of men with records of good conduct were permitted to work outside the prison walls, under a light guard. They were on their honor not to try to escape.   The system has been sometimes criticized as only another privilege granted by the warden to exceptionally well-behaved prisoners.   Nevertheless, it gives the prisoner an opportunity to demonstrate that he can meet some of the demands of conventional society. Many of the present reformatories are regularly run on a system not far different; for example, minimum security institutions of the federal prisons and some state institutions.

Self-Government Programs

An innovation in discipline appeared in the second decade of the twentieth century, when Thomas Mott Osborne organized the Mutual Welfare League first at Auburn Prison and later at Sing Sing, of which he was warden. The antecedent of the Mutual Welfare League was the system of self-government used at the George Junior Republic, with which Osborne was familiar.[14] The George Junior Republic duplicates many features of the normal community; the boys select the cottage where they will live, the jobs they wish to do, and the school courses they will take. An institutional currency is used to pay the boys for work and satisfactory academic marks; the boys in turn pay for their board, room, clothing, and other expenses. The boys organized and operate a town government and their own courts. Inspired by the successful operation of this system, Osborne induced the warden at Auburn Prison to allow him to establish the Mutual Welfare League.

When Osborne became warden of Sing Sing he established a similar system there and brought it to its fullest development. All prisoners could be members of the League, which was governed by delegates elected by them. Within limits set by the warden, the League officers made rules for the conduct of the prisoners, judged disciplinary cases, and assigned punishment. The League had committees for such activities as education, athletics, sanitation, and entertainment. Osborne granted many privileges to the prisoners upon request of the League—visits on Sunday, more latitude in writing letters, the chance to buy stamps instead of depending upon gifts from friends, permission to receive gray sweaters and shoes from the outside, the use of lights until a later hour at night, and reduction of guard supervision while working and going to and from work. Greater yard privileges, more recreation and entertainment, and increased educational classes were granted. Tension between prisoners and guards decreased with the formulation of rules and enforcement of discipline by the League instead of the guards. Breaking a rule no longer meant outwitting a guard or getting even with him, but opposing the prisoner's own organization that had secured many privileges for him.[15]

Osborne's system was a marked change from previous types of prison discipline, which had assumed that all prisoners must be repressed and closely guarded. He assumed that most prisoners would respond to privileges and freedom as any human being would—they would use and enjoy

all prisoners would attempt to escape if given the slightest opportunity; hence the older fortress-like structures.   Open work camps and reformatories have now amply demonstrated that most prisoners do not try to escape if given a reasonably full and varied round of activities.   Nevertheless, certain prisoners are preoccupied with plans for escape and over weeks or months of time will seek to perfect some elaborate scheme that may involve making contacts with people outside of prison to secure tools or weapons or to arrange for safe hiding once the escape is made; or the scheme may involve slowly and secretly tunneling through or under a wall; or the careful study of the habits of guards to discover some laxness in locking cells that may seem to make escape feasible.   Other prisoners simply seize upon some chance incident that makes it possible for them to overpower a guard or snatch keys and weapons and then make a bold and open break for freedom.   Usually only one or a few prisoners are united in these plans or open breaks; mass attempts to escape are unknown, although in some instances additional men might easily join those seeking to escape.

The infrequency of successful escapes is evident from the reports of prisons.   In penal institutions of Pennsylvania during the year ending May 31, 1952, only 27 out of 6,614 male prisoners escaped—a mere 0.4 per cent. No women escaped.[17]   An additional 22 men attempted to escape but were caught and returned.   In California for the year ending June 30, 1952, 80 out of 12,852 prisoners (0.6 per cent) escaped and another 71 made the attempt but were captured and returned to prison.[18]   In Minnesota for the year ending June 30, 1952, 15 out of 2,580 male prisoners escaped, or 0.6 per cent, and another 37 were returned after attempted escape from prison or as fugitives from parole.[19]   No women escaped.

A number of factors operate against attempted escapes.   The procedure is dangerous: the escapee runs the risk of being injured or killed, since in strongly guarded prisons, the guards shoot to kill at an escaping man.   Although we think of crime as calling for great daring, actually most crime does not greatly endanger the life of the criminal; most criminals apparently prefer to wait out their term and secure a safe release.   If the escapee is caught later, he is subject to return to prison and usually heavy penalties. A successful escape, therefore, often is followed by the necessity to avoid family and friends, a change of name, moving to another state—in fact, a change of identity for the rest of the man's life, in order to avoid detection and a return to prison.   The returned escapee loses whatever reduction in sentence he had accumulated for good conduct, and loses his chance at parole; he must serve his full time.   He may be subjected to immediate and severe punishments, for an escape is regarded as the ultimate in defiance of authority and as a threat to the warden's efficiency in keeping prisoners in custody.   He may be placed in solitary confinement in a dark cell with no chance for activity for weeks or months; he may be severely beaten.   If he had previously made a good record and had been transferred to a work camp where he had many privileges, he is returned to prison with its restrictions and repressions.   According to the figures given in the preceding paragraph, there is only about a 50-50 chance that an escape can be made good. A few prisoners take the chance; most prisoners, in the face of the penalties for failure, choose to remain in prison.

Riots

The widespread newspaper publicity given to prison riots (as well as to escapes) gives the erroneous impression that riots are a continuous threat. Actually, they are of rare occurrence, although a riot in one prison is likely to be followed by a series of riots in other prisons.   An outburst of riots in 1952 and early 1953 makes it possible to form some tentative generalizations.[20]

Unlike escapes, which signify the dissatisfaction of a few individuals, riots indicate widespread restlessness and frustrations within the prison population.   Nevertheless, riots rarely involve the entire inmate group, either because guards succeed in locking certain cell blocks and thus confine prisoners not already in the rioting group, or because some prisoners remain orderly and even helpful in the quelling of the riot.

During 1952, 15 state penal institutions experienced riots; in the United States there are 304 state penal institutions.[21]   An estimated 6,400 prisoners participated in the riots; in state penal institutions there are approximately 150,000 prisoners at any one time.   Although it was unusual that so many disturbances occurred in the space of a few months and each disturbance caused great trouble when it occurred, actually in the total prison-life of the country the riots were incidental.   In only a few prisons did a majority of prisoners participate.   In one prison of 3,300 prisoners, 600 ran wild, burning buildings; in contrast, the inmate fire department worked steadily to extinguish the flames.   In another prison of 1,400, the riot involved only 50 men.   In a prison of 600, 43 were rioters.   In South Michigan Prison with 6,500 prisoners, some 2,000 took part in a short, violent riot with burning of buildings, but only 169 participated in the 5 day disturbance during which they locked themselves in their cell block.

Although riots are violent, they are of brief duration.   The various disturbances of 1952 lasted from 2 hours to 5 days.   Only half the disturbances lasted for as long as 24 hours, before the resistance of the prisoners was broken and formal order restored.

The disturbances of a mass nature take a number of different forms, not all of which are violent, although all defy regulations and authority. The difficulties in 1952–53 took these forms in different institutions: prisoners barricaded themselves in cell blocks, sometimes with guards as hostages, while they attempted to force concessions from the prison authorities under threat to harm or kill the guards if their demands were not granted; prisoners destroyed furnishings and equipment of cell blocks or workshops, causing thousands of dollars' worth of damage; prisoners burned buildings, again causing great monetary loss; prisoners "struck" and refused to carry out activities; prisoners milled around, shouting, defying guards, occasionally attacking one of their own number whom they hated.

The riots represent acute social disorganization and temporary loss of control on the part of administration and guards. The immediate reaction of prison officials is to mobilize the entire force of guards and, if necessary, to call upon nearby state police or military forces. All these groups are trained in methods of bringing rioters under control: for instance, in wedge formation, the police force their way into a mob and divide it into smaller groups; by a diagonal advance they may force a mob away from a protecting wall into the open; and by a straight line formation block the advance of a mob, or turn it toward an enclosure. Although guards and police may be ordered by their commanding officers to shoot to kill, as a rule such a procedure is used only as a last resort, and recourse is had to riot guns and tear gas. Firemen may stand by with high pressure hoses to force the mob back if necessary. If the riot occurs in an unwalled institution, police may ring the grounds to prevent escape; or within a prison may ring a building within which prisoners are rioting. Although a few men were killed among both prisoners and police and a number injured in the 1952 riots, the rioters were brought under control with remarkably little injury. When prisoners barricade themselves within a cell block, and especially when they hold guards as hostages, the method becomes one of guarding the building to prevent prisoners from leaving it until they are ready to submit to control; since the prisoners cannot secure food, they are "starved out." From this account it is evident that prisoners who at first seem in control of the prison actually are soon brought under control of police and guards.

During the time when prisoners were able to hold out against police in the 1952 disturbances, they made many demands for changes in prison regulations or in the state policies. Typical were demands for better food, for the removal of certain guards or wardens, for more humane methods of discipline, and for a revision of the parole system. In a few instances, concessions were made to prisoners in order to safeguard hostages; but for the most part, officials simply promised to investigate complaints and recommend or make changes if conditions seemed to call for change. When the promises are made by the warden, they are not necessarily carried out, since state prison officials may overrule him.   In some instances, the warden loses his job as a result of the riots, since one of his functions is to maintain control of the prisoners and a riot may therefore be interpreted as a failure of the warden to fulfill his duties.   Often restrictions are increased for all prisoners with heavy penalties imposed upon the chief rioters, who may be placed in solitary confinement for long periods.   In some instances, prisoners who held guards as hostages are removed to city jails and charged with kidnaping. Heavy-handed wardens may replace ones who have attempted a humanitarian approach.   Riots thus often seem not only to fail in bringing improved conditions but may bring loss of privileges and a more repressive program.

A series of riots, however, stirs up public interest in prisons and leads to inquiries into prison conditions, which bring into the open some of the worst conditions of penal institutions.   As an aftermath of the 1952 riots statements appeared in both popular and professional publications, made by James V. Bennett, director of the Federal Bureau of Prisons, by the wardens of 8 prisons where disturbances occurred, by criminologists, by the deputy warden of one prison, by a state prison commissioner, and by a special committee headed by Richard A. McGee, Director of the California Department of Corrections.   The chief conditions held to be responsible for restlessness and rioting by these specialists and practical administrators were as follows:

1. Large size of some prisons.   The American Prison Association now regards 1,200 as the maximum number of men who can be confined in one institution and receive individual attention.   The South Michigan Prison at Jackson, scene of the 5-day riot, has approximately 6,500 prisoners; the penitentiary at Columbus, Ohio, where heavy damage by fire occurred, has over 3,000 prisoners; Louisiana Penitentiary, Angola, has more than double the ideal number.   Other prisons involved, however, had less than 1,000 prisoners.

2. Overcrowding.   Many prisons have many more inmates than the number for which the prison was built.   If the number of convicted criminals increases in a state that fails to provide additional institutions for them, existing prisons become overcrowded.   Several men are crowded into small cells planned for one man; others may have cots in corridors or be housed in rooms intended for other purposes.   Dissatisfaction grows and tensions develop between closely crowded inmates or between prisoners and guards.

3. Many prisons are outmoded in structure.   Among prisons where riots occurred were some well over 100 years old.   Many such old structures cannot be modernized; they are often dark, damp, and without modern sanitary facilities.   They do not lend themselves to separation of prisoners

Prison standards call for a cell for each inmate, with the cell usually measuring about 6 or 7 feet square. When the number of prisoners exceeds the facilities, the prison administration has no choice but to place more than one man in a cell, as shown above.

The illustration also shows the layout of a typical modern cell. Metal walls and ceiling facilitate cleanliness and prevent escapes. A washbowl and toilet and the minimum necessary furniture are provided. In some prisons the cells remain barren cubicles; in others the prisoners are encouraged to make additional pieces of furniture, such as a bookcase or shelves, and to add such items as a curtain to hide the toilet facilities, or a bedspread. Photographs, a few pictures, hobby material, books, and so forth are permitted in many prisons. In these and other ways many prisons seek to soften the harsh impact of the barred cell, to treat the inmates as human beings, and to help them maintain contact with the world beyond the walls. (Illustration from the Federal Bureau of Prisons.)

into groups graded by responsiveness to rehabilitation, age, or seriousness of offense. Young and old, the hardened criminal and the one who might be rehabilitated are treated alike and usually in terms of the amount of custody required by the most difficult to control.

4. Lack of work. The restrictions on productive work make it impossible for some prisons to keep all men occupied. Idle men or those who can be given only part-time work or minor maintenance jobs that lack interest easily build up resentment and restlessness.

5. Untrained personnel and poor disciplinary methods. The move toward greater freedom of prisoners and rehabilitation for normal community life calls for specially trained personnel. Many wardens and guards are political appointees, changed with every change in state administration. They are unable to maintain order in prison by any methods other than threats and force.

6. Psychopaths. Although seriously psychotic prisoners usually are transferred to a mental institution, psychopaths often remain in the prison. The riot in South Michigan Prison was instigated in the cell block reserved for psychopaths and other incorrigibles. Other prisoners, it is true, had a spontaneous uprising and destroyed and fired the buildings. They were quickly brought under control, whereas the psychopaths locked themselves inside their cell block with guards as hostages, and held out for 5 days. This group of men remained locked in individual cells month after month, while the normal prisoners had many privileges and considerable freedom. The prison was not equipped to treat the psychopaths, but the state had failed to provide a special institution for them.

7. Poor food. Inadequate or poorly prepared food is a standing complaint. In some states the basic reason is that the amount of money allowed for food is too small. But it also seems probable that some of the dissatisfaction stems from the unappetizing way in which the food is served, the inability to eat in small groups with normal conversation, the constant surveillance of the guards.

No one institution is characterized by all the factors listed, but one or two may be enough to create restlessness and repressed hostility. A planned uprising by a few men or a spontaneous event may suddenly release the emotions of a large group and a riot is underway.

It is significant of the present trend in prison administration that when the Committee on Riots of the American Prison Association, consisting of 14 directors of prison systems, wardens of prisons, ministers with experience in prisons, and a professional criminologist, listed preventive measures for riots, very little was said about strictness of rules, punishments for disobedience, or increase of guards. The burden of creating a type of prison life that would not goad prisoners to revolt was placed upon prison administrators. The 5 measures are here summarized.

1. The morale of the prisoners should be kept at a high level through positive measures, such as provision for basic physical needs including adequate food and clothing, proper medical attention, and healthful living conditions; fair and just treatment; and an opportunity to bring their grievances to the attention of prison authorities. When prisoners feel that the administration is mindful of their needs, they respond with an interest in the prison program.

2. Avenues of communication between prisoners and administration are necessary. The administration may learn about the prisoners through contacts with prison activities, observing the daily life at first hand, and casually talking with prisoners. Individual interviews should be arranged for inmates with problems. Informers among the prisoners (stool-pigeons) are now discredited as a means of securing information. The Committee was divided in its opinion as to the advisability of prisoner councils, but it was noted in the report that some wardens had successfully used such councils to establish contact with prisoners.

Administrators need not only to receive information but to be able to transmit to prisoners policies and plans, especially those that will create some change in prison life. Some methods are talks by officials directly or by radio, articles in the prison newspaper, and informal interviews.

3. Discipline should be firm and consistent and should be maintained without relaxation, especially over agitators, aggressive prisoners, drug smugglers, and others calculated to disturb the general order of the prison. It is noted that the best discipline does not rely upon "friction, emotionalism, and punishment."

4. Employee morale also is of major importance. Good judgment on the part of employees, self-discipline, pride in the work, and loyalty to superiors are characteristics of the effective staff.

5. Alertness to real grievances is necessary on the part of the prison administration, so that restlessness and dissatisfaction do not grow, and so that adjustments can be made to eliminate them. The wise warden does not, however, accede to prisoner demands that are not justified, although he explains why they could not be granted.

These recommendations place upon the administration the responsibility of maintaining order firmly and fairly. At the same time the administration must recognize and, so far as is possible within the confines of a prison, satisfy the common human needs of the inmates.

QUESTIONS

1. Reconcile Bates' statement of the warden's need to maintain discipline with modern programs of rehabilitation?

2. What training does the guard need to enable him to fit into the new plans of prison administration and rehabilitation?

3. Contrast repressive measures of discipline (corporal punishment, use of solitary confinement) with incentive measures (good time, privileges). Which measures seem more sound psychologically? What better methods of discipline would you suggest?

4. Is there a place for solitary confinement in the prison program? If so, how should it be used?

5. Why do not more prisoners attempt to escape?

6. How might the probability of riots be reduced?

READINGS

Many of the books listed under Readings for Chapter 15 are applicable to Chapter 16.

Osborne, Thomas Mott, *Prisons and Common Sense* (Lippincott, 1924).
———, *Society and Prisons* (New Haven: Yale University Press, 1916).
———, *Within Prison Walls* (Appleton, 1914). Osborne's attempts to substitute self-government among prisoners for strict control by the warden and his granting of privileges were regarded as radical and dangerous. He became a controversial figure in penal reform and politically. These books relate his efforts at prison reform and his philosophy of treatment.
Tappan, Paul W. (ed.), *Contemporary Correction* (McGraw-Hill, 1951). Excellent discussions of administrative procedures, programs of treatment, and types of institutions, written by specialists in their various fields.

For further reading on prison riots, see the references listed under footnote 20.

FOOTNOTES

[1] *Attorney General's Survey of Release Procedures,* Vol. 5, *Prisons* (Washington: U.S. Department of Justice, 1939), ch. 3.

[2] W. J. Ellis, "Public Control and Supervision of Prisons," *Annals of the American Academy of Political and Social Science,* 57 (1931), 47–48.

[3] C. T. Duffy, "The Function of the Prison to Prepare for Freedom," *Proceedings of the American Prison Association* (1945), 131.

[4] Sanford Bates, *Prisons and Beyond* (Macmillan, 1936), pp. 176ff.

[5] K. J. Scudder, "In-service Training," *Proceedings of the American Prison Association* (1941), pp. 247–54.

[6] *Federal Prisons, 1953* (Washington: Federal Bureau of Prisons, U.S. Department of Justice, 1954), pp. 33–39.

[7] K. J. Scudder, *Prisoners are People* (Doubleday, 1952).

[8] *Federal Prisons, 1953,* pp. 33–39.

[9] W. J. Ellis, "New Jersey's Program for Training Prison and Reformatory Officers," *Proceedings of the American Prison Association* (1941), pp. 277–82.

[10] W. M. Wallack, *The Training of Prison Guards in the State of New York* (New

York: Teachers College, Columbia University, 1938); "Prison Reform in New York," *Journal of Criminal Law, Criminology, and Police Science,* 43 (1952), 223–24.

[11] *Biennial Report for the Period Ending December 31, 1952* (Sacramento: Department of Corrections, State of California, 1952), p. 25.

[12] *Prisoners in State and Federal Prisons and Reformatories, 1943* (Washington: Bureau of the Census, 1946), pp. 30–31.

[13] D. A. Lamson, *We Who Are about To Die* (Scribner's, 1935), pp. 98ff.

[14] Sheldon and Eleanor T. Glueck (eds.), *Preventing Crime* (McGraw-Hill, 1936).

[15] Thomas Mott Osborne, *Society and Prisons* (New Haven: Yale University Press, 1916); Frank Tannenbaum, *Osborne of Sing Sing* (Chapel Hill: University of North Carolina Press, 1933).

[16] Lewis E. Lawes, *Twenty Thousand Years in Sing Sing* (New York: Long and Smith, 1932), pp. 112ff., 194–95.

[17] *Eighteenth Annual Statistical Report of the Department of Welfare,* Bulletin No. 102, *Penal* (Harrisburg: Commonwealth of Pennsylvania, 1952), Section B.

[18] *Biennial Report for the Period Ending December 31, 1952* (California), p. 48.

[19] *Biennial Report for the Period Ended June 30, 1952* (St. Paul: Division of Public Institutions, State of Minnesota, 1952), p. 327.

[20] The discussion of riots is based on the following: Sanford Bates, "The Significance of Prison Riots," *Focus,* 32 (1953), 129–34; James V. Bennett, "Prisons in Turmoil," *Federal Probation,* 16 (Dec. 1952), 3–6; Committee on Riots, *Prison Riots and Disturbances* (New York: American Prison Association, 1953); Vernon Fox and Bill Fay, "How I Broke the Michigan Prison Riot," *Collier's,* 130 (July 12, 1952), 11–13, 48–49; Austin MacCormick, "Behind the Prison Riots," *Annals of the American Academy of Political and Social Science,* 293 (1954), 17–27; D. P. Wilson and H. E. Barnes, "Riot is an Unnecessary Evil," *Life,* 33 (Nov. 24, 1952), 138–40; "Aftermath of Riot," *Prison Journal,* 24 (April, 1954), entire issue; and numerous news reports on the riots of 1952.

[21] Austin MacCormick, "The Prison's Role in Crime Prevention," *Journal of Criminal Law and Criminology,* 41 (1950), 36–37.

Life in Prison: Services and Activities

Within the framework of rules and regulations designed to maintain order, numerous activities and services have been organized for the benefit and welfare of the prisoners. In addition to the programs sponsored by the prison administration there are the informal groupings and social relationships among prisoners and between prisoners and guards that grow spontaneously as imprisoned men seek to fulfill their personal and social needs.

ADMISSION SYSTEMS

The individual prisoner enters the prison world through an admission routine. Simple admission systems make an identification record of each incoming prisoner, discover a few simple facts about physical condition, and assign the man to a cell and some form of work. A slightly more elaborate system explores the prisoner's potential capacities further and gives him some orientation to prison life. The routine followed in a southern prison may be used as illustration.

In this prison a series of interviews continues through the first 8 to 10 days of the prisoner's sentence, culminating in the man's assignment to work. Upon first arriving at the prison, the inmate is registered in the Identification Office, given a prison number, issued an outfit of clothing, and assigned to a cell. The man is then interviewed by the identification officer; he is photographed, fingerprinted, and examined for marks and scars that later might serve to identify him. On the following day, the Department of Records and Personnel secures a short biography and criminal history of the prisoner. A thorough physical examination, including blood and other tests, is given by the prison physician. The educational director talks with each man, and administers psychological and aptitude tests. The prison chaplain discusses the religious services offered and attempts to establish a friendly relationship that may lead to future counseling. Finally, the prison superintendent interviews the prisoner with the purpose of establishing a close contact with him.

After this series of interviews, the new prisoner is assigned to work according to his physical condition; transfers may later be made. The man may be assigned to a farm operated outside the prison grounds or to various industries operated by the prison, such as a shop for automobile license tags, a tannery, saw mill, shoe factory, laundry, tobacco factory, and syrup plant. Other work is provided in maintenance shops, such as the machine shop, electric shop, and ice plant.

Along with the various interviews and testing sessions, the prisoner receives a certain amount of orientation; he is also provided upon his arrival with a booklet of rules and regulations, which opens by telling the prisoner:

You are now in the hands of the State Government. Respect of it will win for you an invisible and powerful friend. Scorn of it may make a terrible and unforgiving foe.

Seventeen rules are listed, emphasizing prompt and unquestioning obedience to the officer in charge of the prisoner, diligence, cleanliness of cell, and absence of weapons, liquor, and playing cards. Mail and visiting regulations are outlined and the various services listed: religious activities, social service, educational training, library, athletics, and recreation. The booklet also states the factors considered for reduction of sentence and the amount by which sentences of different length may be reduced.

This admission system and others of its type make only a rudimentary attempt to deal with the prisoner as an individual personality. They attempt to fit the man into activities to which he seems fitted but do not penetrate into underlying factors or provide very much in the way of rehabilitation programs beyond what the prisoner can gain for himself from work, recreation, such educational classes as he chooses, voluntary attendance at religious services, and such friendly counseling as the chaplain offers. In other prisons the admissions system has been expanded into a classification system.

CLASSIFICATION SYSTEMS

A few states have developed a new type of admission procedure, called a classification system, in which the basic principle is the development of a special program for each prisoner that is most likely to assist him toward rehabilitation. In a rudimentary form, classification may consist simply of placing a prisoner in a special type of institution. As the various states established specialized types of institutions, judges were able to sentence each offender to the institution to which the judge thought he belonged, a procedure still followed in most states.   Wardens may later transfer obvious misfits to other institutions: for instance, a prisoner who exhibits insanity may be transferred to the special institution for the criminal insane; or a youth who is incorrigible when sent to the reformatory may be transferred to an institution of greater security and more rigorous discipline; or an old professional convict, worn out with the years, may be transferred from prison to the penal farm.

Classification Committees

A development of classification that came in the 1930's focused attention on each prisoner after conviction and at the beginning of his prison term.[1] This procedure was authorized not by the judge who sentenced the prisoner but by a state correctional system or an individual prison.   The essence of the procedure was the work of a group or committee of professionally trained people who examined and studied each incoming man.   At first largely merely advisory to the warden, classification committees in some prisons now have advanced to a stage of active program planning with the warden.

The classification committee therefore has a dual aim; diagnosis of the problems of the individual prisoner; and planning of a rehabilitative program for him, compatible with the sentence given by judge or jury. Diagnosis alone is of no value in rehabilitation unless it leads to a practical corrective program.   In the past, group or mass activities have been used in prisons without regard for the needs of individual prisoners and have failed to benefit many prisoners.   The classification committee relates activity to diagnosis in an effort to achieve rehabilitation.

Whereas the conventional prison personnel is made up primarily of guards with a small professional group composed of warden, physician, and chaplain, classification brings to the prison sociologists, social workers, psychiatrists, and psychologists.   These professionals do not replace the older group but add to their special approaches the knowledge of human behavior provided by the behavioral sciences.   Moreover, the classification procedures bring the various professionals into a co-ordinated group.   No one specialist makes the decision that determines the diagnosis and program for a prisoner; all contribute.

When the prisoner enters an institution with a classification committee, he is segregated from older inmates for a period of 6 to 8 weeks.   During this time, he is examined, tested, and interviewed.   Various items are considered: physical condition, age, intelligence, experience, skill, criminal record, attitudes, maturity, trustworthiness, sense of responsibility, the prisoner's own desires and plans, and the type of community and family to which he will return eventually. Reports are prepared that will become part of the file upon the individual prisoner. In a staff conference, the various findings are presented to the professional group and some agreement is reached as to the basic problems involved and the type of program needed. When the classification committee serves only one prison, a preliminary decision may be whether the prisoner will be best aided in that prison or whether he should be transferred. The type of employment, living conditions (cell or prison farm), needed treatment of any sort, education and vocational training, and need for counseling are some of the subjects about which decisions must be made. After the basic decisions have been made, the prisoner often is invited to a staff conference, where the findings are discussed with him and where he may state his opinions and wishes. An effort is made to gain his co-operation without invalidating the program that the specialists regard as necessary.

It is important that the warden and perhaps other administrative personnel should be included on the classification committee. Their inclusion helps to gain full co-operation for the recommendations of the committee. They are also well aware of the limitations and possibilities of the institution and hence prevent idealistic recommendations that could not be carried into effect. In addition, since wardens usually are not trained in psychology or sociology, the meetings have an educational value.

From time to time, each prisoner is restudied and if it seems desirable, changes are made in his program. The entire file on the prisoner is available to the parole board for its use in determining when the prisoner is ready to be released on parole to return under supervision to the community. Thus the classification committee follows the prisoner through his entire period of imprisonment.

During the weeks when the incoming prisoner is segregated from other inmates he often is helped to orient himself to the prison. If the prisoner faces his first prison experience, he often is beset by anxieties, fears, and hostilities; he may look forward with dread to his close association with other criminals; he may have heard or read stories of brutality by guards; and he may be deeply concerned about the welfare of wife and children. Personal interviews and group discussions are used to aid the prisoner to release some of his emotional tensions and come to a more receptive attitude before he enters upon the regular prison routine.

Reception Centers and Youth Authorities

A few states have gone beyond the use of classification committees after the judge has sentenced the prisoner, and have established reception centers to which the judge sentences the prisoner after his conviction.[2]   The staff of the reception center then diagnoses the convicted person's difficulties and comes to a decision regarding the disposition of the person, through probation or imprisonment; if the latter, in which specialized institution; and in that institution, what kind of program and treatment.   The increased value of such a reception and study center over the older type of classification program is that a trained group of diagnosticians replaces the legally trained judge in deciding what procedure will be most likely to rehabilitate the offender and ready him for a return to the community.   Full recognition is given to the fact that the criminal laws define unacceptable types of behavior and establish the rules by which a fair trial may be held; for this procedure the judge is the specialist.   But after guilt has been determined, the offender is given into the care of other specialists, trained in the behavioral sciences, whose task it is to diagnose the basic causes of the criminal behavior and map a program of training and treatment.

Diagnosis by a central group of specialists while the offender is held in a reception center is more often used for young offenders than for older ones.   The system as it operates for youth, therefore, will be described. Since a few states are experimenting with the same plan at the adult level, it may safely be said that the plan will gradually spread to cover more types of offenders as well as into more states.

The new plan for organizing and expanding facilities for treatment of young offenders was proposed in 1940 by the American Law Institute under the title Youth Correction Authority.   California, first to adopt the plan in 1941, changed the title to Youth Authority.   Other states with similar plans call them by widely different names, although they are referred to collectively as Youth Authority programs.   By 1950 five states had created Youth Authorities and since then other states have passed the necessary laws or initiated preliminary investigations and discussions.

Proposed originally for youths from 16 to 21, above juvenile court age, states show a tendency to lower the age limit to include children who come before the juvenile court.[3]   The plan when fully developed envisages the centralization of all phases of treatment in one board for the entire state. The members of the board are appointed by the governor, usually with several or all chosen from a list compiled by a committee of civic-minded persons, thus reducing the probability of political appointments.   The board functions on a full-time basis, with members receiving salaries.   Its duties include both treatment and prevention.

Although the model act devised by the American Law Institute proposed that youths after conviction should be immediately turned over to the Youth

Authority, the actual laws passed by the states leave a certain amount of discretion in the hands of the judge.   Probation is granted by the judge; thus only offenders whom the judge believes unsuitable for probation come under the control of the Authority.   In some states the judge may also fix a definite sentence, although such an act is contrary to the philosophy of the Authority.   With these exceptions, the Authority in most states receives children from the juvenile court who are not granted probation and juvenile felons from other courts whose sentences are less than life.   In general, the duration of control runs to age 21 to 25, with some variation for felons or delinquents.

The first step taken by the Authority is a careful individual study of the offender in some central residential institution.   The diagnosis leads to classification of offenders according to the type of treatment and re-education needed, processes that call either for different types of institutions within the state or for variations in program and services within one institution. The wealthy and populous states will find it possible to provide separate institutions; poor and scantily populated states will be handicapped at this point.   California, in 1950, had one diagnostic clinic for offenders aged 16–19 and provided clinical services at certain institutions.[4]   The Division of Training and Treatment of the California Authority operates 6 correctional schools and 4 forestry camps, each with a distinctive program.   Some of these institutions had been in existence for many years, but were transferred to the control of the Authority; others were newly built by the Authority to receive children from jails and detention homes and to make possible specialized schools.   Each institution receives a certain sex and age group in need of a special type of treatment.   The Youth Conservation Commission of Minnesota assumed the control of the 2 state training schools for boys and girls and soon set in motion proposals for a forestry camp, which was opened in 1951 with a capacity of 60 boys.[5]   The Commission may also use the facilities of the state reformatories for men and women and of state institutions for mentally afflicted and feeble-minded people.

Whether or not new institutions are added to those already existing the general affect of their control by the Youth Authority has been to make possible co-ordination of programs and the establishment of new standards. The institution that has lagged behind the more progressive schools is brought up to standard.   In addition and of great importance, the directives under which the Authority works and the quality of board members have led to a revision of methods of treatment.   Punishments and repressive routines have tended to give way to emphasis upon personal guidance and a well rounded program of education, recreation, and vocational training.

Whereas the tendency often has been to key the institution to the most incorrigible inmate, under the Youth Authority the trend is to make it as free and livable as the average inmate can accept and if necessary to have a special cottage for those who are unable to accept freedom.

With the discarding of the idea of punishment and retribution, the way has been opened for concentration on preparing inmates for a return to the community. A very important phase of the reorganization under the Youth Authority is that the Authority traces the progress of each individual in order to determine when he is ready to accept the restrictions and responsibilities of a free life. Some offenders are returned to the community immediately after diagnosis in the classification center; sometimes their stay in an institution is very short; but if necessary for retraining or to protect the community, the youth may be retained for a number of years—in fact, may be transferred with maturity to an adult institution if all methods of rehabilitation have failed. The length of institutional life, therefore, is not fixed ahead of time by the judge who has tried the case or heard the delinquency proceedings, but by the progress of the offender himself. The return to the community is carefully planned and is made under parole supervision.

In summary, the Youth Authority does not introduce new principles of individual study, retraining, or supervision, but is primarily an administrative device to bring all phases of the handling of delinquents after the court hearing, under a central agency, which may then make a unified plan of study and treatment. If, as at present seems to be true, the board and staff of the Youth Authority represent the best of what we know about rehabilitation, the entire process may be brought to a high level of achievement, not only for youth but for all offenders. California has taken the step of establishing 2 reception centers for adults.

MEDICAL SERVICES

Medical and dental services play three functions in the modern prison: to care for illnesses and diseases that develop while men are in prison; to correct defects with which they enter and which may contribute to their inability to adjust to conventional norms of behavior; and to establish and maintain sanitary and healthful standards in the prison.

The larger prisons maintain a hospital with operating room, X-ray rooms, a pharmacy, and examination rooms for medical specialties, such as eye-ear-nose-and-throat ailments. The hospital differs from one on the outside primarily in special provisions for security so that the patient or prisoner-orderly will not attempt to escape.

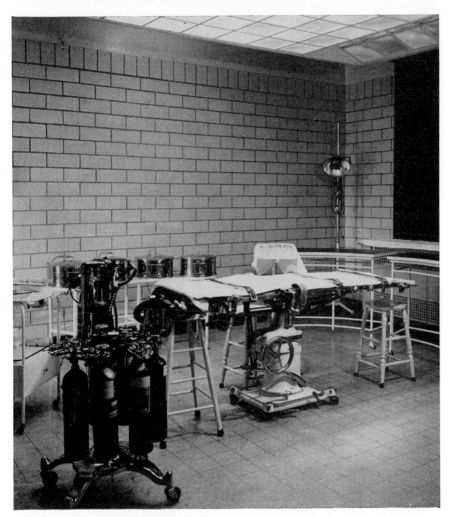

The modern prison with a large number of inmates provides special care for ill or physically handicapped prisoners. The Illinois State Penitentiary at Stateville, from which this illustration of X-ray equipment comes, maintains a complete medical center, including an operating room, sterilizing equipment, fluoroscopic apparatus, a drug dispensary, an emergency room for administration of first aid, and facilities for treatment of eye, ear, nose, and throat infections. Four resident physicians are in charge.

Some states maintain special hospitals for tubercular prisoners or those with other chronic diseases and some prisons become in essence old people's homes where aging and infirm prisoners are congregated.

PSYCHIATRIC SERVICES AND COUNSELING

Some prison systems include special institutions for criminal psychotics; others place mentally abnormal criminals in public mental hospitals; still others maintain one cell block in one prison for deranged criminals. Besides the psychotic criminals there are many other prisoners with mild emotional disturbances or unsocialized attitudes, which have been a factor in their criminal acts or which make them an adjustment problem in prison.

Individual Therapy

To care for these various types of disturbed prisoners, many states employ psychiatrists on a full or part-time basis. The number of psychiatrists is not sufficient, however, to fill all the posts; also, many psychiatrists prefer private practice, which is often more lucrative and which presents fewer problems in the psychiatrist-client relationship.

The practice of psychiatry in prison is difficult. The psychiatrist is often associated in the prisoner's mind with the guards and warden, who symbolize authority and often punishment. The prisoner may maintain the same watchful reserve toward the psychiatrist as toward guards, fearing that any revelation of hostility or abnormality will result in loss of privilege or in punishment. It is also true that many difficult adjustments in prison cannot be changed, such as the lack of female companionship or the restrictions on liberty. Such socially abnormal situations may cause emotional tensions, but must be accepted. The most the psychiatrist can do is help the prisoner to accept them. The psychiatrist, therefore, is limited in the help he can give, even when he breaks through the prisoner's reserves. He may even feel that to help the prisoner adjust to prison life is to create future maladjustments to community life when the prisoner is released.

Group Therapy

Not all prisoners are seriously maladjusted and in need of individual therapy. It is now recognized, however, that all prisoners need some readjustment in attitudes before release. An approach gaining approval since the early 1940's is group counseling and therapy.[6] These services may be carried on by social workers and trained counselors, thus freeing the psychiatrist for supervision and work with deeply disturbed prisoners.

Counseling and group therapy with noninstitutional groups have been discussed in Chapter 10. In prisons these services are being experimented with chiefly in reformatories and correctional schools. The institutional framework of a penal or correctional institution adds elements to group therapy that are not present in the noninstitutional setting. The usual relationship between officers and prisoners creates a wide social distance between them; on the one side are authority, high status, power to control; on the other, low status and at least overt submission.   Attempts to bridge the gulf between the two groups often meet with failure, and usually no attempt is made to close the gap.   The group therapist is identified with the authoritarian official group, not only in the minds of the prisoners but in terms of employment and certain obligations to institutional rules.   He is not a criminal; he is not a prisoner.   If the therapist is successful in establishing rapport with the prisoners, the inmates who compose the therapy group gradually are able not only to express some of their troublesome attitudes but also to talk through and gain some insight into their relationships to each other and to the prison officials and rules.   Thus the therapy tends to help the inmate to adjust better to the institution and also to change underlying attitudes that prevent conformity to normal community life.

Group therapy cannot be simply superimposed upon the prison program in a superficial fashion.   It must have the approval and support of the warden; and other prison personnel must not only recognize it as a part of the prison program but must be prepared to understand what is going on and also the reactions of the prisoners.   McCorkle, with long experience in group therapy among prisoners, states that the prisoners may use the sessions, where they are free to speak their minds, as a threat to guards, hinting that anything unpleasant said to them by the guards will be reported in the therapy sessions, with the implication that the remarks might in time reach the warden.[7]   Also, sometimes hostilities may be brought to the surface in the group sessions and carry over into a free expression of hostility in other relationships instead of the customary repression.   Guards and other personnel must be prepared for such temporary reactions on the part of the prisoners.

Evaluation of group therapy in reformatories is incomplete.   At the Medical Center of the Federal Bureau of Prisons, group therapy was used with two groups with serious problems—psychoneurotics and homosexuals.[8] Some members of each group felt they had benefited, but an objective evaluation was not possible.   At El Reno Reformatory 46 inmates placed in a group therapy program were matched with a control group of 50.   Personality tests and disciplinary records for both groups were kept over a 6 months' period.   The two groups had about the same number of minor infractions but the therapy group had only about half as many major infractions as the control group.   As experimentation continues, measures of changes in attitudes and behavior undoubtedly will be developed, and methods of treatment will be clarified and refined.   In the meantime, group therapy must be regarded as one of the promising developments of the 1940's and 1950's.

WORK FOR PRISONERS

The employment of prisoners has long been accepted as desirable. Prisons in Rome and Ghent and a few jails in Switzerland, Holland, and Germany established handicraft shops as early as the eighteenth century. The Norfolk Prison in England, built in 1784 and modeled on the continental prisons, provided employment for convicts.   When the cell house for felons was opened in the yard of the Walnut Street Jail in Philadelphia in 1790, a wide choice of handicrafts was introduced: weaving, shoemaking, cutting and polishing marble, tailoring, carding various fibers, sawing wood, and so on.   Although overcrowding soon made such work almost impossible, the pattern of providing work in jail and prison had been successfully established as an integral part of prison life.   Six methods of organizing prison work have been used during the past century and a quarter, some of which, although popular in the past, have now been virtually abandoned.

Contract System

The earliest organization of prison work and one that received widespread approval was the manufacture of various articles under the contract system.[9] The Auburn Prison developed contract labor in the 1820's, the period in which the rapid expansion of American industries created a pressing demand for cheap labor.   The success of the contract system at Auburn caused other prisons to institute similar systems.   Under contract labor, a manufacturer contracted with the state for the output of the prisoners, paying the state a small sum—perhaps fifty cents a day—for each prisoner who worked.   The prison administration housed, fed, clothed, and disciplined the prisoners.   The contractor provided needed tools or machinery and the raw material; he also supervised the work and marketed the goods.

It was soon discovered that this system not only made prisons self-supporting but provided a profit to the state.   In 1852, for instance, 9 prisons reported a combined surplus above expenses of $23,000.   The successful warden, who retained his office for any length of time, was able to show a financial profit on the prison operation.   The public approved the system, since it did not need to pay taxes for the support of prisoners.   The work was not regarded as rehabilitation or vocational training, but purely as a financial arrangement for the benefit of the state.

Contract labor provided several beneficial by-products for the prisoners: it relieved the monotony of endless idle days and established or maintained certain work habits. It also benefited the administration: orderliness in the prison increased when inmates were occupied rather than idle. With the introduction of machinery came a limited sociability, since the men worked in shops in company with others instead of with hand tools in their cells. In some prisons necessary talking was permitted; in others silence was imposed, but the men found ways of communication that relieved the isolation. With improved orderliness on the part of the prisoners, other repressive measures were relaxed. Soon wardens were of the opinion that work was valuable not only because it made prisons self-supporting but as an aid to discipline.

The contract system led to certain abuses. In many institutions each prisoner was required to produce a fixed quantity of work each day and failure led to severe punishment. Clark, describing his experiences in 1884, states: [10]

I know that the only foreman who could hold his job was the man who was utterly devoid of sympathy for human suffering. Such a man always held the job and received a good salary for his work; and the keepers employed by the State were about of the same caliber and received each month a certain sum from the contractor, in addition to their pay from the State. So no matter how much work the convict did he never received any thanks, but any man who failed to do the task would be sure to hang in the dungeon half the night and then get up in a weakened condition and do another big day's work or receive the same dose again that night, with perhaps a strapping added, which I received at one time four nights in succession.

The contract system was employed most widely in the northern industrial states, particularly in the East and Middle West. At the time of its most extensive use, the West was still relatively undeveloped and the South was primarily agricultural. The system brought sporadic attacks from both labor and competing manufacturers. Prison contractors paid less for their labor than for free labor; other expenses were also low. Hence the prison contractor flooded the market with cheap prison-made goods to the distress of the independent manufacturer and his workmen. The situation was intensified by the fact that each prison tended to manufacture only one type of article. Thus, although the ratio of prisoners to the total laboring population was extremely low and the ratio of prison-made goods to total goods produced was also low, in one industry the prison-made goods might represent a high proportion of that type of goods produced in a given state or region. By the end of the nineteenth century the protests had gained sufficient force to cause restrictive legislation in various states and political pressure in others. As a result, by 1900 many prisons had reluctantly abandoned contract labor.

The Piece Price System

In the attempt to meet some of the criticisms against contract labor, Zebulon Brockway, the noted prison reformer, proposed the substitution of a piece price system. Under this system, which developed as contract labor declined, the manufacturer supplied the machinery and the raw material and paid the state a certain sum for each article made by the prisoners. The warden assumed responsibility for management of production. The new procedure decreased the pressure for a high rate of production that contractors had customarily placed upon prisoners in the effort to force as much work from them as possible. A humane warden could set a fair production rate, and the manufacturer paid for the resultant output. On the other hand, a warden interested primarily in income could set a high production rate, and the system could be as onerous as the contract system. The prison, of course, still competed with the independent employer, although the cost of production was now slightly higher, and hence the manufacturer who used prison labor could not undercut prices to the extent possible under the contract system.

Leasing of Prisoners

Meantime, in the South another type of employment had come into somewhat general use, in response to conditions immediately following the Civil War. The South lacked finances to rebuild prisons that had been destroyed or damaged during the war or to increase the number of penal institutions. The situation was made more critical by an increase of petty offenses and crime during the reconstruction period. In the absence of sufficient penal institutions, some substitute method of supervision became necessary and was provided by leasing prisoners to employers. This arrangement enabled the South to repair war damage and develop its resources at a time when the chief previous supply of labor—slaves—had disappeared. The 2 problems of what to do with the growing number of prisoners and where to find additional laborers were thus solved by leasing prisoners to private industries or to individuals needing a few workmen. The employer paid the state a set sum for a given number of prisoners, whom he was obligated to house, feed, and clothe; and privileged to work. Since there was no warden or supervision by the state or any disinterested agency, the prisoners were virtually slaves of the employers and at their mercy. Mining and railroad building were the 2 major industries that absorbed many prisoners. In Florida, for example, after some experimentation with leasing, in 1876 a permanent policy was established, whereby 1,100 prisoners were leased to 3 companies on 20 year contracts.[11]

When prisoners were discharged at the termination of their sentences or if they died, they were replaced by others. For the labor of these 1,100 men each of the 3 companies paid $25,000 per year, or $68.18 per capita per year. The companies then maintained the prisoners and retained all profits secured from their work. In 1884 the Tennessee Coal and Iron Railway leased all state prisoners (about 1,000) for $100,000 per year, to work in mining camps. Many of the prisoners were Negroes who had found it difficult to conform to laws in a hostile environment. Without legal restriction or supervision the employer was able to support the prisoners at a mere subsistence level and to force as much work from them as possible. Discipline was maintained at the point of a gun. Medical care, recreation, and sanitation were almost unheard of. These abuses and the gradual development of a free laboring class and of more humanitarian principles of penology gradually undermined the leasing system. In some states, however, it continued until about 1930.

The State Account System

A fourth development was the state account system, a substitute for the contract and the piece price systems. The state itself became the manufacturer, bearing all expenses of production and marketing the articles made by prisoners. The outstanding example was Minnesota, which produced binder twine, for which there was a wide market in the state for agricultural purposes. The state account system abolished the outside supervisor and permitted whatever diversification of employment the prison administration saw fit to introduce. It did not eliminate the criticism of unfair competition, but this criticism grew less with diversification of articles produced so that no single industry bore the brunt.

Objections to Prison Industries

Meanwhile, the combined pressure of labor and competing manufacturers produced restrictive legislation, which varied from state to state. Some states forbade contracting prison labor; others provided that all prison-made goods should be thus labeled, so that consumers opposed to such competition with free labor could refuse to buy them; others restricted the sale of prison-made goods or limited their importation from other states. Under these conditions, production decreased, and financing of prisons gradually shifted from self-support through prison labor to financing by the state from tax funds.

Although this assumption of financial responsibility by the states relieved one problem linked with prison labor, it did not solve another and more crucial difficulty: how to fill the prisoners' time. Wardens generally agreed that they could not maintain discipline without some means of occupying prisoners, since restlessness and monotony found outlets in disorders that ranged from mischief to riots. Maintenance work in the institutions required only a small proportion of the inmates. Making handicraft articles to sell to visitors again provided for only a few and did not appeal to the typical prisoner. Few wardens had any sort of training in the difficult task of creating educational or training programs that might have served as substitutes for work.

State Use System

An answer to the difficult problem was sought in the state use system, whereby the prison manufactured articles as under the state account system, but limited the market to other state institutions. Since institutional demands necessitated a variety of industries, prisoners could be given some choice of occupation. State use also lessened criticism from the outside

A major prison problem is finding occupations for prisoners. Most large prisons operate industrial plants within the prison walls, although the sale of products is usually limited to other state institutions. Stateville, Illinois, has a typical array of industries. Above is shown its largest plant, the furniture factory. The prison also operates a tin shop where ash and garbage cans, kitchen utensils, and fire extinguisher containers are made. Other plants turn out soap chips and mattresses.

since no single industry was placed in full competition with prison production.   One drawback arose from the fact that state institutions were not
required to purchase from the prisons.   For example, in Sing Sing in 1931
about one third of the prison population was employed in the brush and
mattress shop, print, knitting, shoe, and sheet metal shops.[12]   The articles
manufactured were sold to state, county, and city institutions, which were
not, however, compelled to buy them.   Nevertheless, the total sales for the
year ending June 30, 1931 was $801,000, of which about $200,000 was
profit.   Another adaptation of the state use system was the development
of prison farms, the products of which are used in state institutions.

Public Works and Ways

In some parts of the country the state use system did not produce manufactured articles but was known as public works and ways, that is, the
prisoners were employed in public services, as road construction, or fire-
preventive work in forests.   The road camps and forestry camps in the
South and West are examples, and are deeply entrenched despite the protest
of private construction companies.

Legislative Restrictions

Meanwhile, legislation restricting the sale of prison-made goods has continued.   The Hawes-Cooper Act of 1929, which became effective in 1934,
and the Ashurst-Sumner Act of 1935 placed severe penalties on the shipment of prison-made goods into states that forbade sales of such goods
from other states.   The effectiveness of this federal legislation rested on
state statutes forbidding their entrance or sale.   By 1940 every state had
passed some type of restrictive legislation, and in that year federal laws
forbade the shipment of prison-made goods outside the state that manufactured them.

Trends in Prison Industries

The trends in employment are clearly shown in Table 20.   The leasing
of prisoners was at its height about 1885 when it accounted for 26 per cent
of those employed.   After 1905 it showed a sharp decline.   The contract
system, under which 40 per cent of all prisoners were employed in 1885,
also declined, especially after 1914.   The piece price system, never so
extensive as the lease or the contract system, reached its peak about 1895
and continued in use until 1940.   The various systems of production for
the use of public offices (state account, public works and ways, and state
use) have all endured and the last two have increased.

The entry of the United States into World War II brought a temporary

TABLE 20

Percentage of State and Federal Prisoners Productively Employed for
Different Years

System of Work	1885	1895	1905	1914	1923	1932	1940
Engaged in all systems	100.0	100.0	100.0	100.0	100.0	100.0	100.0
Types of work							
State use			18	22	36	42	59
Public works and ways	26	33	8	11	19	23	29
State account			21	31	26	19	12
Piece price	8	14	8	6	7	11	Less than 1
Contract	40	34	36	26	12	5	0
Lease	26	19	9	4	0	0	0
Percentage of prisoners under sentence engaged in productive labor	75	72	65	—	61	52	44

Source: R. F. Jones, "Prison Labor in the United States, 1940," *Monthly Labor Review,* 53 (1941), 582.

increase in prison employment as prisons were able to expand production for the government.   However, with the end of the war, the prisons again faced the problem of devising labor for their inmates.

The problem of prison labor is also reflected in the proportion of the prison population that is productively employed.   The trends in prison employment are shown in Tables 20 and 21.   The most conspicuous figures are those that show the decrease in the proportion of prisoners working.

TABLE 21

Value of Production and Number Employed in State and Federal Prisons,
1923 and 1940

System of Work	Value of Production	
	1923 (per cent of total)	1940 (per cent of total)
State use	18.1	60.2
Public works and ways	20.1	23.7
State account	21.6	15.6
Piece price	16.2	0.5
Contract	24.0	0.0
All systems of work	$76,096,960	$56,731,654
Average number of prisoners under sentence	84,761	191,776
Average number productively employed	51,799	83,515
Percentage of prisoners employed	61	44

Source: R. F. Jones, "Prison Labor in the United States, 1940," *Monthly Labor Review,* 53 (1941), 582.

Table 20, item 8, indicates that in 1885, 75 per cent of all prisoners were employed. A steady decrease followed, until in 1940, only 44 per cent were employed. This 44 per cent, however, represents a larger number of prisoners than the earlier, higher percentages, owing to the increase in number of prisoners from decade to decade. For example, Table 21, items 7, 8, and 9, shows that 51,799 prisoners, or 61 per cent of the total number, were employed in 1923. But in 1940, although only 44 per cent were employed, the number at work greatly exceeded the number employed in 1923. A part of the problem therefore has been to find a constantly increasing source of employment for an increasing number of prisoners.

States vary greatly in their policies.[13] In Nevada in 1940, 7 per cent of prisoners were employed; in North Carolina 81 per cent. In only 15 states were more than 50 per cent of the inmates productively employed.

At Stateville, Illinois, some inmates are employed in maintenance work and in the daily operation of the prison. In large modern prisons food is prepared with the aid of mechanical equipment. The kitchen is equipped with steam-jacketed kettles of 100- and 200-gallon capacity. Much of the food used is produced by other inmates on the prison farm, where all of the pork, 25 per cent of the beef, and 50 per cent of the potatoes are raised.

In addition to productive employment, prisons use inmates for maintenance work: 35 per cent of state prisoners perform some sort of such work. Moreover at any given time small percentages are ill or completely idle. Many of those listed as employed work only for short or intermittent periods, a situation especially true of maintenance work.

Organization of Prison Industries

The most successful program of work for prisoners is carried out when planning and control are removed from the individual institutions and placed in the hands of a central agency that can plan for an integrated and diversified program for an entire state. Some states now have organized their prison industries on a state basis; the Federal Bureau of Prisons also has a centralized organization of industries, which sets the pattern for state practices.

In 1934, faced with idleness of federal prisoners, the federal government passed a law creating the Federal Prison Industries, Inc. to operate all industrial production in federal prisons. Farming, road construction, and forestry were excluded. The policies of the Industries are formulated by a board of directors upon which are represented the Federal Bureau of Prisons, labor, agriculture, industry, and retailer-consumers. This board established 8 policies, as follows: [14]

"1. All inmates not needed for the maintenance of institutions, or not engaged in important educational activities, should be given the opportunity to work in the industries.

"2. In determining the nature of a diversified industrial program, the government market alone will be considered. The industries will engage to supply a pro rata proportion of the demands of other governmental agencies (in addition to an unlimited production for federal correctional institutions).

"3. Industries set up in prisons must be practical of operation within that institution and cannot require skills not available therein.

"4. Industries established must require a maximum of hand labor and have a definite vocational training value.

"5. Industries established must give promise of a fair return on the investment after deducting overhead charges (including depreciation), contingencies and wages to inmate workers.

"6. After providing most institutions in need of employment for their inmates with industrial establishments, the Board will attempt development along lines of diversification 'to eliminate undue competition with free industries and to comply with the language of the statute requiring the more effective diversification of prison industries.'

"7. Production of industries will not be permitted to develop at any time to a degree that is inconsistent with contemporaneous conditions.

"8. No prisoner shall be employed more than 40 hours a week."

The Federal Bureau of Prisons has an advantage not held by any state prison system, a diversity of types of institutions widely scattered over the United States, thus reducing the possibility of competitive pressure on any one industry or region. In 50 shops located in many prisons, over 300 different kinds of products are produced, all for government use and in the 1940's and 1950's, mainly for the armed forces. In 1953, 22 per cent of all federal prisoners were employed in the prison industries, the remainder being employed on prison farms, in road building, forestry projects, and construction, as well as in institutional maintenance and "housekeeping."

California also has diversified, widely scattered institutions. Industries for all California prisons are under the control of an organization called California Correctional Industries.[15] Although only 13 to 14 per cent of the prison population is employed industrially—more being employed on farms, in camps, and for maintenance—the industrial program is regarded as important financially to the state and in the rehabilitation of prisoners. The principles of rehabilitation are stated as follows:

"1. Keep otherwise idle inmates busy and aid in reducing disciplinary problems.

"2. Develop a pattern of good work habits in inmates.

"3. Prevent physical and mental deterioration.

"4. Provide realistic, on-the-job vocational training.

"5. Reduce the cost of the penal program to the taxpayer.

"6. Aid materially in the financial support of inmates."

All products are sold to state agencies, the earnings being used largely for production costs, new equipment, salaries of supervision, and wages to inmates.

As with the Federal Prison Industries, Inc., the California Correctional Industries is guided by a board representing the Department of Corrections, labor, industry, agriculture, and the public. Plans of diversification to avoid undue competition with private industry are worked out through this board.

In other states, also, centralized planning is helping to establish specific aims and policies that take account of the benefit of work to prisoners on the one hand and the need to keep amicable relations with private industries on the other.

EDUCATION FOR PRISONERS

Background of Prison Education [16]

Education for prisoners began as an adjunct of religious teaching. When a reform movement of the 1820's emphasized Sunday schools, Bible reading, and memorizing Biblical passages, chaplains sometimes passed from cell to cell, giving such individual instruction as they could. An official recognition of the need for education came in 1847 when New York State passed a law providing two instructors for each state prison. By the 1860's some half dozen eastern states provided for a limited degree of education taught by special teachers or chaplains. Since this instruction was carried on chiefly in the individual cells, it was very meager as the teacher could visit each prisoner only at long intervals. The education offered was elementary and academic in character.

Elmira Reformatory under Brockway gave impetus to education for young offenders. Unfortunately, Brockway's experiments did not at once affect prisons for adults, which continued to organize activities around work with the motive of making the prisons self-supporting. Such educational classes and activities as were required by law or provided by wardens on their own initiative were regarded as an aid to discipline rather than as a retraining program. With the gradual collapse of the various systems of prison industries, however, classes of various sorts were snatched at as a substitute to keep prisoners occupied. Education was an acceptable substitute because of our great faith in education as a necessary attribute of the citizen and as somehow conducive to the good life. Since many prisoners had had meager schooling, education seemed a justifiable activity on general principles as well as to maintain discipline. Teaching programs were of a makeshift character, however, inadequately financed by the state, understaffed, and carried out under almost impossible conditions. The chaplain, a guard, or even a prisoner was often the instructor; or a teacher gave evening classes after teaching all day in some nearby school. Classes were held in the mess hall, the chapel, or some odd part of the prison structure converted into a schoolroom. Courses were not planned with the needs of the prisoners in mind.

A survey of prisons and reformatories in 1927–28 showed that some reformatories for young offenders, following Brockway's example, offered some form of education.[17] Prisons, however, in general provided for only limited and mediocre education or for none at all. Thirteen prisons had no provision for education; about the same number were required by law to carry prisoners through the third, fourth, or fifth grade. About a dozen prisons had fairly satisfactory programs. In general, the programs were handicapped by lack of suitable books for illiterate adults, poor lighting, and inadequately trained staff. The prisons at San Quentin, California, and at Waupun, Wisconsin, were exceptions. In both institutions during the 1920's qualified prisoners might take correspondence courses offered by the respective state universities. Minnesota and Virginia were also above the average.

Educational Trends Since 1930

Many states still make almost no provision for education of prisoners and those that have a fully developed system are rare. Also, even when state provision exists much depends upon the warden's enthusiasm and ability in encouraging and organizing the work. Nevertheless, since 1930 a new attitude has developed toward education of prisoners, stemming from several situations. (1) The rapid breakdown of prison industries,

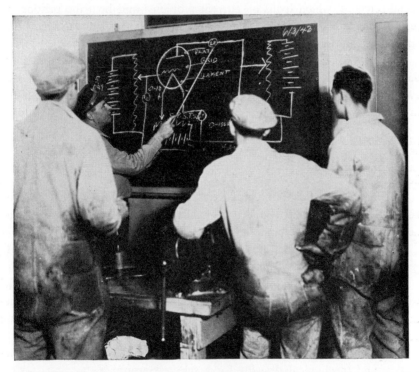

In this photograph an instructor is demonstrating electrical processes to federal prisoners. Education and vocational training are highly developed in the federal prisons, and attain their widest scope in the reformatories and in the Lewisburg and Terre Haute penitentiaries. Academic work extends from elementary school subjects taught to illiterates to correspondence courses and individual instruction at the college level. Vocational training covers many skills and trades.

and since 1940 their virtual abandonment except for temporary war contracts and state use, stimulated the establishment of educational programs, both academic and vocational.   (2) The development of the federal prison system with well-developed educational facilities has set a standard for state institutions.   (3) The recent attention of psychiatrists and sociologists to delinquents and criminals has helped to formulate a new conception of education, as not merely academic or even trade training, but in terms of extensive social education that will help the prisoner to adjust to the community when he is released.   This theory of education, when fully developed, involves preliminary study of the individual prisoner (classification system), and placement in classes and work according to his needs.   It also calls for good equipment, freedom to attend classes and use the prison libraries, and some choice on the part of the prisoner of what he wishes to study.   Courses include not only academic and trade subjects but the social sciences, which focus on current problems and help the prisoner to readjust his views of society, government, law, finance, and the like.   The classes are administered by a special director and trained teachers.

Types of education in some of the more highly developed systems are described, in order to show present trends.   It must be remembered, however, that these systems are still exceptions to the general rule and are found in only a few prisons.

Prisoner Education in Federal Prisons

In the federal prisons, the educational program includes the following fields: [18]

1. Elementary education for illiterates and borderline cases who rank below the fourth or fifth grade on standard achievement tests, but who nevertheless have the ability to learn.

2. Advanced academic education for those who score above the fifth grade on achievement tests and who wish to study.

3. Trades and occupational information for a selected group of industrial workers and for all vocational trainees.   Inmates capable of such instruction are classified as vocational trainees.   The institutional industries are used for on-the-job training.

4. Special classes in such fields as languages, commercial subjects, mathematics, and mechanical drawing for a selected group.

5. Correspondence courses and cell-study courses for men who cannot attend classes or who have special requirements.

The application of this general program varies from one federal institution to another, depending upon the age and needs of the prisoners (see pages 419–25).

Stateville, Illinois

This Illinois state penitentiary houses criminals with long terms, many of whom are repeaters from urban centers. A schoolhouse is one of the newer buildings, in which is provided grade and high school instruction; work of junior college level may be taken by correspondence. Vocational training in a number of trades is available in the classroom; other trades are taught in the well-developed industries.

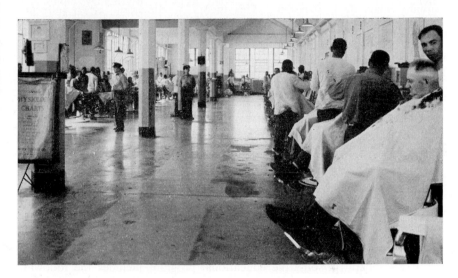

Inmates at Stateville, Illinois may complete the three-year training course for a state license in the 43-chair barbershop shown above. Frequently the probability of earning money immediately after discharge prevents a return to criminal habits.

New York State Prisons

The principles underlying the educational system in New York institutions are stated in the Laws, 1935, Chapter 670, Section 3 and Laws, 1929, Chapter 243, Section 136.[19] The qualifications for teachers and the close relationship of prison education with civil education are also stated and indicate the high quality of education sought for prisoners.

The objective of prison education in its broadest sense should be the socialization of the inmates through varied impressional and expressional activities with emphasis on individual needs. The objective of this program shall be the return of these inmates to society with a more wholesome attitude toward living, with a desire to conduct themselves as good citizens and with the skill and knowledge which will give them a reasonable chance to maintain themselves and their dependents through honest labor. To this end each prisoner shall be given a program of education which, on the basis of available data, seems most likely to further the process of socialization and rehabilitation. The time daily devoted to such education shall be such as is required for meeting the above objectives. The director of education shall develop the curricula and the education programs that are required to meet the special needs of each prison and reformatory in the department. The state commissioner of education, in cooperation with the commissioner of correction and the director of education, shall set up the educational requirements for the certification of teachers in all such prisons and reformatories. Such education requirements shall be sufficiently broad and comprehensive to include training in penology, sociology, psychology, philosophy, in the special subjects to be taught, and in any other professional courses as may be deemed necessary by the responsible officers. No certificates for teaching service in the state institutions shall be issued unless a minimum of four years of training beyond high school has been secured, or an acceptable equivalent. Existing requirements for the certification of teachers in the institutions shall continue in force until changes pursuant to the provisions of this section.

Under this law, education is regarded as either social or vocational in nature. Social education attempts to revise the attitudes that prisoners have acquired toward social institutions and emphasizes the individual's relationships to them. Interests and skills required in acceptable social living are developed. Every effort is made to be realistic and to recognize the actual economic and social conditions that the prisoner will meet when he is released. This modification of the prisoner's attitudes is sought through the following program:

> Academic subjects
> Mental hygiene classes
> Health and physical education programs
> Recreational activities
> Arts
> Classes for the physically and mentally handicapped
> Cultural development

The other division of the over-all program, vocational education, includes teaching special skills to those capable of learning them; a wide variety of less exacting skills for the less capable; and discussion of labor and economic problems. The development of pride and satisfaction in doing good work are also objectives.

Throughout, a definite effort is made to handle the subject matter so that it will have meaning to the prisoners. All material is socialized— that is, it is related to the adjustment that the inmate will have to make after he leaves the institution. Also, all material is vitalized, or made interesting.

Difficulties of Prison Education

The difficulties of introducing and operating a prison educational system should not be minimized. For instance, the range of intelligence, which approximates that of the general population, is wide. In the Illinois State Prison approximately 10 per cent of native-born white prisoners and 45 per cent of foreign-born white prisoners showed inferior (below normal) intelligence test scores according to the army alpha test. These scores are almost identical with the scores for noncriminals of the respective groups.

Moreover, previous educational achievement has a wide range among prisoners. The data in Table 22 show that the median grade achieve-

TABLE 22

Educational Level of Male Prisoners Admitted during One Year to Five State Prisons

Amount of Education	Per Cent
Illiterate	6
Grade school (grades 1–8)	58
Highschool (1 to 4 years)	31
College (1 or more years)	3
Unknown	2
Number	3,434

Source: Annual reports of admissions during 1 year from the courts to state prisons in 1 eastern, 1 middle western, 1 western, and 2 southern states.

ment of prisoners is below the eighth grade and that 6 per cent are illiterate. In the South, and especially among Negro prisoners, the percentage of illiterates is undoubtedly much higher. Prisoners also have many special interests and abilities, and as in the civilian population some are suited for one type of training, some for another.

Several general characteristics of prisoners also make it hard to give them adequate education. They are adults and many have not attended school or studied for many years. Some, no doubt, disliked school. The idea of school and classes may be repugnant to them and learning anew how to study may be almost impossible. Nor is it clear that all prisoners can be aroused to an interest in their own rehabilitation. The professional criminal who regards imprisonment as an "off season" is neither likely to be interested in a trade nor in academic subjects. He is interested primarily in passing the time in prison with as much comfort to himself as possible and hopes for an early release on parole.   Nevertheless, a group remains whose interest can be aroused and who can benefit from an educational and vocational training program.   To be successful, prison education must meet the prisoners at their own level of intelligence, educational achievement, and special abilities or disabilities.   The program must be varied and flexible, and in the hands of skilled teachers.

The Prison Library

The prison library is an adjunct of the educational system.   Beginning with Bibles and religious tracts supplied by chaplains, libraries first consisted of a few shelves of books donated by interested persons—often discarded and with no appeal to prisoners.   By the 1840's a few states had begun to make small appropriations for libraries, and by the 1860's the practice was rather general of making some slight provision for reading material.   The development of libraries has been slow and irregular, however, as a 1937 survey shows.[20]   It is true that of 115 state penal institutions all but 5 had libraries, but in almost half of them libraries were in makeshift quarters, in some corner of the chapel, post office, visiting room, or storage place.   Considerably less than half the prisons included library expense in their budgets.   Only one prison employed a trained civilian librarian.   In many institutions prisoners ordered books from a printed list, to be read in their cells; there was no reading room.

Since 1937, a library has become part of the plan for a standard penal institution and new prisons typically include a special place for a library, with a reading room.

When books are specially selected and some guidance is given to prisoners in the choice of books, reading can become not only a pastime but also a means of informal education and stimulation.

RECREATION IN PRISON

Development of Recreation

For many years after imprisonment became the standard punishment for felonies, recreation was thought to have no place in prison life.   The concept of imprisonment emphasized the belief that the lot of the prisoner should be harsh, uncomfortable, and repellent in effect.   In prisons that practiced confinement in individual cells recreation was limited to solitary exercise in a high-walled yard and to reading the Bible and other religious publications.   Prisons that permitted inmates to work in groups in institutional industries usually required silence unless speech was absolutely necessary; silence was also part of the mealtime regime.   Prisoners became adept, however, at communicating with each other without attracting the attention of guards and thus established a meager type of social contact and interchange of thought.   The overcrowding of prisons that necessitated placing 2 or more prisoners in 1 cell, and sometimes the establishment of dormitories, brought further relaxation of the rule of silence.   As it became apparent that nothing disastrous happened when prisoners met informally and communicated with each other—in fact, orderliness improved under these conditions—a few wardens began to grant freedom of the yard and to permit conversation in the mess hall on national holidays.[21]   Such steps had been taken by some wardens as early as the 1850's.

The next stage in the development of recreation was the introduction of organized sport.   As in the case of education, the reformatories led the way.   Brockway, at Elmira, brought organized games to a high point of development, in the belief that such activities would develop self-control and team spirit.   During the same period, the reformatory at Concord, Massachusetts, organized sports and a series of clubs, to one of which all convicts who were classified as of the first grade were eligible.   The clubs included a Y.M.C.A., Reformatory Prayer Meeting, a Catholic Debating Society, a Saturday Scientific and Literary Club, a Baseball and Literary Society, and a Chautauqua Club.[22]   If some of these clubs seem uninteresting in terms of present-day organizations for young people, it must be remembered that such activities were very popular immediately after the Civil War.   The club meetings were conducted with a great deal of freedom of discussion by the reformatory inmates.

Gradually, more freedom of speech and action as well as more organized recreation were introduced into adult prisons, the degree depending on the attitude of the individual warden, the directives of state political and administrative groups, and public reaction.   Freedom of speech was usually limited to certain brief periods, perhaps on one day a week.   Freedom of the yard was likewise restricted.   Sports, clubs, and lectures that brought prisoners together in groups often were avoided, because they aroused fear of riots.   Gradually, however, occasional privileges became established customs.   By 1910–15 organized sports had become a regular part of prison life in the North.   The prison band provided a concert as part of the Sunday program.   Lectures and music became more frequent.   More recently, motion pictures and radios have been added to the equipment of many prisons, with television in an occasional institution.

The development of recreational activities was stimulated by the decline of prison industries.   They are a way of occupying time and they prevent the accumulation of unrest and resentment occasioned by prolonged idleness.

Hence recreation becomes a form of discipline and is valued by the warden as such. The original reformatory concept of recreation as a means of developing character and teaching co-operation has been largely lost, except in those few institutions that are experimenting with integrated programs of rehabilitation.

Recreational Programs

The more progressive prisons now employ a variety of recreational outlets. In the Illinois prison studied by Clemmer the official recreation consisted of the following: [23]

1. The Saturday afternoon ball game provides actual participation in the game for a few men and gives the spectators a chance to relax, gossip, and enjoy it. Informal sports are also allowed in the yard.

2. Motion pictures, the most popular type of recreation, are shown once a week except during the ball season.

This photograph shows the most recent development in prison library facilities—the comfortable reading room where prisoners may spend some of their free time, such as is found in the United States Penitentiary at Terre Haute, Indiana. In many prisons, especially old ones, the library consists of only a few shelves of books whose titles are listed in a printed catalog from which the prisoner may choose a book to be read in his cell.

3. Radio programs are broadcast over a loud speaker for a half hour each noon and from 7 to 9 at night. The prisoners cannot select their programs and must either listen to the programs that are chosen or train themselves to disregard the sound.

4. Letters may be written on Sunday afternoons. Visits from relatives may occur at stated intervals.

5. Books may be selected from a mimeographed catalogue for reading in the cells.

6. The prisoner may or may not attend church services, as he desires.

Minimum security institutions and many reformatories allow much more freedom of action and informal group interaction than do prisons, but for all there are certain limitations in the interest of custody and orderliness.

The inmates devise some types of recreation for themselves, which either must be carried on secretly or with unofficial sanction of guards. These amusements include gambling on card games, which are allowed. The stakes are necessarily low and consist of small sums of money, tobacco, matches, food, or cleaning the winner's cell. Occasional drinking goes on. Sometimes alcoholic drinks are smuggled in from the outside. In other cases drinks are manufactured from fruit juice, yeast, and sugar brought to the cells by kitchen workers or taken from the dining room. Other inmates occupy their leisure time in daydreaming or in listening to the stories told by other prisoners. All in all, the range of possibilities for recreation is limited and leisure tends to be filled with boredom.

RELIGIOUS SERVICES AND FACILITIES

Religious groups, instructors in religion, and chaplains were active early in American prisons. The concept of behavior as based on free will, and of religion as providing the gateway to personal morality and ethical conduct resulted in the acceptance of religion as the focal point in the reformation of criminals. Early chaplains therefore played an important part in prisons. They were among the few persons other than guards who had any contact with prisoners, and they earnestly tried to guide the prisoners' thoughts along religious lines. They also introduced the first small libraries and attempted to teach illiterates to read the Bible. With the passage of time, the concept of the basis of conduct changed. Conduct is now considered the result of the component forces of innate drives and social pressures. Other specialists have come to the fore as the chief technicians of good conduct.

The chaplain is in the process of reformulating his relationship to prison inmates. He is no longer willing to do odd jobs for the prison administration that interfere with his primary task. A recent statement by the president of the National Chaplain's Association emphasized that the chaplain is not a parole officer, administrator, supervisor, or disciplinarian.[24] His task is to be a spiritual guide and teacher. Personal counseling falls within his realm, as well as maintaining contact with the inmates' own church in order to prepare for the prisoner's reception after release.

An interesting project in vitalizing religion has been reported from a state prison.[25] When the old hospital was replaced by a new structure, one wing of the old building was retained. The chaplains secured permission to convert this wing into a chapel. The prisoners themselves performed the work, and the chapel was then equipped by various churches. The building seats 300 persons; it also provides offices for the Protestant and Catholic chaplains. Previously a large auditorium seating a thousand had been used. In the new, small chapel, the chaplains found it possible to develop a new religious life with the prisoners participating in choirs and on committees.

Prisoners are sometimes permitted to express their ideas through artistic work. The backdrop of the prison chapel at Stateville, Illinois, was painted by inmates. The auditorium, which seats 1,720 persons, is equipped with a public address system, electric organ, and moving picture projector. It is used for recreation, lectures, and religious services. Six chaplains provide religious and counseling advice.

PERSONAL RELATIONSHIPS OF PRISONERS

As rules and punishment enforcing isolation and silence have declined, and contacts, conversations, and group activities among prisoners have increased, the informal life of the prison has become more significant. Prisoners are human beings with the urges, emotions, fears, hates, likes, and de-

Compensations for Lack of Feminine Contacts

Prisoners suffer from two types of isolation that work peculiar hardships upon them: (1) They are separated from their families; and (2) they are segregated by sex and therefore have no contacts with those of the opposite sex.

Table 19 on page 434 shows the percentage of male felons in 5 state prisons who were single, married, widowed, divorced, or separated at the time they entered prison. One third of the men were married and one fourth were widowed, separated, or divorced. It is not known how many had children. During the prison term, the prisoner is allowed to receive visits only at infrequent intervals and then only under supervision. There is rarely opportunity for privacy or display of affection, or even the intimate discussion of family plans. Marriages are likely to suffer strain or disintegration.

Families that were functioning prior to commitment may not survive the strain of the separation or the disgrace of a prison sentence, in those cases in which the offender was not a professional criminal. In 41 states conviction for a felony of husband or wife constitutes grounds for divorce. We do not know how often divorces are granted for this reason or for some other cause that arises from the separation and inability of the husband to support his family during his prison term.

Maintaining and reviving the prisoner's close relationship with his family is regarded as of major importance for the young offender who is soon to leave prison. Counselors, therefore, often act as go-betweens for prisoner and family or secure the aid of community social agencies to help the family. At a few institutions, including the California Institution for Men, families are allowed to come at stated times to visit the men under virtually normal social conditions. At the Institution, Sunday became visiting day, when families including children could bring picnic lunches to the Institution, to spend the day with their prisoner-members.

For many prisoners incarceration means sexual frustration. In the prison population, in addition to those accustomed to normal marital relationships, are many young men at the age when they would normally marry. Some, not interested in marriage, have been accustomed to casual sex relations. A small proportion of each prison population have been imprisoned for sexual offenses. For each of these types, some form of sexual strain is present, and opportunities for normal satisfaction not present.

The possibilities for sexual satisfactions in prison are limited to compensation, autoerotic practices, and physical contacts with those of the same sex.[30]

1. Compensation may be found in the telling of "smutty" stories and in deriding marriage and fidelity to one woman. Daydreaming of past or desired sexual adventures is also common. The lack of activity in prison and the long hours spent in the cells encourage both stories and daydreaming and offer no substitute diversions or interests.

2. Autoerotic practices apparently are common in prison. Among male prisoners, at least, they represent for many merely a reversion to childhood or adolescent practices. If the prison term is short the habit is probably discarded when the prisoner is released and is again able to make normal contacts with women.

3. The amount of actual homosexual activity in prison is unknown. In prison, as in civilian life, homosexual activities are legally forbidden and constitute a crime. They are concealed from guards as much as possible. Homosexuality is found in several degrees of intensity.

At one level is found the relationships established among inmates who, prior to imprisonment, had led normal sexual lives. Homosexuality is of a casual and temporary nature and is discarded when the prisoner is released.

At another level are the confirmed homosexuals. They include a small number who were homosexuals before imprisonment—in fact, whose crime may have been homosexuality—and some who in the course of long terms become habituated to this form of activity. Such men, who prefer contacts with other men to contacts with women, fall deeply in love and pursue an aggressive courtship, and may become a serious problem in the prison community. They represent a very small percentage of the prison population that is in need of special psychiatric diagnosis and treatment.

No adequate solution for frustrated sexual desires has been found. The official view maintains that such desires should be suppressed. Suppression is difficult under the conditions of prison life because of inactivity, the presence of a small group of confirmed homosexuals, and the development of obscene stories and poems that pass from one to another. The effect is to stimulate rather than suppress or divert interest in sex.

Informal Prisoner-Guard Relationships

The work required of the typical guard is obnoxious to many men and also brutalizing in its effect upon the personality. The function of the guard is to enforce the many rules and regulations and to prevent any attempt or even suggestion of an uprising. He must count the men under his charge several times a day, must see that they march in even lines when going from one place to another, that they are silent when talking is forbidden, and that they are locked in their cells at the appointed time. Since the rules call for the repression of many normal impulses (talking, laughing, lounging, playing, informal walking, jumping, running, and so on), the guards must constantly impose the authority of their office upon the prisoners to gain the necessary obedience. They must appear alert, imposing, forceful, and must be ready to enforce obedience by physical means if necessary. They have the power to grant minor privileges, inflict punishment, and report or withhold instances of major violations to higher officials. The prisoner has little recourse to any higher authority if the guard becomes abusive. This extreme power over the prisoners tends to warp many guards, and to make them autocratic and brutal. At best, guards are never able to have normal contacts with prisoners. Both convicts and wardens agree that under the present system of prison life the best guards are men who are able to remain impartial and fair, who enforce the rules uniformly on all prisoners, but who avoid sentimentality. They gain the respect of the prisoners and are able to perform their duties without resorting to physical force, although the threat is always present.[31]

The guards tend to look down upon the prisoners and to regard them as inferior, defective, depraved, dissolute, or incorrigible. Tannenbaum believes that this attitude on the part of the guards develops as a rationalization for their strict and sometimes brutal control over the prisoners.[32] The guards would not be able to treat equals as they treat the prisoners and retain their self-respect; but they may believe that it is both necessary and proper to dominate those who are inferior and incorrigible. Weinberg connects the attitude of the guards with the conflict inherent in the guard-prisoner relationship.[33] Both groups attribute to the other characteristics opposed to those that they believe themselves to have. Thus the guards, regarding themselves as normal, law-abiding people, term the prisoners untrustworthy, degenerate, deficient, and inferior. The prisoners, in turn, regard themselves as normal persons whose misfortune is discovery, whereas others are free not because they are more law-abiding but merely because they have not been caught. They are contemptuous and refer among themselves to guards and prison officials as ignorant, economic failures unable to hold a job elsewhere, or as political hacks. Thus each party to the conflict overlooks its own shortcomings and elaborates upon the defects of the other. Also, each group develops stereotyped concepts of the other, which are passed on from old prisoners to newcomers, from old guards to new recruits.

These concepts, which grow out of a conflict inherent in the prison organization, enable the guards to impose the same treatment on all prisoners and to disregard personal characteristics that otherwise might appeal to their sympathies. The prisoners, on their part, find many small ways to annoy the guards or to break minor rules without detection.   Their pleasure is often not what they obtain by breaking a rule but the satisfaction of knowing that they have successfully outwitted the guards.

More discriminating selection and better training would lay the basis for better prisoner-guard relationships.   But as long as the custodial motive, backed by repressive measures, dominates the prison system, constructive relationships cannot be expected.   As the rehabilitation of the prisoner slowly becomes the primary function of prisons, better understanding between the 2 groups and more helpfulness on the part of guards may be in prospect.   The training given guards in several prison systems to promote a new relationship has been described on pages 439–40.

EFFECT OF IMPRISONMENT

The effect of imprisonment on individuals depends in part upon their attitudes when they enter prison.   The first offender feels lost at first in the depersonalized atmosphere of prison.   He is uncertain, uneasy, fearful. His first experiences do not reassure him.   His personal property is taken away, he is clothed in the standard, uniform prison garb, and he is known by a number instead of his name.   Officially he tends to lose his identity. He also loses his individuality, for he must follow meticulous rules rather than make his own choices, and he must carry out all small personal duties as well as work in unison with a large group of other prisoners.   A few prisoners later reclaim their identity and individuality in the performance of special jobs that they are given about the prison; but the majority are not singled out for special jobs and if they emerge again as distinct personalities they must do so in the informal groups of prisoners rather than in the relationship with guards and prison officials.

Few offenders enter prison with a feeling of penitence and a desire to reform.   They may not claim innocence but they express many justifications for their offenses.[34]   Some of these justifications pertain to personal hardships that they have endured—to the stress of illness or a poverty-stricken childhood, to liquor or the need of food or money.   Other prisoners rationalize their crimes by referring to shady practices in politics or business that go unpunished; their crimes, they say, are no worse.

Many prisoners feel that they have been unjustly treated.   If they have been abused by the police or if they know of others who have committed crimes similar to their own but have been found not guilty, released on probation, or given shorter sentences they are especially likely to feel bitter. They believe that their imprisonment is not a just punishment but is the result of their inability to employ a skillful lawyer or to arrange a "fix." Others, fully as guilty as they, have gone free or have received light sentences. The domination by prison guards increases this feeling of injustice. If the parole board grants paroles to others and not to them, they are further confirmed in their feeling that they are for some reason unfairly treated. This feeling of bitterness is expressed in a verse composed by an inmate of the Massachusetts Reformatory for Women: [35]

> I'm walking about a prison,
>   What do you think I see?
> A lot of dumb-bells doing time,
>   While all the crooks go free.

The effect of prison depends also upon the degree to which the prisoner is steeped in criminal attitudes. The first offender, who is arrested soon after developing criminal activities, may reorient his life during the prison term. If his sentence is short and if he receives assistance after release he may be stopped short at the beginning of his criminal career. If the prisoner has long been associated with a delinquent or criminal group and prior to imprisonment has affiliated himself with the underworld, the probability of reorientation is slight. He enters prison allied with the criminal world and opposed to the police, courts, prisons, and reform. The prison regime, even when it is generally re-educative in effect, makes little impression upon him. He is satisfied with his way of life and does not desire a change.

A few prisoners, unable to adapt themselves to the prison regime, become rebellious and incorrigible. Repressive measures are applied to force at least surface obedience—solitary confinement, the denial of privileges, and other forms of punishment. The prisoner may learn to conform or continue to rebel. He may attempt to escape, incite others to riot or to mass escapes, or attack other prisoners or guards. If he commits some crime in the course of his rebellion he may be tried and given an additional sentence. Otherwise he is ineligible for parole, and is forced to serve the maximum term for his offense.

A few prisoners who are unable to adjust become psychotic, although they may have been previously normal. These prisoners may be placed in a separate ward or transferred to a special institution for the insane.

Most convicts adapt themselves to the prison regime and learn to accept passively the warden's authority, the many rules, and the codes and mores of the prisoners. In fact, in this acceptance they may lose some of their tensions and conflicts and find a form of security. Clemmer describes this process whereby the prisoner is assimilated into prison life as "prisonization." [36] He says it occurs most readily if the following factors are present:

Long sentence
Dearth of positive relationships with people outside of prison
Unstable personality
Ready entrance into primary groups of other prisoners
Blind acceptance of prison dogmas and mores
Readiness to participate in gambling and abnormal sexual behavior
Chance placement among other prisoners with a similar orientation

Once prisonized, the criminal readily adjusts to prison if he must serve a second term.   Professional and habitual criminals frequently become prisonized and accept successive prison terms without resentment.

In another interesting analysis of the process of adjustment, Lindner does not use the term prisonization but discusses essentially the same process.[37] His experience as a psychologist in a federal prison led him to observe 3 general processes:

1. The prisoner accepts the prison regime on the surface, following the routine and refraining from breaking rules.   But his basic personality pattern remains unchanged; his needs and his potentialities for criminal behavior continue.   Such prisoners give guards a minimum of trouble and hence meet official approval.   Their acceptance of the prison routine is regarded as rehabilitation, but in reality they are merely holding their individual needs and desires in a state of suspension.   They leave the prison in the same condition in which they entered it.

2. The other process of adjustment involves regression from a mature personality to infantilism.   The prisoner becomes dependent upon the routine and is unable to make decisions or take the initiative.   These prisoners often fear the date of release and react with sleeplessness and loss of appetite.   They have become so dependent upon the prison to feed and clothe them and to direct their activities that they feel unable to live outside its walls.

3. A third and rather rare process occurs: genuine rehabilitation resulting in the development of new goals and attitudes.   The way of life that the prisoner learns in prison does not aid him when he returns to the community. The institution is too artificial, too far removed from normal modes of living, to serve as a place where the prisoner may learn the new attitudes and social habits that he needs in order to become law abiding.   The fact that adjustment to prison tends to cause maladjustment to the community is a paradox. If the prisoner serves only a short term he may be able to shake off prison habits and return to normal community living.   But if his term is long he may become so inured to prison customs and habits of thought that he cannot readily readjust to conventional society.   Refusal to be absorbed into the mores of the prison gives him a better chance for normal adjustment when

he leaves.   Thus prison, supposed to rehabilitate the offender, does just the opposite in the degree to which the prisoner accepts the regime.   Hayner and Ash, after a study of prison conditions, state: [38]

In general, it is our conclusion that the conventional prison situation is the antithesis of the normal community and does not prepare for it.   Monotonous routine, sex starvation, lack of self-direction, and isolation from law-abiding culture patterns do not rehabilitate.   They demoralize.

It is not possible to judge to what extent the recent educational and vocational training programs will change the situation.   Too often, all the work of the classification committee and the programs to support their recommendations are only superimposed upon the previous repressive prison routine.   So far little seems to have been done to provide training in self-discipline or in responsible community living.

QUESTIONS

1. What are the objectives of a classification system?   What are the elements of a satisfactory system?
2. What are some of the special aspects and problems of group therapy when carried on within a penal institution?
3. Why are many prison administrators unable to supply work for prisoners? Outline a system of prison labor that would be advantageous to prisoners and at the same time not injurious to outside industry or business?
4. Discuss the needs for academic, vocational, and social education in prisons.
5. What is the relation of recreational programs to prison discipline?
6. In what important ways do social contacts within prison differ from those in the conventional community?
7. How can the process of prisonization be avoided?

READINGS

Tappan, Paul W. (ed.), *Contemporary Correction* (McGraw-Hill, 1951). Covers many aspects of prison administration and program, with each chapter written by a specialist.

Sellin, Thorsten (ed.), "Prisons in Transformation," *Annals of the American Academy of Political and Social Science,* Vol. 293 (1954).   A series of articles by experts on the background of prisons and current plans and programs.

    The following references all discuss the informal life of prisoners and are important in giving an understanding of how the formal prison regime affects prisoners.

Clemmer, Donald, *The Prison Community* (Boston: Christopher Publishing Company, 1940).

Foreman, P. B., "Guide Theory for the Study of Informal Inmate Relations," *Southwestern Social Science Quarterly* (Dec., 1953), pp. 34–46.

Hayner, N. S., "The Prisoner Community as a Social Group," *American Socio-logical Review,* 4 (1939), 362–69.

—— and E. Ash, "The Prison as a Community," *American Sociological Review,* 6 (1940), 577–83.

McCorkle, L. W., "Resocialization within Prison Walls," *Annals of the American Academy of Political and Social Science,* 293 (1954), 88–98.

Reimer, Hans, "Socialization in the Prison Community," *Proceedings of the American Prison Association* (1937), pp. 151–55.

Weinberg, S. K., "Aspects of the Prison's Social Structure," *American Journal of Sociology,* 47 (1942), 717–26.

In contrast to the statements of professional staff on the programs offered and to the sociological studies of prisoner reactions are the statements of prisoners themselves.   The following accounts were written by men who had had experience as prisoners: they record their own and their fellow-inmates' reactions to prison administration and official activities.   The reports often lack objectivity.   The older accounts do not always record the present status of the prisons involved.

Clark, Charles L., and Earle E. Eubank, *Lockstep and Corridor: Thirty-five Years of Prison Life* (Cincinnati: University of Cincinnati Press, 1927).   The life story of a professional thief who was in and out of prisons from youth until old age.   Eubank appends a sociological analysis to the account.

Hassler, Alfred, *The Diary of a Self-Made Convict* (New York: Fellowship Publications, 1954).   Imprisoned for violations of federal laws growing out of his objections to fighting, the author describes the influence of prison on criminals.

Lamson, D. A., *We Who Are About to Die; Prison as Seen by a Condemned Man* (Scribner's, 1935).   Sentenced to death for the murder of his wife and confined in death row at California's San Quentin State Prison, Lamson writes an unusually objective although critical account of the prison.   He was later released from prison.   For another view of San Quentin that brings the account up to date, see: Duffy, Clinton T., and Dean Jennings, *The San Quentin Story* (Doubleday, 1950).

Nelson, Victor F., *Prison Days and Nights* (Little, Brown, 1933).   Eastern prisons as they appeared to a drifting habitual thief and drunkard, who was never able to accept a conventional mode of living.

Tasker, R. J., *Grimhaven* (Knopf, 1928).   Another view of prison life by a prisoner.

FOOTNOTES

[1] *Attorney General's Survey of Release Procedures,* 5, *Prisons* (Washington: U.S. Department of Justice, 1939), 143ff.; E. R. East, "Classification Reception Centers," *Journal of Criminal Law and Criminology,* 36 (1945), 243–48; Paul W. Tappan (ed.), *Contemporary Correction* (McGraw-Hill, 1951), ch. 7; annual reports of many state penal systems describing their methods of classification.

[2] Norman Fenton, "The Process of Reception in the Adult Correctional System," *Annals of the American Academy of Political and Social Science,* 293 (1954), 51–58; Tappan, *op. cit.,* ch. 8.

[3] Sol Rubin, "Changing Youth Correction Authority Concepts," *Focus,* 29 (1950), 77–82.

4 Karl Holton, "California Youth Authority, Eight Years of Action," *Journal of Criminal Law and Criminology*, 41 (1950), 1–23.

5 *Progress Report of the Youth Conservation Commission up to July 1, 1950* (St. Paul: State of Minnesota); G. J. Reed, "Minnesota's YCC Program," *Focus*, 32 (1953), 49–51.

6 Lloyd W. McCorkle, "Group Therapy in the Treatment of Offenders," *Federal Probation*, 16 (Dec., 1952), 22–27; F. L. Bixby and Lloyd W. McCorkle, "Guided Group Interaction in Correctional Work," *American Sociological Review*, 16 (1951), 455–61.

7 Tappan, *op. cit.*, ch. 14; F. L. Bixby and Lloyd W. McCorkle, "Applying the Principles of Group Therapy in Correctional Institutions," *Federal Probation*, 14 (March, 1950), 36–40.

8 *Federal Prisons, 1952* (Washington: Federal Bureau of Prisons, U.S. Department of Justice, 1952), pp. 25–26.

9 Blake McKelvey, *American Prisons, a Study in American Social History Prior to 1915* (University of Chicago Press, 1936), p. 40. Throughout this book the history of prison labor is traced. See especially chs. 5 and 8. Most of the historical material in this chapter is from McKelvey.

10 Charles L. Clark and Earle E. Eubank, *Lockstep and Corridor: Thirty-five Years of Prison Life* (Cincinnati: University of Cincinnati Press, 1927), p. 7.

11 McKelvey, *op. cit.*, pp. 174ff.

12 Lewis E. Lawes, *Twenty Thousand Years in Sing Sing* (New York: Long and Smith, 1932), pp. 161ff.

13 R. F. Jones, "Prison Labor in the United States, 1940," *Monthly Labor Review*, 53 (1941), 587.

14 "Gearing Federal Prisons to the War Effort" (Washington: United States Bureau of Prisons, Department of Justice, 1947), pp. 92–94.

15 *Biennial Report for the Period Ending December 31, 1952* (Sacramento: Department of Corrections, State of California, 1952), pp. 21–22; R. A. McGee, "Saving Prison Waste," *Annals of the American Academy of Political and Social Science*, 293 (1954), 59–69.

16 McKelvey, *op. cit.*, pp. 26, 41, 57, 108ff.; Austin H. MacCormick, *The Education of Adult Prisoners* (New York: National Society of Penal Information, 1931), pp. 9, 41.

17 Austin H. MacCormick, "Résumé of Progress in Correctional Education," *Correctional Education Today* (New York: American Prison Association Yearbook, 1939), pp. 23ff.

18 *Federal Prisons, 1953* (Washington; Federal Bureau of Prisons, U.S. Department of Justice, 1954), pp. 20–23.

19 W. M. Wallack, G. N. Kendall, and H. L. Briggs, *Education within Prison Walls* (New York: Bureau of Publications, Teachers College, Columbia University, 1939), pp. 8–9, 22ff.

20 S. H. Souter, "Results of Prison Library Survey," *Proceedings of the American Prison Association* (1941), pp. 322–27.

21 McKelvey, *op. cit.*, p. 41.

22 McKelvey, *op. cit.*, pp. 114–17.

23 Donald Clemmer, *The Prison Community* (Boston: Christopher, 1940), ch. 9.

24 E. C. Krumbholz, "Message from the President of the National Chaplain's Association," *Proceedings of the American Prison Association* (1944), pp. 170–72.

25 A. W. Stremel, "Implementing Religion in Prison," *Prison Journal*, 22 (1942), 245–46.

26 Clemmer, *op. cit.*, p. 107; N. S. Hayner and E. Ash, "The Prisoner Community as a Social Group," *American Sociological Review*, 4 (1939), 367–68.

27 Clemmer, *op. cit.*, ch. 6.

28 Clemmer, *op. cit.*, ch. 5.

29 Clark and Eubank, *op. cit.*

30 Hayner and Ash, *op. cit.*, pp. 368–69; Clemmer, *op. cit.*, ch. 10; Joseph Fulling Fishman, *Sex Life in American Prisons* (New York: National Library Press, 1939).

31 R. J. Tasker, *Grimhaven* (Knopf, 1928), pp. 118ff.; D. A. Lamson, *We Who are about to Die* (Scribner's, 1935), pp. 68–69; Lawes, *op. cit.*, ch. 8.

[32] Frank Tannenbaum, *Wall Shadows: a Study in American Prisons* (Putnam, 1922), pp. 24–26.

[33] S. K. Weinberg, "Aspects of the Prison's Social Structure," *American Journal of Sociology,* 47 (1942), 717–26.

[34] H. E. Field, "The Attitudes of Prisoners as a Factor in Rehabilitation," *Annals of the American Academy of Political and Social Science,* 157 (1931), 150–63; Albert Morris, "Criminals' Views on Crime Causation," *Annals of the American Academy of Political and Social Science,* 217 (1941), 138–44.

[35] Morris, *op. cit.,* p. 138.

[36] Clemmer, *op. cit.,* ch. 12.

[37] Robert M. Lindner, *Stone Walls and Men* (New York: Odyssey, 1946), pp. 420–22.

[38] Hayner and Ash, *op. cit.,* p. 580.

18

The Woman Offender and Her Treatment

Women offenders differ from men in frequency of arrests, types of offenses, type of correctional institution, and treatment-program provided. They are, of course, subject to the same judicial processes as men. Some of these differences have been stated in Chapter 2; for example, in cities of 25,000 and over, 8 men are arrested for every woman. In actual numbers, more men are guilty of each individual crime than are women, except, of course, prostitution and here the reports are misleading, since men patrons are not included. Arrested women most nearly approach men in the commission of murders, aggravated assaults, forgery, embezzlement, larceny, vagrancy, narcotic drug violation, disorderly conduct, and violation of liquor laws (but not drunkenness); men exceed women most in arrests for automobile thefts, burglary, and drunkenness.

WOMEN IN JAILS

Minor female offenders are sentenced to jails, as are male offenders. Except in large cities, separate jails are not provided. In some jails women are placed in cells not completely segregated from men inmates and are under the supervision of men jailers or wardens. This practice is soundly condemned by federal and state inspectors, penologists, and social workers. Good practice calls for complete separation of women from men, on separate floors or separate units of the jail, so that they are not within sight of each other, and for a woman matron on duty both day and night.

In larger jails that provide separate units for women, the construction of the women's unit often differs from that of the men. A common sleeping room may replace cells or if the women are locked into cells at night, they may be allowed considerable freedom in the corridor or a day room during the day. Often only unmanageable women are locked up during the day.

In all except the large cities the women's section of the jail may be empty most of the time or at most have only a very few prisoners. These women occupy themselves with reading, talking, or playing cards. In large jails an attempt is made to provide occupations. The following description of the women's quarters at the county jail of one of the most populous counties in the United States gives a realistic picture.[1]

In this jail, which in the past has rated high in federal inspections, women awaiting trial are separated from those already convicted and serving sentences. The number of women has outgrown the facilities, so that there are 114 women crowded into 59 cells originally planned to accommodate 90 women. Extra cots are crowded into the cells; the hospital, a 15 by 18 foot room, is also filled with beds and at times additional beds for the sick are set up in the corridor. A minority of the cells have toilets and shower facilities are too few for the number of inmates. Women are sentenced for periods up to one year, although most of them have sentences of only a few months.

The staff consists of a head matron and 9 assistants, some of whom are always on duty. They mix firmness with sympathy and encourage both cleanliness and some occupation for inmates. The women care for their own cells, which are neat and clean; they keep washroom and kitchen clean, and twice weekly scrub the corridor upon which the cells open.

The women are out of bed by 7 A.M., tidy their cells, and breakfast at 7:45. From then until 7 P.M. they are locked into the day room, which is furnished with benches and tables. They have a movie on Sunday; otherwise they spend much of their time reading and playing cards. The matron tries to encourage them to sew or embroider, but many have no interest. There are two sewing rooms where they may do institutional sewing and receive some pay for it. Visitors may come twice a month to talk to them in special booths where they are separated from the inmates by glass partitions equipped with sound slits.

Women in jails are guilty primarily of drunkenness or disorderly conduct, which often includes prostitution, and for which they serve sentences of a few months. In some states, women misdemeanants who must serve longer terms are sent to a state farm, house of correction, or women's reformatory that also receives women guilty of major crimes. These institutions provide more livable quarters than do jails and a wider variety of occupations.

CHARACTERISTICS OF WOMEN CRIMINALS

In view of the lack of over-all figures showing the characteristics of women criminals, information given in the annual reports of women's reformatories for a limited number of states is here brought together. In some instances the reformatories include some misdemeanants as well as women guilty of felonies. State laws also differ as to the minimum age of inmates. The summaries of characteristics, therefore, cannot be accepted as valid for major criminals; they show, however, the types of women in reformatories.

Age

New admissions to state reformatories range all the way from girls in their teens to old women. Figure 23 shows the bulking of new arrivals in

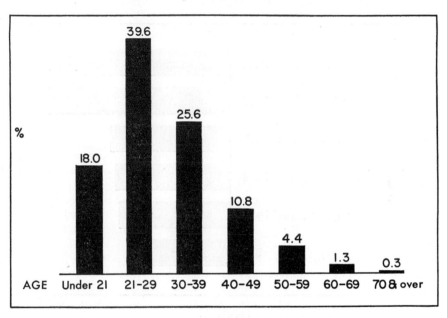

FIGURE 23

Age distribution of women prisoners at admission. The distribution points up the relative youthfulness of most offenders admitted to women's reformatories, as well as the intermixture of a few old women. The distribution is for 1,329 women admitted during one year to women's reformatories in 7 northern states and 1 southern. The reformatories, widely scattered over the United States, were chosen primarily on the basis of the adequacy of their annual reports, from which the information for this and Figures 24 and 25 was selected.

the younger ages but also a small ingredient of older women even into the years of infirmities. The population in institutions at any one time would differ somewhat from the distribution shown in the Figure, since some women are committed for very short terms and others for long terms or life. In individual reformatories the age distribution is affected also by the state laws that set the minimum age for admission. In some women's reformatories girls as young as 15 are admitted; others are reserved for adults, with adolescents being confined in special institutions. As compared with women serving short terms in jail, the reformatory group is much younger.

Offenses

The offenses for which women are committed to prison are primarily of 4 types—thefts of various kinds; drunken, disorderly, or vagrant conduct; neglect of children; and sex offenses.   These offenses account for three fourths of all convictions.   The distribution of offenses for commitments in one year for 12 states is shown in Figure 24.

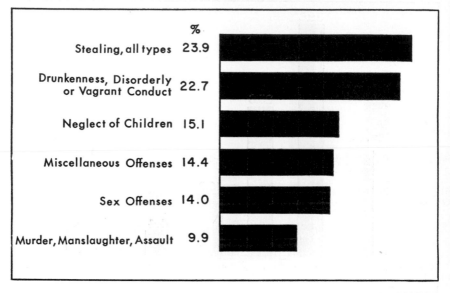

%

Stealing, all types	23.9
Drunkenness, Disorderly or Vagrant Conduct	22.7
Neglect of Children	15.1
Miscellaneous Offenses	14.4
Sex Offenses	14.0
Murder, Manslaughter, Assault	9.9

FIGURE 24

Distribution of offenses of women prisoners in reformatories.   The Figure shows the high proportion of thefts and personal disorderliness (including sex offenses).   The Figure is based on 1,821 admissions during one year to women's reformatories in 10 northern and 2 southern states, according to annual reports.

Although offenses are minor, the offenders are not novices.   According to the report of the Commissioner of Correction for Massachusetts, among the 190 new admissions to the Reformatory for Women in 1950, only 83 were serving their first commitment.[2]   Most of the recidivists had had from 1 to 3 previous commitments to training schools, jails, state farms, or re- formatories; 28 of the women, however, had had more than 3 previous com- mitments, with one having had the phenomenal number of 40 commitments. In California a similar situation exists.[3]   Among the 177 women offenders sentenced to the California Institution for Women in 1951–52, less than half—74—had no prior commitments.   Although most of the remainder had been committed as a misdemeanant or juvenile delinquent only, 18 had previously been confined to prison.   Other state reports show essentially the same situation.   The women's reformatories are confronted, therefore, with women whose criminal habits are well established.

Marital Status

Marital life has been highly disorganized and many have failed to keep their marriages alive, as Figure 25 shows.   Almost a third of women of-

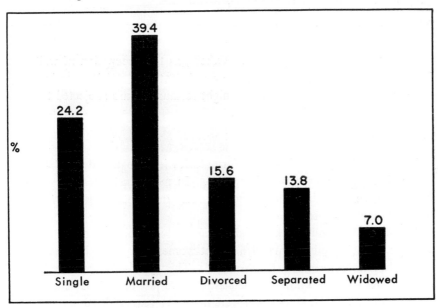

FIGURE 25

Percentage of women prisoners in each marital status.   Marital failure among reformatory women far exceeds that in the general population.   A valid comparison of the marital status of prisoners with that of the general population is difficult to make because of differences between the two groups in age, economic, and regional distributions.   It may be pointed out, however, that among all women aged 14 and over, 66.6 per cent are married (includes separated) as compared with 53.2 per cent married and separated among prisoners.   The most startling difference is in the divorce rate: 2.3 per cent of the general population but 15.6 per cent of the prisoners are divorced.   The Figure is based on 1,001 admissions during one year to women's reformatories in 8 northern states, as given in annual reports.

fenders are divorced or separated at the time of commitment.   Among women 14 years of age and over in the general population, only about 2 per cent are divorced.   Although divorce or separation always involves the husband as well as the wife, it seems certain that these women lack the personal qualities and training necessary to maintain a stable marriage relationship.

Education and Occupation

Educationally women offenders are deficient. Although among women admitted to institutions in 7 northern states there were few illiterates, the median educational level was slightly under the eighth grade. Reformatory reports that include data on previous occupations reveal a high proportion of domestic workers, waitresses, and unskilled workers among the inmates. There are also many housewives. Many of the occupations listed are solitary ones (domestic workers) that do not bring the woman into the close control of a primary group. Others, as the occupation of waitress, may accustom the woman to many casual contacts. Waitresses in some types of taverns, night clubs, or all-night restaurants are subjected to constant sexual proposals from patrons.

Disorganization

The annual reports of some reformatories include a statement on the parental family background of inmates. In many instances, the women have been reared in disorganized homes, sometimes with a parent or sibling having criminal record.

Details of the family background of reformatory women are given by the Gluecks in their study of 500 delinquent women who served terms in the Massachusetts Reformatory for Women.[4]   The women studied were typical of the wider number whose characteristics have just been sketched.   They were poorly educated; 80 per cent were under 31 years old; 78 per cent had been sent to the reformatory for sex offenses, or idle and disorderly conduct. A study of their childhood background reveals that most of them came from typical transitional areas, as described in Chapter 3.   Almost half came from slum-type homes; 77 per cent of the families had been clients of social agencies; 77 per cent of the parents were illiterate or nearly so; half the fathers were day laborers or factory workers and half the mothers worked; slightly more than half the homes were broken.   Although many of these characteristics are not directly conducive to delinquency, they do not provide a stable environment for a child.   More crucial are such facts as the following: 55 per cent of the homes were of poor moral standards; in 45 per cent of the families the parents or siblings had been arrested, and in another 35 per cent there had been some delinquency or crime without arrest.   The inmates of the reformatory themselves, as children, were given to truancy, excessive lying, immorality, stealing, or drinking.

We may safely conclude that the staff of a woman's reformatory has to cope with a large proportion of inmates who are personally disorganized in some respects, with a record of marital and family disorganization, poor education, and work experience that offers little stability.   The short period of imprisonment, even when there is a good program, is not adequate to combat the habits and attitudes of a lifetime.   Increasing the length of sentence, however, breeds hopelessness and isolates the woman from normal community life.

HOUSING WOMEN CRIMINALS

Compared with men criminals who are imprisoned, women criminals are few in number.   Among federal prisoners, 2.7 per cent are women, and among state prisoners, 3.6 per cent.[5]   Federal women prisoners for the entire United States are all concentrated in one institution at Alderson, West Virginia.

Approximately 5,500 women criminals are in state institutions, either independent prisons and reformatories for women or segregated quarters in men's prisons.   Twenty-seven per cent are housed in men's prisons, the number of women sometimes being as small as 5 or 6 per prison.   Twenty-two states place women prisoners in men's prisons; 22 states and the District of Columbia maintain women's reformatories or prisons under state control and administered independently of the men's prisons.   Four states board their few women prisoners in reformatories in other states.   With few exceptions the combined men's and women's prisons are in the South and West, and the independent institutions for women in the northeastern, middle Atlantic, and north central states.

When men and women are in the same institution, there is complete segregation.   The women may have a portion of one cell block, with their own work shops (usually sewing), under supervision of women matrons. They are in a small prison within a prison.   In some of the more populous states with sufficient women prisoners to justify an expanded program, special buildings have been erected at some distance from the men's prison but under the administration of the prison warden.   Such buildings usually are similar to the cottages used in most independent reformatories and the routine of life and work follows the reformatory rather than the prison pattern.   For example, at the Missouri State Penitentiary, the men occupy traditional cell blocks; at a remote part of the prison grounds, within the wall but completely detached from the men's section, are two dormitory cottages for women.   Here the women carry out normal housekeeping procedures and work in a large garden.   At the Colorado State Penitentiary, the 1,400 men are concentrated behind high walls, whereas the 35 women prisoners have their own cottage-type institution outside the wall but within the high wire security fence.   In each case women personnel supervise the women prisoners but the warden of the penitentiary is the administrator.

Aside from these movements toward a special type of housing and program for women, the women in men's prisons seem to be the forgotten prisoners.   Neither annual reports from the various states nor surveys of prisons do more than mention the number of women in each prison.   In report after report nothing is said about their living conditions, recreation, occupations, crimes, or general characteristics, although detailed information covering many pages is usually included about the male prisoners.

WOMEN'S PRISONS AND REFORMATORIES

The two earliest separate penal institutions for women were opened in the 1870's.[6]   Indiana placed its first offenders in what is now called the Indiana Women's Prison in 1873; the Massachusetts Reformatory for Women (originally called Prison Reformatory) was opened at Framingham in 1877. The third women's institution did not open until 1901 and it was really not until after World War I that the movement gathered strength.

Cottage System

When the early women's prisons were built, the model for prisons was tiers of cells two or three stories high, all encased in thick walls for ease of supervision and custody.   Early women's prisons tended to follow this pattern, although none were so grim and forbidding as the typical men's prison of the nineteenth century.[7]   By 1915–20, it was realized that fortresses were not needed to confine women prisoners and that they could be provided with quarters that, though institutional, were comfortable and had many of the amenities of normal living.   Consequently, a cottage system of construction was substituted for the one large building of the earlier period.

In appearance a modern woman's reformatory bears a close resemblance to a nonpenal institution such as a large hospital, old people's home, or even a college.[8]   The only obvious reminders that it is a penal institution are often a high wire fence around the grounds and light bars or heavy screening over the windows.   There is usually an attractive administration building, a unit for classes, one or more industrial buildings, a chapel or assembly building, and a number of housing units adequate for 25 to 60 people euphemistically called cottages.   Grounds are landscaped and bouquets of flowers adorn the administration building in season.   The grim high walls and guard towers and the cell blocks of the men's prison are missing from the modern women's reformatory.

Each cottage typically is an independent living unit with its own living room, dining room, kitchen, and individual bedrooms for the prisoners. The furnishings resemble those of a well kept lower middle-class home.   The women are required to maintain the home, including their rooms, in excellent condition. Encouraged to decorate their rooms individually, they often spend their free time knitting doilies or embroidering bedspreads. The

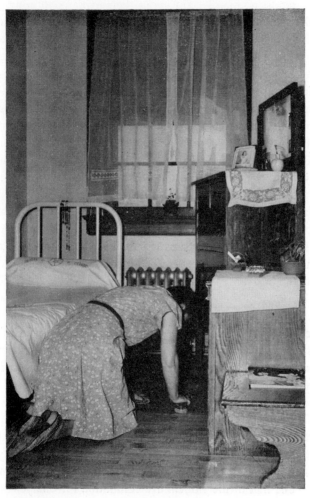

Most women's reformatories are built on the cottage plan, with each cottage containing its own living or recreation room, dining room, kitchen, and sleeping rooms for 30 to 60 inmates. As this picture from an eastern reformatory shows, the rooms, although small and simply furnished, are more comfortable and less prison-like than the barred cells of the typical men's prison. Inmates usually are encouraged to decorate bed spreads and dresser scarves with embroidery or crocheting. Cleanliness and orderliness are emphasized. It is hoped that the women, who often come from meager social backgrounds, will respond to the standards set in their cottages. Windows have steel frames and doors are locked at night to prevent escape.

kitchen is fully equipped and meals are prepared by the inmates, who follow balanced menus.   The dining room usually is equipped with small tables, linen, and china dishes.

Staff

The staff is related to the program offered and in general is primarily composed of women.   A superintendent, appointed by the state agency in charge of reformatories, heads the staff, which includes house matrons, teachers, and work supervisors.   Either full or part-time medical and religious services are provided.   When special emphasis is placed on rehabilitation, counselors and social workers are included in the staff, usually with access to psychiatric services.

State Organization

The state agency in charge of the reformatory varies.   In some states, women's reformatories are part of the prison system and are controlled by the same agency as men's penitentiaries; in others the penitentiaries are under a correctional agency, the women's reformatories and juvenile training schools under a welfare department; and in still others all state institutions, penal and nonpenal, are supervised by one state board.

SERVICES AND ACTIVITIES

Many services and activities are provided in the typical women's reformatory; from the point of view of rehabilitation the program is more adequate than in most of the men's prisons.   What can be done is affected, however, by the length of sentences of women prisoners.

Sentences

Sentences on the whole are short.   Although it is impossible to compile a composite table of sentences because of the different methods of sentencing in different states, an inspection of sentences state by state shows that from one third to one half of the women are committed for one year or less, except in a few institutions that receive only felons.   The short sentences signify the relatively mild quality of offenses; nevertheless, in each institution there is a small group of serious offenders (convicted of murder, assaults, robbery, burglary, and the like) who enter under the burden of a long sentence, 10 to 20 years or even life.   The inclusion in one institution of short- and long-term prisoners creates a serious problem in program-planning. Inmates serving a few years may look forward eagerly to release, plan for the future, and accept with some grace the training program of the institution.

Each inmate enters the program at Alderson through submitting to study by the classification committee and leaves under the protection of a parole officer who is a member of the classification committee. Acceptance of the program and regulations brings a relative amount of freedom; inability to conform brings loss of privileges and if necessary confinement in an isolation building with barred windows.

The modern women's reformatory resembles an educational institution in general style of buildings and in the well-kept grounds. Outstanding among reformatories is the Federal Reformatory for Women at Alderson, West Virginia, which receives women from all parts of the United States who have violated some federal law. In general, the women live in more normal surroundings and enjoy greater freedom in the cottages and unwalled grounds than do men in prisons. Emphasis is placed upon improving education, giving some vocational training, and providing an experience in group living through working, eating, and spending leisure in small groups.

Household skills are emphasized by the cottage routine; in addition, homemaking classes are popular, and besides cooking and sewing include practical nursing, knitting, rug making and a variety of other skills and arts. Academic classes provide both for the poorly educated woman and the one desiring to take business courses or to increase her appreciation of art or music. The principal industry is a sewing project where clothing is made for the inmates of various federal institutions. Many women work on the farm, while others are engaged in smaller projects.

A detailed description of life at Alderson as viewed by an inmate has been provided by Helen Bryan, who served 3 months there in 1950 for contempt

of Congress.[14]   On the one hand was regimentation, with a fixed time schedule, a set program, and minute rules of behavior and procedure.   For example, clothes had to be folded in a certain way before they were put away;
the inmate was instructed never to lie or sit on her bed when the spread was

Women's reformatories, as well as men's prisons, face the difficult task of finding
constructive occupations for their inmates. At the Federal Reformatory for
Women at Alderson, West Virginia, the power sewing shop offers employment
for many women, who make clothing for other government services as well as
the clothing worn in the institution and an outfit for each woman who leaves.

on; all inmates stood in the presence of an officer and addressed her with
"Yes, ma'am" or "No, ma'am."   On the other hand, life in the reformatory
had many amenities.   The locked door at night was preceded by an evening
of gossip and smoking by little groups of girls gathered in one room, or by
larger group sessions in the living room.   The routine and meticulous care
of sleeping rooms was offset by the fact that rooms were decorated in different colors, furniture could be arranged as each inmate pleased, and
family photographs and other personal objects could be used to decorate the
rooms.   Each woman was issued the same set of institutional clothing, but
each had a choice of colors and in addition the women could knit sweaters
and make belts and other ornaments for their own use.   Education and
work filled the day, but with freedom to cross the campus unattended, a time
for shopping at the commissary, freedom to sing when it would not interfere
with the progress of the work, and provision for movies and other recreation.

COMPARISON OF MEN'S AND WOMEN'S PENAL INSTITUTIONS

No matter how attractive the appearance, how varied the program, how comfortable the living arrangements, women's reformatories are still prisons; women are sent to them against their will for the violation of criminal laws. Compared with men's prisons, however, the women's reformatories seem to be institutions of another order. The best of the men's institutions do not equal the best of the women's reformatories in a comfortable mode of living. Men's institutions are built on the congregate plan, with certain buildings devoted to sleeping, others to eating, others to recreation, and so on. The cottage system, which welds a relatively small number into a social group and concentrates much of the routine of living in one building, characteristic of women's institutions, is almost unknown for men.

Another and more fundamental difference is the general tendency for men's institutions to be operated with a punitive attitude, the women's with rehabilitation as the central motive.

The two differences—type of building and motive of program—are related. Men's prisons either were built, or follow the model of ones that were built a hundred years ago when the assumption was that all criminals were dangerous and that reform would be accomplished by rigorous living, severe punishment, and hard work. Medium and minimum security institutions, even of the most modern and best type, are essentially simply modifications of the old style cellular, barred prison, with a congregate (rather than the cottage small-group) type of living. Programs of rehabilitation are imposed upon the outmoded type of structure.

Women's institutions with few exceptions were built after it was recognized (1) that not all criminals need maximum security institutions, and (2) that a better possibility for rehabilitation is to be found in retraining, re-education, and counseling than in a repressive, punitive regime. Women's institutions fall far short of achieving perfection, but they are basically rehabilitative in policy and program and usually flexible enough to incorporate new methods. In structure, they are adapted to the mass of inmates who require only medium or minimum security. The "hardened" women criminals exist, just as "hardened" men criminals do. But in women's prisons, unlike the situation in men's prisons, they are treated as the minority and not allowed to dominate and determine the entire prison program as so often happens in men's prisons.

The smaller number of women than of men also is a factor in the difference. In California, for instance, one institution is sufficient to house all the women criminals in the state and still stay well within the limits of a manageable institution; 5 institutions are required to house the men, with one prison—

San Quentin—having 4,000 prisoners. Four thousand prisoners in one institution cannot be handled in the same way as 400. Many men's prisons run well over 1,000 inmates, whereas only one women's state reformatory has over 400 inmates and most women's reformatories have less than 100 prisoners. To convert men's prisons into something similar to the women's, with cottage living and small groups would entail a tremendous outlay of money, greatly increased staff, and a new program.

Another and vital factor is that there is less fear of women criminals than of men criminals on the part of both public and staff. A woman criminal is still thought of as a woman, with human qualities, whereas a man criminal tends to be stereotyped as a wild and dangerous beast. To what extent this is simply a stereotype and to what extent true is not possible to say. Certainly not all men criminals are dangerous, as the successful minimum security institutions for men are proving. However, since there are more male than female offenders, the number of professional criminals is greater among the men. Congregated together in one prison, they may make a formidable group. It is also probably true that male professional criminals reach a degree of acceptance of criminality and of ruthlessness in dealing with opponents not achieved by many women criminals. For example, when one or several women are attached to a group of organized gangsters, it is the men who force their way into the bank and who kill guards or policemen if they stand in the way of escape, whereas the woman usually stays in the background.

A final factor to consider is the effect on prisoners of the type of prison. Are men sometimes motivated by the nature of the male prison, with its repression and threat of punishment, to engage in riots and other unruliness? Are the frustrations so great that they arouse hostility? Women's reformatories and men's minimum security institutions accept their inmates as essentially human rather than essentially criminal and the ease of operating these institutions may be in part because under these circumstances the inmates react as human beings rather than as outlaws. This would be only one factor, of course, especially among men, since the inmates of the minimum security institutions are carefully selected.

QUESTIONS

1. What are the chief characteristics of women criminals?

2. Contrast women's penal institutions with men's as to living arrangements. Which seems most conducive to rehabilitation?

3. In view of the short sentences, what can the woman's reformatory hope to accomplish in the way of rehabilitation?

4. What is your opinion of policies now followed with reference to babies born to women prisoners?

5. In what ways do men's prisons surpass women's prisons and reformatories?

6. In what ways do women's surpass men's?

READINGS

Bryan, Helen, *Inside* (Houghton Mifflin, 1953). Personal impressions of the Federal Reformatory for Women, Alderson, West Virginia, by a college-trained woman who spent 3 months as a prisoner for contempt of Congress. The book details in narrative form her own progression through admission, quarantine period, and cottage and work life. She describes the relationship between prisoners and officers and relates the life stories of many of the inmates as told by themselves.

Glueck, Sheldon and Eleanor T., *Five Hundred Delinquent Women* (Knopf, 1934). This study gives the most complete objective picture in print of women offenders with reformatory experience. Their social backgrounds, personal characteristics, offenses, reformatory experiences, and post-reformatory lives are all explored and conclusions drawn as to significant factors for successful adjustment and failure to adjust. Of special interest are chapters 2 and 9 giving life histories. Chapter 8 describes the Massachusetts Reformatory for Women prior to 1930.

Harris, Mary, *I Knew Them in Prison* (Viking, 1936). Written by a woman with wide experience as head of 4 women's institutions, the book combines factual observations with interpretations and the author's own philosophy. She had charge of the women's Workhouse, Blackwell's Island, New York City, 1914–18; of the State Reformatory for Women at Clinton, New Jersey; State Home for Girls, Trenton, New Jersey; and Federal Industrial Institution for Women (now Alderson) in the years immediately after its opening in 1927. Her account of Alderson should be read in connection with the Bryan reference, given above—the superintendent's view versus the inmate's view.

Hepner, Arthur W., "Ordeal in Massachusetts, The Vindication of Dr. Van Waters," *Harper's Magazine,* 198 (June, 1949), 81–89. This article might well be used as a follow-up to the Gluecks' account of the Massachusetts Reformatory for Women; it presents the difficulties encountered by Dr. Miriam Van Waters, superintendent of the Reformatory, when she attempted to introduce new methods of rehabilitation and gained the enmity of certain political groups. The conflict between the professionally trained administrator and the politically controlled state officials is clearly drawn.

Monahan, Florence, *Women in Crime* (Ives Washburn, 1941). An account of administrative experiences written by the head of two women's reformatories and one training school for girls. The account is less penetrating than the similar project by Mary Harris.

O'Hare, Kate Richards, *In Prison* (Knopf, 1923). A scathing account of life in the State Penitentiary at Jeffersonville, Missouri, during the period of World War I, written by a woman confined there as a federal prisoner. At this time the Federal Reformatory for Women was not in existence.

Tappan, Paul W. (ed.), *Contemporary Correction* (McGraw-Hill, 1951). Chapter 19 on "Women's Institutions" gives an excellent general discussion of the treatment of women criminals, written by a woman with many years of experience in women's correctional work.

FOOTNOTES

[1] Report in a newspaper in 1954, by a woman journalist who specializes in social problems.

[2] E. E. McDowell, *Statistical Reports of the Commissioner of Correction for the Years Ending December 31, 1949 and December 31, 1950,* Public Document No. 115 (Boston: Department of Corrections, Commonwealth of Massachusetts, undated), p. 127.

[3] *Biennial Report for the Period Ending December 1, 1952* (Sacramento: Department of Corrections, State of California, 1952), p. 52.

[4] Sheldon and Eleanor T. Glueck, *Five Hundred Delinquent Women* (Knopf, 1934), chs. 1–7, 9.

[5] *National Prisoner Statistics,* No. 7 (Washington: Federal Bureau of Prisons, U.S. Department of Justice, Nov., 1953).

[6] Fred E. Haynes, *The American Prison System* (McGraw-Hill, 1939), ch. 5; E. C. Lekkerkerker, *Reformatories for Women in the United States* (Groningen, Netherlands: J. B. Wolters, 1931).

[7] Glueck, *op. cit.* Chapter 8 describes the Massachusetts Women's Reformatory.

[8] Descriptions of reformatories are based on personal visits to several, annual reports, discussions in state publications, and magazine articles. An attempt has been made to give a generalized picture.

[9] E. S. Zemans, "Prison Babies," *The Mother* (Quarterly Bulletin of the American Committee on Maternal Welfare, Chicago), 10 (Oct., 1948), 1–5.

[10] *Biennial Report for the Year Ending December 31, 1952* (California), pp. 42, 47.

[11] Helen Bryan, *Inside* (Houghton Mifflin, 1953).

[12] L. S. Selling, "The Pseudo Family," *American Journal of Sociology,* 37 (1931), 247–48.

[13] *Gearing Federal Prisons to the War Effort* (Washington: U.S. Bureau of Prisons, 1942), pp. 78–81; Bryan, *op. cit.*

[14] Bryan, *op. cit.*

19

Release of the Criminal Without Imprisonment

The readjustment of the criminal to the community after conviction is an important step in the elimination of crime. If the criminal is released without complete personal and social rehabilitation, he will presumably pursue his criminal activities unless he is helped to adjust by community agencies for a transitional period.

Approximately two thirds of the persons convicted of major crimes are sentenced to some type of penal institution. Almost all (about 95 per cent) are eventually released to return to the community. One third of major criminals are released immediately after conviction without the necessity of serving a term in jail or prison (see page 373). The final disposition of the criminal therefore is not imprisonment versus freedom, but when and under what conditions shall he be returned to the community.

DIFFICULTIES OF READJUSTMENT

Specific drawbacks hinder readjustment of criminals in the community.

1. Certain criminals do not readily readjust. The offender whose life habits are firmly set in a delinquent or criminal pattern—the professional or habitual criminal—is not easy to readjust to conventional life. The situation is more hopeful for the inexperienced offender, who is not essentially criminal in attitude or total life organization, or for the child or adolescent whose habits are still in a formative stage. Offenders whose delinquencies or crimes stem from some personality defect cannot be expected to readjust without treatment: for instance, chronic alcoholics, drug addicts, psychopaths, neurotics, and psychotics. Release of these persons in the community does not improve their condition. Criminals whose offenses have aroused public fear and horror are shunned when released; the community refuses to accept them on any terms. And finally, some criminals, for the sake of public safety, should not be at large in the community. Therefore,

521

a serious problem arises in the selection of delinquents and criminals who may be released in the community, with some hope of readjustment on their part and the maintenance of public security.

2. Another drawback is the realization that the offender, if left to his own devices, will probably continue in his old patterns of misconduct. Some form of supervision is necessary during the period of readjustment. For some criminals supervision should include specialized treatment for physical or emotional defects.

3. A third drawback is the fact that neither unconditional release in the community nor imprisonment seems satisfactory treatment for some offenders; instead, some combination of the two is necessary. For instance, deeply ingrained habits that cannot be broken in the community under the degree of supervision possible in this setting might be broken during a period of institutionalization, followed by supervision.

Out of the recognition of all these factors, alternative methods of releasing offenders have arisen: the suspended sentence, probation, parole, pardons, unconditional release of felons at the end of their sentence, and unconditional release of misdemeanants after a short jail term or payment of a fine. These various methods of release have not developed logically, but in a haphazard and piecemeal manner. They are all in a sense grafted onto the older, primary system of punishment by imprisonment. Only two of the methods —probation and parole—provide any form of supervision. Each method of release is discussed in some detail.

SUSPENDED SENTENCE

Both the suspended sentence and probation are alternatives to imprisonment, since the convicted offender is released without serving any part of the sentence that would normally follow. The suspended sentence does not provide for supervision and therefore is not wholly defensible from the point of view of rehabilitation. It is the basis, however, of probation, which does provide supervision.

The suspended sentence originated as a device whereby the judge could avoid imposing upon a convicted person the legal penalty for his crime. It was a reaction to the severe punishment common in England during an early period, which judges did not always like to impose, and indicated a growing consciousness that severity did not lead to reform. In this procedure, the judge released the convict either before or after sentence was passed, to resume civilian life provided that he did not commit another offense. If the person subsequently committed a delinquency or crime the sentence for the previous offense was immediately imposed. The judge was thus able to give a second chance to an offender whom he believed would make a satisfactory adjustment in the community, and when a prison sentence would be an injustice or would probably do more harm than good.

The suspended sentence, employed occasionally in the United States before 1850, came into wider use after that period.[1]   The judges justified their action by reference to the English common law, which permitted certain mitigations of sentences.   Convictions carried to state supreme courts were often sustained.   The Supreme Court of the United States, however, decided in 1916 that the power to suspend sentences was not inherent in the courts but could be granted by state statutes.   Most states therefore have legally provided for suspended sentences, often with various restrictions.

The suspended sentence is important as a forerunner of probation.   Its early use signified a disbelief in the efficacy of reform by imprisonment and a recognition that for many offenders a return to the community might lead to reorganization of their lives along noncriminal lines.   Its weakness is that the only specific motivation toward such reorganization is the threat of imposing the sentence that hangs over the offender.   No one is responsible for assisting him.

The suspended sentence is also susceptible to abuse, inasmuch as the judge may use it to release professional criminals who are connected with a corrupt political machine.   Moreover, it does not imply that the judge seeks or secures the background information necessary in deciding whether punishment should be imposed or a suspended sentence granted.

DEVELOPMENT OF PROBATION

Probation is a type of suspended sentence, buttressed with legal restrictions, and implying study of the offender's personality and background and supervision by a probation officer or volunteer.   If the offender does not make a satisfactory adjustment in the community, probation is revoked and the original sentence is imposed; or if probation was granted prior to imposing sentence, sentence for the original crime is passed.

Although the suspended sentence is chiefly a method of granting leniency, probation is a technique for treatment.   Its importance lies in the emphasis upon treatment and retraining instead of punishment by fine or imprisonment.   It constitutes a major shift in emphasis.   The early philosophy of handling the offender was to equate the offense to punishment on the assumption of the deterrent effect.   The new approach is to readjust the offender to a normal conventional life.   Probation provides an interval of supervised community living, without the onus or detriment of imprisonment, during which readjustment may be accomplished.

Legally, probation developed from the suspended sentence.   Its social origin, however, was not in statutes but in the acts of a socially minded New Englander, John Augustus.[2]   This man was a Boston shoemaker of the mid-nineteenth century who became interested in offenders—chiefly drunkards—who were confined in jail.   He secured the release of many of these men by paying their fines, after which he tried to help them to refrain from drinking.   Other offenders were released to Augustus after conviction and before sentence.   In the interval before they were recalled to the court for sentence Augustus helped them and reported on their progress, with the result that the judge often fined these offenders a nominal sum and released them.   Augustus was in effect a volunteer probation officer, basing his work on his good will and his faith in human nature rather than on any definite technique of investigation and case work.

In other eastern cities during the same period similar efforts were made by a few individuals.[3]   Legal sanction was given to the program when Massachusetts passed the first probation law in 1878; Maryland followed in 1894, Vermont in 1898, and Rhode Island in 1899.   Under these laws paid probation officers were established to succeed volunteers, who had provided the first probation supervision.   The establishment of juvenile courts stimulated the practice for juveniles and the movement grew rapidly in that direction.   All states have now established some provision for probation for juvenile offenders.   Probation for adult felons developed more slowly.   In 1951, 3 states were still without provision for adult probation services.[4]   A federal law for probation of federal offenders was passed in 1925.   Few states provide such supervision for misdemeanants.

ADMINISTRATION OF PROBATION

The supervision of the offender who is placed on probation is in the hands of a probation officer who is generally a court officer, usually appointed by the local court to serve a local community.   Standards therefore vary from one community to another, since (with few exceptions) there is no state supervision.   Although in some communities probation officers are appointed from a civil service list, usually the judge selects them.   Hence the appointments are open to the dangers of political pressure and uncertainty based upon the favor or tenure in office of the appointing officer.   Rural counties, with few probationers, are especially handicapped by the local administration of the procedure.   Ploscowe, writing in 1939, noted that in New York State 14 counties employed only untrained volunteers for the work; and in New Hampshire, although the law required that probation officers should be appointed, only about one third of the local communities had such officers and many of them were part-time employees with other occupations.[5]

Trends

Several trends are evident in the administrative organization of probation. One course is toward state appointment of probation officers or state supervision of local appointments.   State supervision may be justified by the need of financially poor or rural counties for state aid.[6]   Also such supervision permits combining several rural counties under one officer.   Furthermore, standards of selection and training of officers can be uniform.   A further justification lies in the fact that the laws to be enforced are state statutes. On the other hand, under state supervision a probation officer may be sent into a community whose background is unfamiliar to him or may be assigned to work with an incompatible judge.   Local communities are sometimes suspicious of outside officers and resent them.

Another trend is toward combined supervision of probationers and parolees, a common practice when probation is placed under state supervision. In 1950, 11 states had completely unified their adult probation and parole services with no local probation or institutional parole officers.[7]   Six other states had partial state-wide services, with some local probation offices also functioning.   The combined service is especially helpful in rural areas, where combining probationers and parolees may justify the employment of a well-trained supervisor.

Qualifications of Probation Officers

One of the weakest points of the probation system is the variation in qualifications for probation officers and the virtual lack of professional standards in most communities.   Probation procedure, well done, is case work.   The probation officer needs training in social case work and needs to know how to take advantage of specialized medical, psychological, and psychiatric services in the community.   From time to time professional groups issue statements regarding the training and experience deemed necessary for probation officers.   One such statement lists the following desirable prerequisites.[8]

Specialized knowledge needed:

1. The probation officer should have a working knowledge of the principles and practices of social case work.

2. As an administrative agent of the court he should be familiar with the laws of his state and with the powers and limitations of his office.

3. He should be familiar with the functions of related law-enforcement agencies.

Minimum qualifications should include:

1. A bachelor's degree from a recognized college or its equivalent, with courses in the social sciences.

2. Experience of one year under a competent supervisor in an approved social agency, or an additional year of training in field practice, or adequate in-service training.

3. Good character and well-balanced personality.

Salary: comparable to salaries in other social-work positions.

It seems doubtful whether any except the best organized departments, serving large cities, meet these standards.   Certainly attaining such standards throughout a state depends upon state control and some method of combining rural counties.

The lack of adequate probation officers is linked in part with the dearth of male social workers.   Most social workers are women; the relatively few men trained in this field usually hold administrative positions.   It is conceded that most probation officers should be men, inasmuch as most offenders, both juvenile and adult, are male.

Case Load

The number of cases that one probation officer can adequately serve is limited.   Federal agencies recommend 50 cases for each officer, and a smaller number if the probationers are delinquent girls.[9]   This ideal is rarely if ever attained.   In actual practice a single probation officer may have as many as 1,000 or 1,500 cases.   Many carry 4 or 5 hundred.

Functions of Probation Officers

The probation officer has two functions: (1) to make a presentence investigation, that is, to investigate the case before the judge decides whether or not to place the offender on probation, in order to secure the necessary background information; and (2) to supervise probationers.   Legally, only half the states require a presentence investigation, and often only at the discretion of the courts.   It seems certain, therefore, that probation is often granted by the judge solely on the basis of the information revealed during the trial.

Supervision of the probationer is hindered primarily by the large number of cases assigned to the individual officer.   Frequently the probationer is required merely to report at stated intervals for interviews consuming perhaps half an hour.   Genuine individual case work is impossible under these circumstances, although it is the ideal set by those interested in the development of probation.   At present, the probationer must make his own adjustment and frequently continues in his delinquencies until he is arrested again.

When the probation officer is able to do individualized case work he finds himself in a delicate position.   Case work is successful only when the client co-operates—when he is willing to talk over his problems with the case worker and to accept assistance in analyzing them and in constructive planning.[10]   Case work is not a hardship imposed upon the client, but is a method of aiding him to reorganize his attitudes and conduct.   A harmonious relationship is hard to achieve because the client in this situation has not voluntarily sought the assistance of the case worker (probation officer), but has been assigned to his care as an alternative to prison.   The probationer is all too likely to be aware of the threat of imprisonment behind the relationship and to conceal rather than reveal his attitudes and motives.   The probation officer therefore has an especially difficult task in establishing rapport.   He must avoid the threat of punishment or exercise of his authority as a court officer.   At the same time, he is under obligation to report violations and if he fails to do so will incur the ill will of the community and the disapproval of the court.   In order to perform his dual role of guardian of the law and community on the one hand and of confidant of the offender on the other, the probation officer requires not only adequate training in psychology and case work technique but a well-balanced personality.

Since the probationer must be able to manage his life eventually without the sustaining hand of the probation officer, part of the task of the officer is to aid the probationer to become thoroughly incorporated into conventional community life so that his future conduct will be guided and supported by normal types of social interaction.   To function effectively, therefore, the probation officer should extend his full services during the early period of probation and should gradually withdraw as the probationer is able to establish community contacts.   The corollary of this process is the presence in the community of leaders and organizations that are able and willing to bring the probationer into participation in intimate groups, clubs, institutions, and employment that will stabilize him and give him status and self-respect.

THE PROBATIONER

Eligibility for Probation

Eligibility for probation may be limited by legislative restrictions.[11]   In many states persons guilty of crimes of violence and certain sex and mercenary offenses are ineligible.   Persons with criminal records and especially those previously convicted of a felony also are frequently denied probation. For all criminals except these excluded groups, the judge determines whether to place the convicted offender on probation or to sentence him to prison.

Neither the legislative restrictions nor, in most cases, the judge's decision is closely related to a scientific estimate of the probability of success in making a satisfactory adjustment on probation. The legislative restrictions are primarily reflections of popular revulsion and prejudice against certain kinds of crimes. However, there is no evidence that a person once convicted of a crime of violence is more likely to repeat it than the person convicted of a theft is likely to repeat his crime. But more fear and horror are felt toward the perpetrator of a crime of violence. In our present state of lack of specific information on the probability of readjustment on probation, emotion rather than knowledge determines the issue.

Unless the judge has the benefit of a presentence investigation of the offender he does not have the necessary information to decide whether probation will aid a particular criminal. With the present inadequate number of probation officers, many of whom lack training in case work, such presentence investigations are the exception instead of the rule. In the absence of such an investigation the judge has no means of knowing the background data necessary for an intelligent decision. He relies upon common sense, his own prejudices, and the recommendation of the prosecuting attorney, which may or may not be based upon adequate information.

Conditions of Probation

Usually, the offender is placed on probation for a specified period of time, within limits set by the laws of the state. These statutes sometimes set conditions, and the judge may set others. The offender on probation is expected to meet these conditions, or run the risk of forfeiture and a prison sentence. There is no uniformity in the conditions, but some common requirements follow.[12]

The probationer may be required to pay court costs, a fee for the guidance service rendered by the probation officer, or a fine. Any of the 3 conditions constitutes a financial obligation and in a sense is a penalty, although technically only the fine is so considered.

The probationer may be obliged to post a bond for good behavior, a procedure that appears to be of some value when the services of a probation officer are not available. This practice favors the wealthy, however, and places a handicap upon the person unable to post a bond. Thus the financial status of the offender or his friends may become the deciding factor in admission to probation instead of the offender's rehabilitation.

Sometimes the probationer is required to restore money or property stolen or destroyed. If such restitution is related to an offender's earning power while on probation, it has the value of forcing him to face the injury he has done to another and to compensate the victim for his losses. However, if the sum and method of payment are not related to the offender's earning

outlining the duties of probation officers, and in general supervising the work in order to develop an efficient system.   Appropriation of $200,000 was granted, which was to provide 40 probation officers.

In 1939 an administrative office was established for the United States Courts, in connection with the Judicial Conference of Senior Circuit Judges, which acts as a board of directors.[15]   The supervision of probation was placed under this office, as well as supervision of parole.

Since this firm establishment of the federal probation system many changes have occurred.   The number of supervisors has greatly increased and probation is granted to approximately one fourth of all convicted federal prisoners.[16]   Qualifications for probation and parole officers have also been raised.

TABLE 23

Percentage of Criminals Placed on Probation by Type of Crime

Type of Crime	Per Cent
Murder	1.0
Violation of drug laws	8.9
Robbery	18.1
Manslaughter	22.0
Commercialized vice	24.8
Rape	25.7
Other sex offenses	28.6
Aggravated assault	30.2
Burglary	35.0
Carrying concealed weapons	35.1
Forgery and counterfeiting	35.7
Larceny	39.7
Embezzlement and fraud	41.9
Receiving stolen property	43.6
Automobile theft	43.7
Other major offenses	27.3

Source: *Judicial Criminal Statistics* (Washington: Bureau of the Census, Government Printing Office, 1945), p. 7.

ADVANTAGES AND DISADVANTAGES OF PROBATION

The advantages of probation are usually considered in contrast to the limitations of imprisonment and include the following: [17]

1. The offender is spared the enervating experience of imprisonment and isolation from normal community contacts, as well as the abnegation of personal responsibilities.   These conditions, if long continued, may hinder social readjustment, warp the personality, and establish close contacts with other criminals that continue after release from prison.

2. The offender is not labeled a "convict" in the minds of his family, friends, and potential employers.

3. The offender remains in a normal community and continues to lead a normal life.   Hence, the situation is conducive to social adjustment.

4. The offender is able to support himself and to fulfill his responsibilities to his family.

5. The offender is in a position to make reparations if his offense has involved stealing or damage to property.

6. Minor offenders are supervised rather than merely dismissed.

7. Young offenders are especially benefited by probation, since they may have committed their first serious offense and are still not incorporated into the criminal world.

8. Probation is more economical than imprisonment, for the offender continues to support himself and his dependents and the cost of administration of probation is much less per offender than the cost of operating a prison.

9. Probation permits the use of specialized medical and psychiatric services in the community that may not be available to inmates of jails or prisons.

Disadvantages may also be cited, although many of them are not inherent in the system but merely characterize the present stage of development.

1. If the offender does not desist from crime the community is still exposed to his depredations until he is caught again.   He would then be imprisoned.   The contrasting situation is imprisonment immediately after conviction in which case the community would be spared criminal activities during the period of incarceration; however, in many instances the prisoner resumes his criminal activities upon release.

2. The offender is often allowed to return to the same family and community environment that bred him; hence he is exposed to the same influences that preceded his arrest and conviction.

3. Most judges have inadequate information upon which to base the selection of probationers.   This situation is partly because they do not demand presentence investigations from probation officers; partly because the number of officers is inadequate to provide such service; and partly because not enough is known at the present time regarding the characteristics that render a given offender a promising candidate for probation.

4. Many probation officers lack training and are overworked.

5. Probation may be granted to professional criminals if the courts are dominated by a corrupt political machine.

RESULTS OF PROBATION

It is not to be expected, especially in its present state of development, that all offenders placed on probation will make good social adjustments.

Available reports show considerable variation in the proportion estimated to have succeeded on probation.

A study by Beard of 500 probationers from the Boston Juvenile Court shows that 43 per cent of the boys and 76 per cent of the girls were considered to have abandoned their illegal and antisocial activities as a result of probation.[18]   Thirty-four per cent of the boys and 12 per cent of the girls were classified as temporary successes; 21 per cent of the boys and 12 per cent of the girls were failures.

A more comprehensive study by the Gluecks followed 1,000 delinquent boys over a 15 year period, from the time the average age of the boys was 13 until the average age was 29.[19]   During this period, 806 of these youths had been on probation at some time or other.   Their behavior on probation was studied with the results shown in Figure 26.   Failures exceeded successes.

A third study regarding juvenile delinquents on probation was provided by Carr, who reported on 230 juvenile probationers from 16 Michigan counties.   Fifty-four per cent made successful adjustments, 26 per cent doubtful adjustments, whereas 20 per cent failed.[20]   Two thirds of the first offenders were successful but only a little over one third of the recidivists.

Turning to adult offenders, we find that the *Attorney General's Survey of Release Procedures* reported on 19,256 cases in which probation was granted.[21]   In 19 per cent of the cases it was revoked, an indication that the probationer had violated the conditions and that sentence for his original offense had been imposed.

A more rigid definition of failure on probation was used by the Gluecks in their study of 500 male criminals, all of whom had served terms in penal institutions.[22]   Three hundred and ninety of these men had at some time been on probation during the 15-year span of the study.   The criteria of successful behavior on probation were the same as for the study of juvenile delinquents already cited: actual arrest, more than an occasional violation of conditions, commitment to an institution for violation, or a known or recorded offense for which arrest was possible.   According to this inclusive definition of failure, extremely few of the men were found to have made a satisfactory adjustment during their probation periods.   For those on straight probation only 2.4 per cent always behaved satisfactorily; 0.8 per cent succeeded at first and later failed; 4.0 per cent failed at first and later succeeded; 0.4 per cent were erratic as to behavior; and 92.4 per cent always failed.   For those on probation under suspended sentence, the percentages were strikingly similar to these.

A thorough-going study of probation in Essex County (Newark), New

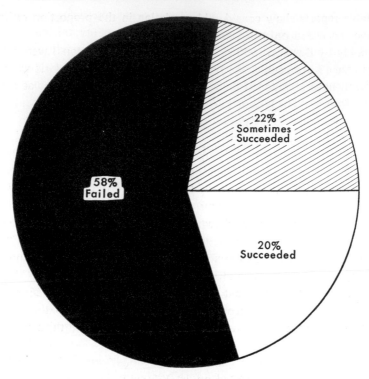

FIGURE 26

Percentage of juvenile delinquents who succeeded or failed during a 15-year period that included probation.   Failure was measured by actual arrest, frequent violation of probation conditions, commitment to an institution for violation, or a known or recorded offense for which arrest was possible, even though it had not occurred.   The Chart suggests that present methods of probation are not adequate to forestall or combat the pressure of adverse influences.   (Based on Sheldon and Eleanor T. Glueck, *Juvenile Delinquents Grown Up* [New York: Commonwealth Fund, 1940], pp. 153, 161.)

Jersey traces the experiences of 1,000 probationers approximately 8 years after their release from probation.[23]   The group studied was a composite one made up of probationers from the criminal court, domestic relations court, juvenile court, and police courts.   For 764 persons, a usable record could be obtained, which gave the following results: 33 per cent showed some improvement and 26 per cent marked improvement, leaving 41 per cent unimproved.   Half of the total number had been arrested at some time during the study period, 31 per cent more than once.   Certain types of offenders were found to do poorly on probation: recidivists, the mentally disordered or potentially disordered, and drug or alcohol addicts.

Various factors in addition to treatment by the probation officer affect the percentages of failures and successes reported: the degree to which the criminal has developed permanent attitudes of criminality; the length of time he has been following criminal activities before he is placed on probation; his personality make-up; the type of community and family activities into which he enters.   These factors and others related to failure on probation are discussed in Chapter 21 in connection with recidivism.

EVALUATION OF PROBATION

Probation is in the chaotic state that any social movement passes through when it develops rapidly and without centralized control.   Therefore it should not be condemned.   The basic philosophy of probation is in line with our present knowledge of the origin and control of criminal conduct. Crime develops from personal maladjustment and a social environment with accepted criminal patterns operating either singly or in conjunction with each other.   The solution appears to lie in careful study of the individual to determine the causes of his criminal conduct, and then in planning a remedial program for him.   Since he will eventually live in a normal community, it seems logical to attempt immediately to work out his adjustment in that community rather than to interpose a term in prison.   Institutionalization (not necessarily imprisonment) is justified only if the offender is so far removed from normal personality or normal social habits that the community is endangered by his release, or if he is in need of intensive retraining.   Institutionalization should be organized, however, not as punishment but as a period of complete rehabilitation.

The shortcomings of probation are not inherent in the basic philosophy, but in the present type of administration and the lack of a sufficient number of trained persons to act as officers.   Better administration and higher personnel standards undoubtedly will come in time, for several agencies are definitely working toward that end.   One of the most aggressive is the National Probation and Parole Association, which holds annual conventions and publishes a quarterly journal and news bulletin.

QUESTIONS

1. What percentage of prisoners returns to the community?
2. Why is probation regarded as an improvement over the suspended sentence?
3. What are some of the deficiencies of probation at the present time?   How might these be eliminated?
4. Describe the functions of the probation officer.   How is his training related to his ability to perform his functions?
5. Why is a presentence investigation a necessary part of the probation system?
6. When should the prisoner be released from probation?

7. What are the advantages of probation?   The disadvantages?   How could the disadvantages be overcome?

8. Should all convicted persons be placed on probation?   Support your statement with arguments.

9. How successful is probation?

READINGS

Attorney General's Survey of Release Procedures, Vol. 2, *Probation* (Washington: U.S. Department of Justice, 1939).   An extensive factual survey of probation principles and practices in the 1930's.

Federal Probation, a quarterly journal published by the Administrative Office of the United States Courts in co-operation with the Federal Bureau of Prisons of the United States Department of Justice.   Articles in this journal are not limited to the subject of federal probation; they also cover preventive and corrective activities in delinquency and crime, carried on by both public and private agencies.

Glueck, Sheldon (ed.), *Probation and Criminal Justice* (Macmillan, 1933).   An authoritative book setting forth many of the principles of probation.

Kawin, Irene, "Therapeutic Use of Authority," *Federal Probation,* 17 (Sept., 1953), 22–26.   A deputy chief probation officer supports the use of authority in probation as a prop to the offender who is not able to exert adequate self-discipline to stay out of trouble.   Within the framework of authority, treatment goes on until the offender is self-sufficient.

Lanzer, I. A., "Forensic Social Case Work: An Analytical Survey," *Journal of Criminal Law and Criminology,* 39 (May–June, 1948), 34–48.   The author attempts to reconcile the permissiveness now advocated in case work with the authoritarianism inherent in probation and parole work.   He believes the authoritarianism can be made beneficial.

Tappan, Paul W. (ed.), *Contemporary Correction* (McGraw-Hill, 1951).   Chapter 24 by Richard A. Chappell and Will C. Turnbladh discusses common misconceptions about probation and case work practices in probation.

Yearbook of the National Probation and Parole Association.   This yearbook carries papers read at the annual meetings of the Association.   The articles are practical in nature and press for better practices.   The Association also publishes *Focus* 6 times a year; this journal has a variety of articles, news notes, and book reviews.

Young, Pauline V., *Social Treatment in Probation and Delinquency* (rev. ed., McGraw-Hill, 1952).   Written from a sociological viewpoint, this book covers both prevention and probation.   Case studies are emphasized and the legal aspects of probation are discussed.

FOOTNOTES

[1] Sheldon Glueck (ed.), *Probation and Criminal Justice* (Macmillan, 1933), p. 26.

[2] N. S. Timasheff, *One Hundred Years of Probation* (New York: Fordham University Press, 1941).

[3] *Attorney General's Survey of Release Procedures,* Vol. 2, *Probation* (Washington: U.S. Department of Justice, 1939); Harry Elmer Barnes, *The Story of Punishment*

(Boston: Stratford, 1930), pp. 224ff.; Gilbert Cosulich, *Adult Probation Laws of the United States* (New York: National Probation Association, 1940).

⁴ Paul W. Tappan (ed.), *Contemporary Correction* (McGraw-Hill, 1951), p. 394.

⁵ Morris Ploscowe, *Crime and Criminal Law,* National Law Library, 2 (New York: Collier, 1939), 301–5.

⁶ R. T. Smith, "Statewide Organization of Probation Service," *Yearbook, National Probation and Parole Association* (1950), pp. 130–38.

⁷ *Ibid.*

⁸ "Standards for Selection of Probation and Parole Officers," *Journal of Criminal Law and Criminology,* 36 (1945), 193–94, abstracted from *Probation* (June, 1945).

⁹ Margaretta Williamson, *The Social Worker in the Prevention and Treatment of Delinquency* (New York: Columbia University Press, 1935), citing the United States Children's Bureau and the National Probation Association; *Attorney General's Survey of Release Procedures,* Vol. 2.

¹⁰ *Attorney General's Survey of Release Procedures,* Vol. 2, pp. 125ff.

¹¹ *Ibid.,* Vol. 2, ch. 4.

¹² *Ibid.,* Vol. 2, ch. 7.

¹³ *Judicial Criminal Statistics,* Bureau of the Census (Washington: Government Printing Office, 1945), p. 5.

¹⁴ Glueck, *op. cit.,* pp. 254–55.

¹⁵ H. P. Chandler, "Plans for the Development of Probation in the United States Courts," *Federal Probation,* 4 (Nov.–Dec., 1940), 4–8.

¹⁶ W. H. Speck, "The Federal Probationer," *Federal Probation,* 16 (June, 1952), 21–23.

¹⁷ Based in part upon Fred R. Johnson, *Probation for Juveniles and Adults* (Century, 1928).

¹⁸ Quoted by Lowell J. Carr, *Delinquency Control* (Harper, 1941), p. 171.

¹⁹ Sheldon and Eleanor T. Glueck, *Juvenile Delinquents Grown Up* (New York: The Commonwealth Fund, 1940), pp. 153, 161.

²⁰ Carr, *op. cit.,* pp. 171–72.

²¹ *Attorney General's Survey of Release Procedures,* Vol. 2, pp. 335ff.

²² Sheldon and Eleanor T. Glueck, *Criminal Careers in Retrospect* (New York: The Commonwealth Fund, 1943), p. 151.

²³ Jay Rumney and Joseph P. Murphy, *Probation and Social Adjustment* (New Brunswick, N.J.: Rutgers University Press, 1952).

Release of the Criminal
after Imprisonment

Almost all offenders sent to prison are eventually restored to the community. Approximately 95 per cent are released after long or short terms in prison; only about 5 per cent die in prison, are executed, or escape. In most states, even those sentenced to life imprisonment are eligible for consideration for parole after a given period of time; or their sentences may be commuted to a stated term of years, at the expiration of which they are released. The question, therefore, is not whether offenders shall remain in prison or be released, but what are the conditions of release.

METHODS OF RELEASE

Figure 27 shows that the most frequently used method of release is conditional—that is, the prisoner is released prior to the end of his sentence but remains at liberty only by observing certain conditions. Usually he is under the supervision of a parole officer, a method of release that has been gaining favor over a long period of time.

The use of parole varies from one state to another. A few states (New Hampshire, Ohio, Colorado, and Washington) release almost all prisoners on parole, according to figures for 1952. Other states in the same year released almost no prisoners on parole. Table 24 shows that the north-

TABLE 24

Percentage of Prisoners Released on Parole from State Prisons, by Regions, 1952

Region	Per Cent
Northeastern states	75.6
North Central states	66.5
Southern states	32.3
Western states	74.2

Source: *Federal Prisons, 1953* (Washington: Federal Bureau of Prisons, U.S. Department of Justice, 1954), pp. 106–7.

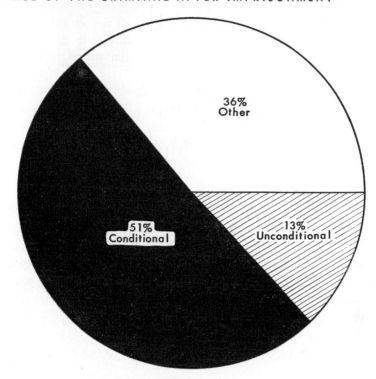

FIGURE 27

Percentage of prisoners with different kinds of release from state penal institutions, 1952. Conditional releases are parole in 96 per cent of the cases; in the other 4 per cent they are conditional pardons or other special releases. Unconditional releases are those that come at the expiration of the sentence, when the prisoner is released without stipulations as to his future behavior and without supervision. Thus conditional, or supervised, releases occur 4 times as often as unconditional, or unsupervised, releases, and indicate the tendency of parole boards to permit the prisoner to prove his ability to conform in the community before he has completed his prison term. If he does not conform he is returned to prison to complete his sentence. "Other" refers to pardons, deaths, executions, escapes, and court orders for discharge, no one of which accounts for very many prisoners. (Based on *Federal Prisons, 1953* [Washington: Federal Bureau of Prisons, Department of Justice, 1954], p. 106.)

eastern and the western states use parole most liberally as a means of release, with the southern states releasing only a third of their prisoners on parole.

THE PAROLE SYSTEM

Parole is a system of releasing prisoners under supervision before the end of their prison sentence; they are not discharged officially from prison until the end of the parole period, and if they violate the conditions of parole they may be returned to prison to complete serving their sentences within the prison walls.   Parole resembles probation in that the convicted criminal is released in the community under supervision.   It differs from probation in that the parolee, unlike the probationer, has served a portion of his prison sentence.

Parole provides a method for releasing prisoners when they seem ready to return to the community, even though their sentences have not expired; it also provides for a period of trial adjustment to the community.

Development of Parole

Although tentative movements toward shortened sentences coupled with some form of supervision had developed earlier, the first definite attempt to apply parole came with the opening of Elmira Reformatory, which was authorized in 1869 and opened in 1876.   By 1900, 20 states had provided for parole, by 1922, 44 states,[1] and by 1944, all states.   The provisions vary greatly from state to state and no specific statement applies generally to the administration of parole in the United States nor the efficiency with which the system is carried out.

Administration of Parole

Parole involves 2 functions: the selection of the prisoners to be paroled; and supervision of those on parole.   In most states the 2 functions are vested in the same agency.

Parole agencies are established in different ways.   Most frequently a central state board has the power to grant paroles, a system used by 26 states, the District of Columbia, New York City, and the federal government at the time of the *Attorney General's Survey of Release Procedures.*[2]   The governor, usually assisted by an adviser or an advisory board, was the sole parole-granting authority in 17 states.   Boards attached to individual penal institutions granted parole in 7 states, sometimes as the only parole-granting authority in the state and sometimes in addition to a state board that served other institutions.   The trend is toward full-time boards that function for all penal institutions in a given state.

Each system deserves more detailed discussion.

1. The central state parole authority has certain advantages.   It can function uniformly throughout the state so that all institutions are handled with the same policies.   It also achieves a certain detachment from the institution and hence from charges of prejudice or favoritism toward some special prisoner.   In addition it has the advantage of representing the opinion of a group of persons rather than of one individual.

In operation, however, the central board often has distinct shortcomings. In some states the board is composed of state officers, such as the governor, attorney general, secretary of state, or justices of the supreme court; in addition there may be one or more citizen members.   These men all have other duties to perform that take most of their time and attention and for which they may be trained.   Since their function as parole-board-members is secondary, they can give only a small amount of time to this work.   In states with a small population and hence a small number of prisoners, part-time boards may be adequate, but in most states the number of prisoners eligible for consideration by the parole board necessitates full-time boards if an adequate study is to be obtained of each prisoner.

The members of parole boards, whether composed of state officials or of citizens, rarely have special training for selection of prisoners for parole or for their supervision.   Some members may be state officers elected to some office other than the parole board; others may be appointed by the governor, often because of political affiliations.   When restrictions are placed upon appointment to the parole board, either by law or custom, the object usually is to "keep the parole board out of politics" rather than to select individuals especially qualified by training and experience to determine which prisoners are capable of readjustment to community living.

2. Allocation of parole authority to the governor is not sound.   The governor not only has many other duties that absorb his time, but he is untrained for parole work.   The advisory board may be appointed by him and hence merely reflect his views.   Usually no legal restriction is placed upon the governor's use of parole, so that a governor may be subject to various types of pressure to release certain prisoners regardless of their fitness for parole.

3. The general local boards attached to institutions are not adequate as parole agencies.   Usually they are untrained in parole work and may be dominated by the wardens of the institutions they serve.   It is generally conceded that the parole authority should be independent of the prison administration.

The best systems, followed by a few states, are built around a full-time state parole board.   Its members are paid an adequate salary, are appointed by the governor for long terms, and are selected not because of political affiliations but by training and experience.

THE PAROLEE

One duty of the parole authority is to determine which prisoners should be paroled and when the parole should start.   This function is usually circumscribed by legal provisions and the sentence that the judge has imposed on the prisoner.

Definite and Indeterminate Sentences

In order to understand parole completely, it is necessary to bear in mind the provisions for different kinds of sentences.   Two systems are employed in the United States.   Under a definite sentence the offender is imprisoned for a specific number of years.   The length of the sentence may be set by law for a particular crime or may be determined by the judge within legal limits.   For instance, the law may provide a penalty of 10 to 20 years for a certain crime; the judge may then set a definite term within these limits.

The second method of sentencing is called the indeterminate sentence, although strictly speaking such sentences are not indeterminate.   On an actual indeterminate sentence the offender would enter prison without having been sentenced by a judge to serve any particular length of time.   Under these circumstances, some other agency would be required to determine the time served.   In a completely integrated system of rehabilitation and parole, such broad powers could be delegated to a specially trained group, but at present approaches to such a system are only tentative.   The so-called indeterminate sentence rests upon laws that set a minimum and a maximum sentence for each type of crime.

In general, the judge states in the sentence the minimum time that the offender must remain in prison, which is either the legal minimum or any longer term not to exceed the maximum set by law.   For instance, if a statute specified that the prison sentence for a certain crime must be not less than 10 years nor more than 20, the judge might sentence the offender to any length of time within this period.   He might, for instance, sentence him to a minimum of 19 years, or a period of not less than 19 nor more than 20 years.   The indeterminate law thus permits the judge to express in the length of sentence his opinion of the proper duration of imprisonment.   The fallacy of this situation, of course, is that no one can determine in advance how long a period in prison will be required to effect rehabilitation in a particular person.   The indeterminate sentence therefore becomes a sliding scale of punishment and enables the judge to impose a light penalty on one offender and a heavy one on another for the same crime, the difference being based upon the offender's previous record, the circumstances surrounding the crime, the attitude of the criminal, the recommendation of the prosecuting attorney, and the personal prejudices and opinions of the judge.

The first statutes granting indeterminate sentences were passed in connection with parole laws, but the 2 provisions have not developed together.

Thus, in 1936, when only 3 states were without some parole system, 11 states had no provision for indeterminate sentences.[3]

States that provide for indeterminate sentences may restrict them to certain crimes, reserving definite sentences for others. Indeterminate sentences usually are not granted to persons convicted of murder, treason, and rape; in some states kidnaping, armed robbery, and other crimes involving violence also are excluded. In some states only first offenders may be given the indeterminate sentence. In other states in which either the indeterminate sentence or a definite sentence might be applied to the same crimes, the definite sentence is more widely used. The *Attorney General's Survey of Release Procedures* found that in 1936 a fifth of the states providing for indeterminate sentences used definite sentences more frequently.[4]

Eligibility for Parole

The agency that grants paroles works within the legal provisions for sentencing and must observe the sentence imposed by the judge in each case. The law specifies when an offender becomes eligible for consideration by the parole board. Where indeterminate sentences are in operation, the law may provide that the prisoner must serve the minimum sentence as set by the judge before he can be considered for parole; or, in some states, he must serve a stated proportion of the minimum or the maximum sentence. When there is no provision for indeterminate sentences and a definite sentence has been set by the judge, the offender may never be eligible for parole or only after a certain portion of the sentence has been served. In the federal system, for example, offenders are eligible for parole after serving one third of a definite sentence.

In a few states the offender becomes eligible for parole after serving one year of his sentence, and in other states at any time that the parole agency determines.[5] In the latter situation, this agency usually sets up rules that are adhered to rather rigidly. All offenders may be required to serve a minimum period before the parole agency will consider them; at that time the agency will determine how much longer each prisoner must serve.

Each state has developed in more or less haphazard manner its own combination of the sentencing powers of judges and the authority of parole agencies. Sometimes these functions work at cross purposes. In all cases, the sentencing power of the judge acts as a brake on the power of the parole agency, since it can function only after the prisoner has served some proportion of the sentence. The parole agency likewise serves as a check on the judge who imposes a long sentence, since the parole agency may support the judge's intention by refusing parole, or may defeat his purpose by granting it as early as possible.

Any system, whether determined by law, the sentencing power of the judge, or the rules of the parole agency, that designates in advance how long a prisoner must serve before he becomes eligible for parole is based more on the theory of punishment than on the theory of rehabilitation.   For it is impossible to know in advance how long a period will be needed for rehabilitation.   The same criticism may be applied to fixed sentences for specific crimes; such sentences are also in the nature of punishment, for we have no reason to think that all persons guilty of stealing, let us say a thousand dollars, may be rehabilitated in the same length of time.

In most states prisoners automatically become eligible for consideration by the parole agency after they have served a specified time.   This fact does not imply, however, that they automatically have the right of parole. It indicates only that they have the right to be considered by this agency, which then decides whether they are suitable subjects for parole.   In some states application for consideration is made by the prisoner or his friends or family; in other states the parole agency takes the initiative and reviews the cases of all prisoners at or near the time when they would be first eligible. The latter is now regarded as the most fair method.

Selection of Parolees

The procedure of the parole agency is often perfunctory and almost meaningless.   The members may review only the record of the crime for which the offender was convicted and his prison record.   They may know little or nothing about his background.   They may not see the prisoner but may depend wholly on a written record, or they may see him for only a few minutes of desultory conversation.   In some states the number of prisoners under consideration is large and only a brief period of time is at the disposal of part-time parole boards, so that only 5 or 10 minutes are given to the merits of each case.   In other states relatives and friends may be present at the hearing.   An emotional and sentimental element then tends to replace objectivity concerning the prisoner's fitness for release, and the board may be inclined to release an offender on parole because of sympathy for his family.   Sometimes a lawyer is permitted to attend the hearing to press the prisoner's claims for parole.   Often the prosecuting attorney who tried the case or the judge who imposed the sentence either recommends parole or protests against it, perhaps years after the crime was committed. The judge and prosecuting attorney base their pleas on the criminal's record prior to conviction regardless of changes in attitude that may have occurred during the prison term.   Selection of parolees, therefore, is influenced by many factors.

A limited number of states provide for study of the offender both before imprisonment and during the time in prison.   Such information is more and more regarded as necessary, to enable the board to judge the readiness of the prisoner for parole and also to give some indication of supportive and destructive factors in his background that may become operative again upon his release from prison.   Illinois also provides for statistical study of the probabilities of successful adjustment on parole.*

When a prison system includes a classification unit, this unit secures information needed by the parole agency.   If the classification unit follows up the initial examinations with successive interviews and observation, a detailed case study of the prisoner is available covering both his preprison and prison life.   To function effectively, the parole agency needs such data as the educational, vocational, and family background of the prisoner, his criminal record, personality type, behavior in prison, new training, chances of employment after release, and the family and social contacts that await him.   Only when such information is available to the parole agency, and only when its membership is made up of persons trained to understand and interpret the content, will selection of prisoners for parole become more than a haphazard procedure.

Conditions of Parole

When the prisoner is released on parole he agrees to limit his activities in certain ways and to report regularly to the agency or officer.   If he does not live up to the conditions imposed he may be declared delinquent and returned to prison even though he has not committed a new crime.   The usual conditions of parole are the following: [6]

1. Abstention from intoxicants.

2. No change of address or employment without the permission of the parole agent.

3. Reporting to the parole agent, employer or sponsor immediately on release from prison and submitting a notice of his arrival to the parole authority.

4. Prompt submission of required written reports.

5. No law violation.

6. Marriage only with the consent of the parole authority.

7. Neither purchasing nor driving an automobile without permission.

8. Leaving the state only with permission.

These restrictions support 2 purposes.   They serve to keep the parole

---

* Prediction of successful adjustment on probation or parole, based upon factors known at the time of sentence or parole, has been a theoretical possibility for a number of years.   As a practical device, such prediction methods are not widely used.   Because of their importance for future selection of offenders for individual treatment, prediction techniques are described in Chapter 21.

agent constantly informed as to the whereabouts and activities of the parolee; and they prevent or lessen the probability of new offenses. It is important to note in this connection that any statement of parole violations is based upon some such list as the above and overstates the number of parolees who have committed known crimes.

Length of Time on Parole

In some states the parolee is legally under the supervision of the parole authority until the date of expiration of his sentence, less any deductions for good behavior. If his original sentence was long and he was paroled soon after entering prison he might therefore be legally on parole for 5 or 10 years. Actually, close supervision is not provided over such long periods, and parole assumes little meaning. A second system, used in other states, fixes the period by law. Still a third system allows the parole authority the right to determine the duration for each case. This last system is the most flexible and permits adjustment of parole to the individual offender.

PREPARATION OF THE PRISONER FOR PAROLE

If the prisoner is to adjust successfully after release from prison changes must occur to him during his prison stay. If he leaves with the same attitudes and habits with which he entered, he will soon be under arrest for some new offense. The statement, therefore, is often made that preparation for release on parole should begin the day the man enters prison. Any retraining or rehabilitative program of the prison is, of course, automatically training for release. In addition to this long-range preparation, some prisons and reformatories give special attention to the prisoner as he nears the day of release. He may be given special counseling or may be transferred to a prison farm or camp for a few months before he re-enters the community.

Not only should the prisoner be prepared for release, but his family should be prepared in advance to receive him.[7] During a prison term, contacts between the prisoner and his family are likely to be infrequent and formal; only a few institutions provide a comfortable place for visiting and semi-privacy for discussion of personal matters. Such institutions usually are of the minimum security type, with a relaxation of close supervision, that houses prisoners who can be trusted not to attempt to escape. It is advisable that the contacts between prisoner and family should be maintained from the beginning of the prison term and that the parole officer should have some contact with the family during the entire period. He may be able to adjust misunderstandings and to interpret the prisoner to his family and vice versa.   When the prisoner is first released he is usually in need of understanding and consideration as he faces the resumption of civilian life.   If possible, the family should be ready to reincorporate the prisoner into its circle.

The community to which the prisoner returns should also be ready to accept him.   Employment is of special importance and often assurance of employment is required by the parole board before they will release a prisoner, otherwise thought to be ready for parole.   The family or the parole officer may act as go-between in securing the job in advance of release.   In some communities the parole staff works with the United States Employment Service.   New York has developed this co-operation to the point that a member of the staff of the employment agency in metropolitan New York has been assigned to the Division of Parole.[8]   He visits the penal institutions (primarily the reformatories) and interviews men ready for parole, securing a record of their assets and skills.   He also reads the prison record on each man.   When he returns to New York he tries to find the job for which each prisoner is best fitted, thus giving the man the best chance for success.

PAROLE SUPERVISION

The basic theory of parole is that the released offender is given some type of supervision, intended to serve two purposes: protection of the community; and assistance to the parolee in adjusting to community life.   In many states the supervision is woefully inadequate.   The parolee may be merely required to report in writing to the parole agency at stated intervals; supervision may be in the hands of untrained volunteers or part-time parole supervisors, also usually untrained.   Full-time parole supervisors may be provided but in too few numbers to give real supervision.   With 50 regarded as the ideal number of parolees for each supervisor if personal rehabilitation is to be effective, hundreds of parolees actually may be assigned to one supervisor.

Since 1930 casework treatment for parolees has gradually been accepted as the ideal and in some places has been put into practice.   Case work necessitates professionally trained parole supervisors and limited case loads. Parole officers usually are appointed by the state parole-granting agency and they may be political appointments made without strict regard for the adequacy of the supervisor for his job.   Only slowly is parole supervision moving into the professional field, with definite qualifications for training, civil service examinations, secure tenure, and adequate salaries.   The focus of parole supervision is shifting also, from mere surveillance of the parolee to individual treatment. A certain amount of surveillance is necessary, since the community is entitled to protection against continued crimes. When the state has established meticulous rules that the parolee must follow, it is the function of the parole supervisor to check on the degree of observance of these rules.   For complete adjustment with some promise of permanence, the supervisor must go beyond surveillance and help the parolee to dissipate such emotional attitudes as fears and hostilities that may accompany his return to the community, to find a social role, and in general to establish himself in the community.

ADVANTAGES AND DISADVANTAGES OF PAROLE

The advantages of parole are similar to the advantages of probation.

1. Parole reduces the time that the offender spends in prison.   In most prisons, as we learned in Chapter 17, long terms unfit the inmate for ready adjustment to the community.   This situation is true because most prisons are operated on the basis of punishment rather than as a means of rehabilitation; even those that have introduced retraining programs have superimposed them upon the old regime.   A short term during which the offender is removed from his former associates and habits may help him to reorganize himself.   The period in prison also gives an opportunity for studying the offender, if means are provided.   After retraining and study parole is advisable.   A few offenders, of course, have become so deeply criminalistic in attitude and habits that they probably cannot be rehabilitated and for them long terms or even permanent institutionalization seems necessary.

2. Parole provides an opportunity for the offender to attempt adjustment to the community under the guidance of the parole officer.   He is expected to obey certain rules that restrict his activities and associates, to seek and retain employment, and to secure the advice of his parole officer. At the same time that the offender is given this opportunity to make a normal adjustment, the community is partially protected from further criminal activities during the parole period, for the offender may be immediately returned to prison without a trial until the expiration of his original sentence if he commits another crime or breaks any of the rules imposed upon him by the conditions.

3. Parole relieves the state and other agencies of certain financial burdens.   Parole is less expensive to the state than imprisonment; also during the period the offender may support any dependents who otherwise might be forced to seek public relief.

The disadvantages of parole lie chiefly in the present system of administration. If the parole authority does not have a complete study of the offender and the training necessary to interpret this information, parolees are often not selected on the basis of their probable ability to adjust on parole. Casual release of prisoners on a common sense basis, because of the pressure of family or political party, or to relieve over-crowded conditions in prisons is not conducive to effective readjustment of the parolee.

When the prisoner is released before the expiration of his term without personal supervision, as he is in many states where he merely reports occasionally by mail to the parole board and experiences no real guidance, the effect of parole is merely to shorten the sentence.   Again, the operation of the system may be criticized when parole officers are untrained in social work or when they have such heavy case loads under their supervision that frequent individual attention is impossible.

The conditions of parole need revision since in some respects they run counter to community mores, so that the parolee who follows them finds himself unable to participate in normal activities.   If officers were better trained and in closer touch with their clients they would be able to help each parolee to plan and follow a constructive course without necessity of so many formal restrictions.

EVALUATION OF PAROLE

The purpose of parole is to aid offenders to reorganize their lives in order to conform to community standards.   Hence evaluation of the system should be on the basis of the degree to which parolees make satisfactory adjustments.   The basis of measurement might be merely the proportion who avoid breaking the law during parole; or the proportion who do not violate the conditions; or satisfactory adjustment might be considered more constructively as including steady employment, personal morale, good family relationships, and the like.

The national statistics for all state penal institutions show that the number of parole violators who are returned to prison each year equals about one fourth of the number of prisoners released conditionally.   Other studies trace the experience of a given group of prisoners over a 5 to 15 year period after release on parole to determine the success or failure of a specific group. One such study was made of prisoners released during 1944–45 from the Minnesota State Reformatory for Men, a maximum security institution for young offenders, mostly aged 20-29.[9]   Not only were parole violations included in the study, but also fingerprint records with the Federal Bureau of Investigation, and the files of the state board of police and of police departments in Minnesota cities.   During the first 5 years after release, many of the 183 men on parole had considerable difficulty in remaining out of prison: 42 per cent maintained their freedom; 15 per cent were fingerprinted (suspected of some crime) but were released; 25 per cent were returned to prison as parole violators; and 18 per cent were convicted on felony charges. Thus a total of 43 per cent failed to adjust as noncriminals.

A study from the New York State Division of Parole gives the percentage of offenders who violated their paroles during a 5-year period after release.[10] Of 1,606 offenders paroled in 1936 and studied in 1941, 7.6 per cent had been convicted of new felonies, 7.1 per cent of misdemeanors, and 20.4 per cent of violations of parole conditions not involving conviction of a crime. Although a total of 35.1 per cent violated their parole, only 7.6 per cent were convicted of a felony. In view of the fact that the original convictions were for felonies, these figures show a low percentage of recidivism for known felonies. It must be recalled that many violations of parole may occur that are not actual crimes, such as failure to notify the officer of changes in address or employment. Violations of the conditions may be delinquencies only because they violate a parole rule and would not be thus considered if performed by someone not on parole. The New York record, therefore, shows a low rate of recidivism for known violations of the criminal law. It is quite possible that other violations occurred, unknown to the parole officers and undiscovered by the police.

Successful adjustment on parole was studied by the Gluecks for 500 men and for 500 women who had served sentences in the state reformatories of Massachusetts.[11] Among the men, 465 had served some time on parole during the 15-year span covered by the study. Of this number, 22.6 per cent always succeeded in making a satisfactory adjustment on parole, 0.9 per cent succeeded at first and later failed, 11.8 per cent failed at first and later succeeded, 1.0 per cent showed erratic adjustment behavior, and 63.7 per cent always failed. Nonadjustment was judged by arrest, violation of parole, and known or recorded offenses for which arrests were possible. The criteria of adjustment are more finely drawn than in the New York study, and it is therefore not surprising that the Gluecks found 63.7 per cent who failed to make adjustment as compared with the 34.7 in New York who failed to the extent of violating their parole.

Among the 500 women, 20.7 per cent violated the conditions of their parole, and were ordered returned to the reformatory.[12] Actually only 13.8 per cent were returned, as the remainder of the violators had disappeared. A more detailed survey revealed that of 256 women whose conduct was checked, 45 per cent were not delinquent during the parole period, 23 per cent were arrested, and 32 per cent, although guilty of gross misconduct, were not arrested. For the purposes of their study the Gluecks defined nondelinquency as no arrests and no misconduct for which the person might have been arrested, such as drinking or stealing.

The high percentages of failure to adjust well on parole are not necessarily indicative of failure of the parole system as a method of release of prisoners. Many factors enter into successful adjustment besides the one of supervision; these factors are discussed in Chapter 21 in connection with recidivism.

PARDONS

Pardons are not extensively used. In 1952, no prisoners in federal prisons were pardoned and only 194 in state prisons.[13] An additional 2,470 state prisoners were released after commutation (shortening) of their sentences. A pardon is an act of clemency, justified by the fact that occasionally a man convicted of a crime is later found to be innocent; or an offender has received an unjust sentence without possibility of parole; or an offender has reformed but no other method of release is open to him. Pardons may also be used to release criminals convicted under laws later repealed, or to release those imprisoned during some period of public hysteria when emotion rather than evidence has influenced convictions. The pardoning power, therefore, serves to prevent or remedy injustices that might arise in the course of the usual legal procedure. Sentences are commuted for much the same reasons.

Unfortunately, there is inadequate restriction of the use of the power. It is possible for criminals who happen to be political favorites to secure pardons when there is no justification for their release. Criticism is also often directed at the granting of pardons to convicted offenders in return for information from them that will lead to the conviction of other and perhaps more dangerous criminals. Such a procedure, although open to criticism, may permit the release of one minor offender in exchange for the imprisonment of several major criminals, which may lessen the total danger to the community.

Another criticism of pardons is that inadequate information is secured on the offender's background and upon the probability that he will make a good adjustment after his release. This criticism does not apply to the innocent person who has been unjustly convicted, but to other categories.

The power to pardon usually rests with the governor, who may have the assistance of a board of pardons. This board may serve in an advisory capacity or the governor may sit on it as one member with no more authority than any other member. However, the President of the United States has unlimited pardoning power.

In some states with inadequate provisions for parole, pardons are used as a substitute and sometimes are granted subject to certain conditions. Such pardons are essentially parole, although they lack the provision for supervision that is inherent in the parole system. The confused situation in some states would be cleared by adequate parole laws and reserving the pardon for cases where injustice exists that cannot be rectified under present laws.

UNCONDITIONAL RELEASE OF FELONS

Almost one third of the prisoners released from state penal institutions in 1952 had completed their prison terms and were given an unconditional release. These men on the whole had served longer sentences than those released on parole and included more professional criminals. They probably had fewer noncriminal associates awaiting them in the community and their longer terms in prison would have weakened these contacts. They would also be more completely out of step with employment trends and more unaccustomed to independent management of their affairs than men who had served shorter terms ending in parole. These men, most in need of assistance both because of their greater acceptance of criminal attitudes and their longer isolation from the community, are the ones released without any supervision, such as that provided by parole. There is no official whose function is to see that they have a place to live, employment, or means of making friends.

Assistance for Released Prisoners

If prisoners released unconditionally have no family to aid them, help may come from 2 sources. Here and there philanthropically minded persons make a practice of giving employment and personal encouragement to discharged criminals. Such help is not reserved for those released unconditionally, but may also be given to convicts on parole. For instance, the millionaire president of a large advertising-specialty firm in a Middle West City, who had himself served a term in federal prison for tax evasion, has provided employment to some 200 ex-convicts over a period of 23 years.[14] Inasmuch as he receives yearly pleas for help from hundreds of prisoners nearing the date of release, it seems evident that the ones given assistance are a selected group. This assumption is further borne out by the fact that only 2 of those aided have failed to meet the expectations of their sponsor. Although such enterprises are to be commended they can reach only a limited number of released convicts and they can provide little assistance to those who have become unfitted for normal employment. These efforts cannot substitute for the systematic assistance to all released prisoners that is necessary.

Prisoners' Aid Societies

The other source of aid for released prisoners, whether on parole or not, is the prisoners' aid society. These societies are private agencies, supported by friends or community fund organizations, that help the released prisoner to adjust to the community. They are located in the larger cities where released convicts congregate.

The earliest of these organizations was the Philadelphia Society for Assisting Distressed Prisoners, established in 1776.[15] Reorganized in 1787 as the Philadelphia Society for Alleviating the Miseries of Public Prisons, it is now incorporated as the Pennsylvania Prison Society. Other similar organizations are the John Howard Association of Chicago, the Connecticut Prison Association, the United Prison Association of Massachusetts, the Wisconsin Service Association, the Jewish Committee for Personal Service in Los Angeles and San Francisco, the Osborne Association of New York City, and the Parting of the Ways Home in Pittsburgh.

Although each association has an individual program of activity, in general the societies assist released prisoners financially until they find employment, or provide lodging and food during this period, help them to find work, give advice and guidance, assist with family problems, promote community understanding of the prisoner's problems, and develop rehabilitation plans during imprisonment. Some of these organizations make their initial contacts with offenders while they are still in prison. One society, the Connecticut Prison Association, is employed by the state to supervise probationers and men who have been released from prison or jail after serving their sentences.

Although we cannot be sure to what extent the work of these societies prevents recurrence of crime, it is probable that they assist in readjusting offenders. Much depends upon the training and skill of those who work with released prisoners and the closeness of contact. A persevering, skillful approach applied to a small group can be successful. The prisoner who has served a long term emerges from prison out of touch with the civilian world, lacking in self-confidence, sensitive to his status as an ex-convict, often scorned by his family, and unable to find work. The released prisoner on parole may secure help from the parole officer if a good system of supervision is provided. When the parole system is not well organized, and for prisoners released at the expiration of their terms, no official aid is available. The volunteer societies step in at this point. Their assistance is in part material—lodging, food, and small sums of money. The society also serves as a link with the community and helps the ex-prisoner find employment. Moreover, it provides emotional security in that it gives a supporting hand during a transitional period and supplies a place where the released prisoner can find understanding and help. The societies to aid prisoners serve as a bulwark between the criminal and the underworld and help to incorporate the offender into the conventional community.

Many prisoners, either unconditionally released or inadequately supervised on parole, do not come under the care of helpful employers or prisoners' aid societies, but must try to make their own adjustment. Often the easiest course is to drift into association with other delinquents and criminals, who share the same attitudes and perhaps have similar prison experiences. The commission of new crimes is then to be expected.

The solution to the problem would be the release of all prisoners under some system of supervision. At present parole takes on the flavor of a reward given to the minor offender or to the obedient prisoner. It should be, rather, a truly rehabilitative method that would be applied to all prisoners to aid them to readjust to the community, in the full recognition that professional criminals and those who have served long prison terms will find readjustment more difficult than those who have had more casual criminal experiences and short terms of imprisonment.

PLACE OF PROBATION AND PAROLE IN REHABILITATION

The trend of opinion of those who are seriously interested in delinquency and crime, as personal and social problems rather than as legal violations, is away from prolonged imprisonment and in support of readjustment in the community with adequate supervision. At present both probation and parole suffer from inadequate administrative devices and from a shortage of trained personnel. These defects are remediable and should not be allowed to impede progress toward a fuller use of both systems. The extension of probation and parole are not advocated as a complete substitute for institutionalization. Certain types of misconduct derive from habits of thought and action so deeply ingrained that the person's entire life pattern is fixed in the mold of criminality. An intensive period of retraining in special institutions may be necessary before readjustment in the community is attempted. Other types of misconduct rest upon equally deep-rooted emotional maladjustments, which also call for intensive investigation and perhaps treatment under custody. These conditions indicate that there is no short cut to the selection of suitable treatment. Each offender to some extent presents an individual problem and the plan for treatment should be adapted to his problem.

QUESTIONS

1. What is the purpose of parole?

2. Contrast the advantages and disadvantages of the 3 main methods of selecting parolees: a central board; the governor; a local board.

3. On what basis should the selection of parolees be made?   What deficiencies are there at present in making selections?

4. What preparation for release should the prisoner have before leaving the prison?

5. How could parole supervision be improved?

6. What do studies of success on parole show regarding the proportion of parolees who "make good" on parole?   Of what do violations consist?

7. Why are pardons criticized as a means of release from prison?   When is a pardon justified?

8. What agencies assist the prisoner who leaves prison with an unconditional release?

READINGS

Attorney General's Survey of Release Procedures, Vol. 4 *Parole* (Washington: U.S. Department of Justice, 1939).   An extensive survey of parole principles and practices in the United States.

Dressler, David, *Probation and Parole* (New York: Columbia University Press, 1951).   The author has had long experience as Executive Director of the New York Parole System.   He presents his view of the philosophy of parole and discusses administrative and supervision problems.   He attempts to straddle the difficult problem of case work vs authoritarianism.

Federal Probation, quarterly journal published by the Administrative Office of the United States Courts in co-operation with the Federal Bureau of Prisons. Many articles on parole in both state and federal systems are published.

Handbook on Pre-release Preparation (New York: American Prison Association, 1950).   A comprehensive discussion of preparation for release while the convict is still in prison.

Tappan, Paul W. (ed.), *Contemporary Correction* (McGraw-Hill, 1951). Chapter 23 on "Parole and Services to the Discharged Offender," by G. C. Killinger, Chairman of the United States Board of Parole, discusses parole generally, using the federal service for concrete data.

Yearbook of the National Probation and Parole Association.   The *Yearbooks* carry a variety of articles, including some on parole.   The Association also publishes *Focus* 6 times yearly.

FOOTNOTES

[1] *Attorney General's Survey of Release Procedures,* 4, *Parole* (Washington: U.S. Department of Justice, 1939), 18ff.

[2] *Ibid.,* Vol. 4, pp. 44ff.

[3] *Ibid.,* Vol. 4, pp. 20ff., 93ff.

[4] *Ibid.,* Vol. 4, pp. 93ff.

[5] *Ibid.,* Vol. 4, pp. 105ff.

[6] *Ibid.*, Vol. 4, p. 212.

[7] J. A. Wallace, "Bridging the Gap between the Prison and the Community," *Yearbook, National Probation and Parole Association* (1952), pp. 41–52.

[8] Jean Long, "Job Placement for Overtime Inmates," *Yearbook, National Probation and Parole Association* (1952), pp. 53–61.

[9] S. B. Zuckerman, A. J. Barron, and H. B. Whittier, "Follow-up Study of Minnesota State Reformatory Inmates," *Journal of Criminal Law, Criminology and Police Science,* 43 (1952–53), 622–36.

[10] David Dressler, "Parole Results," *Proceedings of the American Prison Association* (1941), pp. 416–25.

[11] Sheldon and Eleanor T. Glueck, *Criminal Careers in Retrospect* (New York: The Commonwealth Fund, 1943), p. 151.

[12] Sheldon and Eleanor T. Glueck, *Five Hundred Delinquent Women* (Knopf, 1934), pp. 209, 387.

[13] "Prisoners in State and Federal Institutions," *National Prisoner Statistics,* No. 9 (Washington: Federal Bureau of Prisons, Aug. 1953), Table 2.

[14] "Convicts' Champion," *Life,* 21 (Sept. 30, 1946), 2–8.

[15] B. L. Scott, "The Discharged Prisoner," *Annals of the American Academy of Political and Social Science,* 157 (1931), 113–16; "The Offender Reenters the Community," *Prison Journal,* 25 (Oct., 1945), 113–19; also reports and pamphlets published by the societies.

21

Success and Failure of the Released Criminal

The entire system of Criminal justice, including penal institutions, is sometimes condemned because not all criminals who experience the long process that begins with arrest and ends with release from prison are able to adjust satisfactorily to the social and legal demands of the community. Some criminals again break laws; others avoid legal violations but otherwise fail to meet community standards of steady employment, self-support, care of dependents, and conventional personal conduct. From a rather limited point of view, their failure is a measure of the shortcomings of our system of treating criminals. But considered more broadly their failure is an indication of the inability of our total social organization to produce well-adjusted and law-abiding citizens. An examination of the extent of recidivism and of social factors associated with it will clarify this point.

EXTENT AND TYPES OF RECIDIVISM

Numerous studies show that one half to two thirds of the men and women who become seriously delinquent in youth continue such activities well into adulthood, and are not deterred by serving a sentence in a penal institution.* Moreover, not all of those placed on probation adjust successfully. From one fifth to two thirds of juvenile and adult probationers continued their delinquent or criminal activities, according to several studies.† Among misdemeanants, who are not included in these studies, recidivism is also high. Surveys of jail populations in different cities show that from 40 to 75 per cent, by their own admission, have been arrested previously.‡ The actual percentage undoubtedly would be higher if records could be checked.

Recidivists are not all of the same criminal type. Some few are profes-

* The details of these studies have already been discussed on pages 65–67.
† The details of these studies are given on pages 533–34.
‡ See pages 385–86.

sionals and their entire lives are organized around their criminal activities. These persons, whether they operate alone or in an organized group, at almost any time would be subject to arrest and conviction if evidence could be produced against them.   Because they make a business of crime and turn all their skill to it and because they have often secured political protection and legal advice, they appear less frequently in arrest and prison records than do other types of criminals.

Certain white-collar criminals are also continuously engaged in activities that are outright violations of the law or, although within legal limits, are ethically indefensible.   They also protect themselves from arrest and conviction.

A third type of recidivist, the misdemeanant whose offense is personal vice, may be continuously delinquent.   Unlike the professional and the white-collar criminal, he has no protection and the record of arrests is long and dreary.   He may be in jail for short terms several times a year.

Many other recidivists alternate between conventional activities and an occasional criminal episode.   Their lives are not thoroughly organized around either crime or vice but show instability of organization and vacillation from conventional to illegal activity.

Recidivism frequently exhibits a progression from one type of delinquency and crime to another.   Youthful offenders are characterized by a rather general array of delinquent activities, in which theft predominates among boys and sexual immorality among girls.   Four possibilities are open to these boys and girls as they come into adulthood.

1. They may abandon their youthful delinquencies and assume adult responsibilities.   They may secure employment, marry, buy homes, rear their children properly, and otherwise meet the adult standards of the community.

2. They may continue to commit occasional delinquencies, alternating with periods of conventional living.   In other words, they retain the instability and irresponsibility of their youth.

3. They may progress in illegal activities until they become confirmed criminals whose misconduct is a serious menace to the community.

4. They may slip backward into minor delinquencies and vice and become the typical demoralized misdemeanant.

Statements of the percentages of juvenile delinquents and criminals who become recidivists do not show the different types of recidivism nor the progressive changes that may take place.   A few special studies, however, have attempted to probe into the social as well as the penal factors that are associated with recidivism or with normal adjustment to community standards.

FACTORS RELATED TO RECIDIVISM

Factors of Early Life

Certain effects of early social experiences and individual traits are indelibly marked upon the personality of the delinquent and influence his behavior all through life. Probation, imprisonment, and parole may provide adequate supervision and remedial work, but in some cases they cannot eradicate the effects of early social experiences or the influence of personal traits. Hence the roots of recidivism in adulthood may reach back into childhood and indeed into an individual's physical and mental make-up. Careful studies, based on personal investigation of each criminal, make it possible to select experiences and traits that existed prior to the onset of delinquent behavior and are associated with recidivism or rehabilitation of the adult criminal. The most complete information on the relation of childhood background factors to adult recidivism is supplied by the Gluecks.

One thousand delinquent boys who had passed through the juvenile court and the Judge Baker Foundation (now the Judge Baker Guidance Center) of Boston were studied at 5-year intervals until a total span of 15 years had passed from the time of their first examination.[1] At the end of the 15-year period the average age of these delinquents was 29. One phase of the study compared the background characteristics of the men who reformed with the background of those who continued to recidivate. Certain characteristics were more closely associated with recidivism than with successful adjustment. It is not to be expected, however, that any one characteristic is always associated with reform and never with recidivism, or vice versa. Rather, a given factor is more frequently associated with recidivism than with reform.

Factors associated with recidivism included poor discipline by the parents; mental disease or distortion and marked personality liabilities or unusual adolescent instability; truancy and other school misconduct; and onset of delinquent behavior in the preadolescent years.

A comparison of those who reformed before the age of 21 with those who reformed later reaffirms the association of the above characteristics with recidivism and supplies others. For those who found reform most difficult a longer period had passed between the onset of delinquency and the first arrest than had elapsed for those who reformed early; that is, they were more habituated to delinquent conduct before they came to official attention. Later reform was also more closely associated with poor family moral standards, dull or subnormal intelligence, and school retardation. Membership in supervised recreational groups was more highly associated with later reform, but employment at street trades or night work with early reform.   These two associations are contrary to what one might expect, but the Gluecks point out that those who reformed late were also those who came to the attention of the juvenile court at an average age of 14 years, whereas those who reformed early came to the court at an average age of 12 years and 9 months.   The older group had had more opportunity to become affiliated with recreational groups.   The younger children, not yet able to secure full employment, were naturally more often found in street trades; they were also the ones who reformed earlier.   The authors, therefore, do not regard these two associations as significant in reference to reform.

In another study, the Gluecks traced 500 young male offenders who had been sentenced to the reformatory, from the time of discharge either unconditionally or from parole until a period of 15 years had passed.[2]   At the end of that time they were able to compare 140 reformed offenders with 256 recidivists.   Family background factors more closely associated with recidivism than with reform were these: delinquency of other members of the family; low economic status of parents; employment of the mother outside the home; dependence of the family on welfare agencies; broken homes; incompatibility of parents.   Characteristics of the offender in his prereformatory period that were more closely associated with recidivism than with reform were these: mental deficiency; mental pathology; truancy; first delinquency under the age of 14; first departure from home under the age of 14; ability to do only unskilled work; poor work habits; inability to meet economic responsibilities; and lack of affectional tie with parents and siblings.

In general, the factors in youth that were associated with continued delinquency and crime in adulthood centered around the home, the school, mental defect or instability, and work habits.   The early family life of confirmed adult offenders appeared disorganized, involving conflict between the parents, low moral standards, poor discipline of the children, and often the absence of one parent.   The economic standard was low, and the mother was possibly employed outside the home.   Family ties were weak.   At school frequent factors were truancy, misconduct, and retardation, often linked with low mental ability.   Delinquencies started during childhood.   In adolescence, the delinquent tended to leave home, and failed to learn either good work habits, or a skill or trade.   He found it difficult to meet economic responsibilities.

These factors related to recidivism derive from two studies of male delinquents in Massachusetts.   Caution should be exercised in drawing general conclusions, although it is probable that the findings may be safely applied to criminals in other communities.

relationships, 77.3 per cent recidivated; and among those with poor family relationships, 98.5 per cent did not reform.

Another study, by Healy and Bronner, also throws light on the relation of marriage to recidivism.[6]   Among 420 Chicago male criminals were 164 who were no longer criminals at age 25; 14 per cent of this group were married.   Two hundred and fifty-six of the males were continuing their delinquent or criminal behavior; of these 5 per cent were married.   Among the females who had made a successful adjustment to noncriminal life, 60 per cent were married, the same percentage that is found in the general population; whereas among those continuing in criminality only 32 per cent were married.   The failures among both married males and females had many marital difficulties.   Among the successful males all those who were married were living with their wives at the time of the study; among the failures, of the 14 who were married, 3 were divorced and 4 were deserters or nonsupporters.   Among 83 successful females who were married, 80 were living with their husbands; of 38 failures who were married, 4 were divorced, 2 were immoral, 4 were prostitutes, and 8 had deserted or were neglecting their children.

The evidence is not altogether conclusive, but it seems to point to the fact that criminal conduct and marriages—especially stable marriages—do not mix.   Healy and Bronner suggest that, although marriage probably helps the delinquent to assume and maintain noncriminal conduct, few young male delinquents are sufficiently well established economically and socially to marry, or they are unwilling to assume the responsibility of marriage.[7]   The Gluecks cite cases in which the chief factor in a man's adjustment to conventional behavior was a well-balanced and understanding wife; but in other cases men with equally well-balanced wives relapsed again and again into some form of delinquency in spite of obvious efforts to remain law abiding.[8]   It is impossible to generalize regarding the cause and effect relationship between crime and marriage.   Marriage may occur and succeed because the former delinquent has made an adjustment to conventional living; or a man who otherwise might continue in delinquency may be stabilized by marriage.   However, the pull toward delinquent habits may be so strong that marriage cannot check it.   Further studies are necessary before the interrelation is completely understood.

In the case of girls who have been delinquent, marriage occurs more often than among young men.   Successful marriages are made by many girls who are sex delinquents.   Healy and Bronner point out that marriage legitimatizes the conduct that has brought many of them into the courts; it also offers economic and social security.   Marriage is perhaps a stabilizing element that contributes to the conventional conduct of such girls.

The use of leisure time is perhaps most highly related to continued criminal activity.   Among the Gluecks' 500 women, none who used their leisure constructively continued in delinquency, although all those whose leisure was occupied improperly continued in delinquency.   For the men, none of those who used their leisure constructively became total failures, 16.7 per cent, however, continued certain delinquencies; among those who used their time harmfully, none were completely reformed.

The relationship of criminality to postparole factors is shown by the Gluecks more clearly when personal and social relationships are combined and compared with recidivism.   Among the women, of those who adjusted themselves at least fairly well in all personal and social relationships, only 17.1 per cent continued in delinquency beyond the parole period; of those who failed to adjust in one or more relationships, 98.4 per cent continued in delinquency.   Among the men, of those who were completely or partially successful in personal and social relationships, 26.8 per cent were recidivists in the postparole period; of those who failed in one or more types of personal and social relationships, 98.2 per cent failed to reform (see Figure 28).

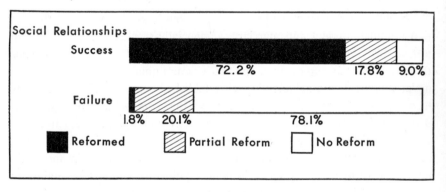

FIGURE 28

Percentage of men with success or failure in social relationships during postparole period who reformed or failed to reform.   Success or failure was measured by degree of industrial stability, of economic responsibility, of family adjustment, and of constructive use of leisure.   The graph shows the close relationship between successful social relationships and reform, or acceptance of a conventional mode of living.   The relationship is probably reciprocal: good behavior brings social acceptance; social acceptance encourages good behavior.   (Based on Sheldon and Eleanor T. Glueck, *Five Hundred Criminal Careers* [Knopf, 1930], p. 222.)

Although these relationships indicate the association of good adjustment with nondelinquency and of poor adjustment with recidivism, we cannot impute a causal relationship.   It is not possible to state that good relationships prevent continued delinquency; nor are we sure that recidivism causes poor personal and social relationships.   Cases presented by the Gluecks, as well as other published studies of delinquents and criminals, indicate that the relationship may function in either direction.   To the extent that the offender is able to establish himself in stable and conforming groups his own behavior improves; if he secures the companionship and approval of these groups he must meet their standards and abandon delinquency and crime. Also, as personal ties are formed, members of the groups may aid the wavering delinquent.   For example, marriage to a stable, law-abiding, and understanding wife may influence the criminal to readjust his attitudes and habits to conventional living; whereas marriage to a woman who is delinquent or weak may reinforce the earlier criminal habits of the husband.   We must remember, however, that criminals may deliberately seek companionship with other criminals rather than in conventional groups.   Possibly those who associate with constructive groups are the ones whose criminal attitudes and habits are not deeply ingrained and are therefore most easily influenced by conventional persons.

The Maturity Factor in Reform

One of the theoretical results of the studies by the Gluecks is their formulation of the hypothesis that at a certain stage of maturity delinquency tends to disappear and offenders assume a conventional pattern of conduct.[9] Maturation is not measured by chronological age, but by the span of time that elapses after the first appearance of delinquent tendencies.   If delinquency first begins in early childhood, such conduct will have run its course by early adulthood; if delinquency begins, however, in adolescence, it will persist until a later period of adulthood.   According to this hypothesis, reform awaits the development of judgment, self-denial, ability to repress or divert antisocial impulses, and integration of personality.   Normally, this process is completed in early chronological adulthood.   But for some, maturation is delayed and in these cases if delinquent conduct has appeared it will continue until maturation checks it.   Other criminals, the Gluecks believe, never become mature and eventually the natural processes of deterioration with age cause criminal activities to decline as the offender loses his energy and daring.   Or major criminal activities are abandoned for delinquencies that do not require sustained effort, and the once youthful criminal sinks into the demoralized habitual petty offender.

This hypothesis is interesting and is compatible with other factors related to recidivism.   At present not enough is known about the processes of maturation to permit dogmatism, but quite probably disintegrating social situations found to be associated with delinquency before and after imprisonment may hinder the development of those mental qualities associated with maturity, and may prevent the integration of interests and roles that typify the well-balanced adult.

Additional studies are needed to test the hypothesis and to relate it to other factors already known to be associated with recidivism. If maturation is proved to be a factor, remedial work with delinquents should be directed not only toward education, vocational instruction, and habit training; but also toward achieving emotional stability, a sense of responsibility, and ability to work for distant, socialized goals of conduct—all attributes of the mature personality.

PREDICTION OF NONCRIMINAL BEHAVIOR

In the 1920's interest developed in the possibility of predicting in advance whether criminals would become recidivists if placed on parole. At that time the system was sharply criticized by many people who believed that dangerous criminals were released on parole before the expiration of their prison terms to continue their criminal activities in the community. If, while the criminal was still in prison, it could be predicted how he would conduct himself after release, authorities would be able to select those criminals for parole who showed the highest probability of reform.

The method of prediction depends upon observing characteristics of successful parolees that distinguish them from those who commit new crimes or who otherwise violate parole conditions. When these characteristics are discovered, the assumption is that other criminals with the same characteristics will be equally successful in adjusting on parole. They must be easily ascertainable, measurable, and evident before the criminal leaves prison. They may be factors from his life prior to imprisonment or related to his conduct in prison.

The material discussed in the earlier sections of this chapter demonstrates that many factors from early life are associated with success or failure on parole. Such factors form the basis of prediction techniques.

An early prediction table for forecasting success on parole was devised by Ernest W. Burgess. It was based on a study of 1,000 parolees each from the Illinois State Reformatory for young male offenders, and the two state penitentiaries at Joliet and Menard.[10] These parolees were classified according to many factors, such as work record prior to commitment, degree of intelligence, type of residential community prior to commitment, marital status at time of commitment, broken homes, and so on. For the subgroups of each factor the percentage was taken of men who adjusted successfully while on parole. When these percentages were compared with the percentage of the total group who adjusted successfully, it was found that some factors showed a high and some a low association with success. Figure 29 illustrates the association with success on parole of different clas-

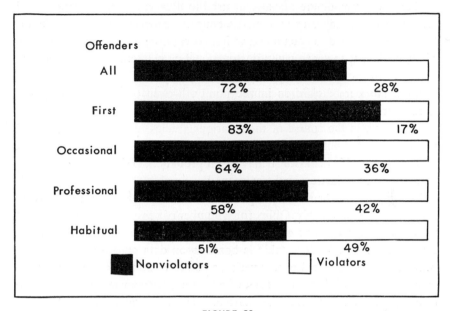

FIGURE 29

Percentage of parole violations of different types of criminals.   First offenders are very good risks on parole; only 17 per cent of this group violate the conditions of parole and are returned to prison.   Habitual offenders have least chance for success on parole.   When a number of factors related to tendency to violate parole are found, they can be made into a useful scale for predicting success on parole, while the criminals are still in prison.   (Based on A. A. Bruce, E. W. Burgess, and A. J. Harno, *The Workings of the Indeterminate-Sentence Law and the Parole System in Illinois* [Springfield: State of Illinois, 1928], p. 224.)

sifications of criminal activities.   Judging from this one factor, the first offender appears to be a much better risk for parole than does the habitual offender.

Twenty-one factors showing an association with success on parole were selected and formed into a prediction scale, whose scores could be compared with the scores in a master expectancy table to show the probability of success on parole of an individual prisoner.

The publication of the Burgess report was followed by experimentation and testing on the part of many others in the effort to establish prediction tables for success on parole and probation.   The most detailed work was performed by the Gluecks.[11]   Their basic assumption was the same as that of Burgess—that experiences and characteristics existing at the time of imprisonment and associated with recidivism could be grouped together and used to predict the probability of successful adjustment on parole.   Their method, however, differed from that used by Burgess, in that they selected only a limited number of factors most highly associated with success and failure and assigned to each one a weighted value determined by the degree of association with successful adjustment.   For predicting behavior during parole from the reformatory they employed these 5 factors: education of parents, number of children in the family, broken or inadequate homes, intelligence, and grade attained in school.

Moreover, in the course of their various studies, the Gluecks published prediction tables not only for parole from several types of institutions, but also for postparole behavior, behavior on probation, and adjustment during different types of institutional treatment.

Building on earlier studies of prediction and especially upon the Bruce, Burgess, and Harno study, Ohlin, for a number of years Research Sociologist with the Illinois Division of Correction, has devised a prediction table for success on parole.[12]   The table is based upon data on more than 17,000 prisoners in 3 Illinois prisons, covering a period of 20 years.   Twelve items compose the prediction table, each of which has been found to be related to degree of success or failure on parole.   The items and their ratings are given in Table 25.   For an individual prisoner under consideration for parole, the appropriate ratings for that prisoner are determined and the individual ratings are then computed into a total score by assigning a weight of 1 to each favorable item, 0 to each neutral, and minus 1 to each unfavorable, and substracting the total minus figure from the total plus figure.   On the basis of years of records, an Experience Table has been constructed which gives for any prediction score the probability of success on parole for the individual with that score.   Table 26 gives the Experience Table. Armed with this or a similar instrument, parole boards may supplement their interviews with the prisoners and their study of case material with an objective prediction score.

Although prediction tables are practical and easy to use, they are employed by only a few institutions that deal with criminals.   Some agencies do not assemble even the simple background data needed for applying prediction tables.   In others the persons who pass upon release are untrained in the use of scientific instruments, do not understand them, and hence distrust them.   The rapid turnover in some parole boards and other agencies prevents the establishment of definite policies and procedures for determining who shall be released, or if such policies are established by one officer or board they may be abandoned by the next one.   Hence old-fashioned, un-

TABLE 25

Rating of Prediction Items, Joliet-Stateville and Menard Divisions, Illinois State Penitentiary System

Prediction Factors and Items	Favorable	Neutral	Unfavorable	Prediction Factors and Items	Favorable	Neutral	Unfavorable
1. Type of offense				Ne'er-do-well		0	
Homicide and assault	1			Floater			−1
Robbery		0		Socially maladjusted			−1
Burglary			−1	Drunkard			−1
Larceny and stolen property		0		Drug addict			−1
Forgery and fraud		0		Sex deviant		0	
Sex offenses	1			**7. Work record**			
Miscellaneous		0		Regular	1		
2. Sentence				Irregular		0	
All definite sentences	1			Casual		0	
All other sentences		0		Student		0	
3. Type of offender				None		0	
First	1			**8. Community**			
Technical first		0		Urban		0	
Occasional		0		Rural		0	
Juvenile recidivist		0		Transient			−1
Recidivist			−1	**9. Parole job**			
Habitual			−1	Adequate		0	
4. Home status				Inadequate			−1
Superior	1			None		0	
Average		0		**10. Number of associates**			
Inferior		0		None		0	
Broken		0		One or two		0	
Institution		0		Three and over	1		
Left home		0		**11. Personality**			
5. Family interest				Normal (no gross defects)	1		
Very active	1			Inadequate		0	
Active		0		Unstable		0	
Sustained		0		Egocentric		0	
Passive		0		Gross personality defects		0	
None			−1	No record		0	
6. Social type				**12. Psychiatric prognosis**			
Erring citizen	1			Favorable	1		
Marginally delinquent	1			Problematic		0	
"Farmer"	1			Doubtful		0	
Socially inadequate	1			Guarded		0	
				Unfavorable		0	
				No record		0	

Source: Lloyd E. Ohlin, *Selection for Parole* (New York: Russell Sage Foundation, 1951), p. 52.

[a] In scoring, each favorable item in an individual's record counts 1, neutral counts 0, and unfavorable −1. The total of the −1's is subtracted from the total of the +1's. Terms used in the table are exactly defined in the appendix to the study.

TABLE 26

Experience Table for 4,941 Parolees, Joliet-Stateville and Menard Divisions,
Illinois State Penitentiary System, Paroled 1940–45

Score Group	Violators per 100 Cases in Each Score Group		
	Total Violators	Minor Violators	Major Violators
5 to 10	3	2	1
4	7	5	2
3	10	7	3
2	18	10	8
1	19	10	9
0	29	16	13
−1	40	25	15
−2	46	27	19
−3 and −4	56	34	22
−5 and −6	75	62	13

Source: Lloyd E. Ohlin, *Selection for Parole* (New York: Russell Sage Foundation, 1951), p. 58.

certain practices continue in use, and the more exact methods of both prediction tables and intensive case studies are neglected.

REDUCTION OF RECIDIVISM

The reduction of recidivism requires an increase in rehabilitative and reformative measures. There are five lines of defense against recidivism.

1. Prevention of delinquency and crime.

2. Humane treatment of offenders by officials and quick and fair trials.

3. Genuinely rehabilitative treatment during the period of incarceration.

4. Release of the criminal as soon as possible from institutionalization, in order to make his adjustment under adequate supervision in the community. For many offenders, community adjustment might be effected without institutionalization, provided adequate supervision were supplied.

5. Acceptance by the community of responsibility for the offender's readjustment, not only by providing an adequate number of well-trained parole and probation officers but by establishing other rehabilitative agencies. A general revision of the public attitude toward criminals is also necessary.

QUESTIONS

1. In the Gluecks' study of juvenile delinquents what background factors were found to be more closely associated with recidivism than with reform?

2. In the Gluecks' study of 500 young male offenders what factors were found more closely associated with recidivism than with reform?

3. What is the effect of many impeding factors (rather than only one) on reform?

4. What is the relation of previous family, school, and community experiences to conduct while in prison? Is the usual treatment in prison suitable for combatting poor prior conditions so that the prisoner emerges improved in attitudes and conduct?

5. In the postprison period, what types of industrial experience, family life, and use of leisure are related to successful adjustment?

6. State the maturation theory of the Gluecks. Criticize this theory.

7. Discuss methods devised to predict successful adjustment on parole. How were the prediction tables set up? How may they be used by a parole board?

READINGS

Bruce, A. A., E. W. Burgess, and A. J. Harno, *The Workings of the Indeterminate-Sentence Law and the Parole System in Illinois* (Springfield: The State of Illinois, 1928), Part 4. An early study of background factors associated with violation and nonviolation of parole.

Glueck, Sheldon and Eleanor T., *Juvenile Delinquents Grown Up* (New York: Commonwealth Fund, 1940); *Five Hundred Delinquent Women* (Knopf, 1934); *Criminal Careers in Retrospect* (New York: Commonwealth Fund, 1943). The Gluecks in their studies of three groups of offenders have paid especial attention to background factors associated with recidivism. Other important data concern institutional treatment and postprison situations and their relationship to recidivism.

Monochesi, Elio D., "American Studies in the Prediction of Recidivism," *Journal of Criminal Law and Criminology,* 41 (1950), 268–89. An excellent survey of prediction studies.

Ohlin, Lloyd E., *Selection for Parole* (New York: Russell Sage Foundation, 1951). The subtitle, *A Manual of Parole Prediction,* indicates the practical nature of this report on the construction and use of the prediction instrument used by the Illinois Division of Correction to aid in selection of parolees.

FOOTNOTES

[1] Sheldon and Eleanor T. Glueck, *Juvenile Delinquents Grown Up* (New York: Commonwealth Fund, 1940), pp. 111ff.

[2] Sheldon and Eleanor T. Glueck, *Criminal Careers in Retrospect* (New York: Commonwealth Fund, 1943), p. 127.

[3] *Ibid.,* p. 190.

[4] Sheldon and Eleanor T. Glueck, *Five Hundred Delinquent Women* (Knopf, 1934), pp. 20–241.

[5] Sheldon and Eleanor T. Glueck, *Five Hundred Criminal Careers* (Knopf, 1930), pp. 217–23.

[6] William Healy and Augusta F. Bronner, *Delinquents and Criminals, Their Making and Unmaking* (Macmillan, 1926), p. 268.

[7] Healy and Bronner, *op. cit.,* pp. 130–31.

[8] Glueck and Glueck, *Criminal Careers in Retrospect,* pp. 10–71.

[9] Glueck and Glueck, *Juvenile Delinquents Grown Up,* pp. 90–106; 264–70.

[10] A. A. Bruce, E. W. Burgess, and A. J. Harno, *The Workings of the Indeterminate-Sentence Law and the Parole System in Illinois* (Springfield: The State of Illinois, 1928), pp. 246–49, 265.

[11] Glueck and Glueck, *Criminal Careers in Retrospect,* p. 244.

[12] Lloyd E. Ohlin, *Selection for Parole* (New York: Russell Sage Foundation, 1951).

22

Treatment of Offenders in the Armed Forces

A discussion of crime and penal and correctional institutions in the United States is no longer complete without the inclusion of the incidence and treatment of offenses among men in military service. The armed forces, especially during time of war, drain out of the civilian population a large number of men from the age group of peak criminal activity. The strength of the Army (including the Air Force) and the Navy swelled from approximately one half million in 1940 to 12,314,000 on June 1, 1945, and another 3 million were in service at some time during this period.[1] In this predominantly male force, the median age was 25.7 years and few were over 35 years old.[2] This concentration of young men in the armed forces led to the estimate that, at the period of peak strength, 30 per cent of the criminal potential was in the armed forces.[3] Between the end of World War II and the beginning of the Korean conflict, the number of men in service fell sharply and the median age decreased to 22.2 years in December, 1948. The Korean War called for increased strength, and 3 million men were drafted or enlisted between June, 1950 and the end of July, 1952. These men were primarily between 18.5 and 26 years—a period of high crime rates.

Although the armed forces reject many men with histories of crime or behavior maladjustment, the withdrawal of so many young men from civilian life cannot help but affect the trends of civilian crime. Table 27 shows the number of civilian prisoners in state and federal prisons for the years 1940–50, and also the numbers of servicemen confined under sentences imposed by military courts. In 1945, when the largest number of military prisoners was confined, military prisoners equaled 25 per cent of the civilian prisoners; in 1950, 4 per cent.

573

TABLE 27

Civilian and Military Prisoners, 1940–50

Year	Civilians in Federal and State Prisons, December 31	Military Prisoners, June 30	Total Prisoners
1940	172,846	1,051	173,897
1941	164,669	1,523	166,192
1942	149,392	2,442	151,834
1943	135,651	7,246	142,897
1944	130,559	18,890	149,449
1945	130,543	32,562	163,105
1946	136,053	21,820	157,873
1947	147,234	13,885	161,119
1948	151,942	8,980	160,922
1949	160,797	7,058	167,855
1950	163,613	6,269	169,882

Sources: Civilian—*Federal Prisons, 1952* (Washington: Federal Bureau of Prisons, U.S. Department of Justice, 1952), p. 104. From the number of prisoners reported in this publication, the number sentenced by courts-martial (military courts) and confined in federal prisons has been deducted for each year, leaving only the civilian prisoners.

Military—*The Army Correctional System* (Washington: Office of The Adjutant General, U.S. Department of the Army, 1952), p. 163. The military prisoners were confined in disciplinary barracks, rehabilitation centers, federal prisons, and other places (guardhouses and overseas installations among others). They include men convicted of both military and civilian offenses.

REJECTION OF CRIMINALS FOR MILITARY SERVICE

Objective of Military Training

The keynote of life in the armed services is found in the following brief statements of the purpose of military training:

The primary purpose of the United States Army is to organize, train, and equip land forces of the United States for the conduct of prompt and sustained combat operations on land in accordance with plans for national security.[4]

Stated in sociological terms, the task that confronts all branches of the armed forces, especially during war time, is the rapid conversion of an "initial aggregate of heterogeneous individuals with widely different civilian backgrounds and experiences" into a "unified combat group." [5]

In selecting men for the service, the armed forces desire, both in the regular forces and among selectees, only those who give definite promise of being able to meet the demands and further the purpose of the armed forces. The classification used screens out criminals and various types of defective persons. Physical disabilities, feeble-mindedness, and emotional disturbances account for many exemptions. Criminals are also unwelcome because men who cannot conform or control their behavior and who reject authority do not make dependable fighting men. It is also felt that they are a moral risk to other, and especially young, servicemen.

The Regular Armed Forces

Army, Navy, and Air Force agree in refusing to accept enlistment for the regular forces of men with convictions of felonies. Other troublemakers also are unwanted. For example, Air Force regulations state that "persons having frequent difficulties with law enforcement agencies, criminal tendencies, a history of antisocial behavior, alcoholism, drug addiction, sexual perversity, or questionable moral character which renders the person unfit to associate with other persons are morally unacceptable." [6]   It is assumed in advance that they will not be able to adapt themselves to the rigorous discipline nor to the responsibilities of military life.

An attempt is made to screen out those misdemeanants who in all probability could not adjust to military regulations. The general assumption is that misdemeanants are not acceptable, but if a reasonable supposition of conformity can be established, waivers may be issued permitting enlistment. Army [7] and Air Force [8] regulations are similar: before applying for enlistment the offender must have abided by the law for at least 6 months following unconditional release from prison, parole, or probation. A complete investigation and recommendations from 3 reputable citizens and the investigating officer may lead to issuance of a waiver by a superior officer.

Conviction by a juvenile court as a delinquent, wayward minor, or youthful offender is not in itself a bar to enlistment. Each such person, however, is thoroughly investigated to determine whether he would be a moral risk. The Air Force, for example, refuses to accept juvenile offenders who "have had frequent difficulties with law enforcement agencies, a history of antisocial behavior, sexual perversity, or questionable moral character." [9]   In any case, 6 months of good behavior must intervene between release from civil authorities and application for enlistment.

In none of the above classifications are waivers granted to female applicants.

Selectees

Under the provisions of the Universal Military Training and Service Act,* unified for all branches of the service, men enter the armed forces for a statutory period of training and service of 24 consecutive months, unless released sooner. Essentially the same classifications of persons are

* Enacted in 1948 as the Selective Service Act of 1948 and amended in 1951.

excluded among selectees as for enlistment in the regular forces. However, persons convicted of felonies may have the disqualification waived by the respective department of the forces into which they are to enter.[10] Men with criminal charges filed and pending against them or who have been released by a court on condition that they apply for induction into the armed forces are not acceptable and no waivers are granted. Occasional exceptions do not violate the general policy that the armed forces may not be used as a substitute for imprisonment.

The usual policy of the armed forces, therefore, is to accept only men with a record of good adjustment in civilian life. Those with physical, mental, moral, and criminal handicaps are eliminated, and the ones accepted would presumably continue to have at least average adjustment.

Among men acceptable by military regulations a few become legal offenders at the time of registration or induction. Some refuse to register at all; others will not comply with necessary procedures. Certain conscientious objectors who fail to substantiate their claims to religious convictions also refuse to complete registration or induction. (Religious conscientious objectors are recognized in law as having a valid reason for refusing to fight and are placed in alternative activities useful to public or military life.) Men who thus refuse to enter service are civil offenders who are tried in the federal (not military) courts and, if convicted, sentenced to federal prisons.

THE UNIFORM CODE OF MILITARY JUSTICE

As soon as a man has been inducted into the armed forces he becomes subject to the Uniform Code of Military Justice, which covers not only the misdemeanors and crimes found in most civilian codes of criminal law but military regulations as well. These regulations are specifically designed to help train men in appropriate military habits and weld them into a cooperating unit. Both officers and privates in the Army and the corresponding groups in other services, therefore, are subject to two sets of laws: civilian-type criminal laws; and military regulations.

Autonomous Character of Military Justice

On May 5, 1950, Congress passed an act * establishing a Uniform Code of Military Justice applicable to all the armed forces of the United States.[11] This act unified, consolidated, revised, and codified the independent codes under which the various departments of the armed forces formerly func-

* Public Law 506, 81st Congress, c. 169, 1, 64 Stat. 108; Title 50 U.S.C. (Chap. 22), pp. 551–736.

tioned, and provided a uniform code for the Department of the Army, the Department of the Navy (including the Marine Corps), the Department of the Air Force, and the Coast Guard. In addition, each branch of the service has special regulations.

The system of military justice operates concurrently with the civilian system but is more comprehensive in character. Courts-martial (military courts) exercise jurisdiction over all types of offenses and crimes when men are overseas or otherwise beyond the range of civil courts. The Uniform Code of Military Justice applies to those in active military service, reserve personnel on active duty, and civilians accompanying the armed forces either in the field or in overseas areas. Jurisdiction ends with discharge from the forces, except with reference to certain serious offenses committed while still in active service, which are not within the jurisdiction of a state or federal court.

Thus military justice follows the serviceman around the world. It applies whether the armed forces are in the United States, on shipboard, or on foreign soil.

The inclusive and comprehensive qualities of the system of military justice give it an autonomous character that has led to the statement, "Nowhere else in our jurisprudence is so much power over law enforcement and the treatment of the offender vested in a single agency" as in the military authorities during wartime.[12]

Offenses

Fifty-eight articles (Nos. 77–134) of the Code of Military Justice are termed the Punitive Articles;[13] they correspond to civilian criminal laws. Many of the articles growing out of military procedures have no equivalent in civilian life. Their purpose is to maintain discipline, train men to fight, and assure that the men put forth their best effort in the face of the enemy— in short, to support the military objective. In order to clarify military regulations as distinct from civilian-type crimes, the articles covering specific offenses are described in some detail.

Articles 85–87 cover absences taken without authority: desertion, absence without leave, and missing the movement of a ship, aircraft, or unit through design or neglect.

Articles 88–92 are concerned with contempt toward government officials, disrespect toward a superior officer, assaulting or wilfully disobeying an officer, insubordination to a noncommissioned officer, and failure to obey an order or a regulation.

Article 93 forbids cruelty toward a subordinate.

Article 94 defines mutiny and sedition.

Articles 95–98 make it an offense to resist apprehension or to escape from custody, to release a prisoner without authority, to detain another unlawfully, and intentionally to neglect procedural rules.

Articles 99–110 are specifically related to behavior that would endanger the United States forces or would aid the enemy: misbehavior before the enemy (chiefly forms of cowardice); surrender without authority; improper use of countersign; forcing a safeguard; not turning over to the proper United States authority property taken from the enemy; aiding the enemy; misconduct as a prisoner (currying favor from enemy captor, or mistreating a fellow prisoner); acting as a spy against the United States; making false official statements; illegally destroying or disposing of United States military property, or other property; and improper hazarding of a vessel.

Articles 111–117 refer to personal conduct of a hazardous nature: drunkenness on duty or when driving, misbehavior of sentinel, dueling, malingering, inciting to riot, or making provocative speeches or gestures.

Articles 118–132 define crimes that are felonies when committed by civilians: murder, manslaughter, rape, larceny, robbery, forgery, maiming, sodomy, arson, extortion, assault, burglary, housebreaking, perjury, and frauds against the government.

Article 133 forbids conduct unbecoming an officer and a gentleman, that is, conduct of an official nature that also disgraces the individual as a gentleman, or conversely, personal behavior that compromises the individual's standing as an officer.   This conduct is interpreted to mean either one of the offenses specifically listed above or any other conduct reflecting upon the person as an officer and a gentleman.   Examples are "dishonorable failure to pay debts; opening and reading the letters of another without authority; being grossly drunk and conspicuously disorderly in a public place; and failing without good cause to support his family." [14]

Article 134, the last of the Punitive Articles, is a blanket article covering all behavior that threatens good order and discipline or brings discredit upon the armed forces.   With few exceptions, this misconduct is of a type that does not threaten security or constitute a felony.   A few examples selected at random follow: [15]

Military personnel who render themselves unfit for duty because of prior indulgence in intoxicants or narcotic drugs.

Appearance in improper uniform.

Violation of local laws or other discreditable conduct.

Various types of assaults.

Disloyal statements that bring discredit to the United States.

A man in service, therefore, may subject himself to military punishment either by committing civilian crimes or by violating special military laws. Table 28 shows the distribution of offenses among Army and Air Force prisoners; military offenses outnumber civil offenses more than 2 to 1.

TABLE 28

Principal Offenses of Army and Air Force General Prisoners

Principal Offenses	World War II and Immediate Postwar Offenders [a] (per cent)	Offenders Committed during Fiscal Years 1949 and 1950 [b] (per cent)
Military offenses	69.5	62.1
Absent without leave	30.1	19.4
Desertion	24.8	31.6
Discreditable conduct toward superior officer	7.1	4.5
Misbehavior of sentinel	1.0	0.8
Violation of escape or arrest	4.5	3.2
Other military offenses	2.0	2.6
Civil offenses	30.5	37.9
Murder or manslaughter	2.0	0.9
Assaults of all types	5.4	5.2
Rape, sodomy	2.1	1.1
Robbery, burglary, larceny	12.2	18.3
Fraud, forgery	5.2	7.4
Other	3.6	5.0
Total number	33,396	14,120

[a] Based on 74 per cent of all general prisoners in confinement at rehabilitation centers, disciplinary barracks, and federal institutions January 1, 1945 and received from that date through June 30, 1946.

[b] For 1949 and 1950, all general prisoners sentenced during the year including those in overseas installations and guardhouses in the United States.

Source: *The Army Correctional System* (Washington: Office of The Adjutant General, U.S. Department of the Army, 1952), p. 153.

It should be noted that military regulations redefine many types of behavior. Conduct that is a matter of personal choice in civilian life may be an offense in the military system and call forth heavy penalties. It has been pointed out that quitting one's job becomes desertion in the military services; going on strike is defined as mutiny; and disobedience to the boss is wilful disobedience of a superior officer.[16] In civilian life, the person guilty of these offenses at most would lose his job; in the armed forces, he is officially punished because these acts interfere with the training of soldiers in the implicit acceptance of regulations, orders, and authority.

Penalties

A maximum punishment is assigned to each Punitive Article by executive order of the President; within this framework, the court-martial directs what punishment shall be given each offender.   Penalties may be slight, such as loss of privileges or restriction to a limited area without confinement; or they may involve long periods of imprisonment or sentence of death.[17] They are related to offenses in such a way that penalties for minor offenses do not prevent performance of duties.   It should be noted also that the death sentence is used sparingly and virtually never for a military offense alone.

Some penalties are unlike those found in civilian laws.   Dismissal from the armed forces because of misconduct is a serious penalty.   In addition to the sense of disgrace that the offender may feel and the scorn exhibited by others toward him, there are practical disadvantages: re-enlistment in the armed forces is forbidden and civilian employment may be difficult to secure. Two types of severe punitive discharge are used.   1) A dishonorable discharge is usually imposed only on persons convicted of offenses that would be classed as felonies under civil law or who have committed a serious military offense.[18]   2) A bad conduct discharge may be imposed upon a first offender when the offense does not merit a dishonorable discharge but justifies punitive separation from the service; or it may be used as a penalty for continued misconduct of a minor nature, no one instance of which alone would merit a dishonorable or bad conduct discharge.   The bad conduct discharge provides the service with a method of disposing of chronic petty offenders. In contrast to the dishonorable and bad-conduct discharges for enlisted men and warrant officers, dismissal from the service constitutes dishonorable separation of officers from the service.

Forfeiture of pay is also used as a punishment, running from a few days to a number of months.   For enlisted men, pay may also be withheld, a less serious penalty than forfeiture, since the offender collects the money when he leaves the service.   Fines are usually imposed only on civilians who are subject to military law or when the offender has secured some financial gain through his offense.[19]

Certain penalties are prohibited: flogging, branding, marking, tattooing, or any other cruel or unusual punishment.[20]   Handcuffs or leg irons may be used only when necessary to ensure safe custody.   Other forbidden punishments include forcing the offender to carry a loaded knapsack, shaving his head, placing him in stocks or pillory, placarding him, or tying him up by the thumbs.

The maximum penalties are often severe, as is true also of penalties for federal and state civilian crimes, but the maximum is not imposed in most cases. As offenses in the armed forces are actually dealt with at present,* many offenders have an opportunity for re-entrance to the service after rehabilitation.   The penalties smack of the earlier punitive methods, which placed in the hands of the military authorities severe penalties to be used in extreme cases.   Practice now tends to be modern, scientific, and experimental, as later discussion in this chapter makes clear.

MILITARY POLICE

The military police serve essentially the same function for the armed forces that civilian police serve in the community.[21]   They enforce laws, investigate crimes, prevent crime, assume custody of prisoners, and undertake a number of duties not related to crime or military offenses.

Emphasis is placed on prevention of offenses. Commanding officers may designate places and areas of doubtful moral influence—for example, known houses of prostitution—as off-limits for soldiers; military police enforce off-limit regulations.   They are also expected to report potential trouble spots—dance halls, taverns, bars, cafes, or skating rinks of doubtful status.   They also take into protective custody any member of the armed forces who is behaving in a way to bring discredit upon the service.   The military police step in before minor misbehavior becomes serious.

Outside of military reservations in the United States an arrangement has been worked out to prevent conflict of jurisdictions between civil and military authorities, when military personnel have violated civil laws.   During peacetime, military authorities may, upon request, turn such offenders over to civil authorities; but in time of war, all except the most serious offenses are tried in military courts.   Violations of military regulations are, of course, tried by the military courts.

THE MILITARY JUDICIAL SYSTEM

Violators of the Uniform Code of Military Justice are tried in a special system of military courts, called courts-martial.   These courts are similar in function to the criminal courts that try violators of state laws, or the federal courts that hear cases of federal offenders.   Three grades of courts-martial handle 3 levels of offenses in terms of their seriousness, just as felonies are tried in criminal courts in the civilian community, with mis-

* 1954.

demeanors falling to the jurisdiction of county, municipal, or police courts. Finally, in the military service, nonjudicial punishment may be imposed for minor offenses by commanding officers.

General Court-Martial

The general court-martial corresponds to the higher courts in civilian life.[22]   Empowered to try all offenses, in practice it tries only the more serious ones—murders, serious assaults, stealing of large amounts, other felonies, and the more serious military offenses.   In general, it tries the cases in which the death penalty, dishonorable discharge, confinement in excess of 6 months, and/or heavy forfeiture of pay might be imposed.

Under the Code the general court-martial has several essential characteristics.   It is composed of at least 5 members, and often more, who usually are senior in rank to the accused.   A law officer with legal qualifications and certified by The Judge Advocate General performs functions similar to those of a civilian judge.   A trial counsel, or prosecutor, and defense counsel, both qualified lawyers, are appointed.   If the accused is an enlisted man and requests it, one third of the members of the court must be enlisted men.   In the Army and the Air Force, the legal counsels are called judge advocates; in the Navy, law specialists.

The trial follows the same general pattern that is found in civilian courts, with presentation of evidence, a decision of guilt or innocence, and sentencing.   The members of the court-martial act much as a jury does in a criminal court in those states in which the jury assesses the punishment; the law officer is the legal authority for the court-martial, but does not sentence the offender, as does the civilian judge in some states.   A system of reviews of the court decision by higher authorities protects the offender from injustice.

Special Court-Martial

The special court-martial consists of at least 3 members, one of whom acts as president and passes upon legal questions, since there is no law officer.[23]   Trial and defense counsels are appointed but are not necessarily lawyers.   The special court-martial handles cases in which the penalty is noncapital and does not involve a dishonorable discharge.   Typical offenses tried are violations of duty on the post; absences without leave for less than 61 days; dereliction in the performance of duties; breaking various regulations; minor thefts or disturbances; and drunkenness.   Penalties include short periods of confinement, forfeiture of pay, or bad conduct discharges under certain conditions of review.

Summary Court-Martial

One officer, appointed by a commanding officer, constitutes the summary court-martial.[24]   The jurisdiction of the summary court-martial extends to minor offenses committed by enlisted men.   Penalties are limited to brief periods of confinement or forfeiture of pay.   There is no law officer, trial counsel, or defense counsel.   This court might be compared to the police magistrate or justice of the peace in civilian life.

Nonjudicial Punishment

For minor offenses, the commanding officer may impose disciplinary corrective measures without a formal trial.[25]   Typical penalties that may be imposed are withholding of privileges for a limited number of weeks, restriction to specified areas, or forfeiture of pay for a short period.

THE PENAL AND CORRECTIONAL SYSTEM OF THE ARMED FORCES

Military penal systems have followed much the same trend as civilian systems in making the transition from severe punishments and repressive measures to re-education and rehabilitation with the objective of returning prisoners either to service in the armed forces or to law-abiding community life.   During World War II, when prisoners overflowed the existing military confinement facilities and when there was great need to improve the rehabilitation program, the War Department drew upon civilian specialists in penal administration and rehabilitation for advice and consultation.   A modern system of correctional treatment was established that allowed for liberal experimentation.   A cross-fertilization of ideas and methods between military and civilian penal systems followed, with enrichment of both systems.

The military forces maintain a series of penal and correctional institutions that correspond roughly to the jails, correctional centers, and prisons in the civilian system.   Military terminology, however, differs from civilian. Corresponding to local jails are the guardhouses and stockades (called brigs by the Navy) that serve posts, camps, and stations; they are used for detention of accused persons awaiting trial and for the confinement of convicted persons serving short terms.   Prisoners with long terms are confined in military prisons, called disciplinary barracks by the Army and retraining commands by the Navy.   Air Force offenders are placed in the disciplinary barracks maintained by the Army, and Coast Guard and Marine offenders in the Navy's retraining commands.   Certain offenders convicted by courts-martial are sent to the federal prisons; they are habitual offenders, those who have committed serious felonies or those whose personality characteristics indicate the need for prison confinement.   Rehabilitation programs are also used and were widely employed during World War II.   For the most part the men selected for rehabilitation training are guilty of military offenses only, and in general, their native ability, civilian and military background, and attitudes indicate that they have a reasonable chance of responding to the training and becoming acceptable military men.

The Army Correctional and Penal System

The administration of the Army disciplinary barracks was placed in the hands of The Adjutant General of the Army in 1915, where it remained until 1954.   During World War II, with the increased number of prisoners and the introduction of modern correctional methods, it became desirable to unify various functions pertaining to prisoners, which were vested in different agencies. Mr. Austin MacCormick, an outstanding penologist who was serving as special consultant on penology, was assigned the task of studying the situation and making recommendations.   Upon his recommendation, a Correction Division was established in the office of The Adjutant General.   The Correction Division brought about the type of integration under a central authority that is necessary for co-ordination of penal activities.   The division was given supervision of disciplinary barracks, rehabilitation centers, guardhouses, and post stockades; authority to formulate a program for military prisoners, and to select and train personnel; the task of establishing civil boards of consultants on correctional policies and procedures for the various service commands; responsibility for assisting in the selection of a correctional officer in each service command; and the duty of maintaining liaison with the Federal Bureau of Prisons.[26]   The basic purpose of the Correction Division was stated as correctional and rehabilitative rather than penal.   With reference to prisoners, its function was " . . . their reformation with a view to their honorable restoration to duty or re-enlistment and their rehabilitation in such a way that they will become useful citizens of the civil community after their release from confinement." Although some changes in functions have occurred since 1944, the basic principles, policies, and procedures continue.   In 1954, the Correction Division was transferred to The Provost Marshal General, but without marked change in function or philosophy.

The disciplinary barracks.   The basic Army correctional institution is the disciplinary barracks, the successor to the older military prison.   The number of disciplinary barracks varies with the needs of the Army.[27]   Prior to World War II, the United States disciplinary barracks at Fort Leavenworth, Kansas, was the only maximum security prison maintained by the Army.

The needs of the war led to the establishment of 3 additional maximum security and 12 medium security disciplinary barracks.   By 1950, the number had been reduced to 3, at Fort Leavenworth; Camp Cooke, Lompoc, California; and New Cumberland, Pennsylvania.   With the increase in army strength occasioned by the Korean hostilities, the prisoner population expanded and 2 additional medium security barracks were activated, at Camp Gordon, Georgia, and Camp Crowder, Missouri.   During World War II, the Air Force was a part of the Army; since their separation, Air Force prisoners continue to be confined in Army disciplinary barracks.

The disciplinary barracks of the Army, the equivalent of a civilian prison, receives prisoners who are initially considered not restorable to military duty.   They have committed the more serious military offenses or are guilty of crimes that would be classified as felonies in civilian criminal law—although the latter crimes may also lead to incarceration in a federal prison. The barracks are of 2 types—maximum security with the usual prison walls, and medium security with the barracks enclosed with wire fences.

The personnel of the disciplinary barracks resembles that of a federal prison, except that almost all prison officers are military officers; hence the terminology differs.   The commandant replaces the warden; the executive officer, the assistant to the warden; an adjutant handles correspondence and records, and so on.   Other officers are provided for needed services of supply, mess, and security.   There are specialists, such as vocational training, farm, medical, psychological, and psychiatric officers, as well as chaplains.

The process of admission includes medical examination, fingerprinting, and photographing, followed by assignment to the reception company for a period of observation and orientation.   The prisoner is studied by the various specialists, information is collected on personal and social background, including any civilian crimes, and tests of various sorts are made. From this intensive study, lasting over a 30 day period, the man's potentialities are discovered and a report is made to the classification board.

The classification board determines whether the prisoner should be placed in minimum, medium, or maximum custody, or transferred to another type of institution.   A work assignment is made and, when indicated, a special program of education, or medical or psychiatric treatment.   A date is set for the man to appear for reclassification.   Annually, prisoners are considered by the classification committee for restoration to military duty and for clemency.

The program of activities resembles that of a modern federal or state prison. Work of various skilled, unskilled, and agricultural types and some vocational training are provided.   A library, motion pictures, hobby shops, various forms of recreation, and religious services are available to prisoners.

Good conduct time, clemency, and parole are part of the system.[28]   The prisoner automatically reduces the length of his sentence materially by his good conduct.   A greater reduction can be made through clemency, which is granted by the Clemency and Parole Board of the Correction Division. The board is composed of a professional civilian penologist, an Army officer, and an Air Force officer, one of whom has legal training.   The classification board at the individual disciplinary barracks usually makes the initial study for clemency, within the first 6 months of the prisoner's confinement, and reviews the situation at intervals thereafter.   The classification committee makes its recommendation to the commandant, who approves or disapproves, and forwards the recommendation to the Correction Division.   The action of the Clemency and Parole Board may reduce the length of sentence and/or change the type of discharge.   Through the action of clemency, inconsistencies in sentencing by different courts-martial can be eliminated, men can be rewarded for rapid adjustment of their behavior, restoration to duty can be quickened, and in general sentences can be adjusted to the individual prisoner.   The work of the local classification boards and the review by the Clemency and Parole Board place the procedure on a professional level.

Parole may also be granted, again with first consideration by the classification board.[29]   A prisoner is eligible to apply for parole after he has served one third of his sentence or a minimum of 6 months, or 10 years if the sentence is for life.   The parolee remains under the legal custody and control of the commandant or the prison from which he was paroled or to which he may be transferred; actual parole supervision is given by a member of the Federal Probation Service.   When a prisoner is not restored to duty but is released at the termination of his sentence or after serving on parole, the military discharge that he receives is usually a dishonorable or a bad conduct discharge.

During the period immediately following World War II, from August, 1945 to June, 1950, 83,119 prisoners were considered for clemency, 43 per cent of whom received reduced sentences.[30]   Clemency policies in general permit greater reductions during peace than during war, since both Army and public opinion oppose the release of nonrestorable prisoners to civilian life while other men are risking their lives in battle.

Rehabilitation and restoration to military service.   Since 1942, the Army has strongly emphasized rehabilitation of offenders with the objective of restoring them to military service.   It should be borne in mind that the objective of rehabilitation differs from the objective in civilian prisons. Military correctional institutions carry on rehabilitation for a specific function—restoration to military service. This objective influences the type of men accepted for rehabilitation programs and the programs used.

During World War II, from December, 1942 to May, 1946, the Army operated special rehabilitation centers, establishing one in each of the 9 service commands, with a capacity of 2,000 in each unit.[31] In these centers, the findings of civilian research and correctional experience were applied in an experimental spirit, to establish a rehabilitation program new to military prisons.

The rehabilitation programs were limited to minor offenders, who usually had violated military regulations that did not have counterparts among civilian crimes, often men who had been absent without leave for a moderate period of time or who had failed to accommodate themselves to other military regulations. The habitual offender, the felon, and the man with a long record of past difficulties, were not normally accepted. The men who entered these programs were only marginal offenders—men who in civilian life might have failed in some of their family, civic, or job responsibilities but who would probably not have become criminals.

To these offenders the rehabilitation centers offered both a hope and a threat. The hope held out was of restoration to duty, suspension of dishonorable discharge, and eventual honorable discharge if the offender fulfilled his obligations in the service without further offenses. The threat was of a term in disciplinary barracks and, at the end of the sentence, usually a dishonorable or bad conduct discharge.

The average length of time that men restored to duty remained in a center was 32 weeks. The first 2 to 6 weeks after arrival were spent in the Receiving Company. The prisoner was photographed, fingerprinted, given physical examinations, interviewed by the psychiatrist, psychologist, and counselor, and instructed in the rules of the center. Finally, he was classified by the classification board and interviewed by the commandant (warden).

Next came about 3 months in the Training Company, which was composed of about 200 prisoners headed by 1 officer and 5 or 6 noncommissioned officers who had charge of the prisoners' daily routine and acted as instructors and advisers. The program consisted of 6 days a week of classes, drill, recreation, and group therapy. Daily records were made of each man's attitudes and progress.

The prisoner passed from the Training Company to the Parolee Company, where he spent about 9 weeks. He received on-the-job vocational training on the post and was permitted to work outside the wire enclosure without a guard.

The Honor Company followed, with emphasis on military training. The

Honor Company lived outside the wire enclosure and was allowed the privileges of the post on an honor basis.   The prisoner was in the Honor Company for approximately 7 weeks.

Upon successful completion of these various stages of training, the remainder of the prisoner's original sentence was suspended and he was returned to duty.   If he became involved in further misconduct, however, the sentence would be reinstated—the same provision that is made in civilian courts for violation of parole, probation, or suspended sentence.   Usually the restored prisoner was assigned to a unit rather than to a replacement center, thus facilitating rapid absorption into active service.   He was not returned to his original organization where his misconduct occurred. Through reports at 3-month intervals, the progress of the man was followed.

During the approximately 3 and one-half years that the rehabilitation centers operated, 39,352 men were received at the centers.   Of this number, 29,944 (approximately three fourths) were considered candidates for rehabilitation; and of these, 17,450 (58 per cent) successfully completed the restoration program and were returned to service.[32]

Among prisoners restored to duty, the rate of recidivism was low.   From January, 1943, to June, 1950, a total of 40,366 soldiers had been restored by the Army from all types of institutions, of whom 11.3 per cent became recidivists within the same period of time.   It may be assumed that some of the ones released toward the end of the period might still become recidivists.[33]

The possibilities of group therapy were explored in the rehabilitation centers—an experiment that has furthered group therapy in civilian penal and correctional institutions.   As described in one center by Joseph Abrahams and Lloyd W. McCorkle, the program of group therapy consisted of daily one-hour sessions for each man.[34]   Half the sessions were in large groups of 125 to 175 men and half in small groups of 15 to 35 men.   The group therapy was closely correlated with individual psychotherapy and was under the guidance of a psychiatrist, although carried out by trained assistants.   The sessions were carried on for a period of 26 weeks.   The chief technique used was free discussion, with the group taking the initiative and the therapist maintaining a very permissive atmosphere.   Discussions were kept on a personal level.   Visual aids were used, such as films, color slides, and posters on simple mental hygiene and sociological principles, preceded by music to enhance the emotional value.   A center newspaper was published through the group therapy department, which also operated a broadcasting system for programs of therapeutic value to the men in the center.   Through discussion and the interpretative aid of the therapist the men were helped to gain insight into their individual problems.   Each group became a social unit, approving or disapproving the men as they expressed their attitudes and brought forth their problems. Gradually emotional tensions were reduced, insight into personal problems was increased, and more conventional and responsible attitudes achieved. The therapists at the center felt that for many men the treatment resulted in improved emotional stability, greater maturity, more initiative, and increased leadership ability. The end result of helping the men adjust to military duty was aided by these emotional and attitudinal changes.

After the rehabilitation centers were closed, certain of the disciplinary barracks instituted a program of rehabilitation for restorable men. The retraining included an intensive course in basic military training, general education, recreation, and religion. Individual and group psychotherapy were also provided. After 8 weeks of intensive training, the men returned to active duty with an opportunity to secure eventually an honorable discharge.

In the spring of 1954 came another change of setting for the rehabilitation program, when disciplinary barracks at Camp Gordon, Georgia were designated as the Rehabilitation Training Center for the retraining of all Army prisoners sentenced to punitive discharge and regarded as restorable to duty.

Rehabilitation in the Air Force *

As stated, Air Force offenders are sometimes committed to Army disciplinary barracks. The Air Force maintains local base detention facilities, and since November, 1951, a special rehabilitation center known as the 3320th Retraining Group, located at Amarillo Air Force Base, Texas, has been in operation.

Offenders are assigned to these 3 types of centers as follows:

In the 185 base institutions are confined 5,300 prisoners.[35] Emphasis is on reclaiming the men for further service, and close custody is deemphasized. Less than 10 per cent of these prisoners are classified as in need of maximum security; 47 per cent require medium security; and 43 per cent minimum security. Only maximum security prisoners have armed supervision. To the Army disciplinary centers are sent prisoners with sentences of 6 months or more, a punitive discharge, and with an initial classification as not restorable to military service. Other serious offenders are committed to the federal prisons.

The 3320th Retraining Group has as its objective restoring selected offenders to active service.[36] The retrainee population is composed of con-

---

* In addition to published sources cited, the author has drawn upon the results of observations and conferences at the Retraining Group during parts of 2 days spent there in August, 1954.

victed offenders who meet certain specifications that are believed to be favorable to rehabilitation: youth, absence of a criminal record, satisfactory military service, and ability to perform military duties. The offender must be in good physical and mental health, and must demonstrate a desire for restoration to duty. Experience has shown that in addition to these rather formal specifications, other attributes are desirable for successful completion of the retraining program. A stable and loyal relationship in the past to some group, such as school, family, or place of employment, is indicative of ability to develop a loyal relationship toward the Air Force. Normal mental ability and literacy are also important attributes for retraining. Conversely, certain characteristics indicate that the man, even with intensive retraining, probably will be unable to adjust to military requirements. Alcoholism, serious criminality, serious psychoneurotic disorder, homosexuality, and desertion in combat make a man unacceptable. Other undesirable traits are narcotics addiction, habitual truancy in earlier life, and repeated convictions for minor offenses. The retraining period in most cases is short (it may be as short as 3 months) and the men who enter it must have potentialities for future useful Air Force duty.

Most of the men who have entered the retraining group have been guilty of violating military regulations; the most frequent military offense is absence without leave. The most frequent nonmilitary offense is larceny.

The retraining center can handle 250 men at one time. Since they stay only a few months as a rule, in the course of a year the center handles many more. Nevertheless, the retrainees represent only a small fraction of all offenders, and therefore are a carefully selected group with good possibilities for restoration. Selections are made by the commands having charge of the prisoners, and men come from base guardhouses or military disciplinary barracks.

The philosophy of the center is correctional and rehabilitative. No part of the program is instituted for punitive purposes. Men are expected, however, to meet the standards of the Air Force, as part of their preparation for restoration to service. The original staff was sent to the unwalled federal correctional institution at Seagoville, Texas, for orientation and training in nonpunitive correctional methods. As staff is transferred, new members are indoctrinated at the center with the correctional principles and practices that have been established.

The Retraining Group occupies a cluster of regular air force buildings in one corner of the Amarillo Air Force Base. In appearance there is no hint that the area houses convicted offenders. There are no high walls, guard towers, or strong wire fences; in fact, there is no physical barrier to complete freedom. Similarly, there are no armed guards. There is, however, a program of activity that fills the entire day and close custody through informal supervision.   Emphasis is placed on the men's status as members of the Air Force rather than upon their status as prisoners under sentence. They wear regulation uniforms without indication of prisoner identity and are called retrainees.   So far as retraining permits, they follow the normal pattern of life on the base.

The retrainee progresses through 4 phases, each carrying him nearer to release and restoration, provided he profits by the retraining.   Men in a given phase are housed together and share common activities.   Phase 1, from 7 to 10 days, is a period of testing, interviewing, and orientation.   The man becomes acquainted with the center and its professional personnel; the professional staff is able to evaluate the man.   Phase 2 concentrates on adjustment to the fundamentals of military and civil life.   Upon entering this phase the man moves to a different barracks where all phase 2 men live.   The men have citizenship training and learn about the history and organization of the Air Force.   They are taught their obligations and rights as airmen.   Drill, athletics, recreation, and hobby work are also scheduled. This program fills 8 hours per day for 6 days of the week, for a period of 2 or 3 weeks, at the end of which time the man meets the correctional classification board in preparation for the next phase, and in planning for the remainder of his stay in the group.   Phase 3 carries the man to another barracks and into specialized technical courses and job assignments, which are made for retraining purposes and not primarily for purposes of maintenance and operation of the base or center.   One objective of the program is to return each man to the service equipped to perform some needed skill or to perform a previously acquired skill better.   Phase 4 is an honor phase for which the man is eligible after about 3 weeks in phase 3; he may not, however, achieve phase 4 if his progress does not merit the transfer.   At each step, progression through the phases brings added privileges, increased freedom of movement, and greater responsibilities.

Paralleling the classes and job assignments, constant help is given the men in personal and social adjustment.   On the professional level, 2 trained social therapists follow the men through their entire stay at the center, regardless of which phase they are in.   Group discussions bring out tensions and problems; individual conferences follow in many cases.   A psychiatrist and a psychologist handle cases of serious maladjustment; chaplains are always available.   Supervisors (Air Force personnel) in the men's barracks are responsible not only for good order but for mixing with the men, settling minor disagreements, and reporting minor difficulties and tensions to their superior officers.   The social therapists and one educational specialist are the only civilians on the staff.   They work closely with the officers to further the purpose of the center but at the same time maintain their civilian status with the retrainees in order to provide a neutral contact for them.

Discipline is handled through counseling and informal adjustments by the supervisors. Custody is unobtrusive in order to maintain a relaxed atmosphere. Nevertheless, orderliness and the meeting of obligations are insisted upon as part of the retraining program, and for serious disciplinary problems there is a disciplinary board, which recommends action to the commander of the center. The hearings are informal and the retrainee is permitted to present his side of the situation.

Clemency and restoration boards review all cases, with recommendations to appropriate authorities. For the successful retrainee the original sentence may be shortened and the man restored to active service. The unsuccessful retrainee may be discharged with a punitive discharge (bad conduct or dishonorable) if originally included as a portion of his sentence, or he may be administratively discharged for ineptness. If the retrainee becomes a disciplinary problem or attempts to escape, he may be returned to the custody of a disciplinary barracks or other security institution, and his opportunity for retraining ends.

The program has not been in operation long enough for a statistical evaluation of the adjustment of the men restored. The evaluation, when it is made, will be pertinent to all correctional systems, for the Retraining Group embodies virtually all features recommended for rehabilitation—small group of retrainees; adequate staff including a psychologist, a psychiatrist, and social therapists; informal, nonpunitive methods and relaxed atmosphere; fully occupied days; well balanced program of activities; progressive granting of freedom; and opportunity for full restoration to service without a stigma. The Retraining Group, therefore, tests, in a practical way, many proposed methods of correction.

The Navy Correctional System [37]

The Navy passed through much the same process as the Army in expanding and reconstructing its prison facilities and treatment program during and after World War II. Prior to the War, the Navy had approximately 200 offenders confined primarily in naval prisons at Portsmouth, New Hampshire, and Mare Island, California. In March of 1944 the problem became numerically significant, and the Secretary of the Navy transferred the management of prisons and prisoners from The Judge Advocate General to the Chief of Naval Personnel. The Corrective Services Division was established in the Bureau of Naval Personnel, in Washington, and, under a Marine Corps Colonel as Director, was staffed largely by men experienced in this field of work and commissioned in the Naval Reserve for the duration of the war. In May, 1944, the first U.S. Naval Retraining Command was established at Camp Peary, near Williamsburg, Virginia. In the 2 years of its existence there, 6,000 general courts-martial prisoners were received as "retrainees." Of these, 5,500 were restored to duty, 100 were transferred to disciplinary barracks or discharged, and 400 moved with the Command to the Naval Base, Norfolk, Virginia. The peak of the naval prisoner population was not reached until November of 1945, after the end of World War II. By that time the Navy and Marine Corps operated nearly 375 brigs in the continental United States; the 2 retraining commands, the 8 disciplinary barracks, and 2 naval prisons held nearly 16,000 Navy, Marine Corps, and Coast Guard general courts-martial prisoners.

Approximately 75 per cent of all naval general court-martial prisoners who were confined during and immediately after the end of World War II were returned to active duty after retraining; of these 68 per cent completed a probationary period of 6 to 12 months satisfactorily and thereafter either continued in the service or were honorably discharged. A random group of 1,200 who were returned to duty March, 1946, showed a somewhat better record, as Table 29 shows.

TABLE 29

Record of Navy and Marine Corps Offenders Returned to Duty

	Navy (per cent)	Marine Corps (per cent)
Successfully completed probation	75.0	74.0
Probation still in effect	3.75	2.0
Failed and awarded disciplinary discharge	7.0	12.5
Failed and reconfined	12.25	9.0
Failed and deserted	2.0	1.5
Number—1,200		

Source: J. Maginnis, "The Navy's Postwar Correctional Program," *Prison World,* 9 (Mar.–Apr., 1947), 32.

With the end of the war, restoration to duty continued to be the chief objective for all men capable of accepting the necessary retraining. In 1954 the Navy operated only 3 prisons, all called retraining commands, located at Norfolk, Virginia; Portsmouth, New Hampshire; and Camp Elliott, California. Eighty-six per cent of the 2,800 prisoners confined in these 3 commands are guilty of military offenses only, chiefly some form of unauthorized absence.

The basic policy of the prison treatment is stated as follows in the *Regulations for Operation of Retraining Commands, 1951:*

The Navy's correctional program is based on the concept that confinement itself is of little value unless it carries with it the objective of reformation.   While it accepts as its first responsibility the enforcement of the sentences of the court as they relate to confinement, it realizes that it also has the additional responsibility for corrective treatment of offenders committed to its care.   This implies that not only the basic needs of the prisoner as a human being shall be met, but that he shall also be given the opportunity, through training, work, and other special programs, to overcome those deficiencies which have contributed to his being confined.

Accordingly, as many men as possible are given an opportunity for restoration to full active duty in the service, after retraining.   Some prisoners, however, cannot be rehabilitated to the point of restoration to duty because of personality defects, rebelliousness, or other qualities.   At each retraining command therefore a screening process lasting 14 days aids officials in classifying prisoners and placing them in appropriate programs.   The procedure includes physical examinations, securing a social history, educational and vocational evaluations, review of religious interests and personal problems, and discovery of recreational interests and skills.   Psychological tests and psychiatric interviews are included.   From these varied and specialized approaches a composite picture of the prisoner's personality, capacities, limitations, needs, and skills is secured.

The Classification and Assignment Board, making use of the material assembled by the screening center, places each prisoner in 1 of 3 categories:

1. Short-term nonrestorable prisoners, who are retained in a segregated detention component at the retraining command, where their program emphasizes work and education preparatory to a return to civilian life.   They are released with a dishonorable, bad conduct, or administrative discharge.

2. Long-term offenders and those who are vicious, violent, serious custody risks, or a menace to other prisoners.   These men are transferred to the federal prisons, where, in 1954, there were 74 naval courts-martial prisoners, a very small proportion of naval prisoners.

3. Prisoners judged to be capable of restoration to duty, who are placed in an intensive retraining program at the retraining command, oriented toward adjusting the offender to active duty in the Navy.   The Assignment Board reviews the classification of each man at least every 4 months and may recommend reclassification to the commanding officer.

Eventually, the Classification and Assignment Board passes its files on each prisoner to the Clemency and Restoration Board, which recommends to the commanding officer whether or not the prisoner should be restored to duty; the Board may also recommend reduction in the length of sentence or a change of the original sentence of discharge to a less onerous type (for example, recommend changing a dishonorable discharge to a bad conduct discharge). Once the man has requested clemency in the form of suspension of the discharge, he may not be discharged until the Secretary of the Navy has acted upon his request. If approved, he is restored to duty on probation; if disapproved, he may be discharged upon completion of confinement and completion of all appellate reviews required by law.

Between the time of initial classification and final release, the retrainee passes through a program of diversified retraining. An orientation phase enables the retrainee to straighten out his thinking about himself, his family, friends, the service, the community, and his military and civilian obligations as a citizen. This period is essentially one of citizenship training, with emphasis on individual responsibility. The professional members of the staff (psychiatrist, chaplain, educator, Red Cross representative, and others) contribute to this program through lectures, group discussions, and individual interviews and counseling. The results, indicated by enhanced morale, good discipline, and apparent rehabilitation, have convinced the administrative staff that this phase is the most important part of the retraining program.

Individual counseling and group therapy have been in operation since 1944. In addition any retrainee may receive permission for an interview with any member of the staff, including the commanding officer, without formality. The way is thus opened for first hand contacts between retrainees and staff members.

Each retrainee has a planned schedule of activities, that includes military drill, physical conditioning, academic training for those who test below sixth grade level, and a work program. Work, regarded as part of the training for restoration, includes maintenance and repairs as well as industries, of which each command operates 2 or 3 major types and a number of minor projects. Some of the larger work projects are a retrainee uniform shop, a printing plant, a mattress renovation plant, an upholstering shop, furniture factory, and an amphibious landing craft repair shop. The retrainee may be transferred from one type of work to another by the Classification and Assignment Board.

The customary special services usually found in civilian prisons are found in the retraining commands—medical, religious, and recreational.

As in all military training institutions, the men are expected to accept and abide by strict discipline as part of their training for restoration to duty. An effort is made to forestall violations by instructing retrainees in what is expected of them and by providing fair and impartial discipline when necessary.   Reprimands, loss of privileges, assignment to extra duty, and reduction in conduct grade or class are the usual methods of discipline.   For the few recalcitrant cases more severe measures may be used, such as solitary confinement with restricted diet for limited periods.   Also, good-conduct or extra good-time reductions of sentence may be forfeited or withheld.   As in all medium or maximum security institutions, precautions are taken against escapes.   The retraining commands are surrounded by wire fences, broken at intervals by towers with armed sentries.

The retraining period tends to be short.   The greatest number of sentences runs from 4 to 6 months, and the average is 7 months.

Trend of Correctional Procedures

Since 1940, under the pressures of war and with the consultation of professional penologists, all branches of the armed forces have radically revised their methods of handling prisoners.   The harsh punishments and repressive prison routines that were formerly the lot of the military as well as the civilian offender have given way to modern correctional methods. The Army and the Navy have each established a special correctional division at the Departmental level, which centralizes authority and co-ordinates the program.   The Army prison system and the Naval prison system, therefore, resemble the Federal Bureau of Prisons in having integrated systems of correction.   Army, Navy, and Air Force all emphasize rehabilitation and restoration to duty for all offenders with the capacity to make the adjustment.

WARTIME MILITARY ACCEPTANCE OF CRIMINALS

The armed forces reject criminals because of the belief that criminals cannot be integrated into the military life.   During time of war, however, there is added demand for servicemen and all sources of manpower are scrutinized.   Furthermore, many people feel that prisoners should not be allowed to sit safely behind prison walls, or ex-prisoners go free in the community when law-abiding men are risking and losing their lives at the front. Consequently, during World War II modifications were made in the regulations governing the selection of inductees to permit the inclusion of certain men with criminal records.   The experiment was significant not only to the armed forces but also to correctional treatment, since criminals, popularly regarded as antisocial, were thrown into a highly regimented situation where they were in close physical and social contact with many men, and under strict authority, but without the coercion of a prison situation.

Criminals were not inducted haphazardly, but were carefully chosen from among parolees or prison inmates.   The regulations were similar to those already outlined on pages 575–76 for induction of persons with criminal records under the Universal Military Training and Service Act, although phrased differently.   Two types of induction of criminals were used during World War II.

Induction of Ex-Convicts

A method for screening and inducting into the Army (including the Air Force) men previously convicted of a crime, but already released from prison or on probation or suspended sentence, was devised after considerable consultation in 1942 among the officials of the Selective Service System, the War Department, and the Bureau of Prisons.[38]   A demonstration of exemplary civilian conduct was necessary: for a period of 6 months for men who had served sentences for heinous crimes (more serious felonies); 30 days for first offenders with less serious crimes who had served sentences of more than 1 year; and 90 days for recidivists.   It was necessary for civil custody to be suspended or terminated when the man was still on parole or on another form of conditional release, in order that the armed forces could exercise their normal authority.

Induction Direct from Prison

The induction of men with criminal records into the armed forces was further expedited by screening men still in prison for their suitability for service.   Special local boards established at 20 federal and 106 state institutions reviewed the records of prisoners, with special attention to men whose parole date had passed or whose parole or release was near at hand.   Many imprisoned convicts whose records were scanned were rejected.   Only those men considered good risks for military training were accepted.   The prisoners selected were classified in the same way as all other registrants.   Each prisoner granted immediate induction signed a voluntary application for such induction and was considered a volunteer.   After release of the prisoners by the civil authorities and issuance of waivers by the military authorities, the men were inducted through regular channels and the fact of imprisonment was not revealed to their immediate officers or associates in the service.

The special boards were discontinued November 6, 1946.

Outcome of Policy Regarding Criminals

Through the procedures outlined above the Army inducted more than 2,000 men directly from prison, and well over 100,000 men, at one time imprisoned for felonies, served in the Army.[39]   In Illinois alone, from October, 1940, to October, 1945, a total of 4,485 men were inducted into the armed forces under the various provisions for acceptance of men with criminal records.[40]

In view of the peacetime regulations that reject persons with a criminal record, the wartime experiences of men with criminal records is extremely important. Is the assumption correct that these men cannot accept military discipline and are a moral risk to other men in the service?

Of the 3,036 felons inducted from the State of Illinois, it was unofficially estimated that approximately 100 became noncommissioned officers and only about 50 were returned to custody. Honors for outstanding services were awarded to many.[41]

Among 2,125 criminals from New Jersey who were inducted into the service (principally the Army) or into the Merchant Marine, 77 were promoted, chiefly to noncommissioned rank, and 7 received citations. On the other hand, 25 received dishonorable discharges, 7 were discharged as undesirable, and 3 were discharged for fraudulent enlistments.[42] The vast majority of both Illinois and New Jersey men with criminal records completed their service with neither promotions nor unfavorable misconduct or discharges. It is to be assumed that their service was satisfactory but not outstanding.

The ability of these men with civilian criminal records to adjust to military regulations, in many ways more exacting than adjustment in a civilian community, strongly suggests the need for experimentation in different types of parole supervision in the community.

CHARACTERISTICS OF MILITARY OFFENDERS

Age

Although prisoners run the full gamut of age of men in service, during World War II the average age of Army and Air Force prisoners was slightly lower than the average age of all men in these branches of the service. During and immediately after World War II, the median age of prisoners was 24.5 years and of enlisted men 25.7.[43] Comparisons for later years show a slightly higher median age for offenders than for regular or enlisted men. But fair comparisons are difficult to make because of changes in policy of induction between the end of the war and the beginning of Universal Military Training and Service in 1948.

Education

The educational level of prisoners was much lower than that of servicemen in general. Table 30 shows that during World War II, especially, the discrepancy was great, with twice as many offenders as servicemen having

TABLE 30

Educational Level, Army and Air Force Prisoner Commitments, Compared
with Educational Level of Enlisted Men

Educational Level	World War II and Immediate Postwar Offenders (per cent)	Enlisted Men as of June 30, 1944, Army and Air Force (per cent)	Prisoner Commitments, Fiscal Year, 1949 (per cent)	Enlisted Men December 31, 1948, Army (per cent)
Up to and including eighth grade	58.6	28.6	49.5	34.0
First to fourth year high school	39.2	60.2	48.9	61.2
Some or complete college	2.2	11.2	1.6	4.8

Source: *The Army Correctional System* (Washington: Office of The Adjutant General, U.S. Department of the Army, 1952), p. 159.

less than a ninth-grade education.   In view of the educational differences, it is not surprising to find that half of the prisoners rank below average on intelligence test scores.   Table 31 shows the tremendous differences in distributions between enlisted men and prisoners.

TABLE 31

General Classification Test Scores of Army and Air Force
Prisoners and Enlisted Men

GCT Score	World War II and Immediate Postwar Offenders (per cent)	Enlisted Men as of March 31, 1945, Army and Air Force (per cent)	Prisoner Commitments, Fiscal Year, 1949 (per cent)	Enlisted Men December 31, 1948 Army (per cent)	Air Force (per cent)
Superior (130 and over)	2.1	6.0	1.4	3.6	6.8
Above average (110–129)	14.9	31.0	14.1	25.5	41.8
Average (90–109)	30.0	31.2	35.5	35.6	34.9
Below average (60–89)	44.4	27.1	44.3	32.6	15.6
Inferior (below 59)	8.6	4.7	4.7	2.7	0.9

Source: *The Army Correctional System* (Washington: Office of The Adjutant General, U.S. Department of the Army, 1952), p. 161.

Absence Without Leave and Desertion

Absences without leave (AWOL) and desertions account for fully half of all Army and Air Force offenses (Table 28, p. 579). These are the most troublesome of all offenses, since it is self-evident that if the armed services are to produce trained men, they must be able to keep the men at their posts. Men who wander off and become absent without leave may be regarded, from one point of view, as unadjusted to military life or, from another point of view, as offenders who have violated one of the most stringent of regulations. Absence of more than 30 days is automatically classified as desertion, a more serious offense than shorter periods of absence, since it involves an intent not to return. During combat any absence is a threat to the precise and efficient functioning of troops. Formerly treated as wilful disobedience, absences and desertions are now sometimes recognized as symptoms of personal maladjustment or of the unendurable stress of combat. The concept of AWOL, therefore, is not completely clear cut, as it may be part of a general pattern of psychoneurosis. At the same time, it is listed as a violation of regulations, punishable by court-martial during training, service in the United States, or service abroad, under conditions of peace or combat.

Just as certain civilian crimes are most frequently found among specific types of people, so with AWOL. Studies during World War II by the Research Branch, Information and Education Division, made about midway of the war, compare several classifications of a sample of soldiers in the United States, with reference to education, age, marital condition, and length of time in the service.[44] Figure 30 shows that AWOL's were disproportionately drawn from the poorly educated. To a slight extent, AWOL's had an over-representation of younger age groups and, as compared with privates, of married men.

Studies of the Research Branch also revealed that marked differences in attitudes distinguished AWOL's in the United States from other, apparently adjusted groups.[45] In some respects AWOL's resembled psychoneurotics more nearly than any other group. According to Figures 31 through 34, a large percentage of AWOL's felt in low spirits most of the time, felt they could be of more use to their country as war workers than as soldiers, felt that the Army did not give them a chance to show what they could do, and thought the Army was poorly run.

A large percentage of AWOL's thought they should have been deferred. Table 32 compares a cross section of soldiers with AWOL's and shows that more than twice as many AWOL's as soldiers in general thought they should have been deferred, primarily because of dependents or health.

TABLE 32

Attitudes Toward Being Drafted Expressed by Soldiers and AWOL's,
in the United States, 1943–44

Question: "At the time you came into the Army did you think you should have been deferred?"

	Cross Section of Soldiers (per cent)	AWOL's (per cent)
I was not drafted—this question does not apply to me	25	25
No, I did not think I should have been deferred	49	16
Yes, I should have been deferred:	26	59
Dependents who needed my support	7	26
The importance of my job	5	4
My health or physical condition	9	20
Other reason or no answer	5	9
Number	3,729	218

Source: S. A. Stouffer, *et al., Studies in Social Psychology in World War II,* 1, *The American Soldier: Adjustment during Army Life* (Princeton: Princeton University Press, 1949), 123.

These attitudes of discouragement, disgruntlement, and resentment suggest that many servicemen who went AWOL were initially not well adjusted personally and were unable to adapt to military life.   The lower educational level may also have made difficult the processes of indoctrination into military philosophy.   Stresses from home life also came into the situation

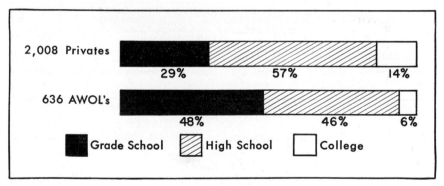

FIGURE 30

Comparison of AWOL's and privates with reference to education.   AWOL's among troops in the United States in 1943–44 had a high percentage of men with no more than grade school education.   (Simplified from S. A. Stouffer, *et al., Studies in Social Psychology in World War II,* 1, *The American Soldier: Adjustment during Army Life* [Princeton, N.J.: Princeton University Press, 1949], 123.)

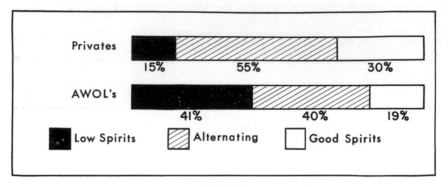

FIGURE 31

"In general, how do you feel most of the time, in good spirits or in low spirits?" Almost 3 times as many AWOL's as privates in the service 6 or more months usually felt in low spirits. (Simplified from S. A. Stouffer, *et al., Studies in Social Psychology in World War II,* 1, *The American Soldier: Adjustment during Army Life* [Princeton, N.J.: Princeton University Press, 1949], 89.)

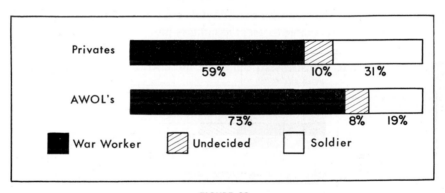

FIGURE 32

"If it were up to you to choose, do you think you could do more for your country as a soldier or as a war worker?" Although more than half of the privates who had been in service 6 months or longer felt they could be of more benefit as war workers, AWOL's outnumbered them in this respect. (Simplified from S. A. Stouffer, *et al., Studies in Social Psychology in World War II,* 1, *The American Soldier: Adjustment during Army Life* [Princeton, N.J.: Princeton University Press, 1949], 89.)

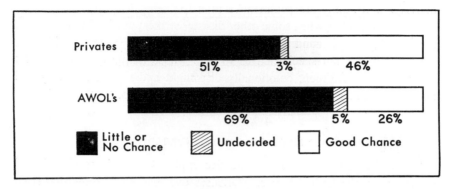

FIGURE 33

"On the whole, do you think the army is giving you a chance to show what you can do?" AWOL's in much larger proportions than privates in service for 6 or more months felt they had little or no chance. (Simplified from S. A. Stouffer, *et al., Studies in Social Psychology in World War II, 1, The American Soldier: Adjustment during Army Life* [Princeton, N.J.: Princeton University Press, 1949], 89.)

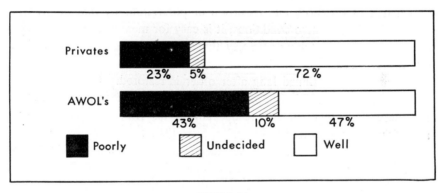

FIGURE 34

"In general, how well do you think the army is run?" Almost twice as many AWOL's as privates with 6 or more months of service expressed general dissatisfaction with the army by checking responses "Very poorly" and "Not so well." (Simplified from S. A. Stouffer, *et al., Studies in Social Psychology in World War II, 1, The American Soldier: Adjustment during Army Life* [Princeton, N.J.: Princeton University Press, 1949], 89.)

in some cases, often creating a conflict of values.   Our customary values of marriage and family life commend a man for being with his family when wife or child is ill or when some other disaster strikes; opposed to this value, the armed forces demand the complete loyalty of men.   The armed forces, when feasible, grant special leaves to men whose families are in distress; nevertheless, some men, emotionally distraught and fearful that they will not be granted leave, go home without authority to do so.

MILITARY JUSTICE ABROAD

The Uniform Code of Military Justice applies to men in service abroad as well as in the United States.   Offenses overseas differ somewhat from those typical in the United States.

Thefts and Allied Activities

One overseas offense is stealing from the enemy, often called looting, "liberating of property," or the collecting of souvenirs.   Although such stealing is severely penalized according to the Code of Military Justice, it is of common occurrence.   When an army first enters a newly subdued area, there may be almost complete social disorganization, partial or complete destruction of property, and desertion of possessions by inhabitants who have fled.   Under these conditions, it is easy for members of the invading army to rationalize taking property that does not belong to them.   The stealing is then easily extended into friendly countries in which armies are stationed and also continued long after order is restored.   One writer, McCallum, states that in his company 80 per cent of the men looted and that the successful looter gained prestige among his fellows.[46]   Other illegal activities consisted in thefts of supplies from their own Army by American soldiers, who then sold the articles to citizens of the war-torn countries, whether friendly or defeated.   An example is given by McCallum of a railroad battalion that engaged in wholesale stealing until caught; a court-martial convicted 6 officers and 182 enlisted men.   The widespread group approval (in contrast to official disapproval) of such activities reduced any sense of guilt felt by the men and led to continuation of thefts.   At other times, soldiers sold articles that were their legitimate possessions but for fantastic prices, or sold supplies intended only for the use of the occupation army.

These various activities—looting, thefts of supplies, and misuse of property—were not necessarily carried on by men with previous criminal records.   Often they were the responses of normally law-abiding men to situations lacking normal social controls.   With confused definitions of ownership, men turned the situation to their own advantage and felt little or no sense of guilt, since the practices were widespread and often participated in by officers.

AWOL and Desertion Under Combat Conditions

During periods of combat, stresses greatly increase.   Although most men fought regardless of personal danger, a few were unable to face the imminence of injury or death and fled.   They were then officially guilty of such charges as being absent without leave, desertion, or misbehavior in the face of the enemy.

The extreme penalty for many frontline offenses is the death sentence. However, in World War II, the death penalty was not used by the Army for military offenses alone.[47]   During the war the Army executed 146 soldiers, all but one for murder or rape.[48]   The one execution for desertion was of a man who deserted twice under fire, and his was the first execution for a purely military crime since the Civil War.   The soldier in the front line therefore, did not face certain death by execution if he avoided a highly probable death at the hands of the enemy by deserting.   There is no official record, of course, of instances in which combat leaders may have forced men at gun point to continue to fight.   The Research Branch of the Information and Education Division turned up few rumors of such compulsion in its extensive research, and it is believed that it is extremely rare.

Other penalties than the death sentence were used, the severity of which varied greatly from time to time and as between divisions of the Army.   The Research Branch cites such varying penalties as 6 months at hard labor; long terms in a stockade or disciplinary center; or use of dishonorable discharge in addition to imprisonment.   In other cases, however, if the deserter agreed to return to combat no charge was made against him.[49]

Since desertions from the front line were usually the result of fear, the attitude of the Army toward feelings of fear is significant.   The Army recognized that fear under threat of injury or death is a natural reaction and early in World War II adopted a permissive attitude toward fear, an attitude explicitly imparted to soldiers.[50]   They were told in official communications they would be afraid just prior to battle, that such fear was not cowardice— and that it would pass as they engaged in combat and began to make use of their training.   The permissive attitude toward fear, of course, did not extend to tolerance toward running away from the field of battle.   Nevertheless, cases of extreme fear and anxiety, often accompanied by inability to fight or a tendency to withdraw from combat or run away, were treated as medical cases, and men were sent to hospitals in the rear or given a few days of rest and medical treatment in an aid station.   The line between uncontrollable fear and cowardice meriting court-martial was very narrow indeed and seems to have consisted largely in whether or not the soldier made an effort to continue in combat in spite of fear.   When symptoms of fear (trembling, faintness, cold sweats, insomnia, nausea, lack of control of elimination, nightmares, and so forth) continued, although the soldier tried to remain in combat, men and officers alike conceded that the man needed medical attention.   When men seemed to evade fighting or ran away without making an effort in spite of fear, the cases were treated as disciplinary and court-martial followed.

COMPARISON OF MILITARY AND CIVILIAN SYSTEMS OF JUSTICE AND CORRECTION

The military system of justice resembles the federal in that it cuts across state lines and applies equally in all parts of the United States.   The military system differs, however, in that it extends beyond United States territory and controls men and women in the armed forces wherever they are stationed. Within the armed forces the codes of justice, including offenses, court systems, and penalties, have been unified since 1951, with only slight differences between the Navy and the land forces, necessitated by conditions on shipboard.   Each branch of the armed services enforces, in addition to the Uniform Code of Military Justice, special regulations.   There is a diversity similar to that found among different branches of the federal government with respect to criminal laws applying to specific crimes of each branch; for example, the Post Office Department, the Bureau of Internal Revenue, the Bureau of Narcotics—each has its own regulations.

Although there are differences in organization between military and civilian police, court, and penal systems, certain principles are common to both systems.   The power of the police is limited to apprehension and custody of an offender.   The rights of the accused person are protected by court procedures, investigation by a psychiatrist when necessary, defense counsel, interrogation of witnesses on both sides, and rights of appeal to higher courts and review by higher authorities.

During the 1940's, the military penal system was revised with emphasis on retraining and rehabilitation.   Both the Navy and the Army (which then included the Air Force) established special institutions for rehabilitation, and modified their penal systems to emphasize correctional education for the more serious offenders.   In establishing the new program, the military services had the assistance of outstanding leaders in civilian penal and correctional work.   Prominent among them were Austin H. MacCormick, Executive Director of the Osborne Association, long a specialist in penal reform; Richard A. Chappell, formerly Chief of Probation, United States Courts, and recently retired from the United States Board of Parole; and Victor H. Evjen, Assistant Chief of Probation of the United States Probation System, United States Courts. These men and others with special training and skills assisted in bringing to military authorities the best that has been learned in correctional methods in civilian institutions.

The results of the military rehabilitation program in turn have added to knowledge that may be applied in civilian institutions. The military services went beyond the civilian provisions for restoring an offender to normal life. Offenders restored to service were given an opportunity to secure an honorable discharge, thus virtually wiping out, by good conduct outside of prison, the stigma of crime. Among civilian criminals the stigma of being an ex-convict and sometimes the loss of certain citizenship rights follow the man back into the community. It was demonstrated also that many offenders could safely have their sentences drastically reduced and after careful training for a specific function and induction into that function could perform normally. Significantly, the training was focused on a specific goal and the transition to that goal (in this case resumption of military service) was not left to the man's initiative but was made for the man in an authoritative manner. The military services provide more supervision than does community life and, in a sense, serve as a special kind of parole. Men who could adjust to this close supervision apparently were then able to make the successful transition to complete freedom in the community. It may also be significant that the service they rendered in the armed forces was important to the country. Again, the men were placed in units where their misdeeds were not known; they started with a clean slate. These factors suggest the need for a restudy of men restored to service with reference to their permanent community adjustment and their attitudes toward the restoration program. Undoubtedly sound suggestions for civilian criminals would result.

QUESTIONS

1. Why is it important to a study of criminology to include offenders in the armed forces?

2. What policy do the armed forces follow in accepting proved offenders for the regular service? As selectees? Are the armed forces justified in using the limitations imposed?

3. What types of behavior are offenses under the Uniform Code of Military Justice but not in civilian life? Why are these differences necessary?

4. Compare the organization and procedures of courts-martial and civilian criminal courts. What policies are followed by both?

5. Discuss the change in treatment of military prisoners that occurred between the 1930's and the period during and since World War II.

6. What military correctional procedures provide valuable suggestions for civilian correctional procedures?

7. How do you account for the concentration of military offenders at the lower educational and intelligence levels?

8. By whom should cases of AWOL and allied misbehavior in combat be handled—medical officers or court-martial?

READINGS

The Army Correctional System (Washington: Office of the Adjutant General, Department of the Army, 1952). A brief history of Army prisons is followed by a detailed discussion of the methods of classification and rehabilitation instituted during World War II. The report covers procedures used through 1951. Included in the appendix are reprints of 6 articles previously published in professional journals on different phases of the Army correctional system. This is a complete and excellent authoritative, but easily read, account of military correctional methods.

The American Journal of Sociology, Vol. 51 (March, 1946). The entire issue is devoted to the armed forces as a special type of social world which the selectee enters. In 21 articles, various phases of military life are sociologically analyzed, the special stresses are pointed up, and methods of handling maladjustment are discussed.

Edwards, M. O., and Charles Decker, *The Serviceman and the Law* (Harrisburg, Pa.: The Military Service Publishing Co., 1951). This is a nontechnical discussion of discipline and violations in the armed forces and of the processes by which the Code of Military Justice is enforced through courts-martial. Planned for the man in service, it is equally valuable for the student.

The following 4 articles by 2 civilian specialists in penology and parole who were closely associated with reforms in the military correctional system enlarge upon many of the problems and procedures discussed in this chapter.

MacCormick, A. H., "Defense Department Policy toward Former Offenders," *Yearbook of the National Probation and Parole Association* (1951), pp. 1–19.

———, and V. H. Evjen, "The Army's Rehabilitation Program for Military Prisoners," *Yearbook of the National Probation Association* (1945), pp. 17–19.

———, "Statistical Study of 24,000 Military Prisoners," *Federal Probation* 10 (April–June, 1946), 6–11.

———, "The Army's Postwar Program for Military Prisoners," *Prison World,* 9 (May–June, 1947), 3–7, 32–34, 38.

The following 3 articles discuss clemency and parole.

Garrison, L. R., "The Military Parolee and the Federal Probation Officer," *Federal Probation,* 14 (June, 1950), 65–70.

Goldberg, H. L. and F. A. C. Hoefer, "The Army Parole System," *Journal of Criminal Law and Criminology,* 40 (1949), 158–69.

———, and L. W. McCorkle, "Post War Clemency and the Military Offender," *Social Service Review,* 21 (1947), 197–207.

The 3320th Retraining Group at Amarillo Air Force Base has been described in 2 popular articles.

Bennett, R. V., "At USAF's New Retraining Center They Treat 'Em Like Men," *Air Training,* 1 (June, 1952), 10–15.   (Published by Air Training Command, U.S. Air Force; editorial office, Room 316, Buder Building, St. Louis 1, Mo.)

Nordyke, Lewis, "These Prisoners Get a Second Chance," *Saturday Evening Post,* 225 (February 7, 1953), 22–23, 86–87, 89.

A discussion of the Navy retraining program is found in the following:

Maginnis, J., "The Navy's Postwar Correctional Program," *Prison World,* 9 (Mar.–Apr., 1947), 3, 25, 28, 32.

Skinner, E. W., "The Navy's Correctional Program," *Prison World,* 7 (Jan.–Feb., 1945), 8–9, 27–30.

FOOTNOTES

[1] L. B. Hershey, *Selective Service and Victory, 4th Report of the Director of Selective Service, 1944–1945, with a Supplement for 1946–47* (Washington: Government Printing Office, 1948), p. 154.

[2] *The Army Correctional System* (Washington: Office of The Adjutant General, Department of the Army, 1952), p. 157.

[3] Delmar Karlen and L. H. Pepper, "The Scope of Military Justice," *Journal of Criminal Law and Criminology,* 43 (1952), 285–98.

[4] *The Army Correctional System, op. cit.,* p. 1.

[5] A. B. Hollingshead, "Adjustment to Military Life," *American Journal of Sociology,* 51 (1946), 375.

[6] *Air Force Regulation,* No. 39–9F, Enlisted Personnel, Change, AFR 39–9F, 8, 13 (Washington: Department of the Air Force, December 3, 1952).

[7] *Special Regulations,* No. 615-105-1, Enlisted Personnel, Change, No. 4 (Washington: Department of the Army, May 18, 1953).

[8] *Air Force Regulation, op. cit.*

[9] *Ibid.*

[10] *Special Regulations,* No. 615-180-1, Enlisted Personnel (Washington: Department of the Army, April 10, 1953).

[11] *Manual for Courts-Martial, United States, 1951* (Washington: Government Printing Office, May 31, 1951).

[12] H. L. Goldberg and L. W. McCorkle, "Postwar Clemency and the Military Offender," *Social Service Review,* 21 (1947), 197–207.

[13] *Manual for Courts-Martial, op. cit.,* pp. 439–49.

[14] *Ibid.,* pp. 380–81.

[15] *Ibid.,* pp. 381–87.

[16] Karlen and Pepper, *op. cit.*

[17] *Manual for Courts-Martial, op. cit.,* pp. 219–28.

[18] *Ibid.,* pp. 122–23.

[19] *Ibid.,* pp. 211, 228.

[20] *Ibid.,* pp. 205–6.

[21] *Military Police,* Department of the Army Field Manual FM 19-5 (Washington: Government Printing Office, September, 1950).

[22] *Manual for Courts-Martial, op. cit.,* pp. 418–23.

[23] *Ibid.,* pp. 421–23.

[24] *Ibid.,* pp. 418–22.

[25] *Ibid.,* pp. 229–35, 417–18.

[26] *The Army Correctional System, op. cit.,* ch. 1.

[27] *Ibid.,* ch. 4

28 *Ibid.,* chs. 6, 8; Goldberg and McCorkle, *op. cit.;* H. L. Goldberg and F. A. C. Hoefer, "The Army Parole System," *Journal of Criminal Law and Criminology,* 40 (1949), 158–69.

29 L. R. Garrison, "The Military Parolee and the Federal Probation Officer," *Federal Probation,* 14 (June, 1950), 65–70.

30 *The Army Correctional System, op. cit.,* p. 151.

31 *Ibid.*

32 *Ibid.,* p. 23.

33 *Ibid.,* p. 150.

34 Joseph Abrahams and L. W. McCorkle, "Group Psychotherapy of Military Offenders," *American Journal of Sociology,* 51 (1946), 455–64.

35 *State and National Correctional Institutions of America, Canada, England and Scotland* (New York: American Prison Association, July, 1954), p. 59.

36 *Air Force Regulation,* No. 125–44, Selection and Reassignment of Prisoners to 3320th Retraining Group (Washington: Air Provost Marshal, Department of the Air Force, December 31, 1952); Lewis Nordyke, "These Prisoners Get a Second Chance," *Saturday Evening Post,* 225 (February 7, 1953), 22–23, 86–87, 89; R. V. Bennett, "At USAF's New Retraining Center They Treat 'Em Like Men," *Air Training,* 1 (June, 1952), 10–15.

37 J. Maginnis, "The Navy's Postwar Correctional Program," *Prison World,* 9 (Mar.–Apr., 1947), 3, 25, 28, 32; *Regulations for Operation of Retraining Commands* (Washington: Bureau of Naval Personnel, Department of the Navy, 1951); E. W. Skinner, "The Navy's Correctional Program," *Prison World,* 7 (Jan.–Feb., 1945), 8–9, 27–30.

38 L. B. Hershey, *Selective Service as the Tide of War Turns, Third Report of the Director of Selective Service, 1943–44* (Washington: Government Printing Office, 1945), pp. 227–28.

39 *Ibid.,* p. 230.

40 Victor Kleber, *Selective Service in Illinois, 1940–47* (Printed by the Authority of the State of Illinois, undated), p. 192.

41 *Ibid.,* p. 195.

42 Hershey, *Selective Service as the Tide of War Turns, op. cit.,* pp. 230–31.

43 *The Army Correctional System, op. cit.,* p. 157.

44 S. A. Stouffer, *et al., Studies in Social Psychology in World War II,* Vol. 1, *The American Soldier: Adjustment during Army Life* (Princeton, N.J.: Princeton University Press, 1949), pp. 116–18.

45 *Ibid.,* p. 89.

46 M. R. McCallum, "The Study of the Delinquent in the Army," *American Journal of Sociology,* 51 (1946), 479–82.

47 Stouffer, *op. cit.,* pp. 112–13.

48 Official Press Release, *Washington Times Herald,* February 9, 1950.

49 Stouffer, *op. cit.,* p. 113.

50 *Ibid.,* pp. 196–207.

23

European Adult Offenders and Prisons*

For centuries there has been an interchange and cross-diffusion of methods of criminal justice and penal philosophy and practices among the countries of Europe, between Europe and the United States, and between Europe and the United States and the Far East.

DIFFUSION OF PENAL METHODS

At first, diffusion was carried on through actual migrations of people from one part of the world to another. Each early wave of Europeans who moved into England carried new methods of punishing criminals. Later, colonization and conquest spread English and European methods around the world, with each nation imposing its own variation of penal philosophy and practices on its colonies, always modified to meet local conditions. New methods devised in these areas later flowed back to Europe.

Special international visits by criminologists and penologists furthered the diffusion of policies and methods, at first chiefly between European countries. John Howard, the great English prison reformer of the eighteenth century, after extensive tours of the continent, incorporated his findings into a book, *The State of Prisons,* published in 1777.[1] Some of Howard's recommendations, including solitary confinement in cells day and night, were written into the English Penitentiary Act of 1779. As a result, Eng-

---

* During the summer of 1953, in part through the kindness of Professor Negley Teeters of Temple University, the author visited 6 prisons and 2 correctional schools in England, Sweden, Norway, Denmark, and France. The discussion in this Chapter is limited to these 5 countries. The information gained from observation and interviews with prison administrators and staff has been supplemented with published material and one original account written by a Norwegian. Nevertheless, a definitive analysis cannot be made because of limited material. It is hoped, however, that this Chapter and the photographs will stimulate interest and suggest changes that might be made in American practices.

611

lish county jails were remodeled with individual cells.   For example, the jail at Wymondham in Norfolk, built in 1785, had solitary cells for use 24 hours of the day.

Later, Europe, especially England, contributed to American penology. A description of Wymondham jail, as well as a copy of Howard's book were in the hands of prison reformers in Philadelphia when they persuaded the state legislature to pass an act on April 5, 1790, providing for the erection of a new building with solitary cells in the yard of the Walnut Street Jail in Philadelphia.   Also borrowed from England was the circular cell house, or panopticon, advocated by Jeremy Bentham, with cells lining the circumference of a circular building, all of which could be readily supervised by someone stationed in the middle.   Never used in England, Bentham's plans for the panopticon influenced several American prisons, notably the prison built at Richmond, Virginia, in 1800, and the Illinois penitentiary at Stateville, built in 1919–27 (see page 422).

Europe continues to the present time to devise new types of treatment. Denmark's psychiatric institution for maladjusted criminals at Herstedvester is attracting the attention of both European and American criminologists and psychiatrists.

Likewise, eastward across the Atlantic, new methods traveled from the New to the Old World.   In the nineteenth century when the Pennsylvania system of isolation and the Auburn system of congregate work (see pages 403–05) were staging their struggle for supremacy as models for prison construction and program, interest in England and Europe was keen. Public-minded visitors and official representatives of the various governments arrived to study the applicability of the systems to their own countries. Today, in many countries of Europe prisons built on the Pennsylvania model can be seen.   Some still use the small, individual exercise yards and the individual stalls in which prisoners sat at chapel, concealed from each other but able to see and be seen by the chaplain.

Brockway in establishing the first reformatory for men at Elmira, New York, borrowed ideas from abroad and also contributed to European penology.   He drew upon experiments in Australia and Ireland in the idea of indeterminate sentences.   Later, the founder of the first English Borstal or training institution for youth visited Elmira and in his turn was stimulated by the new reformatory methods.   The English Borstals in turn became models for other European countries and have been recommended for the United States.

The juvenile court, organized in Chicago in 1899, was based on principles long used in England (see pages 362–69); nevertheless, it preceded the establishment of a juvenile court in England by 9 years, when the Children Act of 1908 provided for juvenile courts that differed somewhat from American courts.

Formal international conferences and associations, which bring together theoretical and practical penologists from many countries, have been organized.   The International Penal and Penitentiary Commission, for many years active in organizing international congresses, in 1951 handed its functions to the Social Affairs Division of the United Nations Secretariat, which organizes world congresses on criminology at 5 year intervals and stimulates regional conferences.

Back and forth across the English Channel and the Atlantic Ocean have traveled criminologists, prison administrators, and reformers seeking new experiments to be applied in their own countries.   The informal visits, the formal inspections, the congresses and conferences with their learned papers and discussions are all supplemented by a vast quantity of printed material in journals, annual reports, and proceedings of meetings.

GENERAL OBSERVATIONS

In most European countries, prisons are operated by the national government.   Each country, therefore, has only one system of prisons, similar to our federal system but covering all types of penal institutions, including local jails.   Since World War II, many countries have modified their laws governing penal institutions.   Although these countries are in the process of remodeling and constructing prisons to serve new purposes, they must also continue to use many old structures not adapted to new methods.   In general, therefore, to the observer prisons seem old, crude, lacking in modern equipment, and with few comforts for the prisoners.   Several factors must be remembered, however.   Europeans do not have our passion for tearing down buildings and erecting new, larger, more modern ones, so long as the old plants can be made to function.   Also, at present they still suffer from the effects of the war and many are rebuilding bombed or burned factories and houses, which are valued more highly than new prisons.

European prisons cannot, in fairness, be compared with American prisons; they should be measured against the mode of living of people in the particular country.   In a French prison, for instance, many men wear wooden shoes in which they noisily stride along the walks in their exercise periods, discarding them indoors for soft slippers.   The shoes are the standard footwear supplied by the prison.   Others wear leather shoes bought out of their earnings or received from family or friends.   Compared to conditions in the

United States, this procedure seems a disregard for the prisoner's comfort. But in France wooden shoes are a normal type of footgear in village and on the farm.   French prisoners are supplied with a rural workingman's type of shoe.   Again, in the old part of a French prison there was no heat, even in the winter.   Inquiry disclosed that in most French homes there is also no provision for central heating.   As a third illustration, in this same prison, the staple article of food for the day was a huge brown-crusted loaf of bread —this too is standard for the working man.   The men in this prison supplement the bread and coffee supplied by the prison with vegetables and fruit that they may buy.   They are also allowed to buy one fourth liter of wine each day.   In a woman's prison the inmates are served wine once a week.   The wine, too, is part of the normal diet of the French man and woman.   The prisons must be viewed against the background of the country and of the times, not against the condition of prisons in the United States.

The following discussion of European prisons presents them in a period of change.   As in the United States, social-psychological methods of correction are replacing repressive primitive methods.   But, as is true here, the transition is not complete.   There is resistance, fear of the new, and the difficulties of outmoded buildings, untrained staff, and inadequate finances.

TYPES OF OFFENDERS

European offenders are startlingly similar to offenders in the United States.   Although an exact comparison cannot be made because of differences in recording, a general comparison is possible.   The similarity among offenders indicates that European countries and the United States face many common problems in penology and rehabilitation.   Experiments carried out in one country may be helpful in suggesting modifications in treatment in another country.   A descriptive rather than an exact statistical comparison is all that can be given.

Types of Offenses

As in the United States, minor offenders far outnumber serious or dangerous criminals, and property crimes greatly exceed homicides and assaults.

The following comparisons for 1950 show the predominance of minor offenses.   In England and Wales, 16 times as many people were fined for minor offenses as were sentenced to all types of jails and prisons.[2]   One third of all indictable (serious) offenses were "simple and minor larcenies"; in contrast, only 5 per cent were homicides and serious assaults.   Violations of liquor laws and drunkenness were the most common of minor misdemeanors, with minor assaults in second place. In Denmark, among offenses exclusive of begging and vagrancy (the number of which is not given), 78 per cent were crimes against property as compared with 11 per cent crimes of violence.[3]   In Norway, there were 11 misdemeanors for every felony.[4]   In addition, for an unrecorded number of cases, usually of first offenders, prosecution was waived.   Two thirds of all misdemeanors were cases of intoxication, and two thirds of all felonies were larceny cases. In Sweden there were 170,000 offenders, the vast majority of whom were petty offenders guilty of such things as traffic violations.[5]   Among 9,972 sentenced for property offenses, 88 per cent were fined and 7 per cent received a waiver of prosecution; only 5 per cent received more serious penalties, an indication of the very small proportion of serious crimes.

In the United States, with the exception of traffic law violations, drunkenness and violations of liquor laws account for more cases than all other offenses put together.   Among serious crimes, various forms of theft far outnumber homicides and assaults; the ratio is approximately 17 to 1.

In both Europe and the United States, therefore, excessive drinking, usually combined with disorderly conduct, is a common problem for the police and courts.   A second similarity is the high proportion of crimes against property as compared with homicide and serious assaults.

However, some differences do exist.   Officials in the countries visited tended to emphasize the scarcity of highly organized criminal groups and juvenile delinquent gangs, both of which are a source of much criminal and disorderly behavior in cities in the United States.   Several possible explanations, based on differences in the social background, may be offered.

In the United States the most powerful adult organized criminal groups are the syndicates that supply illegal pleasures—gambling, prostitution, and, in the past, liquor.   The attitudes toward certain of these activities differ from country to country.   The European policy toward these and similar activities generally is to permit and regulate rather than to stamp out by imposing severe penalties.   Gambling, the source of vast amounts of illegal income for organized criminal groups in the United States, may be used as an example.   Since 1934 Sweden has legally empowered one organization, Tip Service, to handle betting on soccer matches, with limited returns to the shareholders, a stated percentage for expenses, a division of 50 per cent of the profits among the winners, and the remainder to the government.[6] About 1 Swede out of 7 bets through Tip Service.   Since the returns per winner are small, there is little temptation to big-time gamblers to try to control the company.   Lotteries, betting on races, and operation of gambling casinos are legal in European countries.   The famed casino at Monte Carlo in Monaco and the almost equally well-known casinos in France are examples.   These gambling facilities are regulated by law, and often a portion of the profits forms a substantial part of the government's finances.

Nonmarital sex relations are also defined somewhat differently in European countries than in the United States.   Except in England, prostitution usually is omitted from the criminal code.   In Denmark, for instance, there is no crime corresponding to statutory rape, and nonmarital sex relations after the age of 18 are not prosecuted unless there has been violence or public indecency.[7]   In most of the countries, police regulations rather than criminal laws control prostitution.   In France, houses of prostitution are licensed and medical examinations are required once each week; prostitutes not attached to the licensed houses register with the police and are given fortnightly medical examinations.   Nonregistration exposes the woman to the possibility of arrest.   Girls under 18 years old are dealt with as juvenile delinquents.   Acknowledgment of the existence of prostitution and mild regulations reduce the allure that operating brothels might have for organized criminal groups.

Another probable reason for the existence of less organized crime in Europe than the United States, at both the juvenile and the adult level, is the difference in degree of cultural homogeneity.[8]   Ideals, ethics, and standards of conduct in European countries tend to be uniformly accepted, and laws and conduct are adjusted to each other.   In general, immigrants entering the European countries under discussion have come in small numbers and slowly enough to be integrated.   In the United States hordes of European immigrants from many cultural backgrounds have introduced behavior permitted in the home countries but illegal in the United States.   In addition, the rate of integration has been too slow to prevent personal disorganization. Many large cities in the United States contain small foreign-language cities where a hybrid culture develops that often seems to embody the worst of the parent culture and the worst of American culture.   Out of this situation autonomous criminal groups develop, with allegiance to no established social or legal code.   Europe has been less plagued with such conditions. Added to this difficult situation is the derogatory attitude and discrimination exhibited in the United States against certain cultural groups whose members react aggressively by vandalism or assaults.   In homogeneous European countries, such hostile conditions may not exist.

The scarcity of organized crime in Europe, therefore, may be at least partially accounted for by lack of opportunity for syndicates to be profitable, absence of cultural conflicts, social integration, and non-discriminatory attitudes.

It must be noted, however, that crime and delinquency rates in European countries in general increased during the socially disorganized period of World War II, but since have declined. Also, the material in this chapter does not touch upon the countries that experienced destruction of or major changes in their form of government, or great shifts in population.

Sex Ratio

The United States is not unique in its excess of male over female offenders. In England in 1950, the ratio of male to female prisoners was 10.6 to 1; in France in 1946, 4 to 1; in Sweden in 1952, 39 to 1; in Norway in 1950 among felons, 12 to 1; and in Denmark in 1950, 16 to 1.[9] Arrests and imprisonment sometimes have different sex ratios, since women's crimes lead to probation or short jail sentences more often than do men's. In the United States arrests typically run 8 men to 1 woman and imprisonment 30 men to 1 woman. It is significant that in all the countries listed imprisoned men far outnumber women; therefore provision of facilities and treatment of prisoners concern primarily the rehabilitation of men.

Age

Unfortunately, most of the materials available for preparing this chapter do not contain age distributions. The English reports are an exception.[10] In England in 1950, the median age of prisoners in both local and national prisons was 29 years; for indictable (serious) crimes, 28.8 years; for nonindictable but serious offenses, 30.5; and for minor nonindictable offenses, 37.6. Among individual crimes, burglary and housebreaking are the youth's crimes, with the largest number of offenders between 17 and 20 years; drunkenness belongs to middle and old age. In the United States, according to a special survey made in 1952, the median age for arrests (not imprisonment) was 35 years. As in England, burglary and in fact all types of theft involving the threat of force are committed by young persons, while drunkenness is an offense of middle and old age. The most conspicuous crime of youth in the United States is automobile theft. English statistics do not report automobile thefts in a separate category, but it is probable that in a nation with relatively few automobiles, their theft is not a frequent crime.

Recidivism

As in the United States, the treatment of criminals in European countries does not always reform. Seventy-seven per cent of English male prisoners in 1950 and 72 per cent of females had previous proved offenses.[11] The median number of offenses was 5 for men and 3 for women. Some members of each sex had had more than 20 previous proven offenses. It must be remembered that inmates of local prisons are included; like our jails, the local prisons receive minor offenders who often are habitual occupants of the prison cells.   That other European countries also are plagued with recidivism is evident from the practice of establishing special institutions for habitual offenders, sometimes workhouses for habitual misdemeanants, and close custody institutions for criminal recidivists.

Rural-Urban Contrast

In Europe, cities produce more than their share of criminals.[12]   Copenhagen, with one fourth of the population of Denmark in 1950, had contributed 42 per cent of the imprisoned criminals.   In Norway in 1950, Oslo had a felony rate that was 2.5 times the rural rate, although the rate for other cities and towns slightly topped Oslo's rate.   In the United States, also, the tendency is for cities to have higher crime rates than small towns or rural areas.

Similarity of Offenders Abroad and in the United States

The above statistics are sufficient to show that England, certain European countries, and the United States are faced with essentially the same types of offenders, with the exception of criminals in the United States who operate in strongly organized groups and who often avoid conviction.   The prison populations are remarkably similar, as to seriousness of offenses, sex ratio, age, recidivism, and type of community.

ENGLAND AND WALES

Administration

All prisons in England and Wales are administered by a national Prison Commission, which functions under the Secretary of State for the Home Department.[13]   Prisons of Scotland and Ireland are separately administered by their own Home Departments.   The members of the Prison Commission are permanent civil servants appointed by the Crown.   The governors (wardens) of individual prisons are also permanent civil servants appointed by the Secretary of State.   Governors are selected competitively, and an effort is made to induce prison staff members to register in special staff courses to prepare themselves for advancement, including the position of governor. The professional staff must meet standards set by the Civil Service Commission.   The control and operation of the prisons, therefore, are in the hands of persons selected for their qualifications for the work rather than in the hands of men chosen for political affiliations as is so often true in the United States.

Post-War Reforms

The Prison Commission faced many new problems after World War II. Since the prison population had increased from approximately 11,000 before the war, to more than 24,000 by 1952, new facilities were imperative. In addition, during the war years buildings had not had normal repair and were in need of rehabilitation. On the physical side alone, drastic steps had to be taken. Consequently 26 additional prisons of various types were opened. Even with these, some 4,500 men are still housed 3 to a cell.

Moreover, during the 1930's and 1940's many new concepts of treatment had been developing in penal philosophy, some in England, some in other countries. The time seemed ripe to formulate these new concepts into definite principles and to adapt old and new buildings to the new principles of treatment. As a result, the Criminal Justice Act of 1948 and the Prison Rules of 1949 were passed.

Rehabilitation of criminals is emphasized as the primary purpose of imprisonment. Discipline and order are recognized as necessary for the operation of an institution and also as a part of training; they are to be maintained with as little restriction as is necessary. Secure custody is also recognized but again it is to involve only the amount of restriction necessary to prevent escapes. The importance of the prison staff in rehabilitation is affirmed; the staff is expected to provide leadership, set a good example, and treat the prisoners in such a way that they will develop self-respect and a sense of personal responsibility. Work, education, religion, and character improvement are the foundation stones of treatment. Little is said about recreation, although it is not overlooked, and nothing appears in the reports on sports or team games.

Classification

The first step in the process of rehabilitation is classification of prisoners. Unlike the highly developed systems in the United States, classification in England is the grouping of prisoners into types according to a few easily ascertainable characteristics. People awaiting trial are segregated from the convicted, and criminal offenders from civil offenders, who are deficient in meeting certain financial obligations. Women and men are in separate institutions or, if in the same institution, in separate units. Another classification is made on the basis of age and depth of criminal habits. People under 21 years of age form the Young Prisoners' group; first offenders over 21, called Stars, are in another group; the remainder of the prisoners are called Ordinaries. The above groups are further classified by length of sentence: those with sentences of a few months are grouped together; 1 to 3 years form another group; over 3 years (a long sentence in England) a third group. Persistent or habitual offenders are given longer sentences and receive a special type of treatment.

Types of Prisons

Segregation of these groups and distinctive programs for each are achieved through an array of classified prisons, still in process of development.   Many prisons are very old, many have been converted to prisons from other uses, and a few are newly constructed.   In some cases, one prison is made to serve several classes of prisoners, with the groups isolated from each other.

The prisons fall into 5 general types.

1. Local prisons have many of the functions of the county jail in the United States, although, unlike our jails, they come under the control of the national Prison Commission along with other types of prisons.   Twenty-five such prisons distributed about the country house people on remand (detention), those awaiting trial, and sentenced prisoners awaiting transfer to another prison.   Prisoners (both civil and criminal) with very short terms also serve them in the local prisons.   All these various classes of prisoners are kept in separate parts of the local prisons, and further separations are made by sex and age.   In addition, 8 local prisons serve as overflow institutions for Star or civil prisoners.

2. Regional prisons serve criminals sentenced to 1 to 3 years of imprisonment; 60 per cent are Stars.   Two are designated as Young Prisoners' Centers (under 21 years old).   Most of the regional prisons are minimum security institutions, or have an open camp attached.   The prisoners are selected from the local prisons and if they do not conform to the program in the regional prisons, they are returned to the local prisons.

3. Central prisons receive both Stars and Ordinaries who have long sentences to serve (more than 3 years).   Less than 3 per cent of male prisoners have such sentences.

4. Borstal * is the name given to institutions that receive boys and girls between ages 16 and 21, who have been convicted of a crime punishable by imprisonment, or who are on transfer from a corrective school for juvenile delinquents.

5. A fifth type of institution, called a corrective training prison, is de-

---

* The name Borstal comes from Borstal Prison, located at Borstal near Rochester, England.   In a wing of this prison, a reformatory-like program for young male offenders was instituted early in the twentieth century.   With the success of the program, similar types of training were begun in other prisons where young offenders were segregated from the older men.   Borstal became a generic name for the program and, in time, Borstals, which had become separate institutions, were given a prominent place in the English correctional and penal system.

signed for young habitual criminals who have not responded to the programs in other prisons. These offenders are sent to an Allocation Center where they are studied by a staff of specialists, who then decide to what type of prison to send them, whether to a regional prison or the corrective training prison. The maximum sentence possible is 4 years but usually a 3 year sentence is given.

Prison Services and Programs

Medical service is provided for all prisoners, including treatment for venereal disease; when prisoners are willing, routine blood tests are carried out. Special attention is given to pregnant women prisoners.

Three psychiatric treatment centers are maintained, 2 for men and 1 for women, where seriously disturbed prisoners receive individual treatment. The institutional staff also makes diagnoses of prisoners when requested to do so by the courts. In some of the larger prisons psychologists and psychiatric social workers are stationed.

English prisons place great emphasis on work as a means of rehabilitation. All prisoners in all prisons work. During World War II it was possible to provide each inmate with 40 hours of work per week; in 1954 the average was 22 hours in the shops, with perhaps some additional work carried on in the cells. The type of work varies with the prison. In local prisons with many short-termers, almost half the men make or repair mail bags—a type of handwork that does not require elaborate machinery or long training. Other industries in the local prisons include matmaking, picking and sorting oakum, tailoring, and a wide variety of other types of work employing small numbers of prisoners. Although mail bags and mats occupy inmates in prisons other than the local ones, the longer terms served in regional and central prisons permit more emphasis on skilled trades—carpentry, tinsmith and allied work, weaving, and shoemaking. In all prisons new buildings are constructed by prisoners, and "housekeeping" and maintenance work fall to them. A critical statement written by an American penologist in 1951 points out that much of the work is done by hand and that equipment is out of date, thus making vocational training for release difficult.[14] The Prison Commissioners are aware of these shortcomings, and in their *Report for the Year 1951* speak of various improvements in equipment and the establishment of new shops in a number of prisons. Definite vocational training with classes paralleling work have been instituted in prisons where inmates are serving sufficiently long terms to make such training practicable.

An important part of the program is the use of nonfamily visitors who help to keep prisoners in contact with the outside world.[15] For the whole of England there are some 500 men and 150 women visitors who have been approved by prison wardens and the Prison Commission, and who are organized into the National Association of Prison Visitors.   Not professional social workers, these people are interested in the welfare of prisoners and voluntarily visit some 6 to 10 prisoners once a week.   Prisoners are encouraged to talk, made to feel that they are not outcasts, and that people still care about their welfare.   Often the visitors continue their contacts after prisoners are released.

Borstals

Borstals are a distinctive English institution with a program that differs from that of the local, regional, and central prisons.

Borstals receive teenager criminals who are sentenced by the courts for an indeterminate period between 9 and 36 months.   The average term for 1951 was 16.5 months.   The individual Borstals are small and are of several types—reception centers for study and placement, closed and open institutions, and one recall center.   Boys and girls are in separate Borstals.

The stated objective of the system "is the all round development of character and capacities—moral, mental, physical, and vocational, with particular emphasis on the development of responsibility and self-control through trust increasing with progress.   This conception requires conditions as unlike those of a prison as is compatible with compulsory detentions." [16]

A Borstal is neither a prison nor a school.   It is a training center for "adolescents or young men (or women) whose presentence histories show poor work records as a preponderating factor." [17]   It is, nevertheless, a part of the prison system and some Borstals are merely wings of adult prisons. The routine of training places a hard day's work at the head of the program. Manufacturing and farming are carried on at the Borstals.   Farm produce is sold to outside markets and to prisons.   Those who learn trades are encouraged to take the examinations of the City and Guilds of London Institutes; certificates are helpful in securing later employment.

Illiterate or academically poorly prepared inmates are assigned to educational classes during the work hours.   Others are expected to enroll in classes for 6 hours per week outside of work time.   Hobbies and handicrafts are encouraged.

An effort is made in each Borstal to develop responsibility, and inmates are progressively given more responsible tasks and increased freedom.   One form of freedom is work outside the institution.   Carefully selected boys are permitted to work at a newly learned trade outside the Borstal, returning to the Borstal after work.   Also, groups of inmates are taken outside to work, either for private employers or on government projects.

Selected Borstal inmates may leave the institution for short periods without supervision.   These short intervals of freedom, with the necessity of returning to the Borstal on their own responsibility, are regarded as a valuable part of the inmates' training.

Obviously not all boys and girls respond to Borstal training. About 1 in 6 attempts to escape but is usually returned. Repeated attempts to escape or incorrigibility brings transfer to a closed correctional Borstal. A recall center also receives inmates who fail to adjust after their release, and imposes a short period of supplementary training. Approximately half of the released Borstal members of the 1940's did not have a reconviction in 7 years after release; one fourth had one reconviction, and one fourth more than one. Girls have a slightly better record than boys.

For girls there are 3 Borstals, with essentially the same plan of study of the individual, treatment, and release as are found in the boys' Borstals. As is the case in reformatories and prisons for women in the United States, provision must be made for babies born to girls in the institution.

Inmates may be released from Borstal any time after 9 months, provided sufficient progress has been made. Records are carefully kept by the house supervisor and members of the staff and are reviewed by the institution board and a visiting committee. The release is conditional and the young person remains under trained supervision for 4 years. The boy or girl is helped to find a place to live and a job, and is counseled about problems that may arise.

Preventive Detention

Criminals of long standing for whom hope of rehabilitation has been lost may be segregated for long periods of time under a special nonpunitive program called preventive detention. Instituted in 1908 and retained by the Criminal Justice Act of 1948, preventive detention may keep a habitual offender institutionalized for as long as 14 years. In 1954, there were over 1,000 such offenders. These men are not, however, simply placed in prison and forgotten. Eventually they are released, at the end of the sentence or with a slight reduction in time. Certain ones, after two thirds of the sentence has been served, are permitted to live in a special hostel in another city, work, draw wages, pay their own expenses, support their families, and so on. They are under supervision of the Central After-Care Association, as are all released preventive detention prisoners.

Supervision of Prisoners After Release

Supervision of prisoners after release is in the hands of two organizations, both of which are financed partly by private contributions and partly by grants from public funds.[18] The older of the two organizations consists of the National Association of Discharged Prisoners' Aid Societies, with which are affiliated 38 local Discharged Prisoners' Aid Societies.

The Aid Societies, which limit their work to inmates of local prisons, are in a period of transition.   Their original work consisted of small financial grants to released prisoners to tide them over the period between release and employment.   However, the development of welfare programs in England has reduced the need for such financial aid.   Sir Lionel Fox, Chairman of the Prison Commission, in a recent book called attention to the degree to which the released prisoner is immediately eligible (with some legal limitations as compared with the nonprisoner) to receive fare home, maintenance through the Assistance Board (which also aids family finances), medical aid through the National Health Service, assistance in finding a job from the Ministry of Labour, unemployment insurance if he does not find work, and other benefits.[19]   Financial needs, therefore, seem fairly well supplied.   A study of Discharged Prisoners' Aid Societies, made by the Home Office in 1953, points out other types of aid that the Societies should emphasize, such as guidance of prisoners in planning how they will conduct their lives after release, advice about domestic and personal affairs, and moral support during the period of adjustment to the outside community.   Such aid would tend to counteract the social pressures that often immediately assail the released prisoner and force him back into criminal associations and acts.   It seems probable, therefore, that the work of the Societies will be modified in the near future and brought into closer co-ordination with the public financial assistance programs in order to eliminate overlapping and to extend the range of services offered.

The second organization for aiding released prisoners is the Central After-Care Association, whose duties are confined to regional and central prisons and Borstals.   In general, the Association is charged with responsibility for prisoners with terms of more than 3 years.   The Central Association includes the Borstal Association for supervision of released inmates from the Borstals and the Aylesbury Association, which supervises women.   Funds are virtually all supplied by the government.

Summary

Along with many antiquated prison buildings, England retains the vestiges of old, repressive policies.   The movement toward rehabilitation is best seen in programs for young prisoners.

FRANCE

The popular American conception of French prisons is usually limited to semifictional accounts of the prison colonies in French Guiana, to which France transported major criminals and habitual offenders intermittently from 1763 until the 1940's, when, first, war conditions and then prison reforms ended transportation.[20]

Administration

Prisons and their operation are under the control of the French Prison Administration, which administers all prisons in France as an integrated system.

Types of Prisons

At present all criminals and minor offenders remain in France in a series of prisons designed for special types of offenders, as described below.[21]

Local institutions receive persons awaiting trial, those with less than a year to serve, and boys and girls awaiting transfer to a reformatory.

For youthful offenders there is a school prison for boys opened in 1947 and one for girls opened in 1950. A hostel with limited freedom is operated in connection with the boys' school prison.

A training center in mechanical and building trades and 2 open institutions are maintained for men aged 25 to 35.

For habitual offenders there are 3 observation centers opened between 1948 and 1953, where offenders are classified into 3 types, antisocial, asocial, and retrainable. Five treatment institutions are maintained, whose structure and programs range from strict custody to semifreedom. The retrainables enjoy semifreedom or receive conditional release. Eleven central prisons receive major criminals, many of the type formerly sent to prison colonies. Five of these prisons operate on the traditional pattern of strict discipline and labor, while 6 incorporate recently initiated treatment methods. All major criminals with sentences of more than 1 year pass through a study center where an allocation committee assigns them to specific prisons.

Prison Reform

The building of the new institutions mentioned above and the new diagnostic and treatment programs stem from the work of a commission that met in 1945 to consider problems evolving from the war years: the increase in the number of prisoners; inclusion of new types of offenders, such as enemy collaborators and criminals formerly transported; and deterioration or damage to prisons as a result of the war.

The basic principle formulated by the commission states that the purpose of imprisonment is the reformation and social rehabilitation of the offender. This end is to be achieved through humane treatment, work, social and medico-psychological services, conditional release (parole), and both pre- and post-release assistance to facilitate adjustment.

Several old provisions that seem incongruous in the light of the new social-psychological approach were retained.   For the first year of imprisonment the prisoner is in solitary confinement in his cell, leaving it only for daily solitary exercise.   This provision is a carry-over of the Pennsylvania plan for solitary confinement, adopted by France in 1875, and now 75 years later still part of the first stage of a program of rehabilitation.   The present Director of Prisons, Charles Germain, admits that, while solitary confinement prevents contamination of one prisoner by another, it also brings social rejection.   Isolation also makes it difficult to establish certain kinds of treatment or to provide adequate work.[22]

A legal provision that is out of harmony with treatment limits sentences given by the courts to imprisonment at hard labor, strict imprisonment, or simple imprisonment.   In practice, however, the French Prison Administration, in co-operation with the courts, is devising new experimental programs. For instance, short-termers may be placed in any one of a number of programs, depending upon their rehabilitation needs: confinement to cells; assignment to a work gang under guard outside the prison walls; assignment to unguarded work with nights, Sundays, and holidays spent in the prison; or release under a suspended sentence.

Prison Services and Programs

Several principles of treatment run through the entire system.   Suspended sentences have been in use in France since 1891, with the sentence declared null and void after 5 years without conviction of a new crime.   Experimentation has been carried on in supervised probation, for which legal provision is sought.

Postsentence study only is used.   Presentence diagnosis may come in time but to be effective would need to be accompanied by changes in sentencing laws.

Work with pay for all prisoners is strongly emphasized.   When the prisoner is sufficiently responsible, work outside the prison walls is provided, as a means of increasing wages, making possible the support of family, and giving gradual adaptation to community life.   Strict imprisonment thus can be reserved for those who must have constant observation.

The larger institutions have social workers in the staff who aid in the treatment of prisoners.

After serving a certain portion of their sentences, persons may be released under supervision of an Aid Committee for Discharged Prisoners.

The judge's duties do not end with sentencing the offender.   A judge serves as chairman of the allocation committee that determines the specific prison to which a criminal is sent, and he also is responsible for the execution of sentence. Hence a judge is attached to each penal or correctional institution. He sees that the legal rights of prisoners are respected and becomes by practice a criminologist as well as a judge.

The author was privileged to visit 2 prisons in France in 1953, a local institution for women in Paris and a central prison for men, each having the new type of treatment. Unfortunately, both institutions were old, and many physical features were not suited to modern types of treatment. Nevertheless, rehabilitation was the main objective. The two prisons are shown on pages 628 and 630.

Women's Prison in Paris (Maison d'Arrêt de la Roquette)

Formerly a men's prison built in 1811, the women's prison in Paris accommodates about 400 women awaiting trial or serving short terms. Long-termers, after conviction, are sent to one of the 2 women's prisons that serve the whole of France.

The structure of the building lends itself to many small units. It is hexagonal in shape with a four storied building around the edge of the hexagon; each of the six sections is connected with a central building by a long building. Between the connecting sections are spacious triangular outdoor yards with grass and trees. The administration buildings and the superintendent's apartment are attached and the entire institution is enclosed by a high wall. Beyond the wall lies the closely built and populous city of Paris.

In equipment and treatment of prisoners the prison is an odd assortment of old and new. In the kitchen, for instance, coal heat is used in the great built-in ovens, and a copper soup kettle converted into a stove is so huge that a small stepladder must be mounted in order to peer into it. The only modern touch—by American standards—is a large electric refrigerator. A high-domed chapel was in process of remodeling in 1953. For many years the prisoners sat in small separate stalls in the chapel, invisible to each other but with a direct view from prisoner to pastor. Other phases of life are communal: the women eat together at long wooden tables, scrubbed white; they work together; and small groups share one sleeping room. There is a library of donated books, all neatly and uniformly bound in blue by inmates. Each woman may select one book of fiction and one of nonfiction per month; however, many of the inmates cannot read.

The women are segregated within the institution by types: those awaiting trial; those serving short terms for a first arrest; abortionists; "tramps"; and chronic "tramps," who are in and out of prison every few days.

Many services are provided for these women. There is medical and dental care and an infirmary with separate rooms for the "nervous," the ill, and the tubercular. The chapel for religious services has already been

Above, the entrance to the women's prison in Paris (Maison d'Arrêt de la Roquette) leads into the hexagonal-shaped structure, where portions of the connecting buildings are separated by triangular yards. The compactly built, walled prison stands in a closely built-up section of Paris. Inside the walls in the 6 triangular yards (below) women are permitted to walk or sit to embroider on orders received from outside the prison.

Here the inmates of the women's prison in Paris gather for meals. The congregate living in this prison, exemplified by the photograph, contrasts with the custom in numerous European prisons of isolating prisoners for many hours of the day including mealtime when meals are served to prisoners locked in their cells.

mentioned. Prisoners may have visits from their families 3 times weekly. In the winter a movie is shown weekly.

The mainstay of the program is work, both maintenance and filling of orders from outside companies. On the day of the author's visit the "first arrests" were folding and packaging football notices on contract for an outside concern under the watchful eye of a woman supervisor who sat on a platform at one end of the room. On a bench along one side of the room 6 idle women sat; having refused to work, they were required to spend each day in the workroom. Other work is individual: in one of the pleasant, triangular yards, 2 women sat near a small table embroidering to fill orders from outside the prison. On the table lounged a pet cat. The women were unsupervised but the yard was enclosed by the various buildings. The scene might have been any private courtyard where women met to talk and work.

The living quarters consisted of well-lighted rooms, each equipped for 3 inmates. Every woman had her own cot and a small wall cupboard, and the three shared one table. Thick bags filled with excelsior served for mattresses. When the bag becomes soiled, the woman removes the excelsior, washes the bag, and replaces the excelsior. The cells have solid wooden doors, each with a small peephole and barred transom. The general impression is of age and barrenness. Ten or 12 rooms form a unit, which is heated by a stove in the corridor, the heat entering the individual rooms through the transom or by penetrating the walls. Each living unit has lavatory rooms with showers.

The superintendent and medical officers are civilians. All other members of the staff are members of the Order of Saint Joseph, blue garbed women whose demeanor is calm and sympathetic, but firm. These dedicated women live in the prison, accepting a lifetime of service to women offenders, many of whom are depraved women from the streets of Paris.

Central Prison at Melun, France

The central prison at Melun affords an example of the new type of corrective program superimposed upon the traditional regime and handicapped by an old structure. In 1808 a prison was established in the former convent

Central prison in Melun, France, for long-term serious criminals is viewed on its island location across the waters of the Seine. The high wall and guard towers mark it as a maximum security institution, comparable to many state and federal prisons in the United States.

of the Sisters of Saint Nicolas, which was appropriated at the time of the French Revolution.[23] During the next 80 years, the structure was almost completely rebuilt so that today little of the original convent remains. The prison is of the maximum security type, with inner and outer walls and a dozen guard towers. Here approximately 675 prisoners, aged 30 to 60 years, serve sentences of 10 to 20 years for serious crimes. In general, the prison fits the standard for a maximum security prison—administration building, storerooms, kitchen, dining room, chapel, exercise yards, cell blocks, disciplinary cells for isolation, lavatories, and an infirmary. The buildings appear to be old, with some in need of interior paint. In the oldest sections the floors are of wood, and cells are without heat or artificial light. In other sections, the paint is new and there are cell lights and central heat. In general all workrooms and offices, as well as the cell blocks, are of the simplest construction and have a minimum of equipment other than that needed for the work. Each cell, measuring approximately 6 by 8 feet, houses one prisoner and is equipped with an iron bed that folds against the wall when not in use, a folding table, a chair, a wall cupboard, a small toilet table, a toilet bucket, a pitcher of water, floor brush, and in the newer cell blocks a radiator. All articles are of the simplest construction and material.

Cell block for prisoners under observation, central prison, Melun, France. Note the heavy solid doors with small openings that may be bolted shut from the outside, and the shuttered transoms. Some of the cell blocks have four tiers of similarly constructed cells.

Men whose sentences date from before the prison reform of 1945 work in a print shop. Men admitted since the new program went into effect follow a different routine designed to emphasize rehabilitation. The old Pennsylvania principle of complete isolation still dominates the first year of imprisonment, but is progressively modified as the months pass. For 3 months the prisoner remains in his cell day and night, except for a half hour of exercise alone morning and afternoon. During this period his human contacts are limited to the counselors (educateurs) and, if necessary, a psychiatrist. At the end of 3 months the men have some group recreation but otherwise are in isolation. Handwork is provided for them in their cells. The year of solitude is followed by assignment to the first of 3 progressive stages, characterized by different types of work. First, the man

Recreation room at the central prison at Melun, France, for the use of certain classifications of prisoners. Liberty and privileges are increased as the prisoner progresses through various stages of training.

works in the shoe shop; the second stage takes him to the furniture shop; the third is in the tailor shop. Good behavior and good work are rewarded with yellow symbols sewed to the sleeves of the men's jackets. Only a very small group works in the prison without supervision. A plan providing for work outside the walls, but with all other time spent in the prison, has not yet been put into effect. Men receive wages for their work and pay some of their own expenses.

The workshops are large, well-lighted, and equipped with necessary machinery. Most of the work is for the state but a few private contracts are accepted. The atmosphere is relaxed and orderly. The men in each shop take their exercise together and eat together in a large dining room at tables that seat 6. The exercise yard is small and activities are limited to sitting in the sun or walking along paths separated by patches of vegetables that constitute the private project of a staff member who is reluctant to yield the space for recreation. Thus the old tradition of repression hinders the newer program of rehabilitation.

Shoe shop at central prison, Melun, France, where prisoners under the recently instituted progressive system spend the second period of their confinement. The first period consists of isolation in their cells, where they are provided with handwork. The last 2 periods are spent, respectively, in the furniture shop and the tailor shop.

School Prison

In contrast to the central prisons for serious criminals, there are the school prisons for youths aged 18 to 25. The school prison for males, located at Oermingen, as described by Fenton, follows the general pattern of French prisons, but shifts the emphasis from custody and formality to re-education and limited freedom. Built in 1947, the institution follows modern construction plans. Seven guard towers and guarded gates combined with high wire fences prevent escapes, but at the same time permit freedom on the grounds. Supervision of the men comes from professionally trained counselors (educateurs) and professional instructors, neither of whom are

Many prisoners at the central prison, Melun, France, entered prison before the present system of retraining was instituted. They do not receive the counseling and progressive increase of privileges accorded the more recently sentenced prisoners. They are not, however, neglected in the general program of prison life. They spend their days working in a large and well-equipped printing establishment within the prison walls.

in uniform. The counselors, who are constantly in close touch with the inmates, handle most of the disciplinary problems, reporting only serious offenses to the warden. The inmates are in living groups of about 25, each group having its own counselor who lives on the grounds. Each unit has its own dining and recreational rooms, and interaction among the members is encouraged. The recreational rooms have been decorated by the inmates, each group devising its own scheme of decoration; one room has a fountain illumined by lights and another a stage. Retraining is organized around work as the basic activity, with hobbies and recreation for leisure hours.

Summary

France is in the process of converting an old prison regime and a philosophy with punishment as the central motive to a modern program of rehabilitation.   As is true in other European countries and in many states in the United States, the new program has to take form slowly.   Old prisons must still be used and adapted as well as can be.   Money must be appropriated and time allowed for construction of observation centers and open institutions to supplement the old maximum security prisons.   Laws are slowly changing to allow supervised probation, indeterminate sentences, and the discarding of solitary confinement as the first part of the prison regime. Guards and staff accustomed to the old regime require retraining and many new guards and professional staff members must be found and incorporated into the program.   It is noteworthy that France has not thought it necessary to await the completion of new buildings before instituting rehabilitation; in spite of material handicaps the new program is under way.   All in all, decided progress has been made and the way seems open for the development of an integrated national program of rehabilitation.

DENMARK

Administration

Denmark, in common with other European countries, has centralized control of its correctional system.   The Ministry of Justice has supervision over police, court personnel, jails, and prisons.   The professional positions in the Ministry of Justice are held by lawyers, and employees are on civil service.[24]

Types of Prisons

The institutions are of many different types.   Local jails house those in detention before trial, convicted offenders with sentences of less than 5 months, and those awaiting transfer to other institutions.   There are juvenile prisons or Borstals for men between the ages of 17 and 21; open institutions for first offenders under 25; prison camps for men and for women; a penal workhouse for nondangerous habitual criminals; and prisons for adult males, graded as to degree of recidivism or seriousness of crime.   Special institutions for criminal psychopaths provide unusual methods of treatment that are drawing international attention.

All prisons and correctional institutions are small, the maximum capacity of any being under 550.   Many of the prisons house less than 100 inmates.

Each prisoner has his own cell, and overcrowding is not a problem. In open institutions small dormitories for 3 or 4 persons are used.

Prison Services and Programs

Prisoners are received directly from the courts without the intermediate step of a reception center. A thorough presentence investigation is made, however, with a psychiatric examination of almost all women offenders, sex offenders, those convicted of serious crimes, and, when feasible, many others. On the basis of this presentence investigation, offenders are sentenced to specific institutions. In some prisons the new inmate remains in isolation a month, during which time he may be tested and interviewed. He is then assigned his place in the prison program.

As in other European countries, useful work is emphasized. The objective is rehabilitation and the training of the inmates in some useful trade. The prison industries are supervised by a board whose members represent Parliament, the trade unions, and employers. Prison industries are primarily for state use, the major ones being tailoring, printing, weaving, and the manufacture of furniture and envelopes. Other prisoners work in agriculture and forestry or as gardeners; manufacture toys for private concerns; or do maintenance work. All prisoners, including those who are ill or unemployed but with good prison records are paid small amounts, half of which may be spent and half of which is saved for the day of release.

Educational classes are offered evenings on a voluntary basis in the walled prisons and are incorporated into the work day in institutions for young offenders. Vocational training is usually carried out on the job.

For recreation some institutions have pleasant day rooms for indoor games, radio programs, and letter writing. Orchestras and bands, composed of staff and inmates, are organized in some institutions. Libraries are well stocked. Gymnasiums usually are included in the institutional facilities, and outdoor recreation yards are found in both walled and open institutions. Inmates may form clubs for hobbies or other special interests. In general each inmate may have his own small garden plot; he may eat what he raises and carry flowers into his cell. He is also allowed to carry on hobbies and, at least in some institutions, to have a pet.

Attendance at religious services in the institutional chapel is voluntary. Full-time chaplains are generally found on the staff and devote much time to counseling the inmates and their families.

Custody is adapted to the type of institution. The relationship between prison officers and inmates is nonpunitive and accepting. Officers treat prisoners with respect. Norman Fenton, in his visits to Danish prisons, observed that staff and inmates of an institution for young offenders shared a rest period and snack. Officers may also work with prisoners on menial jobs or at maintenance. Nevertheless, discipline and custody are maintained, sometimes by forceful methods in odd contrast to the relationships just noted. In several prisons, Fenton learned that police dogs accompany officers on patrol or are used to track down escapees. Discipline is enforced by fines paid by the prisoner from his earnings, isolation, denial of privileges, or a diet of bread and water for a limited number of days.

Institutions for young, first offenders permit greater freedom than do the walled prisons and emphasize counseling, education, and vocational training. Inmates accompanied by supervisors may visit certain community institutions, such as the theater, zoo, or beach. The relationship is friendly and permissive, a situation fostered by the small number of inmates in an institution (78 in one and 125 in another).

Release

The inmates' preparation for release begins with his entrance into prison. Therefore, only a few special sessions are held with inmates before they leave the prison. The counselor who has been in contact with the prisoner during his term often maintains this contact after release, thus providing continuity of a supportive relationship. The prisoner must have employment awaiting him and he is given the portion of his prison wages that was saved for him. Prior to release many prisoners are gradually reintegrated into the community through assignment to camps; working out by the day on private farms to which they go on bicycles without supervision; furloughs for job-hunting; or attendance at church or theater in civilian clothes. Although no one institution uses all these privileges and methods as preparation for release, the tendency is to allow as much freedom to as many inmates as possible in order to build up responsible community contacts before release.

Parole is supervised privately by trained social workers who are employed by the Danish Welfare Association, a private organization subsidized by the state. This association combines the functions of a prisoners' aid society, a parole agency, and a probation department. It also maintains 2 large farms for homeless parolees and 3 homes for probationers. The police also are co-operative and helpful to paroled prisoners who get into further minor difficulties.

Criminal Psychopaths

The most unusual aspect of the Danish prison system is the series of related institutions for male psychopaths developed by a psychiatrist, Dr. Georg K. Stürup.[25] Offenders are committed to these institutions on indeterminate sentences when their mental abnormalities do not justify commitment to a mental hospital but when it seems evident that the usual prison program will not reform them.

The chief institution is the Asylum for Criminal Psychopaths at Herstedvester, which houses 178 men and also operates an open unit for 29 inmates.* Another unit for about 200 men operates at the state prison at Horsens.

The objective of these institutions is not punishment but treatment and protection of society, since some men have committed serious crimes and there is reason to believe they might repeat them. The 2 most frequent crimes are theft and sexual offences, especially against children. The inmates are sent to the special units, however, not simply because they are criminals, but chiefly because they are also psychopathic.

Committed for an indefinite period, the inmates are held in secure custody in a walled area. Within the institution grounds, however, there are provisions for various degrees of freedom; for those who can accept increased freedom, transfer to the open unit is possible. From the open unit the inmate may be given day parole to work in the community.

The unique feature about the institution for psychopaths is the intensive, individual psychiatric treatment given each inmate and the supportive social program within the institution.

Living units are limited to 15 members, with each man assigned to a psychiatrist and a social worker who remain attached to the case until the man's release. Daily staff meetings are held to acquaint staff members in charge of prisoners with the particulars of each case and how daily problems should be handled. The attitudes of all who deal with the inmates is permissive and nonpunitive; otherwise the treatment would fail. Treatment is not forced on the inmate. He may remain in the institution for months without treatment, but as soon as he indicates his need and willingness to accept help, the psychiatrist steps into the picture.

A full day's work is regarded as an essential part of the program, motivated in part by the payment of small wages. At Herstedvester the work includes agriculture, printing, bookbinding, woodwork, toymaking, tailoring, and repair of buildings. The work, in addition to its current therapeutic value, prepares the inmates for employment after release.

Each man has an individual cell where he may carry on such hobbies as weaving or painting. He may keep birds or fish. Social life among the inmates is encouraged. The men play chess and bridge, have hobby clubs, such as stamp collecting, and put on short plays and skits. In the skits they often release tensions against judges or officials that they would not feel free

* The author was privileged to visit the Asylum at Herstedvester in the summer of 1953.

to release directly. There are also classes and, for those who wish them, correspondence courses.

As men become adjusted they are given increased freedom within the institution's walls and later in work assignments in the community or at the open farm unit. When they have been at the institution one year they may have an 8 hour furlough attended by a nonuniformed guard. At this time the inmate may visit his family, attend a movie, or apply for work.

Special provisions are contained in the laws covering sexual psychopaths, a group that includes those convicted of rape, indecent assaults on girls or boys, and exhibitionism. Castration is permitted for certain types of sexual psychopaths, and over a period of 22 years, 606 cases have been treated by castration. Although the law provides for compulsory castration, in practice all operations have followed written requests from the men to the Minister of Justice. Men under 25 years of age are not permitted to have this treatment. The man is helped to understand the effect that the operation will have on his life, and many accept the limitation it places on sexual activity in order to be freed from the possibility of recidivism of a sexual offense and consequent reincarceration. If the man is married, his wife must also consent to the operation. The man receives psychotherapy to help him adjust to his new status.

The usual length of stay at the Asylum at Herstedvester is 2 or 3 years; however, a few men who show no improvement have been there as long as 20 years. The judge who sentenced the man may release him on parole when he is ready for freedom. The parole, under supervision, lasts from 2 to 4 years.

Summary

Fenton, after careful observation of the institution at Herstedvester, came to the conclusion that the combined approach of psychiatrist, psychologist, and psychiatric social worker points the way to successful treatment, not alone of criminal psychopaths, but of all adult offenders.

SWEDEN

Administration

The Prison Administration, under the Department of Justice, has charge of all penal and correctional institutions.[26] An integrated national system therefore has been developed and is still in process of growth. Prison personnel are civil servants with secure tenure.

Principles

Like many other European countries, Sweden wholeheartedly adopted the Pennsylvania system of individual isolation of prisoners and in the 1840's built new prisons with individual cells to replace older congregate institutions. Gradually the period of isolation was reduced until, in the 1920's, it was 6 months for adult offenders and 3 months for young prisoners. Various modifications continued to be made until 1938 when a Penal Code Commission was appointed to study the entire situation thoroughly. In 1944 the commission submitted its report, upon which the present penal code is based. The code is not a complete break with the past but modifies and co-ordinates earlier practices.

The general principles for correctional treatment, as set forth in the report, make the protection of society the chief objective of penal practices. Protection is interpreted to mean not only relief from crime during the period of a criminal's incarceration but also preparation of the criminal for a responsible and law-abiding life after his release from prison. It is further stated that treatment should be humane and that, so far as is possible, prison life should resemble life in free society, with employment and useful occupation of leisure time.

Penalties and Prisons

Offenders are classified into types, for each of which specialized programs and institutions have been devised.

Imprisonment for nonpayment of fines because of poverty has been abolished. A system of day fines is used, whereby each offense calls for the payment of a fine for a given number of days. The amount of the fine, however, is adjusted to the income of the offender. The rich offender pays heavily per day; the laborer guilty of the same offense, only a small amount. Moreover, payments may be made on the installment plan. The offender who is able to pay but refuses, is sent to jail. Thus Sweden has made a realistic adjustment to the problem of inability to pay fines. The number of prisoners committed for nonpayment of fines dropped from 13,358 in 1932 to 286 in 1946.

Offenders between the ages of 18 and 21 are sentenced to youth prisons, institutions patterned after the English and Danish Borstals. In general an indeterminate sentence is given, with a maximum of 4 years. A new youth prison, opened at Roxtuna in 1954, introduced a reception center for the individual study of the 65 offenders who can be accommodated. Dangerous offenders are segregated in units behind wire fences, whereas others are grouped in housing units of 9 inmates each. Considerable freedom is al-

Types of Penalties

Two degrees of offenses are recognized: misdemeanors, which may result in imprisonment up to 3 months; and felonies, which carry imprisonment for more than 3 months.* Most cases of misdemeanors are handled without a court trial. The police officer makes a written charge against the offender, stating the crime and a certain fine (with a subsidiary term of imprisonment if the fine is not paid). If the offender agrees, this "contract" has the same effect as a court sentence. If he refuses to agree, the police must drop the charge or bring the case before a court. The wide acceptance of the "contracts" is shown by the fact that in 1950, 38,474 misdemeanor cases were settled in this way, whereas only 3,435 cases were taken to court. There is no consistent attempt to adjust the fines to the income of the offender, as in Sweden. When the subsidiary prison term is served (it may be as short as 24 hours), the prisoner may choose to shorten the time by accepting imprisonment on bread and water, since one day of this type of punishment is counted as equivalent to 3 days of straight imprisonment. The limitation to bread and water may not be imposed for more than 20 consecutive days. This retention of a medieval type of punishment is used mostly in cases involving intoxication.

Felonies are handled in a number of different ways. Most lenient of methods comes when the offender admits his guilt and prosecution is waived, without the formality of a trial. For one fifth of male offenders and slightly more than one third of female offenders prosecution is waived. These offenders usually are young first offenders primarily guilty of theft, or older offenders against whom the prosecuting attorney has so strong a case that conviction seems certain. Young offenders often are handed over to the Child Welfare Boards, which assume charge of juvenile delinquents outside the jurisdiction of the courts. The older offenders may be placed on probation for 2 years.

Offenders who are tried in the courts may be given a conditional sentence (probation), fined, or sentenced to prison. Twenty per cent of women felons and 39 per cent of men were imprisoned in 1950. First offenders, youthful offenders, and those guilty of small thefts are most likely to be given conditional sentences, while the older, more serious offenders and recidivists find their way into prison.

Prison sentences may be as short as 21 days or as long as life. In practice the terms are short: for 1949–50, 39 per cent of felons were given sentences of 90 days or less, 32 per cent between 90 days and 6 months, and 18 per

---

* Note that in the United States the dividing line between a misdemeanor and a felony usually is imprisonment of one year or more.

cent from 6 months to 1 year; only 10 per cent received sentences of more than 1 year.   Sentences are for stated periods of time, but it is customary to release the prisoner after he has served two thirds of his sentence and a criminal with a life sentence is held not more than 20 years.   The death penalty is not used for civil crimes; it is reserved for high treason and certain war crimes.

Sentences up to 6 months are served in district prisons; longer sentences in state prisons.*

Special Types of Offenders

Certain classes of offenders are singled out for special attention.   Persons who commit crimes while insane, intoxicated, because of mental defects, or when unconscious of their acts cannot be punished.   If it is probable that they may repeat their crimes because of a continuation or recurrence of any of these conditions, protective measures may be instituted and the offenders may be placed under supervision for the protection of society.   The person may be (1) assigned to a certain place of residence, which he may not leave without a permit, or forbidden to visit certain places; (2) placed under supervision; (3) forbidden to use intoxicating beverages; (4) placed in an asylum, hospital, or workhouse; or (5) sentenced to prison.   The court's decision regarding protective measures rests in part upon prior psychiatric study of the offender.   Since 1945, Norway has had a special institution near Oslo (Ila Sikringsanstalt) for persons sentenced to protective measures.   Understaffing prevents the full measure of treatment needed and the institution therefore tends to resemble a prison.   It does make it possible, however, to remove from the prisons some of the more troublesome inmates, such as psychopaths and those with nervous disorders.

Prolonged custody may be instituted against habitual criminals whose crimes are a serious menace to the public, such as rape, some sexual crimes against minors, assault, homicide, grand larceny, and robbery.   Custody may be maintained at the court's discretion, usually for 3 to 5 years (a lengthy sentence for Norway).   Since the state has not provided a special institution for these offenders, the measure is not used extensively.

The protective measures and the prolonged custody are the most severe sentences that can be given in Norway.   Since they may be prolonged or renewed, these devices make it possible to institutionalize a person for his entire life, in the interest of protection of society.   In 1950, 4 males were sentenced to prolonged custody and 112 males and 7 females to protective measures, primarily in supervised places of residence or on farms.

* The author's personal observations of certain prisons are given later in this section, together with illustrations.

Another troublesome group that does not fall clearly into the class of criminals is composed of able-bodied vagrants who are a burden to society or who beg for a living, and chronic alcoholics who are a public nuisance.

These people usually have a long history of fines and of unsuccessful treatment at clinics for alcoholics, and are well known to relief agencies. They may be sentenced by a court to 18 months' labor on a farm (Opstad tvangsarbeidshus, Jären), with a sentence of 3 years for a second offense. The institution is unable to restore these people with its present program and has many recidivists.

Application for castration or sterilization may be made by a sexual offender to a board composed primarily of medical and legal members, the application being made by the person involved or, if the person is mentally incompetent, by his guardian, a prison director, or the chief of police. Permission for the operation is granted only after careful consideration and as a last resort. In a 15 year period 102 operations were performed upon criminals, only one of whom has become a recidivist in 4 or more years since the operation. From a criminological point of view, the operation is considered successful; but attendant psychological problems have not all been solved.

Although the movement toward change in treatment of offenders in Norway is slow, it is in the direction of more individualized treatment. The attitude that crime must necessarily be paid for by punishment and hard labor is changing toward acceptance of rehabilitation. Nevertheless, Norwegian penologists tend to be conservative and change comes slowly.

Women's State Prison and House of Correction, Oslo *

Four women criminals and 20 vagrants, gathered from various parts of Norway, occupied the women's institution that combines prison and house of correction when the author visited Oslo in the summer of 1953. Most of the vagrants were prostitutes of long standing who had been sentenced to 6 or more months of imprisonment. The two groups of inmates were separated at work and in their various activities—a policy that reduced the possibilities for group activities for the 4 criminals.

The plant dates from 1930, when it was built for boys. In 1940 the women prisoners occupied it, but soon vacated it for the political prisoners who were placed there during World War II. After the end of the war, the women again were placed there. The prison consists of a number of large buildings, in grounds surrounded by a wire fence topped with barbed wire. Although the first impression is of an institution with barren sur-

---

* This and the following prison descriptions are the result of observation and conversations by the author.

roundings, actually there are many amenities and a genuine effort to help the women during the short time they are institutionalized.

Individual sleeping rooms open off a long corridor, and, except for the barred windows, have nothing to suggest a prison.   They are simply furnished.   Each floor also has a small sitting room with gaily checked chair

This snowy scene shows the women's prison and house of correction at Oslo. Note that the grounds are enclosed only by a wire fence.

At the women's prison and house of correction, Oslo, a small living room on each floor provides for group gatherings where the inmates may play games, sing, talk, or do handwork—sometimes joined by members of the staff.   The large and intricately designed doily upon which one woman is working indicates the many hours spent in such handwork as well as the encouragement given to the production of useful and handsome articles.

covers and tablecloth.   Each woman is locked into her room when not at work or in the sitting room.   Since there is no institutional dining room, the women eat alone in their rooms.

As is customary in European prisons, work is provided for all.   In small workshops with women supervisors the inmates sew for the police department, knit men's socks on small hand-operated machines, and weave rugs and toweling.

A large, immaculate building contains a large all-purpose room and a

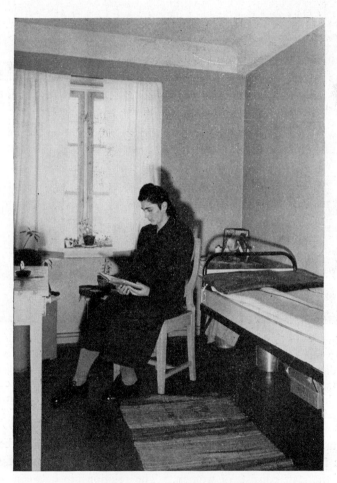

This room at the women's prison and house of correction, Oslo, is simply but adequately furnished.   The austerity of barred windows and plain walls is broken by the photograph on the stand at the foot of the bed, the curtains and small rug, and the potted plants.   The type of furnishings, the neatness and cleanliness equal similar qualities in the American reformatory room shown on page 507.

chapel.   The all-purpose room is used for recreational purposes, although a separate building is also soon to be remodeled for recreation.   Volunteer groups from Oslo visit the prison for recreational activities with the inmates. At Christmas a tree is decorated, and at the time of the writer's visit the inmates were carefully tending 3 pigs that were destined to form the main course of a Christmas feast.

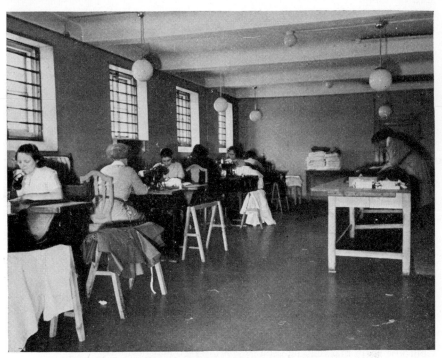

The sewing room in the women's prison and house of correction, Oslo, is well lighted by many windows and ceiling lights.   Note the bars on the windows. An attendant in uniform is at the long work table and another is working at the second machine from the left.   This shop for a small prison may be compared with the large sewing room at the Federal Reformatory for Women in West Virginia, shown on page 516.

The staff numbers almost as many as the inmates—19.   With the exception of a few men who work on the grounds and have no contact with the inmates, the staff consists of women.   The relationship between the staff, including the superintendent, and the inmates seemed to be relaxed and easy.   The inmates acknowledged the difference in status, however, by springing to their feet as soon as the superintendent entered a room where they were working.   Discipline is handled quietly: the superintendent talks to the woman, or she is deprived of some privilege.   When these measures fail, the inmate is placed in a solitary room until she quiets down. Constructive measures are also used. The games and conversation in the sitting rooms, the recreation, and the parties are significant; in these activities staff members join the inmates on a friendly basis.

The chapel at the women's prison and house of correction, Oslo, is a beautiful spot with handsome chandeliers, mural by Maria Vigeland, famed Norwegian church decorator, and altar and pulpit cloths designed by the same artist and embroidered by inmates. Separated from the chapel by sliding doors is an all-purpose room that may be used for parties or other meetings.

Local Prison, Oslo

The local prison visited in Oslo receives men and women offenders serving sentences of less than 6 months. With 200 men and 28 women, the prison had many empty cells. Rebuilt from a brewery in the 1930's, the prison provides each inmate with an individual room measuring about 10 by 15 feet. A barred window separates him from the outside world and a solid wooden door from communication with other inmates. He sleeps, eats, and works in his cell, the food being passed in to him through a small opening in the door; the opening has a covering that can be bolted shut from the outside. The women are housed in one wing of the prison under the same conditions as the men.

In the event that this regime seems severe to the reader, it should be remembered that equal isolation is found in various American prisons and jails, in strange contrast to the community type of living found in others, where dormitories are provided or cells with barred fronts prevent any privacy.   It was in this Norwegian prison that a guard, in reply to a comment about the isolation, stated that he did not believe Norwegians would like the lack of privacy found in United States prisons.

Prison for Long Term Male Offenders, Oslo

Built in the 1850's, the prison for long-term offenders at Oslo is basically isolationist in program and cannot be otherwise because of the physical construction of the prison.   The individual cells are similar to those described for the local prison.   Exercise is limited to solitary walking around a worn path in a small wedge-shaped yard enclosed with a high brick wall.   A num-

In Oslo stands the central prison that receives men from all parts of Norway who are serving sentences of 6 months or more.   Built in the 1850's it has vestiges of provisions for daily solitary confinement in individual exercise yards, stalls in the chapel, and lack of recreation and dining rooms.   However, the prison also uses many modern methods of rehabilitation, such as work shops and occupations in cells.   The prison also operates a farm that is completely unwalled.   Assignment to the farm is used both as a reward for good behavior and for therapeutic purposes.

ber of exercise yards fanned out from the circular end of the prison, thus making it possible for a number of men to exercise in isolation at one time. The men are required to walk for the entire exercise period—they may not stand still nor sit down. The chapel retains the solitary cells or stalls that were adopted from the Pennsylvania system; each man occupies a narrow stall with solid wooden sides, a roof, a half door in front, and a small bench inside to sit on.

The woodwork shop at the men's penitentiary in Oslo provides one of several occupations. The piles of shavings suggest that the prisoners have been only momentarily withdrawn to permit the photograph to be taken. A machine shop is also operated, and toys may be made in the cells.

In contrast to the high degree of cellular isolation imposed by the old structure of the prison are large carpentry and machine shops where numbers of men work together, using modern machinery. (The men also make toys, mats, and other small articles in their cells, from the sale of which they receive money for tobacco and other commodities.) Also in contrast to the isolated living is the freedom allowed on the prison farm, an unwalled institution.

The inmates have medical and psychiatric service, although badly disturbed prisoners are sent to special institutions for the criminal insane.

Summary

Norway impresses the visitor as a country whose leaders in penology have adopted a policy of rehabilitation.   Development of new methods is hindered, however, by the conservatism of other groups.   Also, construction of new prisons is prevented by the pressure of more urgent financial demands during the post war period.

PENOLOGICAL COMPARISONS

Although the comparison of types of offenders given in the first part of this chapter showed many similarities, a comparison of prisons and treatment tends to show marked contrasts between European countries and the United States.

Administration

The general European pattern is centralized national control, which has the same advantages found in the United States Federal Bureau of Prisons. All penal institutions, including local prisons or jails, are integrated into one system, which can be adjusted to the segregation and specialized treatment of many types of offenders.

Another advantage of centralized control is that a progressive prison administration can press for legislation to bring the entire national prison system to a higher level.   In the United States progress is piecemeal and a state with an excellent prison system may be adjacent to one that uses century old penology.   On the other hand, of course, a conservative or indifferent central administration can impede the progress of the entire country.   In the United States, an individual state can experiment with new methods and perhaps become a model for other states.

In any discussion of centralized control it must be recalled that in size and population many European countries are comparable to some of our individual states, and that there is more uniformity of culture than in the United States.   More complete centralization at the state level, in some instances regional administration, and a raising of professional standards are, however, needed in many parts of the United States.

Appointments to the prison administration are made from the Crown or the national governing body for indefinite periods of time.   Appointments in individual prisons are on a competitive or ability basis.   In other words, there is no evidence of the kind of political appointments that prevail in many parts of the United States, where, with a new governor—especially of the opposing party—the heads and often the staff of state prisons are changed overnight, with the new appointees often no better qualified for their duties than were those dismissed for belonging to the deposed political party. The nonpolitical appointments give greater security of tenure, attract people with some interest in the work and encourage staff training.

In some European countries police, jails, and local prisons are under the national administration with all the advantages of high uniform standards, supervision, professional control, and integration into the prison system that the United States generally lacks where jails are concerned.

Size of Prisons

The European countries under consideration lack the mammoth prisons that some states built and have found almost unmanageable without the most rigid supervision and discipline.[27] Only 2 English prisons have accommodations for more than 1,000 prisoners and only 1 of the 2 actually houses more than 1,000 prisoners. Most of the institutions—local and national prisons and Borstals—are built for less than 500 inmates. Although the local prisons are overcrowded, with some 4,500 sleeping 3 to a cell, all the prisons for major criminals that operate on a regional or national basis have fewer prisoners than cells. Plans have been made to relieve the local overcrowding by the building of new prisons for approximately 500 inmates each. In other words, a degree of overcrowding that in the United States would be accepted without comment is regarded as cause for new buildings in England.

Of 12 Danish prisons listed by Fenton, the range in capacity is from 29 to 550, with 7 having capacity for less than 200 inmates each. Few of the prisons in 1952 were filled to capacity.

Although exact figures on individual prison capacity or population cannot be given for other countries, descriptions of prisons and personal observations indicate that usually prisons are limited to a few hundred inmates and are not filled to capacity.

In many instances prisons for several hundred prisoners are classified into smaller units, each with its own living quarters within the prison and its own staff. The small units enable the staff to work personally with the prisoners—a procedure impossible in our large penal institutions. On the other hand, some European prisons are so small that efficient administration and staffing are impossible. Sweden is meeting this situation through regional grouping of prisons, which permits the personal contacts between staff and inmates to continue, and at the same time provides for over-all administration and the provision of special services, such as psychiatric, on a regional basis.

In the United States the tendency has been to meet the increasing numbers of prisoners that automatically occur with increasing population by building larger and larger prisons, thus decreasing the opportunities for staff to know inmates personally and the possibilities for organizing prisoners into small groups. Rigidity and formality, with little opportunity for rehabilitation, have been the result.

Sentences

The statement is often made that sentences in Europe are much shorter than the sentences in the United States. A fair comparison is difficult to make, however. In the countries reviewed in this chapter, local prisons serving the functions of United States jails are part of the national system and in the reports available it was usually not possible to distinguish between sentences given to minor offenders in the local prisons and to major offenders in regional or national prisons. In the United States the thousands of misdemeanants sentenced to jails receive sentences of less than one year, often of only a few weeks or months. If jail and prison sentences could be combined, the median term of imprisonment in the United States would also be very short.

When reports permit a comparison of sentences for felonies abroad and in the United States, there is some indication of shorter sentences in Europe. In Norway, for example, the median sentence for felonies is about 4 months and only 1 per cent of the sentences is longer than 6 years.[28]

However, European countries give long sentences to habitual criminals placed in preventive detention. In Denmark, in 1950, 566 prisoners received sentences of more than 1 year (comparable to our felony sentences), of whom only 22 or 4 per cent were sentenced to 4 or more years. However, an additional 119 offenders were given indeterminate sentences to preventive detention.[29]   These offenders are the persistent criminals and troublemakers. The minimum sentence for preventive detention is 4 years on a first conviction or 8 years on a second, with a possible maximum of 20 years. The average term is 7 years 7 months. In the United States such offenders would be included among the general run of criminals. When the preventive detainees are added to other prisoners in Denmark to make a total of 685 offenders with sentences of 1 or more years, 22 per cent receive sentences of 4 or more years. The actual situation in Denmark seems to be a concentration of short sentences among minor, first, and occasional offenders, and a concentration of long sentences among recidivists.

In England a somewhat similar situation appears.[30]   In 1951, for the average run of prisoners sentenced to more than 1 year, the median was approximately 20 months, and very few received sentences of more than 5 years.   For those assigned to corrective training, sentences must be between 2 and 4 years; in practice over half in 1951 were serving sentences of 3 or 4 years.   Preventive detainees (persistent recidivists) serve not less than 5 nor more than 14 years; in 1951 the median was 8 years.   Although short sentences are prevalent among the great majority of prisoners, the recalcitrant and persistent offenders are subjected to long terms.

Similarly, in other European countries short sentences are liberally given to first or minor offenders, whereas recidivists receive long sentences, served often in special detention institutions.

The short terms have the advantage of preventing institutionalization of prisoners but sometimes have the disadvantage of being so short that rehabilitation is impossible.   The United States too often metes out a long sentence but fails to provide adequately for rehabilitation, or for the termination of the sentence at the point where maximum change has occurred in the prisoner.

Fines and conditional release with suspended sentences or probation are widely used in Europe.   Sweden, in particular, has evolved a system of equating fines to income and accepting payments on the installment plan; only those who refuse to pay are imprisoned.   Much overcrowding of the United States jails comes from imprisoning persons unable (not unwilling) to pay fines.   Sweden's method unclogs the jails, saves money that the state would pay for the maintenance of prisoners, and also makes possible the collection of the fines.

Isolation vs Congregate Living

The struggle between complete cellular isolation and congregate living, at least during the day, which wore itself out in the United States a century ago—with modified congregate living the victor—is at the present still active in Europe.   With newer methods of treatment and recognition of the necessity for communal adjustment, isolation is breaking down in European prisons, where limited group contacts within the prison are cautiously being introduced.

Often a stated number of months at the beginning of a sentence must be served in isolation, with the result that prisoners with short terms often sit out the entire term behind a locked and solid door, whose surface is broken only by a small peephole.   Progressively, the long term prisoner moves toward more and more contact with other prisoners.   Newer prisons, and especially those for young offenders, may have dormitories and complete congregate living at the same time that other prisons in the same system continue to impose isolation.

In general social contacts among prisoners are more widely permitted in United States prisons than in European prisons, some of which still use small exercise yards where the only form of recreation consists of prisoners walking alone or in pairs around and around the yard on paths worn smooth by many prisoner feet over many years of time. Team games and group recreation are little used. The older prisons do not have dining rooms; each prisoner eats in his cell; only fearfully are some prisons experimenting with congregate eating.

It might be said that European prisons are still basically isolationist in attitude, while United States prisons have become basically group-minded, with isolation only for the troublemakers. Old American prisons, to be sure, sometimes make inadequate provision for group activities, but as new prisons replace old, provisions for social contacts are improved, with the women's reformatories providing a reasonably normal method of living.

Attitudes

In many European prisons the attitudes of guards and other staff members toward prisoners is in marked contrast to the attitudes typical of many United States prisons, although not of the smaller institutions that emphasize correction and rehabilitation. In the prisons visited by the author (in Norway, Denmark, and France), the relationships between staff and prisoners were relaxed and nonpunitive. Fenton in his visits to European prisons received the same impression.[31] He offers several possible explanations. Prisoners do not differ in appearance, name, race, language, or cultural attitudes from police, judges, or prison staff. Therefore, prejudices based on such differences do not complicate the staff-prisoner relationship.

Crime is accepted objectively, as a problem to be solved—much as one would accept chronic illness or an epidemic. The small size of prisons also enables the staff to know the prisoners and reduces the need for regimentation.

This attitude of acceptance does not carry over into lack of orderliness or disrespect of prisoners toward the staff. Prisoners are expected to follow through on their daily routines and to show respect for staff members (for example, to stand when a prison officer enters the workshop). Nevertheless, the atmosphere is democratic, nonpunitive, and understanding of the problems of prisoners.

SIGNIFICANT PROCEDURES

Many features of European prisons could be applied to United States prisons.

Furloughs

Short furloughs, either with an officer or unattended, are used in many European prisons. In the United States all except 6 states provide short furloughs in case of severe family illness or a funeral of a close relative.[32] In a few states, selected prisoners who have demonstrated good behavior over a period of several years are allowed to visit their families for a few days at long intervals, and a few states give day furloughs to permit prisoners to work in the community during the day.

In Europe, short furloughs to visit relatives or to secure a job before release or the day furlough for work are more widely used and are regarded as part of the treatment plan.   The furloughs help maintain family contacts and establish community work relationships while the prisoner is still under official control.   The furloughs also test the prisoner's responsibility for control of his personal behavior while away from supervision.   The day furloughs for work are especially useful in giving an opportunity to earn money as well as to gain genuine work experience.

In the United States prison officials are deterred by many fears: that the prisoners on furlough will escape, commit new crimes, become intoxicated, be arrested for disorderly conduct, arouse the antagonism of local police, plot future escapes, or bring contraband articles into the prison.[33]   The warden fears that such events, if they happened, would bring disrepute upon him or create disciplinary problems.   European prisons have not experienced these problems nor have the few United States prisons that permit short furloughs.   Attempted escapes are few and many values accrue to the prisoners.

Visitors

Visitors to inmates at the prison help to maintain contacts with normal community life.   United States prisons allow a limited number of visits per month from approved persons, with the conversation usually carried on through a closely screened window that prevents any physical contact or passing of articles back and forth.   Some institutions permit prison trusties to meet visitors in a supervised lounge where they may sit comfortably and talk.   A few, notably in Florida and California, have a supervised picnic ground where responsible prisoners may join their families for picnics. United States prisons have not systematically provided for nonfamily visitors nor for recreational community contacts.

England, by way of contrast, has a national organization of prison visitors.

Work

Much of the work in Europe, as here, is for state use only.   However, in some countries prisoners are put on contract work from the outside or articles that they make are sold on the open market.   Thus the problem of idle prisoners is reduced.   In none of the prisons visited by the writer and in none described by Fenton was there a tendency to force prisoners to speed up in their work.   The speed of working seemed to be normal.   In contrast to American prisons, which emphasize machine work and communal working conditions, prisons in Europe often use handwork that can be carried on in the cells, thus increasing isolation.   Payment seems more liberal in European than in United States prisons.   Maintenance work is paid for as well as work that actually brings a cash return to the prison.   When the amount earned is adequate, prisoners are encouraged to send money to their families, thus imposing some of the normal community responsibilities upon the prisoners.

Special Groups

Although the United States prides itself on the progress made not only in classification of prisoners into groups for special institutions, but also in individual classification, certain groups have not been singled out as in Europe. Europe tends to regard certain troublesome offenders not as criminals to be punished but as social menaces to be detained for long periods and retrained if possible.   The preventive detention of habitual criminals who seem unable to respond either to punishment or treatment is one method of dealing with recidivists.   Sex offenders whose difficulty is basically maladjustment similarly receive special attention that centers around psychiatric treatment.

CROSS-FERTILIZATION

This brief survey of certain European prison systems shows the common cultural roots for these countries and the United States, the earlier diffusion of principles and procedures, and the persistence of early policies and practices.   World War II created new problems and in the rebirth of social reform in the post war period, one European country after another reformulated its system of justice and penal practices.   The objective now is rehabilitation; each country is engaged in a building program and in revision of prison procedures.   Experiments are underway.   The United States is undergoing a similar process.   The cultural backgrounds of the United States and Europe are sufficiently compatible to make cross-fertilization of ideas a fruitful possibility for all the countries.

QUESTIONS

1. Give examples of cross-fertilization of principles or methods in penology between the United States and Europe; what further exchanges might be fruitful to either side of the Atlantic?

2. Discuss the problems of the minor offender in different countries.

3. What system of control is used in European countries for habitual offenders? How does their system differ from our treatment?

4. Discuss the salient points of the treatment of the criminal psychopath in Denmark.   In the light of Danish success in this field, what modifications might be suggested for the United States?

5. Compare policies on work for prisoners in the United States and Europe. What methods might be exchanged to the advantage of both areas?

6. Why have prisons in the United States gone further than European prisons in expanding recreational programs and sports?   Which approach seems sounder from the point of view of rehabilitation?

READINGS

General

The following suggestions are made for students who may wish to read about penology in other countries than the ones touched upon in this chapter.

Cornil, Paul, "Prison Reform in Belgium since the War," *Annals of the American Academy of Political and Social Science,* 293 (1954), 130–38.

Morris, Norval, *The Habitual Criminal* (Cambridge: Harvard University Press, published for the London School of Economics and Political Science, University of London, 1951).   A comparative study of the habitual criminal in a number of countries, but with the most thorough treatment given to England.

Mueller, G. O. W., "Resocialization of the Young Adult Offender in Switzerland," *Journal of Criminal Law, Criminology, and Police Science,* 43 (1952–53), 578–91.

Sethna, M. J., *Society and the Criminal* (Bombay, India: Leaders' Press, Ltd., 1952).   Intermingled with discussion of criminological theories are accounts of crime and penology in India, including some information on the criminal tribes.

Sutherland, H., "Spanish Penal System," *19th Century,* 143 (Jan., 1948), 38–45; (June, 1948), 316–23.

Teeters, Negley K., *World Penal Systems, A Survey* (Philadelphia: Pennsylvania Prison Society, 1944).   Limited to pre-World War II, this book nevertheless gives good background material for more recent accounts of prison systems the world over.

———, *Penology from Panama to Cape Horn* (Philadelphia: University of Pennsylvania Press, 1946).   An account of South American penology.

Winterburg, D. E., "Penal Institutions in Korea," *Prison World,* 10 (July–August, 1948), 29–33.

England

Fox, Lionel W., *The English Prison and Borstal Systems* (London: Routledge and Kegan Paul, Ltd., 1952; sold in the United States by Grove Press, New York).

———, "English Prisons since the War," *Annals of the American Academy of Political and Social Science,* 293 (1954), 119–29.

Healy, William, and Benedict Alper, *Criminal Youth and the Borstal System* (New York: Commonwealth Fund, 1941).

Patterson, Alexander, "The Prison Visitor in England," *Jail Association Journal,* 2 (Jan.–Feb., 1940), 10–11, 43.

France

Germain, Charles, "Postwar Prison Reform in France," *Annals of the American Academy of Political and Social Science,* 293 (1954), 139–51.

Denmark

Fenton, Norman, *Observations of the Correctional System of Denmark* (Sacramento, California: Department of Corrections, State of California, 1954).

Norway

The author failed to find up-to-date accounts of Norwegian penology published in English.

FOOTNOTES

1 Harry E. Barnes and Negley K. Teeters, *New Horizons in Criminology* (2nd ed. Prentice-Hall, 1951), pp. 385–90. In the course of their historical discussion, Barnes and Teeters give many illustrations of cross-fertilization of principles and practices among different countries.

2 Home Office, *Report of the Commissioners of Prisons for the Year 1951* (London: Her Majesty's Stationery Office, 1952), pp. 147–49.

3 Norman Fenton, *Observations of the Correctional System of Denmark* (Sacramento, California: Department of Corrections, State of California, 1954), p. 11.

4 Knut Sveri, *Nature of the Criminal Law and Treatment of Adult Offenders in Norway* (unpublished manuscript).

5 Torsten Eriksson, "Postwar Prison Reform in Sweden," *Annals of the American Academy of Political and Social Science,* 293 (1954), 154–55.

6 B. Ahrnborg, "Betting on Football Matches in Sweden," *Annals of the American Academy of Political and Social Science,* 269 (1950), 144–49.

7 Fenton, *op. cit.,* p. 27.

8 Fenton, *op. cit.*

9 Home Office, *Report of the Commissioners of Prisons for the Year 1951,* p. 149; S. H. Steinberg, editor, *The Statesman's Yearbook for the Year 1952* (London: Macmillan, 1952), p. 961; Fenton, *op. cit.,* p. 11; Sveri, *op. cit.;* Eriksson, *op. cit.* p. 155.

10 Home Office, *Report of the Commissioners of Prisons for the Year 1951,* pp. 150–51.

11 *Ibid.,* pp. 152–55.

12 Fenton, *op. cit.,* p. 18; Sveri, *op. cit.*

13 Most of the material on English prisons is drawn from Home Office, *Report of the Commissioners of Prisons for the Year 1951.*

14 N. K. Teeters, "The Prison Systems of England," *Journal of Criminal Law and Criminology,* 41 (1951), 578–89.

15 A. Patterson, "The Prison Visitor in England," *Jail Association Journal,* 2 (Jan.–Feb., 1940), 10–11, 43; Home Office, *Report of the Commissioners of Prisons for the Year 1951,* pp. 50–51.

16 *Directory of Probation Officers, Probation Homes and Hostels, Remand Homes, Home Office Schools and Borstal Institutions, 1947,* quoted by Hanne-Marie Tjensvoll, *Child Welfare and Juvenile Delinquency in the United Kingdom* (Oslo, 1950), p. 129.

17 Home Office, *Report of the Commissioners of Prisons for the Year 1951,* pp. 65–70.

[18] *Report of the Committee on Discharged Prisoners' Aid Societies* (London: Her Majesty's Stationery Office, 1953).

[19] Lionel W. Fox, *The English Prison and Borstal Systems* (London: Routledge and Kegan Paul, Ltd., 1952; sold in the United States by Grove Press, New York).

[20] Blair Niles, *Condemned to Devil's Island* (London: Jonathan Cape, Ltd., 1928); René Belbenoit, *Dry Guillotine* (Dutton, 1938).

[21] Charles Germain, "Postwar Prison Reform in France," *Annals of the American Academy of Political and Social Science,* 293 (1954), 139–51; —— *Le Traitement des Récidivistes en France* (Paris: Prison Administration, Department of Justice, 1953). Steinberg, *op. cit.,* pp. 960–61.

[22] Germain, "Postwar Prison Reform in France."

[23] *Notice sur la Maison Centrale de Melun* (Melun, France, 1950).

[24] Most of the material about Danish prisons is drawn from Fenton, *op. cit.*

[25] Fenton, *op. cit.,* chapters 10, 11, 12; Louis le Maire and Georg K. Stürup, *The Treatment of Psychically Abnormal Delinquents at Herstedvester* (Herstedvester, Denmark: Asylum for Criminal Psychopaths, 1950); personal visit to Herstedvester by the author, 1953.

[26] The material on Sweden is variously drawn from the following 3 references and from a visit to Sweden in 1953. Eriksson, *op. cit.;* Thorsten Sellin, *Recent Penal Legislation in Sweden* (Stockholm, Sweden: Isaac Marcus Boktryckeri-Aktiebolag, 1947); —— "The Treatment of Mentally Abnormal Offenders in Sweden," chapter 12 of *Vårdorganisation för Förvarade och Internerade* (Stockholm, Sweden: K. L. Berkmans Boktryckeri, 1953).

[27] Home Office, *Report of the Commissioners of Prisons for the Year 1951,* pp. 1, 134–36; Fenton, *op. cit.,* p. 127.

[28] Sveri, *op. cit.*

[29] Fenton, *op. cit.,* p. 19.

[30] Home Office, *Report of the Commissioners of Prisons for the Year 1951,* pp. 16–17, 34, 36.

[31] Fenton, *op. cit.,* ch. 4.

[32] *Handbook on the Inmate's Relationship with Persons from Outside the Adult Correctional Institution* (New York: American Prison Association, 1953) ch. 5.

[33] *Ibid.,* p. 55.

24

Trends and Future Objectives

The survey of criminal justice and penal institutions provided in Part Two exposes a system grounded in an outmoded philosophy of rational choice and deterrent punishment; organized by small geographical units; permeated with political graft; and tolerated by indifferent public opinion. Nevertheless, the slow ferment of change has begun to work. Here and there, in individual institutions, or in an occasional state penal system, current theories of criminal causation and rehabilitation are finding their counterpart in specialized personnel and a new type of program. The change is observable, also, in the writings of both theoretical and practical criminologists. For some years now, leaders in the fields of law, police administration, penal treatment, parole, and probation have urged the need for rehabilitation of offenders and a reorganization of courts and penal systems to effect it.

Part Two covered each phase of the criminal's treatment in detail. As the police, court procedures and officials, penal institutions, probation, and parole were discussed, criticisms, limitations, and suggestions for changes in each system were included. The task now remaining is to draw together these specific criticisms into a general summary; to determine trends of change in thought and practice; and to seek future objectives.

CHANGES IN POINT OF VIEW

The basic change in point of view destroys the conception of criminal behavior as deliberate or wilful. Crime is now recognized as human conduct that differs from conventional conduct primarily in that it is disapproved by the dominant and lawmaking social group. It develops as other conduct develops—by interaction of the individual with other persons or groups. Its purpose is the same—to satisfy human needs. In general, criminal behavior follows one of two lines of development.

1. Criminality consists of habits of thought and action that grow out of group affiliations and are associated with loyalty to the group. Examples are the offenses of the gang boy, the professional criminal, the member of a gang, the racketeer, the corrupt politician, or the white-collar criminal. The processes involved seem to be the same as those that go into the making of the well-behaved boy or girl, or the responsible man or woman. But the content of learning is nonconforming, criminal attitudes and habits instead of law-abiding codes of behavior.

2. In other cases crime is the effort of someone temporarily distraught to solve a practical problem; or of someone chronically disorganized to relieve himself of inner emotional tensions. The distraught person may be illustrated by the episodic criminal or some occasional criminals who face a difficult practical problem that they do not know how to handle. In fear, panic, or anger they overstep the bounds of responsible conduct, and commit theft, assault, or murder. The chronically disorganized—a small proportion of all major criminals but a large proportion of misdemeanants—include both the mentally disturbed person whose crime has some symbolic meaning and the unorganized or immature individual who drifts into vagrancy or alcoholism. Many of the difficulties of these two groups arise because they are unable to meet the social expectations of the community they live in.

Criminal behavior, therefore, is closely allied with the failure of society to meet social and personal needs of people and with the presence of criminal groups and criminal patterns of conduct. The indifference and tolerance of society in general and of the local community in particular are largely responsible for the development of personal stresses and strains and for the existence of criminal modes of conduct, in which individuals may seek satisfaction for such varied needs and interests as the desire for food, shelter, companionship, social recognition, dominance, sexual expression, revenge, and release from fear or emotional tension. Crime must be recognized as a social and community issue as well as a personal problem.

Criminal conduct is also no longer considered a unitary act performed by a special type of individual, called the criminal. There is no one type of conduct that may be called criminal and no one type of personality that can be designated as criminal. Rather, there are many kinds of conduct that are violations of criminal laws, performed by many sorts of persons from a variety of motives.

This approach to crime as a socially learned, personally motivated, and varied type of behavior leads to several conclusions:

1. Since criminal behavior is a response to special social contacts or frustrations, it may be prevented from developing by removal of criminal

patterns of conduct on the one hand and of frustrating situations on the other.   In place of these destructive factors, society needs to develop constructive agencies directed toward specific problems.   Such a program is difficult to inaugurate, as it cannot be carried out by grafting a few new agencies upon the community but involves a reconstruction of the community itself.

2. Since criminal habits are learned, they may be modified or replaced by law-abiding habits through a process of retraining.   When criminality is in response to an emotional drive, it may be modified by uncovering and healing the emotional disturbance underlying the criminal acts.   Whatever the type of crime a specific program of rehabilitation is required.

3. Since the successful treatment of criminals is rehabilitative, there is little place for punishment unless it is incorporated into a general and integrated program of rehabilitation.

4. Since crime results from various motives and criminals are not all of the same personality type, individualized treatment is necessary.

Turning now from theory to practice, we shall consider trends and objectives of preventive and rehabilitative programs and their administration.   We must also discuss the relation of the community to these programs and some of the barriers to their achievement.

PREVENTION OF CRIME

Prevention has been thoroughly discussed in Chapter 10.   Two general points may be re-emphasized: the preventive attack must come from many angles—schools, homes, recreational groups, clinics, and other specialized agencies.   All the efforts of these organizations should be co-ordinated in order to close as many loopholes as possible.

REHABILITATION AND TREATMENT

Identification of Potential Offenders

Among children progress has been made in identifying those who are potential offenders before their conduct becomes sufficiently serious to be called criminal or even delinquent.   We use the terms "problem children" and "predelinquents" to describe these boys and girls.   Parents, teachers, social workers, other professional persons, or interested friends bring these children to the attention of child guidance clinics when such clinics are provided by the community.   There is no corresponding service for the adult, who consequently may hover on the edge of criminal behavior for a long time.   Not until he actually oversteps the bounds is official notice taken of him.   The agency that then takes charge of him is not the teacher, the social worker, the clinician, or anyone in fact who is interested in helping him solve his problem.   It is the police force, which is not linked with a rehabilitative program but with a punitive, law-enforcement policy.

The police are charged with taking offenders into custody.   The main problem, however, is not actually the performance of this task but of identifying the offender.   Many crimes are committed in secret, or the offender flees immediately afterward, and no one is sure of his identity.   In the case of juvenile offenders, the child himself is referred to the corrective agency; but among adults the crime is reported to the police, who then must find the criminal.   Many of the criticisms of the police hinge on this fact.   Their failure to make arrests, arrests on suspicion, holding suspects without bringing them before a judge, and attempts to force confessions all grow out of the necessity to identify the offender.   Inasmuch as the police are assigned this task, they should also be provided with the equipment and the authority to carry it out.

In order to identify offenders the police force needs officers and men who are of a high level of intelligence and who are well trained in crime detection.   Initial steps have been taken in more adequate selection of men and in better training, but much remains to be done especially in rural areas and in all communities in which the police force is under the domination of machine politics.

The police also need the support of laws that will enable them to retain custody of persons reasonably suspected of committing some crime, until they are able to assemble evidence.   The complexity of crime, especially in large cities, often makes it incompatible for the police to obey the law regarding immediate appearance of the arrested person before a judge and at the same time trace evidence.   If the police are not allowed to retain custody, the judge should be empowered to place the suspect under some form of supervision until the question of probable guilt is solved.

The police should have better support from the public.   With better selection and training of police, public support will probably increase.   At present the public does not respect the police force and often does not report suspected criminals.   People fear the criminal may be mistreated, they do not believe effective action will follow, or they may secretly sympathize with the offender.

The police should extend their activities to cover all types of crimes.   At present certain criminals are seldom molested, either because they pay police officers or their superiors for the privilege of operating illegal businesses, or because they enjoy high prestige in the community.

Some agency, whether the police or some other organization, should have the power to bring potential adult criminals to the attention of corrective agencies, in the same way that problem children are brought to a clinic or to the juvenile court.   The object should not be punishment but corrective treatment to forestall criminal behavior.

Function of Trials in the Identification Process

At present trials have two stated purposes: to complete the process of the offender's identification by conviction or acquittal; and to impose a penalty upon the convicted person.   Unfortunately, however, criminal trials often resemble verbal gladiatorial contests between the prosecuting and the defense attorneys.   The desire of each side to win, regardless of the merits of the case, does not result in the spirit of impartial inquiry that should surround a criminal trial.   The purpose of a trial should be to discover the true facts of a crime.   It may be argued that a trial as such should not be held, but that a board of competent judges should direct an impartial investigation into crimes and then on the basis of the evidence come to their decision.   This procedure is in essence followed by most juvenile courts, in which the delinquent, the complainant, parents, teachers, social workers, and police are interrogated in an effort to learn the truth, and without the battle of wits between opposed attorneys.

When the offender pleads guilty, he usually does so on the basis of a confession to the police or prosecuting attorney.   On the surface, this procedure may resemble the impartial inquiry advocated as a substitute for trial. It is rarely the consequence of such an inquiry, however.   The confession may be obtained by excessive pressure from the police, or it may result from an agreement with the prosecuting attorney, whereby the offender pleads guilty to a less serious crime than he actually committed.   Under both circumstances, the true facts of the crime may be obscured.

For a number of years students of crime and of our criminal courts have repeatedly advanced the suggestion that the second function of the courts— imposing penalties—should be withdrawn from the courts and entrusted to a special board.   This board would be composed, not of specialists in the law, but of specialists in human nature.   Serving on it might be a sociologist, a psychiatrist, a psychologist, an educator, and a physician.   Diagnosis of the underlying cause of the criminal conduct and a plan of treatment would thus substitute for infliction of punishment.   The offender would be placed on probation, sent to vocational school, summer camp, a special reformatory institution, a colony for the feeble-minded, a hospital for drug addicts, or undergo some other designated treatment, as the case might demand.   Arrangements would be necessary for reconsideration of each case at intervals, in order that the board might determine when the person had become sufficiently well socialized and conforming in conduct to be released from supervision and allowed complete freedom of action.   Moreover, the same procedure is desirable for misdemeanants in order that treatment and rehabilitation may be substituted for fines and jail sentences.

Such a procedure would necessitate drastic revisions of laws, based on a complete abandonment of the attempt to equate a given crime to a specific fine or to length of prison sentence.   It would also require new types of institutions and a greatly expanded system of community supervision.

A beginning has been made in consigning a convicted person to a special board for individual study and planning in the various forms of youth commissions that a small number of states have established.   An expansion of the plan to adult offenders is also under experimentation in a few states. As these ventures prove their worth and practicality, there is reason to believe that additional states will turn away from sentencing the convicted criminal to definite years of imprisonment and place his treatment in the hands of a board of specialists.

Provisions for Treatment of Offenders

There is general agreement that jails, reformatories, and prisons do not often effect a change in criminal attitudes and habits.   Built at a time when solitude, meditation, and repression were regarded as the keystone to repentance and reform, prisons are not adapted to present-day programs of rehabilitation.   Not all criminals require the same type of rehabilitation, but in general they need to learn responsible social customs and to achieve affiliation with noncriminal groups; many of them need to learn the skills and techniques for earning a living; some of them need help with emotional problems.   Herding criminals together into one large institution builds up their allegiance to each other, although they need to find a foothold in noncriminal groups.   Repression of normal tendencies and denial of responsibility and independent action within the prison render the criminal still less able than before his entrance to carry on normal adult life in the community.   As far as possible with safety to the community, rehabilitation should take place in that environment.   Within the community setting, however, special plans should be made for criminals.   Probation, whether under that name or not is immaterial, should be expanded.   Probation should be accompanied by willingness on the part of the offender to participate in programs of rehabilitation, by an active effort on his part to become a member of the conventional community, and by co-operation in attending whatever schools or other community institutions are prescribed by the treatment program.   In other words, the probation experience should not be haphazard and indifferent but should be active, vital, and purposeful.

Some prisons would undoubtedly still be needed, in the sense of institutions for full-time custody of offenders who are unable or unwilling to co-operate in community rehabilitation. But they should resemble colonies or residential schools, in order to provide a constructive experience in controlled community living in the hope that reform might be brought about under an intensive program. For some, especially those whose personalities are hardened into a criminal pattern, permanent custody might be necessary. Many special institutions would be needed. Some would resemble the better reformatories in which offenders are removed for a time from community life. Others would be semiresidential: the offenders would live in them but would go each day to work or attend school in the community, returning to the institution to spend their free time. Still others would provide special programs for offenders who would remain at home and come to the institution for special types of treatment or training.

Special institutions would probably be needed also for those whose offenses stem from a personality maladjustment, such as drug addicts and chronic alcoholics. Recent trends in the treatment of alcoholics, however, do not recommend institutionalization but special treatment centers within the community.

Regardless of the treatment, release from it should be a progressive process, based upon the changes evident in the offender. Gradually decreasing supervision should be maintained until the criminal is able to live a normal, law-abiding life without the support of supervision.

This program may seem visionary and impracticable. A movement in this direction is under way, however. Evidences of it may be found in such functioning agencies as the following: the classification clinics that diagnose each convict and decide upon his general program of treatment; the few, full-time competent parole boards that determine the length of time the offender must remain in prison; the increased interest in both parole and probation; and the establishment of unwalled reformatories, chiefly for women and young male offenders, where a semblance of community life may be maintained.

CHANGES IN ADMINISTRATION

Running through the discussion of all phases of penal administration certain criticisms appear. They may be summarized briefly, since they point out shortcomings in the present system and obstacles to its revision.

Politics

At every point, from the appointment of a new policeman to the selection of a parole officer, politics prevent the best functioning of the present system.

Public Attitude Toward Offenders

Rehabilitation is impeded by the social stigma attached to one who has been arrested and convicted. Even an arrest without conviction is regarded as almost evidence of guilt. Epithets such as "jailbird" or "convict" set the offender apart from the normal community. People withdraw from him and do not want to associate with him. Employers do not want to give him a job. Segregation during jail or prison term serves to break community ties and to make the offender in some degree a hostile stranger. As a stranger he finds some difficulty in re-establishing old associations; with the stigma of convict he may find it impossible. Rejected by the conventional groups in the community, he turns to other nonconformers like himself and associates with the group least able to help him in reorganizing his life.

A part of the difficulty rests in the stereotype of the convict in the public mind. The criminal is regarded as a different order of being from the conventional adult, moved by abnormal impulses, and likely at any moment to commit a crime. Actually, the great majority of criminals are little different from law-abiding people; for most of them crime is not a continuous activity but intermittent acts, with intervening periods of conventional activity. The need is to prolong the law-abiding periods and to strengthen noncriminal associations and habits. Understanding and willingness to help the offender on the part of the public will swing many criminals into the ranks of the law abiding.

HINDRANCES TO ACHIEVEMENT OF GOALS

Although we can point out goals toward which to direct changes in the method of handling delinquents and criminals and can detect faint trends toward their achievement we must also recognize some obstacles. One barrier is public ignorance regarding rehabilitation of criminals, coupled with indifference. The attitude that the offender is different from other people and destined to remain so prevents an active interest in reform. Public indifference is marked. Some community institutions are well known to the public because they entertain and their clients proudly present exhibits and programs. The inmates of jails and prisons are not paraded before the public. Most persons who have not been sentenced to these institutions have never been inside either of them. They have no direct experience with criminals and penal institutions and they are hazy and indifferent toward the entire problem.

Another barrier is the resistance of vested interests to change. As long as positions in the penal system can be used as rewards to members of the ruling political party, and as long as the present system protects political graft, there will be little official agitation for change. Also, certain changes advocated would reduce the authority of some officials—for example, the criminal judge—and are resisted because they seem to lower the status of the office.

A third obstacle is the fear that a revised system would cost more money. Although comparative figures between the present and the prospective systems are not available, it seems doubtful whether the revisions suggested would add to the total cost. The present type of prison is highly expensive to build; unwalled institutions and special hospitals and schools would cost less. Supervision of offenders in the community by parole or probation officers is known to cost less than maintenance in prison. Also, while in the community offenders usually earn money and support dependents who otherwise might require relief from public agencies. Decreased public expenditures would result, too, from the reduction in recidivism that would accompany the new type of training.

A fourth hindrance is our admittedly imperfect knowledge of the causes of criminal conduct and of procedures to change behavior when attitudes and habits are firmly established. However, the knowledge of educators, psychiatrists, psychologists, and sociologists has never been pooled and thoroughly applied to offenders. There is every reason to believe that concentration of available knowledge would both benefit offenders and add to knowledge of the causes of crime and the rehabilitative process. It would also point the way for research directed at crucial problems.

The intricacy and complexity of the entire problem of crime present great difficulties. The present system attempts to simplify the problem by assuming that all crime may be cured by imprisonment and that the only differentiation needed is in the length of sentence. The new approach would recognize many motivations and processes, each of which might require a somewhat different treatment. Every criminal would be viewed as a distinct personality, to be studied, his assets appraised, his handicaps revealed. It is assumed, however, that offenders would fall into such well-defined classes that much of the treatment and retraining could be carried out in groups, a procedure that would reduce the complexity of the program.

A major difficulty at the present time is the lack of trained personnel to carry out this new type of program. Police need training in better methods of crime detection. Judges and lawyers need special training in criminal law and psychology. The entire prison personnel needs overhauling. In fact, with the hoped for future revision of many prisons into training institutions, the present type of warden and guard would disappear altogether, to be replaced by a minimum of guards for custodial purposes and a diagnostic and training staff of specialists.   These institutions would open a new field for sociologists, psychiatrists, psychologists, and social workers on the one hand and for educators, teachers, and recreational workers, on the other.   At present, trained persons are not available to staff such institutions.   Probably special methods of applying the skills of the various specialists to the task of retraining criminals must be developed.   It is well known that there are not enough male social workers at present to supply the need for parole and probation officers.   Here again, there is need to stimulate training in the social techniques needed by parole and probation supervisors.   Certainly if positions were created in these fields, demanding careful preparation and providing adequate salaries and the promise of professional careers unhampered by political tampering, candidates for the positions would appear, and colleges and universities would supply the necessary training.

Finally, there is the social inertia of the complex, locally centralized system of criminal law and penal institutions.   The leaven of change must work, not in one unified and co-ordinated order, but in 48 states (and the District of Columbia), 3,000 counties, and thousands of cities.   Law-enforcement agencies are naturally conservative, for they rely upon the precedents and customs of the past.   Change will come slowly and unevenly.   But the first steps have already been taken.

QUESTIONS

1. What improved methods do we need to identify offenders and especially potential criminals?

2. What type of treatment should be substituted for the usual prison experience for most criminals?

3. With expanded use of probation, would prisons still be needed?   For whom?

4. How could law enforcement and the treatment of criminals be taken out of politics?

5. Suggest a plan for co-ordinating police, courts, penal institutions, probation, and parole.

6. What responsibilities should the community assume in the rehabilitation of criminals?

7. What are the chief hindrances to achievement of the goals set forth in this chapter?

APPENDIX A

Theories of Criminality

The history of theories of criminality is the history of man's effort to find a general explanation of why men commit crimes. In the past 150 years, first one explanation and then another has been formulated by scientists, expanded, publicly acclaimed and defended, accepted by laymen, and contested and possibly refuted by other scientists who presented conflicting theories or data. Most of these theories have contained at least a modicum of truth, and traces of their influence are found in present-day theories. In general, concepts of crime have suffered from these defects:

1. They are apt to assume that criminality is based on one trait or characteristic. Such an assumption overlooks the fact that there are many types of criminal, each of which may act from a different motivating force. Even when common sense and practical observation have forced theorists to concede the existence of types of criminals, they have tended to overemphasize the one in which they were interested.

2. Many theorists have assumed that at least some criminals—the real criminals—were different in some basic physical or psychological respect from noncriminals. Criminals were special human beings.

3. Also, until recently, little effort was made to relate the supposed cause of crime to the ultimate criminal act. The process by which the cause was translated into human action was not studied.

4. The theories have largely reflected dominant trends in philosophy and scientific knowledge. Each advance in science has been hailed as supplying the key wherewith to unlock the secret of criminality. Not one science alone, but many sciences have at some time purported to have uncovered the basic cause of criminal activities.

A complete history of theories of crime would necessarily go back many centuries. The present discussion includes approximately 150 years. This limitation does not mean that earlier conceptions of causes of criminal behavior have completely dropped out of sight. At one time man was regarded as the battleground for the conflict between the forces of good and evil. Men sinned and committed crimes when they allied themselves with the devil. This point of view is still current in certain groups and is implied in many popular conceptions of crime. The doctrine of free will and voluntary choice of good or evil is still inherent in much of our legal machinery and forms of punishment.

The phrenological approach to crime causation was espoused by Franz Joseph Galt (1758–1828).[1] According to his theory the conformation of the brain followed the external shape of the skull; various faculties of the mind could be discovered by studying the shape of the skull. He measured the heads of inmates of jails and asylums and concluded that the shapes of their heads, and therefore their mental faculties, differed from those of non-criminal and normal people. Charles Caldwell introduced phrenology to the United States in 1821 and expanded the theory to the point of explaining definite types of crime, such as infanticide, murder, theft, kleptomania, and moral insanity by peculiarities in the shape of the skull, which he thought indicated defective mental or moral tendencies. Phrenology, at one time widely acclaimed, even by some scientists, as the key to criminal behavior, still crops up here and there, although it had begun to decline in popularity in this country by the 1840's.

Theories of crime that had some basis in factual studies, rather than in philosophy or pseudo science, fall into four general classes: sociological, physical or biological, psychological, and psychiatric. In western Europe and the United States, the theories first appeared in much the same order. At present all four approaches are represented in theories that sometimes overlap and corroborate each other and sometimes contradict. As in the past, there is still no single, generally accepted point of view regarding the causation of criminal behavior.

EARLY SOCIOLOGICAL APPROACH

Statistical and Ecological Studies

The early sociological approach—although not called by this name—developed in France in the 1830's through the work of A. Quetelet and A. M. Guerry.[2] Their research stimulated similar approaches in Germany, Belgium, and England. One source of information was the official crime statistics that were published in France in 1825 and in other countries shortly thereafter. These statistics lent themselves to an analysis of the geographic distribution of crime and its association with other social factors. In 1829 Guerry and an associate used shaded maps to represent crime rates, a technique that was eagerly adopted by other students of crime. After crime rates were broken down according to small geographic areas, attempts to account for differences in rates followed naturally. General social conditions, variations in legislation, as well as sex, age, and climatic differences were noted.

Juvenile delinquency was also of enormous interest in England and Europe during the early and middle parts of the nineteenth century. The failure of the family and society to provide adequate care was recognized, and attempts to remedy the situation led to the establishment of hundreds of reformatories and agricultural colonies.

The professional criminal had also been isolated as a type that originated with the breakdown of the feudal system and the freeing of serfs without adequate social control or means of support. Many special studies and articles on professional criminals appeared in England, Germany, and France. These studies recognized the origin of the professional thief, his relation to the anonymity of the city where he thrived, and the fact that children were inducted into the philosophy, skills, and argots of professional crime in much the same way that they were trained to other trades or professions. In attempting to understand the lives of criminals (in contrast to the study of variation of crime rates) several persons began the study of individual criminals and secured from them accounts of their careers. The implication of these studies was that crime was a social phenomenon, a type of activity originating in general social conditions or in specific life experiences of criminals.

The value of much of this sociological approach to crime was abrogated by the emphasis on physical and biological factors during the latter part of the nineteenth century. In the United States, especially, these early studies seem to have contributed but little to an understanding of criminal behavior. Lindesmith and Levin believe there were several reasons for this failure of the English and European studies to receive attention in the United States.[3] One explanation is that the continental studies were not translated and made easily available. Another is that the United States did not have well-developed bodies of statistics making possible similar studies in this country. Other probable reasons exist, that these authors do not mention. The science of sociology was not far advanced, especially in the United States, and therefore no organized or trained group was in a position to accept and further sociological studies. Also, no definite theory of social causation was developed from the English and European studies. A body of data was slowly accumulating but no specific theory had been formulated. Nor had an aggressive spokesman arisen to insist that crime was based on social causation. Later theories often owed their wide acceptance to the activity of some one or two enthusiastic propagandists. Finally, before the social theories were well developed, they were overshadowed by the next wave of theories, biological in nature. However, in England and western Europe, regardless of biological theories, crime as a social phenomenon continued to receive attention.

Crime by Imitation

Gabriel Tarde, the French sociologist, regarded crime as strictly a social phenomenon. According to Tarde's general theory, all social interaction was a process of imitation, whereby some activity or belief originated and was then imitated or copied, according to rather definite rules.[4] Imitation worked most effectively in crowds or mobs, hence in cities where people could easily congregate. Imitation spread from the city into the rural areas, and also from those with prestige to those of lower social status. Thus crimes that originated in the cities were imitated in rural areas, and antisocial acts that once were the prerogative of the aristocracy later became the criminal acts of the masses. It seems unnecessary to go further into Tarde's detailed discussion, inasmuch as his general theory of imitation as the basic type of social interaction is no longer accepted. Tarde's contribution to criminology was not his specific theory, but the fact that he upheld a social origin of crime at a time when the trend of thought was toward acceptance of a biological differentiation of criminals from noncriminals.

Crime as a By-Product of Capitalism

Certain criminologists viewed crime as closely related to the economic system. William A. Bonger, the Dutch criminologist, took his theory from Marx and found the roots of crime in the capitalist system. Bonger discussed many types of crime and in virtually all found the economic system either the primary or a secondary factor.[5] A few examples of his reasoning will clarify his position. In his opinion vagrancy arose because many workingmen, under a capitalistic system, could not sell their labor. In a time of crisis, especially, they became unemployed and, unable to meet their needs, drifted into vagrancy. Failure of the economic system to care for the old and sick, and for abandoned children, was also a cause. Theft was directly related to the division of people under capitalism into the rich and the poor. Those who were actually poverty stricken stole to acquire the necessities of life. Those with moderate incomes envied the luxuries of the rich and wished to emulate them; they stole as a means of fulfilling this ambition. Professional criminals also envied the rich, and seeing them live comfortably without working, wished to do the same. In other crimes, according to Bonger, the economic system was less directly involved but nevertheless was an important factor. Many sexual crimes were the result of poverty that prevented or postponed marriage. Alcoholism contributed to crime and was a result of such economic factors as excessive hours of work, uncertainty of employment, and the efforts of producers of alcohol to encourage drinking in order to increase their profits. Bonger's general conclusion was that "we have a right to say that the part played by economic conditions in criminality is preponderant, even decisive." [6] Bonger's proposed solution to crime was a reorganization of society so that the "means of production" are held "in common," in other words, some form of socialism or communism.

Bonger used statistics to support his thesis, but in general his reasoning is a priori and deductive. His presentation is therefore not convincing but it represents a sensitiveness to social factors in crime and an antidote to the theories that emphasize biological factors as the cause of criminology.

PHYSICAL AND BIOLOGICAL APPROACH

During the latter half of the nineteenth century the biological sciences made great strides, and the imaginations of physicians and of scientists in other fields elaborated some of the new biological discoveries and theories into general explanations of social behavior. Darwin's theories of evolution, and Von Baer's and Haeckel's theories of the recapitulation of evolutionary development of life in the embryonic development of the human being, especially stimulated a transfer of these theories to group and individual behavior in the social realm. In view of the trend of thought of the times it is natural that someone should have seized upon them and adapted them to explain the existence of criminal activity.

Criminals as Atavists and Degenerates

Cesare Lombroso and his student and ardent follower, Enrico Ferri, were the leaders in the attempt to connect criminal behavior with biological causes. They developed what came to be known as the Positive School of criminology. Lombroso was an Italian physician who as an army doctor had speculated upon physical differences between conforming and disorderly soldiers. His interest led to studies of prisoners in Italian penitentiaries and of inmates of asylums for the insane. He appeared to make little progress until he had an opportunity to examine after death the skull and brain of a famous brigand. He discovered a series of physical anomalies in the structure of the brain and believed he had determined the primary cause of criminal behavior. He examined other criminals and as often as possible the skulls and brains of prisoners after death. Soon he elaborated a theory of the biological origin of crime, which was set forth in 1876 in *L' Uomo Delinquente.*

Lombroso's theory was that criminals were an anthropological type. They were an atavistic type of human being—a throwback to a primitive, savage stage of human development. In fact, he believed that the criminal was so low in the evolutionary scale that he retained certain animal characteristics of savagery not found in noncriminal persons. In the examination of 383 skulls of criminals he found fifteen anomalies that he believed distinguished them from the skulls of noncriminals.[7] These anomalies included small capacity of the skull, fusion of its bones instead of normal sutures, retreating forehead, asymmetrical development, various deformities, irregular development of the teeth, and exaggerations of facial bones. He also claimed to have found differences in the convolutions of the brain and in the development of the heart, skeleton, genital organs, and stomach. In addition to studies of cadavers, he measured and observed many living criminals. He came to the conclusion that in criminals the measurement of the outstretched arms from finger tip to finger tip exceeded the height, and that there was a predominance of left-handedness, a prehensile foot, precocious wrinkles, hairiness, low and narrow forehead, large jaws and cheekbones, outstanding ears, and so forth. These observable physical characteristics were regarded as stigmata of crime.

Lombroso argued that a person with these various structural anomalies of the brain could not have the same impulses and sentiments as a normal person. He identified them with early man, whom he believed to have been a savage, with primitive peoples whom he believed to be a type of early man, and with animals. The criminal thus was a type of undeveloped and, by inference, only partial human being.[8]

It was soon pointed out that many of the anomalies listed by Lombroso were the result of abnormalities of development, perhaps before birth, rather than of congenital factors. Lombroso therefore expanded his theory to include degeneracy as a cause of crime and in his later books emphasized degeneracy more than atavism. He believed that degeneracy was revealed in certain anatomical and physical characteristics, such as prominent ears, jaw, and cheekbones, a thin upper lip, and a ferocious look with a squint. He compared the degenerate criminal to a moral imbecile (insane person) and to an epileptic.

This criminal who was atavistic and/or degenerate was the true or "born" criminal. About 40 per cent of all criminals were born criminals, according to Lombroso. They could be recognized by their physical type and were not really responsible for their acts. Eventually, Lombroso added other types of criminals: occasional criminals, criminals by contracted habit, criminal madmen, and criminals of passion.

In Lombroso's later formulations considerable space is given to a discussion of the etiology of crime, including such physical features as climate and geological factors, economic conditions, education, religion, occupation, and the like. He also strongly advocated fitting the punishment to the type of criminal, rather than to the crime committed. A born criminal and an occasional criminal should not be treated similarly, even though they had committed the same crime.

Ferri, who was twenty-one years younger than Lombroso, accepted Lombroso's thesis with only minor modifications. He regarded Lombroso as the first person to oppose the earlier "classical" school of criminal law, which proposed a specific punishment for each crime, and the first to distinguish criminals by types, each of which should be given distinctive treatment.[9] Ferri's chief interest was the disposition of criminals. He advocated that one or more experts in criminal anthropology should be attached to each court, whose duty it would be to determine to which class a given criminal belonged. This method, rather than the verbal tilting of lawyers, would determine the degree of culpability. Punishment as retribution would be entirely discarded and penalty and treatment suited to the class of criminal substituted. Thus born criminals, who committed their crimes because of inborn traits based on physical anomalies, would receive a different treatment from habitual criminals who had learned their behavior from childhood associations. It should be noted that criminals were still thought of as motivated by some definite impulse, inborn or acquired, and at least the born criminals were considered to be different from noncriminals.

Criticism of Lombroso's Theories

Many criticisms may be aimed at Lombroso's work. He used the term atavism loosely and included as symptoms many personal and social customs, as well as anomalies in physical development. He also regarded primitive peoples as in a lower stage of evolution than civilized man and thought that any presumable similarity between criminals and primitive peoples indicated atavism. He also assumed a direct connection between physical structure of brain and body and exact forms of emotion and conduct. He regarded criminality as a unified type of behavior and did not distinguish between criminals, except to make certain broad classifications into born criminals, occasional criminals, and so on. He did not understand crime as an element in the process of human living, attributable to social and physical factors, and produced by the same processes that lead to noncriminal behavior.

Lombroso is believed both to have hindered and to have helped the development of criminology. Lindesmith and Levin believe that he hindered the progress of the science;[10] others hail him as the "father" of a scientific approach to criminology, in that he emphasized the study of the individual criminal.   His forceful insistence upon his point of view certainly called the attention of physicians and biologists to the problem of crime and brought new attention to it.   Undoubtedly, this trend delayed the progress of the sociological approach.

Crime as the Result of Mental Anomalies

Baron Raffaele Garofalo, who wrote in the 1880's, accepted the general thesis of Lombroso, that criminals were a distinct type of human being.[11] He related crime to mental irregularities, rather than to physical anomalies. These mental characteristics were hereditary and a deviation from the traits of normal civilized man.   They were not atavistic, but rather denoted moral degeneracy—a regression to some extremely early savage type of ancestor or to an animal stage of development.   He also believed that criminals had certain physiognomic expressions that distinguish them from noncriminal persons and that it was possible to differentiate murderers from thieves and both of these from violent or impulsive criminals and from noncriminals. He implied that this expression probably rested in part upon physical factors and in part upon early experiences and education.

As a corollary to his thesis that criminals were the result of innate mental anomalies, Garofalo proposed a system of punishment containing a specific penalty for each class of criminal.   In general, he urged that murderers be "eliminated" by execution, as they were beyond any possibility of reform; that violent criminals be interned under supervision for an indefinite period; that criminals committing crimes against property be colonized and forced to work for a living; and that lascivious criminals be sent to overseas colonies.

Although Garofalo seems to have discarded much of Lombroso's theory, he retained the basic point of view—that crime arose from inborn and heritable anomalies that set off the criminal as a distinct anthropological type. Social factors were minimized and reform or re-education was regarded as doubtful.

Refutation of the Anthropological Type

The opposition to Lombroso and the Positive Italian School of criminology stimulated research in England in the first decade of the twentieth century, which rather definitely disposed of both physical and mental anomalies.   In 1902 a project was initiated whereby British prison physicians made careful measurements of prisoners and detailed reports on mental qualities.   Eventually chief responsibility for the work was assumed by Charles Goring, with the result that a report was published in 1908.[12]

Measurements and observations were secured for three thousand prisoners and for control groups of noncriminals consisting of university undergraduates, inmates of a general hospital, insane persons, and soldiers. Also, habitual and nonhabitual criminals were compared. Cephalic measurements were taken, and hair and eye color, defective hearing, left-handedness, and tattooing were observed and recorded. Goring's information is presented in detail with statistical exactitude. He concluded that there was no evidence of a physical criminal type. Criminals differed among themselves as did noncriminals, but there were no physical traits typical of criminals that set them apart as a class from noncriminals.[13]

Goring did report, however, two differences between criminals (about 90 per cent of whom were thieves) and the general population. He found that thieves were less well developed physically than the general population, that criminals of violence were better developed, and that the intelligence of criminals tended to be lower than that of the general population.[14] It should be noted that whereas the conclusions on physical factors were based on exact measurements, the conclusions on mental differences were based on considered judgments. Intelligence tests were not sufficiently well developed at that time to be used. It is not surprising therefore that although Goring's data on physical characteristics have not been seriously refuted, his observations on differences in intelligence have been reversed by recent studies in which standardized intelligence tests were used.

Although Goring denied the existence of an anthropological criminal type, he did not tear himself away from the current philosophy that criminality was based on physical and inheritable differences. He posited a "criminal diathesis," or constitutional factors causing criminal behavior, and maintained that this criminal diathesis was inherited at much the same rate as were physical and mental qualities and pathological conditions. Parental influences were secondary and "inconsiderable" in relation to the influence of inheritance and mental defectiveness, which were "by far the most significant factors" discovered by the study of the etiology of crime.[15]

In addition to his presentation of material relative to the Lombrosian theory, Goring presented an analysis of his data with reference to education, employment, alcoholism, family life, standard of living of the parents, age of the criminal at the death of his mother, order of the subject in his family, the number in the family, marriage, and number of children.

Recent Biological Studies

Periodically, interest revives in possible physical differences of criminals from noncriminals. An impressive study of the 1930's was made by E. A. Hooton, an anthropologist, who analyzed measurements and observations on 14,477 inmates of jails, prisons, reformatories, and asylums for insane and mentally defective criminals, and on 1,976 sane and 1,227 insane noncriminals.[16]   Hooton and his associates took more than 100 physical measurements, including minute measurements of the head, nose, forehead, chin, shape of the features, and classification of hair color and abundance of hair.   Stature and body build were also noted.   The prisoners were classified into various types and compared.   For example, men convicted of different forms of crime were compared with respect to individual measurements; Old American criminals (whites whose ancestors had lived in the United States one or two generations), Negroes, and various nationality groups were compared; criminals and civilians were contrasted.

Hooton came to the conclusion that, although there were no physical stigmata, criminals were biologically inferior.   For example, among the Old American white stock, a comparison of criminals with noncriminals showed that the criminal was of smaller size, with a smaller head.   He had straighter hair, broader face, more prominent nose, narrower jaws, and smaller but broader ears.   Hooton admits that it is not possible on the basis of physical differences to distinguish an individual criminal from an individual noncriminal.   There is no single distinguishing physical mark or no one combination of traits common to all criminals.   Criminals as a group merely have a higher percentage of members with these physical traits than do noncriminals as a group.[17]   It should also be noted that usually the percentages of the two groups that have the same degree of a characteristic are greater than the percentages that differ.   In other words, criminals and noncriminals are more similar than different.

Hooton was also much interested in the physical types among criminals of different racial stocks.   Anthropologists have long since separated mankind into a limited number of races (Caucasian, Negroid, Mongoloid) and subraces on the basis of the particular combination of differing physical traits.   It has been a moot question, however, whether the races differed psychologically.   Psychological differences, if they existed, might be of two types.   Races might actually have psychological traits that would constitute qualitative differences; or they might have the same traits but in different degrees of intensity, which would constitute quantitative differences.   If races differ psychologically, either qualitatively or quantitatively, it is reasonable to presume that they would differ in conduct, including criminal conduct.   The alternative explanation is that races, since they all belong to the same species, do not differ psychologically although they do differ in external physical coloring and structure.   Differences in conduct, including criminal conduct, are then explained on the basis of accidental differences in culture.   Hooton comes out strongly for qualitative psychological differences, inferring them from physical differences rather than proving them on the basis of psychological tests.[18]   He argues that "racial physical differences should naturally be associated with racial psychological differences, and that the social behavior of distinct racial stocks should vary in accordance with their physiological and psychological divergences."   He classified the white prisoners into 9 racial types, 4 of which were "pure" and 5 mixed or composite.   The details of his comparisons cannot be given but some of his conclusions are that the blond, longheaded Pure Nordic type is "an easy leader in forgery and fraud, a strong second in burglary and larceny, and last or next to last in all crimes against persons." [19]   The brunet, round-headed Alpine type "ranks first in robbery but last in forgery and fraud." The blond, roundheaded East Baltic type stands first in burglary and larceny, but is low in offenses against the person, except rape.   He modifies the implications that some races might be more inclined to criminal activity than others by saying that his data do not prove this assumption, and that in each racial group are biologically inferior persons who form the criminal group in that race.

Unfortunately, Hooton did not cover either psychological or sociological differences.   It is natural, therefore, that with his interest in physical anthropology and the complete failure to consider other factors than the physical, he should have over-emphasized the relatively minor differences in physical characteristics as indicative of underlying psychological differences and hence divergences in conduct.   The study is also weak in that the prisoners and noncriminals were not well matched; many of the noncriminals were firemen and members of the militia, groups that must meet certain physical standards and hence are probably above the general civilian population in physical development.   The author makes many unwarranted assumptions in addition to the one that social conduct rests on physical differences.   He assumes that the physical differences found are hereditary, thus that criminals form a segment of the population containing the seeds of criminal conduct in their germ plasm; actually, many of these physical differences may be the result of malnutrition or accidental failures in normal development.

The general trend in studies purporting to relate physical structure to crime has been away from the idea of definite physical stigmata by which the individual criminal can be identified.   But the protagonists of this point of view persist in the idea of inherited physical anomalies of some type that mark the criminal as a class and in the unproved theory that psychological traits and social conduct are the result of these inherited characteristics.

Two studies of juvenile delinquents conducted with a broader viewpoint and hence with less bias in interpretation deserve mention.   One was made by 4 scientists (a physician, a sociologist, a physical anthropologist, and a statistician) of 4,000 boys in 2 delinquency areas.[20]   Delinquents were compared with nondelinquents.   To avoid the criticism that delinquents who have been arrested constitute only a fraction—and perhaps the less efficient—of the total delinquents in a community, delinquents known to social agencies but never arrested were included.   The selection of both delinquents and nondelinquents from the same communities forestalls criticisms of the adequate social matching of the 2 samples.   For each subject, 63 anthropomorphic measurements were taken, a medical and neurological examination was given, and social and morphological data were assembled. The conclusion was reached that there were no significant differences between delinquents and nondelinquents among whites but that among Negroes some differences existed.   Interestingly, the delinquent Negroes exhibited fewer of the so-called stigmata of crime than the nondelinquents and were superior to them in health.   No differences in intelligence were found.

The second study is that by Healy and Bronner, in which 105 juvenile delinquents were compared with an equal number of nondelinquent brothers and sisters.[21]   The delinquents exhibited excess of physical defects when compared with the control group, but not of structural anomalies.   Each group contained 6 members with Lombrosian stigmata of crime.   The types of physical defect are interesting.   They included such conditions as defective vision, enlarged or diseased tonsils, nasal obstruction, carious teeth, and endocrine disorders.   The delinquents also exceeded the nondelinquents in being either extremely tall or short, in being overweight, and in showing either premature or retarded sexual development.[22]   The authors do not regard the physical differences as direct causes of criminal behavior; rather, physical defects made adjustment difficult and hence led to divergent conduct.   Thus, the overgrown boys tended to be restless and to need "larger physical self-expression" than was provided by schools and community institutions for boys of a given age.   Their attempts to fulfill their needs led to delinquent behavior.   Likewise, girls who matured early became interested in sex and were drawn into sexual activities at an age when most girls were not interested in these matters.[23]   Thus, physical defects and divergences are not viewed as a direct cause of crime but rather as making social adjustment at home, in school, and among friends difficult and thus leading indirectly to delinquency, as the puzzled adolescent seeks some outlet for his energies or some compensation for his defects.   Healy and Bronner state explicitly that physically "the delinquent group of young people is closely similar to the general group of young people in so far as standards for comparison exist.   Physically the delinquent does not form a separate group.   Nor is any particular physical condition found to be significant in relation to the later career of the offender." [24]

The middle-of-the-road point of view is expressed in the following terms by a biologist, and may serve as a conclusion of this summary of attempts to find the basic cause of crime in inherited physical characteristics that set criminals apart as a separate class: [25]

Mind is a social product. It represents the social organization of previously unorganized nervous tissue, and the expression of that nervous tissue according to the cultural pattern of its organization, that is, in behavior . . . Genes do not create mind, but they do provide every individual with a somewhat different basic morphological pattern of cellular tissues . . . Man, alone among the members of the animal kingdom, is more dominantly and prominently a creature influenced by his cultural history than by his ancestral or individual biological history.

PSYCHOLOGICAL APPROACH

The psychological approach has focused chiefly on the attempt to relate crime to feeble-mindedness. It will be recalled that Goring, on the basis of observations and comparsions between prisoners and civilians, came to the conclusion that prisoners tended to be of lower intellectual capacity than noncriminals. Soon after Goring made his study, intelligence tests were available to provide a more exact comparison. Interest in intelligence levels swept the United States like an epidemic. Estimates of the intelligence of criminals were freely made; tests were given with more or less care, not always by persons adequately trained to administer or interpret them. The results were published in journals and books. Here at last seemed to be an easy way to distinguish the criminal from the noncriminal. Physical differences as the basis for criminal conduct had fallen into disrepute. Psychological differences appeared to be one step nearer the answer to criminal conduct than physical differences.

In many respects, however, the interest in intelligence levels was identical with the interest in physical differences. Scientists were still trying to find one cause for all crime; they still regarded the cause of criminality whether physical or mental as inheritable; the implication remained that criminals were a definite subclass of human beings who could be identified by some special symbol of their criminality.

Criminals and Mental Defect

The most ardent advocate in the United States of mental defect as the cause of crime was Henry H. Goddard, Director of the Research Laboratory of the Training School at Vineland, New Jersey, for Feeble-Minded Girls and Boys. He was not alone, however, but was merely the most prolific writer of the group and is here regarded as the representative of a common viewpoint that flourished between 1910 and 1920. Goddard divided criminals into 2 types: those who committed crime as a result of some defect and who were not wholly responsible for their conduct; and those who became criminals from carelessness, indifference, or wilful refusal to comply with the demands of society and who were responsible for their acts.[26] This mild statement is modified, however, by the assertion that the "greatest single cause of delinquency and crime is low-grade mentality, much of it within the limits of feeble-mindedness." He based this assertion upon the numerous tests of prisoners that showed from 10 to 80 per cent of the inmates of various institutions to be of low mentality. He attributed the wide range in percentage partly to the way in which the groups tested were selected, and partly to the degree of conservatism of the person who interpreted the tests. In an earlier publication, Goddard asserted that "every feeble-minded person is a potential criminal." [27] He did not believe, however, that characteristics that were inherited and hence innate in the criminal constituted a propensity for crime; rather inherited traits caused lack of judgment and self-control and the inability to distinguish right from wrong. Therefore the feeble-minded person, especially if of a nervous or impulsive temperament, was almost sure to become a criminal.

Goddard's supreme effort to support his thesis was the careful tracing of the histories of 327 families that had children confined at the Vineland School.[28] However, only 10 per cent of the families showed criminality in any of their members and when the incidence of crime was computed as a percentage of the individuals in the families rather than of family units, only one third of 1 per cent had committed crimes. Goddard regarded this degree of criminality as surprisingly small and attempted to account for it in several ways. He stated that the percentage of crime was higher in families in which feeble-mindedness seemed definitely hereditary than in those in which it arose from some other cause. He believed that the low percentage of crime resulted from the fact that many of these families lived in rural communities where misconduct was tolerated rather than reported to the authorities; that opportunities for crime and temptations were low in such areas; that criminally inclined members may have left the community and hence were unrepresented in the family histories. Goddard weakened his study by the tendency to group many aberrant types of behavior with feeble-mindedness as general symptoms of its hereditary character. Thus immorality, insanity, alcoholism, and crime were indiscriminately discussed in the family histories as evidences of low mentality, as well as direct symptoms of mental incapacity.

In line with earlier students of crime who attempted to fit punishment to the type of criminal, Goddard suggested specific treatment of feeble-minded criminals. He believed that feeble-mindedness was a unit character inherited in accordance with Mendelian principles—a doctrine since modified. As such, there seemed to be no way to rid society of the feeble-minded potential criminals except to eliminate the strains carrying mental deficiency. He advocated either colonization with the sexes segregated to prevent propagation, or sterilization of the feeble-minded after which they could be allowed to live in the community.[29]

Similarity of Intelligence of Criminals and Noncriminals

During the 1920's intelligence tests were interpreted with more understanding of what the tests really revealed, and also of external factors that modified the performance of certain individuals on tests. Moreover, comparative studies between prisoners and civilians were undertaken, which greatly changed the contentions of Goddard and other early testers.

An unprecedented opportunity for a comparative study came after the First World War, which made available the scores on intelligence tests of soldiers in the United States Army as a cross section of young male noncriminals. Carl Murchison, who was Chief Psychological Examiner at Camp Sherman, Ohio, was invited by the Warden of the Ohio Penitentiary to examine the prisoners, using the same test given to the soldiers. From this beginning Murchison was enabled to secure tests from inmates of 4 penal institutions in Ohio, 2 in Illinois, 2 in Indiana, 1 in New Jersey, and 1 in Maryland.[30] Murchison used 3 groups, native-born whites, foreign-born whites, and Negroes. Criminals in each state studied were compared with the corresponding group in the army draft for that state. For the foreign-born, the groups were further classified by country or origin. The criminals and soldiers were then compared as to the distribution of scores made on the army alpha intelligence test. This comparison showed that both criminals and soldiers made scores that ranged from extremely low to superior. For the Negroes and certain of the white groups, the distribution of intermediate scores was almost identical for criminals and soldiers; that is, the 2 groups had essentially the same percentage of low normal scores, medium or normal scores, and high or superior scores. For most of the white groups, however, the criminals had higher proportions in the moderately high (but not the superior scores) and lower proportions in the moderately low (but not the lowest scores). Murchison concluded that on the whole criminals tended to have higher degrees of intelligence, as measured by the army alpha intelligence test, than did noncriminals.

Various criticisms might be aimed at Murchison's study; Murchison himself discusses some of them in the opening pages of his book. For example, certain essential industrial workers were excluded from the draft; if they were of high intelligence their omission from the groups of soldiers tested would have lowered the scores for the soldiers; on the other hand, obviously feeble-minded persons were also excluded from the draft, which would have had the opposite effect. Although such omissions would have made some difference, certainly on the whole Murchison's study was valid, and it seems to have laid for all time the contention that criminals are drawn heavily from the ranks of the feeble-minded.

Later studies have sought to refine the methods of comparison used by Murchison by more exactly delimiting the groups compared and thus eliminating factors that might influence the test scores. These studies minimize Murchison's conclusion that criminals tended to include a larger proportion of persons of high intelligence than was found among noncriminals. They indicate that criminals and the general population exhibit essentially the same distribution of intelligence levels.[31] The army alpha scores for the First World War were used as the indication of intelligence in the general population for these later studies as for Murchison's.

OTHER ATTEMPTS TO FIND A UNITARY CAUSE OF CRIME

Several other attempts have been made to link criminal conduct with some one specific physical or mental cause. As they have been more or less short lived and have not aroused great controversy, they are mentioned only briefly.

The development of endocrinology and the discovery that diseases of the glands affected emotional reactions, and to some extent behavior, led some persons to jump to the conclusion that criminal conduct was the result of malfunctioning of the glands. But more conservative students of the subject maintain that little is known of the relation of glandular disturbances to conduct and that to erect a system of criminology upon the basis of glandular malfunctioning is ludicrous.[32]

The effect of the diseased glands was assumed to operate through the emotions. Other attempts also were made to uncover emotional differences between criminals and noncriminals, although not necessarily to link such differences with physical factors. Slawson, in his study of male juvenile delinquents, used a psychoneurotic inventory and reached the conclusion that delinquent boys differed in emotional reactions from nondelinquents.[33] Excitability, aggressiveness, introversion, extroversion, and other emotional temperamental traits have been studied from time to time. Also, the attempt has been made to discover total personality patterns typical of the criminal.[34] Periodically some one type of mental disease is set forth as the primary cause of crime.   Perhaps the cause most often suggested and held responsible for the largest proportion of crimes is the psychopathic personality.   This mental disease is the most amorphous of the various categories—the catchall for miscellaneous or abnormal cases that do not fit any of the more rigidly defined classifications.   It is therefore the most difficult to diagnose, as psychopaths exhibit many different and often contradictory traits.   Therefore a psychiatrist who inclines to the belief that mental abnormality is the chief cause of crime may find in prisoners relatively easily some of the many traits of the psychopath.   The diagnosis was especially easy at one time because of the assertion that crime itself was a symptom of psychopathy, even though no other symptoms existed.   Some surveys reported that 40 or 50 per cent of the prisoners in certain institutions were psychopathic.[35]

The attempt to find an emotional reaction or a personality type closely linked with crime in a causal relationship is part and parcel of the trend started by Lombroso, when he attempted to find anomalies in physical structure that would account for criminal conduct.   The emphasis has shifted from physical to emotional traits, but the hope persists to find some one cause of crime.

THE PSYCHIATRIC-PSYCHOANALYTIC APPROACH

It remained for a psychiatrist to turn the trend of studies away from the search for some physical or mental trait indelibly marking the criminal toward a new approach—the study of all factors in one case of delinquency or crime.   This service was performed by Dr. William Healy, head of the Juvenile Psychopathic Institute (now the Institute for Juvenile Research) in Chicago.   In 1915 he published *The Individual Delinquent,* which presented an analysis of a thousand cases of delinquent boys and girls examined and treated at the Institute.[36]   In view of his training, it is natural that Dr. Healy should lay greatest emphasis on mental factors; but the examination of each delinquent included investigation of heredity, home situations, companions, and physical conditions.   The average number of causative factors in each case was 3.5.   Healy did not find reliable evidence either of hereditary criminal tendencies or of stigmata of crime.   He did not use a control group of nondelinquent children and it is therefore not possible to determine to what extent the factors that he listed as causative occurred more frequently among delinquents than nondelinquents.   But regardless of this deficiency, Healy's book stimulated the study of delinquents and criminals not as a class set apart by some definite criminal tendency, but as ordinary people who exhibited criminal behavior because of one or more mental or physical conditions operating in conjunction with social experiences. Working as he did with individual cases, Healy recognized that many factors operated to cause criminal behavior and that it was not all of one type.

Criminal Conduct, Conflicts, and Frustrations

In *Mental Conflicts and Misconduct,* Healy discussed a group of children, constituting about 11 per cent of the total number of delinquents handled at the Institute, whose delinquencies developed as an attempt on their part to find some solution to mental conflicts.[37] Delinquency thus was viewed as an element in the process by which the children sought to satisfy certain inner needs and to relieve themselves of inner tensions. Their delinquency was not deliberate or planned, but was nevertheless purposive in that it was a part of an attempted adjustment on the part of the child. In his later studies of delinquents, Healy has elaborated on this theory.

Although Healy makes the general statement that the primary human desires are for ego-satisfaction and affection from others, he does not discuss these two urges but pins his discussion to more specific desires.[38] These specific desires are: to feel secure, in the family and other social relationships; to be accepted by some person or group; to obtain recognition and status; to feel personally adequate. Somewhat lesser urges that also demand satisfaction are for accomplishments satisfying to the self, for new experiences, for outlets for physical and mental energies, and for ownership of possessions. As the child grows toward adulthood he wants more opportunity for self-assertion and independence from the restrictions of the family. If the customary satisfaction of these urges is interfered with in any way, the child feels thwarted and frustrated. He reacts emotionally with jealousy, anger, or hatred. And he tries to find some direct or substitutive satisfaction for the compulsive urges within him. For instance, the child usually finds affection in his relationship with family and close friends. When, for some reason, he has no family relationships or they are remote and cold, the desire for affection is not satisfied and a feeling of frustration results. In his random attempts to find satisfaction for thwarted desires that have not been satisfied by socially approved channels, the child sometimes hits upon methods of satisfaction that are regarded by the community (but not by himself) as delinquent. Healy classified these attempts as follows: [39]

(a) Attempt to avoid, even as a temporary measure, the unpleasant situation by *escape* or *flight* from it.

(b) Attempt to achieve substitutive *compensatory satisfactions* through delinquent activities. These satisfactions include the thrill of delinquent adventure and the gratification at obtaining special recognition or attention, perhaps even notoriety, as a delinquent. In some instances material gains figure as compensation for deprivation.

(c) Attempt to strengthen or *bolster up the ego* wounded by feelings of inadequacy or inferiority. The aim then is to obtain *recognition and status* with the delinquent crowd; or, if the offender is more solitary in tendencies, by the individual proving to himself that he really is courageous and can in some way play a spirited role. This "masculine protest" we found to be a not uncommon reaction with some previously effeminate or feminized boys. Said one such lad, "They thought I was no good so I went out to show a cock-eyed world that I was a regular guy."

(d) Attempt to get certain ego-satisfactions through direct and conscious or even unconscious expression of *revenge attitudes*—perhaps through hidden desire to punish parents or others by conduct that will make life difficult for them.

(e) Attempt to gain a *maximum of self-satisfaction,* to inflate the ego, by generally aggressive, antisocial attitudes, that is, by the exhibition of definite hostilities and antagonisms to authority.

(f) *Response to the instinctual urges* felt to be thwarted. While this response may be exhibited in sexual misbehavior, more notably in our delinquents we have discovered the attempt to satisfy the urge for independence and emancipation which normally flares up as an adolescent phenomenon.

(g) The wish for punishment was clearly discernible in a few instances and suspected in others. This *seeking punishment*—delinquent behavior possibly offering an opportunity for being punished—was always a response to a conscious or unconscious sense of guilt.

Thus the delinquent acts contain meaning for the child, although not the implication that the community attaches to them. For instance, a boy who has been rejected in other groups may be acceptable to a boys' gang if he participates in their activities, including stealing. In order to satisfy his need for inclusion in a group he steals. On the other hand, a boy may feel personally inadequate and may steal alone in order to prove to himself that he is not a coward. Thus the delinquent act, stealing, has meaning for the boy in terms of the emotional need that it satisfies.

Another formulation comes from Richard L. Jenkins, formerly with the Michigan Child Guidance Institute.[40] He describes three types of personality structure:

1. The over-inhibited child whose internal conflicts arise from excessive parental repressions. Among the cases at the Institute these children came from families above the clinic average in education and social status. They suffered from parental disapproval and lack of affection.

2. The unsocialized, aggressive child. This child generally came from an unhappy home in a deteriorated neighborhood. He exhibited undisguised hostility and had overly developed sex interests. He showed little remorse for his misdeeds.

3. The pseudo-social child, who was often the gang boy, loyal to his own group but hostile to the out-group.

The origin of delinquent acts is no mystery. The child does not invent new ways of behaving but finds around him examples and patterns of delinquency and crime that he is free to follow. The boy who is not able to find satisfaction for his desires in socially approved forms is most likely to experiment with delinquent ways. Thus Healy attempts to synthesize the personal and social factors in delinquency: the community offers patterns of crime but the motivating force that causes the boy or girl to seek antisocial groups and acts is the failure to find socially approved satisfactions for strongly urgent innate desires.[41]

Psychoanalytic Approach

The psychoanalytic approach also views crime as significant in terms of a person's inner emotional urges and as a part of the process by which he seeks inner peace and self-approval. But the theoretical structure of needs and processes differs from that just presented; in fact, the theoretical framework differs from one psychoanalyst to another. One well-developed formulation places stress upon deviations in the process by which the child passes from interest in his own physical reactions to a sense of social responsibility; or, stated in psychoanalytic terms, from supremacy of the id in control of behavior to supremacy of the super-ego or ego-ideal.

In psychoanalytic theory, the id consists of the unsocial instinctive impulses possessed at birth, which dominate infancy and early childhood. As social pressures and training are brought to bear on the child, he represses the more crude and unsocial aspects of the id or finds acceptable ways of expressing these instinctive impulses. Gradually he develops ideals and moral standards, which are called the super-ego. The super-ego is another term for what most people call conscience. Between the unsocial id and the idealistic super-ego is the ego—the active, organized, socially adjusted part of the personality that functions in everyday activity. In poorly organized persons the id attempts to encroach upon the ego and to cause the person to act in accord with selfish unsocial native impulses; the super-ego also exerts an influence upon the ego. Therefore if a person has not successfully tamed the id, his ego may be a kind of battleground for the struggle between id and super-ego. After this brief general explanation, a more specific analysis of the failure of the ego to become socially adjusted and the relation of this failure to crime may be discussed.

Under the influence of the id the young child seeks first his own pleasure and is restrained primarily by pain of some sort. The instinctive source of pleasure is first the child's own body and its physical functions. As the child's experiences broaden, he becomes attached to the mother. This attachment is called the oedipus complex, which arouses in the son a dual emotional reaction to his father.* He feels himself to be a rival of the father and fears castration at the father's hands, if the father becomes aware of his attachment to the mother. This fear causes anxiety and tends to inhibit the masculine drive. As a result, the boy develops a more feminine attitude and craves the love of the father. Thus he is torn between fear and hatred of the father as a rival for the mother's affection on the one hand and desire for the father's love and approbation on the other. The solution is that the son identifies himself with the father as far as he can. The identification is not complete as the son lacks the father's capacities for sexual fulfillment and also retains the hidden fear of castration. But this partial identification enables the boy to inhibit his instinctive sexual impulses (the id) hoping for later fulfillment in maturity (socially organized ego). The new concepts that he develops are part of the super-ego. As the boy matures, his desire for the love of the father is transformed into a desire for harmony with his own ideals, which in turn are in harmony with social standards. When these three components of the personality are not well balanced, the id rather than the super-ego dominates and delinquent or criminal conduct may result. As the super-ego is never entirely inactive, the ego, having deviated from the ideal pattern, feels guilty. For this reason, the delinquent or criminal may seek punishment, as the punishment relieves the sense of guilt. This conflict does not always show itself in criminal action. The psychoneurotic suffers from the same conflict but expresses his maladjustment symbolically, whereas the criminal expresses his maladjustment in disapproved action that will be punished and thus bring him relief.[42]

Other psychoanalysts, although accepting the general thesis of development from instinctual unsocial impulses to socially formulated action accompanied by maladjustment when the process is incomplete, do not link delinquency only with failure to socialize sexual drives. Aichhorn in his stimulating and interesting book, *Wayward Youth,* discusses at various points other situations that may result in delinquency: a painful or traumatic experience in which the emotion is too great to be assimilated; the oedipus complex, already discussed; an excessive attachment between brother and

* It is one of the peculiarities and weaknesses of the psychoanalytic theory that personality development is almost invariably discussed in terms of the son's attachment to the mother and rivalry for the father. The opposite of the oedipus complex, the electra complex, whereby the daughter is attracted to the father, is almost never discussed in detail, although it is asserted to exist and from time to time some particularly striking example of the electra complex is reported. In view of the low rate of delinquency and crime among females, a psychoanalytic study of the electra complex and its relation to female delinquency would be especially helpful.

sister; harsh early treatment that forces the child to face reality too soon; or extreme indulgence and love that protect the child from reality; severity and indulgence at the same time, representing different treatment by the two parents; conflict between parents; emotional rejection of children by parents; and a succession of foster homes that prevents the child from identifying himself with any one adult.[43]

Psychoanalysts do not necessarily claim that all crime is based upon this inner maladjustment of the personality. Alexander and Staub concede 4 types of criminal: the neurotic criminal, whose criminality is the result of personal maladjustment; the normal criminal whose super-ego is properly developed but in terms of the standards of criminal groups (the professional criminal); the defective criminal who suffers from biological or organic mental defect or psychoses; and the acute criminal who commits a crime under certain special circumstances but is not a chronic criminal, like the first 3 types.[44]

Limitations of Psychiatric and Psychoanalytic Theories

The student may be confused by the divergence of opinion among psychiatrists and psychoanalysts. The usual procedure is for the specialist in these fields to set forth his theory and to offer as supporting evidence a limited number of cases that illustrate the theory. The process of psychoanalyzing a person or giving therapeutic psychiatric treatments covers a long period of time, and probably most of the cases that come to the attention of these specialists are not criminals but persons whose maladjustment has expressed itself in other ways. Few psychiatrists or psychoanalysts therefore have a large number of complete studies of criminals. The exception is found in the files of clinics, such as those for juvenile delinquents or for adult criminals in connection with criminal courts and some prisons. Few well-considered studies have come from these sources, except those by Dr. Healy and his associates. It seems worth noting, therefore, that the theories of Dr. Healy are less extreme in nature and less prone to link all delinquency with one process of maladjustment than are the theories of those with a less well-grounded experience. Until psychiatrists and psychoanalysts, who deal with the same types of problem although applying somewhat different methods and theories, iron out their differences, the best advice that can be given to students in adjacent fields is to read widely among the publications of psychiatrists and psychoanalysts and to pin their faith upon those who offer a wide body of objective data and who draw their conclusions from it, rather than upon those who set up an elaborate theoretical structure illustrated by a few appropriate case studies.

Value of Psychiatric and Psychoanalytic Approach

Regardless of present confusion in theories, the point of view and approach of psychiatrists and psychoanalysts to delinquency and crime are important. These specialists have centered attention upon the delinquent as a person whose physical make-up and psychological functions are no different from those of noncriminal persons; the old attempt to establish a criminal class has been discarded—unless such an attempt can be seen in the tendency of some psychoanalysts to connect crime with one fixed process of maladjustment. Psychiatrists and psychoanalysts have emphasized the origins of maladjustment in the childhood years—the same years in which delinquency begins to develop. They have also related the outward acts of crime to inward urges and have found that criminal acts have a psychological meaning to the criminal understandable only in terms of his inner needs. The less didactic of the group attach a certain importance to social influences —in establishing the norms of approved conduct and in providing criminal patterns. Some limit the concept of crime as the outward symptom of maladjustment to only certain types of criminal, conceding that other criminals are well-adjusted personally but adjusted to a criminal group rather than a socially minded community.

CURRENT SOCIOLOGICAL APPROACH

Throughout the history of the attempt to establish tenable theories of criminality 2 trends have appeared: to find basic causes within a person himself; and to find those causes in the impact of society upon an individual. At present the cleavage between these 2 points of view is rather well marked. The preceding section presented the attempt to find basic causes in the unsatisfied urges of the individual. This section presents the other point of view.

The search for social concomitants of delinquency and crime received great impetus through the studies made by Clifford Shaw and his associates, as part of the work of the Institute for Juvenile Research and the Behavior Research Fund. These carefully objective studies, made first in Chicago and later duplicated by Shaw and others in many other cities, established the existence of areas in cities in which rates of delinquency and crime were many times higher than rates in other areas of the same cities. These so-called delinquency areas always coincided with physically and socially disintegrated communities adjacent to commercial or industrial sections, regardless of the nationality or race of the residents.[45]

When factors, such as delinquency and evidences of social and physical deterioration, are found to exist in close proximity, the temptation is always strong to assume a causal relationship. In this case the temptation is to assume that the social and physical deterioration has caused delinquency and crime. It should be noted, however that the areal studies by Shaw and others merely show that delinquency and social disintegration exist in the same communities. Evidence is not presented to show that individual boys and girls who become delinquent live in the neighborhoods or blocks with the greatest disintegration or come from families and small social groups that are disorganized.

Other studies, however, have shown that juvenile delinquents do, in fact, have membership in various types of disorganized groups and are personally in a position to pattern their conduct after established modes of crime. Thrasher's study of boys' gangs in Chicago demonstrated not only the prevalence of delinquent and semidelinquent gangs in the delinquency areas, but also the process by which boys were inducted into gangs, and, activated by such motives as restlessness and the desire for companionship and prestige, adopted the gang's way of life.[46] Shaw's studies of individual boys again show the way in which they are inducted into criminal patterns, first through association with older and more experienced delinquent boys and later adult criminals.[47] Although these cases present some information on the family background and personality of the delinquent boy (Shaw has not published any case studies of delinquent girls), the chief elaboration and point of emphasis is in community contacts. Commenting on a case study selected as typical of a long series, Shaw states: [48]

This case study sums up in a concrete manner many of the major points brought out in this report. It shows the successive steps in the development of a criminal career, which had its beginning in various forms of petty stealing in the neighborhood and truancy from school. These early patterns of delinquency were acquired through the boy's contacts in his play groups and community. As far as could be ascertained, he never became incorporated into any conventional group in the neighborhood which might develop socially accepted types of behavior or correct his early tendency toward delinquency. While his relationships to his parents were congenial, the family control was not sufficiently effective to counteract the more powerful demoralizing influences in the area in which he resided.

This case history suggests that the attitudes and habits underlying Jack's later delinquent and criminal behavior developed gradually in the course of his participation in the various activities prevailing in his play groups and neighborhood. They were, presumably, the end result of a long succession of social experiences extending back into the period of his early childhood. It is clear that an appreciation of the factors involved in a criminal career such as Jack's necessitates an understanding of the early childhood experiences of the offender and the situations in which these experiences occur.

In the same report, the authors state that "delinquent patterns of behavior develop as a product of a long process of interaction between the individual and the successive social situations in which he lives. This process in which criminal habits and attitudes are formed usually involves a continuity of experiences, extending over a long period of time. From this standpoint, a delinquent or criminal act is a part of a dynamic life process and should be considered as such in the analysis and treatment of cases." [49]

E. H. Sutherland, also, has come out strongly in support of social interaction of the individual with criminal groups as the source of criminal behavior. Sutherland's original work in the field of criminology concerned the white-collar criminal, and his formulation of the causative factors in crime is obviously dictated in part by his attempt to find a theory applicable to white-collar criminals as well as to underworld criminals.[50] He states that "systematic criminal behavior" is acquired through the same processes as "systematic lawful behavior." Criminal behavior occurs, he writes, when a person's associations are in criminal rather than in lawful groups, and the probability that such behavior will develop is conditioned by the frequency and consistency of the individual's contacts with criminal patterns. Factors often regarded as direct causes of criminal behavior, such as family disintegration or temperamental traits of the individual, are influential only indirectly; that is, if such factors lead the individual into association with criminal rather than law-abiding groups. Thus the criminal behavior arises fundamentally from contact with criminal groups. At the basis of criminal patterns lie cultural conflict and social disorganization, which make possible the existence of a number of divergent and often conflicting standards of behavior and scales of moral values. Thus in the social organization criminal patterns are supported and perpetuated and offer a philosophy and techniques of crime to the person who comes in contact with them. Since unethical and criminal practices are carried on in commercial, industrial, and professional life, the novice in these fields is exposed to criminal patterns in the same way that the slum boy is exposed to those of the underworld. It should be noted that Sutherland qualifies his theory as applying to "systematic criminal behavior," by which he apparently means criminal behavior that has become integrated into the general life-pattern of the individual and has been more or less accepted by him and rationalized into an acceptable type of conduct. Later in the same text, Sutherland discusses briefly the relation of mental and emotional factors to crime, but points out the extremely small percentage of criminals who have been found to suffer from such defects.

The studies by the Gluecks also support the theory of delinquency and crime as the result of social interaction with disorganized and criminal groups.

And in fact some of the factual material in Healy's studies might be so interpreted, although Healy evaluates it somewhat differently.

SYNTHESIS OF PRESENT-DAY APPROACHES

Unfortunately certain psychiatrists and sociologists have disparaged each other's studies, a situation that has prevented a necessary joint approach to the study of crime.   Actually, both the psychiatric-psychoanalytic and the sociological approaches agree on certain important points.   Both agree that the development of delinquent and criminal behavior is a process that has its roots in the experiences of early childhood.   Both agree that no child is a born criminal but that he adopts criminal behavior as a result of experiences that begin early in life.   Thus both agree that there is no easy way to understand crime; the attack must be made upon the individual boys and girls or men and women who exhibit criminal behavior.   Both agree, also, that there is no quick and sure cure for crime; the process of elimination of crime or of reform of criminals is slow and uncertain.

Points of disagreement are marked.   The psychiatric-psychoanalytic group places the origin of crime at a much earlier age than do the sociologists. At least one psychoanalytic case study pushes the initial conflict that later led to confirmed criminal behavior back to the first year of life.[51]   Sociologists, however, place the origin of crime at the point when contacts are developed with persons of established delinquent and criminal habits.   Sometimes these initial contacts are in the family, but more often they are in the community.   Thus delinquent behavior may originate at the age of 5 or 6 years, but is unlikely to occur much earlier.

The psychiatric-psychoanalytic group regards criminal behavior as significant to a person in terms of his unfulfilled inner drives and unresolved emotional conflicts.   These drives have failed to find socially acceptable outlets and have a heavy emotional content.   Crime serves to satisfy them: it may represent rebellion and revenge upon society's restraints; or a way of a person's proving to himself that he is not inferior to some hated rival; or a means of symbolically satisfying an urge in a manner less repugnant than direct expression.   The fact that a guilt-feeling accompanies many of these emotional conflicts also leads an individual to criminal behavior, since he will then be punished and thus relieved of his sense of guilt.   It is conceded that criminal behavior exists in the social organization and to this extent furnishes a ready-made pattern for a person to follow; but the reason for adopting a life of crime is to provide inner emotional satisfaction.

The sociologist, on the other hand, views the typical criminal as no more or less disorganized emotionally than the typical noncriminal.   Criminal behavior is learned through group associations just as politeness, tennis, or banking are learned through other types of association, and for the same reasons—the common desire for companionship, participation, and approval.

The problem always arises as to why some people become criminals and others do not. Even in the most starkly delinquent of the delinquency areas, about three fourths of the boys and a much higher proportion of the girls are not delinquent in the course of any one year. The psychiatrist or psychoanalyst would say that those who become delinquent have emotional conflicts engendered by their early life experiences; the sociologist would say that the choice is in part accidental and in part determined by whether or not conventional groups have absorbed the individual and thus prevented association with delinquent groups.

Several reasons can be found for this great divergence in theory and interpretation. The more moderate statements of each group make certain concessions to the other. Thus Alexander and Staub, although they discuss only the neurotic or personally maladjusted criminal, list 4 types of criminal, one of which is the normal person whose super-ego functions properly but has been developed in a criminal group. Sociologists often present case studies that reveal emotional conflicts, although they minimize this aspect and elaborate on the effects of social interaction in delinquent community groups. They also frequently discuss poor family relationships as found in case histories of delinquents but do not probe into any possible emotional concomitants of such situations.

Thus, in a way, each group recognizes the approach of the other, but in any given discussion minimizes the opposite approach and overemphasizes its own theory. The reason for this state of affairs lies largely in the intensive and therefore limited professional training of each group. The psychiatrist and the psychoanalyst do not fully appreciate and cannot evaluate the effect of group associations because they lack the techniques for a sociological study. Similarly, the sociologist undervalues the emotional factors because he is not trained to probe deeply into the personality problems of the individual. As a result each group studies intensively the factors that each is trained to observe, and eventually tends to study only the cases most clearly dominated by the chosen factors. Thus the psychiatrists and psychoanalysts, partly by selection of cases and partly by overemphasis on emotional factors, present a clear-cut case for criminal activities as the direct result of emotional conflicts; the sociologists, by the same process, present an equally valid case for social interaction as the basis for criminal activities.

Both groups tend to overlook the complexity of activities that come under the heading of criminal. In the last analysis such activities are arbitrarily designated. Criminals violate some of the established moral values of a given community, but they do not all violate the same values.   Some acts called criminal are offenses against the right of individuals to be secure from physical assault; others are infringements of personal property values; still others are breaches of community rights.   Beating, stabbing, and murder are examples of the first type of violation; stealing, embezzlement, forgery, and fraudulent accounting are examples of the second; destroying public property, misuse of public funds, and treason are examples of the third. Obviously the motives for these many kinds of behavior are not identical; therefore it is a mistake to seek a general cause or a general process to explain criminal behavior.   Rather one should expect to find several processes, which is the result achieved by psychiatrists, psychoanalysts, and sociologists.

FOOTNOTES

[1] Arthur Fink, *Causes of Crime* (Philadelphia: University of Pennsylvania Press, 1938), pp. 1–19.

[2] For a discussion of criminological studies prior to 1870, see A. Lindesmith and Y. Levin, "The Lombrosian Myth in Criminology," *American Journal of Sociology,* 42 (1937), 653–71.   This article is the basis for the present discussion of early studies. Excerpts from many early writers will be found in W. A. Bonger, *Criminality and Economic Conditions,* translated from the 1905 Amsterdam edition (Little, Brown, 1916), Part I.

[3] *Op. cit.,* pp. 666–67.

[4] *Penal Philosophy* (Little, Brown, 1912). This book was first published in France in 1890.

[5] *Op. cit.,* pp. 545ff.

[6] *Op. cit.,* pp. 669–70.

[7] Cesare Lombroso, *Crime, Its Causes and Remedies,* Modern Criminal Science Series (Little, Brown, 1912), pp. xiff, Introduction by M. Parmelee. This translation is not of Lombroso's original publication but of a later one in which he gives weight to social as well as biological factors. In the Introduction, however, Parmelee outlines Lombroso's original theories.   For other publications in English of Lombroso's theories, see Gina Lombroso-Ferrero, *Criminal Man, according to the Classification of Cesare Lombroso* (Putnam, 1911); Cesare Lombroso and William Ferrero, *The Female Offender* (Appleton, 1895).

[8] Lombroso, *op. cit.,* pp. 365–66.

[9] Enrico Ferri, *Criminal Sociology* (Appleton, 1896).

[10] *Op. cit.,* pp. 669–70.

[11] *Criminology,* The Modern Criminal Science Series (Little, Brown, 1914).

[12] *Abridged Edition of the English Convict* (London: His Majesty's Stationery Office, 1919).

[13] *Ibid.,* pp. 34–97.

[14] *Ibid.,* pp. V, 98–122, 162–84.

[15] *Ibid.,* p. 268.

[16] *Crime and the Man* (Cambridge: Harvard University Press, 1939). This book is a popular but thorough treatment of the complete report, published in three volumes under the title of the *American Criminal: An Anthropological Study* (Cambridge: Harvard University Press, 1939).

[17] *Ibid.,* pp. 127–28.

[18] *Ibid.,* pp. 6–7.

[19] *Ibid.,* pp. 250–78.

[20] B. Boshes, S. Kobrin, E. Reynolds, and S. Rosenbaum. The study is outlined in

M. F. A. Montagu, "The Biologist Looks at Crime," *Annals of the American Academy of Political and Social Science,* 217 (1941), 51–52.

21 William Healy and Augusta F. Bronner, *New Light on Delinquency and Its Treatment* (New Haven: Yale University Press, 1936).

22 *Ibid.,* pp. 56, 73–74.

23 *Ibid.,* pp. 133, 138.

24 *Op. cit.,* p. 145.

25 Montagu, *op. cit.,* pp. 47–48.

26 *Human Efficiency and Levels of Intelligence* (Princeton, N.J.: Princeton University Press, 1920), pp. 63ff.

27 *Feeble-Mindedness, Its Causes and Consequences* (Macmillan, 1914), p. 514.

28 *Op. cit.,* pp. 515–16.

29 *Feeble-Mindedness, Its Causes and Consequences,* pp. 566–567; *The Criminal Imbecile* (Macmillan, 1915), pp. 106–7.

30 *Criminal Intelligence* (Worcester, Mass.: Clark University, 1926).

31 A. A. Hartman and A. W. Brown, "A Survey of the Intelligence of Illinois Prisoners," *Journal of Criminal Law and Criminology,* Vol. 28 (1938). Simon H. Tulchin, *Intelligence and Crime* (Chicago: University of Chicago Press, 1939). For a summary and evaluation of studies up to 1933, see L. D. Zeleny, "Feeble-mindedness and Criminal Conduct," *Journal of Criminal Law and Criminology,* 38 (1933), 564–76. Another summary is given by E. H. Sutherland, chapter 15 in *Social Attitudes,* edited by Kimball Young (Holt, 1931).

32 In support of the glandular theory, see Louis Berman, *The Glands Regulating Personality* (Macmillan, 1921); M. G. Schlapp and E. H. Smith, *The New Criminology* (Boni and Liveright, 1928). For a more conservative and moderate statement, see R. G. Hoskins, *The Tides of Life* (Norton, 1933); *Human Biology and Racial Welfare,* edited by E. B. Cowdry (Hoeber, 1930).

33 *The Delinquent Boy* (Badger, 1926), p. 268.

34 References are: J. W. Bridges and K. M. Banham, "A Psychological Study of Juvenile Delinquents by Group Methods," *Genetic Psychology Monographs,* 1 (1926), 411–506; M. S. Covert, "Excitability in Delinquent Boys," *Journal of Delinquency,* 5 (1920), 224–39; R. J. Ball, "Introversion and Extroversion in a Group of Criminals," *Journal of Abnormal and Social Psychology,* 26 (1932), 422–28; A. Courthial, "Emotional Differences of Delinquent and Nondelinquent Girls of Normal Intelligence," *Archives of Psychology,* No. 133 (1931); R. J. Ball, "The General Emotionality of the Prisoner," *Journal of Applied Psychology,* 15 (1931), 436–61.

35 For a more complete treatment of the characteristics of psychopaths, see pages 242–46. For a detailed discussion of the tendency to attribute crime to psychopathy, see Morris Ploscowe, "Some Causative Factors in Criminality," *Report on the Causes of Crime,* No. 13, Vol. I of the reports of the National Commission on Law Observance and Enforcement (Washington: Government Printing Office, 1931), 49–60.

36 (Little, Brown, 1915).

37 (Little, Brown, 1917).

38 William Healy and Augusta F. Bronner, *New Light on Delinquency and Its Treatment* (New Haven: Yale University Press, 1936), pp. 3–7; 132–34.

39 Healy and Bronner, *op. cit.,* pp. 133–34.

40 R. L. Jenkins, "A Psychiatric View of Personality Structure in Children," *The Delinquent and the Wartime Community* (National Probation Association Yearbook, 1943).

41 Another formulation of Healy's point of view will be found in Franz Alexander and William Healy, *Roots of Crime: Psychoanalytic Studies* (Knopf, 1935).

42 For an elaboration of this theory, see Franz Alexander and Hugo Staub, *The Criminal, the Judge, and the Public, a Psychological Analysis* (London: Allen and Unwin, 1931). For general statements of psychoanalytic theory, not related to crime, see Ives Hendrick, *Facts and Theories of Psychoanalysis* (Knopf, 1934); William Healy, A. F. Bronner, and A. M. Bowers, *The Structure and Meaning of Psychoanalysis* (Knopf, 1930). For an analysis of cases, see Alexander and Healy, *op. cit.;* Franz Alexander and L. J. Saul, "Three Criminals," *Psychoanalytic Review,* 124 (1937), 113–30; and the *Journal of Criminal Psychopathology,* which was first issued in 1939.

[43] (Viking, 1939), pp. 8–9, 41ff., 63ff., 120–21, 200ff., 225–226.

[44] *Op. cit.*, pp. 50–69.

[45] These studies are discussed in detail in Chapter 3.

[46] Frederic Thrasher, *The Gang* (Chicago: University of Chicago Press, 1936).

[47] *The Jack-Roller* (University of Chicago Press, 1930); *The Natural History of a Delinquent Career* (Chicago: University of Chicago Press, 1931); *Brothers in Crime* (Chicago: University of Chicago Press, 1938).

[48] Clifford R. Shaw and Henry D. McKay, *Social Factors in Juvenile Delinquency*, No. 13, Vol. II of the reports of the National Commission on Law Observance and Enforcement (Washington: Government Printing Office, 1931), 379–80.

[49] Shaw and McKay, *op. cit.*, p. 393.

[50] *Principles of Criminology* (Lippincott, 1939), pp. 4–9.

[51] R. M. Lindner, *Rebel without a Cause, The Hypoanalysis of a Criminal Psychopath* (New York: Grune and Stratton, 1944).

APPENDIX B

Definitions of Crimes[*]

Part I Offenses

1. Criminal homicide.—(a) Murder and non-negligent manslaughter includes all wilful felonious homicides as distinguished from deaths caused by negligence. Does not include attempts to kill, assaults to kill, suicides, accidental death, or justifiable homicides. Justifiable homicides excluded from this classification are limited to the following types of cases: (1) the killing of a felon by a peace officer in line of duty; (2) the killing of a hold-up man by a private citizen. (b) Manslaughter by negligence includes any death that police investigation establishes was primarily attributable to gross negligence on the part of some individual other than the victim.

2. Rape.—Includes forcible rape, statutory rape (no force used—victim under age of consent), assault to rape, and attempted rape.

3. Robbery.—Includes stealing or taking anything of value from the person by force or violence or by instilling fear, such as strong-arm robbery, stickups, robbery, armed. Includes assault to rob and attempt to rob.

4. Aggravated assault.—Includes assault with intent to kill; assault by shooting, cutting, stabbing, maiming, poisoning, scalding, or by the use of acids. Does not include simple assault, assault and battery, fighting, etc.

5. Burglary—breaking or entering.—Includes burglary, housebreaking, safecracking, or any unlawful entry to commit a felony or a theft, even though no force was used to gain entrance. Includes attempts. Burglary followed by larceny is included in this classification and is not counted again as larceny.

6. Larceny—theft (except auto theft).—(a) Fifty dollars and over in value; (b) under $50 in value—includes in one of the above subclassifications, depending upon the value of the property stolen, thefts of bicycles, automobile

* Uniform Crime Reports for the United States and Its Possessions, 1953, 24, No. 1 (Washington: Government Printing Office, 1953), 64–65.

accessories, shoplifting, pocket-picking, or any stealing of property or article of value which is not taken by force and violence or by fraud. Does not include embezzlement, "con" games, forgery, worthless checks, etc.

7. Auto theft.—Includes all cases where a motor vehicle is stolen or driven away and abandoned, including the so-called joy riding thefts. Does not include taking for temporary use when actually returned by the taker, or unauthorized use by those having lawful access to the vehicle.

Part II Offenses

8. Other assaults.—Includes all assaults and attempted assaults which are not of an aggravated nature and which do not belong in class 4.

9. Forgery and counterfeiting.—Includes offenses dealing with the making, altering, uttering, or possessing, with intent to defraud, anything false which is made to appear true. Includes attempts.

10. Embezzlement and fraud.—Includes all offenses of fraudulent conversion, embezzlement, and obtaining money or property by false pretenses.

11. Stolen property; buying, receiving, possessing.—Includes buying, receiving, and possessing stolen property as well as attempts to commit any of those offenses.

12. Weapons; carrying; possessing, etc.—Includes all violations of regulations or statutes controlling the carrying, using, possessing, furnishing, and manufacturing of deadly weapons or silencers and all attempts to violate such statutes or regulations.

13. Prostitution and commercialized vice.—Includes sex offenses of a commercialized nature, or attempts to commit the same, such as prostitution, keeping bawdy house, procuring, transporting, or detaining women for immoral purposes.

14. Sex offenses (except rape and prostitution and commercialized vice).—Includes offenses against chastity, common decency, morals, and the like. Includes attempts.

15. Offenses against the family and children.—Includes offenses of nonsupport, neglect, desertion, or abuse of family and children.

16. Narcotic drug laws.—Includes offenses relating to narcotic drugs, such as unlawful possession, sale, or use. Excludes federal offenses.

17. Liquor laws.—With the exception of "drunkenness" (class 18) and "driving while intoxicated" (class 22), liquor law violations, state or local, are placed in this class. Excludes federal violations.

18. Drunkenness.—Includes all offenses of drunkenness or intoxication. .

19. Disorderly conduct.—Includes all charges of committing a breach of the peace.

Index

Abbott, Grace, 375
Abrahams, Joseph, 588, 610
absence without leave, 600-06
administration:
  of European prisons, 618, 625, 635, 639, 642
  of parole, 540-41
  of prison industries, 474-75
  of prisons, 426-28, 434-36
admission:
  to prison, 456-57
  to women's reformatories, 509-11
age:
  of European offenders, 617
  of military offenders, 598
  of offenders, 41-49, 432, 501
Ahrnborg, B., 660
Aichhorn, August, 109, 111, 124
alcoholism, 210-16
Alexander, Franz, 249, 698, 703, 705
Alexander, M. E., 396, 397
Alinsky, Saul, 271, 272, 282, 284
Alper, Benedict, 660
Anderson, D., 69
Anderson, J. Fay, 69
Anderson, Nels, 149, 226, 228
Angell, R. C., 189-202
Arieff, A., 37, 68
armed forces:
  characteristics of offenders in, 598-604
  court-martial in, 181-83
  induction of criminals into, 597-98
  offenders in, 573-74
  offenses by members of, 579
  offenses in, abroad, 604-06
  police in, 581
  rejection of criminals by, 574-76
Arnold, D. S., 302, 335
arrests:
  and convictions, 370
  offenses cleared by, 330-33
  on suspicion, 321-22

Asbury, Herbert, 149, 178, 179
Ash, E., 496, 497, 498
Axelrad, S., 59, 69
Auburn system, 404-05

babies in prison, 511
Baarslag, Karl, 148, 317, 336
Bacon, G. R., 397
Bacon, S. D., 397
bail, 340-43
Baker, N. F., 374, 375
Ball, R. J., 705
Banay, R. S., 216, 227
Banham, K. M., 705
banishment, 291
Barnes, Harry Elmer, 299, 455, 536, 660
Barnes, R. D., 428
Barron, A. J., 556
Bates, Sanford, 428, 436, 454, 455
Beeley, Arthur L., 374
Beier, E. G., 265, 284
Belbenoit, René, 661
Bennett, James O'Donnell, 31
Bennett, James V., 395, 455
Bennett, R. V., 609, 610
Berger, M., 179
Berman, Louis, 705
Bettelheim, B., 30
Bixby, F. L., 497
Black, Jack, 148
Blanche, E. E., 223, 228
Blumer, Herbert, 74, 103, 104
Bok, Curtis, 375
Bonger, William A., 680, 681, 704
Borstals, 622-23
Boshes, B., 704
Bowers, A. M., 705
Bowery, L. E., 227
Bowle, C., 37, 68
Bowman, K. M., 226
Bridges, J. W., 705
Briggs, H. L., 497

711

Brockway, Zebulon R., 414, 415, 468, 476, 483, 612
Bromberg, Walter, 249, 250
Bronner, Augusta, 56, 69, 109, 110, 111, 114, 123, 124, 262, 284, 563, 571, 688, 705
Brown, A. W., 705
Brownell, E. A., 375
Bruce, A. A., 202, 567, 568, 571, 572
Bryan, Helen, 515, 519, 520
Bulger, J. E., 179
Burgess, Ernest W., 79, 194, 195, 202, 284, 566, 567, 568, 571, 572
Burns, Robert E., 429
Bushong, E. M., 118
Butler, M., 105

Cahill, J. C., 375
Caldwell, Charles, 678
Caldwell, M. G., 105, 118
Callender, Clarence N., 201
camps:
   road, 408-13
   work, 408, 424-25
Carpenter, N., 105
capital punishment, 288-90, 399
Carr, Lowell J., 87, 91, 104, 105, 533, 537
Casey, Roy, 395, 396
Cassidy, J. H., 202
casual offender, 23, 180-81
Caswell, George, 104
Cavan, Ruth Shonle, 105, 118, 283
Chandler, H. P., 537
Chappell, Richard A., 536, 607
Charlesworth, James C., 201
Chicago Area Project, 270-71
churches, see religious training
Chute, C. L., 374, 375
cities (see also delinquency areas):
   arrests in, 332
   crime in European, 618
   crime rates in, 41, 43
   police systems in, 301-10
Claghorn, K. H., 105
Clark, Charles L., 148, 149, 467, 496, 497
classification systems, 457-62:
   in Europe, 619-20, 640-41, 644
   in military correction, 585, 587, 589, 594-95
   in women's institutions, 510-11
Clemmer, Donald, 429, 484, 493, 495, 497, 498
Clinard, M. B., 30, 105, 178, 179, 183, 196, 197, 198, 199, 201, 202
clinics (see also counseling and therapy), 275-78
comic books, 75
community, 90-94, 112-13, 122, 671-73
Conboy, M., 178

Conn, J. H., 228
convictions, 369-73
Cooper, R. Weldon, 335
co-ordination:
   in law enforcement, 295-97, 669-71
   of police systems, 312-15
   of preventive programs, 266-73, 281-82
Corey, Herbert, 178
correctional institutions, 423-24
Corwin, E. H. L., 397
Cosulich, Gilbert, 537
counseling, school, 256
Courthial, A., 705
courts, 337-73:
   criminal, 345-46
   functions of, 287, 293-94
   juvenile, 362-69
   lower, 384
   military, 581-83
courts-martial, 581-83
Covert, M. S., 705
Cowdry, E. B., 705
Crawford, Paul L., 284
Cressey, Donald R., 73, 104
crime:
   control of, 199-200
   defined, 3
   interest in, 70-75, 78-86
   rates of, 42-45, 80-87
crimes:
   arrests for different types of, 330-33
   classified, 4-6, 8, 21, 40-42, 707-09
   comparison of, for Europe and the United States, 614-18
   unreported, 36-38
criminal, defined, 4
criminal behavior:
   learned, 12-17
   and maladjustment, 17-20
   theories of, 11-20, 662-64, 677-704
criminal law, 7-8, 287-88
criminals (see also prisoners):
   characteristics of, 41-64, 67
   classified, 21-29
   rejection of, by armed forces, 574-76
cultural influences, 70-75
Cunningham, E. V., 397

Davis, Jerome, 396
Decker, Charles, 608
defense attorney, 358-62
delinquency areas, 78-98
De Long, E. H., 374, 375
Denmark, prison system in, 635-39
depression, economic, 76-77
disciplinary barracks in army, 584-86
discipline:
   in jail, 387-88

in prison, 440-46, 453
for women, 513-14
disorganization, social, 75-78, 504-05, 678-81, 699-702
Dolton, I., 283
Doshay, L. J., 186, 187, 202
Douglas, Paul H., 193, 195, 200, 201, 202
Dressler, David, 555, 556
drug addiction, 216-20
Duffus, R. L., 179
Duffy, Clinton T., 428, 429, 454, 496
Dumpson, J. R., 284
Dunham, H. W., 246, 248, 249, 250

economic status, 88, 114-15
education:
    for female prisoners, 512
    of female prisoners, 504
    for male prisoners, 476-82
    of male prisoners, 481-82
    of military offenders, 598-99
Edwards, M. O., 608
Eissler, K. R., 31, 123, 124
Elliott, M. A., 103
Ellis, W. J., 454
England, prison system in, 618-24
episodic criminal, 23-24, 189-90
Erickson, M. H., 250
Eriksson, Torsten, 660, 661
escapes, 446-48, 513
Eubank, Earle E., 148, 149, 497
Evjen, Victor H., 607, 608

Fabricant, Louis, 375
family:
    influence of, 13-14, 107-22
    and recidivism, 559-61
    reorganization of, 274-75
Fay, Bill, 455
Federal Bureau of Investigation, 317-19:
    methods of, 326-29
    training by, 308
federal prison system, 419-26:
    education in, 478
    group therapy in, 465-66
    industries in, 474-75
    women's reformatory in, 514-16
Federn, Paul, 31
fee system, 383-84
felonies:
    and age, 48
    arrests for, 331-32
    and convictions, 371
    rates for, 44
    and sex, 50-51
    types of, 707-08
Fenton, Norman, 496, 636, 637, 653, 658, 660, 661
Ferrero, William, 704

Ferri, Enrico, 11, 681, 683, 704
Field, H. E., 498
fines, 294-95, 385:
    in Sweden, 640
Fink, Arthur, 704
Fishman, Joseph Fulling, 497
Fishmann, J. T., 227
Floch, M., 334, 336
foreign-born, 60-64, 80
Foreman, P. B., 495
Fox, Sir Lionel, 624, 659, 661
Fox, Vernon, 455
Fraenkel, O. K., 336
France, prison system in, 624-35
Frank, S., 335
Frazier, E. Franklin, 59, 69
Freeman, J., 179

Galt, Franz Joseph, 678
gambling, 223-24
gangs:
    boys, 14, 94-96, 151-52
    criminal, 26-28, 151-54
Garofalo, Baron Raffaele, 684
Garrett, E. W., 334
Garrison, L. R., 608, 609
Gerlach, E. M., 395
Germain, Charles, 626, 660, 661
Gerrity, J., 228
Gillin, J. L., 57, 69
Gilmore, Harlan W., 14, 31
girls (see also women): 49-53, 96-97, 127-30, 131-33, 135-36
Glane, S., 105
Glueck, Bernard, 244, 250
Glueck, Eleanor T., 44, 56, 65, 66, 68, 69, 95, 96, 97, 105, 108, 111, 113, 114, 118, 120, 123, 124, 125, 149, 183, 184, 186, 201, 202, 228, 258, 283, 284, 297, 455, 519, 520, 533, 534, 537, 550, 556, 560, 561, 562, 563, 564, 565, 567, 568, 570, 571, 572, 701
Glueck, Sheldon, 44, 56, 65, 66, 68, 69, 95, 96, 97, 105, 108, 111, 113, 114, 118, 120, 123, 124, 125, 149, 183, 184, 186, 201, 202, 227, 228, 258, 283, 284, 297, 455, 519, 520, 533, 534, 536, 537, 550, 556, 560, 561, 562, 563, 564, 565, 567, 568, 570, 571, 572, 701
Goddard, Henry H., 689, 690, 691
Goldberg, H. L., 608, 609
Goldberg, Louis P., 375
Goldman, M. C., 375
Goldman, M. M., 191, 192, 202
Goring, Charles, 684, 685, 689
Gossett, W. T., 202
Gross, Fred, 396
group work, 262-66

guards, 437-40, 490-92
Guerry, A. M., 678
Gurfein, M. I., 179
Guttmacher, M., 228

habitual offenders, 28, 203-26:
    in Europe, 623, 625, 641, 644-45
Haenszel, W. M., 105
Hall, J., 227, 336
Hall, Livingston, 374
Hallowitz, E., 282
Hampton, P. J., 226
Harno, A. J., 374, 375, 367, 568, 571, 572
Harris, Mary, 227, 519
Hartman, A. A., 705
Hartshorne, Hugh, 258, 284
Hartsough, Mildred, 104
Hartung, F. E., 299
Hassler, Alfred, 496
Hauser, Philip M., 74, 103, 104
Hayes, M. M., 227
Hayner, N. S., 68, 69, 86, 90, 104, 105,
    106, 124, 496, 497, 498
Haynes, Fred E., 520
Healy, William, 56, 69, 109, 110, 111,
    114, 123, 124, 249, 262, 284, 563,
    571, 660, 688, 693, 694, 696, 698,
    702, 705
Hendrich, Ives, 705
Henry, Nelson B., 283
Hepner, Arthur W., 519
Hershey, L. B., 609, 610
Hightower, P. R., 258, 284
Hillman, Arthur, 284
Hoefer, F. A. C., 608
Hoffer, F. W., 396
Hollingshead, A. B., 609
Holton, Karl, 497
homes, broken, 115-20
Hooton, E. A., 685, 686, 687
Hoover, J. Edgar, 178, 318, 334, 336
Hoskins, R. G., 705
House, F. N., 396
house of correction, 391
housing, 87
Howard, John, 611
Hubermann, Leo, 179
Hurlbert, H. S., 250
Hynd, Alan, 284

Imbau, F. E., 336
industries, prison, see work for prisoners
insanity, 353-54
intelligence, 53-56, 689-92:
    of military offenders, 599
investigation, criminal, 325-30

jails, 376-95:
    women in, 499-500
Jellinek, E. M., 227

Jenkins, Richard L., 695, 705
Jennings, Dean, 428, 496
Johnson, B., 228
Johnson, Fred R., 537
Johnson, G. B., 69
Johnston, James A., 428
Jones, R. F., 472, 497
Josephson, Matthew, 103
judge:
    criminal, 350-53
    municipal, 399-40
judicial powers and police, 320-21
jury:
    grand, 294, 344-45
    petit, 294, 349-50
justice of the peace, 338-39
juvenile delinquency, 29, 59, 63-64, 64-65,
    71, 74-75, 183-87:
    and courts, 362-69
    and crime, 126-37, 174-76
    defined, 364-65
    in delinquency areas, 78-86, 92
    and drugs, 220
    and jails, 387
    prevention of, 251-82
    and probation, 532-34

Kahn, Alfred J., 283, 284
kangaroo court, 388
Kaplan, Benjamin, 374
Karlen, Delmar, 609
Karpman, Benjamin, 226, 228
Kawin, Irene, 536
Kefauver, Estes, 38, 69, 178, 179
Kendall, G. N., 497
Key, V. O., 334, 336
Killinger, G. C., 555
Kimball, R. A., 335
Kinberg, O., 227
Kinsella, Nina, 396
Kirchwey, G., 288, 299
Kirk, P. L., 334
Kleber, Victor, 610
Kobrin, S., 704
Kolb, L., 218, 227
Konopka, Gisela, 283
Krumbholtz, E. C., 497
Kvaraceus, W. C., 69, 258, 283

Lamson, D. A., 455, 496
Landesco, J., 148, 149, 178
Lane, Clem, 31
Lanzer, I. A., 536
Larson, John A., 329, 336
law enforcement, 293-97
Lawes, Lewis E., 428, 429, 435, 445, 455,
    497
Lejins, P. P., 299
Lekkerkerker, E. C., 520
le Maire, Louis, 661

Lenroot, Katherine F., 368, 375
Levenson, Eleanore, 375
Levin, Y., 679, 683, 704
libraries in prisons, 482
lie detector, 329-30
Liggett, W. W., 179
Lindner, R. M., 224, 228, 243, 249, 250, 498, 706
Lindesmith, A. R., 178, 226, 227, 679, 683, 704
Locke, Harvey J., 227, 228
lockups, 379-81
Lockwood, P. E., 179
Lohman, J. D., 284
Lombroso, Cesare, 11, 681, 682, 683, 684, 693, 704
Lombroso, Gina, 704
Long, Jean, 556
Longmoor, E., 86, 104, 105
Loth, David, 178
Lottier, S., 105
Lukas, Edwin J., 179, 227
Lumpkin, K. D., 108, 113, 124

McCallum, M. R., 610
McCarthy, R., 179
McCorkle, Lloyd W., 465, 496, 497, 588, 608, 609, 610
MacCormick, A. H., 396, 455, 497, 584, 606, 608
McDowell, E. E., 396, 520
McEvoy, F. P., 182, 201
McGee, Richard A., 450, 497
McKay, H. D., 14, 30, 31, 89, 103, 104, 105, 115, 116, 119, 123, 124, 284, 706
McKelvey, Blake, 429, 497
MacNamara, Donald E., 305, 334, 335
Madden, J. W., 375
Maginnis, J., 593, 609, 610
maladjustment, 17-20, 28-29, 204-07, 229-48
Malamud, D. I., 284
Mann, D. M., 396
Marston, W. M., 329, 336
Martin, John, 179
Maurer, D. W., 149, 228
May, Mark A., 258, 284
marital status, 56-58, 140-41:
  of female prisoners, 503
  of male prisoners, 433-34
  and recidivism, 563-64
maximum security, 400-01, 420-21
medical services:
  in jail, 388
  in prison, 462-63
medium security, 421
Meltzer, B. D., 375
Michelson, T., 227
military correctional system, 583-96:

comparison of, with civilian, 606-07
Miller, Justin, 375
Miller, M. H., 397
Millspaugh, Arthur C., 334, 335, 336
minimum security, 415-19
misdemeanants, characteristics of, 385-86
misdemeanors, 8, 93:
  and age, 48
  and convictions, 372
  and habitual offenders, 203-26
  rates of, 45
  sentences for, 385
  and sex, 52
  types of, 708-09
Mishkin, Charles, 375
mobility, 89, 97-98
Moberg, D. O., 69
Moley, Raymond, 311, 335, 374, 375
Monahan, Florence, 519
Monochesi, Elio D., 571
Monroe, David Geeting, 336
Montagu, M. F. A., 705
motion pictures, 74-75
Moore, F. D., 375
Moore, M. E., 148
Moos, Malcom C., 429
Morris, Albert, 498
Morris, Norval, 659
Morris, Richard W., 335
Mowrer, Ernest R., 64, 69, 82, 83, 84, 85, 86, 104, 105
Mowrer, Harriet R., 205, 227
Muehlberger, C. W., 334, 336
Mueller, G. O. W., 659
Murchison, Carl, 53, 54, 55, 69, 691, 692
Murphy, F. J., 37, 68
Murphy, Joseph P., 537

Negroes, 59-60, 90
Nelson, Victor F., 496
Niles, Blair, 661
Nolting, O. F., 302, 335
nonconformity, 9-10, 22
Nordyke, Lewis, 609, 610
Norway, prison system in, 642-52

occasional criminal, 23, 181-89
Odegard, P. H., 179
O'Hare, Kate Richards, 519
Ohlin, Lloyd E., 568, 569, 570, 571, 572
Oldigs, W., 397
organized crime, 26-28, 150-77
Osborne, Thomas Mott, 444, 445, 454, 455
Overholser, Winfred, 375

pardons, 551-52
Park, Robert E., 79
Parker, Alfred E., 334, 336
Parmelee, M., 704

parole, 287, 442-43, 538-51:
 in Europe, 623-24, 626, 637
 in military correctional system, 596
Patterson, Alexander, 660
Pennsylvania system, 403-05
People's Organization, 271-73
Pepper, L. H., 609
Perlman, V. T., 227
personal relationships of prisoners, 486-92
Peterson, V. W., 335
Phelps, H. A., 104
Phleger, M., 105
physical factors, 681-89
planning, residential, 273-74
Ploscowe, Morris, 23, 31, 178, 179, 189,
 202, 227, 250, 299, 374, 400, 429,
 524, 537, 705
police, 300-33:
 arrest policies of, 38
 federal, 316-20
 functions of, 287, 293
 needs of, 665-66
 military, 581
 and prevention, 259-62
 state, 315-16
policewomen, 308-10
political corruption, 27-28, 166-72, 173-
 74, 193, 323-24
Pollak, Otto, 50, 68, 69
Porterfield, A. L., 37, 68, 185, 186, 202
Pound, Roscoe, 5, 31, 375
prediction of parole success, 566-70
prevention, 251-82
prisons, 398-428:
 administration of, 419-20, 426, 434-37
 in Air Force, 589-92
 in Army, 584-89
 compared, for Europe and United
 States, 652-58
 in Denmark, 635-39
 early development of, 291-92, 399-404
 effect of, on prisoners, 492-95
 in England and Wales, 618-24
 in France, 624-35
 life in, and recidivism, 561-62
 for men and women compared, 517-
 18
 in Navy, 592-96
 in Norway, 642-52
 in Sweden, 639-42
prisoners (see also criminals):
 characteristics of, 431-34, 481, 500-05
 and marital status, 57-58, 433-34
 number of, 398
 on parole, 541-45
 on probation, 523-35
prisoners' aid societies, 553-54:
 in England, 623-24
prison farms, 407-08

probation, 523-35:
 amount of, 373, 531
 functions of, 287
 for misdemeanants, 391-92
probation officers, 524-27
professional criminal, 25-28, 125-47
prosecuting attorney, 354-58
prostitution, see sex offenders
psychiatric services:
 in Denmark, 637-39
 in jail, 388
 in prison, 464-66
 for women, 513
psychological factors, 53-56, 689-99
psychoneurotic criminals, 28-29, 238-40
psychopathic criminals, 29, 240-44:
 in Denmark, 637-39
psychotic criminals, 29, 232-37, 353-54
public opinion, 7, 155, 208-10
public, responsibility of, 278-80, 671-73
public defenders, 362
punishment, physical, 289-90

Quetelet, A., 678

race, 58-60, 90
racket, criminal, 159-64
Radzinowicz, L., 249
Rappaport, Mazie F., 397
reception centers, 459-60
recidivism:
 extent of, 557
 in Europe, 617-18
 factors in, 559-66
 among male prisoners, 432-33
 of military offenders, 588, 593
 of parolees, 549-51
 of probationers, 532-35
 reduction of, 570
 types of, 558
Reckless, Walter C., 93, 105, 223, 227, 228
recreation:
 for male prisoners, 482-85
 and prevention, 262-66
 for women prisoners, 512-13
Reed, Ellery F., 284
Reed, G. J., 497
reform, see rehabilitation
reformatories:
 education in, 476-77
 for men, 413-15, 421-28
 recreation in, 483
 for women, 425, 505-08
rehabilitation (see also, treatment, discipline), 64-67:
 among Air Force offenders, 589-92
 among Army offenders, 586-89
 lack of, in prison, 492-95
 among Navy offenders, 592-96

methods of, 297-99, 459-62, 664-68
and probation, 532-35, 549-51
Reimer, Hans, 496
Reinemann, John Otto, 375
release:
from jail, 393-94
unconditional, 552-53
religious services:
in prison, 485-86
in women's reformatories, 513
religious training, 257-59
retaliation, 288-89
retraining center in Air Force, 589-92
retraining command in Navy, 593-96
Reuter, Edward B., 69
Reynolds, E., 704
Ridley, C. E., 302, 335
Riemer, S. H., 187, 202
Rinck, Jane E., 283
riots, 448-53
Robinson, L. N., 375, 377, 395, 396
Robinson, Sophia, 36, 68
roles, 13, 16-17
Romano, F. A., 284
Rose, M., 226
Rosenbaum, S., 704
Rubin, Sol, 496
Rumney, Jay, 537
rural areas, 100-102:
crime rates in, 41, 43, 99
police in, 310-12

Sain, F. G., 396
Sait, E. M., 179
Salter, J. T., 178
Sanders, R. C., 179
Saul, L. J., 705
Schilder, P., 250
Schlapp, M. G., 705
schools, 254-57
Schroeder, C. W., 105
Schroeder, P. L., 69, 91
scopolamine, 330
Scott, B. L., 556
Scudder, Kenyon J., 418, 429, 430, 438,
454
Seaberry, Samuel, 168, 179
segmental crime, 24-25, 190-200
self-government in prison, 444-45
Sellin, T., 30, 37, 69, 104, 429, 495, 661
Selling, L. S., 520
sentences:
of criminals, 373
of minor offenders, 385
of prisoners, 432
of women, 508-09
Senturia, J. J., 179
Sethna, M. J., 659
settlements, see group work

sex:
deprivation of, in prison, 489-90
in Europe, 617
and types of crime, 49-53, 502-03
sex offenders, 186-87, 220-23
Shalloo, J. P., 335
Shaw, Clifford, 13, 31, 64, 79, 80, 81, 86,
89, 90, 94, 95, 103, 104, 105, 115,
116, 117, 119, 123, 124, 146, 148, 149,
270, 271, 284, 699, 700, 706
sheriff, 310-11, 383-84
Sherwin, R. V., 228
Shulman, H. M., 105
Silk, S. A., 250
sin, 10
Skinner, E. W., 609, 610
Slawson, J. 692
slum, see delinquency areas
Smith, Alfred E., 311
Smith, Bruce, 334, 335, 336, 374
Smith, E. H., 705
Smith, F. S., 396
Smith, R. H., 375
Smith, R. T., 537
sociological factors, see disorganization,
social
Souter, S. H., 497
Speck, W. H., 537
statistics:
basis of, 38-40
limitations of, 35-38
sources of, 32-35
Staub, Hugo, 698, 703, 705
Steinberg, S. H., 660
Stenton, Doris May, 299
Stevens, A., 227
Stevenson, C., 179
Stouffer, S. A., 601, 602, 603, 610
Stremel, A. W., 497
Stroup, Herbert H., 283, 284
Stuart, J., 105
Stullken, E. H., 283
Stürup, Georg K., 637, 661
Sullenger, T. E., 227
suspended sentences, 391-92, 522-23
Sutherland, E. H., 105, 148, 149, 191, 192,
194, 199, 200, 201, 202, 227, 228,
659, 701, 705
Sveri, Knut, 642, 660, 661
Sweden, prison system in, 639-42
syndicates, criminal, 154-59, 207-08

Taber, Robert C., 283
Tannenbaum, Frank, 455, 491, 498
Tappan, Paul W., 30, 194, 202, 395, 429,
454, 495, 496, 497, 520, 536, 537,
555
Tarde, Gabriel, 680

Tasker, R. J., 496, 497
Taylor, E. A., 105
Teeters, Negley K., 229, 375, 611, 659, 660
television, 71
theories of criminal behavior, 11-20, 662-64, 677-704
therapy, 264-65:
  in Air Force retraining center, 591
  in Army rehabilitation centers, 588-89
  group, 264-65, 464-66
  individual, 464
  in Navy retraining command, 595
thieves, petty, 225-26
third degree, 322-23
Thompson, C. B., 250
Thrasher, Frederic M., 14, 31, 94, 95, 103, 105, 149, 178, 262, 284, 700, 706
Timasheff, N. S., 536
Tjensvoll, Hanne-Marie, 660
Tough, R., 375
treatment (*see also* rehabilitation):
  in jail, 387-91
  in the past, 287-99
  by police, 320-24
trial:
  criminal, 346-54
  of juveniles, 365-66, 367-69
  by jury, 349-50
  and rehabilitation, 666-67
Tulchin, Simon, H., 54, 55, 68, 69, 705
Turnbladh, Will C., 536
Turner, J. W. C., 249

underworld, 137-47
Uniform Code of Military Justice, 576-81

vagrants, 224-25
Van Cise, Philip S., 148, 149, 158, 174, 179
Van Vechten, C. C., 69, 396
Vaughn, Wayland F., 104
vice, 10-11, 205-06
Vold, G. B., 104
Vollmer, August, 178, 179, 260, 334, 335, 336
voluntary defenders, 361

Wait, John Barber, 336, 375
Wall, J. H., 227
Wallace, J. A., 556
Wallack, W. M., 454, 497
war, 77-78

warden, 435-37, 449-50
Warner, S. B., 336
Wattenberg, W. W., 258, 283
Weeks, H. A., 118, 119, 120, 124
white collar crime, *see* segmental crime
Weihofen, H., 228
Weinberg, S. K., 491, 496, 498
Weintraub, R. G., 375
Wertham, Frederic (also, Fredric), **75,** 104, 230, 231, 235, 249
White, C. W., 335
White, R. C., 86, 87, 104
Whittier, H. B., 556
Wiers, P., 105
Willbach, H., 76, 104
Williams, Carol M., 335
Williamson, Margaretta, 537
Wilson, D. A, 455
Wines, Frederick Howard, 299
Winston, S., 105
Winterburg, D. E., 659
Witmer, Helen L., 284
Wolff, P. O., 227
Wolters, J. B., 520
women offenders (*see also* girls), 499-518:
  and drug addiction, 219-20
  institutions for, in Europe, 627-30, 645-49
  institutions for, in United States, 425, 505-08
  and intoxication, 211
  and prostitution, 222-23
  rates for, 49-53, 83
Wood, A. L., 105
work for prisoners, 466-75:
  for women prisoners, 511-12
workhouse, 391
Wortes, J., 249
Wright, Roberts J., 395

Yeomans, R. F., 249
Yoke, H. L., 105
Youell, R. M., 396
Young, E. F., 86, 104, 105
Young, Kimball, 705
Young, Pauline V., 536
Youth Authority, 367, 459-62

Zeleny, L. D., 705
Zemans, E. S., 396, 520
Zink, Harold, 335
Zuckerman, S. B., 556